THE **OFFICIAL**
NATIONAL
FOOTBALL
LEAGUE

FOOTBALL ENCYCLOPEDIA

THE **OFFICIAL
NATIONAL
FOOTBALL
LEAGUE**

FOOTBALL ENCYCLOPEDIA

BY **ROGER TREAT**

**A. S. BARNES & CO.
NEW YORK**

TO

Peter and John Treat

WITH WARM, PATERNAL CONFIDENCE THAT THEIR NAMES
WILL SOMEDAY BE INSERTED IN THIS RECORD AS THE
SAMMY BAUGH AND BRONKO NAGURSKI OF THE 1960's.

FOREWORD

by BERT BELL

Commissioner of the National Football League

For their efforts in producing the OFFICIAL NATIONAL FOOTBALL LEAGUE FOOTBALL ENCYCLOPEDIA, A. S. Barnes & Company deserve the thanks and congratulations of everyone associated with the National Football League.

Roger Treat, as editor, and his associates have brought forth a monumental amount of information about major league football that will be a welcome addition to the book shelves of all sports-loving Americans.

The painstaking manner in which the names of players, clubs and coaches; the history of the game, individual and team statistics and other information was collected, edited and placed in this volume is evident in each of its pages. It was truly a tremendous task.

We of the National Football League are proud of this book. It bears witness to the sound growth of the sport that had its inception in 1895. Along the way to its present position, it once numbered among its believers "Mr. Baseball," Connie Mack, who guided a professional team in 1902.

From the formation of the American Professional Football League in 1920, until today, the growth has been phenomenal. The problems of development created many failures, caused many heartbreaks, but they also served to make more determined those who saw ahead the brilliant future of professional football.

Whatever success the National Football League has had is due, in no small measure, to the wholehearted support it has received through the years from newspapermen, radio announcers and commentators, and, more recently, television announcers and commentators.

To the spectator whose passage through the turnstiles brought the wherewithal to make it possible to continue, we owe a special tribute. The fan, whose loyalty, year in and year out, has contributed his support to our teams, calls for the gratitude of all who are interested in this great game.

The publication of the OFFICIAL NATIONAL FOOTBALL LEAGUE FOOTBALL ENCYCLOPEDIA is, in itself, a tribute to all those who have, in small or large measure, played a part in making major league football one of the nation's most popular sports.

"It's like a lightning-fast chess game with pawns weighing 250 pounds. I make my gambit; the defense makes the counter-play. If all my pawns, castles, knights and bishops do what they are supposed to do, my king—that's the ball carrier—goes over for a touchdown. The tiniest mistake means disaster. A guard shifts his feet and gives the play away. A halfback takes a peek at the defensive end and tells him, 'Here I come, brother, get ready.' Brains win in this league; brains and psychology."

That, to a veteran quarterback in the National Football League, is major league football, a kingdom where men of intense competitive fire play the game for pay, but would play it for free if no salary were forthcoming. They deny this, but this ancient observer, who knows them well, would bet on it.

For these men are a race apart. Football is as essential to them as breathing. Their *esprit de corps* is tremendous; their personal valor is majestic. The painful, blue-black bruises they carry from August to December, the shoulder separations, the twisted bone-joints and mangled muscles are minor annoyances to be overcome each Sunday afternoon with gallons of novocaine. The blackened eyes and lost teeth are part of the fun.

For more than a decade the writer has known these players. In the dressing rooms before and after victory and defeat; at the training camps where the All America rookie learns with dramatic suddenness that he knows very little about football; through the long train rides from coast to coast; in their homes with their wives and children; in the hospitals where they mend their broken bones. His admiration grew until it had to pour out on paper.

Thus this history.

Who were (and are) they? What did they do? Who taught them how to do it? These were the simple questions proposed by John Lowell Pratt, president of A. S. Barnes and Company, as the project started. The answers covered 1,132 pages of manuscript.

It was decided to begin the formal listing of statistics with the season of 1920. But the league itself kept no records until 1933. After that the material was available and the collecting of it routine. Before that was a fourteen-year void that had to be filled through excavations and research which might not have bewildered the FBI but were certainly a catastrophic experience for an amateur.

A card system was created to pick up the playing records of each man. One by one these entries were gleaned from flaky, old programs, brittle newspaper clippings, microfilms, record books and the memories of many men until nearly thirty thousand individual "years played" were accumulated.

Without monumental help from many sources, this volume could never have been completed. The list of contributors follows, and if any have been shuffled aside in the confusion of ceiling-high piles of data, an apology is offered in advance.

A frantic SOS was broadcast in all directions, endorsed by Commissioner Bert Bell of the NFL. The response was heart-warming. George Calhoun of Green Bay, Wisconsin, forwarded his precious, and massive, files and proved to be a true triple-threat on digging up facts which once seemed as inaccessible as the vital statistics on the population of Mars. Edward Caswell checked in from Buffalo, New York, with proof that he had been a major league football fanatic for years and years, keeping records and files of his own just for the fun of it. These two men have been the main sources of supply, the arsenals of difficult data. They are both fervent football fanatics and the writer is eternally grateful for the hours of work they have contributed to this production.

The office of the Commissioner of the National Football League has been drained of its records of the past twenty years. Commissioner Bert Bell himself; Joe Labrum, his assistant; Denny Shea, league secretary and treasurer; Harry Standish and Al Ennis, league trouble shooters; Ruth McClennen and Elaine Emerson of the office staff, all have been loyal co-workers.

Several who were active in the league in by-gone days have contributed. Robert Haines of the old Frankford Yellowjackets; Val Ness of the Minneapolis Maroons; Ed Simandl of Orange and Newark; Ole Haugsrud of Duluth in the days of the Eskimos;

GEORGE CALHOUN   EDWARD CASWELL

Ned Kornaus of Chicago, another statistical maniac; Carroll Sollars of Mansfield, Ohio; Jim Schlemmer, Akron, Ohio, sports editor, an expert on the times when Canton, Dayton, Columbus, Hammond, Racine and Rock Island fielded their teams; Eddie Cook, once my frantic assistant in the Sports Department of the Washington *Daily News,* who found himself working once more for his old boss.

Jim Conzelman, the "Mad Genius" of the Chicago Cardinals' days of glory spearheaded by the "Dream Backfield" of a few years ago, dug into his memory of less abundant years with the Rock Island Independents, the Milwaukee Badgers, the Detroit Panthers, the Providence Steamrollers and the original Chicago (Staley) Bears, to fill in many gaps in the records. All the charter members, such as Steve Owen, Curly Lambeau, George Halas and Paddy Driscoll, who took their lumps before the days of novocaine, did their share as co-editors.

The story and statistics of the All America Football Conference came by courtesy of Joe Petritz, former publicity director of Notre Dame and the AAFC. To Arch Ward, sports editor, and Ed Prell, major league football writer, of the Chicago *Tribune,* my thanks for the story of the All Star games at Chicago.

The owners, publicity directors, coaches and other officials of the twelve active clubs were harassed with inquiries, bombarded with questionnaires. They responded as nobly from the front office as their more muscular co-workers do on the playing fields.

Gratitude goes, therefore, to Walter Wolfner, Arch Wolfe, Ed McGuire, Joe Kuharich and Bob Nussbaumer of the Chicago Cardinals; to Arthur "Mickey" McBride, Paul Brown and Russ Gestner of the Cleveland Browns; to James Clark, Vince McNally, Ed Hogan and Wayne Millner of the Philadelphia Eagles; to Art Rooney, Ray Byrne, Ed Kiely, Joe Bach and Walt Kiesling of the Pittsburgh Steelers; to George Preston Marshall,

Dick McCann, Dick Todd and Herman Ball of the Washington Redskins; to Tim, Jack and Wellington Mara, Steve Owen and Bill Lauder of the New York Giants; to George Halas, Frank Korch, Clark Shaughnessy, Paddy Driscoll and Luke Johnsos of the Chicago Bears; to Nick Kerbawy and Buddy Parker of the Detroit Lions; to Emil Fischer, Lee Joannes, Jug Earp, Gene Ronzani, Tarzan Taylor, and Scooter McLean of the Green Bay Packers; to Dan Reeves, Tex Schramm, and Joe Stydahar of the Los Angeles Rams; to Giles Miller, Al Ennis, Tex Maule and Jimmy Phelan of the Dallas Texans; to Tony and Victor Morabito, Dan McGuire and Buck Shaw of the San Francisco 49ers. Each did all that was asked—and a little more.

To the registrars of more than four hundred colleges who searched their records for minor facts and reported them promptly, a salute.

Finally, for countless hours of clerical drudgery, reshuffling of lists, addressing of hundreds of envelopes, thanks to my own personal "staff": my mother, Mrs. Esther Treat Mills; my wife, Gerda Dahl Treat—who now know more about major league football than many "experts" I have encountered.

Source books included: *The New Encyclopedia of Sports* by Frank Menke (A. S. Barnes, New York); *The Chicago Bears* by Howard Roberts (G. P. Putnam's Sons, New York); *My Life with the Redskins* by Corinne Griffith Marshall (A. S. Barnes, New York); *The Green Bay Packers* by Arch Ward (G. P. Putnam's Sons, New York); *Football Facts and Figures* by Dr. L. H. Baker (Farrar & Rinehart, New York); *My Greatest Day in Football* by Murray Goodman and Leonard Lewin (A. S. Barnes, New York); *The Greatest Sports Stories from the New York Times* by Allison Danzig and Peter Brandwein (A. S. Barnes, New York); *Professional Football* by Dr. William March; *Record and Rules Manual of the National Football League* from 1941 through 1951; *The National Football Guide* from 1937 through 1940; *Record Manuals of the All America Football Conference* from 1946 through 1949.

CONTENTS

THE OFFICIAL NATIONAL FOOTBALL LEAGUE

FOOTBALL ENCYCLOPEDIA

CHAPTER I
THE STORY OF THE GAME

THE EVOLUTION OF FOOTBALL

The celestial spirit of an unknown Dane who died in England soon after the year 1,000 A.D. may be strutting around the universe at this moment claiming that he is responsible for the game of football. He never played any version of the game as it is known today and the credit due him stems from an episode in which others used his head.

This Dane, whose name, under the circumstances, could not have been recorded for posterity, was a member of the armed forces of the "dastardly aggressor" of the moment. England was occupied by the victorious Danes, a condition which lasted from 1016 to 1042, and during that period, this unknown father of football died, and was buried on the battlefield. Time passed. The British rose again to drive the aggressors into the sea and the unknown Danish GI mouldered in his grave.

Some time later, an Englishman, digging in the old battlefield, unearthed the skull of this Dane, and, muttering about unpleasant memories of the days of the occupation, proceeded to kick the skull around the pasture. Other Englishmen joined in the fun and some youngsters, watching this new pastime, dug farther, until other Danish skulls were found. Soon, everyone in the township was kicking a skull and this sport continued until toes became more painful than the smoldering hatred of the Danes. It was not long before some minor inventive genius of the time produced the inflated bladder of a cow to take the place of the skulls, and thus the head of the unknown Dane had been used to create the embryo of football. There was a long road to travel from that pasture pastime to the passing skill of Redskin Sam Baugh, the elusive wizardry of Packer Don Hutson and the devastating black magic of T-formations. It would take nearly a thousand years to produce the lightning thrusts and bewildering deception of American Professional Football, but an ever-increasing multitude of major league fans in the United States of America is fanatically grateful that an unnamed Englishman did unearth a certain skull and did proceed to boot it for that first field goal attempt in history.

As if to set the pattern for later days, or perhaps to prove that there is nothing new, ever, anywhere, "Over-emphasis" blossomed within the first century of football history. Those who howled in 1952 that football must be abolished to preserve the good way of life, merely parroted the words of King Henry II (1159–1189), who not only threatened banishment of the sport, but did indeed ban it forever during his reign.

The ban followed a national craze which had developed over the joys of booting the inflated bladders in contests which were a combination of soccer, vandalism and mass modified-homicide. For the "big game" of those days was played in no stadium, but around, over and through two townships. The entire population of each contestant met at a point between the towns, the bladder was tossed in the middle, and chaos broke loose. The touchdown was scored when the ball was kicked into the center of the opposing town and there were no further rules to confuse the issue. If children, gentle old ladies and valuable livestock were trampled in the process, there were no referees to step off penalties. Gardens, crops, fences and even dwellings were flattened as the valiant athletes gave it the "old college try." Nor were there any gate receipts; the fans were taking part in the game. It would have been a glorious spectacle for television with no one to dictate restrictions. The celebrations which took place in the conquered village formed a pattern for American Legion conventions of later years and King Henry soon learned that the Danish occupation had been less devastating than one season of "futballe" as it was then called.

Futballe brought on its own banishment for still another reason. National preparedness in those days required each male citizen to put in a certain number of hours of archery practice, even as his descendants would practice running into burrows to escape the weapons of the future. When King Henry found that his soldiers were too busy playing futballe to tend to their bow and arrow exercises he blew the whistle. "No more futballe," he said. "We must build our national security with such a formidable fighting force that no aggressor will dare attack."

Futballe immediately "went underground" and was played only in those communities where the big-shot hoodlums of the time were able to corrupt the local police. This condition prevailed for the next four hundred years.

The invention of firearms bailed futballe out of official disgrace early in the sixteenth century, and James I revoked the ban at the request of thousands of sportsmen who had been playing all the time anyway, but wanted to make the game respectable. The game spread to all sections of the British Isles, and, unlike its namesake of modern times, it was a sport concerning a foot and a ball. There was no running with the ball; there was no forward passing. The previous assaults between townships were now confined to a standard-sized playing field and points were scored for driving the ball across the opponent's goal. Later refinements produced goal-posts and restrictions of the number of players. Eventually, this game became known as "Association Football" to distinguish it from other varieties. This designation was shortened to "Assoc." and, through slang, to "soccer," which it is called today.

In this same period, futballe drifted over into Ireland where it was immediately condemned as a sissy game, sorely in need of a strong injection of manliness, Irish style. The denizens of Ireland added some features of their own, mainly punching with the fists. This punching was supposedly aimed at the ball with intent to propel it toward the goal-line, but it was so much more satisfying to miss the ball and punch the opponent in the head that Gaelic football, as it is played today, is still a cross between boxing and soccer with emphasis on the former. It has changed little in nearly six hundred years.

The first variation from soccer, which pointed the way to the pattern of American football, took place at Rugby College in England in 1823. During an inter-class game of soccer, a player named William Ellis, discouraged with his lack of success at kicking the ball, was inspired to pick it up in his hands and run with it, thus scoring the first touchdown in history. Ellis was temporarily disgraced by his breach of sportsmanship, but soon, more adventurous souls decided to change the rules to permit running with the ball—and thus the game of Rugby was born.

In the ranks of the Pilgrim Fathers there were plenty of soccer players. There may even have been a few soccer balls, as well as cricket equipment, on the *Mayflower* when she made her momentous trip to these shores. But, strangely enough, there is no sign that any of the early immigrants to this country were Rugby players. The game was apparently unknown, or little appreciated, until 1875, when Harvard College, feeling its muscles at soccer, and unable to find a contender among the other American colleges, challenged McGill University to come down from Montreal to play a match of football. McGill came, but, unfortunately it was a Rugby team which showed up. A compromise was reached by playing half the game under soccer rules, half under Rugby, and the American boys liked the foreign game so much that they forgot all about soccer.

The next year Harvard sold the idea of playing Rugby to Yale to start a rivalry which is still renewed annually. Six years before, Rutgers had played Princeton in a football (soccer) game, enabling these universities to lay claim to being the pioneers of intercollegiate gridiron warfare, which was to be periodically accused of over-emphasis, and also periodically forgiven by the American public which loved the game.

For many years, Yale, Harvard and Princeton, then called "The Big Three," dominated the collegiate game, with the balance of the present members of the Ivy League assuming the secondary roles. It was not until well after World War I that the public became aware that football was not the exclusive property of the Eastern seaboard.

Early All America teams were dominated by the Big Three. Occasionally a West Point player, or a member of the Carlisle Indians, would get his name on the list, but seldom.

In present times there are nearly as many "All" teams as there were players in the early days of American football. Even now these mythical line-ups seldom include the first college rookies to be selected by the major league clubs when it comes to the annual player drafts. As many big stars in the major leagues have come from such unlikely campuses as Western Michigan State, Abilene Christian, St. Anselm's, Grambling and West Louisiana Teachers as have checked in from the Big Ten and similar highly publicized collegiate leagues.

Scoring originally paid off most highly on the field goal, which counted 5 against 1 for a touchdown. As late as 1884, a safety was 1 point, a touchdown 2, a point-after-touchdown 4, and a field goal 5. Later a touchdown was awarded 5 points, the same as a field goal, with the point-after-touchdown dropping to 1 and the safety becoming 2. Finally, in 1910 the field goal was dropped to 3 points, and, in 1912 the touchdown became 6 to set up the entire scoring routine as it is today. At present there is a movement led by Commissioner Bert Bell of the National Football League to make the touchdown equal to 7 points, to eliminate the point-after-touchdown altogether, and to provide for a sudden-death play-off in case of a tie. Bell believes that the point-after-touchdown is an unnatural sideline of football which depends too much on the skill of a few players, and that the fans deserve a decision at the end of any football game—as well as the players, owners and coaches.

The pattern of football strategy has progressed rapidly within seventy-five years from an offense which consisted mostly of "grab-it-and-run" to the intricate refinements of T-formation which can produce upward of ten thousand variations, counting individual blocking assignments, flankers, decoys and men-in-motion.

The first dramatic innovation was the so-called "flying-wedge," in which a phalanx of blocking linemen hung on to suitcase handles sewed to the pants of the man in front, and thundered down the field thus tied together with the ball carrier flitting along behind waiting for the opposition to be rolled up in a broken heap along the way.

This led to so many serious injuries—and deaths—and brought on such a savage game that President Teddy Roosevelt threatened to send football to Siberia if adequate safety precautions were not taken. In 1905, a gigantic Swarthmore tackle named Bob Maxwell, apparently the key-man in Swarthmore's defense, was seriously manhandled by the little gentlemen from Pennsylvania. A photograph of the bleeding Maxwell leaving the field incensed President Roosevelt and it was then that he waved the big stick at collegiate football.

The next year (1906) the forward pass was legalized in an effort to open up the game, the flying wedge was banished, and football had entered its next phase of growth.

It was not until 1913, however, that Gus Dorais (later to be coach of the Detroit Lions) and Knute Rockne, as Notre Dame players, brought the forward pass into a game with West Point and scored a sensational triumph. From that moment until the mid-1930's, the forward pass was something that a daring quarterback might demand on third down or when a game was hopelessly lost. It was a desperation measure for extreme circumstances.

And then, at little-known (at the time) Texas Christian University, there appeared a halfback named Samuel Adrian Baugh, and football, particularly the professional game, was about to make the most revolutionary change in its format to date. For Baugh, easily the most sensational passer of record, made the forward pass a routine offensive performance, a natural development of football warfare. Parenthetically, Baugh began to strike through the air at the same time that aircraft became the dominant factor of the bigger game known as "war," a fact that may have deeper meaning to deeper thinkers. This innovation led to further ramifications of football, until, in current times, roughly half of all offensive football is the forward pass.

Other changes have concerned themselves with offensive backfield formations: the single-wing, double-wing, punt, short-punt, Notre Dame box, the A and double A, and, finally and most important, the T.

The origin of the T is not entirely clear. It existed as far back as 1920, probably before that. But its devastating deception and all-around possibilities were not fully realized until George Halas, owner-coach of the Chicago Bears, and Clark Shaughnessy went to work on it in the late 1930's with the immortal Sidney Luckman as T quarterback. It was Halas who realized fully the possibilities of creating another effective blocker in the forward line by the almost too simple device of permitting the center to hand back the ball while he kept his eyes on his opponent, not looking back between his own legs. It was Halas—and Luckman—who worked out the pantomime of hand-faking that is now routine to the expert T quarterbacks. It was Halas who developed more plays now used by the other professional teams, as well as hundreds of college squads, than any other coach. Halas now claims that the Bears can call more than ten thousand different plays—and that there are still many realms in the higher strata of T-formation that he has not had time to develop as yet.

The man-in-motion, and the flankers were developed in the National Football League and their deadly possibilities have loosened up the defense so that football has become a whirlwind operation of speed combined with crushing power.

At the same time defense has been catching up with the T, and now it is almost mandatory for a professional team to have an offense which combines wing formations, short-punts, and other variations, with the T, so that the fan reaps a full menu of offensive fireworks whenever two of the major league teams tangle their talents in a showdown.

The result of this development has been higher, faster scoring. It is not unusual for a team to score more points in one game (the record of 70 is held by the Los Angeles Rams) than some teams scored in an entire season not many years ago. (The Philadelphia Eagles scored 51 points in 12 games in 1936.) Through statistical studies, training of officials and other innovations, the National Football League has speeded up its game until it now gives the fans approximately twenty more plays per game than the fastest college teams, and the average figure goes higher each season. It has also added the fifth official in the interest of better officiating and has introduced many other regulations to make its version of football the most enjoyable.

Steadily increasing attendance figures, despite the drain-off to television, radio, and the ever-present problem of bad weather in late fall, prove that major league football is the healthiest young sport in America. More and more fans are realizing each year that big league football, so far as skill and ability is concerned, bears the same relation to the college game that big league baseball does to minor league baseball.

With its rosters a listing of the finest players the thousands of colleges can produce, it is a tornado of touchdown thrills.

THE BEGINNING ERA, 1895-1920

The first professional football team to be recognized as such played in the township of Latrobe, in Westmoreland County, Pennsylvania, forty miles southeast of Pittsburgh. It was sponsored by the local YMCA. Latrobe made its artistic debut on August 31, 1895, by defeating Jeannette, another township ten miles away, by the impressive score of 12–0. For the next ten years, Latrobe fielded a powerful team which played wherever and whenever it could, for whatever cash it could get.

Dr. John Brallier, who was to become a dentist in Latrobe, is awarded the distinction of having become one of the first "confessed" professionals when he deserted the University of West Virginia team to play for Latrobe. Fielding Yost, who later denounced professional football, played for Greensburg; and "Doggie" Trenchard of Princeton, Walter Okeson of Lehigh, Walter Howard of Cornell were a few of the early college stars to join the early rampages. In 1897, the entire Lafayette backfield (Best, Barclay, Bray and Walbridge) played for Greensburg.

1894   DR. JOHN BRALLIER   1934

During the next few years, other professional teams began to appear. The city of Pittsburgh developed the Duquesne County and Athletic Club, and its rosters listed some of the finest collegiate players of the time. Arthur Poe of Princeton, "Pudge" Heffelfinger of Yale; Bemus and Hawey Pierce, the two magnificent Indians from Carlisle; G. H. Brooke and P. D. Overfield of Pennsylvania, Fred Crolius of Dartmouth, all as prominent then as the current swarms of All Americans are now, played with the Pittsburgh club.

Upper New York State followed Pennsylvania into the joys of professional football soon after the turn of the century. Teams existed in Buffalo, Syracuse, Watertown, Auburn, Corinth, Clayton, Oswego, Alexandria Bay and Ogdensburg. One of the outstanding players for Watertown and Syracuse was Phil Draper, former miracle-man back of Williams College, another great player who was born fifty years too soon to reap the gold and glory that would have been his today.

On December 28, 1902, Syracuse, with Draper, Glenn "Pop" Warner, and his brother Bill, along with the peripatetic Pierce brothers, Bemus and Hawey, played the Philadelphia Nationals to a 6–0 defeat in Madison Square Garden, New York. The officials worked in full dress, including high silk hats and white gloves. Thirty years later, the Chicago Bears defeated the Portsmouth Spartans, 9–0, indoors at Chicago Stadium. That, up to 1952, was the end of indoor football.

Also in 1902, Connie Mack organized a football team which he named the "Athletics."

He put the spectacular playboy pitcher, Rube Waddell, in the line-up, much to the Rube's confusion, and claimed the championship of the world after beating Pittsburgh, which had a fullback by the name of Christy Mathewson who had once been a line-crasher at Bucknell. The Indian Pierces played for Mack—and for almost everybody else.

Starting in 1904, and lasting until 1920 when the American Professional Football Association, the father of the National Football League, was formed, Ohio was the battleground, and the nursery, for major league football. Canton, Massillon, Akron, Columbus and Dayton contained many violent and valiant men, ever ready for some periodic bloodletting against any team which cared to show up. It was at Canton that Jim Thorpe first appeared to play for many years until he finished his career with the New York Giants in 1925.

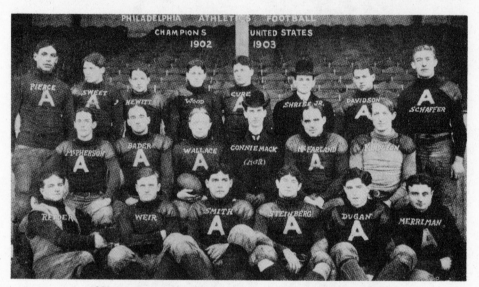

1902 PHILADELPHIA ATHLETICS MANAGED BY CONNIE MACK.

When Billy Heston, an all-time Michigan backfield ace, expressed a willingness to pick up some pocket money after finishing his college career in 1904, Canton, Massillon and Akron got themselves into a bidding auction for his services. Heston, believing he had the three teams over a barrel, lifted his demands to the point where all three rebelled and refused to hire him at any price. A year later, Heston did play one game for Canton for a fabulous $600, was massacred on the first play by the Massillon defense and never gained another inch. He played one more game in Chicago, collected a broken leg early in the game, and that was the end of his professional career.

Charlie Moran, major league umpire of renown, was a great back for Massillon in the same era. From the Carlisle Indian school came the Pierce brothers, Bemus and Hawey, and the great players called Frank Mt. Pleasant and Albert Exendine. Later, Jim Thorpe organized an entire team of Indians, who called themselves the "Oorang Indians" and played in the NFL in 1923. Before that, Jim went through the glory, and the heart-break, of his experiences at the 1912 Olympic games at Stockholm, where he and George Patton of West Point dominated the scene.

As time went on, Columbus and Shelby in Ohio had teams. The Columbus Pan-handles, managed by Joe Carr, who later became president of the National Football League (from 1921 until his death in 1939), had the distinction of fielding one of the strangest line-ups in football history. In 1906, eight of its eleven positions were filled by men named "Nesser." Seven of these amazing players were brothers, and the eighth was Fred Nesser, the son of Ted, the oldest. None of them had ever accepted any of the offers made by many colleges. They played with many teams for many years, brother Al finally writing an end to the family saga with the Cleveland team in 1931.

In the late teens, Knute Rockne and Charles "Gus" Dorais, whose forward-passing act had recently flabbergasted a highly touted West Point team, moved into professional football. They played with so many teams, jumping from one high bidder to another, that it would be impossible to trace their careers with any degree of accuracy. It is reported that the Columbus team found itself facing Rockne in six different uniforms during one season. Dorais later became coach of the Detroit Lions from 1943 through 1947.

Men who were destined to make their fame as coaches, rather than players, appeared in the Canton-Massillon line-ups of 1919. "Tuss" McLaughry, now of Dartmouth; and the

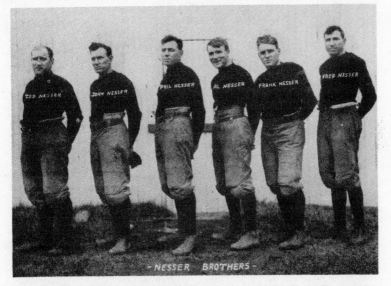

TED IS THE FATHER OF FRED. ONE BROTHER WHO PLAYED WITH THEM IS MISSING FROM THE PICTURE.

late "Jock" Sutherland and Earle "Greasy" Neale took part in those bitter struggles. Charlie Brinkley, the great Harvard drop-kicker, tried it for a while with little success. "Fido" Kempton, a tiny quarterback from Yale, joined Canton for a few games in 1921.

War must be given some credit for the birth, or at least the conception, of what is now known as the National Football League. For, in 1918, the team representing the Great Lakes Naval Training Station was chosen to play in the Rose Bowl, where it proceeded to wallop the Mare Island squad. On that Great Lakes team were the men who would mold and nurse major league football to its present burgeoning prosperity. George Halas, fresh from the University of Illinois, was its brilliant end. Jim Conzelman, John "Paddy" Driscoll, Harold Erickson were in its backfield. Hugh Blacklock, a fine Bear tackle to be, was there, as were two excellent guards from Notre Dame, Jerry Jones and Emmett Keefe, who would play in the league to come.

There were many truly magnificent players in this early era of growth, many almost unknown to current fans who have been conditioned to believe that major league football "began" with the spectacular unveiling of Harold "Red" Grange in 1925. Only the name of Jim Thorpe seems to carry over from those dark days of guerrilla warfare on the fields of Pennsylvania, Ohio and upper New York, although the eyes of the old-timers will light up with a strange fire when they talk of these "good, old days" when each man either played the sixty minutes or was carried off on a stretcher. Not for them are the tactics of specialists and platoons.

Thorpe was, without doubt, a superlative back who could kick, crash or run in the open. He was a physical freak, who could, like Babe Ruth, Walter Hagen and Harry Greb, ignore all the rules in the fitness manuals and still perform at a peak efficiency beyond the reach of lesser athletes. Thorpe used an open field running technique all his own, not dodging violently, but moving with a deceptive hip-twist that seemed to make him almost impossible to drop. Jim himself explains it thus: "I gave them a leg for a second, then took it way." Another weapon Thorpe used in the early days was an illegal, and decidedly lethal, shoulder-pad which had an outer covering of sheet metal concealed

STEVE VAN BUREN POWERS OVER A FALLEN REDSKIN IN A GAME BETWEEN WASHINGTON AND PHILADELPHIA AT WASHINGTON IN 1948.

under his uniform jersey. When he crashed into optimistic tacklers with this device, devastation set in. Not until he joined the New York Giants in 1925 did anyone persuade Jim that he was not allowed to carry such murderous concealed weapons onto a football field. It is generally conceded by all the deeper thinkers of the current National Football League that, if Jim Thorpe were coming out of college in the year 1952, he would be the highest-paid rookie the league had ever known, and, perhaps, its greatest star.

All these warriors of old, many gone on to the gridirons of Valhalla, were the pioneers of America's most exciting sport. They would have played for nothing if they had to—and often did, even as "professionals." The dynamic drive of these men, joined with that of other men of similar courage and aggressiveness, made the league what it is today, and pointed the way toward the greater triumphs of the future.

THE MODERN ERA

The actual birth of the National Football League took place during the hot afternoon of September 17, 1920, as its founders gathered in the automobile agency of Ralph Hays, in Canton, Ohio. Hays also managed the Canton Bulldogs of that year. Jim Thorpe was there, and was elected president of the new American Professional Football Association.

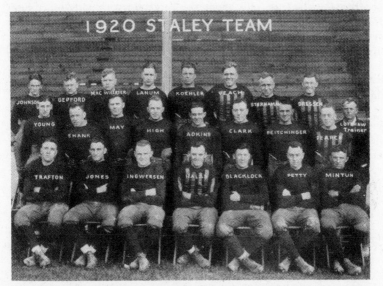

THE 1920 STALEY TEAM WHICH BECAME THE CHICAGO BEARS TWO YEARS LATER.

George Halas, back from the New York Yankees baseball team which had farmed him out to St. Paul, was there, representing the Staley Starch Company of Decatur, which had named him its athletic director. Stanley Cofall, one-time Notre Dame star, then running the Massillon Tigers, was on hand to be elected vice-president. A. F. Ranney, sponsor of the Akron team, was made secretary-treasurer.

The $50,000 fee now paid by each would-be member of the NFL would have paid for no less than 500 franchises that hot afternoon, as they sold for $100 each. Eleven teams signed up for the season to come: Canton Bulldogs; Cleveland Indians; Dayton Triangles; Akron Professionals; Massillon Tigers; Rochester, New York; Rock Island, Illinois; Muncie, Indiana; Hammond, Indiana; the Chicago Cardinals; and the Staleys, who were to become the Chicago Bears two years later.

The league had a perilous beginning that fall with confusion abounding and starvation threatening. The less hardy were discouraged and the survivors concluded that there must be administrative, as well as artistic talent, to create healthy growth. In April of the next year, the league reorganized and elected Joe Carr, an experienced sports promoter, as its new president. It was the smartest move major league football had made to date. Carr guided the league with a wise and sure hand until his death in 1939. He was professional football's balance wheel through the stormy years of its first two decades, a fair and impartial ruler.

There was an immediate realignment of teams in that second year. Massillon, Muncie and Hammond dropped out; Green Bay, Buffalo, Detroit, Columbus and Cincinnati came in, although Cincinnati never did get around to playing a league game that fall.

This shifting of franchises, moving to new frontiers, testing fan support in different areas, was a healthy habit the league had practiced through all its history. The NFL is continually trying for the best possible spread of its teams. Even in this year of 1952, it moved one of its teams to Texas, thus opening up new territory and relieving the overload in New York.

The appearance of the Green Bay Packers in 1921 was the beginning of the saga of the most fabulous football town in the world. Its population in 1920 was slightly over 31,000, but it supported its football team then better than 7,000,000 New Yorkers supported the Giants in 1951. Its stadium seats about 25,000 and the SRO sign has been worn out for nearly every home game during the past thirty-two years. Its newspaper, the Green Bay *Press-Gazette,* tells about the Packers first, reports other news if it has room. Nearly 50,000 wild-eyed football maniacs make up its population today and they know more about football than any other 50,000 people on the face of the earth. Its housewives meet each Monday during the season at the Quarterback Club. The coach of the team is torn to shreds after a losing performance. Any psychopath, seeking an early death by extreme torture, can reach his goal by appearing in Green Bay and praising any member, past or present, of that hated enemy, the Chicago Bears.

The Green Bay Packers—Curly Lambeau—and George Calhoun: through the years they have become synonymous. As a young man Curly dreamed a dream. He went to Charles Peck, an official in the Acme Packing Company of Green Bay, and explained his dream. The magnificent sum of $500—for equipment and expenses—changed hands, and the Green Bay Packers were on the way to glory. Earl Louis Lambeau would be their coach and star back. He'd get the other players somehow. They would challenge any team in the world.

Big league football was a part-time job that year. Curly's twenty-one athletes worked all day, practiced until darkness made practice impossible. They won their first ten games, beating such formidable opponents as Menominee, Marinette, Sheboygan, Racine, New London, Oshkosh, Stambaugh, and Ishpeming. They were ready to claim the championship of Wisconsin, or the whole world, until Beloit whipped them late in the season, creating 30 days of official mourning, and financial embarrassment for almost every citizen of Green Bay. But Curly Lambeau couldn't be stopped. He played until 1929, coached the Packers through 1949, when Gene Ronzani replaced him as head coach.

During Curly's long leadership, the Packers put Green Bay on the map as the home of rough, rugged football, boasting some of the best players in all football history. The names of Don Hutson, Lavvie Dilweg, Clark Hinkle, Cecil Isbell, August Michalske, Baby Ray and Tony Canadeo gained luster at Green Bay, to be remembered as long as football shall live. The blazing rivalry which has developed between the Packers and the Chicago Bears provides two contests each fall that combine all the explosive ingredients of an atom bomb.

The dynamo of the Packers, other than Lambeau, has been a man whose name is never printed in the programs but who has been, from the beginning, and still is, the senior adviser, the patriarchal statesman, the father confessor, the defender of the faith, the only official Monday-morning quarterback, and the historian of all things Packer. George Whitney Calhoun is his name and he is known wherever major league football has been played, from Boston to San Francisco. Even though Lambeau has moved on to other fields, Calhoun is still there, on the telegraph desk of the *Press-Gazette,* and the Packers would be lost without him.

There was a moment in the early days when the Packers came within a wink of giving up the battle because of financial problems. It was then that George Calhoun directed the move which joined together five of Green Bay's outstanding citizens in an organization which called itself the "Hungry Five" and was pledged to keep the Packers going at all costs. Their names were Earl Lambeau, Lee Joannes, Dr. W. Webber Kelly, Andy Turnbull and Gerry Clifford. They sold stock in the Packers—at $5 a share—to hundreds of Wisconsin people. They guaranteed the Packers' debts. They fought the financial warfare—always with Calhoun lurking along the sidelines, working at thankless jobs, goading the others into action, and reaping his reward in the pleasure derived from sending his hymns of Packer praise over the world in his capacity as publicity director of the team.

Occasionally, through the years, more financing has been necessary, and the Hungry Five has always produced it to make Green Bay one of the strongest franchises in the NFL.

NEW YORK GIANTS, CHAMPIONS 1927. (NOTE THAT AL NESSER, WHO PLAYED FOR COLUMBUS IN 1906, IS NOW WITH THE GIANTS. HE WILL PLAY UNTIL 1931, A TOTAL OF 25 YEARS.)

Football fans who have watched metropolitan teams play their home games before audiences too small to play craps among themselves will get a tremendous thrill by traveling to this picturesque town in upper Wisconsin on a zero day, when snowbanks line the Packers' field waist deep. There they will find a sell-out crowd rooting their heroes home. It is one of the most heart-warming pictures in the world of American sports.

For more than a decade, the National Football League, as it was renamed in 1922, battled its way along with little support from the fans and even less from some newspapers. New teams joined, dropped out; some teams moved to other cities. Players shuffled around the league, playing wherever they could find paychecks. Only the Chicago (Staley) Bears, the Chicago Cardinals and the Green Bay Packers are left in 1952 from among those that made up the league roster under Joe Carr's leadership in 1921.

The take-off to true prosperity began in 1925, after Tim Mara had established the Giants in New York's Polo Grounds. It happened when Harold "Red" Grange, his collegiate career finished under screaming headlines, signed with the Chicago Bears. Grange was the biggest name in the country at the time. People who couldn't have named the Vice-President of the United States (by the way, who was he?) knew all about the fabulous redhead from Wheaton, Illinois. It was the flash-spark that major league football needed. His debut in Wrigley Field against the Chicago Cardinals drew 36,000 fans, all the park would hold at that time. Seven days later, 68,000 watched him play against the New York Giants in the Polo Grounds. At last the big league game was off and running after several false starts.

Grange established himself as one of the all-time greats of professional football before he retired in 1935. Just before hanging up his uniform for good, Red wrote a letter to

RED GRANGE SIGNS HIS PROFESSIONAL CONTRACT

Arch Ward, sports editor of the Chicago *Tribune,* containing some remarks that might be of interest to fans who may still believe that a good college team would be a match for a major league squad. It stated:

> I say that a football player, after three years in college, doesn't know any-thing about football, Red wrote. Pro football is the difference between the New York Giants baseball team and an amateur nine. College players not only do not know how to play football, but they don't take as much interest in the game as the pros. In college you have studies to make up, lectures to attend, scholastic requirements to satisfy. In pro ball you are free from all this. You have nothing to do but eat, drink and sleep football and that is just what the boys do.
>
> Pro football is smart. It is so smart you can rarely work the same play twice with the same results. Competition is keen. There are no set-ups in pro football. The big league player knows *football,* not just a theory or system.

In 1933, with prosperity finally peeking from around the corner where it had been hiding for five years, professional football became firmly established as a major league sport. It was in this year that the league split itself into two divisions—East and West—and thereby established a championship play-off. It also began to form an apparatus to keep official statistical records and, generally, came of age.

More than a small part of this development sprang from the agile brain of George

TIM MARA OF THE NEW YORK GIANTS TURNS OVER $115,163 TO MAYOR JAMES WALKER FOLLOWING A CHARITY GAME BETWEEN THE GIANTS AND NOTRE DAME ALL-STARS

Preston Marshall, who, with Vincent Bendix, Jay O'Brien and M. Dorland Doyle, had taken over the Boston franchise the previous year. Marshall, a dynamic and controversial gentleman, was to be the cause of many changes during the next two decades. With the help of his wife, Corinne Griffith Marshall, one-time motion-picture star, he created the greatest series of half-time entertainments ever seen in major league parks. His Redskin band of more than one hundred precision trained musicians became an annual favorite wherever it appeared. Marshall's yowling battle against the All America Football Conference was always rich with witty denunciations which delighted newspapermen and fans alike.

In 1933, Art Rooney took over the Pittsburgh franchise, while Bert Bell, later to become Commissioner, and Ludlow Wray, absorbed the old Yellowjacket Club and created the Philadelphia Eagles. Brooklyn was sold to Chris Cagle and John (Shipwreck) Kelly and Charles Bidwill bought the Chicago Cardinals. The league had received a wholesale .transfusion of new, and wealthy, blood.

With prosperity in sight, membership fees were increased to $10,000; seven years later they would go to $50,000.

Within a year, after the Chicago Bears beat the New York Giants in the first divisional play-off championship, G. A. Richards bought the Portsmouth franchise and transferred it to Detroit and Dan Topping took over the Brooklyn squad. The Cincinnati franchise was transferred to St. Louis where it died of financial malnutrition. Also in 1934, the selective draft and waiver rule was devised to absorb graduating collegians and the player limit was increased to twenty-four men. Jay Berwanger, the great University of Chicago halfback, was the first player chosen—by the Philadelphia Eagles—under the draft plan, but declined the honor and did not play major league football. In the early fall of 1934, the champion Chicago Bears were held to a scoreless tie by the College All-Stars in the first of an annual series sponsored at Soldier Field by the Chicago Tribune Charities.

George Marshall, convinced that Boston preferred the pattern of college football to the professional game, transferred his Redskins from Boston to Washington in 1937 and began to play to capacity crowds. The fabulous Samuel Adrian Baugh appeared from Texas Christian the same fall to start the skein of records which may always be the goal of all football passers. The same fall, the Cleveland franchise was established for Homer Marshman by league president Joseph F. Carr, who died the following spring and was replaced by Carl L. Storck.

There was more franchise juggling during the next two years. Fred J. Mandel, Jr., took over at Detroit, buying out George Richards, and Alexis Thompson bought the Pittsburgh Steeler team from Art Rooney, who, in turn, bought a half interest in the Philadelphia Eagles. The next year, 1941, Thompson transferred his entire club to Philadelphia, which Rooney and Bell vacated in order to take their franchise to Pittsburgh. At the same time, Dan Reeves and Fred Levy, Jr., bought the Cleveland franchise from Marshman to stay in Cleveland until the 1946 season (when they would move the Rams to Los Angeles, making way for the Cleveland Browns).

The league appointed its first Commissioner on March 1, 1941, naming Elmer Layden. Carl Storck resigned as president a month later and Layden was given that post also. He resigned on January 11, 1946, and Bert Bell was elected to replace him. By successive re-appointments, Bell's term is now scheduled to run until January 20, 1959.

The gate receipts were climbing all through these years. The *Tribune* All-Star game at Chicago each fall was selling out to crowds of nearly ninety thousand and the championship games were playing to tremendous gatherings. More and more big-name college rookies were joining the league and it was a long road back to the days of playing for $10 per game. Public interest was rocketing, and after the fabulous Bears of 1940 devastated the Washington Redskins by 73–0 in the championship game, the deeds of the major league footballers were the top topic of conversation in sporting circles for weeks afterward. It is still accepted as gospel in football circles that the Chicago Bears of that amazing afternoon were the most lethal sports aggregation that ever appeared anywhere.

Then came Pearl Harbor and 638 National Football League members went into service in every theater of action. This wholesale departure of top-flight players weakened every team and caused the Cleveland Rams to suspend operations for the season of 1943. And, to take up the slack further, the Pittsburgh Steelers merged their squad with the Philadelphia Eagles to form a Phil-Pitt combination in 1943, then (after Phil-Pitt was dissolved) merged with the Chicago Cardinals for the 1944 season, which welcomed the return of the Cleveland Rams to active play, and also witnessed the debut of the Boston Yanks under the ownership of Ted Collins.

Collins soon learnd that Boston still preferred college ball, even as George Marshall had discovered long before, and moved his team to New York as the "Bulldogs" for the 1949 season. This was a disastrous maneuver, putting three teams in the city which barely supports one properly (the New York Yankees of the All America Football Conference were operating out of Yankee Stadium that fall). The next year brought the merging of the NFL and AAFC. Topping's Yankees gave up the ghost and Collins took over at Yankee Stadium with the "New York Yanks." Some years earlier, in 1945, Topping and Collins had merged the Brooklyn franchise with the Boston club, and the next year Topping deserted to the All-America, thus leaving Brooklyn open for the AAFC to put a franchise there, which Branch Rickey did. It was one of the few disasters (financial) Rickey ever brought upon himself; some games were played before fewer customers than had watched the early warfare of the Chicago Staleys nearly thirty years before.

With the war ended in 1946 and two leagues containing 18 teams in operation, the players had a financial feast for a few seasons, but it was soon apparent that the United States would not support that many major league teams. But it was growth, and the growing pains were lessened by the realization, four years later, that the big league game was solidly on the road to prosperity. New attendance records were broken each year until, in both 1950 and 1951, more than two million cash customers went through the gates.

The merger of the NFL and AAFC brought about a 13-team league for the 1950 season with the Baltimore Colts acting as the "swing" club, playing one game against each member team while the rest played normal schedules against divisional and traditional rivals. The Colts swung themselves into a sea of red ink and disappeared after a disastrous season in which they won one game.

A further settling down took place in 1951, with gate receipts rising all over the circuit. The championship game between the Rams and Browns, telecast from coast to coast, was, fortunately, a hair-raiser, and created thousands of new fans for the future.

At the annual meeting in January, 1952, Ted Collins sold his New York Yanks franchise back to the league, which immediately transferred it to a group of men, headed by Giles Miller of Dallas, Texas, which had been begging for major league football for many years. Dallas was expected to become one of the most successful clubs in the league. And this transfer to Dallas of a team with several Negro stars seemed on the way to breaking, at last, all racial restrictions on sports in Texas.

Bidwill, Halas, Joannes, Lambeau, Mara, Marshall, Rooney, Bell and other survivors from the beginning days have watched developments with fascinated wonder as they remember playing a more brutal game for what would now be considered lunch money. They have witnessed a great change in playing methods. They have seen the greatest stars of thirty years come and go, a few remaining as coaches in the league, many returning to college ball to try to teach the rookies how to play the bigger game. They have learned that few All America players are ever ready for the big time until they have had a season or two of grooming.

The indomitable competitive spirit which is strong in the heart of every successful major league player battled the frightening odds through thirty long years to give America its most exciting game.

If these veterans took a few bows in the solitude of their souls, they had them coming.

FORTY-FIVE CITIES WHICH WERE AFFILIATED WITH THE NFL AND THE YEARS OF THEIR ENTRANCE AS OF 1952

Akron, Ohio (7)   1920, 21, 22, 23, 24, 25, 26.

Baltimore, Md. (1)   1950

Boston, Mass. (11)   1929, 32, 33, 34, 35, 36, and 1944 to 1948 inclusive.

Brooklyn, N.Y. (16)   1926 only, and 1930 thru 1944 inclusive.

Buffalo, N.Y. (8)   1921, 22, 23, 24, 25, 26, 27, 29.

Canton, Ohio (6)   1920, 21, 22, 23, 25, 26.

Chicago Bears (32)   1921 to present time.

Chicago Cards (33)   1920 to present time. (Longest period for team.)

Cincinnati, Ohio (3)   1921 only and 1933, 34:

Cleveland, Ohio (18)   1920, 21, 23, 24, 25, 27, 31, 37, 38, 39, 40, 41, 42, 44, 45, 50, 51, 52.

Columbus, Ohio (6)   1921, 22, 23, 24, 25, 26.

Dallas, Texas (1)   1952

Dayton, Ohio (10)   1920 to 1929 inclusive.

Decatur, Ill. (1)   1920

Detroit, Mich. (23)   1921, 25, 26, 28, 1934 to present time.

Duluth, Minn. (5)   1923 to 1927 inclusive.

Evansville, Ind. (1)   1922

Frankford, Pa. (8)   1924 to 1931 inclusive.

Green Bay, Wis. (32)   1921 to present time.

Hammond, Ind. (6)   1920, 22, 23, 24, 25, 26.

Hartford, Conn. (1)   1926

Kansas City, Mo. (3)   1924 to 1926 inclusive.

Kenosha, Wis. (1)   1924

Los Angeles, Cal. (8)   1926 only, and also 1946 to present time.

Louisville, Ky. (3)   1922, 23, 26.

Marion, Ohio (2)   1922, 23.

Massillon, Ohio (1)   1920

Milwaukee, Wis. (5)   1922 to 1926 inclusive.

Minneapolis, Minn. (5)   1922, 23, 24, 29, 30.

Muncie, Ind. (1)   1920

Newark, N.J. (1)   1930

N.Y. Bulldogs (1)   1949

N.Y. Giants (28)   1925 to present time.

N.Y. Yanks (4)   1927, 28, and 1950, 51.

Orange, N.J. (1)   1929

Philadelphia, Pa. (20)   1933 to present time.

Pittsburgh, Pa. (20)   1933 to present time.

Portsmouth, Ohio (4)   1930 to 1933 inclusive.

Pottsville, Pa. (4)   1925 to 1928 inclusive.

Providence, R.I. (7)   1925 to 1931 inclusive.

Racine, Wis. (4)   1922, 23, 24, 26.

Rochester, N.Y. (6)   1920 to 1925 inclusive.

Rock Island, Ill. (6)   1920 to 1925 inclusive.

San Francisco, Cal. (3)   1950 to present time.

Stapleton, N.Y. (4)   1929 to 1932 inclusive.

St. Louis, Mo. (2)   1923 only, and also 1934.

Toledo, Ohio (2)   1922, 23.

Washington, D.C. (16)   1937 to present time.

SEVENTEEN STATES, PLUS DISTRICT OF COLUMBIA, REPRESENTED IN THE NFL

California (2): Los Angeles and San Francisco

Connecticut (1): Hartford

Illinois (3): Chicago, Decatur, Rock Island

Indiana (3): Evansville, Hammond, Muncie

Kentucky (1): Louisville

Maryland (1): Baltimore

Massachusetts (1): Boston

Michigan (1): Detroit

Minnesota (2): Duluth, Minneapolis

Missouri (2): Kansas City, St. Louis

New Jersey (2): Newark, Orange

New York (5): Brooklyn, Buffalo, New York City, Rochester, Stapleton

Ohio (10): Akron, Canton, Cincinnati, Cleveland, Columbus, Dayton, Marion, Massillon, Portsmouth, Toledo

Pennsylvania (4): Frankford, Philadelphia, Pittsburgh, Pottsville

Rhode Island (1): Providence

Texas (1): Dallas

Wisconsin (4): Green Bay, Kenosha, Milwaukee, Racine

District of Columbia (1): Washington

NOTE: 1 District, 17 states, 45 cities.

A CHRONOLOGY
OF PROFESSIONAL FOOTBALL

(From the *Record and Rules Manual*, National Football League)

1895—First professional football game played at Latrobe, Pa., August 31, sponsored by the local YMCA. Latrobe 12, Jeannette 0.

1902—Connie Mack claimed the professional football championship of the United States for his "Philadelphia Athletics," with Rube Waddell in the line-up, after they defeated Pittsburgh, with Christy Mathewson playing, 12–6. The game was played at Pittsburgh.

First night football game at Elmira, N.Y., November 18. Philadelphia Athletics (39) vs Kanaweola A.C. (0).

First indoor football game at Madison Square Garden, December 28. Syracuse, with Glenn Warner playing guard, defeated Philadelphia Nationals, 6–0.

1905—Canton Bulldogs and Massillon Tigers organized.

1920—American Professional Football Association formed September 17 at Canton, Ohio, with the following membership: Canton Bulldogs, Cleveland Indians, Dayton Triangles, Akron Professionals, Massillon Tigers, Rochester (N.Y.), Rock Island (Ill.), Muncie (Ind.), Staleys of Decatur (Ill.), Chicago Cardinals, and Hammond (Ind.).

Jim Thorpe (Canton) elected president; Stan Cofall (Massillon), vice-president; A. F. Ranney (Akron), secretary and treasurer. Membership fee was set at $100.

1921—American Professional Football Association reorganized April 30 at Akron, Ohio. Joe F. Carr elected president; M. O'Brien (Decatur), vice-president; Carl L. Storck (Dayton), secretary and treasurer.

J. E. Clair of Acme Packing Company granted franchise for Green Bay, Wisconsin, August 27.

1922—Franchise of George Halas for Staley A.C. transferred to Chicago and team renamed Chicago Bears, January 28.

J. E. Clair turned Green Bay franchise back to league following discussion over alleged use of ineligible players, January 28.

Professional football gets first eight-column newspaper headline, Chicago *Herald & Examiner,* January 30. It says: "Stagg Says Conference Will Break Professional Football Menace."

Earl Lambeau granted franchise for Green Bay, Wis., June 24.

Name of American Professional Football Association changed to National Football League.

1924—Frankford Yellow Jackets (Philadelphia) awarded franchise.

1925—Timothy J. Mara and Will Gibson granted franchise for New York for $2,500, August 1.

James Conzelman granted franchise for Detroit, August 1.

Harold "Red" Grange signed with Chicago Bears, November 22.

1926—Rule adopted February 6 making all players ineligible for NFL competition until they have graduated from college.

Adoption of maximum (18) and minimum (15) player limit, February 7.

Edward Butler granted franchise for Brooklyn, N.Y., July 10.

Milwaukee fined $500 on July 10 for using four high school boys against the Chicago Cardinals, and ordered to dispose of franchise within ninety days.

1927—National Football League reorganized with withdrawal of Brooklyn, Detroit and nine other clubs, July 27.

Brooklyn franchise transferred to C. C. Pyle for New York Yankees team.

JOE CARR, FIRST PRESIDENT OF THE NATIONAL FOOTBALL LEAGUE

1928—Detroit's application for re-instatement approved; Cleveland withdrew, August 12. Duluth and Buffalo franchises dropped.

1929—Sale of Chicago Cardinal franchise by Chris O'Brien to Dr. David J. Jones, July 27.
C. C. Pyle surrendered Brooklyn franchise to Stapleton, Staten Island, July 27.
Pottsville (Pa.) franchise awarded to Boston syndicate, July 28.
Adoption of rule to use a fourth official, field judge, July 28.
Chicago Cardinals became first professional team to attend out-of-town training camp—at Coldwater, Mich., August 21.

1930—Player limit increased on January 25 to maximum of 20, minimum of 16.
Portsmouth franchise awarded to Harold Griffen, July 12.
Dayton franchise purchased for Brooklyn by William B. Dwyer and John Depler from Carl L. Storck, July 12.
New York Giants raised $115,163 for New York Unemployment fund by beating Notre Dame All-Stars, 21–0, December 14.

1931—Chicago Bears, Green Bay Packers and Portsmouth Spartans fined $1,000 each on July 11 for having players on their rosters who had not yet been graduated from their college classes.

1932—Inactive Boston franchise transferred to new syndicate composed of George Preston Marshall, Vincent Bendix, Jay O'Brien and M. Dorland Doyle, July 9.
Chicago Bears defeated Portsmouth Spartans, 9–0, for championship. Game played indoors at Chicago Stadium.

1933—Clipping penalty increased to 25 yards, February 25.
Goal posts returned to goal-line, February 25.
Forward passing legalized from any spot behind line of scrimmage, February 25.
Membership fee increased to $10,000, July 8.

A resolution by George P. Marshall setting up a divisional system and a championship play-off adopted, July 8.

A. J. Rooney and A. McCool awarded franchise for Pittsburgh, July 8.

Frankford Yellowjackets franchise declared forfeit and awarded to Bert Bell and Lud Wray of Philadelphia, July 9.

Chicago Cardinals franchise sold to Charles Bidwell by Dr. David J. Jones, October 24.

William Dwyer and John Depler transferred Brooklyn franchise to Christian Cagle and John Kelly, July 9.

1934—G. A. Richards purchased Portsmouth franchise and moved team to Detroit, June 30.

Chris Cagle and John Kelly transferred Brooklyn franchise to Daniel Topping, June 30.

Chicago Bears held to scoreless tie by Collegiate All-Stars in first annual All-Star game sponsored by the Chicago Tribune Charities at Soldier Field, Chicago, August 31.

Franchise of Cincinnati transferred to St. Louis, November 5.

Player selective draft and waiver rule adopted, December 10.

1935—Player limit increased to 24 men, September 4.

1936—Jay Berwanger, University of Chicago halfback, first player selected in NFL draft. Chosen by Philadelphia, February 8.

Player limit increased to 25 men, February 9.

1937—Homer Marshman granted franchise for Cleveland, February 12.

Boston franchise transferred to Washington, February 13.

1938—Player limit increased to 30 men, February 19.

1939—Kick-off out-of-bounds ruled receiving team's ball on its 45-yard line, February 11.

Joe F. Carr, NFL president since 1921, died at Columbus, Ohio, May 20.

Carl L. Storck named president of NFL, May 25.

1940—Detroit Lions fined $5,000 for tampering with Clyde "Bulldog" Turner, Hardin-Simmons center, drafted by the Chicago Bears, February 2.

Fred J. Mandel, Jr., purchased Detroit Lions franchise from G. A. Richards, February 10.

Membership fee increased to $50,000, April 12.

Player limit increased to 33 maximum and 22 minimum, April 12.

Clipping penalty reduced to 15 yards, April 12.

All distance penalties enforced from spot on field of play limited to half the distance to the goal, April 12.

Dennis J. Shea elected treasurer of the league, April 12.

Alexis Thompson purchased Pittsburgh Steelers franchise from Arthur J. Rooney, who then purchased half-interest in Philadelphia Eagles, December 9.

Adoption of rule prohibiting sale or trading of team's first two selections in player draft without unanimous consent of league until one playing season after player's selection.

1941—Elmer F. Layden, head coach and athletic director at Notre Dame, named Commissioner of professional football for five years, March 1.

Carl L. Storck resigned as president-secretary, April 5.

Elmer F. Layden elected president for five years, April 5.

Philadelphia franchise and club transferred to Pittsburgh and Pittsburgh franchise and club transferred to Philadelphia, April 5.

Umpire made official timer of league games, April 6.

Cleveland franchise transferred from Homer Marshman and associates to Daniel F. Reeves and Fred Levy, Jr., June 1.

1942—National Football League raised $680,384.07 for War Relief charities.

1943—Cleveland Rams, with co-owners Fred Levy and Daniel Reeves in service, granted permission to suspend operations for one season, April 6.

Free substitution rule adopted for duration, April 7.

Fred Levy transferred his stock to Daniel Reeves, April 16.

Philadelphia Eagles and Pittsburgh Steelers granted permission to merge under name of Phil-Pitt Eagles, June 13.

Ted Collins granted franchise for Boston, to become active in season of 1944, or as soon thereafter as league deems advisable, June 20.

Adoption of ten-game schedule, June 20.

Player limit reduced to 28 men for one year, August 25.

Philadelphia Eagles and Pittsburgh Steelers merger automatically dissolved on last day of season, December 5.

1944—Boston Yanks granted permission to activate franchise in season of 1944, April 19.

Cleveland Rams granted permission to resume operation in season of 1944, April 19.

Player limit of 28 reaffirmed for one year, April 20.

Free substitutions adopted for another year, April 20.

Adoption of rule assessing penalty of 5 yards for kick-offs out-of-bounds, obligating kicking team to re-kick after each offense, April 20.

Coaching from bench legalized, April 20.

Dennis J. Shea re-elected treasurer of league for three years, April 20.

Chicago Cardinals and Pittsburgh Steelers requested by league to merge for one year under the name of Card-Pitt, April 21.

Card-Pitt merger dissolved automatically on last day of season, December 3.

1945—Striking an opponent with forearm or elbow (flying elbow blocks) barred, April 9.

Inbounds spot changed from 15 to 20 yards in from side-lines for one year, April 9.

Free-substitution rule renewed for one year, April 9.

Wearing of socks in league games made mandatory, April 9.

Defensive team permitted to advance with muffed snap from center, April 9.

Brooklyn Tigers and Boston Yanks merged for one year under name of "The Yanks," April 10.

Committee named to confer with colleges on all matters pertaining to eligibility of players, April 11.

1945—By V-J Day (August 14), the National Football League's service roster for World War II, limited to men who had participated in league games, totaled 638 men, 355 of whom were commissioned, 69 decorated and 21 had lost their lives.

Pre-war player limit of 33 men restored, September 15.

National League, in special executive session at Cleveland, ratified action of Commissioner Layden in which Brooklyn's franchise was declared forfeited and all players on its active and reserve lists were assigned to Boston Yanks, December 17.

1946—Elmer F. Layden resigned as Commissioner of professional football and President of the NFL, January 11.

Bert Bell, co-owner of Pittsburgh Steelers named to succeed Layden and given three-year contract, January 11.

Substitutions limited to no more than three men at a time, January 11.

Receiving team permitted to run punts and unsuccessful field goal attempts out from behind goal-line, January 11.

Forward passes made incomplete automatically upon striking either team's goal post, January 11.

Cleveland Rams franchise and club transferred to Los Angeles, January 12.

National League entered three-year, major-minor league agreement with American Association (later renamed American League), Dixie League and Pacific Coast League, January 13.

Dan Topping announced he was abandoning Brooklyn franchise to enter a new league, December 6.

World Championship game, December 15, between Chicago Bears and New York Giants in the Polo Grounds, N.Y., drew an attendance of 58,346 and gross receipts of $282,955.25, highest in league history. Each Bear got $1,975.82; each Giant $1,295.57, a new high for players.

1947—Bert Bell's contract as Commissioner of the NFL renewed for five years, January 1. An amendment to the constitution imposing a major penalty for anyone not reporting the offer of a bribe, an attempt to fix a game or any other infraction of the rules having to do with gambling, January 1.

Addition of a fifth official, with primary duties as prescribed, to be used on the field and known as back judge—adopted January 24.

Charles W. Bidwell, owner of the Chicago Cardinals, died after brief illness, April 19. Revised use of observers by Hugh L. Ray, National Football League technical adviser, resulted in 162.1 plays per game, and all-time record. It also resulted in a new record of total yards per game—542.4.

1948—A clarification of the clipping rule, permission to use an artificial tee on the kickoff, and the equipping of all officials with whistles were among the important items passed by the Rules Committee and approved at the annual meeting, January 14. Player limit increased to 35 for the entire season.

A syndicate headed by D. Lyle Fife purchased the Detroit franchise from Fred L. Mandel, Jr., Januuary 15.

Dr. John B. "Jock" Sutherland, coach of the Pittsburgh Steelers, died on April 11 after an operation.

Hugh L. Ray, NFL technical adviser, reported that another new all-time high in plays per game had been reached in 1947 with 165.5, and that total yards had climbed to a new mark of 643.3.

1949—A syndicate headed by James P. Clark purchased the franchise of the Philadelphia Eagles from Alexis Thompson, January 15.

Bert Bell, as Commissioner-President, and Dennis Shea, as vice-president and treasurer of the NFL, appointed for ten-year terms, January 20.

Player limit of 32 adopted, January 20.

Free- substitution rule adopted for one year, January 20.

Unanimous consent of the league given for the cancellation of the Boston franchise and a new franchise award to Ted Collins in New York City under the name of the New York Bulldogs, January 21.

Hugh L. Ray, technical adviser, announced that 29 new records had been set during 1948, with 174.5 plays per game, 659 yards per game and many individual marks.

Bert Bell, Commissioner of the NFL, and Arthur Friedlund, representing the All America Football Conference, announced a merger of the two leagues. Baltimore, Cleveland and San Francisco joined the ten teams in the NFL with the balance of AAFC players placed in a pool from which they would be drafted by the 13 teams in the new organization.

1950—Free-substitution rule adopted for an indefinite time, January 23.

Upon advice of counsel and the unanimous consent of the member clubs the commissioner announced that the league would use the name National Football League, divided into National and American conferences. The American Conference to include: Chicago Cardinals, Cleveland Browns, New York Giants, Philadelphia Eagles, Pittsburgh Steelers, Washington Redskins. The National Conference: Baltimore Colts, Chicago Bears, Detroit Lions, Green Bay Packers, Los Angeles Rams, New York Yanks, San Francisco 49ers.

Carl L. Storck, secretary-treasurer of the NFL from 1921 to 1939 and president from 1939 to 1941, died in Dayton, Ohio, March 13.

A new all-time record for attendance during the regular playing season was established. A total of 1,977,556 fans witnessed the 78 games. Two play-off games drew 106,896. The championship game was attended by 29,751.

1951—The first Pro Bowl game was played, January 14, under the auspices of the Los Angeles Publishers' Association before 53,676 spectators in Los Angeles Coliseum, the American Conference All-Stars beating the National Conference All-Stars, 28–27. George P. Marshall fostered the adoption of the game by the league.

Player limit of 33 voted. A minimum of 25 men must be dressed for a championship game, January 18.

No tackle, guard or center may become eligible for a forward pass, January 18.

Baltimore Colt franchise cancelled.

Frank J. Jonet, pioneer in professional football and active with Green Bay since its inception, died at the age of 69 (August 17).

1952—The assets and franchise of the New York Yanks were purchased by the National Football League, January 19.

A new franchise was awarded the Dallas Texans after they purchased the assets of the New York Yanks from the National Football League, January 24.

The tackle eligible rule was made permanent January 18.

On pass interference on the part of the offense, the penalty shall be fifteen yards from the previous spot and not loss of down. Adopted January 18.

CHAPTER 2
THE COMMISSIONER'S OFFICE

THE FUNCTIONS OF
THE COMMISSIONER'S OFFICE

The Office of the Commissioner of the National Football League is the clearing house through which passes all the business of the organization. It is the keystone of the arch around which the member teams have built their own business structures.

A recital of all that the league office does would fill many pages. A brief summary of its activities will give the reader some idea of its functions as the headquarters of the league.

The Commissioner must approve every contract made between a club and a player, also all trades and sales of players. A card bearing the complete playing record of each player is kept as part of the permanent records of the league office. The eligibility of every player, according to the Constitution and By-Laws, must be proved to the Commissioner's satisfaction.

All officials, referees, umpires, field judges, back judges and linesmen are appointed by the Commissioner and assigned by him to teams of officials. For pre-season and regular season games the officiating teams are assigned to games by the Commissioner.

The Commissioner must approve all contracts for pre-season games. This involves an investigation of promoters of proposed contests, the sites of the games and other matters directly related to the games.

Every employee of every club in the league must be approved by the Commissioner. This includes not only the coaches but those responsible for management, trainers and other personnel.

The Commissioner drafts a schedule of games for each season, a task that requires several hundred hours of work.

From the Commissioner's office are sent bulletins of information to each club: the list of players signed and those being waived by teams: facts about the sale of players, which must have the Commissioner's approval before being consummated. The office compiles a reserve list of players numbering about 1,500 names and sends master questionnaires to every player whose contract is approved.

The Commissioner presides at the annual business meeting of the league. He is also the final court of appeal in any dispute between club and player. He enforces the Constitution and By-Laws of the league. He has the power to suspend and/or fine any player or executive of the league who violates the Constitution and By-Laws. The Commissioner also has sole power over the World Championship football game played each year between the winners of the Conference championships.

The Office of the Commissioner includes a treasurer, a publicity director and such assistants as the Commissioner requires for the proper conduct of his office. A technical assistant who interprets rules and keeps records of officials is a member of the Commissioner's staff.

All the statistical records of the teams and individual players are kept in the Commissioner's office. During the season these are released weekly to the press, radio and television. At the conclusion of the season the final statistics are compiled and released.

The annual *Record and Rules Manual* of the league, which contains the league's records, history, statistics, rules and other information, is edited in the office of the Commissioner.

THE ROSTER OF
NATIONAL FOOTBALL LEAGUE OFFICIALS

DOWNES' CREW

Downes, William, Referee, Illinois Tech.
Brubaker, Carl H., Umpire, Ohio Wesleyan
Pecoraro, Samuel, Headlinesman, Dallas University
Mettler, Victor, Back Judge, Notre Dame
Sweeney, Charles, Field Judge, Notre Dame

GIANGRECO'S CREW

Giangreco, Samuel, Referee, Manhattan College
Castree, Gilbert, Umpire, Univ. of Virginia
Cooperman, Samuel E., Headlinesman, Muhlenberg
Rebele, Carl, Back Judge, Penn State
Palazzi, Louis J., Field Judge, Penn State

GIBBS' CREW

Gibbs, Ronald, Referee, St. Thomas
Beiersdorfer, James, Umpire, None
Tehan, Dan, Headlinesman, Xavier University
Austin, Robert C., Back Judge, St. Ambrose
McHugh, William F., Field Judge, De Paul University

GLASCOTT'S CREW

Glascott, John, Referee, Pennsylvania
Wilson, Samuel M., Umpire, Lehigh
Berry, Charles F., Headlinesman, Lafayette
Jaworowski, Stanley, Back Judge, Georgetown
Lisetski, Michael, Field Judge, Muhlenberg

HEINTZ'S CREW

Heintz, Emil, Referee, Pennsylvania
Carter, W. Joe, Umpire, Austin (Texas)
Evans, Lon, Headlinesman, Texas Christian
O'Brien, David, Back Judge, Texas Christian
Looney, Don, Field Judge, Texas Christian

TIMLIN'S CREW

Timlin, Thomas A., Referee, Niagara University
Crowley, Joseph G., Umpire, Muhlenberg
Kane, James A., Headlinesman, Loyola College (Md)
Hamer, James E., Back Judge, California St. Tchrs
Brazil, Lloyd, Field Judge, Univ. of Detroit

WALLACE'S CREW

Wallace, Yans, Referee, None
Connell, Joseph L., Umpire, Univ. of Pittsburgh
Highberger, John M., Headlinesman, Carnegie Tech.
Haines, Henry, Back Judge, Penn State
Grimberg, William H., Field Judge, Villanova

ALTERNATES

Hale, I. B., Texas Christian
Vergara, George, Notre Dame

COAST OFFICIALS
BOWEN'S CREW

Bowen, Rawson, Referee, U.C.L.A.
Terremere, Albert J., Umpire, Santa Clara
Hutchison, Elvin, Headlinesman, U.S.C.
Rothert, Harlow P., Back Judge, Stanford
Underhill, James T., Field Judge, St. Mary's (Calif.)

H. BRUBAKER'S CREW

Brubaker, Harry, Referee, Loyola (L.A.)
Gardner, Cletus, Umpire, Villanova
Grenier, Jacques, Headlinesman, U. of New Hampshire
Duncan, Norman D., Back Judge, U.C.L.A.
Houston, Lawrence, Field Judge, U.C.L.A.

ALTERNATE

Ebding, Harry J., St. Mary's (Calif.)

THE OFFICIALS' SIGNALS

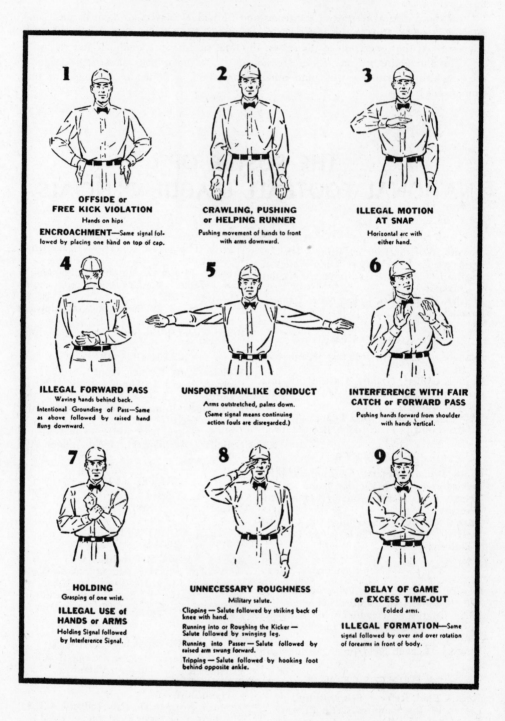

1

OFFSIDE or FREE KICK VIOLATION
Hands on hips

ENCROACHMENT—Same signal followed by placing one hand on top of cap.

2

CRAWLING, PUSHING or HELPING RUNNER
Pushing movement of hands to front with arms downward.

3

ILLEGAL MOTION AT SNAP
Horizontal arc with either hand.

4

ILLEGAL FORWARD PASS
Waving hands behind back.
Intentional Grounding of Pass—Same as above followed by raised hand flung downward.

5

UNSPORTSMANLIKE CONDUCT
Arms outstretched, palms down.
(Same signal means continuing action fouls are disregarded.)

6

INTERFERENCE WITH FAIR CATCH or FORWARD PASS
Pushing hands forward from shoulder with hands vertical.

7

HOLDING
Grasping of one wrist.

ILLEGAL USE of HANDS or ARMS
Holding Signal followed by Interference Signal.

8

UNNECESSARY ROUGHNESS
Military salute.

Clipping — Salute followed by striking back of knee with hand.
Running into or Roughing the Kicker — Salute followed by swinging leg.
Running into Passer — Salute followed by raised arm swung forward.
Tripping — Salute followed by hooking foot behind opposite ankle.

9

DELAY OF GAME or EXCESS TIME-OUT
Folded arms.

ILLEGAL FORMATION—Same signal followed by over and over rotation of forearms in front of body.

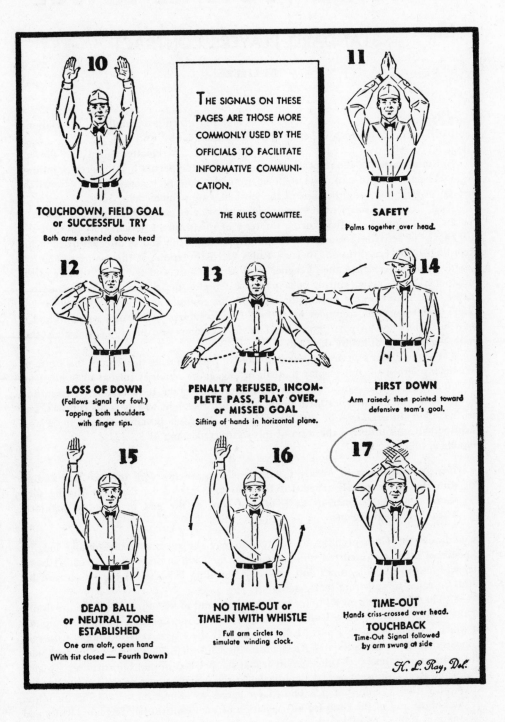

10

TOUCHDOWN, FIELD GOAL or SUCCESSFUL TRY

Both arms extended above head

THE SIGNALS ON THESE PAGES ARE THOSE MORE COMMONLY USED BY THE OFFICIALS TO FACILITATE INFORMATIVE COMMUNICATION.

THE RULES COMMITTEE.

11

SAFETY

Palms together over head.

12

LOSS OF DOWN

(Follows signal for foul.) Tapping both shoulders with finger tips.

13

PENALTY REFUSED, INCOMPLETE PASS, PLAY OVER, or MISSED GOAL

Sifting of hands in horizontal plane.

14

FIRST DOWN

Arm raised, then pointed toward defensive team's goal.

15

DEAD BALL or NEUTRAL ZONE ESTABLISHED

One arm aloft, open hand
(With fist closed — Fourth Down)

16

NO TIME-OUT or TIME-IN WITH WHISTLE

Full arm circles to simulate winding clock.

17

TIME-OUT

Hands criss-crossed over head.

TOUCHBACK

Time-Out Signal followed by arm swung at side

H. L. Ray, Del.

NATIONAL FOOTBALL LEAGUE

STANDARD PLAYERS CONTRACT

BETWEEN

....

....

which operates ...., and which is a member of the National Football League, and which is hereinafter called the "Club," and ....
.... of .... hereinafter called the "Player."

In consideration of the respective promises herein the parties hereto agree as follows:

1. The term of this contract shall be from the date of execution hereof until the first day of May following the close of the football season commencing in ....
................., subject however, to rights of prior termination as specified herein.

2. The Player agrees that during the term of this contract he will play football and will engage in activities related to football only for the Club and as directed by the Club according to the Constitution, By-laws, Rules and Regulations of the National Football League, hereinafter called the "League," and of the Club, and the Club, subject to the provisions hereof, agrees during such period to employ the Player as a skilled football player. The Player agrees during the term of this contract to report promptly for the Club's training seasons, to render his full time services during the training seasons and at the Club's direction to participate in all practice sessions and in all League and other football games scheduled by the Club.

3. For the Player's services as a skilled football player during the term of this contract, and for his agreement not to play football or engage in activities related to football for any other person, firm, corporation or institution during the term of this contract, and for the option hereinafter set forth giving the Club the right to renew his contract, and for the other undertakings of the Player herein, the Club promises to pay the Player each football season during the term of this contract the sum of $...............to be payable as follows:

75% of said salary in weekly installments commencing with the first and ending with the last regularly scheduled League game played by the Club during such season and the balance of 25% of said sum at the end of said last regularly scheduled League game.

In addition, the Club promises and agrees to pay the reasonable board and lodging expenses of the Player incurred while playing for the Club in other than the Club's home city and also to pay all proper and necessary travelling expenses of the Player and his meals en route to and from said games.

4. The Player agrees at all times to comply with and to be bound by all the provisions of the Constitution, By-laws, Rules and Regulations of the League and of the Club, all of which are hereby made a part of this contract. If the Player fails to comply with said Constitution, By-laws, Rules and Regulations the Club shall have the right to terminate this contract or to take such other action as may be specified in said Constitution, By-laws, Rules and Regulations, or as may be directed by the Commissioner of the League, hereinafter called the "Commissioner." The Player agrees to submit himself to the discipline of the League and of the Club for any violation of such Constitution, By-laws, Rules and Regulations subject however, to the right to a hearing by the Commissioner. All matters in dispute between the Player and the Club shall be referred to the Commissioner and his decision shall be accepted as final, complete, conclusive, binding and unappealable,

by the Player and by the Club. The Player hereby waives any and all rights of action against the Commissioner, the League, the Club or any of its members or stockholders, and against any officer of the Club or of the League arising out of or in connection with decisions of the Commissioner, except to the extent of awards made by the Commissioner to the Player. The Player hereby acknowledges that he has read said Constitution, By-laws, Rules and Regulations and that he understands their meaning.

5. The Player promises and agrees that during the term of this contract he will not play football or engage in activities related to football for any other person, firm, corporation or institution except with the prior written consent of the Club and the Commissioner, and that he will not during the term of this contract engage in any game or exhibition of baseball, basketball, hockey, wrestling, boxing or any other sport which endangers his ability to perform his services hereunder, without the prior written consent of the Club. The Player likewise promises and agrees that during the term of this contract, when, as and if he shall receive an invitation to participate in any All-Star football game which is approved by the League, he will play in said game in accordance with all the terms and conditions relating thereto, including the player compensation there in set forth, as are agreed to between the League and the Sponsor of such game.

6. The Player represents and warrants that he is and will continue to be sufficiently highly skilled in all types of football team play to play professional football of the caliber required by the League and by the Club, that he is and will continue to be in excellent physical condition, and agrees to perform his services hereunder to the complete satisfaction of the Club and its Head Coach. If in the opinion of the Head Coach the Player does not maintain himself in excellent physical condition or fails at any time during the football seasons included in the term of this contract to demonstrate sufficient skill and capacity to play professional football of the caliber required by the League and by the Club, or if in the opinion of the Head Coach the Player's work or conduct in the performance of this contract is unsatisfactory as compared with the work and conduct of other members of the Club's squad of players, the Club shall have the right to terminate this contract upon written notice to the player of such termination.

7. Upon termination of this contract the Club shall pay the Player only the balance remaining due him for travelling and board and lodging expenses and any balance remaining due him for football seasons completed prior to termination, and, if termination takes place during a football season, any balance remaining due him on that portion of his total compensation for that season as provided in paragraph 3 hereof which the number of regularly scheduled League games already played by the Club during that season bears to the total number of League games scheduled for the Club for that season.

8. The Player hereby represents that he has special, exceptional and unique knowledge, skill and ability as a football player, the loss of which cannot be estimated with any certainty and cannot be fairly or adequately compensated by damages and therefore agrees that the Club shall have the right, in addition to any other rights which the Club may possess, to enjoin him by appropriate injunction proceedings against playing football or engaging in activities related to football for any person, firm, corporation or institution and against any other breach of this contract.

9. It is mutually agreed that the Club shall have the right to sell, exchange, assign and transfer this contract and the Player's services to any other Club of the League and the Player agrees to accept such assignment and to report promptly to the assignee club and faithfully to perform and carry out this contract with the assignee club as if it had been entered into by the Player with the assignee club instead of with this Club.

10. On or before the date of expiration of this contract, the Club may, upon notice in writing to the Player, renew this contract for a further term until the first day of May following said expiration on the same terms, including rate of compensation to the Player, as are provided by this contract, except that after such renewal this contract shall not include a further option to the Club to renew the contract; the phrase 'rate of

compensation' as above used shall not be understood to include bonus payments or payments of any nature whatsoever other than the precise sum set forth in paragraph '3' hereof.

11. Player acknowledges the right and power of the Commissioner of the National Football League (a) to fine and suspend, (b) to fine and suspend for life or indefinitely, and/or (c) to cancel the contract of, any player who accepts a bribe or who agrees to throw or fix a game or who, having knowledge of the same, fails to report an offered bribe or an attempt to throw or fix a game, or who bets on a game, or who is guilty of any conduct detrimental to the welfare of the National Football League or of professional football; and the Player hereby releases the Commissioner of the National Football League, individually and in his official capacity, and also the National Football League and every club and every officer, director and stockholder of the League and of every club thereof, jointly, and severally, from all claims and demands for damages and every claim and demand whatsoever he may have arising out of or in connection with the decision of said Commissioner of the National Football League in any of the aforesaid cases.

12. This agreement contains the entire agreement between the parties and there are no oral or written inducements, promises or agreements except as contained herein. This agreement shall become valid and binding upon party hereto only when, as and if it shall be approved by the Commissioner.

13. This agreement has been made under and shall be governed by the laws of the State of ....

IN WITNESS WHEREOF the Player has hereunto set his hand and seal and the Club has caused this contract to be executed by its duly authorized officer on the date set opposite their respective names.

WITNESS:

....
....   Club
                             Date   By ....

....
....
                             Date   Player

Approved ....
        Commissioner   Date   Player's Address
           This Copy to be Sent to Commissioner for Approval
                        Return to Member Club

THE 1952 LEAGUE SCHEDULE

SUNDAY, SEPTEMBER 28
1. Chicago Bears at Green Bay   1:30
2. Detroit at San Francisco   2:30
3. Los Angeles at Cleveland   2:00
4. New York Giants at Dallas   2:00
5. Philadelphia at Pittsburgh   2:00

MONDAY, SEPTEMBER 29 (NIGHT)
6. Washington at Chicago Cardinals 8:30

FRIDAY, OCTOBER 3 (NIGHT)
7. Detroit at Los Angeles   8:30

SATURDAY, OCTOBER 4 (NIGHT)
8. Cleveland at Pittsburgh   8:30
9. New York Giants at Philadelphia 8:30

SUNDAY, OCTOBER 5
10. Chicago Bears at Chicago
    Cardinals   1:30

11. San Francisco at Dallas   2:00
12. Washington vs. Green Bay at
    Milwaukee   1:30

SUNDAY, OCTOBER 12
13. Chicago Cardinals at Washington 2:00
14. Dallas at Chicago Bears   1:30
15. Los Angeles vs. Green Bay at
    Milwaukee   1:30
16. New York Giants at Cleveland   2:00
17. Pittsburgh at Philadelphia   2:00
18. San Francisco at Detroit   2:00

SATURDAY, OCTOBER 18 (NIGHT)
19. Green Bay at Dallas   8:30

SUNDAY, OCTOBER 19
20. Chicago Cardinals at New York
    Giants   2:05
21. Cleveland at Philadelphia   2:00

22. Los Angeles at Detroit — 2:00
23. San Francisco at Chicago Bears — 1:30
24. Washington at Pittsburgh — 2:00

SUNDAY, OCTOBER 26

25. Chicago Bears at Los Angeles — 2:00
26. Dallas at San Francisco — 2:30
27. Detroit at Green Bay — 1:30
28. Philadelphia at New York Giants — 2:05
29. Pittsburgh at Chicago Cardinals — 1:30
30. Washington at Cleveland — 2:00

SUNDAY, NOVEMBER 2

31. Chicago Bears at San Francisco — 2:00
32. Cleveland at Detroit — 2:00
33. Dallas at Los Angeles — 2:00
34. New York Giants at Chicago Cardinals — 1:30
35. Philadelphia vs. Green Bay at Milwaukee — 1:30
36. Pittsburgh at Washington — 2:00

SUNDAY, NOVEMBER 9

37. Chicago Cardinals at Cleveland — 2:00
38. Detroit at Pittsburgh — 2:00
39. Green Bay at Chicago Bears — 1:30
40. Los Angeles at Dallas — 2:00
41. San Francisco at New York Giants — 2:05
42. Washington at Philadelphia — 2:00

SUNDAY, NOVEMBER 16

43. Chicago Cardinals at Philadelphia — 2:00
44. Dallas at Detroit — 2:00
45. Green Bay at New York Giants — 2:05
46. Los Angeles at Chicago Bears — 1:30
47. Pittsburgh at Cleveland — 2:00
48. San Francisco at Washington — 2:00

SUNDAY, NOVEMBER 23

49. Chicago Cardinals at Pittsburgh — 2:00
50. Dallas at Green Bay — 1:00
51. Detroit at Chicago Bears — 1:30
52. New York Giants at Washington — 2:00
53. Philadelphia at Cleveland — 2:00
54. San Francisco at Los Angeles — 2:00

THURSDAY, NOVEMBER 27 (THANKSGIVING)

55. Green Bay at Detroit — 12:00

SUNDAY, NOVEMBER 30

56. Chicago Bears at Dallas — 2:00
57. Cleveland at Washington — 2:00
58. Los Angeles at San Francisco — 2:00
59. New York Giants at Pittsburgh — 2:00
60. Philadelphia at Chicago Cardinals — 1:30

SUNDAY, DECEMBER 7

61. Chicago Bears at Detroit — 2:00
62. Cleveland at Chicago Cardinals — 1:00
63. Dallas at Philadelphia — 2:00
64. Green Bay at Los Angeles — 2:00
65. Pittsburgh at San Francisco — 2:00
66. Washington at New York Giants — 2:05

SUNDAY, DECEMBER 14

67. Chicago Cardinals at Chicago Bears — 1:00
68. Cleveland at New York Giants — 2:05
69. Detroit at Dallas — 2:00
70. Green Bay at San Francisco — 2:00
71. Philadelphia at Washington — 2:00
72. Pittsburgh at Los Angeles — 2:00

SUNDAY, DECEMBER 21

World's Championship Playoff Game in home city of American Conference Champion.

CHAPTER 3
THE COACHES

If one basic truth has been established in more than thirty years of major league football, it is that playing experience, plus an apprenticeship of assistant coaching in the big time, is necessary before any man can become a successful coach in the National Football League. In all the years there has been but one exception to that truth, namely, Paul Brown of the Cleveland Browns. Others without these two items of experience have never ranked better than mediocre. The historic trail of the record books is strewn with the whitening bones of "brilliant" college coaches who ventured across the borders of the major league and were immediately scalped, skinned and skunked by tactics they never knew existed. They found that defenses which are air-tight in the college game are wide open to big league attack. They found that veteran brain trusts circulate around George Halas, Steve Owen, Jim Conzelman, Curley Lambeau and Greasy Neale, licking their chops and reveling in new brands of mayhem to be practiced against outraged beginners. Many of them "resigned in mid-season"; some finished one or two years before fleeing back from whence they came.

A second basic truth has been established—that psychology, which stems from the head coach, has become the vital difference between winning and losing; that there is only a microscopic difference in playing ability between the team that wins the championship and the team which finishes in last place; that the difference is the head coach's ability to get his squad psychologically "up" for the important games.

Team spirit, when it is running near the crest in major league football, is the strongest, most devastating and unbeatable factor in any American sport. Men who can stand up and survive in this most violent contact battle must possess to high degree the qualities which produce the finest ideals of team spirit. There can be no malingering, no half-throttle courage, no playing for self alone. The head coach must blend the violent personalities of more than thirty adult males, all full of their own idiosyncrasies, into one unit. Each major league club is made up of thirty-three outstanding stars. There are no "bush-leaguers" around.

As the NFL moves into its thirty-second season in 1952, only George Halas, of those who were there when it started, still remains in a head coaching capacity. Steve Owen, who first appeared as a player in 1924, and has coached the New York Giants since 1932, adds further glory to his record each season. Curly Lambeau, another charter member, has dropped out after thirty-one years as player and coach, but may be back any minute. Jimmy Conzelman, who fled to the less nerve-wracking field of advertising after taking the Chicago Cardinals into two consecutive division titles and one championship in 1947–48, is a proven top man who could come back to do it again with any squad in the league. Earle "Greasy" Neale has won his Master's Degree but is in temporary hiding from the murderous nerve strain that a season of big league football demands.

Behind these veterans a new generation is moving up, properly hardened on the field of battle and with adequate experience as assistants. Gene Ronzani at Green Bay, Buddy Parker at Detroit, Joe Stydahar at Los Angeles, Wayne Millner at Philadelphia,

Joe Bach at Pittsburgh, Dick Todd at Washington and Joe Kuharich at the Chicago Cardinals have shown that they know what they are doing as head coaches in the major league game, that they need only the talent and a few lucky bounces to put them on top. Back in the ranks, piling up priceless experience, are many who are nearly ready to step into the front row. And on all successful teams you find unsung, veteran assistants, busy each season teaching the basic principles of football to college rookies, scouting the opponents, calling plays from their observation posts, inventing, in split-seconds, new

Fran Byrne

CHICAGO BEAR COACHING STAFF, 1951 (LEFT TO RIGHT: LUKE JOHNSOS, ENDS; GEORGE HALAS, HEAD COACH; CLARK SHAUGHNESSY, STRATEGY; PADDY DRISCOLL, BACKS)

strategies of attack and defense to meet new situations. Their names would be Walter Kiesling, Clark Shaughnessy, Tarzan Taylor, Luke Johnsos, Ed Kolman, Hampton Pool, Chuck Cherundulo, Paddy Driscoll, Jim Trimble, Herman Ball and many others.

As mentioned before, Paul Brown has been the only one who has skipped the routine apprenticeships and sailed firmly into the top bracket. During his four years in the All America Football Conference, when Brown and his Browns won 47 of 54 games, National League coaches watched smugly, believing, with considerable wisdom, that he wasn't beating much. When Cleveland moved into the NFL in 1950, they were grinning tigers waiting for a little rabbit named Paul Brown.

But Paul Brown did not choose to be a rabbit. He served notice of his intentions during the pre-season games by walloping the Chicago Bears in a contest that was blood-and-thunder from the opening whistle. When the season was over, Paul Brown had led his team to the championship and had made it look just as easy as it had been in the old All America. Veterans of the NFL have never quite recovered.

Within the list of coaches that follows are the names of the men responsible for nearly all football innovations that have stood the test of time and experience to become part of the game as it is played, not only in the major leagues, but also in thousands of colleges and schools all over the United States. George Halas, with occasional help from Clark Shaughnessy, has developed the T-formation to its present spectacular effectiveness. Steve Owen, although best known as a master of defense and father of the "umbrella," which is actually a variation of the 6-1-4 alignment, also came up with the "A" and "double A" offenses. Greasy Neale harassed his opponents during recent years with his eight-man defensive line, a maneuver which drove T quarterbacks crazy as they tried to avoid that extra man. Ronzani at Green Bay developed some new spread ideas during 1951 which will be stolen and used to supplement the T on other squads in the years to come.

At Los Angeles, blessed with two passers who ranked first and second in the league in 1951, Joe Stydahar has been throwing the ball as it has never been thrown before to win his division title twice and the championship in 1951. Not all teams have Waterfield and Van Brocklin to back up a similar policy—nor receivers like Hirsch and Fears and Glenn Davis. Paul Brown's specialty, with Otto Graham doing the pitching, is a pass to the sidelines that stops the clock as soon as it is caught, and is a chronically successful maneuver which has saved the Browns time and again.

These coaches are the men who have made major league football into the fastest growing, most evenly matched season of combat the American sports world can offer. They live football 365 days a year, planning, scheming, inventing new blocking, new decoys, new maneuvers to thrill the fans in the years to come. They have the courage and mental stability to take the bad breaks and come back for more. They have lost games—and championships—by one freak bounce of the erratic football. And not one of them will disagree with the favorite statement of George Halas, dean of them all, who says: "I'd rather be lucky than good." That is their eternal creed.

THE COACHES IN 1951 AND 1952

Chicago Bears

GEORGE S. HALAS

George Stanley Halas, aged twenty-two, his football career finished at the University of Illinois, sat at his team's banquet in the early winter of 1917 and listened to the farewell speech of Bob Zuppke, his coach, who was complaining bitterly about certain traditional patterns of life.

"Why is it," Zup demanded, "that just when you players are beginning to know something about football after three years, I lose you—and you stop playing? It makes no sense. Football is the only sport that ends a man's career just when it should be beginning."

That remark by Bob Zuppke might well be credited with starting a series of cosmic reactions which resulted, thirty-five years later, in more than two million rabid major league football fans scrambling into National Football League parks to watch America's most thrilling sport. For the words made something click in the brain of Left End Halas, Navy-bound at the moment, but unhappy because he still had a lot of football left in his system and he didn't want it to rot there.

Halas had been an all-round athlete at Illinois, which he chose for an engineering course after graduating from Crane Tech in his native Chicago. He'd been so good at baseball that the New York Yankees wanted him as soon as the war was over. At basketball he had sparkled, becoming team captain in his senior year. But football was his own first choice, and he had become an end instead of a halfback as he had planned, because, as Zuppke once said, "he ran so hard I was afraid he'd get killed as a halfback."

It was a happy surprise to George Halas when he reported to Great Lakes Naval Training Station to learn that the Navy was going to have football too, and that there were plenty of stars on hand to make it roll. Emmett Keefe, a guard from Notre Dame, was captain of the team. John "Paddy" Driscoll, a flashy back from Northwestern, was part of the backfield which included the versatile Jim Conzelman, Harold Erickson, Dutch Lauer and many others. Hugh Blacklock was a roadblock at tackle next to end George Halas, a neighborly pairing which was to endure long after the war was over.

Great Lakes was good enough to tie Notre Dame, to beat the Naval Academy at Annapolis, to be chosen to play in the Rose Bowl on New Year's Day, 1919, where they caused a sensation by upsetting the tremendous team from the base at Mare Island.

Halas was discharged as an ensign and soon reported to the Yankee baseball team in Florida, depressed once more because he still had lots of football left in his fuel-system and it seemed that now it must surely be over for him. He soon won a permanent job with the Yankees. Then he sustained a leg injury in a thundering slide into third base after belting one of Rube Marquard's slants through the outfield during an exhibition game. The injury sidelined him and eventually caused his release to St. Paul. He finished an impressive rookie season there and was headed back to the Yankees the next spring. But he was still restless for more football; he still remembered Bob Zuppke's remarks.

He managed to play a few football games that fall with the independent team of Hammond, Indiana, and then came the break which led the way to the Chicago Bears and the National Football League.

Mr. A. E. Staley, owner of a corn products company in Decatur, Illinois, was a sports fan who wanted his firm to be represented by teams in all possible sports. Joe "Iron Man" McGinnity managed the strong Staley baseball team. Why shouldn't George Halas, the young firebrand who would play football twenty-four hours a day if he could arrange it, be the Staley football leader?

It was all right with Halas. He worked full hours at the plant, played on its baseball team and started recruiting football players with the same acumen and fervor he still employs. When the American Professional Football Association was organized in Ralph Hays's garage at Canton, Ohio, that fall, Halas was there, ready to go with a roster of players that scared the other owners half to death. He proposed to line up with Guy Chamberlain and himself at end; Hugh Blacklock and Bert Ingwerson at tackle; Hubbard Shoemaker and Jerry Jones at guard; George Trafton, center; and the backs would be Ed "Dutch" Sternaman, Jake Lanum, Bob Koehler, Walter "Pard" Pearce and Charlie Dressen. They were the cream of the college crop. His only disappointment was the fact that Paddy Driscoll had joined the Chicago Cardinals and it would be six years before Halas could sign him to a contract.

The Staleys were indeed loaded with talent and end-coach-manager George Halas was a clever field general. They won every game until the Cardinals dumped them, 7–6. Then they came back to whip the Cards, 10–0, to finish a glorious season.

Papa Bear was on his way.

During the ensuing three decades, Halas and his Monsters of the Midway have dominated football. They have won the most championships, 7; they have won the most games, over 400; they have scored the most points, more than 11,000; they have gained the most yards, nearly 25 miles; they have scored the most touchdowns, nearly 1,600; have played to most fans, nearly 15,000,000. They have probably made the most money. And they have definitely been penalized the most.

Individually, too, they have sparkled. Their Sid Luckman holds records for most TD passes in one season (28) and in one game (7). George Halas himself holds a twenty-nine-year-old record that still stands —a 98-yard run with a recovered fumble. The entire tribe of Jim Thorpe's Oorang Indians was whooping in pursuit. He had to make the touchdown or get scalped.

The list of Bear players shines brighter than all the rest in the honor rolls of football. They have been noted for team spirit and have won many games with inferior teams because of this spirit, which originates in the explosive violence and the competitive drive of their owner-coach. Since he retired as a player in 1932 ("When they began to run over me, under me, around me and through me"), Halas has prowled the sidelines through every game, except during World War II when he served in the Navy as a commander. Every cell in his body is in every play, and his spectacular rages against officiating lapses have bemused hundreds of thousands of fans.

Halas made a habit of writing "first" into the record book from the start. The Bears were the first official champions of the reorganized league in 1921 when they moved to Chicago to play that season as the Staleys and to become the Bears a year later. They were the first professional team to practice daily; the first big league team to travel coast-to-coast (the Red Grange Unveiling Tour, which started in Chicago on Thanksgiving Day, 1925, ended three months later after playing in New York, Washington, Providence, Pittsburgh, Detroit, Chicago again, Tampa, Jacksonville, Miami, New Orleans, Los Angeles, San Diego, San Francisco, Portland and Seattle). Other minor firsts were a band and a team song, and a club newspaper; and they were the first to have their games broadcast on radio, and to take movies of games for study and strategy.

Nearly every team which plays football under the banner of T-formation in 1952, whether it be professional, college or grade school, will be using plays which were first diagrammed by the Chicago Bears, which means by George Halas and his Bear-trained staff, all former Bear stars, with occasional help from the brilliant theorist, Clark Shaughnessy, now a Bear vice-president. Halas added the man-in-motion to the ineffective T of older days and made it come alive. In 1937, he bet the future of his team on the ability of an awkward young halfback named Sidney Luckman to make it work. Luckman floundered for a few weeks, but suddenly, through unbeatable determination and endless hours of practice, he got it and a new era was born in football. Halas, Luckman and the T grew to maturity together.

Luckman went on to rank himself as the smartest field general of them all. His nickname, "Mr. Quarterback," was well earned. Today George Halas will testify under oath that Sid Luckman never called a wrong play during twelve years of action; that he was always thinking so far ahead of his opponents, his teammates and everyone else, that he drove most of them crazy, including George Halas himself.

It was inevitable that someday George Halas would come up with a performance that would live forever as the mark of perfection. It happened in Griffith Stadium, Washington, D.C. on December 8, 1940, and when it was over, Steve Owen, coach of the New York Giants, which team had finished third in the Eastern division behind the Redskins, had this to say, "Now I'm glad we didn't win the Eastern championship. In fact, I'm glad we didn't finish second. Even that would have been too close to the Bears today."

For the story of that spectacle, unparalleled in football history and unlikely to be repeated, this encyclopedia will borrow from that fine book, *The Chicago Bears,* written by Howard Roberts, pro football expert of the Chicago *Daily News,* and published by G. P. Putnam's Sons, the complete story of the cold-blooded, premeditated massacre of a sorrowful group of young men known as the Washington Redskins. It was a crime committed with well-planned malice aforethought. In sixty minutes of official play, George Halas made his team do everything lethal a football team can do a little better than it has ever been done before or since, to score a staggering 73-0 humiliation over one of the strongest teams Washington has ever had —and they have had some dandies; to annihilate a team which had beaten the Bears, 7-3, only three weeks before.

It was the masterpiece of football, fashioned by George Halas. This is the way Roberts saw it:

Sunday, December 8, 1940, was a beautiful day in Washington. The sun shone brilliantly and with a warmth surprisingly pleasant for the time of year. The sky was blue and cloudless. Scarcely a breeze rippled the flags over Griffith Stadium where 36,034 people clustered in quivering anticipation as their Redskins prepared to face the Bears for the championship.

Two hours later, although the sun still shone, it was the darkest day the nation's capital would know until another Sunday, 364 days later, when Jap bombs fell on Pearl Harbor to plunge the United States into war.

The events that filled those two hours are unparalleled in sports history. They were so beyond comprehension that even those who saw them or took part in them have difficulty believing it wasn't a dream. To all but a handful of those 36,034 the dream was a nightmare, yet they left the park content. They were disappointed, certainly, but not unhappy. After all, they could tell their grandchildren that they had witnessed the impossible; that they had looked on perfection.

The Bears were perfection that day. There is no other explanation for the score that reads like a misprint in the record books: Chicago Bears 73; Washington Redskins 0.

The score itself is a story, but back of it is another one, a tale of psychology, of emotional uplift, of planning so meticulous that almost nothing was left to chance— except the fervent hope the Redskins would employ the same defense that had kept their goal line inviolate three weeks before.

Halas and his board of strategy knew from bitter experience that Washington was not a team to be taken lightly, for with Slingin' Sammy Baugh pitching passes, the Redskins were almost certain to score against the best of defenses. The trick was to keep Baugh from passing, in so far as that could be achieved. And the best way to keep Sammy from throwing touchdowns was to keep his hands off the ball as much as possible. If the Bears could control the ball throughout most of the afternoon, they might be able to outscore the enemy.

With that in mind, the faculty of Halas U. set about polishing their T until it shone. Movies of the Redskin defeat were studied over and over again. So were films of other Bear-Redskin games. From these showings and from the penciled notes in the coach's little black book were culled only the plays that had worked against Washington. These were perfected and refined; new variations were added; plays the Redskins had stopped were discarded and replaced by new ones calculated to take advantage of Ray Flaherty's defense.

The players saw the movies almost as many times as did the coaches. Every play was analyzed—why this one worked, why that one didn't, what this mistake cost, what that good block accomplished. The Bears, seeing their previous mistakes pointed out on the screen, vowed they wouldn't happen again. Morning practice on the field was followed by chalk talks, lectures, written examinations on individual assignments, more movies. Clark Shaughnessy was brought in to discuss strategy with the quarterbacks—Luckman, Masterson and Solly Sherman.

The greatest weapon Halas brought into play was psychology. The Redskins had made what Halas termed some "tactical vocal errors" after the earlier 7–3 victory, and now they were deftly turned against them. It seems that a club official with a careless disregard for the interpretation that might be placed on his words, had been quoted in the public prints as referring to the Bears by such uncomplimentary terms, as "front-runners" and a "first-half ball club." The Redskins themselves had called the Bears "crybabies" in the final minute of their earlier meeting.

When the Bears came to practice the Monday morning preceding the championship game, their eyes fell upon these disparagements of their courage and staying power plastering the walls of the clubhouse. The reaction was terrific. Mutterings grew to shouts of revenge. The boys were mad clean through. Halas kept them that way, reminding them that Washington regarded them as quitters a final time in his between-halves speech even though the score at that time was Bears 28; Washington 0.

Get one of the 1940 Bears into conversation today about that week of drill and the game itself, and you'll find him turning slightly hysterical, his voice rising in excitement and his eyes flashing.

"I've never experienced anything like it," Luckman admits with a look almost of wonder. "There was a feeling of tension in the air as though something tremendous was about to happen."

That feeling was apparent on the train en route to Washington. Ball players customarily while away train rides by playing cards or sitting around swapping stories. There is laughing, joking, wisecracks, fun. But not this time. There was no laughter, no frolicking, not a single deck of cards in sight. The Bears sat huddled in their seats, notebooks on their laps, studying.

One bit of superstition crept in, too. For luck the Bears moved from their usual Washington hotel to another, a shift Secretary Frank Halas believes entitles him to a share of credit for the momentous events that were in store.

The opening whistle unleashed a Bear attack that was concentrated fury. The kick-off sailed into the arms of Nolting, who sprinted back twenty-two yards to the twenty-four yard line. In the huddle Luckman called a "feeler," the first of four Bear offensive plays having been charted long before to test the Redskin defense. Was it the same as before? Everything depended on the answer to that question.

Kavanaugh, at left end, went 18 yards out on the flank, and the Washington right halfback followed him out. Nolting, at left half, went in motion to the right, and the Redskin backerup trailed him out. That was all Luckman wanted to see. The Washington defense was unchanged. On the play McAfee bolted between guard and tackle for eight yards.

On the next play the left end went wide again, but McAfee, the right half, went in motion to his left. Luckman, making a reverse pivot, gave the ball to Osmanski on a run to the spread side.

"Bill was really driving when I handed off that ball to him," Luckman grins. "I knew he was going someplace in a hurry."

That someplace was sixty-eight yards to a touchdown.

Here, however, is a secret never before revealed about the play—it didn't go according to plan or blueprint. Actually it called for a straight slant off tackle, but McAfee's block hadn't flattened the Redskin right end.

"George had him blocked off," says Osmanski, "but he was reaching out with his hands, and I was afraid he could grab me, so I just made a sort of dip and went out wide around end." That dip, incidentally, is now a charted play in the Bears' book.

Osmanski, who was possessed of jet-propulsion acceleration, streaked away, as Musso, pulling out from right guard to join the interference, flattened the up man in the secondary. Near the Washington thirty-five yard line Osmanski was walking a tightrope down the south sideline with Ed "Chug" Justice and Jimmy Johnston closing in on him. Osmanski saw them, but what neither he nor the two Redskins saw was George Wilson, cutting across from his position at right end, whizzing like a tornado into their path. Just as Justice set himself to tackle Osmanski, Wilson hurtled into him from the blind side with such force the impact could be felt in the stands.

"I've never seen a block like it," Halas maintains.

It knocked Justice into Johnston and both of them into a cartwheel that sent them rolling out of the field of play. Both had to be helped to their feet. As a parlay it was a knockout.

Osmanski, of course, simply kept running. As he flashed over the last white line and into the end zone with a touchdown, the big scoreboard clock showed just fifty-five seconds of playing time elapsed. Jack Manders kicked the extra point, but the parade wasn't on—not quite yet.

Max Krause, who is so much a Redskin at heart that he served as their water boy at times while he was in the Navy and too old and too busy to play football, took the next kickoff and promptly scared the Bears half to death. Straight down the field he raced for sixty-two yards before he was finally tackled on the Bear thirty-two yard line. Then came the play that turned the ball game and set the Bear adding machine in motion.

Baugh faded back and shot a long pass to Charlie Malone. The big end was in the clear with a touchdown and an almost certain tie score in his grasp—but he dropped the ball. And, as that pass trickled off his finger tips, Fate turned her back on the Redskins. Had Malone caught the ball the game might have been the nip-and-tuck, slam-bang affair a championship game is supposed to be. As it was, the Redskins never again were a factor.

No one suspected that such was the case when Bob Masterson missed a field goal attempt from the thirty-two yard line, but the handwriting soon became legible on the wall. The Bears put it there with a magnificent display of power football that swept eighty yards in seventeen plays and four first downs without the use of a pass. Luckman scored the touchdown on a sneak of about a foot under Bulldog Turner. Bob Snyder came in for Osmanski to add the point and make the score 14–0.

The Redskins, startled and shocked into desperation, tried three fruitless passes after receiving the kickoff, then were forced to punt, Luckman coming back to the Washington forty-two. Here Luckman called for almost the identical play on which Osmanski had made his great run. This time, however, Joe Maniaci was the fullback, and instead of taking the ball on a handoff, he got it on a shovel pass. Otherwise the pattern was almost identical, for Maniaci didn't stop running until he had touchdown number three. Phil Martinovich converted, making it three different Bears to add a point after each of three scores.

Twelve minutes and forty seconds had been ticked off on the clock, and the scoreboard read: Bears 21; Redskins 0.

Still another touchdown was added before the end of the half, Kavanaugh leaping in the corner of the end zone behind Frank Filchock and Andy Farkas to catch Luckman's thirty-yard pass. Bob Snyder kicked the twenty-eighth point.

The Redskins still refused to concede defeat and came out for the second half charged with new spirit. Wee Willie Wilkin, the gigantic blond tackle, in particular, was a heroic figure until he was led off the field late in the game, crying in anger and humiliation.

But if the Redskins were fired by the half-time revival, so were the Bears. Halas' brief oration dwelt solely on the premise that Washington regarded the Bears strictly as a "first-half ball club" and "quitters."

They quickly proved this to be a myth. On the second play of the third period Baugh attempted a short pass to fullback Johnston in the flat, but Hampton Pool, the Bear end, sensed the play, batted the ball into the air, caught it, and sped fifteen yards to a touchdown. He had scored before most of the Redskins knew anything was amiss.

That was the coup de grace. The Redskins were done. You could see them wilt before your eyes as the fire and spark and spirit drained out of them like air from a punctured tire.

Three more Bear touchdowns clattered across in the third period. Nolting collected the first when he bolted through a quick-opening hole inside the Washington right tackle and scooted twenty-three yards. Two plays after the ensuing kickoff McAfee intercepted a pass by Roy Zimmerman and zigzagged thirty-four yards behind fine blocking to plant the ball in the end zone. Another Zimmerman pass boomeranged later, Turner intercepting this one and going twenty-one yards to score, aided by a furious block with which Pool removed the unhappy Zimmerman from the picture.

The fourth quarter brought more of the same as the "first-half ball club" made it seven touchdowns for the second half. Harry Clark started it with a forty-four-yard run in the course of which he powered his way right out of Filchock's tackle on the ten yard line.

The Redskins received once more, and immediately things went wrong for them again. A pass from center got away from Filchock and Turner recovered only two yards from the goal line. Famiglietti bridged this gap in one drive.

At just about this moment the public address loudspeakers boomed forth with what was probably the most ill-advised and poorly timed announcement ever made. "Those who wish to purchase season tickets

for next year . . ." came the brassy voice, only to be lost in a cascade of boos and catcalls. Strangely enough those boos meant nothing for the Redskins advance sale for the '41 season had set a new record high by Christmas.

Again the Bears kicked off, and this time the Redskins held possession of the ball for only one play. The second was a pass by Filchock, and Maniaci stepped into its path, returning twenty-one yards to Washington's forty-two yard line. From there the Bears turned on the power, with Clark picking up the final yard and the last points of an historic afternoon.

Dick Plasman and Joe Stydahar added extra points from placement in this half with Maniaci getting another on a pass from Sherman. By this time the Bears didn't care much whether they kicked extra points or not, while the officials and the Washington ball club were hoping they wouldn't. Every placement kick propelled by the strong and accurate toes of the Bears, sailed into the stands and didn't return. So it was that after the last two TDs officials asked the Bears please not to kick for points. Sherman, an obliging fellow, tried passing for two points, one of which scored.

In the course of compiling this astronomical score the Bears gained 372 yards rushing to Washington's 3. But this wasn't the only unusual phase of the statistics. The Redskins, the top offensive team in the league, had been held scoreless for the first time. The Bears divided their eleven touchdowns among ten men, Clark being the only repeater. In all, sixteen Bears shared in the point production, six having a hand (or toe) in conversions. Eight Washington passes were intercepted.

The Bears never let up. So tensely were they keyed for this game that even late in the fourth period players leaving the field would whack their substitutes on the seats of their silk pants and exhort: "Pour it on. Don't let up. Pour it on." They kept on pouring their T until the cup ran over.

Superlatives fairly drooled off the typewriters of the nation's top sports writers as they reached in vain for words to describe the game. Typical of the accolades was that given a Washington newspaper by

"Dutch" Bergman, then coach at Catholic University.

"I saw the perfect football team in the Bears," Bergman wrote. "I have been associated with the game as player and coach for twenty-five years, but never in that time did I ever see a team that did everything perfectly, with such flawless execution, as did the Bears in humbling the Redskins."

Phil Handler, line coach of the Chicago Cardinals, shook his head and muttered, "I've never seen anything like it and never will again."

Halas, over the radio, came up with his second masterpiece of the afternoon, this time one of understatement. "My team played a great game," he told the armchair spectators. "I think they deserved to win."

The bark of the gun ending the massacre caused some pressbox wit to remark, "George Marshall (Redskin Owner) just shot himself." The Redskin man hadn't gone to such lengths, but he was heartbroken, shamefaced, and completely at a loss to account for the holocaust.

The next day as the Bears rode triumphantly home with bruises, a championship, and a few hangovers, a Pullman passenger looked with interest at the rainbow decorating Danny Fortmann's left eye.

"My, my," he clucked sympathetically. "That's a terrible black eye you have there."

"Yes," Fortmann agreed, "but it will disappear in a day or two. Think of the Redskins—that seventy-three-to-nothing score is in the record books for all time."

George Halas, independently wealthy now, has founded a dynasty of sport. His Bears stand for quality, spirit and a dramatic ability. They are entirely his creation. The National Football League can be credited more to him than to any other man. His innovations on the T-formation dominate football in every league.

It is with restraint, rather than overenthusiasm, that the hungry Bohemian lad who listened, thirty-five years ago, to a querulous complaint by Bob Zuppke, is now called "Mr. Football" as often as he is "Papa Bear." For it was his dream alone that has grown into spectacular reality; his courage and determination that would not let it die.

Cleveland Browns
PAUL E. BROWN

With five championships in two professional football leagues on his record, Paul Brown could be accused of making a habit of winning. All the way back through his short but spectacular career as a coach he has scored impressively with high school, college and major league teams.

His own playing experience began as a quarterback at Massillon (Ohio) High. This led him to Ohio State, where he found that was not big enough for varsity football, so he transferred to Miami where he was big enough, and good enough to hold the first string job.

After a year of coaching Severn Prep, he returned to Massillon High as head coach in 1932 and stayed through 1940. In that period he fashioned a fabulous parade of high school teams and set his pattern of winning and winning and winning.

Ohio State called him up as its head coach in 1941 and his three-year term there was another record of success. In 1942, he was given recognition as "College Coach of the Year."

Brown enlisted in the Navy in 1944 and spent two years at Great Lakes coaching its powerful football squad.

When the All America Football Conference was formed in 1946, Paul Brown took over the Cleveland team as coach and general manager. During the next four years, the Browns won 47, lost 4, tied 3.

The only champion the AAFC ever had was the Cleveland team which took the title four years straight.

Paul Brown continued his pattern in 1950 when the Cleveland team joined the National Football League and whipped the Los Angeles Rams in a hair-raising 30–28 rodeo for the world championship. He plastered the College All-Stars, 33–0, to start the 1951 season and then won his divisional title for the second year only to lose the championship to the Los Angeles Rams in the first such game to be telecast from coast to coast.

Detroit Lions
RAYMOND K. "BUDDY" PARKER

Although he is one of the youngest head coaches in the league at the relatively tender age of thirty-seven, Buddy Parker packed in twenty-four years of football, including personal action with three championship teams, before he was named head coach of the Lions to start the 1951 season.

He was one of the nation's leading collegiate ground gainers at Centenary College in 1934, joined the Detroit Lions as a halfback the next year, and was one of the more potent factors which led to the Lions winning the world championship that season. After one more season with the Lions he was traded to the Chicago Cardinals and continued to play brilliantly through the 1943 season. He stayed on with the Cardinals and was assistant coach to Jim Conzelman when the Cardinals won their world championship in 1947 and the

divisional title in 1948. When Conzelman resigned the next spring, Buddy assumed a co-coaching position with Phil Handler for the Cardinals and took over the full job in the middle of the 1949 campaign when Handler was diverted to other duties.

Buddy, along with George Wilson and Aldo Forte of the Bears, went to Detroit as assistants to Alvin "Bo" McMillin in the fall of 1950, and, when McMillin was relieved of his contract, Parker became head coach to start the highly successful year of 1951. He retained Wilson and Forte and added Earle Brown, a collegiate coach with no previous major league experience.

Buddy Parker, with his sound training, delightful personality and ability to handle personnel, is being touted as one of the great coaches of the future.

Green Bay Packers
GENE RONZANI

Gene Ronzani, one of the younger generation of major league coaches, is another graduate of "Halas U" who is carrying the gospel of the Chicago Bear style of football to other squads. Gene was a Bear, both as player and coach for sixteen years. His life is football through twelve months every year. It has been since he first went to Marquette from his home town of Iron Mountain, Michigan, in 1929 to become a nine-letter man and one of the great Marquette backs of history.

He became a Bear in the fall of 1933, to join Bronko Nagurski, Beattie Feathers

and Carl Brumbaugh in one of the most lethal backfields in the history of the league. He switched to quarterback in 1937 and 1938, then took over the coaching of the Newark Bears, a farm club, in 1939. Gene came back to active playing during 1943 and 1944 to help out Sid Luckman. In 1946, he went back to the farm system as head coach of the Akron Bears, then came back to the home club as quarterback coach from 1947 through 1949.

Ronzani was ready then for bigger opportunities and "Papa Bear" George Halas was his loudest booster when the opportunity to coach the Green Bay Packers was offered to Gene to start the 1950 season. Ronzani has gone into battle to do a complete rebuilding job on the Green Bay team, and it is not surprising that all four of his assistants—Dick Plasman, Tarzan Taylor, Scooter McLean and Chuck Drulis —are former Chicago Bears.

The Packers, always a dynamic power in the league since its birth, are on their way up the road to another championship with a young, scrappy club under a young, fighting coach.

Los Angeles Rams
JOSEPH STYDAHAR

Big Joe, a leading candidate for all-time honors as a major league tackle, got his advanced education in football under George Halas, headmaster of the Chicago Bears. Since taking over the top job with the Rams to start the season of 1950, he has returned to haunt his former teacher with sensational scoring units sparked by the bristling passing attacks of Bob Water-

field and Norman Van Brocklin. Joe also showed the versatility of imagination to switch from air war to devastating three-fullbacks offense in 1951.

Stydahar emerged in 1932 to become a spectacular college player at West Virginia and graduated to the Bears in 1936. In those days an official all-pro team was named each season and Stydahar was at tackle in 1937, 1938, 1939, 1940. He left the Bears for Navy service in 1943 and returned late in 1945 to finish that season, and one more, before quitting as an active player. He had established a reputation with his teammates, coaches and opponents as one of the best tackles of history. He had added to his team value by specializing in conversions on five division, and three world champion, teams.

In 1947, Joe joined the coaching staff of the Rams as line coach under Bob Snyder. For two more years he served in the same capacity under Clark Shaughnessy. In 1950, he assumed the top job and led the team to a divisional championship, losing the world title to the Cleveland Browns in a thriller that was not decided in favor of the Browns until eighteen seconds before the final gun. In 1951 the Rams won the World's Championship.

Stydahar uses the Bears' T with variations of his own. With two brilliant passers on his firing line, he has set new records in almost every phase of the aerial attack.

New York Giants
STEPHEN OWEN

Steve Owen, behind only George Halas and Curly Lambeau in length of service as

a head coach in the National Football League, has been one of the most versatile strategists in all football history. His reputation as a master of defense was well earned through more than twenty seasons. His versatile and spectacular diversions of an offense which features T mixed with A and double A have received too little praise. Both of his current quarterbacks handle the variations with equal deftness, and building a defense against the "defensive" Giants is one of the major headaches for opposing coaches.

Steve first appeared in the league as a tackle for the Kansas City Cowboys and played brilliantly with them from 1924 through 1926 after starring for Phillips University at Enid, Oklahoma. He switched to the Giants late in 1926 and played through 1932 with a bruising skill which made him one of the ten best tackles the league has ever known. He began coaching in 1931 and has moved to the top of his profession where he commands the highest respect of every man in football. His team's cyclonic encounters with the Cleveland Browns during the seasons of 1950 and 1951 have been masterpieces on the part of two brilliant coaches; and his endless war with the Chicago Bears has made spectacular league history.

Owen's records as both player and coach will live as long as there is football. He has earned his place on every possible honor roll.

New York Yanks
Dallas Texans

JAMES M. PHELAN

Jim Phelan served his first year as a National Football League head coach in 1951, taking over the New York Yanks a few days before the season opened. His previous major league experience was gained as head coach of the Los Angeles Dons in the All America Football Conference in 1948 and 1949.

He first blossomed in the football world as a high school quarterback at Portland, Oregon, his home town, from 1911 through 1913. Next stop was Notre Dame, under Coach Knute Rockne, where Phelan finished as captain of the team in 1917.

When he returned from Army service in World War I he took over the head coaching of the University of Missouri and led that school to spectacular success from 1919 to 1921. That job well done led to the top job at Purdue, where Jim served from 1922 through the 1929 season.

Next stop was his home country, where he became head coach at the University of Washington for twelve years ending in 1941. St. Mary's of California was his next position, from 1942 through 1947. After that it was the big leagues and his short career with the Los Angeles Dons.

Phelan took over a Yank squad loaded with talent, but disorganized as a result of several of its stars jumping to Canadian football for the 1951 season. He grappled with a serious morale problem and produced a spectacular offensive team, always on the verge of winning.

When the franchise was transferred to Dallas to start the season of 1952, Phelan went along as head coach.

Philadelphia Eagles

WAYNE V. MILLNER

Wayne Millner, a recent addition to the list of young head coaches, got his chance at the top spot with the Eagles when Alvin "Bo" McMillin was stricken with a fatal illness early in the 1951 season. It was a fitting reward for fifteen years of faithful service in the major leagues, which had followed a sparkling performance as an end at Notre Dame, where Millner made All-American in 1935.

Cal Pictures

He joined the Redskins for the following season and, through 1946, with two years lost to the Navy, was one of the primary targets for the passing of Sammy Baugh as well as one of the better defensive ends in league history. He graduated to an assistant coaching position with the Redskins which he held from 1947 through 1948 and then moved over to the All America Football Conference to assist Ray Flaherty with the Chicago Hornets. Flaherty had been his coach through most of his pre-war Redskin career. He moved on to the Baltimore Colts as assistant in 1950 and was responsible for the small amount of success the Colts enjoyed.

When the Eagles eliminated Earle Neale after the 1950 season, Millner was sought immediately for the number two spot in the strategy department, being called, technically, the coach of ends and backs. When McMillin was forced to resign, Millner was ready and willing to try the big job. His performance for the balance of the season was more than adequate.

San Francisco 49ers
LAWRENCE T. "BUCK" SHAW

Buck Shaw, a product of Knute Rockne's powerful Notre Dame teams of 1919–21, and all-time tackle in Notre Dame history, has coached the San Francisco team through four seasons in the All America Football Conference and two in the National Football League. He has been busy with football since 1914, when he first became a star player at the high school in Stuart, Iowa, where he was born.

Creighton University at Omaha, Nebraska, was his first choice for higher education, and he played on its varsity in 1918 until the schedule was scrubbed by the influenza epidemic. The next fall he switched to Notre Dame.

When Buck graduated in 1922, Rockne's recommendation won him the head coaching job at North Carolina State. The next year he filled the same position at the University of Nevada and he stayed there until he moved on to Santa Clara to become assistant to Maurice "Clipper" Smith in 1929.

Smith left to take over the Villanova team in 1936, so Buck Shaw moved into the top spot. His 1936 and 1937 teams went to the Sugar Bowl to win twice over Louisiana State University, both victories being upsets. Buck continued at Santa Clara through 1942, when football was abandoned. He remained on the campus to assist in the physical education program for military students.

Buck coached the University of California through the 1945 season and then moved up to the professional league in 1946 when he assumed the head coaching duties for the San Francisco 49ers. For the next four years he suffered the frustration of always being second-best to the nearly-invincible Cleveland Browns. His consolation: of the four games the Browns lost during that period, Shaw's 49ers won two.

Buck is a T-formation man and his team has always played dramatic football with Frankie Albert directing the attack and passing brilliantly.

Washington Redskins
RICHARD TODD

Dick Todd shares with Buddy Parker of the Detroit Lions the distinction of being one of the youngest coaches in the National Football League. They were both thirty-seven in the 1951 season. Todd is a top favorite in Washington, where, as a halfback, he shared glory with fellow Texan Sam Baugh for several years.

Dick started his football career at Crowell (Texas) High School, where he scored an incredible 318 points in one season and 664 in four years. He played four years with Texas A & M and joined the Redskins in 1939 to become one of the most dangerous scat-backs in league history —particularly effective on the receiving end of passes from his roommate, Mr. Baugh.

Dick played through 1948—with two years lost to Navy duty—then returned to Texas A & M as backfield coach through 1949 and 1950. He came back to the Red-

Nate Fine Photo

skins as backfield coach at the start of the 1951 season, and, thanks to a mid-season shake-up, was named head coach to succeed Herman Ball, who returned to scouting duties. Dick recovered from the shock of finding himself head coach of his old roommate, Sam Baugh, and led the Washington team to a strong finish after a disastrous start of the season. A big, strong and rough Redskin line, reminiscent of the team's days of glory a decade ago, plus a bruising bunch of young backs led by the eternal Baugh and veteran Bill Dudley, gave Todd

the start of a promising coaching career.

He is expected to be one of the most successful members of the younger generation of National League coaches.

THE COACHES IN 1951

Chicago Cardinals
EARL LOUIS "CURLY" LAMBEAU

At the end of the 1951 season, Curly Lambeau could check off his thirty-first year as a major league coach, a record that may stand for a long time. He, along with George Halas and Paddy Driscoll of the Chicago Bears, are the sole survivors of the ambitious group of football fanatics who founded the parent organizations of the National Football League in 1920 and 1921. Even before that, in 1919, Curly Lambeau was player-coach of a team in Green Bay, Wisconsin, where he was born in 1898.

After starring through high school days as a halfback, Curly proceeded to

Notre Dame in 1918, where he played fullback under Coach Knute Rockne. He stayed for only one year and returned to Green Bay to organize a team, sponsored by the Acme Packing Company, which was to become famous as the Green Bay Packers. He sold football so well to his native township that its population has habitually filled its twenty-six-thousand-seat stadium although the town itself has less than twice that number total population. On the same ratio, New York City should send four million fans to each game of the New York teams.

For the next thirty-one years (the first two years of which the Packers played independently), Lambeau was the Packers' coach and the Packers were a fearsome team. They won six championships, three of them consecutively, from 1929 to 1931. They have shown through all the years a remarkable ability to win and keep the support of their fans despite a combination of adversities that would have eliminated any but the most worthwhile and courageous sports enterprises.

Curley left Green Bay to take over the head coaching job for the Chicago Cardinals at the start of the 1950 season. He faced a tremendous job of rebuilding a squad upon only an aged scattering of players from the great Cardinal teams of 1947 and 1948. One of his assistants was Cecil Isbell, great passing star of Green Bay teams; the others chosen to assist were Cardinal products, Phil Handler and Garrard "Buster" Ramsey, heroic linemen of other days.

Pittsburgh Steelers
JOHN P. MICHELOSEN

The only team in 1951 major league football which ran primarily from the single-wing and depended on brutal blocking for its success was coached by Johnny Michelosen, a blocking back himself, and a student of the big league game under Dr. John P. "Jock" Sutherland, also an advocate of single-wing.

Johnny played his college football at Pittsburgh, where he was the block and the quarterback. After he graduated in 1938, he toured with an exhibition team through Europe, then returned to become an assistant coach under Sutherland.

From that time until Sutherland's death in 1947, Johnny Michelosen was Jock's assistant, absorbing the theory of football now called "old-fashioned" in an era of passing from the T. When Sutherland resigned from Pitt and went to the Brooklyn Dodgers, Johnny went with him. When Jock came home to take over the leadership of the Steelers from 1946 to 1947, Michelosen was his top assistant.

In 1947, his first year at the controls, Johnny led the Steelers to a tie for the

divisional championship but lost the play-off to the Philadelphia Eagles.

Michelosen's teams established a reputation as rugged spoilers who won or lost the hard way; smashing power, rather than deception, made them difficult to stop, and Michelosen proved a master of defense. All his assistants were either former Steeler players or asssitants during Sutherland's regime.

THE COACHES IN 1952

Chicago Cardinals
JOSEPH KUHARICH

Joe Kuharich, who played guard for the Chicago Cardinals in 1940 and 1941, steps into the toughest head coach assignment the National Football League can offer to start the season of 1952. Since 1947–48, when Jim Conzelman led the

Cards to two divisional titles and a championship, the erratic "Big Red" team of Chicago's Southside has been on the skids through internal dissension and lack of firm guidance. Kuharich will need all the experience he has gathered in the years since he played guard at Notre Dame (1936–37) to survive.

He was an assistant coach at Notre Dame in 1938; head coach at Vincentian Institute, a Buffalo preparatory school, in 1939. After playing with the Cardinals through the next two seasons, he joined the Navy and coached the 1945 Fleet City, California, Navy team to a service championship. He gained his only previous professional coaching experience as line coach of the Pittsburgh Steelers in 1946, then went to the University of San Francisco as assistant to Ed McKeever in 1947. From 1948 through 1951 he was very successful as head coach at San Francisco, scouting on the side for the Pittsburgh Steelers and Detroit Lions.

His first momentous act as top man of the Cardinals was to choose Ollie Matson, his star back at San Francisco in 1951, as his first draft choice for the Chicago team.

Pittsburgh Steelers

JOSEPH BACH

Joe Bach, a veteran of twenty-six years of coaching, returns to the Pittsburgh Steelers to open the 1952 season. He was hired by owner Art Rooney to install the T-formation after several years of mediocrity achieved by the single-wing under Jock Sutherland and Johnny Michelosen. Thus the single-wing as a basic attack dis-

appears from the National Football League, at least temporarily.

Bach first hopped into the headlines at Notre Dame, from which he graduated in 1924 after playing a sparkling right tackle as one of the "Seven Mule" line which operated in front of the immortal "Four Horsemen." He never played professional football, but did coach the Pittsburgh team, known then as the Pirates, in 1935 and 1936.

He has also been line coach at Syracuse, 1925–28; assistant coach at Duquesne, 1929–31; head coach at Duquesne, 1934; head coach at Niagara University, 1937–41; head coach of the Fort Knox Army team, 1942; line coach of the Detroit Lions, 1943–47; line coach of the Boston Yanks, 1948; line coach of the New York Bulldogs, 1949. During 1950 and 1951, Bach was head coach at St. Bonaventure College.

Bach faces a titanic task in revising the entire Pittsburgh offense, but hopes that within a season or two he will have the Steelers winging high.

THE COACHES' ASSIGNMENTS (Active Teams)

*Co-Coach;   †Part season

Alexander, Joseph
1926 New York Giants

Anderson, Heartley
1942–45 Chicago Bears*

Andrews, Leroy
1929–30 New York Giants
1931 Chicago Cardinals*

Bach, Joseph
1935–36 Pittsburgh Steelers
1952 Pittsburgh Steelers

Ball, Herman
1949 Washington Redskins†
1950–51 Washington Redskins†

Barry, Norman
1925–26 Chicago Cardinals

Bell, Bert
1938–40 Philadelphia Eagles
1941 Pittsburgh Steelers†

Bergman, Arthur
1943 Washington Redskins

Bezdek, Hugo
1937 Cleveland Rams
1938 Cleveland Rams†

Brown, Paul
1950–52 Cleveland Browns

Casey, Edward
1935 Boston Redskins

Chamberlain, Guy
1928 Chicago Cardinals

Chevigny, Jack
1932 Chicago Cardinals

Clark, Earl "Dutch"
1937–38 Detroit Lions
1939–42 Cleveland Rams

Clark, George "Potsy"
1930–36 Detroit Lions
1940 Detroit Lions

Conzelman, James
1940–42 Chicago Cardinals
1946–48 Chicago Cardinals

Creighton, Milan
1935–38 Chicago Cardinals

Crowe, Clement
1950 Baltimore Colts

DeGroot, Dudley
1944–45 Washington Redskins

Dietz, William
1933–34 Boston Redskins

DiMelio, Luby
1934 Pittsburgh Steelers

Donelli, Aldo
1941 Pittsburgh Steelers†
1944 Cleveland Rams

Dorais, Charles
1943–47 Detroit Lions

Douds, Forrest
1933 Pittsburgh Pirates

Driscoll, John
1921–22 Chicago Cardinals

Edwards, Albert Glen
1946–48 Washington Redskins

Edwards, William
1941–42 *Detroit Lions

Ewart, Charles
1949 New York Bulldogs

Flaherty, Ray
1936–42 Washington Redskins

Folwell, Robert
1925 New York Giants

Gillies, Fred
1927 Chicago Cardinals

Halas, George
1920–29 Chicago Bears
1932–42 Chicago Bears
1946–52 Chicago Bears

Handler, Philip
1943 Chicago Cardinals
1949 Chicago Cardinals*

Henderson, Gus
1939 Detroit Lions

Horween, Arnold
1923–24 Chicago Cardinals

Johnsos, Luke
1942–45 Chicago Bears*

Jones, Ralph
1930–32 Chicago Bears

Karcis, John
1942 Detroit Lions*

Kiesling, Walter
1939 Pittsburgh Steelers*
1940 Pittsburgh Steelers
1941 Pittsburgh Steelers†
1942 Pittsburgh Steelers
1943 Philadelphia Eagles†
1944 Pittsburgh Steelers*

Kopf, Herbert
1944–46 Boston Yanks

Kuharich, Joseph
1952 Chicago Cardinals

Lambeau, Earl
1921–49 Green Bay Packers
1950–51 Chicago Cardinals

Leonard, James
1945 Pittsburgh Steelers

Lewis, Arthur
1938   Cleveland Rams†

McMillin, Alvin
1948–50   Detroit Lions
1951   Philadelphia Eagles†

McNally, John
1937–38   Pittsburgh Steelers
1939   Pittsburgh Steelers†

Michelosen, John
1948–51   Pittsburgh Steelers

Millner, Wayne
1951   Philadelphia Eagles†
1952   Philadelphia Eagles

Neale, Earle
1941–42   Philadelphia Eagles
1943   Philadelphia Eagles†
1944–50   Philadelphia Eagles

Nevers, Ernest
1929–30   Chicago Cardinals
1931   Chicago Cardinals
1939   Chicago Cardinals

Owen, Stephen
1931–52   New York Giants

Parker, Raymond
1949   Chicago Cardinals
1951–52   Detroit Lions

Phelan, James
1951   New York Yanks
1952   Dallas Texans

Potteiger, Earl
1927–28   New York Giants

Ronzani, Gene
1950–52   Green Bay Packers

Schissler, Paul
1933–34   Chicago Cardinals

Shaw, Lawrence
1950–52   San Francisco 49ers

Shaughnessy, Clark
1948–49   Los Angeles Rams

Smith, Marshall
1920   Chicago Cardinals

Smith, Maurice
1947–48   Boston Yanks

Snyder, Robert
1947   Los Angeles Rams

Strader, Norman
1950–51   New York Yanks

Stydahar, Joseph
1950–52   Los Angeles Rams

Sutherland, John
1946–47   Pittsburgh Steelers

Todd, Richard
1951   Washington Redskins†
1952   Washington Redskins

Walsh, Adam
1945   Cleveland Rams
1946   Los Angeles Rams

Whelchel, John
1949   Washington Redskins†

Wray, Ludlow
1932   Boston Braves
1933–37   Philadelphia Eagles

THE COACHING HISTORY OF THE NATIONAL FOOTBALL LEAGUE

BALTIMORE COLTS

1950   Clem F. Crowe

CHICAGO BEARS

*Retired October 25 to re-enter Navy
†Co-coach

1920–1929   George S. Halas
1930–1932   Ralph Jones
1933–1941   George S. Halas

1942   George S. Halas*
         Heartley Anderson†
         Luke Johnsos†
1943–1945   Heartley Anderson†
         Luke Johnsos†
1946–1952   George S. Halas

CHICAGO CARDINALS

*Resigned after first two games
†Co-coach

1920   Marshall Smith

1921–1922	John "Paddy" Driscoll
1923–1924	Arnold Horween
1925–1926	Norman Barry
1927	Fred Gillies
1928	Guy Chamberlain
1929–1930	Ernie Nevers
1931	Leroy Andrews*
	Ernie Nevers
1932	Jack Chevigny
1933–1934	Paul Schissler
1935–1938	Milan Creighton
1939	Ernie Nevers
1940–1942	James Conzelman
1943	Phil Handler
1944	(Merged with Pittsburgh)
1945	Phil Handler
1946–1948	James Conzelman
1949	Phil Handler†
	Raymond "Buddy" Parker†
1950–1951	Earl "Curly" Lambeau
1952	Joseph Kuharich

CLEVELAND BROWNS

| 1950–1952 | Paul E. Brown |

DALLAS TEXANS

| 1952 | James Phelan |

DETROIT LIONS

(Formerly Portsmouth Spartans, 1930–33)

*Released after third game, October 4

1930–1936	George "Potsy" Clark
1937–1938	Earl "Dutch" Clark
1939	Gus Henderson
1940	George "Potsy" Clark
1941	William Edwards
1942	William Edwards*
	John Karcis
1943–1947	Charles "Gus" Dorais
1948–1950	Alvin N. "Bo" McMillin
1951–1952	Raymond "Buddy" Parker

GREEN BAY PACKERS

| 1921–1949 | Earl "Curly" Lambeau |
| 1950–1952 | Gene Ronzani |

LOS ANGELES RAMS

(Formerly Cleveland Rams, 1937–45)

*Resigned in mid-season

1937	Hugo Bezdek
1938	Hugo Bezdek*
	Arthur Lewis
1939–1942	Earl "Dutch" Clark
1943	(Suspended operation)
1944	Aldo Donelli
1945–1946	Adam Walsh
1947	Robert A. Snyder

| 1948–1949 | Clark Shaughnessy |
| 1950–1952 | Joe Stydahar |

NEW YORK GIANTS

1925	Robert Folwell
1926	Joseph Alexander
1927–1928	Earl Potteiger
1929–1930	Leroy Andrews
1931–1952	Steve Owen

NEW YORK YANKS

(formerly New Yorks Bulldogs 1949;
Boston Yanks 1944–48)

1944–1946	Herb Kopf
1947–1948	Maurice J. "Clipper" Smith
1949	Charles D. Ewart
1950	Norman "Red" Strader
1951	James Phelan

PHILADELPHIA EAGLES

*Merged with Pittsburgh

†Co-coaches

‡Illness after first two games

1933–1937	Ludlow Wray
1938–1940	Bert Bell
1941–1942	Earle "Greasy" Neale
1943	Earle "Greasy" Neale*
	Walter Kiesling†
1944–1950	Earle "Greasy" Neale
1951	Alvin N. "Bo" McMillin‡
	Wayne Millner
1952	Wayne Millner

PITTSBURGH STEELERS

*Resigned in mid-season

†Retired after 2nd game

‡Banned by Commissioner

§Merged with ChiCardinals

¶Co-coaches

1933	Forrest Douds
1934	Luby DiMelio
1935–1936	Joseph Bach
1937–1938	John "Blood" McNally
1939	John "Blood" McNally*
	Walter Kiesling
1940	Walter Kiesling
1941	Bert Bell†
	Aldo Donelli‡
	Walter Kiesling
1942	Walter Kiesling
1943	(Merged with Philadelphia)
1944	Walter Kiesling§
	Phil Handler¶
1945	Jim Leonard
1946–1947	Dr. John B. Sutherland
1948–1951	John B. Michelosen
1952	Joseph Bach

SAN FRANCISCO 49ers

1950–1952 Lawrence T. "Buck" Shaw

WASHINGTON REDSKINS

(formerly Boston Redskins, 1932–36)

*Retired in 1942 to enter Navy
†Resigned November 7
‡Resigned October 18

1932 Ludlow Wray

1933–1934 W. "Lone Star" Dietz
1935 Edward Casey
1936–1942 Ray Flaherty*
1943 Arthur "Dutch" Bergman
1944–1945 Dudley DeGroot
1946–1948 A. Glen "Turk" Edwards
1949 John E. Whelchel†
        Herman Ball
1950 Herman Ball
1951 Herman Ball‡
        Richard Todd
1952 Richard Todd

CHAPTER 4
THE PLAYERS

In more than thirty years of major league football since the American Professional Football Association was formed in 1920, nearly five thousand players have galloped onto various fields to write their stories into the record books. Some have become what the sport world chooses to call "immortal"; others, often grounded by injuries, have spurted briefly through the headline sky; a few, although heavily endowed with All-American honors and glorified by collegiate publicity, have proved to be colossal failures when they really had to play football.

Many, particularly in the lean years of the 1920's, fled to professions which provided habitual eating, and disappeared into the shadows of athletic obscurity, where even their brief claims to fame are difficult to trace. In those days professional football was lucky when its line-ups, and results, were printed—even down among the goitre ads—in the papers. The names were often spelled incorrectly; the scorers of points were not even listed.

Therefore, the roster which follows in these pages is guaranteed only to 99.9% for accuracy. The confusion of similar names such as "Swede" Johnson, and the inevitable swarms of men named Smith, may have resulted in one man's getting credit for playing where he didn't play at all, and another's being missing, although his honorable bruises may still be painful.

The writer begs for clemency in these circumstances. "He done," as they say around the race tracks, "the best what he could" with available material. He asks that any reader spotting flaws report them as calmly as possible so that future revisions of the *Encyclopedia* may make amends for these errors of fact. No one with less than the tracking apparatus of the FBI could have solved some of these mysteries by deadline time.

The study of names becomes an obsession as the search is made through flaky programs, brown newspaper clippings, league manuals, library microfilms, piles of full-length books which may yield no more than a half-dozen names not already known. As the strained vision drops from 20-20 to little better than 0-0, the world becomes a swirling cloud of names. The researcher wakes in the deep night murmuring such terrifying items as "Zygmont Peter Czarobski," or sometimes "Zvonimir Kvaternick," or even "Ventan Constantine Yablonski." Timid remarks by his befuddled wife bring no more reply than a snarling "Ugoccioni and I'll Golembeski." More than four hundred tear-stained pleas go out to registrars of colleges, begging for first names. The writer sent to "Sing Sing University" to learn that the given name of "Alabama" Pitts, of the Philadelphia Eagles, was "Edwin," a fact Commissioner Bert Bell, who coached Mr. Pitts, will learn for the first time on reading this.

One plea was returned with this rather timorous reply: "Since we have only women students, I am sure this is some error." Madam, it was, and Plumridge and Salemi remained first-nameless for several months.

Finally it is done, as far as it can be, until the players themselves, or those who knew them when, tell us where we are wrong.

It would be interesting to know what has become of them all. What, for example, has happened to Wrinkle Meat, who played guard for the Oorang Indians in 1923? Where are Little Twig and Arrowhead and Red Fox and Pete Calac and Joe Guyon, from those days when the American Indians were a big factor in the big game? Only Jim Thorpe remains, flitting in and out of the news. And the last full-blooded brave of record was Jack Jacobs, who played with Green Bay and Washington after World War II before moving on to Canadian football.

Where are you, Mr. Bruncklacher, Louisville Colonels' lineman of 1922 and 1923? Where are you hiding, defying all efforts to trace you? Why is it that the name of Davis and particularly Robert Davis seems almost to predestine the man to become a professional football player? The Davis team of the years would be a most formidable challenger; three Robert Davises have sparkled in recent history. There have been two Ray McLeans, both backs, both little fellows, twenty-five years apart, no relation. There have been two Christmans twenty years apart, both backs, no relation; two Pritchards, twenty years apart, both backs, no relation. In the fall of 1951, two warriors carried the name of Don Paul—not related. Players and fans who have shuddered during recent seasons over the defensive mayhem of the Bears' end, Ed Sprinkle, should know that there was another Sprinkle—Hubert—playing nearly thirty years ago, tactics and ethics unknown. We wait, breathlessly, the appearance of the second Baugh.

There was no problem finding the data on Baugh, Don Hutson, Sid Luckman, Bronko Nagurski, Ernie Nevers, Paddy Driscoll, Red Grange, Dutch Clark, Ken Strong and dozens of others whose names flash automatically when anyone speaks the word "football." Their records have become part of eternity. Nor were the players of the past fifteen years too difficult to find. The league got down to business and began to keep records in the mid-1930's.

Hundreds of stars of the past have gone on to continued success, many, of course, in football. Halas, Driscoll, Lambeau, Steve Owen, of the older generation, are still in the top-flight, climbing higher. A second generation group of coaches—Joe Stydahar, Raymond Parker, Gene Ronzani, Wayne Millner, Dick Todd, Luke Johnsos, George Wilson, Joe Kuharich and Hampton Pool—are coming along, some of them already head coaches in the major league. Countless colleges and high schools are being tutored by men who learned their lessons in the big time. Bert Bell, who once coached some of the weirdest characters in early Philadelphia days, has become Commissioner of the National Football League, with a record already behind him of brilliant handling of many difficult episodes and a surprising control over the explosive and strange souls who have owned some of his teams. Few, if any, commissioners in any sport, have handled their jobs with similar efficiency.

Other players have gone into politics. Lavvie Dilweg, the great Green Bay end of early days, became a state Senator; Chet Chesney, Bear center before World War II, went to Washington as a Representative of his Chicago district. Red Grange has galloped into a political job in Illinois and is headed for bigger things. Others have been mayors, or lesser city officials; they have become bank presidents like Ed McGinley of the New York Giants (whose son was drafted by the Philadelphia Eagles in 1952 to establish the first father-son combination in league history). They have climbed to leadership in industry as did Fred Gillies, the old-time Cardinal and Hammond tackle, who was sent to Europe by President Truman to re-organize German industry (although Fred's best game in the old days was disorganizing, which he practiced against opposing teams when he played the opposite tackle with Fred "Duke" Slater, the first Negro to be appointed a judge in the city of Chicago).

The first quarterback of the Chicago (Staley) Bears was a little fellow named Charlie Dressen, who spent the fall of 1951 wishing he had stayed with football while his baseball Brooklyn Dodgers needed touchdowns, rather than runs, to keep them out of disgrace. One of his players was Jackie Robinson, who played in an All-Star football game at Soldier Field and might have climbed as high in the gridiron world as he has on the diamond.

Tom Harmon, the unforgettable Los Angeles Rams back, has become a top TV and radio sports reporter on the West Coast. Irv Kupcinet, who once slipped the hand-offs to Alabama Pitts for the 1935 Eagles, is a syndicated columnist at the Chicago *Sun & Times.* Jim Conzelman, player, coach, master psychologist of the game, who once sold the Detroit franchise for $50 and was glad to get it, is now an advertising executive and continues to prove himself one of the most versatile human beings of the century with his music, his writing, his speaking, but fights a chronic battle with himself about coming back to the game.

Some big league players became big time boxers—heavyweights of course—like Steve Hamas and "Sully" Montgomery. George Trafton, legendary center of the early Bears, went into boxing for a while before quitting football. His "Battle of the Century" with Art "The Great" Shires of the baseball world was one of the most hilarious tussles of all time. Later he reached enough fistic prominence to become one of the many first-round victims of Primo Carnera during "Old Satch's" triumphant, and completely phoney, march to the heavyweight title. Trafton also dabbled in "rassling," where several more former players have found pots of gold. Eddie Michaels of the Eagles, Redskins and Bears; Bronko Nagurski and Jim McMillen of the older Bears; Leo Nomellini of the 49ers; Fred Davis of the Redskins and Bears—all have tried the grunt-and-groan pastime with varying success. At least one, Lou Gordon of the older Packers and Cardinals, is a wrestling referee. Sam Baugh and Ken Kavanaugh, who might have become one of the immortal passing combinations if they had played on the same team, have invested their pay checks in cattle ranches, to switch from pigskin to cowhide when their playing days are done. Earl Audet of the Redskins and Dons, and Howie Livingston of the Giants and Redskins, have dabbled in Hollywood affairs in their spare time, setting up careers for the future.

Following exhaustive study of football major leaguers, the writer has endeavored in this book to salute those who have been outstanding as players. The author and publisher decided, however, that our All-Time All-Star Team must be three deep in each position, otherwise author and publisher would be leaving by fast plane for a distant hide-out soon after publication to escape the combined wrath of fans and players.

A "Consensus of Opinion" squad of thirty-three players has been gathered and is printed with the sure knowledge that the hide-out is still very much in order. We wait behind a barricade for the smoking accusations that nobody but God's Greatest Knuckle-head could have left So-and-so off any All-Star team. Point granted. Although coaches,

---

THE ALL-TIME ALL-STAR TEAM

DON HUTSON	LAVERN DILWEG	WAYNE MILLNER	END
WILLIAM HEWITT	RAY FLAHERTY	GUY CHAMBERLAIN	END
WILBUR HENRY	FRED DAVIS	ALBERT GLEN EDWARDS	TACKLE
ROBERT HUBBARD	RUSSELL BEHMAN	JOSEPH STYDAHAR	TACKLE
AUGUST MICHALSKE	WALTER KIESLING	WILLIAM WILLIS	GUARD
DANIEL FORTMANN	GEORGE MUSSO	RAY BRAY	GUARD
MELVIN HEIN	CLYDE TURNER	NATHAN BARRAGER	CENTER
SAMUEL BAUGH	ROBERT WATERFIELD	SIDNEY LUCKMAN	Q'BACK
JOHN DRISCOLL	KENNETH STRONG	HAROLD GRANGE	H'BACK
EARL CLARK	WILLIAM DUDLEY	GEORGE McAFEE	H'BACK
BRONKO NAGURSKI	ERNEST NEVERS	CLARK HINKLE	F'BACK

ALTERNATES—End: George Halas; Tackle: Roy Lyman, Stephen Owen; Guard: Riley Matheson, Heartley Anderson; Center: George Trafton, Victor Lindskog; Backs: Clifford Battles, Ernest Caddel, Anthony Canadeo, Alphonse Leemans, Verne Lewellen, John "Blood" McNally, James Thorpe, Steven Van Buren.

owners, players of different decades, writers and just plain "people" were put through a third degree, there are still but thirty-three positions open on this mythical team and the candidates run to the hundreds. Its like Baseball's Hall of Fame—there are plenty on the outside who should be on the inside. All but two of the players in the Helms Athletic Foundation's Football Hall of Fame have made our squad and the Helms list is printed in these pages.

Therefore, as our team lines up, readers and fans will have little difficulty, and a great deal of pleasure, composing rosters of other names which they believe could wallop our squad—maybe by 73–0. There will be no rebuttal from here.

And so, on the following pages are the men who really wrote this book. To each one, from Wrinkle Meat to Baugh, from Abbey, Joseph to Zyntell, James, goes the author's most sincere gratitude for memories beyond price and a deep regret that he could not have watched, from some frigid press-box, every play, of every game, that made this history.

HEARTLEY ANDERSON
Guard—210—5:11—Notre Dame

"Hunk" Anderson, a rock-'em-sock-'em type of player, made his name when sixty minutes of battle was standard procedure and substitutes came in only if the top man had to be carried off. He was a strong and shrewd product of Knute Rockne's squads and has reproduced himself through hundreds of Chicago Bear linemen who have been noted through the years as the best in the book.

He was the top work horse of the Bears through the early 1920's and the famous Red Grange coast-to-coast tour when a murderous game was almost a daily chore.

Fran Byrne

Since playing days, Hunk has been assistant and co-coach of the Bears, head coach at Notre Dame.

NATHAN BARRAGER
Center—220—6:00—Southern California

Barrager first appeared in the league in 1930 when he played for the Minneapolis Redjackets and Frankford Yellowjackets. He started the 1931 season at Frankford, then switched to Green Bay, where

he remained through 1935. Small for a big league center, he was a fierce competitor who substituted brains for brawn. A "player's player," he was outstanding on defense and a terrific blocker. All-League center in 1932.

CLIFFORD BATTLES
Halfback—195—6:01—
West Virginia Wesleyan

Battles was an outstanding back with the Redskins from 1932 through 1937, leading the team to two divisional titles and

Wide World Photo

In his rookie year, 1937, he was named All-League halfback, and again in 1940. When the league discontinued the All-League team in 1943, Baugh was named by both the Associated Press and United Press. In 1945, U.P. and International News Service called him the best quarterback. Two years later, in 1947, U.P. put him in the top halfback spot although he had been a T quarterback all season. U.P. named him best quarterback in 1948, his twelfth season in the league.

Official statistics made him the top passer six times (1937, 1940, 1943, 1945, 1947, 1949). He was the best punter from 1940 through 1942. In 1943, to break the monotony, he led the league in interceptions.

one league championship in his last two years of play. He could smash and he could go through the open field. He was a great defensive player. Baugh, at the other halfback spot in 1937, and he made a devastating duo, both being chosen All-League. Battles was All-League in 1933 and 1936 and led the league in rushing in 1937.

SAMUEL BAUGH
Halfback and Quarterback—185—6:2—
Texas Christian

Baugh, starting his sixteenth season in 1952 to add the "Length of Service" record to his long list of honors, proved long ago that he is in a class by himself as a passer, and is the most lethal offensive player in all football history. It is sometimes forgotten that Baugh has also been a great punter and one of the finest defensive players in the game.

He has now reached the point where, every time he throws the ball to complete a pass, to gain a yard, to score a touchdown, or even to be intercepted, he breaks a world record—his own.

His entire professional career has been with the Washington Redskins.

Baugh's Records

(15 Seasons, 1937–51)

Most Passes Completed	1,689
Most Passes Completed (One season)	210
Most Passes Attempted	2,983
Most Passes Attempted (One season)	354
Most Passes Intercepted	204
Most Yards Gained on Passes	21,913
Most Yards Gained on Passes (One season)	2,938
Most Touchdown Passes	185
Best Passing Efficiency (500 or more attempts)	57.3
Best Passing Efficiency (One season)	70.3
Most Punts (One game)	14
Best Punting Average (One season) —30 punts	48.7

Championship Game Records

Most Passes Completed	42
Most Passes Attempted	81
Most Yards Gained on Passes (One game)	335

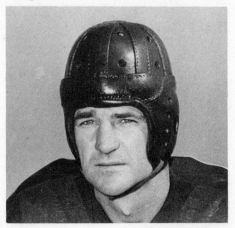

Wide World Photo

Baugh's Record Annually

	Atts.	Com.	Pct. Com.	Yds. G.	Ave. G. Com.	Td. P.	Lng. Gn.	Intrc.	Pct. Intrc.
1937	171	81	.473	1,127	13.9	7	59	14	.081
1938	128	63	.492	853	13.5	5	60	11	.086
1939	96	53	.552	518	9.7	6	*44	9	.093
1940	177	111	.627	1,367	12.3	12	*81	10	.056
1941	193	106	.549	1,236	11.6	10	55	19	.098
1942	225	132	.541	1,524	11.5	16	53	11	.049
‡1943	260	149	.573	1,953	12.9	24	72	21	.080
1944	146	82	.562	849	10.3	4	*71	8	.054
1945	182	128	†.703	1,669	13.0	11	*70	4	.022
1946	161	87	.540	1,163	13.3	8	51	17	.105
1947	†354	†210	.593	†2,938	14.0	25	74	15	.042
1948	315	185	.587	2,599	14.0	22	86	23	.073
1949	255	145	.569	1,903	13.1	18	*76	14	.055
1950	166	90	.542	1,130	12.6	10	56	11	.066
1951	154	67	.435	1,104	7.8	7	53	17	.110
TOTAL	†2,938	†1,689	†.574	†21,933	12.8	†185	86	†204	.066

* Touchdown pass   † League record   ‡ Includes divisional playoff

RUSSELL BEHMAN
Tackle—230—5:10—Dickinson

"Bull" Behman is a name that pops up immediately when early generation veterans of the National Football League start talking about the toughest tackles they ever tangled with. He played with the Frankford Yellowjackets from 1924 through 1931. No All-League selections were made until his final year, which is the only reason the Bull's name is not in the honor rolls several times.

A monstrous man who could stand firm as Gibraltar or move like a cat, Behman was almost impossible to block. Coaches had to assign so many extra blockers to him alone that plays came apart.

He was another "player's player" who never got a fraction of the credit he earned.

RAYMOND BRAY
Guard—245—6:0—Western Michigan

Bray is one of many players in the NFL who came out of a little-known college to make a mockery of the annual insanity of All-American selections. He began his career with the Bears in 1939, lost four years in service, and was still a powerhouse on both offense and defense in 1951. He was chosen All-League guard by the United Press in both 1948 and 1949.

Bray is stocky, tremendously strong and

INP

unusually fast for a man of his build. Under the coaching of "Hunk" Anderson, he has learned to mix smartness with muscle and he plays sixty minutes if necessary. One of Bray's amazing extra-curricular activities is doing one-arm push-ups, fifty at a time.

He played his entire career with the

Chicago Bears until traded to Green Bay at the start of the 1952 season.

ERNEST CADDEL
Halfback—198—6:2—Stanford

Caddel was the slam-bang, smashing type of halfback who had to have a stake driven through his heart to pin him down. He was a smaller version of Nagurski when running. His pet play was a delayed reverse that sent him crashing around the "other" side like a mad bull.

Wide World Photo

He first came up with the strong Portsmouth Spartans in 1933. The team moved to Detroit the following year and Caddel was one of its heroes through 1938. He was a big factor in the powerhouse backfield of 1935 that murdered the New York Giants, 26–7, in the championship game.

Caddel was chosen All-League halfback in the same year.

ANTHONY CANADEO
Halfback—190—6:0—Gonzaga

Tony Canadeo, one of the major heroes of the Green Bay Packers, pounded away through ten seasons, beginning in 1941, to grind out 4,006 yards in 960 attempts, an average of 4.2. He had tremendous speed and deceptive power and was outstanding defensively. His gains amounted to nearly 200 more yards in 200 less attempts than those which Clark Hinkle, another Green Bay titan, racked up.

In 1949, Canadeo galloped for 1,052, gaining an all-time second in the record book. Unfortunately for Tony, the all-time record of 1,146 was made the same season by Steven Van Buren of Philadelphia.

Canadeo played ten years for the Packers, missing the 1945 season. He was named All-League halfback in 1943 by the Associated Press and in 1949 by the United Press. His steady, dependable play has made him one of the all-time greats.

GUY CHAMBERLAIN
End—210—6:2—Nebraska

Chamberlain was the other end, opposite George Halas on the original Staley team in 1920. He is described by his former teammate as the greatest two-way end of all time. Like Halas, he went on the next year to become a player-coach, first with Canton, then with Cleveland, later with Frankford. He finished his career in 1927

INP

with the Chicago Cardinals, then coached the same team in 1928.

Chamberlain was fast, deceptive, impossible to cover on pass plays, which were few at the time. He was a fine blocker and an octopus on defense.

EARL CLARK
Halfback—205—6:1—Colorado

"Dutch" Clark, all-time number one man in Portsmouth and Detroit football history, began his career with the Spartans in 1931. He was an All-League choice in his second year and was chosen on the mythical All-League team five times before he retired at the end of the 1938 season. During the last two seasons he was head coach as well as star of the Lions. From 1939 to 1942 he coached the Cleveland club.

Detroit Free Press

Clark was a blistering broken field runner, a smasher when necessary, an excellent passer and field goal artist, kicking most of his team's conversions. He was the league's leading scorer in 1935, when the Lions won the championship, and in 1936.

Teamed with Ace Gutowsky, Ernie Caddel, Frank Christensen and Raymond Parker, Clark led the Lions into all-time glory with one of the most devastating backfields of record. He is a unanimous choice of every football expert for all-time honors.

FREDERICK LEE DAVIS
Tackle—260—6:3—Alabama

Fred Davis, after three years with the Washington Redskins and six more with the Chicago Bears, might be described as the "ball-player's ball-player." During his career, which started in Washington in 1941 and 1942, lapsed during three years of Army service, resumed in 1945 with the Redskins, and has continued since 1946 with the Bears, Davis has been named only once, in 1947, on the United Press All-League team.

However, those who have played against him both on offense and defense call him the best since 1935 despite greater publicity given to a few others. Davis is strong, agile, rough and smart. He can outsprint many halfbacks; he has a file system memory for the idiosyncrasies of his opponents;

he has smeared more passers than any other tackle; he has been invaluable to the Bears as an unofficial coach of younger linemen as they come up to the ranks.

As his great career draws to a close, many teams are expected to seek him as a line-coach so that he can spread the gospel of the rough and devastating type of forward play that has been the habit of the Bears for so many years.

During the off-season, like many other players, he keeps in shape on the wrestling circuit, sometimes under his own name, sometimes as "Alabama Lee."

LAVERN DILWEG
End—202—6:3—Marquette

Lavvie Dilweg played in an era when an end was a blocker and a defender rather than the catching part of a forward

pass and his name is not prominent in statistical records. But, in the days of the highest glory of the Green Bay Packers, for whom he played for eight seasons, 1927 through 1934, after one year with the Milwaukee Badgers, he made a name for himself as one of the finest ends the Green Bay team, or the league has known.

He was elected All-League the first year that team was named, 1931, and was a sixty-minutes player through all his career, a crashing blocker, impregnable on defense.

JOHN DRISCOLL
Halfback—170—5:11—Northwestern

"Paddy" Driscoll zoomed through the football world in the days when statistical records were just a happy dream of the future. Otherwise, his name might still be sprinkled through the pages that make up the official manual of the NFL, which has been kept efficiently only since 1932.

His 27 points (4 touchdowns, 3 extra points) scored against Rochester for the Chicago Cardinals on October 7, 1923, is fifth highest one-game mark of record. The same 4 touchdowns put him in a tie for fourth place on the most TDs in one game list. He is second to the league mark with 11 field goals in one season, all drop-kicks in his day. His 4 field goals in one game

against Columbus, October 25, 1925, were a league record until Bob Waterfield booted 5 against Detroit in 1951. Twice he drop-kicked from 50 yards away to share a mark today with Wilbur Henry who did it once. His precision punting exhibition,

designed to hold Red Grange in check the day the Redhead made his professional debut, was one of the most deft performances the league has known. Paddy was a brilliant runner and a flawless defensive back as well as a toe artist.

Six years with the Chicago Cardinals beginning in 1920 led to four more with the Bears ending in 1929. Since then Paddy has been an assistant coach of the Bears, one of the strongest factors in their continued success.

WILLIAM DUDLEY
Halfback—175—5:10—Virginia

Dudley is the kind of back that beats teams, because he is always in the right place, always doing the right thing. This dynamic competitor more than once has been stretchered off the field in complete exhaustion.

His first year up, with the Pittsburgh Steelers in 1942, gave him the rushing championship and All-League selection. He devoted the next three years to the Air Force and returned to Pittsburgh in 1946 to lead the league in both rushing and interceptions and to be chosen All-League by United Press. He starred for feeble Detroit teams from 1947 through 1949 and then joined the Washington Redskins for 1950 and 1951.

He made the league's second longest punt return, 96 yards to a touchdown, for the Redskins against Pittsburgh, December 3, 1950; is sixth in lifetime touchdowns with 44; has placed his name among the top six halfbacks of all time despite the fact that he has never played for a title contender.

Dudley does everything—runs, passes, punts, kicks field goals and conversions and is one of the toughest defensive halfbacks ever seen. His personal and team spirit have carried his teammates much higher than they could ever have gone without him. An inspirational player who is expected to become one of the best coaches, he retired after 1951 to join the staff at Yale University under Herman Hickman, another veteran of NFL competition.

ALBERT GLEN EDWARDS

Tackle—256—6:2—Washington State

"Turk" Edwards, a giant in a world of large men, was a tower of strength with the Redskin teams of the late 1930's when they were always either title contenders or very close by.

Turk played at Boston from 1932 through 1936, and continued until 1940 in Washington. He was named to the All-League teams of 1932, 1933, 1936 and 1937.

He was power rather than speed, but was agile enough to play his position as it has seldom been played. He is number one man at his job so far as Washington goes, and no worse than sixth in league history.

After playing days were over, Turk stayed on with the Redskins as assistant coach for several years and took over the head coaching duties from 1946 through 1948.

RAY FLAHERTY

End—187—6:1—Gonzaga

Ray Flaherty came into the league in 1927 with the New York Yankees, survivors of the outlaw league of 1926, played with the Yankees through 1928, and then joined the New York Giants in 1931, to stay through 1935.

Flaherty was one of the finest both-way ends, a breed of player which has almost disappeared from the game since the growth of forward-passing. He was an elusive pass-receiver, a bone-crushing blocker, and was masterful on defense. In 1932, he was chosen All-League end.

Fron 1936 to 1942 he coached the Boston-Washington Redskins, leading them to four division titles and two world championships. In the short run of the All America Football Conference, he was head coach of the New York Yanks for three years, the Chicago Hornets for one season.

DANIEL FORTMANN
Guard—207—6:0—Colgate

Fortmann was one of the smallest of the great linemen, but he ranks no worse than third on the consensus list of guards and he has been called the best by more than one student of the game.

He played eleven consecutive seasons for the Chicago Bears, starting in 1936, and more than a small part of his success can be attributed to the coaching of Hunk Anderson, himself an all-time guard of an earlier day.

Fortmann was chosen All-League five straight times from 1938 through 1942 and, when official All-League teams were discontinued, both the Associated Press and United Press named him again in 1943.

Although he is now one of the most highly regarded surgeons in California, Danny stays close to football in an unofficial capacity through the Los Angeles Rams, whose coaching staff is made up of several former teammates of his playing days.

HAROLD GRANGE
Halfback—190—6:1—Illinois

Grange was the biggest "name" of them all when he came out of college in 1925 to give major league football the shot in the arm which sent it winging on its way to success. But few fans realize that the famous Redhead was valued more as a master defensive player than for his undeniable running ability. For Red's defense alone, one veteran of the league would choose him over all other backs, a strange tribute to the "Galloping Ghost."

He was picked for the first All-League team, named in 1931, late in a career which lasted through 1934.

His entire professional career was played with the Chicago Bears except for 1926 and 1927, when Grange and his manager, the late C. C. Pyle, attempting to operate a rival league, formed the New York Yankees. One year finished the league. The Yankees played in the NFL during 1927, then folded forever and Grange went back to the Bears.

He has stayed close to major league football ever since, recently became a respected radio and television broadcaster of both college and professional games.

GEORGE HALAS
End—200—6:1—Illinois

George Halas has managed to submerge his great ability as a football player in his reputation as a coach and owner of the

most successful team in football history. But it was Halas the player who kept the Bears going back in the early days when the league held onto its lifeline by a slim flow of dollar-plasma from the grandstands. Halas was a smashing, crashing end who showed no regard for life and limb—his or his opponents'.

He played from 1920 through 1930 and found time on the side to coach, collect money, keep the organization alive.

MELVIN HEIN
Center—230—6:3—Washington State

Mel Hein is named unanimously by experts as the top center of history. He played fifteen years, longer than any one else with the exception of John McNally and Sam Baugh. He was known as the man who did best with a minimum of coaching.

Hein started with the New York Giants in 1931, finished with the same

team in 1945. From 1933 he was named All-League center for eight consecutive years, giving way to young Clyde Turner after 1941.

Hein did everything a little better than any other center and did it automatically. He was a great blocker and interference leader, magnificent on defense, a sure handler of the ball. His sparkling qualities of leadership made him the team leader through all of his career.

He has been an assistant coach of the Los Angeles Rams and is now gaining experience in college ball. Football men expect him to be one of the best coaches of the future.

WILBUR HENRY
Tackle—245—6:2—Washington and Jefferson

"Fats" Henry, who died suddenly in February 1952, is named by many as the best tackle of them all. Marvelously mobile

for a man of his weight and build, Henry put his name in the record books as one of the finest punters of history. His booming boots kept rival teams continually back on their heels in the early days of earthbound football. One of them, kicked for the Canton Bulldogs against Akron in 1923, was officially measured at 94 yards, the all-time record for distance.

Henry started with the league at Canton in 1920, played there through 1923; skipped 1924; was with Canton and Akron in 1925; went to the New York Giants in 1926; went on to Pottsville for 1927 and

1928; was with the Staten Island Stapletons in 1930.

In addition to playing spectacularly at tackle, Henry occasionally shifted into the backfield to run with the ball.

At the time of his death he was athletic director at Washington and Jefferson.

WILLIAM HEWITT
End—195—5:11—Michigan

Bill Hewitt became famous for two things: he played without a head-guard and he anticipated the snap of the ball so well that he was accused of being off-side most of the time by all of his opponents— but by none of the officials.

He first came to the Chicago Bears in 1932 and was good enough to be chosen All-League in 1933 and 1934. He was traded to the Philadelphia Eagles early in 1936 and was All-League for them that year and the next, thus becoming the only player who was All-League for two dif

ferent teams. He played with the Eagles through 1939, retired, then came back for one more round with the Phil-Pitt combination in 1943.

Hewitt was admired most for his vicious blocking and tackling and an uncanny ability to outguess the enemy. He was always in the right place at the right time, usually a split-second ahead of schedule.

Bill Hewitt died as the result of an automobile accident, on January 14, 1947.

CLARK HINKLE
Fullback—198—5:11—Bucknell

Hinkle is always named in the first three of all-time fullbacks because he was an indestructible thunderbolt who would plow his way through a brick wall.

He first came to the Green Bay Packers in 1932, was their power man through

1941. He was chosen All-League fullback from 1936 through 1938, an honor that might have been his in his earlier years had there not been a man named Nagurski playing at the same time. When these two met it was like two wild bulls locking horns in a death battle.

Hinkle was the leading scorer in 1938, and top man with field goals in 1940 and 1941. His all-time yardage of 3,860 in 1,171 attempts is third highest in the records, the number of attempts being second only to those made by Steve Van Buren. Hinkle's 42 touchdowns rank seventh.

He was small for a major league fullback, but a magnificent pair of legs gave him tremendous acceleration and driving power and he was a violent competitor.

ROBERT HUBBARD
Tackle—265—6:5—Geneva

"Cal" Hubbard, as well known as a major league baseball umpire as he is for his football career, played first with the New York Giants in 1927 and 1928. His partner at the other tackle position was Steve Owen, still with the Giants as head coach. Cal joined the Green Bay Packers in 1929, played with them through 1935.

He split his final year of 1936 between the Pittsburgh Pirates and his old friends, the Giants.

When All-League selections started in 1931, Cal was chosen for that year. He also was All-League in 1932 and 1933.

He was a tremendous man, but agile and mobile. He did everything right and his huge bulk made him a chronic headache to opposing teams on both offense and defense.

DONALD HUTSON

End—185—6:1—Alabama

Don Hutson wore out all the superlatives in the football reporters' vocabulary early in his career and kept them busy inventing new ones until he retired. After Sam Baugh he holds more records than any other player.

He came first to the Green Bay Packers in 1935, played with the same team through 1945. He was All-League end in 1936 and from 1938 through 1942. When this honor was dropped by the league, he was awarded the same spot by both the Associated Press and United Press from 1943 through 1945, his last year of competition.

Besides being the greatest scoring threat of all time through his uncanny ability to lose up to three frantic defenders, he was versatile enough to win the field goal championship in 1943 and excelled as a defensive halfback throughout his career.

He was number one pass receiver in 1936 and 1937, missed the honor in 1938, and was top man again in 1939 and from 1941 through 1945, leading the league eight times in eleven seasons. This leadership resulted in his being high scorer three times, 1941, 1942 and 1944; all-time leading scorer with 329 points than his nearest competitor; and holder of enough records to command a chapter all his own in the league manual, an honor only Hutson and Baugh have earned.

Other Hutson records follow:

Lifetime

Most Passes Caught	489
Most Touchdown Passes Caught	101
Most Yards Gained on Passes	8,010
Most Points Scored	825
Most Touchdowns Scored	105
Most Consecutive Games Scored,	41
Shortest Touchdown Pass Caught, Inches	4

Season

Most Touchdown Passes Caught	17
Most Points Scored	138

Game

Most Touchdown Passes Caught	4

Miscellaneous

Most Years Named Most Valuable Player	2
Most Years Leading Pass Receiver	8
Most Years Leading Scorer	5
Most Consecutive Years Leading Scorer	5
Most Consecutive Years Leading Pass Receiver	5

WALTER KIESLING
Guard—235—6:3—St. Thomas

Walt Kiesling, a true work horse guard of the old school, a chronic sixty-minute man of the days of the rugged game, is the favorite choice of men who have watched the league from the beginning. Kiesling was quick and smart, equally deadly on offense and defense, the unspectacular type that gets the job done thoroughly without benefit of headlines.

He played with the Duluth Eskimos in 1926 and 1927, the Pottsville Maroons in 1928. Then came five years with the Chicago Cardinals from 1929 through 1933, one with the Bears in 1934, two with Green Bay in 1935 and 1936, and a final with the Pittsburgh Pirates in 1937. This diversified experience was ideal training for major league coaching, which Kiesling has followed successfully ever since. In 1932 he was named All-League guard.

He was head coach of the Pittsburgh Steelers from 1939 through 1942, co-coach of the Pittsburgh combination in 1943 and 1944. He has also served as an assistant with the Green Bay Packers and the more recent Pittsburgh teams, finishing his first twenty-five years in the league at Pittsburgh in 1951.

ALPHONSE LEEMANS
Halfback—200—6:0—George Washington

"Tuffy" Leemans came up with the New York Giants in 1936 and moved into the honor rolls immediately by becoming the leading ground gainer in his freshman year, a performance which earned him an All-League position.

From then until 1943, when he retired, Tuffy was the leading figure in a consistently powerful Giant backfield. At no time was the team lower than third in its division, while it won a world championship and three division titles.

Leemans was All-League again in 1939, and his 926 attempts are third in the league. He gained 3,117 yards, an average of 3.3. He could do everything required in the running department and was a smashing blocker. His defensive play sparkled all through his career.

VERNE LEWELLEN
Halfback—181—6:2—Nebraska

Verne Lewellen's claim to fame is strong enough to overcome the handicap of having been fashioned in the era before

official records were kept. He was the type of football player who needs no certified evidence in the statistical department to command the highest honors. A rangy speedster who could do anything and everything well, he played in the days when a man never left the field until he was carried off.

He first came to the Green Bay Packers in 1924 and was the big gun of the backfield for the next eight years. In 1929, 1930 and 1931, the Packers were champions, the only team to win three times consecutively. Green Bay patriarchs will claim that Lewellen, more than any other man, was responsible for those titles.

Many veterans name him as the finest punter in history.

VICTOR LINDSKOG
Center—200—6:2—Stanford

Vic Lindskog played eight years with the Philadelphia Eagles, from 1944 through 1951, and announced his retirement to join the Eagles' coaching staff before he was recognized as the best center on the Associated Press All-League team in his last season. For years he was overshadowed by the great "Bulldog" Turner of the Chicago Bears, but Turner himself always declared that Lindskog had no superior.

Although his lack of bulk was a serious handicap, as he always faced a man from twenty to sixty pounds heavier than himself, Lindskog, who was drafted by the Eagles as a defensive center, became even more efficient on offense and played both ways.

Philadelphia officials expect his flair for team uplift to carry him high in the ranks of professional coaching.

SIDNEY LUCKMAN
Quarterback—195—6:0—Columbia

Sid Luckman gets a unanimous rating as the smartest field general football has ever known. His teammates and opponents both attest that he won more games with his head than most teams do with their muscles. He was an excellent open-field runner, a top-flight passer, an adequate punter; also an accurate extra-point man, although he seldom performed as such.

Fran Byrne

Luckman came to the Bears in 1939 and played a prominent part in their switch to T-formation. He was All-League quarterback in 1941 and 1942. He was named to the same honor in 1943 by both the Associated Press and United Press, again by the A.P. in 1944, and by the U.P. in 1947. He was the league's "Most Valuable Player" in 1943.

Although Sam Baugh left few passing records lying around for others to cherish, Luckman tied Baugh for league passing honors in 1945; is second to Baugh with most passes completed, in passes attempted and in yardage gained by passing. He holds second place in yards gained passing in one season and in all-time touchdown passes. His 28 TD passes in one season and his 7 in one game lead them all.

ROY LYMAN
Tackle—240—6:2—Nebraska

"Link" Lyman's name appears on no All-League teams and the story of his deeds is destined to die without benefit of statistics, but he is a demand choice of the men who played against him through the 1920's as a tackle who belongs on every possible all-star team.

Wide World Photo

He did it all a little bit better than anyone else of his era, and there seems to be little doubt that he would have done it just as well in any era.

He started with the Canton Bulldogs in 1922, switched to Cleveland with them in 1923, back to Canton in 1924. Then he went to the Chicago Bears in 1925 and stayed there through the rest of his playing days, which ended in 1933. In the realm of the Bears he is known as no worse than the best they ever had, high praise when the all-time list of Bear tackles is contemplated.

RILEY MATHESON
Guard—210—6:3—Texas Mines

Riley Matheson, mean, smart and able, was one of the finest of defensive guards as well as a powerhouse on offense. He had a surprising ability to outguess the attacking team, seemed able to scent the intended pass-receiver. More than once he amazed everyone by fading back from his linebacking position to intercept passes behind his own safety man.

Matheson came up with the Cleveland Rams in 1939, played with them steadily through the championship win over the Redskins in 1945. Then on to Los Angeles with the same team through two more seasons. In 1948 he went over to the All America Football Conference to star with the San Francisco 49ers.

He was named All-League guard in 1944 by both the Associated Press and

Vic Stein & Assoc.

United Press; and again by both in 1945. In 1946, U.P. voted him into the honor once more.

GEORGE McAFEE
Halfback—180—6:0—Duke

"One-Play" George McAfee, within a span of eleven years, during three of which he was absent on service duty, probably caused more stark panic among defensive football players than any other halfback of record. The nickname was no exaggeration. If they gave him an inch he took a mile, or whatever part of it was necessary to cross their goal-lines.

He came to the Chicago Bears in 1940, was chosen All-League in 1941, then lost the three years that might have been his best of all to the Navy. He was back in 1945 to sparkle until 1950, when a chronically painful bone trouble in his heel forced him to retire.

McAfee, whether running wide or going through the middle, either as pass-receiver or decoy, was a constant headache to the defense. On punt returns he often

whizzed through the entire kicking team on blinding speed alone. Late in his career he became an outstanding safety man on defense. He could punt when necessary and was an accurate left-handed passer for trick plays. If there is anything he couldn't do on a football field, it hasn't been invented.

JOHN McNALLY
Halfback—190—6:1—
Notre Dame, Minnesota, St. John

"Johnny Blood," the almost legendary figure of early days, rolled up plenty of mileage in the NFL, but, unfortunately, few records were kept before 1932. Otherwise he might rank as high on many lists as he does on the one called "Most Years Active Player" where he shows for fifteen years, second only to Baugh—if Baugh plays in 1952.

He was a back who could do everything on the field, a tireless competitor who hated only one thing—the final whistle

of any game. He switched teams even more than he had in college days and added new jewels to his crown with each one.

He played with the Milwaukee Badgers from 1925 through 1927, with side trips to star for the Duluth Eskimos. He split 1928 between the Pottsville Maroons and the Green Bay Packers, then stayed with the latter through 1936. Pittsburgh was the next stop for him, as player coach for 1937 and 1938, then as head coach in 1939.

He was an All-League halfback in 1931 with the Packers and an all-time champion in the memories of those who watched his career.

AUGUST MICHALSKE
Guard—210—6:0—Penn State

"Mike" Michalske received more votes than any other man as the number one guard of all time. He was comparatively small for a lineman, but made up for that with explosive spirit, brains, speed and an

almost inhuman ability to outguess the opposing teams. He did everything a guard can do and did it a little better than all the rest.

He played first with the ill-fated New York Yankees in 1927 and 1928, then went to the Green Bay Packers to stay through the 1937 season. Twice, in 1931 and 1935, he was chosen All-League guard in an era when truly great guards were a dime a dozen.

Michalske thus contributed ten years of sparkling play which demanded honor recognition. Without question, he belongs in the all-time starting line-up.

WAYNE MILLNER
End—190—6:2—Notre Dame

Wayne Millner was one of the few college "hot-shots" who immediately lived up to his All America reputation in the big leagues. He was a prominent factor in the drive of the Boston Redskins to the divisional title the first year he played, 1936. The next year, with the team located in Washington, and rookie Sam Baugh in the line-up, it was Baugh-to-Millner all season long on the way to the eastern title, then Baugh-to-Millner twice in the championship game for long touchdowns and a victory over the Chicago Bears.

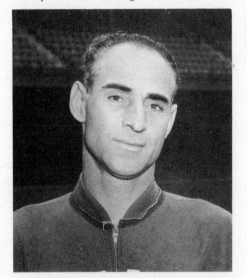

Millner starred on another divisional winner with the Redskins in 1940 and took part in that game all Redskins would like to forget, the 73–0 whipping by the Bears. After the 1941 season, he, like so many other players, wasted three years in the nonsense of war, but returned to play one more season with the 'Skins in 1945.

He turned then to assistant coaching with Washington, with Baltimore and Philadelphia. When illness knocked out "Bo" McMillin early in the season of 1951, Millner stepped into the head coaching spot with the Eagles and performed so well that he was signed for another season.

In playing days he was the ideal two-way type of end, fast and elusive enough for offense, rugged and powerful when the other team had the ball.

GEORGE MUSSO
Guard—255—6:2—Milligan

When George Musso, a gigantic hulk of a youngster, played his first game for the

Chicago Bears in 1933 against the Green Bay Packers, he was so terrible that George Halas wanted to give him his release. A compromise was arranged and, before midseason, Halas would have sold his right eye rather than part with his star rookie.

Musso went on to become one of the all-time heroes of the Bears. Constant practice and determination changed his unwieldy bulk into sure-footed grace. He had a fighting spirit that overflowed to all his teammates.

He was chosen All-League as a tackle in 1935, again as a guard in 1937. He played twelve years with the Bears through 1944, and they wish he could come back to play twelve more. Musso is another example of the unknown player from the unknown college who came up to the majors to create a wave of snickers about All America teams.

BRONKO NAGURSKI
Fullback, Tackle—230—6:2—Minnesota

The Bronk, the legend, the symbol of terrifying, crashing power, the back once described with reverence by coach Steve Owen of the Giants as "the only back I ever saw that ran his own interference."

"The guy could have been an All-American at eleven positions," said Dr. Clarence Spears, who coached him at Minnesota.

"There was something strange about tackling Nagurski," Red Grange recalls. "When you hit him it was almost like getting an electric shock. If you hit him above the ankles you were likely to get killed."

"He was seventy-five percent of an opposing team's worry," declared Harry Newman, former Michigan star, quarterback of the New York Giants. "I was never hit so hard in my life as one time when I tried to stop him in the open field. I hit him as hard as I could and all it did was throw him off pace a little. Dale Burnett nailed him further on and Dale was picked up mumbling about a pile driver."

"Defense him?" Steve Owen said in another discussion. "There's only one defense that could stop him—shoot him before he leaves the dressing room."

"Here's a check for $10,000, Nagurski," said G. A. Richards, owner of the Detroit club. "Not for playing with the Lions, because you belong to the Bears, but just to quit and get the hell out of the league. You're ruining my team."

Thus grew the legend of the Bronk. Nagurski came to the Chicago Bears in 1930 and played consecutively through 1937. In 1932, 1933 and 1934 he was named All-League fullback, taking over the honor from Ernie Nevers who preceded him, and giving way to Clark Hinkle who followed. Thus the three all-time all-star fullbacks crowded their playing careers into the same period.

In 1943, after six years of retirement, Nagurski, who had been farming and wrestling as an old man should, came back to help the war-shredded Bears, played

tackle for a while, then switched to fullback to mangle the Cardinals almost single-handed, leading the Bears to a title and a championship win over the Washington Redskins. None of his opponents of that younger generation could be convinced that the Bronk was nearing forty at the time.

Part of his playing career was in the days before records were kept. Unofficially he is credited with 4,031 yards in 872 attempts, which would place him second only to Van Buren in mileage. His average, unofficial gain, of 4.6 yards per try is highest of all. He could pass, completed 38 of 80; he was a block of reinforced concrete on defense.

No one connected with major league football dares to hope there will ever be another fullback like him.

ERNEST NEVERS
Fullback—205—6:1—Stanford

They'll always talk about that game of November 28, 1929, when Ernie Nevers, fullback of the Chicago Cardinals, lowered his head and plunged into that Chicago Bear line, until even the fans were bruised all over. Smash—crash—smash—Ernie kept it up, with the ball tucked into his belly, until he plowed over the Bear goal-line six times, kicked four extra points himself. Final score: Nevers 40, Bears 6.

It's a record that still stands; William "Dub" Jones of the Cleveland Browns scored an equal number of touchdowns against the same Bears on November 25, 1951, but did not kick any points and thus

is second in most points per game with 36.

Nevers didn't play long in the NFL as compared to many, but the impact of his tremendous plunging power leaves him rivaling Nagurski in the memory of football. He played one year with an independent team in Jacksonville, Florida, before joining the Duluth Eskimos for 1926 and 1927. He went to the Chicago Cards and played through 1931, when he was picked All-League fullback the first time the honor roll was chosen.

He was head coach of the Cards in 1929 and 1930 and again in 1939.

STEPHEN OWEN

Tackle—235—6:1—Phillips

Steve Owen, like George Halas and Curly Lambeau, has been a coach in the major league so long that most fans forget that he was a top-flight player of the early days. Blocky Steve was another of the rare, big men who could move around like a cat when necessary, or stand as firm as the grandstand at the Polo Grounds, where he has spent each football season committing assault and battery on his opponents since 1926.

Before that, Steve played three seasons with the Kansas City Cowboys, who had a lot of fun even though they didn't win many games in the NFL.

Steve played a titanic tackle for the New York team until the end of 1932, coaching also through his last two years as a player. He is still at it as the season of 1952 opens and eleven rival coaches rue-

OWEN

fully admit that he gets a little smarter and harder to beat every season.

KENNETH STRONG

Halfback—210—6:1—New York University

Ken Strong is the number one choice of many coaches and players as the halfback they'd want for one super-colossal game that they had to win. He did everything: ran, plunged, passed, punted, kicked field goals, scored extra points and starred on defense. He did them all about as well as they can be done over a long period of time.

In twelve official seasons (his last few years with the Giants he did nothing but place-kick), Strong scored 35 touchdowns, 169 extra points and 39 field goals, a total of 496 points to wind up second only to Don Hutson in points scored and far ahead of any player still active. Van Buren, next in line and near the end of the road, needs 32 points to catch him.

Strong joined the Staten Island Stapletons 1929, played with them until 1932. He went to the New York Giants the next season, 1933, and played for three years. He retired, played again in 1939, retired and returned for kicking duties from 1944 through 1947. In 1944, he led the league in the field goal department.

JOSEPH STYDAHAR

Tackle—230—6:4—West Virginia

"Jumbo Joe," another physical giant who was able to add brainwork to his mus-

Vic Stein & Assoc.

cular ability, is one more of a long list of great tackles. In the hallowed halls of "Halas U" he ranks with the best of all the honored alumni.

Stydahar came out of West Virginia in 1936. The next year he was a unanimous choice for All-League tackle and an automatic choice for the same distinction through four consecutive seasons. After 1941, he went into the armed forces for three years, and returned to the Bears to play in 1945 and with the 1946 championship team.

For the next three years he served an apprenticeship as an assistant coach at Los Angeles, took over the top job to start the 1950 season. In two years he has won his conference title twice and the championship once (in 1951), which is a little better than par for the course. He, along with Gene Ronzani at Green Bay, are two graduates of the Chicago Bears who are making life difficult for their old headmaster, George Halas.

JAMES THORPE
Halfback—190—6:0—Carlisle

Jim Thorpe was born at least thirty years too soon to make the records to which his ability entitled him in the National Football League. That's the only reason he didn't make the first team in our line-up. In 1920, when the league was founded, Jim was already a veteran, slowing down for that last, painful grind through the home-stretch of his career. By 1926, when he finally retired, he was getting by on his

reputation and a pair of weary, wobbly legs. It would be unfair to hundreds of other players to credit Jim's pre-1920 feats against the players who followed.

Thorpe led the Canton Bulldogs in the first year of the league, played with the Cleveland Indians, so-named in his honor the next season. In 1922 he was back with Canton.

He organized, coached and starred for the Oorang Indians in 1923. It was a squad made up entirely of American Indians, or reasonable facsimiles thereof, and it had little artistic success. Jim went on to play with Rock Island through 1924 and 1925,

then joined the New York Giants. In 1926 he was back with the Canton Bulldogs for his final season.

GEORGE TRAFTON
Center—220—6:2—Notre Dame

George Trafton saw to it that the Chicago Bears had no worries about the middle of the line for the first thirteen years of the team's existence. From 1920, when they played the first official league game as the "Staleys," until the end of 1932, he was in there for nearly sixty minutes each game.

Trafton, with "Hunk" Anderson playing beside him, established the slam-bang, "rock-'em-sock-'em" system of line play that has been the tradition of the Bears all

Acme

through their history. In their day, with no platoons to back them up, they had to be the toughest to survive.

Trafton's extracurricular activities, which included short but spectacular excursions into the world of boxing and wrestling, were sometimes more highly publicized than his long service as the herd-bull of the early Bear days. But his record for long service cannot be denied.

During recent years he had served as assistant coach to different teams in the league, last with the Los Angeles Rams. He was connected with Canadian football during the season of 1951.

CLYDE TURNER

Center—240—6:2—Hardin-Simmons

"Bulldog" Turner never runs worse than one-two-three as the choice for the best center of all time. Some pick Turner as the best of them all. Strangely enough, Turner himself thinks Vic Lindskog of Philadelphia was the best.

After one year of rookie training with the Chicago Bears in 1940, Bulldog ousted the aging Mel Hein from the All-League honor and held it for three consecutive years until the choosing was discontinued after 1942. He was chosen best center by both the Associated Press and United Press in 1943 and 1944. U.P. named him again in 1946 and 1948.

As defensive line backer in 1942, the Bulldog was the league's best interceptor of passes, a rare distinction for a center. He is one of the fastest runners in football,

often sprinting away from halfbacks in sprint competitions. Coaches and players alike attest that he is one of the smartest players in history with an ability to diagnose a play on the field, or on the blackboard, in a split-second.

The year 1952 will be Turner's thirteenth season with the Bears, which will give him a tie for length of service with George Trafton and Alex Wojciechowicz, both centers, one year behind Mel Hein, also a center. Apparently it is a position for men who wear well.

STEVEN VAN BUREN

Halfback—205—6:0—Louisiana State

Eight years in the NFL with the Philadelphia Eagles has given Steve Van Buren nearly all the mileage records in the book. Steve is strictly a specialist; most of his yardage has been gained on one play, through his own right tackle. Although this is common knowledge to all his opponents, they still have been unable to stop him.

He has carried the ball more than anyone else, 1,320 times. He is second to Eddie Price of the New York Giants for most attempts in one season with 263 against Price's 272; second to Harry Newman for most in one game (35). He has gained most yards in one season, 1,146, and his all-time mark is 5,860, nearly 2,000 ahead of his nearest competitor, Tony Canadeo, who has retired.

Steve has scored 464 points which puts him in third place among pros, only 32 behind Ken Strong for second, but hopelessly astern of Don Hutson's incredible 825. He has scored the second most touchdowns—77—28 behind Hutson. Steve has the most TDs in one season, 18.

He was chosen All-League halfback by the Associated Press in 1944, by A.P., United Press and International News Service in 1945, by U.P. in 1947, 1948 and 1949.

ROBERT WATERFIELD
Quarterback—190—6:1—UCLA

Bob Waterfield, with only seven years of NFL play behind him, demands recognition as number two quarterback of all time. In this short period he has led the Rams to four division titles and two championships and has done everything a quarterback can do. His passing has been good enough to lead the league, despite Mr. Baugh, in 1946 and 1951. Twice, in 1949 and 1951, Waterfield won the field-goal crown, his 13 in the latter year tieing the league record, and containing one spurt

of five-goals-in-one-game which beat Paddy Driscoll's all-time record of four which had been standing for twenty-six years. He is a long and accurate punter, runs like a halfback and is one of the best defensive men in the league.

He was awarded the Joe Carr trophy as Most Valuable Player his first year with the Cleveland Rams (1945) and would probably have had it again in 1951 had it not been discontinued. He was All-League choice of both the Associated Press and United Press in 1945; again of U.P. in 1946 and 1949.

He is third in yardage gained by passing with 11,238 yards (10,000 behind Baugh but only 3,000 behind Luckman); third in touchdown passes with 96. He has kicked 271 points after touchdown, nearly a hundred more than retired Don Hutson, the closest competitor for all-time high. His 54 PAT's in one season are the most. His 49 field goals give him a tie for that title with Paddy Driscoll. He has the second longest punt—88 yards.

With many playing years ahead, Waterfield is the only quarterback in sight who may be able to challenge Baugh for the top spot. Like Baugh, he does everything to near perfection. His only weakness has been too many interceptions; a point he holds over Baugh is his marvelous place-kicking.

WILLIAM WILLIS
Guard—216—6:3—Ohio State

Bill Willis, a rare combination of size, strength and pantherine leg-spring, is one

Vic Stein & Assoc.

of the finest guards developed in the All-America Football Conference and the National Football League. For the past six years he has been the advance scout into enemy backfields as the Cleveland Browns have built up a fabulous record of success.

Willis is better known for his defensive play, but is a true two-way guard of blistering speed. He was chosen All-League by United Press in 1950. In 1951, both the Associated Press and U.P. named him on their defensive teams. He is, without doubt, one of the most durable and active linemen in the history of the league.

WILBUR MOORE (35), WASHINGTON REDSKINS, SCRAPES THE CLOUDS IN A RECKLESS LEAP OVER A GREEN BAY BLOCKER TO GET AT TED FRITSCH (64), PACKER FULLBACK. GRIFFITH STADIUM, SEPTEMBER 30, 1945

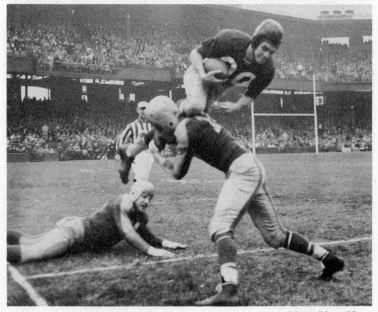

Nate Fine Photo

STEVE BAGARUS (00), WASHINGTON REDSKINS, TAKES THE HIGH ROAD AGAINST THE GREEN BAY PACKERS. GRIFFITH STADIUM, DECEMBER 1, 1946

THE HELMS HALL PROFESSIONAL FOOTBALL HALL OF FAME

(Twenty-nine men have been chosen by the Helms Hall board, composed of Ned Cronin, George T. Davis, Rube Samuelson, Al Santoro, Sid Ziff, Paul Zimmerman, Bill Schroeder and Paul H. Helms, Chairman.)

BATTLES, Clifford—Back. Boston and Washington, 1932–37.

BAUGH, Samuel—Back. Washington, 1937–52.

BLOOD, John (McNally)—Back. Milwaukee, Green Bay, and Pittsburgh, 1925–39.

CARR, Joseph—First President NFL, 1921–39.

CLARK, Earl—Back. Portsmouth and Detroit, 1931–38.

DRISCOLL, John—Back. Chicago Cardinals and Bears, 1921–28.

EDWARDS, Albert Glen—Tackle. Washington, 1932–40.

FLAHERTY, Ray—End. New York Giants and Yankees, 1927–35.

FORTMANN, Daniel—Guard. Chicago Bears, 1936–42.

GRANGE, Harold—Back. Chicago Bears and New York Yankees, 1925–35.

HALAS, George—End, coach. Chicago Bears, 1921–52.

HEIN, Melvin—Center. New York Giants, 1932–45.

HENRY, Wilbur—Tackle. Canton, New York Giants and Pottsville, 1920–28.

HERBER, Arnold—Back. Green Bay and New York Giants, 1930–45.

HEWITT, William—End. Chicago Bears and Philadelphia, 1932–39, 1943.

HINKLE, Clark—Back. Green Bay, 1932–41.

HUBBARD, Robert—Tackle. Green Bay and New York Giants, 1927–36.

HUTSON, Donald—End. Green Bay, 1935–45.

LAMBEAU, Earl—Back, coach. Green Bay, 1921–49.

LEEMANS, Alphonse—Back. New York Giants, 1936–43.

LUCKMAN, Sidney—Back. Chicago Bears, 1939–50.

NAGURSKI, Bronko—Back. Chicago Bears, 1930–37, 1943.

NEVERS, Ernest—Back. Duluth and Chicago Cardinals, 1926–31.

OWEN, Stephen—Tackle, coach. New York Giants, 1926–52.

STRONG, Kenneth—Back. Stapletons and New York Giants, 1929–47.

STYDAHAR, Joseph—Tackle, coach. Chicago Bears and Los Angeles Rams, 1936–52.

THORPE, James—Back. Canton, Cleveland, Oorang, Rock Island, and New York Giants, 1920–26.

TRAFTON, George—Center. Chicago Bears, 1920–32.

TURNER, Clyde—Center. Chicago Bears, 1940–51.

ALL-LEAGUE SELECTIONS

1931
L.E.—Dilweg—Green Bay
L.T.—Hubbard—Green Bay
L.G.—Michalske—Green Bay
C.—McNally—Cardinals
R.G.—Gibson—New York
R.T.—Christensen—Portsmouth
R.E.—Badgro—New York
Q.B.—Clark—Portsmouth
L.H.—Blood—Green Bay
R.H.—Grange—Bears
F.B.—Nevers—Cardinals

1932
L.E.—Flaherty—New York
L.T.—Hubbard—Green Bay
L.G.—Carlson—Bears
C.—Barrager—Green Bay
R.G.—Kiesling—Cardinals
R.T.—Edwards—Boston
R.E.—Johnsos—Bears
Q.B.—Clark—Portsmouth
L.H.—Herber—Green Bay
R.H.—Lumpkin—Portsmouth
F.B.—Nagurski—Bears

1933

L.E.—Hewitt—Bears
L.T.—Hubbard—Green Bay
L.G.—Hickman—Brooklyn
C.—Hein—New York
R.G.—Kopcha—Bears
R.T.—Edwards—Boston
R.E.—Badgro—New York
Q.B.—Newman—New York
L.H.—Presnell—Portsmouth
R.H.—Battles—Boston
F.B.—Nagurski—Bears

1934

L.E.—Hewitt—Bears
L.T.—Christensen—Detroit
L.G.—Gibson—New York
C.—Hein—New York
R.G.—Kopcha—Bears
R.T.—Morgan—New York
R.E.—Badgro—New York
Q.B.—Clark—Detroit
L.H.—Feathers—Bears
R.H.—Strong—New York
F.B.—Nagurski—Bears

1935

L.E.—Smith—Cardinals
L.T.—Morgan—New York
L.G.—Kopcha—Bears
C.—Hein—New York
R.G.—Michalske—Green Bay
R.T.—Musso—Bears
R.E.—Karr—Bears
Q.B.—Clark—Detroit
L.H.—Danowski—New York
R.H.—Caddel—Detroit
F.B.—Mikaluk—Cardinals

1936

L.E.—Hewitt—Philadelphia
L.T.—Smith, E.—Green Bay
L.G.—Evans—Green Bay
C.—Hein—New York
R.G.—Emerson—Detroit
R.T.—Edwards—Boston
R.E.—Hutson—Green Bay
Q.B.—Clark—Detroit
L.H.—Battles—Boston
R.H.—Leemans—New York
F.B.—Hinkle—Green Bay

1937

L.E.—Hewitt—Philadelphia
L.T.—Stydahar—Bears
L.G.—Evans—Green Bay
C.—Hein—New York
R.G.—Musso—Bears
R.T.—Edwards—Washington
R.E.—Tinsley—Cardinals
Q.B.—Clark—Detroit
L.H.—Battles—Washington
R.H.—Baugh—Washington
F.B.—Hinkle—Green Bay

1938

L.E.—Hutson—Green Bay
L.T.—Widseth—New York
L.G.—Fortmann—Bears
C.—Hein—New York
R.G.—Letlow—Green Bay
R.T.—Stydahar—Bears
R.E.—Tinsley—Cardinals
Q.B.—Parker—Brooklyn
L.H.—Danowski—New York
R.H.—Cardwell—Detroit
F.B.—Hinkle—Green Bay

1939

L.E.—Hutson—Green Bay
L.T.—Stydahar—Bears
L.G.—Fortmann—Bears
C.—Hein—New York
R.G.—Dell Isola—New York
R.T.—Barber—Washington
R.E.—Poole—New York
Q.B.—O'Brien—Philadelphia
L.H.—Leemans—New York
R.H.—Farkas—Washington
F.B.—Osmanski, W.—Bears

1940

L.E.—Hutson—Green Bay
L.T.—Stydahar—Bears
L.G.—Fortmann—Bears
C.—Hein—New York
R.G.—Wiethe—Detroit
R.T.—Kinard—Brooklyn
R.E.—Schwartz—Brooklyn
Q.B.—Parker—Brooklyn
L.H.—Baugh—Washington
R.H.—White—Detroit
F.B.—Drake—Cleveland

1941

L.E.—Hutson—Green Bay
L.T.—Kinard, F.—Brooklyn
L.G.—Fortmann—Bears
C.—Turner—Bears
R.G.—Kuharich—Cardinals
R.T.—Wilkin—Washington
R.E.—Schwartz—Brooklyn
Q.B.—Luckman—Bears
L.H.—Isbell—Green Bay
R.H.—McAfee—Bears
F.B.—Hinkle—Green Bay

1942

L.E.—Hutson—Green Bay
L.T.—Wilkin—Washington
L.G.—Fortmann—Bears
C.—Turner—Bears
R.G.—Edwards—New York
R.T.—Artoe—Bears
R.E.—Masterson—Washington
Q.B.—Luckman—Bears
L.H.—Isbell—Green Bay
R.H.—Dudley—Pittsburgh
F.B.—Famiglietti—Bears

Official selection discontinued in 1943.

1943
ASSOCIATED PRESS
L.E.—Hutson—Green Bay
L.T.—Kinard, F.—Brooklyn
L.G.—Farman—Washington
C.—Turner—Bears
R.G.—Fortmann—Bears
R.T.—Blozis—New York
R.E.—Rucinski—Cardinals
Q.B.—Luckman—Bears
L.H.—Baugh—Washington
R.H.—Clark—Bears
F.B.—Canadeo—Green Bay

UNITED PRESS.
L.E.—Hutson—Green Bay
L.T.—Sears—Phil-Pitt
L.G.—Farman—Washington
C.—Turner—Bears
R.G.—Fortmann—Bears
R.T.—Blozis—New York
R.E.—Rucinski—Cardinals
Q.B.—Luckman—Bears
L.H.—Baugh—Washington
R.H.—Clark—Bears
F.B.—Cuff—New York

1944
ASSOCIATED PRESS
L.E.—Hutson—Green Bay
L.T.—Wistert—Philadelphia
L.G.—Younce—New York
C.—Turner—Bears
R.G.—Matheson—Cleveland
R.T.—Kinard, F.—Brooklyn
R.E.—Aguirre—Washington
Q.B.—Luckman—Bears
L.H.—Sinkwich—Detroit
R.H.—Van Buren, S.—Philadelphia
F.B.—Paschal—New York

UNITED PRESS
L.E.—Hutson—Green Bay
L.T.—Wistert—Philadelphia
L.G.—Younce—New York
C.—Turner—Bears
R.G.—Matheson—Cleveland
R.T.—Cope—New York
R.E.—Aguirre—Washington
Q.B.—Zimmerman—Philadelphia
L.H.—Sinkwich—Detroit
R.H.—Cuff—New York
F.B.—Paschal—New York

1945
ASSOCIATED PRESS
L.E.—Hutson—Green Bay
L.T.—Wistert—Philadelphia
L.G.—Matheson—Cleveland
C.—Brock—Green Bay
R.G.—Radovich—Detroit
R.T.—Cope—New York
R.E.—Benton, J.—Cleveland
Q.B.—Waterfield—Cleveland
L.H.—Van Buren, S.—Philadelphia
R.H.—Bagarus—Washington
F.B.—Westfall—Detroit

UNITED PRESS
L.E.—Hutson—Green Bay
L.T.—Wistert—Philadelphia
L.G.—Matheson—Cleveland
C.—Brock—Green Bay
R.G.—Radovich—Detroit
R.T.—Uremovich—Detroit
R.E.—Pritko—Cleveland
Q.B.—Baugh—Washington
L.H.—Waterfield—Cleveland
R.H.—Van Buren, S.—Philadelphia
F.B.—Fritsch—Green Bay

INTERNATIONAL NEWS SERVICE
L.E.—Aguirre—Washington
L.T.—Wistert—Philadelphia
L.G.—Lio—Boston
C.—Brock—Green Bay
R.G.—Radovich—Detroit
R.T.—Schultz—Cleveland
R.E.—Pritko—Cleveland
Q.B.—Baugh—Washington
L.H.—Van Buren, S.—Philadelphia
R.H.—Gillette—Cleveland
F.B.—Akins, F.—Washington

1946
UNITED PRESS
L.E.—Benton, J.—Los Angeles
L.T.—Wistert—Philadelphia
L.G.—Lio—Philadelphia
C.—Turner—Bears
R.G.—Matheson—Los Angeles
R.T.—White—New York
R.E.—Kavanaugh—Bears
Q.B.—Waterfield—Los Angeles
L.H.—Dudley—Pittsburgh
R.H.—Filchock—New York
F.B.—Fritsch—Green Bay

1947
UNITED PRESS
L.E.—Kavanaugh—Bears
L.T.—Wistert—Philadelphia
L.G.—Younce—New York
C.—Banonis—Cardinals
R.G.—Moore, Wm.—Pittsburgh
R.T.—Davis, F.—Bears
R.E.—Kutner—Cardinals
Q.B.—Luckman—Bears
L.H.—Van Buren, S.—Philadelphia
R.H.—Baugh—Washington
F.B.—Harder—Cardinals

1948
UNITED PRESS
L.E.—Pihos—Philadelphia
L.T.—Wistert—Philadelphia
L.G.—Bray—Bears
C.—Turner—Bears
R.G.—Ramsey, G.—Cardinals
R.T.—Huffman—Los Angeles
R.E.—Kutner—Cardinals
Q.B.—Baugh—Washington
L.H.—Van Buren, S.—Philadelphia
R.H.—Trippi—Cardinals
F.B.—Harder—Cardinals

1949
UNITED PRESS
L.E.—Pihos—Philadelphia
L.T.—Sears—Philadelphia
L.G.—Bray—Bears
C.—Naumetz—Los Angeles
R.G.—Ramsey, G.—Cardinals
R.T.—Huffman—Los Angeles
R.E.—Fears—Los Angeles
Q.B.—Waterfield—Los Angeles
L.H.—Van Buren, S.—Philadelphia
R.H.—Canadeo—Green Bay
F.B.—Harder—Cardinals

1950
ASSOCIATED PRESS
L.E.—Fears—Los Angeles
L.T.—Connor—Bears
L.G.—Barwegan—Bears
C.—Bednarik—Philadelphia
R.G.—Signaigo—New York Yanks
R.T.—Weinmeister—New York Giants
R.E.—Edwards, D.—New York Yanks
Q.B.—Lujack—Bears *Notre Dame*
L.H.—Walker, D.—Detroit
R.H.—Geri—Pittsburgh
F.B.—Motley—Cleveland *wow*

UNITED PRESS
L.E.—Fears—Los Angeles
L.T.—Connor—Bears
L.G.—Barwegan—Bears
C.—Tonnemaker—Green Bay
R.G.—Willis—Cleveland
R.T.—Weinmeister—New York Giants
R.E.—Speedie—Cleveland
Q.B.—Lujack—Bears
L.H.—Walker, D.—Detroit
R.H.—Geri—Pittsburgh
F.B.—Motley—Cleveland

1951
ASSOCIATED PRESS
Offensive Team
E.—Elroy Hirsch—Rams
T.—George Connor—Bears
G.—Lou Creekmur—Lions
C.—Vic Lindskog—Eagles
G.—Dick Barwegan—Bears
T.—Leo Nomellini—49ers
E.—Leon Hart—Lions
B.—Otto Graham—Browns
B.—Doak Walker—Lions
B.—William "Dub" Jones—Browns
B.—Eddie Price—Giants

Defensive Team
E.—Larry Brink—Rams
T.—Arnie Weinmeister—Giants
G.—Bill Willis—Browns
G.—Les Bingaman—Lions
T.—Al Derogatis—Giants
E.—Len Ford—Browns
L.B.—Chuck Bednarik—Eagles
L.B.—Paul Younger—Rams
H.B.—Jerry Shipkey—Steelers
H.B.—Otto Schnellbacher—Giants *49ers*
Safety—Emlen Tunnell—Giants

UNITED PRESS
Offensive Team
E.—Elroy Hirsch—Rams
T.—Lou Groza—Browns
G.—Dick Barwegan—Bears
C.—Frank Gatski—Browns
G.—Lou Creekmur—Lions
T.—DeWitt Coulter—Giants
E.—Dante Lavelli—Browns
B.—Otto Graham—Browns
B.—Doak Walker—Lions
B.—William "Dub" Jones—Browns
B.—Dan Towler—Rams

Defensive Team
E.—Len Ford—Browns
T.—Arnie Weinmeister—Giants
G.—Bill Willis—Browns
G.—Jon Baker—Giants
T.—George Connor—Bears
E.—Leon Hart—Lions
L.B.—Tony Adamle—Browns
L.B.—Chuck Bednarik—Eagles *PENN 60-0*
H.B.—Otto Schnellbacher—Giants *over BROWN*
H.B.—Warren Lahr—Browns *1950*
Safety—Emlen Tunnell—Giants

OFFICIAL LEAGUE
MOST VALUABLE PLAYERS
(Winners of Joe F. Carr Trophy)

1938	Mel Hein	New York	center
1939	Parker Hall	Cleveland	halfback
1940	Ace Parker	Brooklyn	halfback
1941	Don Hutson	Green Bay	end
1942	Don Hutson	Green Bay	end
1943	Sid Luckman	Bears	quarterback
1944	Frank Sinkwich	Detroit	quarterback *Georgia*
1945	Bob Waterfield	Los Angeles	quarterback
1946	Bill Dudley	Pittsburgh	halfback

Award discontinued

ARMED SERVICE RECORDS

1945—By V-J Day (August 14, 1945) the service roster of the National Football League for World War II, limited to men who had participated in league games, totaled 638 men, 355 of whom were commissioned; 69 were decorated and 22 had lost their lives.

The Honor Roll:

Cpl. Michael Basca (Philadelphia Eagles halfback): Killed in France on Armistice Day, 1944, with Gen. Patton's 3d Army.

Lt. Charles Behan (Detroit Lions end): Killed by Japanese machine-gun fire on Okinawa, May 18, 1945.

Maj. Keith Birlem (Chicago Cardinals and Washington Redskins end): Killed in England, May 7, 1943, attempting to land crippled B-17 after raid over Europe.

Lt. Al Blozis (New York Giants tackle): Killed by German machine-gun fire in the Vosges Mountains of France, Jan. 31, 1945.

Charles Braidwood, Red Cross (Portsmouth Spartans, Cleveland Indians, Chicago Cardinals and Cincinnati Reds end): Killed in action in South Pacific, winter of 1944–45.

Lt. Young Bussey (Chicago Bears quarterback): Killed leading landing party on first day of Lingayen operation in Philippines.

Lt. Col. J. W. Hinton (Staten Island Stapletons back): Killed in East Indies on flight mission, Dec. 10, 1944.

Capt. Howard Johnson (Green Bay Packers guard): Killed on ninth day of Iwo Jima invasion.

Sgt. Alex Ketzko (Detroit Lions tackle): Killed in France, Dec. 23, 1944, with Gen. Patch's 7th Army.

Lt. John Lummus (New York Giants end): Killed by land-mine leading infantry-tank attack against last Japanese stronghold in Iwo Jima.

Capt. William McCaw (Racine Legions and Louisville Colonels end): Died during Korean War while assigned to ROTC at Indiana University.

Lt. John O'Keefe (Philadelphia Eagles director): Killed piloting Navy plane on patrol mission in Canal Zone.

Lt. Leonard Supulski (Philadelphia Eagles end): Killed in plane crash during maneuvers in Nebraska.

Lt. Donald Wemple (Brooklyn Dodgers end): Killed piloting Army transport plane in India.

Lt. Chester Wetterlund (Chicago Cardinals and Detroit Lions halfback): Killed flying Navy Hellcat on night patrol along New Jersey coast, Sept. 5, 1944.

Capt. Walter Young (Brooklyn Dodgers end): Killed piloting B-29 when he dropped out of formation to cover a crippled colleague during return from first B-29 raid over Tokyo, Jan. 9, 1945.

Lt. John Chevigny (Chicago Cardinals coach): Killed in second day of Iwo Jima invasion by direct shell hit on a bomb crater.

Capt. Ed Doyle (Pottsville Maroons end): First American officer killed in African invasion.

Lt. Edward Kahn (Boston Redskins guard): Died of wounds suffered in Leyte invasion, Feb. 17, 1945.

Capt. Lee Kizzire (Detroit Lions halfback): Leader of flight formation shot down over New Guinea area, Dec. 5, 1943.

Pvt. James Mooney (Chicago Cardinals, Brooklyn Dodgers and Chicago Bears end): Killed by sniper's bullet in France, Aug. 12, 1944.

Chief Spec. Gus Sonnenberg (Providence Steamrollers tackle): Died at Great Lakes Naval Training Station, Sept. 13, 1944.

PLAYERS IN ARMED FORCES FOR THE KOREAN WAR

CLEVELAND
Kenneth Gorgal—tackle—U.S. Army
Weldon Humble—guard—U.S. Marines
Kenneth Kanz—back—U.S. Army

DETROIT LIONS
Cloyce Box—end—U.S. Marines
James Cain—end—U.S. Army
Wallace Triplett—back—U.S. Army

WASHINGTON REDSKINS
Joseph Bartos—back—U.S. Marines
Hall Haynes—back—U.S. Army
Edward LeBaron—back—U.S. Marines (returned 1952)
John Steber—guard—U.S. Navy
Robert Goode—back—U.S. Army

GREEN BAY PACKERS
Clayton Tonnemaker—center—U.S. Army
Robert Forte—back—U.S. Army
Lawrence Coutre—back—U.S. Army
Leonard Szafaryn—tackle—U.S. Army

SAN FRANCISCO 49ers
Samuel Cathcart—back—U.S. Army
Clay Matthews—tackle—U.S. Army
Peter Schabarum—back—U.S. Air Force
Verl Lillywhite—back—U.S. Navy
James Monachino—back—U.S. Navy

NEW YORK GIANTS
Randall Clay—back—U.S. Army
William Milner—guard—U.S. Army
William Austin—tackle—U.S. Army

LOS ANGELES RAMS
Paul Barry—back—U.S. Army
George Sims—back—U.S. Army
Robert Boyd—end—U.S. Navy

PHILADELPHIA EAGLES
Hosea Rodgers—back—U.S. Marines
Toy Ledbetter—back—U.S. Army
Roscoe Hansen—tackle—U.S. Marines
Ray Romero—guard—U.S. Army

PITTSBURGH STEELERS
Thomas McWilliams—back—U.S. Army
Frank Rogel—back—U.S. Army
Walter Szot—tackle—U.S. Army

CHICAGO CARDINALS
John Hock—tackle—U.S. Army
Fred Wallner—guard—U.S. Army

CHICAGO BEARS
Col. Sam Francis—back—U.S. Army
Gerald Weatherly—guard—U.S. Army

DALLAS TEXANS
Andrew Hillhouse—end—U.S. Army
Edward Sharkey—guard—U.S. Marines

ALL-TIME INDIVIDUAL RECORDS

BALL CARRYING

ATTEMPTS

Most Attempts

1,320 Steven Van Buren, Philadelphia Eagles, 1944–1951 (eight seasons).

(Gained 5,860 yards, averaged 4.4.)

1,171 Clarke Hinkle, Green Bay, 1932–1941 (ten seasons). (Gained 3,860 yards, averaged 3.29.)

960 Tony Canadeo, Green Bay, 1941–1944; 1946–51 (ten seasons).

(Gained 4,006 yards, averaged 4.2.)

926 Alphonse Leemans, New York
     Giants, 1936–1943 (eight seasons).
     (Gained 3,117 yards, averaged 3.3.)

917 Leroy Gutowsky, Portsmouth, De-
     troit, Brooklyn, 1932–1939 (eight
     seasons). (Gained 3,278 yards,
     averaged 3.5.)

Most Attempts (one season)

271 Edward Price, New York Giants,
     1951. (Gained 971 yards, averaged
     3.61.)

263 Steven Van Buren, Philadelphia,
     1949. (Gained 1,146 yards, aver-
     aged 4.4.)

217 Steven Van Buren, Philadelphia,
     1947. (Gained 1,008 yards, aver-
     aged 4.6.)

Most Attempts (one game)

39   Harry Newman, New York Giants
     vs Green Bay, Nov. 11, 1934.
     (Gained 114 yards, averaged 2.9.)

35   Steven Van Buren, Philadelphia vs
     New York Bulldogs, Nov. 20, 1949.
     (Gained 174 yards, averaged 5.0.)
     George Grosvenor, Chicago Cardi-
     nals vs Green Bay, Dec. 6, 1936.
     (Gained 100 yards, averaged 2.8.)

GAINS

Total Yards Gained

5,860 in 1,320 attempts (average 4.4
       yards), Steven Van Buren, Phila-
       delphia, 1944–1951 (eight seasons).

4,006 in 960 attempts (average 4.2
       yards), Tony Canadeo, Green
       Bay, 1941–1944, 1946–1951 (ten
       seasons).

3,860 in 1,171 attempts (average 3.29
       yards), Clarke Hinkle, Green Bay,
       1932–1941 (ten seasons).
       (Note: Bronko Nagurski, Chicago
       Bears, credited with 4,031 yards in
       872 attempts (average 4.6 yards)
       in nine seasons—1930–1937 and
       1943—including seasons of 1930
       and 1931, two years before official
       statistics were recorded.)

Most Yards Gained (one season)

1,146 Steven Van Buren, Philadelphia,
       1949

1,052 Tony Canadeo, Green Bay, 1949

Most Yards Gained (one game)

218 in 26 attempts, Eugene Roberts,
     New York Giants vs Chicago Car-
     dinals, Nov. 12, 1950

LONGEST RUNS

Longest Run from Scrimmage

97   Andy Uram, Green Bay vs Chi-

cago Cardinals, Oct. 8, 1939 (TD)
     Robert Gage, Pittsburgh vs Chi-
     cago Bears, Dec. 4, 1949 (TD)

Longest Return of Kickoff

105 Frank Seno, Chicago Cardinals vs
     New York Giants, Oct. 20, 1946
     (TD)

103 Russell Craft, Philadelphia vs Los
     Angeles, Oct. 7, 1950 (TD)

102 Douglas Russell, Chicago Cardi-
     nals vs Cincinnati, Sept. 23, 1934
     (TD)

Longest Return with Intercepted Forward Pass

102 J. Robert Smith, Detroit vs Chi-
     cago Bears, Nov. 24, 1949 (TD)

100 Vern Huffman, Detroit vs Brook-
     lyn, Oct. 17, 1937 (TD)

99   Martin Kottler, Pittsburgh vs Chi-
     cago Cardinals, Sept. 27, 1933
     (TD)

Longest Return with Missed Field Goal

99   Jerry Williams, Los Angeles vs
     Green Bay, Sept. 16, 1951 (TD)

Longest Punt Return

98   Gilbert LeFebvre, Cincinnati vs
     Brooklyn, Dec. 3, 1933 (TD)

96   William Dudley, Washington vs
     Pittsburgh, Dec. 3, 1950 (TD)

90   Andy Uram, Green Bay vs Brook-
     lyn, Oct. 12, 1941 (TD)

Longest Run with Fumble

98   George Halas, Chicago Bears vs
     Oorang Indians, Nov. 4, 1923
     (TD)

92   Joseph Carter, Philadelphia vs
     New York Giants, Sept. 25, 1938
     (TD)

88   Robert Pylman, Philadelphia vs
     New York Giants, Sept. 25, 1938
     (TD)

Longest Run with Intercepted Lateral Pass

93   Richard Poillon, Washington vs
     Philadelphia, Nov. 21, 1948 (TD)

PASSING

COMPLETIONS

Most Passes Completed

1,689 Samuel Baugh, Washington, 1937–
       1951 (fifteen seasons), plus 58 in
       one Play-off and 5 Championship
       games

904   Sidney Luckman, Chicago Bears,
       1939–1950 (twelve seasons), plus
       45 in one Play-off and 5 Cham-
       pionship games

763   Robert Waterfield, Los Angeles

Rams, 1945–1951 (seven seasons),
plus 46 in 4 championship games.
732 Thomas Thompson, Pittsburgh
1940; Philadelphia 1941–42, 1945–
50 (nine seasons), plus 45 in one
Play-off and 3 Championship games

Most Passes Completed (one season)

210 Samuel Baugh, Washington, 1947
(attempted 354)
185 Samuel Baugh, Washington, 1948
(attempted 315)
176 Sidney Luckman, Chicago Bears,
1947 (attempted 323)
162 Charles Conerly, New York Giants,
1948 (attempted 299)
John Lujack, Chicago Bears, 1949
(Attempted 312)

Most Passes Completed (one game)

36 Charles Conerly, New York Giants
vs Pittsburgh, Dec. 5, 1948
33 David O'Brien, Philadelphia vs
Washington, Dec. 1, 1940
29 John Lujack, Chicago Bears vs
New York Giants, Oct. 23, 1949
Samuel Baugh, Washington vs Los
Angeles, Dec. 11, 1949
28 James Hardy, Los Angeles vs Chicago Cardinals, Oct. 31, 1948

ATTEMPTS

Most Passes Attempted

2,983 Samuel Baugh, Washington, 1937–
1951 (fifteen seasons), plus 102 in
one Play-off and 5 Championship
games
1,744 Sidney Luckman, Chicago Bears,
1939–1950 (twelve seasons) plus
85 in one Play-off and 5 Championship games
1,509 Robert Waterfield, Cleveland
Rams, 1945; Los Angeles, 1946–
1951 (seven seasons), plus 116 in
one Playoff and 4 Championship
games

Most Passes Attempted (one season)

354 Samuel Baugh, Washington, 1947
(completed 210)
336 Robert Layne, Detroit, 1950 (completed 152)
332 Robert Layne, Detroit, 1951 (completed 152)
323 Sidney Luckman, Chicago Bears,
1947 (completed 176)
315 Samuel Baugh, Washington, 1948
(completed 185)
Yelverton Tittle, Baltimore, 1950
(completed 161)
312 John Lujack, Chicago Bears, 1949
(completed 162)
306 Frank Albert, San Francisco, 1950
(completed 155)

Most Passes Attempted (one game)

60 David O'Brien, Philadelphia vs
Washington, Dec. 1, 1940 (completed 33)

INTERCEPTIONS

Most Passes Had Intercepted

204 Samuel Baugh, Washington, 1937–
1951 (fifteen seasons) (2,938 attempts)
130 Sidney Luckman, Chicago Bears,
1939–1950 (twelve seasons)

*Fewest Passes Had Intercepted (600 or more
attempts)*

42 Ed Danowski, New York Giants,
1934–1939, 1941 (seven seasons)

*Fewest Passes Had Intercepted (100 or more
attempts) (one season)*

3 Dwight Sloan, Detroit, 1939 (102
attempts)
4 Samuel Baugh, Washington, 1945
(182 attempts)
Paul Christman, Chicago Cardinals, 1948 (114 attempts)

*Most Yards Returned Intercepted Passes
(one season)*

301 Don Doll, Detroit, 1949 (11 interceptions; 1 TD)

Most Passes Had Intercepted (one game)

8 James Hardy, Chicago Cardinals
vs Philadelphia, Sept. 24, 1950 (39
attempts)
7 Parker Hall, Cleveland vs Green
Bay, Nov. 8, 1942 (25 attempts)
Frank Sinkwich, Detroit vs Green
Bay, Oct. 24, 1943 (26 attempts)
Robert Waterfield, Los Angeles vs
Green Bay, Oct. 17, 1948 (35 at-
tempts)

Most Passes Had Intercepted (one season)

31 Sidney Luckman, Chicago Bears,
1947 (323 attempts)
25 Frank Filchock, New York Giants,
1946 (169 attempts)
27 Wilson Schwenk, Chicago Cardinals, 1942 (295 attempts)
24 Robert Waterfield, Los Angeles,
1949 (296 attempts)

Most Passes Intercepted (one season)

13 Dan Sandifer, Washington, 1948
(258 yards; 2 TD's)
Orban Sanders, New York Yanks,
1950 (199 yards)

GAINS

Most Yards Gained on Passes

21,933 Samuel Baugh, Washington, 1937–

1951 (fifteen seasons), plus 831 in one Play-off and 5 Championship games

14,683   Sidney Luckman, Chicago Bears, 1939–1950 (twelve seasons), plus 711 in one Play-off and 5 Championship games)

11,238   Robert Waterfield, Los Angeles (Cleveland) Rams, 1945–1951 (six seasons), plus 932 in one Play-off and 4 Championship games)

10,400   Thomas Thompson, Pittsburgh, 1940, Philadelphia 1941–1942, 1945–1950 (nine seasons), plus 503 yards in one Play-off and 3 Championship games

Most Yards Gained on Passes (one season)

2,938   Samuel Baugh, Washington, 1947 (12 games)

2,712   Sidney Luckman, Chicago Bears, 1947 (12 games)

2,658   John Lujack, Chicago Bears, 1947 (12 games)

2,599   Samuel Baugh, Washington, 1948 (12 games)

2,403   Robert Layne, Detroit Lions, 1951 (12 games)

2,323   Robert Layne, Detroit, 1950 (12 games)

2,251   George Ratterman, New York Yanks, 1950 (12 games)

2,194   Sidney Luckman, Chicago Bears, 1943 (10 games)

2,191   Paul Christman, Chicago Cardinals, 1947 (12 games)

2,175   Charles Conerly, New York Giants, 1948 (12 games)

Most Yards Gained on Passes (one game)

554   Norman Van Brocklin, Los Angeles vs New York Yanks, Sept. 28, 1951 (27 completions)

468   John Lujack, Chicago Bears vs Chicago Cardinals, Dec. 11, 1949 (24 completions)

446   Samuel Baugh, Washington vs Boston, Oct. 31, 1948 (17 completions)

433   Sidney Luckman, Chicago Bears vs New York Giants, Nov. 14, 1943 (21 completions)

Longest Completed Pass

99   Frank Filchock, Washington, to Andy Farkas, vs Pittsburgh, Oct. 15, 1939 (includes pass and run) (TD)

98   Douglas Russell, Chicago Cardinals, to Gaynell Tinsley, vs Cleveland Rams, Nov. 27, 1938 (includes pass and run) (TD)

97   Pat Coffee, Chicago Cardinals, to Gaynell Tinsley, vs Chicago Bears, Dec. 5, 1937 (includes pass and run) (TD)

Shortest Completed Pass (for TD)

4   inches, Cecil Isbell, Green Bay, to Don Hutson, vs Cleveland, Oct. 18, 1942 (TD)

TOUCHDOWN PASSES

Most Touchdown Passes

185   Samuel Baugh, Washington, 1937– 1951 (fifteen seasons)

139   Sidney Luckman, Chicago Bears, 1939–1950 (twelve seasons)

96   Robert Waterfield, Los Angeles, 1945–1951 (six seasons)

90   Thomas Thompson, Pittsburgh 1940, Philadelphia 1941–1942, 1945–1950 (nine seasons)

Most Touchdown Passes (one season)

28   Sidney Luckman, Chicago Bears, 1943 (10 games)

26   Robert Layne, Detroit Lions, 1951

25   Samuel Baugh, Washington, 1947
     Thomas Thompson, Philadelphia, 1948

24   Sidney Luckman, Chi. Bears, 1947
     Cecil Isbell, Green Bay, 1942

23   Samuel Baugh, Washington, 1943
     John Lujack, Chicago Bears, 1949

Most Touchdown Passes (one game)

7   Sidney Luckman, Chicago Bears vs New York Giants, Nov. 14, 1943

6   Samuel Baugh, Washington vs Brooklyn, Oct. 31, 1943
     Samuel Baugh, Washington vs Chicago Cardinals, Nov. 23, 1947
     John Lujack, Chicago Bears vs Chicago Cardinals, Dec. 11, 1949
     James Hardy, Chicago Cardinals vs Baltimore, Oct. 2, 1950

Most Consecutive Games Throwing TD Passes

23   Cecil Isbell, Green Bay (12 in 1941, 11 in 1942)

19   Sidney Luckman, Chicago Bears (3 in 1942, 10 in 1943, 6 in 1944)

10   Samuel Baugh, Washington (2 in 1942, 8 in 1943)
     Samuel Baugh, Washington (10 in 1947)
     Charles Conerly, New York Giants (9 in 1948, one in 1949)
     George Ratterman, New York Yanks (10 in 1950)
     Robert Layne, Detroit (1951)

EFFICIENCY

Best Passing Efficiency (500 or more attempts)

56.6%   Samuel Baugh, Washington, 1937– 1951 (15 seasons) (1,689 completions in 2,983 attempts)

52.1   Thomas Thompson, Pittsburgh

1940, Philadelphia , 1941–1942, 1945–1950 (9 seasons) (732 completions in 1,424 attempts)

51.8 Sidney Luckman, Chicago Bears, 1939–1950 (12 seasons) (904 completions in 1,744 attempts)

50.5 Robert Waterfield, Cleveland 1945, Los Angeles 1946–1951 (7 seasons) (163 completions in 1,509 attempts)

Best Passing Efficiency (one season)

70.3% Samuel Baugh, Washington (128 completions in 182 attempts) 1945

62.7 Samuel Baugh, Washington (111 completions in 177 attempts) 1940

61.7 Frank Filchock, Washington (55 completions in 89 attempts) 1939

59.3 Samuel Baugh, Washington (210 completions in 354 attempts) 1947

58.7 Samuel Baugh, Washington (185 completions in 315 attempts) 1948

58.7 Samuel Baugh, Washington (132 completions in 225 attempts) 1942

PASS RECEIVING

ALL PASSES

Most Passes Caught

489 Don Hutson, Green Bay, 1935–1945 (eleven seasons)

Most Passes Caught (one season)

84 Thomas Fears, Los Angeles, 1950

77 Thomas Fears, Los Angeles, 1949

74 Don Hutson, Green Bay, 1942

66 Elroy Hirsch, Los Angeles, 1951

65 Robert Mann, Detroit, 1949

64 James Keane, Chicago Bears, 1947

Most Passes Caught (one game)

18 Thomas Fears, Los Angeles vs Green Bay, Dec. 3, 1950 (189 yards)

14 Don Looney, Philadelphia vs Washington, Dec. 1, 1940 (180 yards)

Don Hutson, Green Bay vs New York Giants, Nov. 22, 1942 (134 yards)

James Keane, Chicago Bears vs New York Giants, Oct. 23, 1949 (193 yards)

Ralph Heywood, New York Bulldogs vs Detroit, Dec. 4, 1949 (151 yards)

13 Don Hutson, Green Bay vs Cleveland, Oct. 18, 1942 (209 yards)

12 James Benton, Los Angeles vs New York Giants, Dec. 1, 1946 (202 yards)

Cloyce Box, Detroit vs Baltimore, Dec. 3, 1950 (302 yards)

TOUCHDOWN PASSES

Most Touchdown Passes Received

101 Don Hutson, Green Bay, 1935–1945 (eleven seasons)

Most Touchdown Passes Received (one season)

17 Don Hutson, Green Bay, 1942

17 Elroy Hirsch, Los Angeles, 1951

14 Malcolm Kutner, Chicago Cardinals, 1948

13 Kenneth Kavanaugh, Chicago Bears, 1947

Most Touchdown Passes Received (one game)

5 Robert Shaw, Chicago Cardinals vs Baltimore, Oct. 2, 1950

4 Joseph Carter, Philadelphia vs Cincinnati, Nov. 6, 1934

Don Hutson, Green Bay vs Detroit, Oct. 7, 1945

Robert Shaw, Los Angeles vs Washington, Dec. 11, 1949

Cloyce Box, Detroit vs Baltimore, Dec. 3, 1950

Elroy Hirsch, Los Angeles vs New York Yanks, Sept. 28, 1951

YARDAGE GAINED

Most Yards Gained Catching Passes

8,010 Don Hutson, Green Bay, 1935–1945 (eleven seasons)

Most Yards Gained Catching Passes (one season)

1,495 Elroy Hirsch, Los Angeles, 1951

1,211 Don Hutson, Green Bay, 1942

1,116 Thomas Fears, Los Angeles, 1950

Most Yards Gained Catching Passes (one game)

303 James Benton, Cleveland Rams vs Detroit, Nov. 22, 1945 (10)

302 Cloyce Box, Detroit vs Baltimore, Dec. 3, 1950 (12)

237 Don Hutson, Green Bay vs Brooklyn, Nov. 21, 1943 (8)

Longest Completed Pass

99 Andrew Farkas, Washington, from Frank Filchock, vs Pittsburgh, Oct. 15, 1939 (includes pass and run) (TD)

98 Gaynell Tinsley, Chicago Cardinals, from Douglas Russell, vs Cleveland Rams, Nov. 27, 1938 (includes pass and run) (TD)

97 Gaynell Tinsley, Chicago Cardinals, from Pat Coffee, vs Chicago Bears, Dec. 5, 1937 (includes pass and run) (TD)

Shortest Completed Pass (for touchdown)

4 inches Don Hutson, Green Bay, from Cecil Isbell, vs Cleveland Rams, Oct. 18, 1942 (TD).

PUNTING

Most Punts (one season)

92 Howard Maley, Boston Yanks, 1947
81 Adrian Burk, Baltimore, 1950
71 Earl Girard, Green Bay, 1950
   Orban Sanders, N. Y. Yanks, 1950

Most Punts (one game)

14 Samuel Baugh, Washington vs Philadelphia, Nov. 5, 1939
   John Kinscherf, New York Giants vs Detroit, Nov. 7, 1943
   George Taliaferro, N. Y. Yanks vs Los Angeles, Sept. 28, 1951

Longest Punt (Yards)

94 Wilbur Henry, Canton vs Akron, Oct. 28, 1923
88 Robert Waterfield, Los Angeles vs Green Bay, Oct. 17, 1948
86 Ralph Kercheval, Brooklyn vs Chicago Bears, Oct. 20, 1935
   Robert Waterfield, Los Angeles vs Green Bay, Oct. 5, 1947

Best Punting Average (one season)

48.7 yards, Sammy Baugh, Washington, 1942 (30 punts)

PUNT RETURNS

Most Punt Returns (one season)

34 Emlen Tunnell, New York Giants, 1951 (ret. 489 yards)
33 George McAfee, Chicago Bears, 1950 (ret. 284 yards)
31 Emlen Tunnell, New York Giants, 1950 (ret. 305 yards)

Most Punt Returns (one game)

7 Abisha Pritchard, Philadelphia vs Green Bay, Nov. 29, 1942 (ret. 81 yards)

KICKOFF RETURNS

Most Kickoff Returns and Most Yards Returned (one season)

29 Edward Saenz, Washington, 1947 (797 yards, average 27.4)
28 Don Paul, Chicago Cardinals, 1950 (693 yards, average 24.8)

Most Kickoff Returns and Most Yards Returned (one game)

4 Wallace Triplett, Detroit vs Los Angeles, Oct. 29, 1950 (294 yards, average 73.6)

SCORING

POINTS

Total Points

825 Don Hutson (105 TD's, 174 extra points, 7 field goals) Green Bay 1935–1945 (eleven seasons)
496 Kenneth Strong (35 TD's, 169 extra points, 39 field goals) Stapleton 1929–1932, New York Giants 1933, 1935, 1939, 1944–1947 (twelve seasons)
490 Robert Waterfield (12 TD's, 279 extra points, 49 field goals) Cleveland 1945, Los Angeles 1946–1951 (seven seasons)
464 Steven Van Buren (77 TD's, 2 extra points) Philadelphia 1944–1951 (eight seasons)
426 Bill Dudley (44 TD's, 96 extra points, 22 field goals) Pittsburgh 1942, 1944–1945; Detroit 1947–1949; Washington 1950–1951 (eight seasons)
411 Ward Cuff (21 TD's, 156 extra points, 43 field goals) New York Giants 1937–1945, Chicago Cardinals 1946, Green Bay 1947 (eleven seasons)

Most Points (one season)

138 Don Hutson (17 TD's, 33 extra points, 1 field goal) Green Bay, 1942
128 Doak Walker (11 TD's, 38 extra points, 8 field goals) Detroit, 1950
117 Don Hutson (12 TD's, 36 extra points, 3 field goals) Green Bay, 1943
110 Steven Van Buren (18 TD's, 2 extra points) Philadelphia, 1945
   Marlin Harder (6 TD's, 53 extra points, 7 field goals) Cardinals, 1948
109 John Lujack (11 TD's, 34 extra points, 3 field goals) Chicago Bears, 1950

Most Points (one game)

40 Ernest Nevers (6 TD's, 4 extra points) Chicago Cardinals vs Chicago Bears, Nov. 29, 1929
36 William Jones (6 TD's) Cleveland Browns vs Chicago Bears, Nov. 25, 1951
31 Don Hutson (4 TD's, 7 extra points) Green Bay vs Detroit, Oct. 7, 1945
30 Robert Shaw (5 TD's) Chicago Cardinals vs Baltimore, Oct. 2, 1950
27 John Driscoll (4 TD's, 3 extra points) Chicago Cardinals vs Rochester, Oct. 7, 1923

26 Gordon Soltau (3 TD's, 5 extra points, 1 field goal (San Francisco vs Los Angeles, Oct. 28, 1951

24 Don Hutson, Green Bay, 1942; Robert Shaw, Los Angeles, 1949; Cloyce Box, Detroit, 1950; Doak Walker, Detroit, 1950

Most Consecutive Games Scoring One or More Points

41 Don Hutson, Green Bay (2 in 1940, 12 in 1941, 11 in 1942, 10 in 1943, 6 in 1944)

TOUCHDOWNS

Most Touchdowns

105 Don Hutson, Green Bay, 1935–1945 (eleven seasons)

77 Steven Van Buren, Philadelphia, 1944–1951 (eight seasons)

52 Kenneth Kavanaugh, Chicago Bears, 1940–1941, 1945–1950 (eight seasons)

50 Vern Lewellen, Green Bay, 1924–1932 (nine seasons)

48 James Benton, Cleveland Rams, 1938, 1940, 1942, 1944, 1945; Chicago Bears, 1943; Los Angeles, 1946, 1947 (nine seasons)

44 William Dudley, Pittsburgh, 1942, 1945, 1946; Detroit, 1947–1949; Washington, 1950–1951 (eight seasons)

42 John "Blood" McNally, Milwaukee, 1925–1927; Green Bay, 1928–1936; Pittsburgh, 1937–1939 (fifteen seasons)
    Clarke Hinkle, Green Bay, 1932–1941 (ten seasons)

Most Touchdowns (one season)

18 Steven Van Buren, Philadelphia, 1945

17 Don Hutson, Green Bay, 1942
    Eugene Roberts, New York Giants, 1949
    Elroy Hirsch, Los Angeles, 1951

15 Malcolm Kutner, Chicago Cardinals, 1948

14 Steven Van Buren, Philadelphia, 1947

Most Touchdowns (one game)

6 Ernest Nevers, Chicago Cardinals vs Chicago Bears, Nov. 28, 1929

6 William Jones, Cleveland Browns vs Chicago Bears, Nov. 25, 1951

5 Robert Shaw, Chicago Cardinals vs Baltimore, Oct. 2, 1950

4 John Driscoll, Chicago Cardinals vs Rochester, Oct. 7, 1923
   Joseph Carter, Philadelphia vs Cincinnati, Nov. 6, 1934

Don Hutson, Green Bay vs Detroit, Oct. 7, 1945
Robert Shaw, Los Angeles vs Washington, Dec. 11, 1949
Cloyce Box, Detroit vs Baltimore, Dec. 3, 1950
Elroy Hirsch, Los Angeles vs N.Y. Yanks, Sept. 28, 1951

FIELD GOALS

Most Field Goals

49 Robert Waterfield (Place Kicks) Cleveland-Los Angeles Rams 1945–1951 (eight seasons)
    John Driscoll (Drop Kicks) Chicago Cardinals (37) 1921–1925, Chicago Bears (12) 1926–1928 (eight seasons)

43 Ward Cuff (Place Kicks) New York Giants (31) 1937–1945, Chicago Cardinals (5) 1946, Green Bay (7) 1947 (eleven seasons)

Most Field Goals (one season)

13 Robert Waterfield (Place Kicks) Los Angeles Rams 1951

13 Louis Groza (Place Kicks) Cleveland 1950

12 Ray Poole (Place Kicks) New York Giants 1951

11 John Driscoll (Drop Kicks) Chicago Cardinals 1925

10 (Twice) John Driscoll, Chicago Cardinals 1923, Chicago Bears 1926
    Jack Manders (Place Kicks) Chicago Bears 1934

Most Field Goals (one game)

5 Robert Waterfield (Place Kicks) Los Angeles Rams vs Detroit, Dec. 9, 1951 (17, 40, 25, 20, 39 yards)

4 John Driscoll (Drop Kicks) Chicago Cardinals vs Columbus, Oct. 11, 1925 (23, 18, 50, 25 yards)

3 Several players

Longest Field Goal
Place Kick (Yards)

54 Glenn Presnell, Detroit vs Green Bay, Oct. 7, 1934

52 Lee Artoe, Chicago Bears vs New York Giants, Oct. 27, 1940

52 Ted Fritsch, Green Bay vs New York Yanks, Oct. 19, 1950

Drop Kick (Yards)

50 John Driscoll, Chicago Cardinals vs Milwaukee, Sept. 28, 1924

50 John Driscoll, Chicago Cardinals vs Columbus, Oct. 11, 1925

50 William Henry, Canton vs Toledo, Nov. 12, 1922

EXTRA POINTS

Most Points after Touchdown

271   Robert Waterfield, Cleveland Rams 1945, Los Angeles Rams 1946–1951 (seven seasons)

174   Don Hutson, Green Bay, 1935–1945 (eleven seasons)

Most Points after Touchdown (one season)

54   Robert Waterfield, Los Angeles Rams, 1950 (missed four)

53   Marlin Harder, Chicago Cardinals, 1948 (missed none)

Most Points after Touchdown (one game)

9   Marlin Harder, Chicago Cardinals vs New York Giants, Oct. 17, 1948 Robert Waterfield, Los Angeles vs Baltimore, Oct. 22, 1950

8   Robert Snyder, Chicago Bears vs New York Giants, Nov. 14, 1943 Richard Poillon, Washington vs Boston Yanks, Oct. 31, 1948 Marlin Harder, Chicago Cardinals vs New York Bulldogs, Nov. 13, 1949

Most Consecutive Points after Touchdown

84   John Patton, Philadelphia (3 games in 1947, 12 in 1948, 7 in 1949)

81   Marlin Harder, Chicago Cardinals (12 games in 1948, 8 in 1949)

LENGTH OF SERVICE

MOST YEARS ACTIVE PLAYER IN LEAGUE

16   Samuel Baugh, back, Washington, 1937–52

15   John "Blood" McNally, back, Milwaukee 1925–27, Green Bay 1928–36, Pittsburgh 1937–39

15   Melvin Hein, center, New York Giants 1931–45

13   George Trafton, center, Chicago Bears 1920–32

Alex Wojciechowicz, center, Detroit 1938–45, Philadelphia 1946–50

MOST CONSECUTIVE YEARS PLAYED IN EVERY GAME

11   Sid Luckman, back, Chicago Bears 1939–49 (Record started Sept. 15, 1939, ended Oct. 16, 1949)

MOST YEARS COACH IN NATIONAL LEAGUE

31   Earl Lambeau, Green Bay 1921–49, Chicago Cardinals 1950–51

27   George Halas, Chicago Bears, 1920–29, 1933–42, 1946–52

22   Stephen Owen, New York Giants, 1931–52

INDIVIDUAL DEPARTMENTAL CHAMPIONS

BALL CARRYING

*League Record

			Yds.	Atts.
1951	Edward Price	New York Giants	971	271*
1950	Marion Motley	Cleveland	810	140
1949	Steven Van Buren	Philadelphia	1,146*	263
1948	Steven Van Buren	Philadelphia	945	201
1947	Steven Van Buren	Philadelphia	1,008	217
1946	William Dudley	Pittsburgh	604	146
1945	Steven Van Buren	Philadelphia	832	143
1944	William Paschal	New York	737	196
1943	William Paschal	New York	572	147
1942	William Dudley	Pittsburgh	696	162
1941	Clarence Manders	Brooklyn	486	111
1940	Byron White	Detroit	514	146
1939	William Osmanski	Chicago Bears	699	121
1938	Byron White	Detroit	567	152
1937	Cliff Battles	Washington	874	216
1936	Alphonse Leemans	New York	830	206
1935	Douglas Russell	Cardinals	499	140
1934	Beattie Feathers	Chicago Bears	1,004	101
1933	Cliff Battles	Boston	737	146
1932	Robert Campiglio	Stapleton	504	104

FIELD GOALS

*League Record

1951	Robert Waterfield	Los Angeles	13*
1950	Louis Groza	Cleveland	13*
1949	John Patton	Philadelphia	9
	Robert Waterfield	Los Angeles	9
1948	John Patton	Philadelphia	8
1947	Marlin Harder	Cardinals	7
1946	Ted Fritsch	Green Bay	9
1945	Joseph Aguirre	Washington	7
1944	Kenneth Strong	New York	6
1943	Don Hutson	Green Bay	3
1942	William Daddio	Cardinals	5
1941	Clarke Hinkle	Green Bay	6
1940	Clarke Hinkle	Green Bay	9
1939	Ward Cuff	New York	7
1938	Ward Cuff	New York	5
	Ralph Kerchavel	Brooklyn	5
1937	Jack Manders	Chicago Bears	8
1936	Jack Manders	Chicago Bears	7
	Armand Niccolai	Pittsburgh	7
1935	Armand Niccolai	Pittsburgh	6
	William Smith	Cardinals	6
1934	Jack Manders	Chicago Bears	10
1933	Jack Manders	Chicago Bears	6
	Glenn Presnell	Portsmouth	6
1932	Earl Clark	Portsmouth	3

FORWARD PASSING

*League Record

			Passes	Comp.	Yds.	Intercpt.
1951	Robert Waterfield	Los Angeles	176	88	1,566	10
1950	Norman Van Brocklin	Los Angeles	233	127	2,061	14
1949	Samuel Baugh	Washington	255	145	1,903	14
1948	Thomas Thompson	Philadelphia	246	141	1,965	11
1947	Samuel Baugh	Washington	354*	210*	2,988*	15
1946	Robert Waterfield	Los Angeles	251	127	1,747	17
1945	Samuel Baugh	Washington	182	128	1,669	4*
1944	Frank Filchock	Washington	147	84	1,139	9
1943	Samuel Baugh	Washington	239	133	1,754	19*
1942	Cecil Isbell	Green Bay	268	146	2,021	14
1941	Cecil Isbell	Green Bay	206	117	1,479	11
1940	Samuel Baugh	Washington	177	111	1,367	10
1939	Parker Hall	Cleveland	208	106	1,227	13
1938	Ed Danowski	New York	129	70	848	8
1937	Samuel Baugh	Washington	171	81	1,127	14
1936	Arnold Herber	Green Bay	173	77	1,239	13
1935	Ed Danowski	New York	113	57	795	9
1934	Arnold Herber	Green Bay	115	42	799	12
1933	Harry Newman	New York	132	53	963	17
1932	Arnold Herber	Green Bay	101	37	639	9

PASS RECEIVING

*League Record

			Caught	Yds.	TD
1951	Elroy Hirsch	Los Angeles	66	1,495*	17*
1950	Tom Fears	Los Angeles	84*	1,116	7
1949	Tom Fears	Los Angeles	77	1,013	9
1948	Tom Fears	Los Angeles	51	698	4
1947	James Keane	Chicago Bears	64	910	10
1946	James Benton	Los Angeles	63	981	6
1945	Don Hutson	Green Bay	47	834	9
1944	Don Hutson	Green Bay	58	866	9
1943	Don Hutson	Green Bay	47	776	11
1942	Don Hutson	Green Bay	74	1,211	17*
1941	Don Hutson	Green Bay	58	738	10
1940	Don Looney	Philadelphia	58	707	4
1939	Don Hutson	Green Bay	34	846	6
1938	Gaynell Tinsley	Cardinals	41	516	1
1937	Don Hutson	Green Bay	41	552	7
1936	Don Hutson	Green Bay	34	526	9
1935	Tod Goodwin	New York	26	432	4
1934	Joseph Carter	Philadelphia	16	237	3
1933	John Kelley	Brooklyn	21	219	3
1932	Luke Johnsos	Chicago Bears	24	321	2

SCORING

*League Record

			TD	X Pt	FG	Total
1951	Elroy Hirsch	Los Angeles Rams	17	0	0	102
1950	Doak Walker	Detroit	11	38	8	128
1949	Marlin Harder	Cardinals	8	45	3	102
	Eugene Roberts	Giants	17	0	0	102
1948	Marlin Harder	Cardinals	6	53	7	110
1947	Marlin Harder	Cardinals	7	39	7	102
1946	Ted Fritsch	Green Bay	10	13	9	100
1945	Steven Van Buren	Philadelphia	18	2	0	110
1944	Don Hutson	Green Bay	9	31	0	85
1943	Don Hutson	Green Bay	12	36	3	117
1942	Don Hutson	Green Bay	17	33	1	138*
1941	Don Hutson	Green Bay	12	20	0	95
1940	Don Hutson	Green Bay	7	15	0	57
1939	Andy Farkas	Washington	11	2	0	68
1938	Clark Hinkle	Green Bay	7	7	3	58
1937	Jack Manders	Chicago Bears	5	15	8	69
1936	Earl Clark	Detroit	7	19	4	73
1935	Earl Clark	Detroit	6	16	1	55
1934	Jack Manders	Chicago Bears	3	31	10	79
1933	Ken Strong	Giants	6	13	5	64
	Glenn Presnell	Portsmouth	6	10	6	64
1932	Earl Clark	Detroit	4	6	3	39

CHAMPIONSHIP GAME RECORDS

BALL CARRYING

Most Yards Gained

320 Steven Van Buren, Philadelphia (75 attempts; played in 3 games)

214 Bronko Nagurski, Chicago Bears (57 attempts; played in 4 games)

192 Elmer Angsman, Chicago Cardinals (20 attempts; played in 2 games)

178 William Osmanski, Chicago Bears (36 attempts; played in 4 games)

Most Yards Gained (one game)

196 Steven Van Buren, Philadelphia vs Los Angeles, Dec. 18, 1949 (31 attempts)

159 Elmer Angsman, Chicago Cardinals vs Philadelphia, Dec. 28, 1947 (10 attempts)

109 William Osmanski, Chicago Bears vs Washington, Dec. 8, 1940 (10 attempts)

101 James Gillette, Cleveland Rams vs Washington, Dec. 16, 1945 (17 attempts)

99 Otto Graham, Cleveland Browns vs Los Angeles, Dec. 24, 1950 (12 attempts)

Longest Run from Scrimmage

70 Elmer Angsman, Chicago Cardinals (made 2 of 70 yards each) Chicago Cardinals vs Philadelphia, Dec. 28, 1947

68 William Osmanski, Chicago Bears vs Washington, Dec. 8, 1940

49 Steven Van Buren, Philadelphia vs Los Angeles, Dec. 18, 1949

FORWARD PASSING

Most Passes Completed

46 Robert Waterfield, Los Angeles (Attempted 95; played in 4 games)

42 Samuel Baugh, Washington (Attempted 81; played in 5 games)

41 Sidney Luckman, Chicago Bears (Attempted 76; played in 5 games)

41 Otto Graham, Cleveland Browns (Attempted 72; played in 2 games)

Most Passes Completed (one game)

27 Thomas Thompson, Philadelphia vs Chicago Cardinals, Dec. 28, 1947 (Attempted 44)

22 Otto Graham, Cleveland Browns vs Los Angeles, Dec. 24, 1950 (Attempted 32)

19 Otto Graham, Cleveland Browns vs Los Angeles, Dec. 23, 1951 (Attempted 40)

18 Samuel Baugh, Washington vs Chicago Bears, Dec. 12, 1937 (Attempted 33)

Robert Waterfield, Los Angeles vs Cleveland Browns, Dec. 24, 1950 (Attempted 31)

15 Sidney Luckman, Chicago Bears vs Washington, Dec. 26, 1943 (Attempted 26)

Most Passes Attempted

95 Robert Waterfield, Cleveland and Los Angeles Rams (Completed 46 in 4 games)

81 Samuel Baugh, Washington (Completed 42 in 5 games)

76 Sidney Luckman, Chicago Bears (Completed 41 in 5 games)

Most Passes Attempted (one game)

44 Thomas Thompson, Philadelphia vs Chicago Cardinals, Dec. 28, 1947 (Completed 27)

40 Otto Graham, Cleveland Browns vs Los Angeles, Dec. 23, 1951 (Completed 19)

33 Samuel Baugh, Washington vs Chicago Bears, Dec. 12, 1937 (Completed 18)

32 Otto Graham, Cleveland Browns vs Los Angeles, Dec. 24, 1950 (Completed 22)

31 Robert Waterfield, Los Angeles vs Cleveland Browns, Dec. 24, 1950 (Completed 18)

Most Yards Gained Passing

672 Robert Waterfield, Cleveland and Los Angeles Rams (46 completions in 4 games)

670 Sidney Luckman, Chicago Bears (41 completions in 5 games)

632 Samuel Baugh, Washington (42 completions in 5 games)

Most Yards Gained Passing (one game)

335 Samuel Baugh, Washington vs Chicago Bears, Dec. 12, 1937 (18 completions)

312 Robert Waterfield, Los Angeles vs Cleveland Browns, Dec. 24, 1950 (18 completions)

298 Otto Graham, Cleveland Browns vs Los Angeles, Dec. 24, 1950 (22 completions)

Most Passes Had Intercepted

13 Frank Filchock, Washington and New York Giants (Played in 3 games)

9 Robert Waterfield, Cleveland and Los Angeles Rams (Played in 4 games)

8   Arnold Herber, Green Bay and New York Giants (Played in 4 games)
    Samuel Baugh, Washington (Played in 5 games)

Most Passes Had Intercepted (one game)

6   Frank Filchock, New York Giants vs Chicago Bears, Dec. 15, 1946 (Attempted 26, completed 9)
5   Frank Filchock, Washington vs Chicago Bears, Dec. 8, 1940 (Attempted 13, completed 7)
4   Arnold Herber, New York Giants vs Green Bay, Dec. 17, 1944 (Attempted 22, completed 8)
    Robert Waterfield, Los Angeles vs Cleveland Browns, Dec. 24, 1950 (Attempted 31, completed 18)
3   Several

Most Touchdown Passes

7   Sidney Luckman, Chicago Bears (Played in 5 games)
6   Samuel Baugh, Washington (Played in 5 games)
5   Otto Graham, Cleveland Browns (Played in 2 games)
4   Frank Filchock, Washington and New York Giants (Played in 3 games)
3   Robert Waterfield, Cleveland and Los Angeles Rams (Played in 4 games)
2   Several

Most Touchdown Passes (one game)

5   Sidney Luckman, Chicago Bears vs Washington, Dec. 26, 1943
4   Otto Graham, Cleveland Browns vs Los Angeles, Dec. 24, 1950
3   Samuel Baugh, Washington vs Chicago Bears, Dec. 12, 1937
2   Several

Longest Completed Pass (Yards)

82 Robert Waterfield to Glenn Davis, Los Angeles vs Cleveland Browns, Dec. 24, 1950 (TD)
77 Samuel Baugh to Wayne Millner, Washington vs Chicago Bears, Dec. 12, 1937 (TD)
73 Norman Van Brocklin to Thomas Fears, Los Angeles vs Cleveland Browns, Dec. 23, 1951 (TD)

PASS RECEIVING

Most Passes Caught

16 Wayne Millner, Boston and Washington Redskins (Played in 4 games)
15 Dante Lavelli, Cleveland Browns (Played in 2 games)
    Thomas Fears, Los Angeles (Played in 3 games)
10 James Benton, Chicago Bears and Cleveland Rams (Played in 2 games)
9   Don Hutson, Green Bay (Played in 4 games)

Most Passes Caught (one game)

11 Dante Lavelli, Cleveland Browns vs Los Angeles, Dec. 24, 1950
9   Wayne Millner, Washington vs Chicago Bears, Dec. 12, 1937
    James Benton, Cleveland Rams vs Washington, Dec. 16, 1945
    Thomas Fears, Los Angeles vs Cleveland Browns, Dec. 24, 1950
8   Jack Ferrante, Philadelphia vs Chicago Cardinals, Dec. 28, 1947

Most Yards Gained

297 Thomas Fears, Los Angeles (15 receptions in 3 games)
270 Wayne Millner, Washington (16 receptions in 4 games)
193 Dante Lavelli, Cleveland Browns (15 receptions in 2 games)
155 Wilbur Moore, Washington (8 receptions in 3 games)
154 James Benton, Chicago Bears and Cleveland Rams (10 receptions in 2 games)

Most Yards Gained (one game)

160 Wayne Millner, Washington vs Chicago Bears, Dec. 12, 1937 (9 receptions)
146 Thomas Fears, Los Angeles vs Cleveland Browns, Dec. 23, 1951 (4 receptions)
136 Thomas Fears, Los Angeles vs Cleveland Browns, Dec. 24, 1950 (9 receptions)

Most Touchdown Passes

2   Several

Most Touchdown Passes (one game)

2   Several

Longest Completed Pass

82 Glenn Davis from Robert Waterfield, Los Angeles vs Cleveland Browns, Dec. 24, 1950 (TD)
77 Wayne Millner from Samuel Baugh, Washington vs Chicago Bears, Dec. 12, 1937 (TD)
73 Thomas Fears from Norman Van Brocklin, Los Angeles vs Cleveland Browns, Dec. 23, 1951 (TD)

PASSES INTERCEPTED

Most Passes Intercepted By

4   Joseph Laws, Green Bay (Played in 4 games)
    Clyde Turner, Chicago Bears (Played in 5 games)
3   George McAfee, Chicago Bears (Played in 3 games)
    Sidney Luckman, Chicago Bears (Played in 5 games)

Warren Lahr, Cleveland Browns (Played in 3 games)
2 Several

Most Passes Intercepted By (one game)
3 Joseph Laws, Green Bay vs New York Giants, Dec. 17, 1944
2 Several

Most Yards Interceptions Returned
55 Clyde Turner, Chicago Bears (4 interceptions, 5 games)
49 Dante Magnani, Chicago Bears (2 interceptions, 2 games)
48 George McAfee, Chicago Bears (3 interceptions, 3 games)
42 Sidney Luckman, Chicago Bears (3 interceptions, 5 games)
41 Garrard Ramsey, Chicago Cardinals (1 interception, 2 games)

Most Yards Interceptions Returned (one game)
49 Dante Magnani, Chicago Bears vs New York Giants, Dec. 15, 1946 (2 interceptions)
41 Garrard Ramsey, Chicago Cardinals vs Philadelphia, Dec. 28, 1947 (1 interception)
39 Sidney Luckman, Chicago Bears vs Washington, Dec. 26, 1943 (2 interceptions)
    Dante Magnani, Chicago Bears vs New York Giants, Dec. 15, 1946 (2 interceptions) (1 TD)
35 Marvin Johnson, Los Angeles vs Cleveland Browns, Dec. 23, 1951 (1 interception)
34 George McAfee, Chicago Bears vs Washington, Dec. 8, 1940 (1 interception) (TD)

Longest Return of Intercepted Pass—Yards
41 Garrand Ramsey, Chicago Cardinals vs Philadelphia, Dec. 28, 1947
39 Dante Magnani, Chicago Bears vs New York Giants, Dec. 15, 1946 (TD)
35 Marvin Johnson, Los Angeles vs Cleveland Browns, Dec. 23, 1951
34 George McAfee, Chicago Bears vs Washington, Dec. 8, 1940 (TD)
33 Kenneth Gorgal, Cleveland Browns vs Los Angeles, Dec. 24, 1950

PUNTING
Most Punts
26 Robert Waterfield, Cleveland and Los Angeles Rams (Played in 4 games)
19 Joseph Muha, Philadelphia (Played in 3 games)
16 Ray Mallouf, Chicago Cardinals (Played in 2 games)
14 Samuel Baugh, Washington (Played in 5 games)
13 Keith Molesworth, Chicago Bears (Played in 3 games)

Most Punts (one game)
11 Kenneth Strong, New York Giants vs Chicago Bears, Dec. 17, 1933
10 Keith Molesworth, Chicago Bears vs New York Giants, Dec. 17, 1933

Best Punting Average
41.0 Robert Waterfield, Cleveland and Los Angeles Rams (Played in 4 games)

Best Punting Average (one game)
50.8 Robert Waterfield, Los Angeles vs Cleveland Browns, Dec. 24, 1950 (4 punts)

Longest Punt (Yards)
85 Samuel Baugh, Washington vs Chicago Bears, Dec. 13, 1942
69 Joseph Muha, Philadelphia vs Chicago Cardinals, Dec. 28, 1947
68 Horace Gillom, Cleveland Browns vs Los Angeles, Dec. 24, 1950

Shortest Punt (Yards)
4 Joseph Muha, Philadelphia vs Chicago Cardinals, Dec. 28, 1947

PUNT RETURNS
Most Punt Returns
8 Keith Molesworth, Chicago Bears (Played in 3 games)
5 Harry Newman, New York Giants (Played in 3 games)
4 Sidney Luckman, Chicago Bears (Played in 5 games)
   Charles Trippi, Chicago Cardinals (Played in 2 games)
   Irving Comp, Green Bay (Played in 1 game)
   Steven Bagarus, Washington (Played in 1 game)
   Verda Smith, Los Angeles (Played in 3 games)
3 Several

Most Punt Returns (one game)
4 Irving Comp, Green Bay vs New York Giants, Dec. 17, 1944
   Steven Bagarus, Washington vs Cleveland Rams, Dec. 16, 1945
3 Several

Most Yards Punts Returned
113 Charles Trippi, Chicago Cardinals (4 returns in 2 games)
55 Irving Comp, Green Bay (4 returns in 1 game)
52 Steven Bagarus, Washington (4 returns in 1 game)
42 Sidney Luckman, Chicago Bears (4 returns in 5 games)
38 Alphonse Leemans, New York Giants (2 returns in 3 games)

Most Yards Punts Returned (one game)
102 Charles Trippi, Chicago Cardinals vs Philadelphia, Dec. 28, 1947 (2 returns)

55   Irving Comp, Green Bay vs New York Giants, Dec. 17, 1944 (4 returns)
52   Steven Bagarus, Washington vs Cleveland Rams, Dec. 16, 1944 (4 returns)

Longest Punt Return (Yards)

75   Charles Trippi, Chicago Cardinals vs Philadelphia, Dec. 28, 1947
37   John Cochran, Chicago Cardinals vs Philadelphia, Dec. 28, 1947
35   Jerry Williams, Los Angeles vs Cleveland Browns, Dec. 24, 1950
26   Harry Newman, New York Giants vs Chicago Bears, Dec. 17, 1933

SCORING

Most Points Scored

36   Kenneth Strong, New York Giants (Played in 5 games) (4 touchdowns; 9 extra points; 1 field goal)
33   Jack Manders, Chicago Bears (Played in 4 games) (2 touchdowns; 6 extra points; 5 field goals)

Most Points Scored (one game)

17   Kenneth Strong, New York Giants vs Chicago Bears, Dec. 9, 1934 (2 touchdowns; 2 extra points; 1 field goal)
15   Jack Manders, Chicago Bears vs Washington, Dec. 12, 1937 (2 touchdowns; 3 extra points)

Most Touchdowns

4   Kenneth Strong, New York Giants (Played in 5 games)
     Harry Clark, Chicago Bears (Played in 4 games)
3   Kenneth Kavanaugh, Chicago Bears (Played in 3 games)
     Andrew Farkas, Washington (Played in 3 games)
     Dante Magnani, Chicago Bears (Played in 2 games)
     Richard Hoerner, Los Angeles (Played in 3 games)
2   Several

Most Touchdowns (one game)

2   Several

Most Touchdowns Running

2   Several

Most Touchdowns Running (one game)

2   Several

Most Touchdowns Passing

2   Several

Most Touchdowns Passing (one game)

2   Several

Most Extra Points

9   Kenneth Strong, New York Giants (Played in 5 games)

8   Robert Waterfield, Cleveland and Los Angeles Rams (Played in 4 games)
     Robert Snyder, Chicago Bears (Played in 3 games)
6   Jack Manders, Chicago Bears (Played in 4 games)
     John Patton, Philadelphia (Played in 3 games)

Most Extra Points (one game)

5   Robert Snyder, Chicago Bears vs Washington, Dec. 26, 1943
4   Marlin Harder, Chicago Cardinals vs Philadelphia, Dec. 28, 1947
     Robert Waterfield, Los Angeles vs Cleveland Browns, Dec. 24, 1950
     Riley Smith, Washington vs Chicago Bears, Dec. 12, 1937
3   Several

Most Field Goals

5   Jack Manders, Chicago Bears (Played in 4 games)
3   Robert Snyder, Chicago Bears (Played in 3 games)

Most Field Goals (one game)

3   Jack Manders, Chicago Bears vs New York Giants, Dec. 17, 1933 (16, 40, 18 yards)
     Robert Snyder, Chicago Bears vs New York Giants, Dec. 21, 1941 (14, 39, 37 yards)

Most Field Goals Attempted

10   Jack Manners, Chicago Bears (Played in 4 games)
5   Ward Cuff, New York Giants (Played in 3 games)

Most Field Goals Attempted (one game)

4   Jack Manders (twice), Chicago Bears vs New York Giants, Dec. 17, 1933 and Dec. 9, 1934
3   Robert Snyder, Chicago Bears vs New York Giants, Dec. 21, 1941
     John Patton, Philadelphia vs Chicago Cardinals, Dec. 19, 1948

Longest Field Goal (Yards)

52   Louis Groza, Cleveland Browns vs Los Angeles, Dec. 23, 1951
42   Ward Cuff, New York Giants vs Green Bay, Dec. 11, 1938
     Ernest Smith, Green Bay vs New York Giants, Dec. 10, 1939
40   Jack Manders, Chicago Bears vs New York Giants, Dec. 17, 1933

KICK-OFF RETURNS

Most Kick-off Returns

8   Kenneth Carpenter, Cleveland Browns (Played in 2 games)

5 Verda Smith, Los Angeles (Played in 3 games)
3 Several

Most Kick-off Returns (one game)

5 Kenneth Carpenter, Cleveland Browns vs Los Angeles, Dec. 23, 1951
3 Several

Longest Kick-off Return (Yards)

62 Max Krause, Washington vs Chicago Bears, Dec. 8, 1940

46 Boris Dimancheff, Chicago Cardinals vs Philadelphia, Dec. 28, 1947
40 Harry Newman, New York Giants vs Detroit, Dec. 15, 1935

Most Yards Gained Kick-off Returns (Yards)

190 Kenneth Carpenter, Cleveland Browns (Played in 2 games)
99 Verda Smith, Los Angeles (Played in 3 games)
90 Boris Dimancheff, Chicago Cardinals (Played in 2 games)

THE ALL-TIME ROSTER

ABBREVIATIONS

G—Leader Ground Gaining
S—Leader Scoring
P—Leader Passing
R—Leader Pass Receiving
F—Leader Field Goals

K—Leader Punting
I—Leader Intercepting
V—Winner of Joe F. Carr Trophy as Most Valuable Player. Awarded 1938–1946 only.

ABBEY, JOSEPH—End—North Texas College
1948–49 Chicago Bears
1949 New York Bulldogs

ABBOTT, L.—Back—Syracuse
1921–27 Dayton Triangles
1929 Dayton Triangles

ABBRUZZI, LOUIS—Back—Rhode Island State
1946 Boston Yanks

ABELL, EARL—Back—Colgate
1926 Milwaukee Badgers

ABERSON, CLIFFORD—Back—None
1946 Green Bay Packers

ABRAMS, NATHAN—End—None
1921 Green Bay Packers

ABRAMSON, GEORGE—Tackle—Minnesota
1925 Green Bay Packers

ABRUZZINO, FRANK—Center—Colgate
1931 Brooklyn Dodgers
1933 Cincinnati Reds

ACHUI, WALTER—Back—Dayton
1927–28 Dayton Triangles

ADAMLE, ANTHONY—Back—Ohio State
1947–51 Cleveland Browns

ADAMS, ?—Tackle—?
1924 Rochester Kodaks

ADAMS, CHESTER—Tackle—Ohio
1939–42 Cleveland Rams
1942–43 Green Bay Packers
1946–48 Cleveland Browns
1948 Buffalo Bills

ADAMS, JOHN—Tackle—Notre Dame
1945–49 Washington Redskins

ADAMS, O'NEAL—End—Arkansas
1941–45 New York Giants
1946–47 Brooklyn Dodgers

ADAMS, PETER—Center—Pittsburgh
1939 Chicago Cardinals

ADAMS, VERLIN—Tackle—Morris Harvey
1942–45 New York Giants

ADDAMS, ABRAHAM—End—Indiana
1949 Detroit Lions

ADKINS, ROBERT—End—Marshall
1940–41 Green Bay Packers
1945–46 Green Bay Packers

AFFLIS, RICHARD—Guard—Nevada
1951 Green Bay Packers

AGAJANIAN, BENJAMIN—Guard—New Mexico
1945 Pittsburgh Steelers
1945 Philadelphia Eagles

1947–48   Los Angeles Dons
1949   New York Giants

AGASE, ALEXANDER—Guard—Illinois
1947   Los Angeles Dons
1947   Chicago Rockets
1948–51   Cleveland Browns

AGEE, SAMUEL—Back—Vanderbilt
1938–39   Chicago Cardinals

AGLER, HARRY—End—California
1948   Los Angeles Dons

AGLER, ROBERT—Back—Otterbein
1948–49   Los Angeles Rams

AGUIRRE, JOSEPH—End—St. Mary's (Cal.)
1940–44   Washington Redskins
1945   Washington Redskins—F (7)
1946–49   Los Angeles Dons

AIELLO, ANTHONY—Back—Youngstown
1944   Detroit Lions
1944   Brooklyn Tigers

AILINGER, JAMES—Tackle—Buffalo Univ.
1924   Buffalo All Americans

AKIN, LEONARD—Guard—Baylor
1942   Chicago Bears

AKINS, ALBERT—Back—Washington State
1946   Cleveland Browns
1947–48   Brooklyn Dodgers
1948   Buffalo Bills

AKINS, FRANK—Back—Washington State
1943–46   Washington Redskins
1947   Baltimore Colts

ALBANESE, VINCENT—Back—Syracuse
1937–38   Brooklyn Dodgers

ALBERT, FRANK—Back—Stanford
1946–48   San Francisco 49ers
1949   San Francisco 49ers—K (AAFC)
1950–51   San Francisco 49ers

ALBRECHT, ARTHUR—Tackle—Wisconsin
1941   Green Bay Packers
1942   Pittsburgh Steelers
1943   Chicago Cardinals
1944   Boston Yanks

ALBRIGHT, WILLIAM—Guard—Wisconsin
1951   New York Giants

ALDRICH, CHARLES—Center—TCU
1939–40   Chicago Cardinals
1940–43   Washington Redskins
1945–47   Washington Redskins

ALDRIDGE, BENJAMIN—Back—Oklahoma A & M
1950–51   New York Yanks

ALEXANDER, JOHN—Tackle—Rutgers
1926   New York Giants

ALEXANDER, JOSEPH—Guard—Syracuse
1921–22   Rochester Kodaks
1922   Milwaukee Badgers
1925   New York Giants
1926   New York Giants (Head Coach)
1927   New York Giants

ALFONSE, JULES—Back—Minnesota
1937–38   Cleveland Rams

ALFORD, EUGENE—Back—Texas Tech.
1931–33   Portsmouth Spartans
1934   Cincinnati Reds
1934   St. Louis Gunners

ALFORD, HERBERT BRUCE—End—TCU
1946–49   New York Yankees
1950–51   New York Yanks

ALFSON, WARREN—Guard—Nebraska
1941   Brooklyn Dodgers

ALLEN, CARL—Back—Oklahoma City Univ.
1948   Brooklyn Dodgers

ALLEN, EDWARD—Back—Pennsylvania
1947   Chicago Bears

ALLEN, ERMAL—Back—Kentucky
1947   Cleveland Browns

ALLEN, LOUIS—Tackle—Duke
1950–51   Pittsburgh Steelers

ALLISON, JAMES—End—Texas A & M
1926–27   Buffalo Bisons
1928   New York Giants

ALLMAN, STANLEY—End—Michigan State
1936   Chicago Bears
1936   Cleveland Rams

ALLTON, JOSEPH—Tackle—Oklahoma
1941   Chicago Cardinals

AMBERG, JOHN—Back—Kansas
1951   New York Giants

AMBROSE, JOHN—Guard—Catholic
   Univ.
1932   Brooklyn Dodgers

ANANIS, VITO—Back—Boston
   College
1945   Washington Redskins

ANDERSON, EDWARD—End—Notre
   Dame
1923   Rock Island Independents
1923   Chicago Bears
.1923–25 Chicago Cardinals

ANDERSON, EZZRET—End—
   Kentucky State
1947   Los Angeles Dons

ANDERSON, HEARTLEY—Guard—
   Notre Dame
1922–25 Chicago Bears

ANDERSON, OSCAR—Back—Colgate
1920–22 Buffalo All Americans
1922   Rochester Kodaks
1923   Cleveland Indians
1924   Rochester Jeffersons
1925   Rock Island Independents

ANDERSON, STANLEY—End—
   Stanford
1940–41 Cleveland Rams
1941   Detroit Lions

ANDERSON, WILLIAM—End—
   West Virginia
1945   Boston Yanks

ANDERSON, WINSTON—End—
   Colgate
1937   New York Giants

ANDRAKO, STEPHEN—Center—
   Ohio State
1940   Washington Redskins

ANDREWS, LEROY—Back—Kansas
   State Teachers
1923   St. Louis Browns
1924–25 Kansas City Cowboys
1927   Cleveland Bulldogs
1934   Philadelphia Eagles
1934   St. Louis Gunners
1931   Chicago Cardinals (Head Coach)

ANDROS, PLATO—Guard—
   Oklahoma
1947–50 Chicago Cardinals

ANDRULEWICZ, THEODORE—
   Back—Villanova
1930   Newark

ANDRUSKING, SIGMUND—Guard—
   Detroit
1936   Cleveland Rams
1937   Brooklyn Dodgers

ANGSMAN, ELMER—Back—Notre
   Dame
1946–51 Chicago Cardinals

ANNAN, DUNCAN—Back—Brown
1923–25 Hammond Independents
1925   Akron Steels
1926   Hammond Independents

APOLSKIS, CHARLES—End—DePaul
1938–39 Chicago Bears

APOLSKIS, RAYMOND—Guard—
   Marquette
1941–42 Chicago Cardinals
1945–50 Chicago Cardinals

APSIT, MARGER—Back—Southern
   California
1931   Frankford Yellowjackets
1931   Brooklyn Dodgers
1932   Green Bay Packers
1933   Boston Redskins

ARCHOSKI, JULIUS—End—Syracuse
1930   Staten Island Stapletons

ARENAS, JOSEPH—Back—Omaha
   Univ.
1951   San Francisco 49ers

ARENZ, ARNOLD—Back—St. Louis
1934   Boston Redskins

ARGUS, ROBERT—Back—None
1921–23 Rochester Kodaks
1924–25 Rochester Jeffersons

ARIAL, DAVID—End—Alabama
   Polytech.
1934   Brooklyn Dodgers

ARMS, LLOYD—Guard—Oklahoma
   A & M
1946–48 Chicago Cardinals

ARMSTRONG, ?—Tackle—?
1931–32 Portsmouth Spartans

ARMSTRONG, CHARLES—Back—
   Mississippi
1946   Brooklyn Dodgers

ARMSTRONG, GRAHAM—Tackle—
   John Carroll
1941   Cleveland Rams
1945   Cleveland Rams
1947–48 Buffalo Bills

ARMSTRONG, JOHN—Back—
   Columbia
1923–25 Rock Island Independents

ARMSTRONG, NEIL—End—
Oklahoma A & M
1947–51 Philadelphia Eagles

ARNDT, ALFRED—Guard—South
Dakota State
1935 Pittsburgh Pirates

ARNOLD, JAY—Back—Texas
1937–40 Philadelphia Eagles
1941 Pittsburgh Steelers

ARROWHEAD—End—None
1923 Oorang Indians

ARTMAN, CORWAN—Tackle—
Stanford
1931 New York Giants
1933 Pittsburgh Pirates

ARTOE, LEE—Tackle—Santa Clara
1940–42 Chicago Bears
1945 Chicago Bears
1946–47 Los Angeles Dons
1948 Baltimore Colts

ASCHENBRENNER, FRANK—
Back—Northwestern
1949 Chicago Hornets

ASH, JULIAN—Guard—Oregon State
1926 Los Angeles

ASHBAUGH, WILLIAM—Back—
Pittsburgh
1924 Rock Island Independents

ASHBURNE, CLIFFORD—Guard—
Nebraska
1929 New York Giants

ASHMORE, ROGER—Tackle—
Gonzaga
1926 Milwaukee Badgers
1927 Duluth Eskimos
1927 Chicago Bears
1928–29 Green Bay Packers

ASPATORE, EDWARD—Tackle—
Marquette
1934 Cincinnati Reds

ATTY, ALEXANDER—Guard—
West Virginia
1939 Cleveland Rams

ATWOOD, JOHN—Back—Wisconsin
1948 New York Giants

AUDET, EARL—Tackle—Southern
California
1945 Washington Redskins
1946–48 Los Angeles Dons

AUER, HOWARD—Tackle—Michigan
1933 Chicago Cardinals
1933 Philadelphia Eagles

AUGUST, EDWARD—Back—
Villanova
1931 Providence Steamrollers

AUGUSTERFER, EUGENE—
Guard—Catholic Univ.
1935 Pittsburgh Pirates

AULT, WAYNE—Tackle—Oklahoma
A & M
1924 Cleveland Bulldogs
1925 Cleveland Indians

AUSTIN, JAMES—End—St. Mary's
(Cal.)
1937–38 Brooklyn Dodgers
1939 Detroit Lions

AUSTIN, WILLIAM—Tackle—
Oregon State
1949–50 New York Giants

AVEDISIAN, CHARLES—Guard—
Providence
1942–44 New York Giants

AVERNO, SISTO—Guard—
Muhlenberg
1950 Baltimore Colts
1951 New York Yanks

AVERY, DONALD—Tackle—Alabama
1946–47 Washington Redskins
1948 Los Angeles Dons

BABARTSKY, ALBERT—Tackle—
Fordham
1938–42 Chicago Cardinals
1943–45 Chicago Bears

BABCOCK, SAMUEL—Back—
Michigan
1926 Canton Bulldogs

BACCHUS, CARL—End—Missouri
1927 Cleveland Bulldogs
1928 Detroit Wolverines

BACHMAIER, ?—Guard—None
1921–23 Rochester Kodaks
1924 Rochester Jefferson

BACON, FRANCIS—Back—Wabash
1920–24 Dayton Triangles

BADACZEWSKI, JOHN—Guard—
Western Reserve
1946–48 Boston Yanks
1948 Chicago Cardinals
1949–51 Washington Redskins

BADGRO, MORRIS—End—Southern
California
1927–28 New York Yankees
1929–36 New York Giants

BAGARUS, STEPHEN—Back—Notre Dame
1945–46 Washington Redskins
1947 Los Angeles Rams
1948 Washington Redskins

BAGBY, HERMAN—Back—Arkansas
1926 Brooklyn Dodgers
1927 Cleveland Bulldozers

BAGDON, EDWARD—Guard—Michigan State
1950–51 Chicago Cardinals

BAHAN, LEONARD—Back—Notre Dame
1923 Cleveland Indians

BAILEY, EDGAR—End—Duke
1940–41 Brooklyn Dodgers
1946 Boston Yanks

BAILEY, JAMES—Guard—West Virginia State
1949 Chicago Hornets

BAILEY, RUSSELL—Center—West Virginia
1920–21 Akron Steels

BAISI, ALBERT—Guard—West Virginia
1940–41 Chicago Bears
1946 Chicago Bears
1947 Philadelphia Eagles

BAKER, CONWAY—Tackle—Centenary
1936–43 Chicago Cardinals
1944 Card-Pitt
1945 Chicago Cardinals

BAKER, FRANK—End—Northwestern
1931 Green Bay Packers

BAKER, JON—Guard—California
1949–51 New York Giants

BAKER, ROY—Back—Southern California
1927 New York Yankees
1928–29 Green Bay Packers
1930 Chicago Cardinals
1931 Staten Island Stapletons

BALATTI, EDWARD—Tackle—None
1946–48 San Francisco 49ers
1948 New York Yankees
1948 Buffalo Bills

BALAZS, FRANK—Back—Iowa
1939–41 Green Bay Packers
1941 Chicago Cardinals
1945 Chicago Cardinals

BALDWIN, ALTON—End—Arkansas
1947–49 Buffalo Bills
1950 Green Bay Packers

BALDWIN, BURR—End—UCLA
1947–49 Los Angeles Dons

BALDWIN, GEORGE—End—Virginia
1925 Cleveland Indians

BALDWIN, JOHN—Center—Centenary
1946–47 New York Yankees
1947 San Francisco 49ers
1948 Buffalo Bills

BALOG, ROBERT—Center—Denver
1949–50 Pittsburgh Steelers

BANAS, STEPHEN—Back—Notre Dame
1935 Detroit Lions
1935 Philadelphia Eagles

BANCROFT, ?—End—?
1923 Rochester Kodaks

BANDUCCI, BRUNO—Guard—Stanford
1944–45 Philadelphia Eagles
1946–51 San Francisco 49ers

BANET, HERBERT—Back—Manchester
1937 Green Bay Packers

BANJAVIC, EMIL—Back—Arizona
1942 Detroit Lions

BANONIS, VINCENT—Center—Detroit
1942–43 Chicago Cardinals
1946–50 Chicago Cardinals
1951 Detroit Lions

BANTA, HERBERT JACK—Back—Southern California
1941 Washington Redskins
1941 Philadelphia Eagles
1944–45 Philadelphia Eagles
1946–48 Los Angeles Rams

BARABEE, ROBERT—End—New York Univ.
1931 Staten Island Stapletons

BARBER, BENJAMIN—Tackle—Virginia Military Inst.
1925 Buffalo Bisons

BARBER, ERNEST—Center—San Francisco Univ.
1945 Washington Redskins
1945 New York Giants

BARBER, JAMES—Tackle—San Francisco Univ.
1935–36 Boston Redskins
1937–41 Washington Redskins

BARBER, MARK—Back—South Dakota State
1937 Cleveland Rams

BARBOLAK, PETER—Tackle—
Purdue
1949 Pittsburgh Steelers

BARBOUR, WESLEY—Back—
Wake Forest
1945 New York Giants

BARBUTI, RAYMOND—Back—
Syracuse
1930 Staten Island Stapletons

BARCLAY, GEORGE—Guard—North
Carolina
1935 Brooklyn Dodgers

BARIL, ADRIAN—Tackle—St.
Thomas
1923–24 Minneapolis Marines
1925 Milwaukee Badgers

BARKER, HUBERT—Back—
Arkansas
1942–45 New York Giants

BARKER, RICHARD—Guard—Iowa
State
1921 Chicago Bears
1921 Rock Island Independents

BARKMAN, RALPH—Back—Albright
1929 Orange

BARLE, LOUIS—Back—None
1938 Detroit Lions
1939 Cleveland Rams

BARNA, GEORGE—End—Cornell
1929 Frankford Yellowjackets

BARNARD, CHARLES—End—Texas
Tech.
1938 New York Giants

BARNES, WALTER—Guard—LSU
1948–51 Philadelphia Eagles

BARNETT, SOLON—Tackle—Baylor
1945–46 Green Bay Packers

BARNHART, DANIEL—Back—
Houston
1934 Philadelphia Eagles

BARNUM, ROBERT—Back—West
Virginia
1926 Columbus Tigers

BARNUM, LEONARD—Back—West
Virginia Wesleyan
1938–40 New York Giants
1940–42 Philadelphia Eagles

BARR, WALLACE—Back—Wisconsin
1923–24 Racine Legion
1925 Milwaukee Badgers
1926 Racine Legion

BARRAGER, NATHAN—Center—
Southern California
1930 Minneapolis Redjackets
1930–31 Frankford Yellowjackets
1931–35 Green Bay Packers

BARREL—Center—Carlisle
1923 Oorang Indians

BARRETT, EMMETT—Center—
Portland
1942 New York Giants
1944 New York Giants

BARRETT, JEFFREY—End—LSU
1936–38 Brooklyn Dodgers

BARRETT, JOHN—Tackle—Detroit
1924–25 Akron Steels
1926 Detroit Panthers
1928 Detroit Wolverines

BARRON, JAMES—Tackle—
Georgetown
1921 Rochester Kodaks

BARRY, NORMAN—Back—Notre
Dame
1921 Green Bay Packers
1923–24 Hammond Independents
1925–26 Chicago Cardinals—Head Coach

BARRY, PAUL—Back—Tulsa
1950 Los Angeles Rams

BARTAANEN, WILLIAM—Tackle—
None
1938 Pittsburgh Pirates

BARTHOLOMEW, SAMUEL—
Back—Tennessee
1941 Philadelphia Eagles

BARTOS, HENRY—Guard—North
Carolina
1938 Washington Redskins

BARTOS, JOSEPH—Back—
Annapolis
1950 Washington Redskins

BARWEGAN, RICHARD—Guard—
Purdue
1947 New York Yankees
1948–50 Baltimore Colts
1950–51 Chicago Bears

BARZILAUSKAS, FRANCIS—
Guard—Yale
1947–48 Boston Yanks
1949 New York Bulldogs
1951 New York Giants

BASCA, MICHAEL—Back—Villanova
1941 Philadelphia Eagles
Killed in France on Armistice
Day, 1944 with Patton's Third
Army

BASING, MYRTON—Back—
Lawrence
1923–27 Green Bay Packers

BASRAK, MICHAEL—Center—
Duquesne
1937–38 Pittsburgh Pirates
1939 Pittsburgh Steelers

BASS, WILLIAM—Back—Kentucky
State
1947 Chicago Rockets

BASSETT, HERBERT—Tackle—
Nebraska
1924 Kansas City Cowboys

BASSI, RICHARD—Guard—Santa
Clara
1938–39 Chicago Bears
1940 Philadelphia Eagles
1941 Pittsburgh Steelers
1946–47 San Francisco 49ers

BASSMAN, HERMAN—Back—
Ursinus
1936 Philadelphia Eagles

BASTON, ALBERT—End—Minnesota
1920 Buffalo All Americans

BATCHELLOR, ?—Tackle—?
1923 Toledo Maroons

BATINSKI, STANLEY—Guard—
Temple
1941–47 Detroit Lions
1948 Boston Yanks
1949 New York Bulldogs
1949 New York Yankees

BATORSKI, JOHN—End—Colgate
1946 Buffalo Bisons

BATTLES, CLIFFORD—Back—West
Virginia Wesleyan
1932 Boston Braves
1933–36 Boston Redskins
1937 Washington Redskins—G

BAUER, H.—Tackle—Baldwin-
Wallace
1923 Racine Legion
1925 Cleveland Indians

BAUGH, SAMUEL—Back—TCU
1937 Washington Redskins—P
1938 Washington Redskins
1939 Washington Redskins
1940 Washington Redskins—P–K
1941 Washington Redskins—K
1942 Washington Redskins—K
1943 Washington Redskins—P–K–I
1944 Washington Redskins
1945 Washington Redskins—P
1946 Washington Redskins
1947 Washington Redskins—P
1948 Washington Redskins

1949 Washington Redskins—P
1950 Washington Redskins
1951 Washington Redskins

BAUJAN, HARRY—End—Notre
Dame
1921 Cleveland Indians

BAUMAN, ALFRED—Tackle—
Northwestern
1947 Chicago Rockets
1947 Philadelphia Eagles
1948–50 Chicago Bears

BAUMGARDNER, MAX—End—
Texas
1948 Detroit Lions

BAUMGARTNER, WILLIAM—
End—Minnesota
1947 Baltimore Colts

BAUSCH, FRANK—Center—Kansas
1933 Cincinnati Reds
1934–36 Boston Redskins
1937–40 Chicago Bears
1940–41 Philadelphia Eagles

BAXTER, ERNEST—Back—Centre
1923 Racine Legion

BAXTER, LLOYD—Tackle—SMU
1948 Green Bay Packers

BAYLEY, JOHN—Tackle—Syracuse
1927 New York Yankees

BAZE, WINFORD—End—Texas Tech.
1937 Philadelphia Eagles

BEALS, ALYN—End—Santa Clara
1946–48 San Francisco 49ers
1949 San Francisco 49ers—S (AAFC)
1950–51 San Francisco 49ers

BEASEY, JOHN—Back—South Dakota
1924 Green Bay Packers

BEASLEY, TURMAN—Guard—
Vanderbilt
1923 Dayton Triangles

BEATTIE, ROBERT—Tackle—
Princeton
1927 New York Yankees
1929 Orange
1930 Newark

BECHTOL, HUBERT—End—Texas
1947–49 Baltimore Colts

BECK, CARL—Back—West Virginia
1921 Buffalo All Americans
1921 Akron Steels
1924 Akron Steels
1925 Pottsville Maroons

BECKER, JOHN—Tackle—Denison
1926–29 Dayton Triangles

BECKER, WAYLAND—End—
Marquette
1934   Chicago Bears
1934–35   Brooklyn Dodgers
1936–38   Green Bay Packers
1939   Pittsburgh Steelers

BECKLEY, ARTHUR—Back—
Michigan State
1926   Dayton Triangles

BEDFORD, WILLIAM—End—SMU
1925   Rochester Jeffersons

BEDNAR, ALBERT—Guard—
Lafayette
1924–25   Frankford Yellowjackets
1925   New York Giants

BEDNARIK, CHARLES—Center—
Pennsylvania
1949–51   Philadelphia Eagles

BEEBE, KEITH—Back—Occidental
1944   New York Giants

BEEMING, ?—Guard—?
1924   Dayton Triangles

BEHAN, CHARLES—End—DeKalb
1942   Detroit Lions
        Killed by Japanese gunfire on
        Okinawa, May 18, 1945, Lt. in
        U.S. Army

BEHMAN, RUSSELL—Tackle—
Dickinson
1924–31   Frankford Yellowjackets

BEIL, LAWRENCE—Tackle—
Portland
1948   New York Giants

BEINOR, J. EDWARD—Tackle—
Notre Dame
1940–41   Chicago Cardinals
1941–42   Washington Redskins

BELANICH, WILLIAM—Tackle
Dayton
1927–29   Dayton Triangles

BELDEN, CHARLES—Back—None
1927   Duluth Eskimos
1930–31   Chicago Cardinals

BELDING, LESTER—End—Iowa
1925   Rock Island Independents

BELICHECK, Stephen—Back—
Western Reserve
1941   Detroit Lions

BELL, EDWARD—Guard—Indiana
1946   Miami Seahawks
1947–49   Green Bay Packers

BELL, KAY—Tackle—Washington
State
1937   Chicago Bears
1942   New York Giants

BELLINGER, ROBERT—Tackle—
Gonzaga
1934–35   New York Giants

BENKERT, HENRY—Back—Rutgers
1925   New York Giants
1926   Pottsville Maroons
1929   Orange
1930   Newark

BENNETT, CHARLES—Back—
Indiana
1930   Portsmouth Spartans
1936   Chicago Bears

BENNETT, EARL—Guard—Hardin-
Simmons
1946   Green Bay Packers

BENSON, ALVIN—Guard—Western
Maryland
1935   Philadelphia Eagles

BENSON, GEORGE—Back—
Northwestern
1947   Brooklyn Dodgers

BENTON, ?—End—?
1922   Rochester Kodaks

BENTON, JAMES—End—Arkansas
1938–42   Cleveland Rams
1943   Chicago Bears
1944–45   Cleveland Rams
1946–47   Los Angeles Rams

BENTZ, ROMAN—Tackle—Tulane
1946–48   New York Yankees
1948   San Francisco 49ers

BENTZIEN, ALFRED—Guard—
Marquette
1924   Racine Legion

BEREZNEY, PAUL—Tackle—
Fordham
1942–44   Green Bay Packers
1946   Miami Seahawks

BEREZNEY, PETER—Tackle—Notre
Dame
1947   Los Angeles Dons
1948   Baltimore Colts

BERGERSON, GILBERT—Tackle—
Oregon State
1932–33   Chicago Bears
1933–34   Chicago Cardinals
1935–36   Brooklyn Dodgers

BERGIN, WILLIAM—Guard—
Marquette
1922   Toledo Maroons

BERNARD, ?—Guard—?
1926   Racine Legion

BERNARD, CHARLES—Center—
Michigan
1934   Detroit Lions

BERNARD, DAVID—Back—
Mississippi
1944–45   Cleveland Rams

BERNOSKI, DANIEL—Guard—
Indiana
1926   Louisville Colonels

BERNHARDT, GEORGE—Guard—
Illinois
1946–48   Brooklyn Dodgers
1948   Chicago Rockets

BERNS, WILLIAM—Guard—Purdue
1922–23   Dayton Triangles

BERNSTEIN, JOSEPH—Guard—
Tulsa
1923–24   Rock Island Independents
1924   Hammond Pros
1925   Rock Island Independents

BERQUIST, JAY—Guard—Nebraska
1924   Kansas City Cowboys
1926   Kansas City Cowboys
1927   Chicago Cardinals

BERRANG, EDWARD—End—
Villanova
1949–50   Washington Redskins
1951   Detroit Lions

BERREHSEN, WILLIAM—Tackle—
Washington & Jefferson
1926   Columbus Tigers

BERRY, CHARLES—End—Lafayette
1921   Rochester Kodaks
1923   Hammond Pros
1924–25   Akron Steels
1925–26   Pottsville Maroons
1926   Akron Steels

BERRY, CORNELIUS—End—North
Carolina
1939   Detroit Lions
1940   Cleveland Rams
1941–46   Chicago Bears
1947   Chicago Rockets

BERRY, GILBERT—Back—Illinois
1935   Chicago Cardinals

BERRY, REX—Back—Brigham Young
1951   San Francisco 49ers

BERRYMAN, ROBERT—Back—
Cornell
1924   Frankford Yellowjackets

BERTAGNOLLI, LIBERO—Guard—
Washington (St. Louis)
1942   Chicago Cardinals
1945   Chicago Cardinals

BERTELLI, ANGELO—Back—Notre
Dame
1946–47   Los Angeles Dons
1947–48   Chicago Rockets

BERTOGLIO, JAMES—Back—
Creighton
1926   Columbus Tigers

BERWICK, EDWARD—Center—
Loyola (Chicago)
1926   Louisville Colonels

BESON, WARREN—Center—
Minnesota
1949   Baltimore Colts

BESTA, ?—Back—?
1924   Hammond Pros

BETTENCOURT, LAWRENCE—
Center—St. Mary's (Texas)
1933   Green Bay Packers

BETTRIDGE, JOHN—Back—Ohio
State
1937   Cleveland Rams
1937   Chicago Bears

BIANCONE, JOHN—Back—Oregon
State
1936   Brooklyn Dodgers

BIEBERSTEIN, ADOLPH—Guard—
Wisconsin
1926   Racine Legion

BIENEMANN, THOMAS—End—
Drake
1951   Chicago Cardinals

BIERCE, BRUCE—End—Akron Univ.
1920–22   Akron Steels
1923   Cleveland Indians
1923   Buffalo All Americans
1924   Cleveland Bulldogs
1925   Akron Steels

BIG BEAR—Tackle—None
1923   Oorang Indians

BIGGS, CARL—Center—Syracuse
1927   New York Giants

BIG TWIG—Guard—None
1929   Buffalo Bisons

BILBO, JONATHAN—Tackle—
Mississippi
1938–39   Chicago Cardinals

BILDA, RICHARD—Back—
Marquette
1944   Green Bay Packers

**BILLMAN, JOHN—Guard—
Minnesota**
1946 Brooklyn Dodgers
1947 Chicago Rockets

**BINGAMAN, LESTER—Guard—
Illinois**
1948–51 Detroit Lions

BINOTTO, JOHN—Back—Duquesne
1942 Pittsburgh Steelers
1942 Philadelphia Eagles

BIOLO, JOHN—Guard—Lake Forest
1939 Green Bay Packers

BIRK, FERDINAND—Back—Purdue
1922 Hammond Pros

**BIRLEM, KEITH—Back—San Jose
State**
1939 Chicago Cardinals
1939 Washington Redskins
      Killed in England, May 7, 1943,
      attempting to land crippled
      B-17 after raid over Europe.
      Major, U.S.A.F.

BISBEE, BERTIN—End—Minnesota
1922 Milwaukee Badgers

**BISSELL, FREDERICK—End—
Fordham**
1925–26 Akron Steels

**BIZER, HERBERT—Back—Carroll
(Wis.)**
1929 Buffalo Bisons

BJORK, DELBERT—Tackle—Oregon
1937–38 Chicago Bears

**BJORKLAND, ROBERT—Center—
Minnesota**
1941 Philadelphia Eagles

BLACK, CHARLES—End—Kansas
1925 Duluth Kelleys

**BLACK, JOHN—Back—Mississippi
State**
1946 New York Yankees
1946 Buffalo Bisons
1947 Buffalo Bills
1947 Baltimore Colts

BLACK BEAR—End—None
1923 Oorang Indians

**BLACKBURN, WILLIAM—Center—
Rice**
1946–50 Chicago Cardinals

**BLACKLOCK, HUGH—Tackle—
Michigan State**
1920–21 Chicago Bears (Staleys)
1922–23 Chicago Bears
1923 Milwaukee Badgers

1924–25 Chicago Bears
1925 Akron Steels

**BLACKWELL, HAROLD—Back—
Southern Carolina**
1945 Chicago Cardinals

**BLAKE, THOMAS—Tackle—
Cincinnati**
1949 New York Bulldogs

**BLANDA, GEORGE—Black—
Kentucky**
1949–50 Chicago Bears
1950 Baltimore Colts
1951 Chicago Bears

**BLANDIN, ERNEST—Tackle—
Tulane**
1946–47 Cleveland Browns
1948–50 Baltimore Colts

**BLAZINE, ANTHONY—Tackle—
Illinois Wesleyan**
1935–40 Chicago Cardinals
1940–41 New York Giants

**BLEEKER, MALCOLM—Center—
Columbia**
1930 Brooklyn Dodgers

**BLEEKER, MELVIN—Back—Southern
California**
1944–46 Philadelphia Eagles
1947 Los Angeles Rams

**BLESSING, PAUL—End—Nebraska
State Teachers**
1944 Detroit Lions

**BLISS, HOMER—Guard—Washington
&. Jefferson**
1928 Chicago Cardinals

**BLONDIN, THOMAS—Guard—West
Virginia Wesleyan**
1933 Cincinnati Reds

**BLOODGOOD, ELBERT—Back—
Nebraska**
1925–26 Kansas City Cowboys
1927 Cleveland Bulldogs
1928 New York Giants
1930 Green Bay Packers

**BLOUNT, LAMAR—End—Mississippi
State**
1946 Miami Seahawks
1947 Buffalo Bills
1947 Baltimore Colts

**BLOZIS, ALBERT—Tackle—
Georgetown**
1942–43 New York Giants
      Killed by German machine-
      gun fire in Vosges Mountains
      of France, Jan. 31, 1945. Lt.
      in U.S. Army.

BLUMENSTOCK, JAMES—Back—
Fordham
1947 New York Giants

BLUMENTHAL, MORRIS—Back—
Northwestern
1925 Chicago Cardinals

BLUMER, HERBERT—Tackle—
Missouri
1925–30 Chicago Cardinals
1933 Chicago Cardinals

BODENGER, MAURICE—Guard—
Tulane
1931–33 Portsmouth Spartans
1934 Detroit Lions

BOEDECKER, WILLIAM—Back—
DePaul
1946 Chicago Rockets
1947–49 Cleveland Browns
1950 Green Bay Packers
1950 Philadelphia Eagles

BOENSCH, FRED—Guard—Stanford
1946–47 Washington Redskins

BOETTCHER, FRED—Back—Rice
1926 Racine Legion

BOHLMANN, FRANK—Guard—
Centenary
1941 Chicago Cardinals

BOHREN, KARL—Back—Pittsburgh
1927 Buffalo Bulldogs

BOLAND, GEORGE—Back—Purdue
1921–24 Chicago Bears

BOLDT, S.—Back—?
1922–23 Louisville Colonels

BOLLINGER, EDWARD—Guard—
Bucknell
1930 Frankford Yellowjackets

BOMAR, LYNN—End—Vanderbilt
1925–26 New York Giants

BOND, CHARLES—Tackle—
Washington
1937–38 Washington Redskins

BOND, RANDALL—Back—
Washington
1938 Washington Redskins
1939 Pittsburgh Steelers

BONELLI, ERNEST—Back—
Pittsburgh
1945 Chicago Cardinals
1946 Pittsburgh Steelers

BONOWITZ, ELLIOTT—Back—
Wilmington
1923 Columbus Tigers
1924–25 Dayton Triangles

BOOKS, ROBERT—Back—Dickinson
1926 Frankford Yellowjackets

BOONE, J. R.—Back—Tulsa
1948–51 Chicago Bears

BOONE, ROBERT—Back—Elon
1942 Cleveland Rams

BOOTH, CLARENCE—Tackle—
SMU
1943 Chicago Cardinals
1944 Card-Pitt

BOOTH, RICHARD—Back—Western
Reserve
1941 Detroit Lions
1945 Detroit Lions

BORAK, FRITZ—End—Creighton
1938 Green Bay Packers

BORDEN, LESTER—End—Fordham
1935 New York Giants

BORRELLI, NICHOLAS—Back—
Muhlenberg
1930 Newark

BOSTICK, LEWIS—Guard—Alabama
1939 Cleveland Rams

BOSWELL, CHARLES—Tackle—
Pittsburgh
1933 Portsmouth Spartans
1934 Boston Redskins

BOULEY, GILBERT—Tackle—
Boston College
1945 Cleveland Rams
1946–50 Los Angeles Rams

BOVA, ANTHONY—End—St. Francis
1942 Pittsburgh Steelers
1943 Phil-Pitt
1944 Card-Pitt
1945–47 Pittsburgh Steelers

BOVE, JOHN—Guard—Stanford
1930 Newark

BOWDOIN, JAMES—Guard—
Alabama
1928–31 Green Bay Packers
1932 New York Giants
1932 Brooklyn Dodgers
1933 Portsmouth Spartans
1934 Brooklyn Dodgers

BOWSER, ARDA—Back—Bucknell
1922 Canton Bulldogs
1923 Cleveland Indians

BOX, CLOYCE—End—West Texas
State Teachers
1949–50 Detroit Lions

BOYD, ROBERT—End—Loyola
1950–51 Los Angeles Rams

BOYD, SAMUEL—End—Baylor
1938 Pittsburgh Pirates
1939–40 Pittsburgh Steelers

BOYD, WALTER—Back—
Westminister
1930–31 Chicago Cardinals

BOYDA, MICHAEL—Back—
Washington & Lee
1949 New York Bulldogs—K

BOYER, VERDI—Guard—UCLA
1936 Brooklyn Dodgers

BOYLE, WILLIAM—Tackle—None
1934 New York Giants
1934 Pittsburgh Pirates

BOYNTON, BENJAMIN—Back—
WILLIAMS
1920 Buffalo All Americans
1921–22 Rochester Kodaks
1923 Pottsville Maroons
1924 Buffalo Bisons

BRACE, ROBERT—Guard—Brown
1920–22 Buffalo All Americans

BRADEN, DAVID—Guard—
Marquette
1945 Chicago Cardinals

BRADLEY, R. T.—Guard—Ohio State
1928 Chicago Cardinals

BRADLEY, EDWARD—End—Wake
Forest
1950 Chicago Bears

BRADLEY, HAROLD—End—Elon
1938 Chicago Cardinals
1938–39 Washington Redskins
1939 Chicago Cardinals

BRADSHAW, WESLEY—Back—
Baylor
1924 Rock Island Independents

BRAHM, LAWRENCE—Guard—
Temple
1942 Cleveland Rams
1943 New York Giants

BRAIDWOOD, CHARLES—End—
Chattanooga
1930 Portsmouth Spartans
1931 Cleveland Indians
1932 Chicago Cardinals
1933 Cincinnati Reds
     Killed in action in South Pacific in winter of 1944–45.
     Member of Red Cross.

BRAMHALL, ARTHUR—Back—
None
1931 Chicago Bears

BRANDAU, ARTHUR—Center—
Tennessee
1945–46 Pittsburgh Steelers

BRANEY, JOHN—Guard—Syracuse
1925–26 Providence Steamrollers

BRANNAN, ??—Tackle—??
1923 Racine Legion
1925 Cleveland Indians

BRATT, GEORGE—End—Duluth
Cathedral
1924 Duluth Kelleys

BRAWLEY, EDWARD—Guard—
Holy Cross
1921 Cleveland Indians

BRAY, MAURICE—Tackle—SMU
1935–36 Pittsburgh Pirates

BRAY, RAYMOND—Guard—Western
Michigan
1939–42 Chicago Bears
1946–51 Chicago Bears

BRAZELL, CARL—Back—Baylor
1938 Cleveland Rams

BRAZINSKY, SAMUEL—Back—
Villanova
1946 Buffalo Bisons

BREEDON, WILLIAM—Back—
Oklahoma
1937 Pittsburgh Pirates

BRENKHART, WILLIAM—Back
Washington & Lee
1923–24 Akron Steels

BRENNAN, JOHN—Guard—
Michigan
1939 Green Bay Packers

BRENNAN, LEO—Tackle—Holy
Cross
1942 Philadelphia Eagles

BRENNAN, MATTHEW—Guard—
Lafayette
1920–25 Chicago Cardinals
1925 New York Giants
1926–27 Chicago Cardinals

BRENNAN, PAUL—Back—Fordham
1925 Canton Bulldogs

BRETT, EDWARD—End—
Washington
1936 Chicago Cardinals
1936–37 Pittsburgh Pirates

BREWER, BROOKE—Back—
Maryland
1922 Akron Steels
1929 Dayton Triangles

BREWSTER, JAMES—End—West
Virginia
1929 Buffalo Bisons

BRIAN, HARRY—Back—Grove
City
1926 Hartford

BRIAN, WILLIAM—Tackle—
Gonzaga
1935 Chicago Cardinals
1935–36 Philadelphia Eagles

BRIANTE, FRANK—Back—New
York Univ.
1929 Staten Island Stapletons

BRICK, SHIRLEY—End—Rice
1920 Buffalo All Americans

BRIDGEFORD, LANE—Back—Knox
1921–22 Rock Island Independents

BRIGGS, PAUL—Tackle—Colorado
1948 Detroit Lions

BRILL, HAROLD—Back—Wichita
1939 Detroit Lions

BRILL, MARTIN—Back—Notre Dame
1931 Staten Island Stapletons

BRINDLEY, WALTER—Back—Drake
1921–22 Rock Island Independents

BRINK, LAWRENCE—End—
Northern Illinois State
1948–51 Los Angeles Rams

BRISTOW, Gordon—Back—
Oklahoma
1925 Kansas City Cowboys

BRITO, EUGENE—End—Loyola
(Los Angeles)
1951 Washington Redskins

BRITT, EDWARD—Back—Holy
Cross
1936 Boston Redskins
1937 Washington Redskins
1938 Brooklyn Dodgers

BRITT, MAURICE—End—Arkansas
1941 Detroit Lions

BRITT, OSCAR—Guard—
Mississippi
1946 Washington Redskins

BRITT, RANKIN—End—Texas
A & M
1939–40 Philadelphia Eagles
1941 Detroit Lions

BRITTON, EARL—Back—Illinois
1927 Frankford Yellowjackets
1927–28 Dayton Triangles
1929 Chicago Cardinals

BROADLEY, KARL—Guard—Bethany
1925 Cleveland Indians

BROADSTONE, MARION—Tackle—
Nebraska
1931 New York Giants

BROCK, CHARLES—Center—
Nebraska
1939–47 Green Bay Packers

BROCK, J. LOUIS—Back—Purdue
1940–45 Green Bay Packers

BROCKMAN, EDWARD—Back—
Oklahoma
1930 Chicago Bears

BRODA, HAROLD—End—Brown
1927 Cleveland Bulldogs

BROVELLI, ANGELO—Back—St.
Mary's (Cal.)
1933–34 Pittsburgh Pirates

BROWN, DANIEL—End—Villanova
1950 Washington Redskins

BROWN, DAVID—Back—Alabama
1943 New York Giants
1946–47 New York Giants

BROWN, FREDERICK—Back—New
York Univ.
1923 Akron Steels
1926 Pottsville Maroons
1927–29 Dayton Triangles
1930 Portsmouth Spartans
1930 Staten Island Stapletons

BROWN, GEORGE—Guard—TCU
1949 New York Yankees
1950 New York Yanks

BROWN, HARDY—Back—Tulsa
1948 Brooklyn Dodgers
1949 Chicago Rockets
1950 Baltimore Colts
1950 Washington Redskins
1951 San Francisco 49ers

BROWN, HOWARD—Guard—
Indiana
1948–50 Detroit Lions

BROWN, JOHN—Center—North
Carolina College
1947–49 Los Angeles Dons

BROWN, THOMAS—End—William &
Mary
1942 Pittsburgh Steelers

BROWN, WILLIAM—Back—Marshall
1943 Brooklyn Dodgers
1944 Brooklyn Tigers

BROWN, WILLIAM—Guard—
Arkansas
1951   Washington Redskins

BROWNING, GREGORY—End—
Denver
1947   New York Giants

BRUCE, GAIL—End—Washington
1948–51   San Francisco 49ers

BRUCKNER, LESLIE—Back—
Michigan State
1945   Chicago Cardinals

BRUDER, HENRY—Back—
Northwestern
1931–39   Green Bay Packers
1940   Pittsburgh Steelers

BRUDER, WOODIE—Back—West
Virginia
1925–26   Frankford Yellowjackets

BRUMBAUGH, BOYD—Back—
Duquesne
1938   Brooklyn Dodgers
1939–41   Pittsburgh Steelers

BRUMBAUGH, CARL—Back—
Florida
1930–36   Chicago Bears
1937   Cleveland Rams
1937–38   Brooklyn Dodgers
1938   Chicago Bears
1939   Brooklyn Dodgers

BRUMBAUGH, JUSTIN—Back—
Bucknell
1931   Frankford Yellowjackets

BRUMLEY, ROBERT—Back—Rice
1945   Detroit Lions

BRUMM, ROMAN—Guard—
Wisconsin
1922   Racine Legion
1924   Racine Legion
1925   Milwaukee Badgers
1926   Racine Legion

BRUNCKLACHER, ??—Guard—??
1922–23   Louisville Colonels

BRUNSKI, ANDREW—Center—
Temple
1943   Phil-Pitt

BRUTZ, JAMES—Tackle—Notre
Dame
1946   Chicago Rockets
1948   Chicago Rockets

BRYAN, JOHN—Back—Chicago
1922   Chicago Cardinals
1923–25   Chicago Bears
1925–26   Milwaukee Badgers
1927   Chicago Bears

BRYANT, LOWELL—Back—
Clemson
1940   Detroit Lions

BRYANT, ROBERT—Tackle—Texas
Tech
1946–49   San Francisco 49ers

BUCCHIANERI, AMADEO—Guard—
Indiana
1941   Green Bay Packers
1944–45   Green Bay Packers

BUCEK, FELIX—Guard—Texas
A & M
1946   Pittsburgh Steelers

BUCHANAN, STEPHEN—Back—
Miami (Ohio)
1929   Dayton Triangles

BUCHER, FRANK—End—Detroit
1925   Detroit Panthers
1925–26   Pottsville Maroons

BUCK, ARTHUR—Back—John
Carroll
1941   Chicago Bears

BUCK, HOWARD—Tackle—
Wisconsin
1920   Canton Bulldogs
1921–25   Green Bay Packers

BUCKEYE, GARLAND—Guard—
Beloit
1921–24   Chicago Cardinals

BUCKLER, WILLIAM—Guard—
Alabama
1926–28   Chicago Bears
1931–33   Chicago Bears

BUCKLEW, PHILIP—End—Xavier
1937   Cleveland Rams

BUCKLEY, EDWARD—Back—New
York Univ.
1930   Staten Island Stapletons

BUCKLIN, THOMAS—Back—Idaho
1927   Chicago Cardinals
1931   New York Giants

BUDA, CARL—Guard—Tulsa
1945   Pittsburgh Steelers

BUDD, JOHN—Tackle—Lafayette
1926   Frankford Yellowjackets
1927–28   Pottsville Maroons

BUFFALO—Guard—None
1923   Oorang Indians

BUFFINGTON, HARRY—Guard—
Oklahoma A & M
1942   New York Giants
1946–48   Brooklyn Dodgers

BUHLER, LAWRENCE—Back—
Minnesota
1939–41   Green Bay Packers

BUIVID, RAYMOND—Back—
Marquette
1937–38   Chicago Bears

BUKANT, JOSEPH—Back—
Washington (St. Louis)
1938–40   Philadelphia Eagles
1941–43   Chicago Cardinals

BUKSAR, GEORGE—Back—Purdue
1949   Chicago Hornets
1950   Baltimore Colts
1951   Washington Redskins

BULAND, WALTER—Tackle—None
1921   Rock Island Independents
1924   Rock Island Independents
1924   Green Bay Packers
1926   Duluth Eskimos

BULGER, CHESTER—Tackle—
Alabama Polytech.
1942–43   Chicago Cardinals
1944   Card-Pitt
1945–49   Chicago Cardinals
1950   Detroit Lions

BULLMAN, GAIL—End—West
Virginia Wesleyan
1925   Columbus Tigers

BULTMAN, ARTHUR—Center—
Marquette
1931   Brooklyn Dodgers
1932–34   Green Bay Packers

BUMGARDNER, REX—Back—
West Virginia
1948–49   Buffalo Bills
1950–51   Cleveland Browns

BUNYAN, JOHN—Guard—New York
Univ.
1929–30   Staten Island Stapletons
1932   Staten Island Stapletons

BURDICK, LLOYD—Tackle—Illinois
1931–32   Chicago Bears
1933   Cincinnati Reds

BURGESS, GLEN—Tackle—Tulsa
1945   Chicago Bears

BURGNER, EARL—Back—Wittenberg
1923   Dayton Triangles

BURK, ADRIAN—Back—Baylor
1950   Baltimore Colts
1951   Philadelphia Eagles

BURKE, CHARLES—Back—
Dartmouth
1925   Providence Steamrollers

BURKE, DONALD—Back—Southern
California
1950–51   San Francisco 49ers

BURKETT, JEFFREY—End—LSU
1947   Chicago Cardinals

BURKHARDT, A. ??—Guard—Rutgers
1928   New York Giants

BURKS, JOSEPH—Center—
Washington State
1926   Milwaukee Badgers

BURMEISTER, FORREST—Back—
Purdue
1937   Cleveland Rams

BURNETT, DALE—Back—Emporia
Teachers
1931–38   New York Giants
1938   Pittsburgh Pirates
1938   Chicago Cardinals
1939   New York Giants

BURNETTE, THOMAS—Back—
North Carolina
1938   Philadelphia Eagles

BURNHAM, STANLEY—Back—
Harvard
1925   Frankford Yellowjackets

BURNSIDE, ??—Back—??
1926   Racine Legion

BURRIS, PAUL—Guard—Oklahoma
1949–51   Green Bay Packers

BURRUS, HARRY—End—Hardin-
Simmons
1946–47   New York Yankees
1948   Brooklyn Dodgers
1948   Chicago Rockets

BURT, RUSSELL—Guard—Canisius
1924   Cleveland Bulldogs
1925   Canton Bulldogs
1925   Buffalo Bisons

BUSH, R. M.—End—Loyola (Chicago)
1926   Louisville Colonels

BUSHBY, SHERRILL—End—
Alabama
1940   Brooklyn Dodgers

BUSHBY, THOMAS—Back—Kansas
1934   Cincinnati Reds
1935   Philadelphia Eagles

BUSICH, SAMUEL—End—Ohio State
1936   Boston Redskins
1937   Cleveland Rams

BUSLER, RAYMOND—Tackle—
Marquette
1941   Chicago Cardinals
1945   Chicago Cardinals

BUSS, ARTHUR—Tackle—Michigan State
1934–35   Chicago Bears
1936–37   Philadelphia Eagles

BUSSE, ELLIS—Back—Chicago
1929   Chicago Cardinals

BUSSEY, YOUNG—Back—LSU
1940–41   Chicago Bears
Killed leading landing party on first day of Lingayen operation in Philippines. Lt. in U.S. Marines

BUTCHER, WENDELL—Back—Gustavus-Adolphus
1938–42   Brooklyn Dodgers

BUTKUS, CARL—Tackle—George Washington
1948   Washington Redskins
1948   New York Yankees
1949   New York Giants

BUTLER, FRANK—Center—Michigan State
1934–36   Green Bay Packers
1938   Green Bay Packers

BUTLER, JOHN—Back—Tennessee
1943   Phil-Pitt
1944   Card-Pitt
1944   Brooklyn Dodgers
1945   Philadelphia Eagles

BUTLER, JOHN—End—St. Bonaventure
1951   Pittsburgh Steelers

BUTLER, WILLIAM—Back—Marquette
1923   Rock Island Independents
1923–24   Hammond Pros
1926   Canton Bulldogs

BYLER, JOSEPH—Tackle—Nebraska
1946   New York Giants

* * *

CABRELLI, LAWRENCE—End—Colgate
1941–42   Philadelphia Eagles
1943   Phil-Pitt
1944–47   Philadelphia Eagles

CABRINA, AUGUST—Back—Dayton
1927   Dayton Triangles

CADDEL, ERNEST—Back—Stanford
1933   Portsmouth Spartans
1934–38   Detroit Lions

CAFEGO, GEORGE—Back—Tennessee
1940–42   Brooklyn Dodgers
1943   Washington Redskins
1944–45   Boston Yanks

CAGLE, CHRISTIAN—Back—West Point
1930–32   New York Giants
1933–34   Brooklyn Dodgers

CAHILL, RONALD—Back—Holy Cross
1943   Chicago Cardinals

CAHOON, IVAN—Tackle—Gonzaga
1926–29   Green Bay Packers

CAIN, JAMES—End—Alabama
1949   Chicago Cardinals
1950   Detroit Lions

CALAC, PETER—End—Carlisle
1920   Canton Bulldogs
1921   Cleveland Indians
1922   Canton Bulldogs
1923   Oorang Indians
1924   Buffalo Bisons
1925–26   Canton Bulldogs

CALCAGNI, RALPH—Tackle—Pennsylvania
1945–46   Boston Yanks
1947   Pittsburgh Steelers

CALDWELL, BRUCE—Back—Yale
1928   New York Giants

CALDWELL, CYRIL—Tackle—Baldwin-Wallace
1925   Akron Steels

CALHOUN, ERIC—Tackle—Denison
1926   Dayton Triangles

CALLAHAN, J. R.—Back—Texas
1946   Detroit Lions

CALLAHAN, ROBERT—Center—Michigan
1947   Brooklyn Dodgers
1948   Buffalo Bills

CALLAHAN, WILLIAM—Back—Nebraska
1940–45   Detroit Lions

CALLEN, FRANK—Guard—St. Mary's (Cal.)
1947   New York Yankees

CALLIGARO, LEONARD—Back—Wisconsin
1944–45   New York Giants

CALVELLI, ANTHONY—Center—Stanford
1939–40   Detroit Lions

CAMERON, EDMUND—Guard—Washington & Lee
1926   Detroit Panthers

CAMP, JAMES—Back—North
Carolina
1948 Brooklyn Dodgers

CAMPANA, ALBERT—Back—
Youngstown
1950-51 Chicago Bears

CAMPBELL, DONALD—Tackle—??
1935 Pittsburgh Pirates
1939-40 Pittsburgh Steelers

CAMPBELL, GLENN—End—Emporia
Teachers
1929-33 New York Giants

CAMPBELL, LEON—Back—Arkansas
1950 Baltimore Colts

CAMPBELL, WILLIAM—Back—
Oklahoma
1945-49 Chicago Cardinals
1949 New York Bulldogs

CAMPIGLIO, ROBERT—Back—West
Liberty Teachers
1932 Staten Island Stapletons
1933 Boston Redskins

CAMPION, THOMAS—Tackle—
Southeastern Louisiana
1947 Philadelphia Eagles

CAMPOFREDA, NICHOLAS—
Center—Western Maryland
1944 Washington Redskins

CAMPORA, DONALD—Tackle—
College of the Pacific
1950 San Francisco 49ers

CANADEO, ANTHONY—Back—
Gonzaga
1941-44 Green Bay Packers
1946-51 Green Bay Packers

CANADY, JAMES—Back—Texas
1948 Chicago Bears
1949 New York Bulldogs

CANALE, ROCCO—Guard—Boston
College
1943 Phil-Pitt
1944-45 Philadelphia Eagles
1946-47 Boston Yanks

CANNADY, JOHN—Back—Indiana
1947-51 New York Giants

CANNAVA, ANTHONY—Back—
Boston College
1950 Green Bay Packers

CANNELLA, JOHN—Tackle—
Fordham
1933-34 New York Giants
1934 Brooklyn Dodgers

CANTOR, LEO—Back—UCLA
1942 New York Giants
1945 Chicago Cardinals

CAPPS, WILBUR—Tackle—East
Central
1929-30 Frankford Yellowjackets
1930 Minneapolis Redjackets

CARA, DOMINIC—End—North
Carolina
1937-38 Pittsburgh Pirates

CARANCI, ROLAND—Tackle—
Colorado
1944 New York Giants

CARAPELLA, ALBERT—Tackle—
Miami (Fla.)
1951 San Francisco 49ers

CARBERRY, GLENN—End—Notre
Dame
1923 Buffalo All Americans
1924 Buffalo Bisons
1925 Cleveland Indians

CARD, J. HARPER—Tackle—??
1922 Louisville Colonels

CARDARELLI, CARL—Center—None
1924 Akron Steels

CARDINAL, FRANK—Back—Notre
Dame
1947 New York Yankees

CARDWELL, JOSEPH—Tackle—
Nebraska
1937-38 Pittsburgh Pirates

CARDWELL, LLOYD—Back—
Nebraska
1937-43 Detroit Lions

CAREY, JOSEPH—Guard—None
1920 Chicago Cardinals
1921 Green Bay Packers

CARLSON, IRVIN—Guard—St. Johns
1924 Kenosha
1924-25 Duluth Kelleys
1926 Duluth Eskimos
1926 Green Bay Packers

CARLSON, JULES—Guard—Oregon
State
1928-36 Chicago Bears
1937 Chicago Cardinals

CARLSON, RAYMOND—Back—
Marquette
1947 Buffalo Bills

CARLSON, ROY—End—Bradley
1929 Dayton Triangles

CARMAN, EDMUND—Tackle—Purdue
1922 Hammond Pros
1925 Hammond Pros
1925 Buffalo Bisons

CARNELLY, RAYMOND—Back—Carnegie Tech.
1939 Brooklyn Dodgers

CARNEY, ARTHUR—Guard—Navy
1925-26 New York Giants

CARPE, JOSEPH—Tackle—Milligan
1926-27 Frankford Yellowjackets
1929 Minneapolis Redjackets
1929 Boston Braves
1933 Philadelphia Eagles

CARPENTER, JOHN—Tackle—Missouri, Michigan
1947-49 Buffalo Bills
1949 San Francisco 49ers

CARPENTER, KENNETH—Back—Oregon
1950-51 Cleveland Browns

CARR, EDWIN—Back—None
1947-50 San Francisco 49ers

CARR, HARLAN—Back—Canisius
1927 Buffalo Bisons
1927-28 Pottsville Maroons

CARROLL, EDWARD—End—Washington & Jefferson
1921-23 Canton Bulldogs
1925 Canton Bulldogs

CARROLL, VICTOR—Tackle—Nevada
1936 Boston Redskins
1937-42 Washington Redskins
1943-47 New York Giants

CARTER, JOSEPH—End—SMU
1933 Philadelphia Eagles
1934 Philadelphia Eagles—R
1935-40 Philadelphia Eagles
1942 Green Bay Packers
1944 Brooklyn Tigers
1945 Chicago Cardinals

CARTER, ROSS—Guard—Oregon
1936-39 Chicago Cardinals

CARTON, CHARLES—Tackle—Holy Cross
1925 Frankford Yellowjackets

CARY, JOSEPH—Guard—Armour Inst.
1921 Green Bay Packers

CASANEGA, KENNETH—Back—Santa Clara
1946 San Francisco 49ers
1948 San Francisco 49ers

CASE, ERNEST—Back—UCLA
1947 Baltimore Colts

CASEY, ALBERT—Back—Arkansas
1923 St. Louis Browns

CASEY, EDWARD—Back—Harvard
1920 Buffalo All Americans

CASEY, THOMAS—Back—Hampton Inst.
1948 New York Yankees

CASON, JAMES—Back—LSU
1948 San Francisco 49ers
1949 San Francisco 49ers—I (AAFC)
1950-51 San Francisco 49ers

CASPER, CHARLES—Back—TCU
1934 St. Louis Gunners
1934 Green Bay Packers
1935 Pittsburgh Pirates

CASSIANO, RICHARD—Back—Pittsburgh
1940 Brooklyn Dodgers

CASSIDY, WILLIAM—End—Detroit
1924 Kenosha

CASTEEL, MILES—Back—Kalamazoo
1922 Rock Island Independents

CASTIGLIA, JAMES—Back—Georgetown
1941 Philadelphia Eagles
1945-46 Philadelphia Eagles
1947 Baltimore Colts
1947-48 Washington Redskins

CATHCART, ROYAL—Back—Santa Barbara
1950 San Francisco 49ers

CATHCART, SAMUEL—Back—Santa Barbara
1949 San Francisco 49ers

CATO, RALPH—Center—Arkansas
1946 Miami Seahawks

CAVELLI, ANTHONY—Center—Stanford
1939 Detroit Lions
1947 San Francisco 49ers

CAVOSIE, JOSEPH—Back—Butler
1931-33 Portsmouth Spartans
1936 Cleveland Rams

CAYWOOD, LESTER—Guard—St. John's
1927 Cleveland Bulldogs
1927 Pottsville Maroons
1928 Detroit Wolverines
1929-32 New York Giants
1933-34 Cincinnati Reds

CEARING, LLOYD—Back—
Valparaiso
1922–23 Hammond Pros

CELERI, ROBERT—Back—California
1951 New York Yanks

CEMORE, ANTHONY—Guard—
Creighton
1941 Philadelphia Eagles

CHALMERS, GEORGE—Center—
New York Univ.
1933 Brooklyn Dodgers

CHAMBERLAIN, GARTH—Guard—
Brigham Young
1945 Pittsburgh Steelers

CHAMBERLAIN, GUY—End—
Nebraska
1920–21 Chicago Bears (Staleys)
1921–23 Canton Bulldogs—Player-coach
1924 Cleveland Bulldogs—Player-coach
1925–26 Frankford Yellowjackets—Player-
coach
1927 Chicago Cardinals
1928 Chicago Cardinals—Head Coach

CHAMBERS, WILLIAM—Tackle—
Alabama
1948–49 New York Yankees

CHAMPAGNE, EDWARD—Tackle—
LSU
1947–50 Los Angeles Rams

CHAMPION, JAMES—Guard—
Mississippi State
1950–51 New York Yanks

CHANDNOIS, LYNN—Back—
Michigan State
1950–51 Pittsburgh Steelers

CHANTILES, THOMAS—Tackle—
Southern California
1942 Detroit Lions

CHAPMAN, HARMON—Tackle—
Oregon
1925 Pottsville Maroons

CHAPPUIS, ROBERT—Back—
Michigan
1948 Brooklyn Dodgers
1949 Chicago Hornets

CHARLES, WINSTON—Back—
William & Mary
1927 Pottsville Maroons
1928 Dayton Triangles

CHASE, BENJAMIN—Guard—
Annapolis
1947 Detroit Lions

CHASE, RALPH—Tackle—Pittsburgh
1926 Akron Steels

CHEATHAM, LLOYD—Back—
Alabama Polytech
1942 Chicago Cardinals
1946–48 New York Yankees

CHERNE, HAROLD—Tackle—
DePaul
1933 Boston Redskins

CHEROKE, GEORGE—Center—Ohio
State
1946 Cleveland Browns

CHERRY, EDGAR—Back—
Hardin-Simmons
1938–39 Chicago Cardinals

CHERUNDULO, CHARLES—
Center—Penn State
1937–39 Cleveland Rams
1940 Philadelphia Eagles
1941–42 Pittsburgh Steelers
1945–48 Pittsburgh Steelers

CHESBRO, MARCEL—Guard—
Colgate
1938 Cleveland Rams

CHESNEY, CHESTER—Center—
Pennsylvania
1939–40 Chicago Bears

CHEVERKO, GEORGE—Back—
Fordham
1947–48 New York Giants
1948 Washington Redskins

CHICKEN, FRED—Back—None
1921 Rock Island Independents

CHICKERNEO, JOHN—Back—
Pittsburgh
1942 New York Giants

CHIPLEY, WILLIAM—End—
Washington & Lee
1947–48 Boston Yanks
1949 New York Bulldogs

CHISICK, ANDREW—Center—
Villanova
1940–41 Chicago Cardinals

CHRISTENSEN, GEORGE—Tackle—
Oregon
1931–33 Portsmouth Spartans
1934–38 Detroit Lions

CHRISTENSEN, FRANK—Back—
Utah
1934–37 Detroit Lions

CHRISTENSON, ??—End—??
1922–24 Minneapolis Marines

CHRISTENSON, MARTIN—Back—Minnesota
1940   Chicago Cardinals

CHRISTIANSEN, JOHN—Back—Colorado A & M
1951   Detroit Lions

CHRISTMAN, FLOYD—Back—Thiel
1925   Buffalo Bison

CHRISTMAN, PAUL—Back—Missouri
1945–49   Chicago Cardinals
1950   Green Bay Packers

CHURCHMAN, CHARLES—Back—Virginia
1925   Columbus Tigers

CIAGO, WALTER—End—Detroit
1922   Rock Island Independents

CIBULAS, JOSEPH—Tackle—Duquesne
1945   Pittsburgh Steelers

CICCONE, BENJAMIN—Center—Duquesne
1934–35   Pittsburgh Pirates
1942   Chicago Cardinals

CIFELLI, AUGUST—Tackle—Notre Dame
1950–51   Detroit Lions

CIFERS, EDWARD—End—Tennessee
1941–42   Washington Redskins
1946   Washington Redskins
1947–48   Chicago Bears

CIFERS, ROBERT—Back—Tennessee
1944   Detroit Lions
1946   Detroit Lions
1947–48   Pittsburgh Steelers
1949   Green Bay Packers

CIVILETTO, FRANK—Back—Springfield
1923   Cleveland Indians

CLAIR, FRANK—End—Ohio State
1941   Washington Redskins

CLANCY, STUART—Back—Holy Cross
1931–32   Staten Island Stapletons
1933–35   New York Giants

CLARK, ARTHUR—Back—Nevada
1927   Duluth Eskimos
1927   Frankford Yellowjackets

CLARK BERYL—Back—Oklahoma
1940   Chicago Cardinals

CLARK, BUTCH—End—??
1922–23   Rochester Kodaks
1924–25   Rochester Jeffersons

CLARK, CHARLES—Guard—Harvard
1920   Chicago Bears
1920   Chicago Cardinals

CLARK, DONALD—Guard—Southern California
1948–49   San Francisco 49ers

CLARK, EARL—Back—Colorado
1931–33   Portsmouth Spartans
1934   Detroit Lions
1935   Detroit Lions—S
1936   Detroit Lions—S
1937–38   Detroit—Player-coach
1939–42   Cleveland Rams—Head Coach

CLARK, HARRY—Back—West Virginia
1940–43   Chicago Bears
1946–47   Los Angeles Dons
1948   Chicago Rockets

CLARK, JAMES—Back—Pittsburgh
1931   Cleveland Indians
1932   Boston Braves
1933–34   Pittsburgh Pirates

CLARK, MYERS—Back—Ohio State
1930   Brooklyn Dodgers
1931   Cleveland Indians
1933–34   Cincinnati Reds
1934   Philadelphia Eagles

CLARK, WAYNE—End—Utah
1944–45   Detroit Lions

CLARKSON, STUART—Center—Texas A & M
1942   Chicago Bears
1946–51   Chicago Bears

CLATT, CORWIN—Back—Notre Dame
1948–49   Chicago Cardinals

CLAY, BOYD—Tackle—Tennessee
1939   Pittsburgh Steelers
1940–42   Cleveland Rams
1944   Cleveland Rams

CLAY, RANDALL—Back—Texas
1950   New York Giants

CLAY, ROY—Back—Colorado State
1944   New York Giants

CLAY, WALTER—Back—Colorado
1946–47   Chicago Rockets
1947–48   Los Angeles Dons

CLAYPOOL, RALPH—Center—Purdue
1925–26   Chicago Cardinals
1928   Chicago Cardinals

CLAYTON, DONALD—Tackle—None
1936   Philadelphia Eagles

CLEARY, PAUL—End—Southern
California
1948 New York Yankees
1949 Chicago Hornets

CLEMENS, CALVIN—Back—Southern
California
1936 Green Bay Packers

CLEMENT, Alex—Back—Williams
1925 Frankford Yellowjackets

CLEMENT, JOHN—Back—SMU
1941 Chicago Cardinals
1946–48 Pittsburgh Steelers
1949 Chicago Hornets

CLEMENTS, GEORGE—Tackle—
Washington & Jefferson
1925 Akron Steels

CLEMONS, RAYMOND—Guard—St.
Mary's (Cal.)
1939 Detroit Lions
1947 Green Bay Packers

CLEVE, ??—Back—??
1922–24 Minneapolis Marines

CLIME, BENJAMIN—Tackle—
Swarthmore
1920 Rochester Kodaks

CLINE, OLIVER—Back—Ohio State
1948 Cleveland Browns
1949 Buffalo Bills
1950–51 Detroit Lions

CLOUD, JOHN—Back—William &
Mary
1950–51 Green Bay Packers

CLOW, H.—Back—Minnesota
1924 Duluth Kelleys

CLOWES, JOHN—Tackle—William &
Mary
1948 Brooklyn Dodgers
1949 Chicago Hornets
1950–51 New York Yanks
1951 Detroit Lions

COATES, RAYMOND—Back—LSU
1948–49 New York Giants

COBB, ALFRED—Guard—Syracuse
1920–22 Akron Steels
1923 Cleveland Indians
1924 Cleveland Bulldogs

COCHRAN, JOHN—Back—Wake
Forest
1947–50 Chicago Cardinals

COCHRAN, THOMAS—Back—
Albama Polytech.
1949 Washington Redskins

CODY, EDWARD—Back—Purdue
1947–48 Green Bay Packers
1949–50 Chicago Bears

COFFEE, JAMES—Back—LSU
1937–38 Chicago Cardinals

COLE, EMERSON—Back—Toledo
1950–51 Cleveland Browns

COLE, PETER—Guard—Trinity
(Texas)
1934 Cincinnati Reds
1937–40 New York Giants

COLELLA, THOMAS—Back—
Canisius
1941–43 Detroit Lions
1944 Cleveland Rams
1946 Cleveland Browns—I (AAFC)
1947 Cleveland Browns—I (AAFC)
1948 Cleveland Browns
1949 Buffalo Bills

COLEMAN, HERBERT—Center—
Notre Dame
1946–48 Chicago Rockets
1948 Baltimore Colts

COLHOUER, JACOB—Guard—
Oklahoma
1946–48 Chicago Cardinals
1949 New York Giants

COLLIER, FLOYD—Tackle—San Jose
State
1948 San Francisco 49ers

COLLIER, ROBERT—Tackle—SMU
1951 Los Angeles Rams

COLLINS, ALBIN—Back—LSU
1949 Chicago Hornets
1950 Baltimore Colts
1951 Green Bay Packers

COLLINS, JOHN—Guard—Canisius
1924 Buffalo Bisons

COLLINS, PAUL—End—Pittsburgh
1932 Boston Braves
1933–35 Boston Redskins

COLLINS, PAUL—Back—Missouri
1945 Chicago Cardinals

COLLINS, RAYMOND—Tackle—LSU
1950–51 San Francisco 49ers

COLLINS, WILLIAM—Guard—Texas
1947 Boston Yanks

COLMER, JOHN—Back—Miramonte
Jr. College
1946 Brooklyn Dodgers
1947 Brooklyn Dodgers—K (AAFC)
1948 Brooklyn Dodgers
1949 New York Yankees

COLO, DONALD—Tackle—Brown
1950 Baltimore Colts
1951 New York Yanks

COMBS, WILLIAM—End—Purdue
1942 Philadelphia Eagles

COMER, ??—Back—??
1926 Canton Bulldogs

COMER, MARTIN—End—Tulane
1946 Buffalo Bisons
1947–48 Buffalo Bills

**COMP, H. IRVIN—Back—
St. Benedict's (Kan.)**
1943–49 Green Bay Packers

**COMPAGNO, ANTHONY—Back—
St. Mary's (Cal.)**
1945–49 Pittsburgh Steelers

**COMSTOCK, RUDOLPH—Guard—
Georgetown**
1923 Canton Bulldogs
1924 Cleveland Bulldogs
1925 Canton Bulldogs
1926–29 Frankford Yellowjackets
1929 Buffalo Bisons
1930 Brooklyn Dodgers
1930 New York Giants
1931 Staten Island Stapletons
1931–33 Green Bay Packers

**CONCANNON, ERNEST—Guard—
New York Univ.**
1934–36 Boston Redskins

**CONDIT, MERLYN—Back—Carnegie
Tech.**
1941–43 Brooklyn Dodgers
1945 Washington Redskins
1946 Pittsburgh Steelers

CONE, FRED—Back—Clemson
1951 Green Bay Packers

**CONERLY, CHARLES—Back—
Mississippi**
1948–51 New York Giants

CONGER, MELVIN—End—Georgia
1946–47 New York Yankees
1947 Brooklyn Dodgers

**CONKWRIGHT, WILLIAM—
Tackle—Oklahoma**
1937–38 Chicago Bears
1939–42 Cleveland Rams
1943 Washington Redskins
1943 Brooklyn Dodgers
1944–45 Cleveland Rams

**CONLEE, GERALD—Center—
St. Mary's (Cal.)**
1938 Cleveland Rams
1943 Detroit Lions
1946–47 San Francisco 49ers

**CONLEY, JOHN—Tackle—Ohio
Northern**
1922 Columbus Tigers
1926 Columbus Tigers

**CONNAUGHTON, HARRY—
Guard—Georgetown**
1927 Frankford Yellowjackets

**CONNELL, JAMES—Back—Catholic
Univ.**
1926 Chicago Cardinals

**CONNER, EMERSON—Guard—
Texas**
1935 Detroit Lions

**CONNOLLY, HARRY—Back—Boston
College**
1946 Brooklyn Dodgers

**CONNOLLY, WILLIAM—Guard—
Texas**
1946 Chicago Cardinals

**CONNOR, GEORGE—Tackle—Notre
Dame**
1948–51 Chicago Bears

**CONNOR, WILLIAM—Tackle—
Catholic Univ.**
1929 Boston Braves

CONNORS, ??—End—??
1925 Rochester Jeffersons

**CONOVER, LAWRENCE—Center—
Penn State**
1923 Canton Bulldogs
1924 Pottsville Maroons
1924 Cleveland Bulldogs
1925 Cleveland Indians

CONRAD, ??—Center—Kalamazoo
1922–23 Toledo Maroons
1924 Kenosha
1925 Akron Steels

**CONSTANTINE, IRVING—Back—
Syracuse**
1931 Staten Island Stapletons

CONTI, ENIO—Guard—Bucknell
1941–42 Philadelphia Eagles
1943 Phil-Pitt
1944–45 Philadelphia Eagles

**CONZELMAN, JAMES—Back—
Washington (St. Louis)**
1920 Chicago Bears (Staleys)
1921–22 Rock Island Independents
1923–24 Milwaukee Badgers—Player-coach
1925–26 Detroit Panthers—Player-coach
1927–29 Providence Steamrollers—Player-
coach
1940–42 Chicago Cardinals—Head Coach
1946–48 Chicago Cardinals—Head Coach

COOK, DAVID—Back—Illinois
1934–36 Chicago Cardinals
1936 Brooklyn Dodgers

COOK, EUGENE—Back—Washington
1928 Dayton Triangles

COOK, JAMES—Guard—Wisconsin
1921 Green Bay Packers

COOK, TED—End—Alabama
1947 Detroit Lions
1948–50 Green Bay Packers

COOKER, ??—Tackle—??
1924 Rochester Jeffersons

COOMER, JOSEPH—Tackle—Austin (Texas)
1941 Pittsburgh Steelers
1945–46 Pittsburgh Steelers
1947–49 Chicago Cardinals

COON, EDWARD—Guard—North Carolina State
1940–41 Brooklyn Dodgers

COOPER, HAROLD—Guard—Detroit
1937 Detroit Lions

COOPER, JAMES—Center—North Texas State
1948 Brooklyn Dodgers

COOPER, KENNETH—Guard—Vanderbilt
1949–50 Baltimore Colts

COOPER, NORMAN—Center—Howard
1937–38 Brooklyn Dodgers

COOPER, WILLIAM—Tackle—Oregon
1937 Cleveland Rams

COPE, FRANK—Tackle—Santa Clara
1938–47 New York Giants

COPLEY, CHARLES—Tackle—Missouri
1920 Akron Steels

COPPAGE, ALTON—End—Oklahoma
1940–42 Chicago Cardinals
1946 Cleveland Browns
1947 Buffalo Bills

CORBETT, GEORGE—Back—Milligan
1932–38 Chicago Bears

CORBITT, DONALD—Center—Arizona
1948 Washington Redskins

CORBO, THOMAS—Guard—Duquesne
1944 Cleveland Rams

CORCORAN, GERALD—Center—Illinois
1930 Minneapolis Redjackets

CORCORAN, THOMAS—Back—Georgetown
1920 Canton Bulldogs
1921 Cleveland Indians
1922 Akron Steels
1923 Buffalo All Americans

CORDILL, OLIVER—Back—Rice
1940 Cleveland Rams

CORDOVANO, SAMUEL—Guard—Columbia
1930 Newark

CORGAN, CHARLES—End—Arkansas
1924 Kansas City Cowboys
1925 Louisville Colonels
1926 Hartford
1927 New York Giants

CORGAN, MICHAEL—Back—Notre Dame
1943 Detroit Lions

CORLEY, ELBERT—Center—Mississippi State
1947 Buffalo Bills
1948 Baltimore Colts

CORMIER, ULYSSES—Back—LSU
1929 Buffalo Bisons

CORN, JOSEPH—Back—None
1948 Los Angeles Rams

CORNSWEET, ALBERT—Back—Brown
1931 Cleveland Indians

CORTEMEGLIA, CHRISTOPHER—Back—None
1927 Frankford Yellowjackets

CORZINE, LESTER—Back—Davis & Elkins
1933–34 Cincinnati Reds
1934 St. Louis Gunners
1935–37 New York Giants
1938 Chicago Bears

COSGROVE, THOMAS—Tackle—Pittsburgh
1935 Pittsburgh Pirates

COSNER, DONALD—Tackle—Montana State
1939 Chicago Cardinals

COSTER, FREDERICK—Center—Texas A & M
1939 Philadelphia Eagles

COTTON, FORREST—Tackle—Notre Dame
1923 Rock Island Independents
1925 Rock Island Independents

COTTON, RUSSELL—Back—Texas Mines
1941 Brooklyn Dodgers
1942 Pittsburgh Steelers

COUGHLIN, FRANK—Tackle—Notre Dame
1921 Green Bay Packers
1921 Rock Island Independents
1923 Minneapolis Marines

COULTER, DeWITT—Tackle—West Point
1946–49 New York Giants
1951 New York Giants

COUPPEE, ALBERT—Guard—Iowa
1946 Washington Redskins

COURTNEY, GERARD—Back—Syracuse
1942 Brooklyn Dodgers

COUTRE, LAWRENCE—Back—Notre Dame
1950 Green Bay Packers

COWAN, LESLIE—Tackle—McMurry
1951 Chicago Bears

COWAN, ROBERT—Back—Indiana
1947–48 Cleveland Browns
1949 Baltimore Colts

COWHIG, GERARD—Back—Notre Dame
1947–49 Los Angeles Rams
1950 Chicago Cardinals
1951 Philadelphia Eagles

COX, JAMES—Guard—Stanford
1948 San Francisco 49ers

COX, NORMAN—Back—TCU
1946–47 Chicago Rockets

COX, ROBERT—End—Oklahoma
1936 Cleveland Rams

COX, WILLIAM—End—Duke
1951 Washington Redskins

CRABTREE, CLEMENT—Tackle—Wake Forest
1940–41 Detroit Lions

CRABTREE, CLYDE—Back—Florida
1930 Frankford Yellowjackets
1930 Minneapolis Redjackets

CRAFT, RUSSELL—Back—Alabama
1946–51 Philadelphia Eagles

CRAIG, C. W.—End—Pennsylvania
1925 Frankford Yellowjackets

CRAIG, LAWRENCE—Back—South Carolina
1939–49 Green Bay Packers

CRAIN, MILTON—Back—Baylor
1944 Boston Yanks

CRAKES, JOSEPH—End—South Dakota
1933 Cincinnati Reds

CRAMER, CARL—Back—Hamline
1921–25 Akron Steels

CRANGLE, JOHN—Back—Illinois
1923 Chicago Cardinals

CRAWFORD, DENVER—Tackle—Tennessee
1948 New York Yankees

CRAWFORD, FREDERICK—Tackle—Duke
1935 Chicago Bears

CRAWFORD, KENNETH—Back—Miami (Ohio)
1920 Akron Steels
1923 Dayton Triangles
1925 Hammond Pros
1927 New York Yankees
1927 Chicago Bears

CRAYNE, RICHARD—Back—Iowa
1936–37 Brooklyn Dodgers

CREEKMUR, LOUIS—Guard—William & Mary
1950–51 Detroit Lions

CREGAR, WILLIAM—Guard—Holy Cross
1947–48 Pittsburgh Steelers

CREIGHTON, MILAN—End—Arkansas
1931–34 Chicago Cardinals
1935–37 Chicago Cardinals—Player-coach

CREMER, THEODORE—End—Alabama Polytech.
1946–48 Detroit Lions
1948 Green Bay Packers

CRIMMINS, BERNARD—Guard—Notre Dame
1945 Green Bay Packers

CRISLER, HAROLD—End—San Jose State
1946–47 Boston Yanks
1948–49 Washington Redskins
1950 Baltimore Colts

CRITCHFIELD, LAWRENCE—
Guard—Grove City
1931 Cleveland Indians
1933 Pittsburgh Pirates

CROFT, ??—Guard—??
1924 Racine Legion

CROFT, ABRAHAM—End—SMU
1944-45 Chicago Bears

CROFT, MILBURN—Tackle—Ripon
1942-47 Green Bay Packers

CROFT, THURMAN—Guard—
Carnegie Tech.
1936 Pittsburgh Pirates

CROFT, WINSTON—Guard—Utah
1935 Brooklyn Dodgers
1936 Pittsburgh Pirates

CRONIN, JOHN—Back—Boston
College
1927 Duluth Eskimos
1928-30 Providence Steamrollers

CRONIN, THOMAS—Back—
Marquette
1922 Green Bay Packers

CRONIN, WILLIAM—Back—Boston
College
1927-30 Providence Steamrollers
1932 Brooklyn Dodgers

CRONKHITE, HENRY—End—
Kansas State
1934 Brooklyn Dodgers

CROOK, ALBERT—Center—
Washington & Jefferson
1925-26 Detroit Panthers
1926 Kansas City Cowboys

CROSS, WILLIAM—Back—West
Texas State
1951 Chicago Cardinals

CROW, ORIEN—Center—Haskell
1933-34 Boston Redskins

CROWDER, EARL—Back—Oklahoma
1939 Chicago Cardinals
1940 Cleveland Rams

CROWE, PAUL—Back—St. Mary's
(Cal.)
1948-49 Los Angeles Dons
1949 San Francisco 49ers
1951 New York Yanks

CROWELL, ODIS—Tackle—
Hardin-Simmons
1947 San Francisco 49ers

CROWL, R. ??—Center—Rutgers
1930 Brooklyn Dodgers

CROWLEY, JOSEPH—End—
Dartmouth
1944-45 Boston Yanks

CROWTHERS, RAE—Tackle—
Colgate
1925 Frankford Yellowjackets

CROWTHERS, SAVILLE—End—
Colgate
1925-26 Frankford Yellowjackets

CUBA, PAUL—Tackle—Pittsburgh
1933-35 Philadelphia Eagles
1938 Pittsburgh Pirates

CUFF, WARD—Back—Marquette
1937 New York Giants
1938 New York Giants—F (Tie with R. Kercheval) (5)
1939 New York Giants—F (7)
1940-42 New York Giants
1943 New York Giants—F (Tie with D. Hutson) (3)
1944-45 New York Giants
1946 Chicago Cardinals
1947 Green Bay Packers

CULLEN, RONALD—Tackle—
Oklahoma
1922 Milwaukee Badgers

CULLEN, THOMAS—Guard—
Georgetown
1931 Cleveland Indians

CULLOM, JAMES—Guard—
California
1951 New York Yanks

CULVER, ALVIN—Tackle—Notre
Dame
1932 Chicago Bears

CULVER, FRANK—Center—Syracuse
1923 Buffalo All Americans
1924 Buffalo Bisons
1925 Canton Bulldogs

CULWELL, VAL—Guard—Oregon
1942 New York Giants

CUMISKY, FRANK—End—Ohio State
1937 Brooklyn Dodgers

CUNEO, EDWARD—Guard—
Columbia
1929 Orange
1930 Brooklyn Dodgers

CUNNINGHAM, HAROLD—End—
Ohio State
1927 Cleveland Bulldogs
1929 Chicago Bears
1931 Staten Island Stapletons

CUPPOLETTI, BREE—Guard—Oregon
1934–38   Chicago Cardinals
1939   Philadelphia Eagles

CURE, ARMAND—Back—Rhode Island State
1947   Baltimore Colts

CURRIVAN, DONALD—End—Boston College
1943   Chicago Cardinals
1944   Card-Pitt
1945–48   Boston Yanks
1949   Los Angeles Rams

CURTIN, DONALD—Back—Marquette
1926   Milwaukee Badgers

CURZON, ??—End—??
1925   Buffalo Bisons
1925–26   Hammond Pros
1928   Chicago Cardinals

CYRE, HECTOR—Tackle—Gonzaga
1926   Green Bay Packers
1928   Green Bay Packers

CZAROBSKI, ZYGMONT—Tackle—Notre Dame
1948   Chicago Rockets
1949   Chicago Hornets

* * *

DADDIO, WILLIAM—End—Pittsburgh
1940–41   Chicago Cardinals
1942   Chicago Cardinals—F (5)
1946   Buffalo Bisons

DADMAN, HARRIE—Guard—Harvard
1920   Canton Bulldogs

DAGATA, FREDERICK—Back—Providence College
1931   Providence Steamrollers

DAHLGREN, GEORGE—Guard—Beloit
1924   Kenosha
1925–26   Hammond Pros

DAHMS, THOMAS—Tackle—San Diego State
1951   Los Angeles Rams

DAILEY, T. ??—End—Pittsburgh
1933   Pittsburgh Pirates

DALE, ROLAND—End—Mississippi
1950   Washington Redskins

DALEY, WILLIAM—Back—Minnesota, Michigan
1946   Miami Seahawks
1946   Brooklyn Dodgers
1947   Chicago Rockets
1948   New York Yankees

D'ALONZO, PETER—Back—Villanova
1951   Detroit Lions

DAMIANI, FRANCIS—Tackle—Manhattan
1944   New York Giants

DANCEWICZ, FRANCIS—Back—Notre Dame
1946–48   Boston Yanks

DANAHE, RICHARD—Tackle—Southern California
1947–48   Los Angeles Dons

DANIELL, AVERELL—Tackle—Pittsburgh
1937   Green Bay Packers
1937–38   Brooklyn Dodgers

DANIELL, JAMES—Tackle—Ohio State
1945   Chicago Bears
1946   Cleveland Browns

DANOWSKI, EDWARD—Back—Fordham
1934   New York Giants
1935   New York Giants—P
1936–37   New York Giants
1938   New York Giants—P
1939   New York Giants
1941   New York Giants

DARBY, ??—Guard—??
1924   Rochester Jeffersons

DARLING, BERNARD—Center—Beloit
1927–31   Green Bay Packers

DAUGHERTY, RICHARD—Guard—Oregon
1951   Los Angeles Rams

DAUGHTERY, RUSSELL—Back—Illinois
1927   Frankford Yellowjackets

DAUKAS, LOUIS—Center—Cornell
1947   Brooklyn Dodgers

DAUKAS, NICHOLAS—Tackle—Dartmouth
1946–47   Brooklyn Dodgers

DAUM, CARL—End—Akron Univ.
1922–25   Akron Steels

DAVENPORT, WAYNE—Back—Hardin-Simmons
1931 Green Bay Packers

DAVID, ROBERT—Guard—Notre Dame
1947–48 Los Angeles Rams
1948 Chicago Rockets

DAVIDOVITZ, ARTHUR—Tackle—Lehigh
1930 Frankford Yellowjackets

DAVIDSON, GARRISON—Guard—West Point
1928 Chicago Cardinals

DAVIDSON, WILLIAM—Back—Temple
1937–38 Pittsburgh Pirates
1939 Pittsburgh Steelers

DAVIS, CORBETT—Back—Indiana
1938–42 Cleveland Rams

DAVIS, FREDERICK—Tackle—Alabama
1941–42 Washington Redskins
1945 Washington Redskins
1946–51 Chicago Bears

DAVIS, GAINES—Guard—Texas Teachers
1932–33 Portsmouth Spartans
1935 Brooklyn Dodgers
1936 New York Giants

DAVIS, GLENN—Back—West Point
1950–51 Los Angeles Rams

DAVIS, HARPER—Back—Mississippi State
1949 Los Angeles Dons
1950 Chicago Bears
1951 Green Bay Packers

DAVIS, JEROME—Back—Southeastern Louisiana
1948–51 Chicago Cardinals

DAVIS, JOSEPH—End—Southern California
1943 Brooklyn Dodgers
1946 Brooklyn Dodgers

DAVIS, R. LAMAR—End—Georgia
1946 Miami Seahawks
1947–49 Baltimore Colts

DAVIS, PAUL—Guard—Marquette
1920–21 Dayton Triangles
1922 Green Bay Packers

DAVIS, PAUL—Back—Otterbein
1947–48 Pittsburgh Steelers

DAVIS, RALPH—Guard—Wisconsin
1947–48 Green Bay Packers

DAVIS, RAYMOND—End—Alabama
1925–26 Columbus Tigers
1927 Frankford Yellowjackets
1932 Portsmouth Spartans
1935 Chicago Cardinals

DAVIS, ROBERT—End—Penn State
1946–50 Pittsburgh Steelers

DAVIS, ROBERT—Back—Kentucky
1936 New York Giants
1938 Cleveland Rams
1942 Philadelphia Eagles
1944–47 Boston Yanks

DAVIS, ROBERT—Tackle—Georgia Tech.
1948 Boston Yanks

DAVIS, SYLVESTER—Back—Geneva
1933 Portsmouth Spartans
1933 Philadelphia Eagles

DAVIS, VAN—End—Georgia
1947–49 New York Yankees

DAVIS, WILLIAM—Tackle—Texas Tech.
1940–41 Chicago Cardinals
1942 Brooklyn Dodgers
1946 Miami Seahawks

DAWLEY, FREDERICK—Back—Michigan
1944 Detroit Lions

DAYHOFF, HARRY—Back—Bucknell
1924 Frankford Yellowjackets
1925 Pottsville Maroons

DEADEYE—Tackle—None
1923 Oorang Indians

DEAL, RUFUS—Center—Alabama Polytech.
1942 Washington Redskins

DEAN, HAROLD—Guard—Ohio State
1947–49 Los Angeles Rams

DEAN, THOMAS—Tackle—SMU
1946–47 Boston Yanks

DECARBO, NICHOLAS—Guard—Duquesne
1933 Pittsburgh Pirates

DECLERE, ??—Center—??
1921–25 Rock Island Independents

DeCORREVONT, WILLIAM—Back—Northwestern
1945 Washington Redskins
1946 Detroit Lions
1947–48 Chicago Cardinals
1948–49 Chicago Bears

DEEKS, DONALD—Tackle—
Washington
1945–47   Boston Yanks
1948   Green Bay Packers

DeFILIPPO, DAVID—Guard—
Villanova
1940–41   Philadelphia Eagles

DEFILIPPO, LOUIS—Center—
Fordham
1941   Philadelphia Eagles
1941   New York Giants
1945–48   New York Giants

DeFRUITER, ROBERT—Back—
Nebraska
1945–47   Washington Redskins
1947   Detroit Lions
1948   Los Angeles Rams

DEIBEL, ARTHUR—Tackle—
Lafayette
1926   Canton Bulldogs

DEKDEBRUN, ALLEN—Back—
Cornell
1946   Buffalo Bisons
1947   Chicago Rockets
1948   New York Yankees
1948   Boston Yanks

DeLAUER, ROBERT—Center—
Southern California
1945   Cleveland Rams
1946   Los Angeles Rams

DELL ISOLA, JOHN—Center—
Boston College
1934–40   New York Giants

DELLERBA, SPIRO—Back—Ohio
State
1947   Cleveland Browns
1948–49   Baltimore Colts

DELLINGER, ??—Guard—Dayton
1921–23   Dayton Triangles

DeMAO, ALBERT—Center—
Duquesne
1945–51   Washington Redskins

DeMARCO, MARIO—Guard—Miami
(Fla.)
1949   Detroit Lions

DEMAS, GEORGE—Guard—
Washington & Jefferson
1932   Staten Island Stapletons
1933   Philadelphia Eagles
1934   Brooklyn Dodgers

DEMMY, ??—Tackle—None
1930–32   Staten Island Stapletons

DeMOSS, ROBERT—Back—Purdue
1949   New York Bulldogs

DEMPSEY, FRANK—Tackle—Florida
1950–51   Chicago Bears

DEMPSEY, JOHN—Tackle—Loyola
1934   Pittsburgh Pirates
1934   Philadelphia Eagles
1937   Philadelphia Eagles

DENFIELD, FREDERICK—Tackle—
Navy
1925   Duluth Kelleys

DENNERLEIN, GERALD—Tackle—
St. Mary's (Cal.)
1937   New York Giants
1940   New York Giants

DENNERY, VINCENT—End—
Fordham
1941   New York Giants

DePAUL, HENRY—Guard—Duquesne
1945   Pittsburgh Steelers

DEPLER, JOHN—Center—Illinois
1921   Hammond Pros
1929   Dayton Triangles
1929   Orange

DEREMER, ARTHUR—Center—
Niagara
1942   Brooklyn Dodgers

DeROGATIS, ALBERT—Tackle—
Duke
1949–51   New York Giants

DeSANTIS, DANIEL—Back—Niagara
1941   Philadelphia Eagles

DeSHANE, CHARLES—Back—
Alabama
1945–49   Detroit Lions

DesJARDINS, PAUL—Guard—
Chicago
1921   Rock Island Independents

DESKIN, VERSIL—End—Iowa
1935–39   Chicago Cardinals

DeSTEFANO, FREDERICK—Back—
Northwestern
1924–25   Chicago Cardinals

DETWILER, JOHN—Back—Kansas
1923–24   Hammond Pros

DEWAR, JAMES—Back—Indiana
1947   Cleveland Browns
1948   Brooklyn Dodgers

DeWEESE, BYRNE—Guard—Kent
State (Ohio)
1927–28   Dayton Triangles
1930   Portsmouth Spartans

DEWELL, WILLIAM—End—SMU
1940–41   Chicago Cardinals
1945–49   Chicago Cardinals

DeWITZ, HERBERT—Back—
Nebraska
1924 Kansas City Cowboys
1926 Kansas City Cowboys
1927 Cleveland Indians

DIBB, JOHN—Tackle—West Point
1930 Newark

DIBBLE, DORNE—End—Michigan
State
1951 Detroit Lions

DICKENS, MARION—Back—Georgia
1932 Boston Braves

DICKEY, LEONARD—Tackle—
Kilgore Jr. College
1947 New York Yankees

DIEHL, CARL—Back—Dartmouth
1928–30 Frankford Yellowjackets
1930–31 Chicago Cardinals
1933 Cincinnati Reds
1934 St. Louis Gunners

DIEHL, DAVID—End—Michigan State
1939–40 Detroit Lions
1944–45 Detroit Lions

DIETER, HERBERT—Guard—
Pennsylvania
1922 Buffalo All Americans

DIGRIS, BERNARD—Tackle—Holy
Cross
1943 Chicago Bears

DIMANCHEFF, BORIS—Back—
Purdue
1945–46 Boston Yanks
1947–50 Chicago Cardinals

DiPIERRO, RAYMOND—Guard—
Ohio State
1950–51 Green Bay Packers

DISEND, LEO—Tackle—Albright
1938–39 Brooklyn Dodgers
1940 Green Bay Packers
1943 Philadelphia Eagles

DIXON, FELIX—Tackle—Boston
Univ.
1938 Brooklyn Dodgers

DOANE, JOSEPH—Back—Tufts
1922–24 Milwaukee Badgers
1925–26 Detroit Panthers
1927 Pottsville Maroons
1927 Providence Steamrollers

DOBBS, GLENN—Back—Tulsa
1946 Brooklyn Dodgers—P–K (AAFC)
1947 Brooklyn Dodgers
1948 Los Angeles Dons—K (AAFC)
1949 Los Angeles Dons

DOBELSTEIN, ROBERT—Guard—
Tennessee
1946–48 New York Giants
1949 Los Angeles Dons

DOBLIET, ??—Back—??
1925–26 Dayton Triangles

DOBREY, E. A.—End—??
1928 Frankford Yellowjackets

DOBRUS, PETER—Tackle—Carnegie
Tech.
1941 Brooklyn Dodgers

DODRILL, DALE—Guard—Colorado
A & M
1951 Pittsburgh Steelers

DODSON, LESLIE—Back—Mississippi
1941 Pittsburgh Steelers

DOEHRING, JOHN—Back—None
1932–35 Chicago Bears
1935 Pittsburgh Pirates
1936–37 Chicago Bears

DOHERTY, GEORGE—Guard—
Louisiana Tech.
1944 Brooklyn Dodgers
1945 Boston Yanks
1946 New York Yankees
1946 Buffalo Bisons
1947 Buffalo Bills

DOLOWAY, CLIFFORD—Back—??
1935 Pittsburgh Pirates

DOLL, DONALD—Back—Southern
California
1949–51 Detroit Lions

DOLLY, JOHN—End—West Virginia
1941 Pittsburgh Steelers
1945 Pittsburgh Steelers

DOMNANOVICH, JOSEPH—
Center—Alabama
Alabama
1946–48 Boston Yanks
1949 New York Bulldogs
1950 New York Yanks
1951 New York Yanks

DONAHUE, JAMES—Tackle—Boston
College
1926 Providence Steamrollers

DONAHUE, W. ??—Back—Carnegie
Tech.
1927 Frankford Yellowjackets

DONALDSON, JOHN—Back—
Georgia
1949 Chicago Hornets
1949 Los Angeles Dons

DON CARLOS, J. E.—Center—Drake
1931   Green Bay Packers

DONELLI, ALDO—Back—Duquesne
1941–42   Pittsburgh Steelers—Player-coach
1944   Cleveland Rams—Head Coach

DONOVAN, ARTHUR—Tackle—
   Boston College
1950   Baltimore Colts
1951   New York Yanks

DOOLAN, ??—Center—??
1922   Racine Legion

DOOLAN, JOHN—Back—Georgetown
1945   Washington Redskins
1945–46   New York Giants
1947–48   Chicago Cardinals

DOOLEY, JOHN—Guard—Syracuse
1922   Rochester Kodaks
1923   Milwaukee Badgers
1924–25   Rochester Jeffersons

DORAN, JAMES—End—Iowa State
1951   Detroit Lions

D'ORAZIO, JOSEPH—Tackle—Ithaca
   College
1944   Detroit Lions

DORFMAN, ARTHUR—Guard—
   Boston Univ.
1929   Buffalo Bisons

DOSS, NOBLE—Back—Texas
1947–48   Philadelphia Eagles
1949   New York Yankees

DOTTLEY, JOHN—Back—Mississippi
1951   Chicago Bears

DOUDS, FORREST—Tackle—
   Washington & Jefferson
1930   Providence Steamrollers
1930–31   Portsmouth Spartans
1932   Chicago Cardinals
1933   Pittsburgh Pirates—Player-coach
1934   Pittsburgh Pirates

DOUGHERTY, PHILIP—Back—Santa
   Clara
1938   Chicago Cardinals

DOUGLAS, ASTYNAX—Center—
   TCU
1926   Frankford Yellowjackets

DOUGLAS, BENJAMIN—Back—
   Cornell
1933   Brooklyn Dodgers

DOUGLAS, GEORGE—Center—
   Marquette
1921   Green Bay Packers

DOUGLAS, OTIS—Tackle—William &
   Mary
1946–49   Philadelphia Eagles

DOVE, ROBERT—End—Notre Dame
1946–47   Chicago Rockets
1948–51   Chicago Cardinals

DOW, ELWOOD—Back—Oregon
   State
1938–40   Philadelphia Eagles
1941   Washington Redskins

DOW, HARLEY—Guard—San Jose
   State
1950   San Francisco 49ers

DOWD, GERALD—Center—St. Mary's
   (Cal.)
1939   Cleveland Rams

DOWDA, HARRY—Back—Wake
   Forest
1949–51   Washington Redskins

DOWELL, GWYN—Back—Texas
   Tech.
1935–36   Chicago Cardinals

DOWLING, PATRICK—End—DePaul
1929   Chicago Cardinals

DOYLE, EDWARD—End—Canisius
1924   Frankford Yellowjackets
1925   Pottsville Maroons
1927   Buffalo Bisons
         Killed—First officer killed in
         African invasion, 1943. Cap-
         tain, U.S. Army.

DOYLE, THEODORE—Tackle—
   Nebraska
1938–42   Pittsburgh Pirates
1943   Phil-Pitt
1944   Card-Pitt
1945   Pittsburgh Steelers

DRAKE, JOHN—Back—Purdue
1937–41   Cleveland Rams

DRAVELING, LEO—Tackle—
   Michigan
1933   Cincinnati Reds

DRAYER, CLARENCE—Tackle—
   Illinois
1925   Dayton Triangles

DRAZENOVICH, CHARLES—Back—
   Penn State
1950–51   Washington Redskins

DREHER, FERDINAND—End—
   Denver
1938   Chicago Bears

DRESSEN, CHARLES—Back—None
1920   Chicago Bears (Staleys)
1922–23   Racine Legion

DREWS, THEODORE—End—
Princeton
1926 Brooklyn Dodgers
1928 Chicago Bears

DREYER, WALTER—Back—
Wisconsin
1949 Chicago Bears
1950-51 Green Bay Packers

DILWEG, LAVERN—End—Marquette
1926 Milwaukee Badgers
1927-33 Green Bay Packers

DRISCOLL, JOHN—Back—
Northwestern
1920 Chicago Cardinals
1921-22 Chicago Cardinals—Player-coach
1923-25 Chicago Cardinals
1926-29 Chicago Bears

DRULIS, ALBERT—Back—Temple
1945-46 Chicago Cardinals
1947 Pittsburgh Steelers
1948 Washington Redskins

DRULIS, CHARLES—Guard—Temple
1942 Chicago Bears
1945-49 Chicago Bears
1950 Green Bay Packers

DRURY, LYLE—End—St. Louis Univ.
1930-31 Chicago Bears

DRUZE, JOHN—End—Boston
College
1938 Brooklyn Dodgers

DRYDEN, ??—Back—Maryland
1930 Staten Island Stapletons

DUBOFSKY, MAURICE—Guard—
Georgetown
1932 New York Giants

DUBZINSKI, WALTER—Guard—
Boston College
1941 Detroit Lions
1943 New York Giants
1944 Boston Yanks

DUCKWORTH, JOSEPH—End—
Colgate
1947 Washington Redskins
1948 Boston Yanks

DUDEN, RICHARD—End—Navy
1949 New York Giants

DUDISH, ANDREW—Center—
Georgia
1946 Buffalo Bisons
1947 Baltimore Colts
1948 Brooklyn Dodgers
1948 Detroit Lions

DUDLEY, WILLIAM—Back—
Virginia
1942 Pittsburgh Steelers—G
1945 Pittsburgh Steelers
1946 Pittsburgh Steelers—G—I—V
1947-49 Detroit Lions
1950-51 Washington Redskins

DUFFT, JAMES—Guard—Colgate
1922 Milwaukee Badgers

DUFFY, PATRICK—Back—Dayton
1929 Dayton Triangles

DUFORD, WILFRED—Back—
Marquette
1924 Green Bay Packers

DUGAN, LEONARD—Center—
Wichita
1936 New York Giants
1937-39 Chicago Cardinals

DUGGAN, EDWARD—Back—Notre
Dame
1921 Rock Island Independents

DUGGAN, GILFORD—Tackle—
Oklahoma
1940 New York Giants
1941-43 Chicago Cardinals
1944 Card-Pitt
1945 Chicago Cardinals
1946 Los Angeles Dons
1947 Buffalo Bisons

DUGGER, JOHN—End—Ohio State
1946 Buffalo Bisons
1947-48 Detroit Lions
1949 Chicago Bears

DUGGINS, HERBERT—End—
Purdue
1933-34 Chicago Cardinals

DUHART, PAUL—Back—Florida
1944 Green Bay Packers
1945 Pittsburgh Steelers
1945 Boston Yanks

DUKE, PAUL—Center—Georgia Tech.
1947 New York Yankees

DUMOE, WILLIAM—End—Beloit
1921 Green Bay Packers
1921 Rochester Kodaks

DUNCAN, JAMES—End—Wake
Forest
1950 Detroit Lions
1950-51 New York Giants

DUNIGAN, MERTON—Tackle—
Minnesota
1924 Minneapolis Marines
1925-26 Milwaukee Badgers

**DUNLAP, ROBERT—Back—
Oklahoma**
1935   Chicago Bears
1936   New York Giants

**DUNN, COYE—Back—Southern
California**
1943   Washington Redskins

DUNN, JOSEPH—Back—Marquette
1923   Duluth Kelleys
1924–25   Milwaukee Badgers
1925–26   Chicago Cardinals
1927–31   Green Bay Packers

DUNN, R. ??—Center—New York Univ.
1929   Staten Island Stapletons

**DUNNIGAN, WALTER—End—
Minnesota**
1922   Green Bay Packers

**DUNSTAN, W. ELWYN—Tackle—
Portland**
1938–39   Chicago Cardinals
1939–41   Cleveland Rams

**DURDAN, DONALD—Back—Oregon
State**
1946–47   San Francisco 49ers

**DURISHAN, JACK—Tackle—
Pittsburgh**
1947   New York Yankees

DURKO, JOHN—End—Albright
1944   Philadelphia Eagles
1945   Chicago Cardinals

**DURKOTA, JEFFREY—Back—Penn
State**
1948   Los Angeles Dons

**DUTTON, WILLIAM—Back—
Pittsburgh**
1946   Pittsburgh Steelers
1947   New York Yankees

DUVALL, EARL—Guard—Ohio
1924–26   Columbus Tigers
1928   Chicago Bears

**DWORSKY, DANIEL—Back—
Michigan**
1949   Los Angeles Dons

**DWYER, JOHN—Back—Loyola
(Los Angeles)**
1951   Washington Redskins

**DWYER, ROBERT—Back—
Georgetown**
1929   Orange

DYE, LESTER—End—Syracuse
1944–45   Washington Redskins

* * *

**EAGLE, ALEXANDER—Tackle—
Oregon**
1935   Brooklyn Dodgers

EAGLE FEATHER—Back—None
1923   Oorang Indians

EAKIN, KAY—Back—Arkansas
1940–41   New York Giants
1946   Miami Seahawks

**EARHART, RALPH—Back—Texas
Tech.**
1948–49   Green Bay Packers

**EARP, FRANCIS—Guard—
Monmouth**
1921–22   Rock Island Independents
1922–27   Green Bay Packers
1927   New York Giants
1928–32   Green Bay Packers

EASON, ROGER—Tackle—Oklahoma
1945   Cleveland Rams
1946–48   Los Angeles Rams
1949   Green Bay Packers

**EATON, LOUIS—Tackle—
California**
1945   New York Giants

**EBDING, HARRY—End—St. Mary's
(Cal.)**
1930–33   Portsmouth Spartans
1934–37   Detroit Lions

EBERDT, JESS—Center—Alabama
1932   Brooklyn Dodgers

EBERSOLE, H. L.—Guard—Cornell
1923   Cleveland Indians

**EBERTS, BERNARD—Guard—
Catholic Univ.**
1924   Minneapolis Marines

**EBLI, RAYMOND—End—Notre
Dame**
1942   Chicago Cardinals
1946   Buffalo Bisons
1947   Chicago Rockets

**ECKER, ENRIQUE—Tackle—John
Carroll**
1947   Chicago Bears
1948   Chicago Rockets
1949   Chicago Bears
1950–51   Green Bay Packers

ECKHARDT, OSCAR—Back—Texas
1928   New York Giants

ECKL, ROBERT—Tackle—Wisconsin
1945   Chicago Cardinals

**ECKLUND, BRADLEY—Center—
Oregon**
1949   New York Yankees
1950–51   New York Yanks

ECKSTEIN, ALDOPH—Center—Brown
1925 Providence Steamrollers

EDGAR, WILLIAM—Back—Pittsburgh
1923 Buffalo All Americans
1923 Akron Steels

EDLER, ROBERT—Back—Ohio Wesleyan
1923 Cleveland Indians

EDMONDSON, VAN—Center—Oklahoma
1926 Buffalo Bisons

EDWARDS, ALBERT GLEN—Tackle—Washington State
1932 Boston Braves
1933–36 Boston Redskins
1937–40 Washington Redskins
1946–48 Washington—Head Coach

EDWARDS, C. H.—Back—Brown
1930 Providence Steamrollers
1931 Providence

EDWARDS, DANIEL—End—Georgia
1948 Brooklyn Dodgers
1949 Chicago Hornets
1950–51 New York Yanks

EDWARDS, EUGENE—Guard—Notre Dame
1920–21 Canton Bulldogs
1922 Toledo Maroons
1923 Cleveland Indians
1924 Cleveland Bulldogs
1926 Detroit Panthers

EDWARDS, LESLIE—Back—Washington & Jefferson
1930 Providence

EDWARDS, WELDON—tackle—TCU
1948 Washington Redskins

EDWARDS, WILLIAM—Back—Baylor
1941–42 New York Giants
1946 New York Giants

EGAN, RICHARD—End—Wilmington
1922–23 Chicago Cardinals
1924 Kenosha
1924 Dayton Triangles

EHRHARDT, CLYDE—Center—Georgia
1946 Washington Redskins
1948 Washington Redskins
1949 Washington Redskins

EIBNER, JOHN—Tackle—Kentucky
1941–42 Philadelphia Eagles
1946 Philadelphia Eagles

EICHENLAUB, RAY—Back—Notre Dame
1925 Columbus Tigers
1925 Cleveland Indians

EIDEN, ??—Tackle—??
1926 Louisville Colonels

EIDEN, EDMUND—Back—Scranton
1944 Philadelphia Eagles
1944 Detroit Lions

EIKENBERG, VIRGIL—Back—Rice
1948 Chicago Cardinals

ELIASON, DONALD—End—Hamline
1942 Brooklyn Dodgers
1946 Boston Yanks

ELKINS, FAIT—Back—Haskell
1929 Frankford Yellowjackets
1929 Chicago Cardinals
1933 Cincinnati Reds

ELLENSON, EUGENE—Tackle—Georgia
1946 Miami Seahawks

ELLIOTT, ALVAH—Back—Wisconsin
1925 Rock Island Independents

ELLIOTT, BURTON—Back—Marquette
1921 Green Bay Packers

ELLIOTT, CARLTON—End—Virginia
1951 Green Bay Packers

ELLIOTT, CHARLES—Tackle—Oregon
1947 New York Yankees
1948 Chicago Rockets
1948 San Francisco 49ers

ELLIOTT, WALLACE—Back—Lafayette
1922 Racine Legion
1922–23 Canton Bulldogs
1923–24 Racine Legion
1924 Cleveland Bulldogs
1925 Cleveland Indians

ELLIS, DREW—Tackle—TCU
1938–39 Philadelphia Eagles

ELLIS, HERBERT—Center—Texas A & M
1944 Brooklyn Dodgers
1949 New York Bulldogs

ELLIS, LAWRENCE—Back—Syracuse
1948 Detroit Lions

ELLIS, WALTER—Tackle—Detroit
1924–25 Columbus Tigers
1927 Chicago Cardinals
1930 Newark

ELLOR, A. W.—Guard—Bucknell
1930   Newark

ELLSTROM, MARVIN—Back—Oklahoma
1934   Boston Redskins
1934   Philadelphia Eagles
1935   Pittsburgh Pirates
1936   Chicago Cardinals

ELSER, EARL—Back—Butler
1933   Portsmouth Spartans
1934   Cincinnati Reds
1934   St. Louis Gunners

ELSEY, EARL—Back—Loyola (Los Angeles)
1946   Los Angeles Dons

ELSTON, ARTHUR—Center—Southern California
1942   Cleveland Rams
1946–48   San Francisco 49ers

ELY, HAROLD—Tackle—Iowa
1932   Chicago Bears
1933–34   Brooklyn Dodgers

EMERICK, ROBERT—Tackle—Ohio State
1934   Detroit Lions
1937   Cleveland Rams

EMERSON, GROVER—Guard—Texas
1931–33   Portsmouth Spartans
1934–37   Detroit Lions
1938   Brooklyn Dodgers

EMMONS, FRANKLIN—Back—Oregon
1940   Philadelphia Eagles

EMSLIE, ??—Guard—??
1923   Rochester Kodaks

ENGEBRETSEN, PAUL—Guard—Northwestern
1932   Chicago Bears
1933   Pittsburgh Pirates
1933   Chicago Cardinals
1934   Brooklyn Dodgers
1934–41   Green Bay Packers

ENGELMANN, WUERT—Back—South Dakota
1930–33   Green Bay Packers

ENGLUND, HARRY—End—None
1921   Chicago Bears (Staleys)
1922   Chicago Bears
1924   Chicago Bears

ENGSTROM, G. ??—Guard—Superior State
1924   Duluth Kelleys

ENICH, STEPHEN—Guard—Marquette
1945   Chicago Cardinals

ENKE, FREDERICK—Back—Arizona
1948–51   Detroit Lions

ENRIGHT, REX—Back—Notre Dame
1926–27   Green Bay Packers

ERDLITZ, RICHARD—Back—Northwestern
1942   Philadelphia Eagles
1945   Philadelphia Eagles
1946   Miami Seahawks

ERICKSON, CARLETON—Center—Washington
1938–39   Washington Redskins

ERICKSON, MICHAEL—Center—Northwestern
1932   Boston Braves

ERICKSON, WELDON—End—South Dakota
1922   Minneapolis Marines
1923   Green Bay Packers
1923–24   Milwaukee Badgers
1925   Chicago Bears
1925–27   Chicago Cardinals
1927   Pottsville Maroons
1928   Chicago Cardinals
1929–30   Minneapolis Redjackets
1930–31   Chicago Cardinals

ERICKSON, WILLIAM—Guard—Mississippi
1948   New York Giants
1949   New York Yankees

ERNST, JOHN—Back—Lafayette
1925   Frankford Yellowjackets
1925–28   Pottsville Maroons
1929   Boston Braves
1930   Frankford Yellowjackets

ESCHBACH, HERBERT—Center—Penn State
1930–31   Providence Steamrollers

ESHMONT, LEONARD—Back—Fordham
1940–41   New York Giants
1946–49   San Francisco 49ers

ESSER, CLARENCE—End—Wisconsin
1947   Chicago Cardinals

ETHRIDGE, JOSEPH—Tackle—SMU
1949   Green Bay Packers

ETTINGER, DONALD—Guard—Kansas
1948–50   New York Giants

EVANS, EARL—Tackle—Harvard
1925   Chicago Cardinals
1926–29   Chicago Bears

EVANS, FREDERICK—Back—Notre Dame
1946 Cleveland Browns
1947 Buffalo Bills
1947–48 Chicago Rockets
1948 Chicago Bears

EVANS, JOHN—Back—California
1929 Green Bay Packers

EVANS, LON—Guard—TCU
1933–37 Green Bay Packers

EVANS, MURRAY—Back—Hardin-Simmons
1942–43 Detroit Lions

EVANS, RAY—Back—Kansas
1948 Pittsburgh Steelers

EVANS, RAYMOND—Tackle—Texas Mines
1949–50 San Francisco 49ers

EVANS, RICHARD—End—Iowa
1940 Green Bay Packers
1941–42 Chicago Cardinals
1943 Green Bay Packers

EVANSEN, PAUL—Guard—Oregon State
1948 San Francisco 49ers

* * *

FAGIOLI, CARL—Guard—None
1944 Philadelphia Eagles

FAHAY, JOHN—End—Marquette
1926 Racine Legion
1929 Minneapolis Redjackets

FAILING, ??—Guard—??
1930 Chicago Cardinals

FAIRCLOTH, ARTHUR—Back—North Carolina
1947–48 New York Giants

FALASCHI, NELLO—Back—Santa Clara
1938–41 New York Giants

FALCON, GILBERT—Back—None
1921 Canton Bulldogs
1922–23 Toledo Maroons
1924–25 Hammond Pros
1925 Akron Steels

FALKENSTEIN, ANTHONY—Back—St. Mary's (Cal.)
1943 Green Bay Packers
1944 Brooklyn Dodgers
1944 Boston Yanks

FALLON, MICHAEL—Guard—Syracuse
1922 Milwaukee Badgers

FAMIGLIETTI, GARY—Back—Boston Univ.
1938–45 Chicago Bears
1946 Boston Yanks

FARKAS, ANDREW—Back—Detroit
1938 Washington Redskins
1939 Washington Redskins—S
1940–44 Washington Redskins
1945 Detroit Lions

FARMAN, RICHARD—Guard—Washington State
1939–43 Washington Redskins

FARMER, THOMAS—Back—Iowa
1946 Los Angeles Rams
1947–48 Washington Redskins

FARRAGUT, KENNETH—Center—Mississippi
1951 Philadelphia Eagles

FARRAR, VINCENT—Guard—North Carolina State
1939 Washington Redskins
1939 Pittsburgh Steelers

FARRELL, J. T.—Back—Lafayette
1938 Pittsburgh Pirates
1938–39 Brooklyn Dodgers

FARRIS, THOMAS—Back—Wisconsin
1941 Chicago Bears
1946–47 Chicago Bears
1948 Chicago Rockets

FARROTT, SHIPLEY—Guard—Iowa
1938 Pittsburgh Pirates

FAUNCE, EVERETT—Back—Minnesota
1949 Baltimore Colts

FAUST, GEORGE—Back—Minnesota
1939 Chicago Cardinals

FAUST, RICHARD—Tackle—Otterbein
1924 Dayton Triangles
1928–29 Dayton Triangles

FAWCETT, JACOB—Tackle—SMU
1942 Cleveland Rams
1943 Brooklyn Dodgers
1944 Cleveland Rams
1946 Los Angeles Rams

FAYE, ALLEN—End—Marquette
1922 Green Bay Packers

FEARS, THOMAS—End—UCLA
1948 Los Angeles Rams—R
1949 Los Angeles Rams—R
1950 Los Angeles Rams—R
1951 Los Angeles Rams

**FEASTER, WILLIAM—Tackle—
Fordham**
1929 Orange
1930 Newark

**FEATHER, E. E.—Back—Kansas
State Agr.**
1927 Cleveland Indians
1928 Detroit Wolverines
1929–30 New York Giants
1931 Staten Island Stapletons
1932–33 New York Giants
1933 Philadelphia Eagles
1934 Cincinnati Reds

**FEATHERS, BEATTIE—Back—
Tennessee**
1934 Chicago Bears—G
1935–37 Chicago Bears
1938–39 Brooklyn Dodgers
1940 Green Bay Packers

**FEDEROVICH, JOHN—Tackle—
Davis & Elkins**
1941 Chicago Bears
1946 Chicago Bears

**FEDORA, WALTER—Back—George
Washington**
1942 Brooklyn Dodgers

**FEENEY, FRANCIS—Center—Notre
Dame**
1920–21 Canton Bulldogs

**FEHER, NICHOLAS—Guard—
Georgia**
1951 San Francisco 49ers

FEIST, LOUIS—Tackle—Canisius
1924–26 Buffalo Bisons

FEKETE, EUGENE—Back—Ohio State
1946 Cleveland Browns
1946 Buffalo Bisons

**FELBER, FREDERICK—End—
North Dakota**
1932 Boston Braves
1933 Philadelphia Eagles

**FELDHAUS, WILLIAM—Tackle—
Cincinnati**
1937–40 Detroit Lions

**FELKER, ARTHUR—End—
Marquette**
1951 Green Bay Packers

FENA, JOSEPH—Guard—Colorado
1937 Detroit Lions

**FENCL, RICHARD—End—
Northwestern**
1933 Philadelphia Eagles

**FENENBOCK, CHARLES—Back—
UCLA**
1943 Detroit Lions
1945 Detroit Lions
1946–48 Los Angeles Dons
1948 Chicago Rockets

**FENIMORE, ROBERT—Back—
Oklahoma A & M**
1947 Chicago Bears

**FENNEMA, CARL—Center—
Washington**
1948–49 New York Giants

FERGUSON, ??—Guard—??
1932 Chicago Bears
1935 Brooklyn Dodgers

FERNIA, ??—Center—??
1927 Pottsville Maroons

**FERKO, JOHN—Guard—Mt. St.
Mary's**
1937–38 Philadelphia Eagles

FERRANTE, JACK—End—None
1941 Philadelphia Eagles
1944–50 Philadelphia Eagles

**FERRIS, NEIL—Back—Loyola
(Los Angeles)**
1951 Washington Redskins

FERRY, LOUIS—Tackle—Villanova
1949 Green Bay Packers
1951 Chicago Cardinals

FETZ, GUSTAVE—Back—None
1923 Chicago Bears
1923 Canton Bulldogs

FICHMAN, LEON—Tackle—Alabama
1946–47 Detroit Lions

**FIEDLER, WILLIAM—Guard—
Pennsylvania**
1938 Philadelphia Eagles

FIELD, HARRY—Tackle—Oregon
1934–36 Chicago Cardinals

FIELD, RICHARD—Guard—
1939–40 Philadelphia Eagles

FIFE, RALPH—Guard—Pittsburgh
1942 Chicago Cardinals
1945 Chicago Cardinals
1946 Pittsburgh Steelers

FILAK, JOHN—Tackle—Penn State
1926–29 Frankford Yellowjackets

FILCHOCK, FRANK—Back—Indiana
1938 Pittsburgh Pirates
1938–41 Washington Redskins
1944 Washington Redskins—P
1945 Washington Redskins
1946 New York Giants
1950 Baltimore Colts

FILIPOWICZ, STEPHEN—Back—
 Fordham
1945–46 New York Giants

FINCH, OLIN—Back—Whittier
1926 Los Angeles

FINKS, JAMES—Back—Tulsa
1949–51 Pittsburgh Steelers

FINLAY, JOHN—Guard—UCLA
1947–51 Los Angeles Rams

FINN, JOHN—Back—Villanova
1924 Frankford Yellowjackets
1930 Staten Island Stapletons
1930 Newark

FIORENTINO, ALBERT—Guard—
 Boston College
1943–44 Washington Redskins
1945 Boston Yanks
1947 Boston Yanks'

FISCHER, CLETUS—Back—Nebraska
1949 New York Giants

FISCHER, WILLIAM—Tackle—
 Notre Dame
1949–51 Chicago Cardinals

FISHEL, RICHARD—Back—Syracuse
1933–34 Brooklyn Dodgers

FISHER, DARRELL—Back—Iowa
1925 Buffalo Bisons
1925 Canton Bulldogs
1926 Milwaukee Badgers

FISHER, EVERETT—Back—??
1938–39 Chicago Cardinals
1940 Pittsburgh Steelers

FISHER, ROBERT—Tackle—
 Southern California
1940 Washington Redskins

FISK, WILLIAM—End—Southern
 California
1940–43 Detroit Lions
1946–47 San Francisco 49ers
1948 Los Angeles Dons

FISKE, MAX—Back—DePaul
1936–37 Pittsburgh Pirates
1937 Chicago Cardinals
1938 Pittsburgh Pirates

FITZGERALD, DONALD—Center—
 Holy Cross
1930 Staten Island Stapletons

FITZGERALD, FREEMAN—Back—
 Notre Dame
1921 Rock Island Independents
1923 Toledo Maroons

FITZGIBBONS, PAUL—Back—
 Creighton
1926 Duluth Eskimos
1927 Frankford Yellowjackets
1928 Chicago Cardinals
1930–32 Green Bay Packers

FITZKE, ROBERT—Back—Idaho
1925 Frankford Yellowjackets

FLAGERMAN, JOHN—Center—St.
 Mary's (Cal.)
1948 Los Angeles Dons

FLAHERTY, RAY—End—Gonzaga
1927–28 New York Yankees
1929–35 New York Giants
1936–42 Washington Redskins—Head
    Coach

FLAHERTY, RICHARD—End—
 Marquette
1923 Chicago Bears
1926–27 Green Bay Packers

FLANAGAN, LATHAM—End—
 Carnegie Tech.
1931 Chicago Bears
1931 Chicago Cardinals

FLANAGAN, RICHARD—Guard—
 Ohio State
1948–49 Chicago Bears
1950–51 Detroit Lions

FLANAGAN, WILLIAM—Back—
 Pittsburgh
1925–26 Pottsville Maroons

FLATTERY, WILLIAM—Back—
 Wooster
1925–26 Canton Bulldogs

FLAVIN, JOHN—Back—Georgetown
1923 Buffalo All Americans
1924 Buffalo Bisons

FLECKENSTEIN, WILLIAM—
 Center—Iowa
1925–30 Chicago Bears
1930 Portsmouth Spartans
1931 Frankford Yellowjackets

FLEISCHMAN, GODFREY—Guard—
 Purdue
1925–26 Detroit Panthers
1927–29 Providence Steamrollers

FLEMING, MALCOLM—Back—
 Washington & Jefferson
1925 Canton Bulldogs

FLENNIKEN, MAX—Back—
 Centenary
1930 Chicago Cardinals
1930–31 New York Giants

**FLETCHER, ANDREW—Back—
Maryland State**
1920   Buffalo All Americans

**FLETCHER, OLIVER—Guard—
Southern California**
1949   Los Angeles Dons

**FLOWERS, JAMES—Tackle—Ohio
State**
1921–24   Akron Steels

**FLOWERS, ROBERT—Center—
Texas Tech.**
1942–49   Green Bay Packers

FLYNN, FRANK—End—Cornell
1922–23   Minneapolis Marines
1926   Hartford

**FOLDBERG, HENRY—End—West
Point**
1948   Brooklyn Dodgers
1949   Chicago Hornets

FOLEY, JAMES—Back—Syracuse
1926   Hartford

FOLK, RICHARD—Guard—Clemson
1939   Brooklyn Dodgers

**FOLLET, BERYL—Back—New York
Univ.**
1930–31   Staten Island Stapletons

**FOLTZ, VERNON—Center—St.
Vincent's**
1944   Washington Redskins
1945   Pittsburgh Steelers

FOLZ, ARTHUR—Back—Chicago
1923–25   Chicago Cardinals

FORD, ADRIAN—Back—Lafayette
1922   Louisville Colonels
1927   Pottsville Maroons
1927   Frankford Yellowjackets

FORD, LEONARD—End—Michigan
1948–49   Los Angeles Dons
1950–51   Cleveland Browns

FORDHAM, JAMES—Back—Georgia
1944–45   Chicago Bears

**FORKOVITCH, NICHOLAS—
Back—William & Mary**
1948   Brooklyn Dodgers

**FORREST, EDWARD—Center—
Santa Clara**
1946–47   San Francisco 49ers

**FORSYTH, CHARLES—Center—
Syracuse**
1920   Rochester Kodaks

FORTE, ALDO—Guard—Montana
1939–41   Chicago Bears
1946   Chicago Bears
1946   Detroit Lions
1947   Green Bay Packers

FORTE, ROBERT—Back—Arkansas
1946–50   Green Bay Packers

**FORTMANN, DANIEL—Guard—
Colgate**
1936–46   Chicago Bears

**FORTUNE, BURNELL—Guard—
DePaul**
1924–25   Hammond Pros

FOSDICK, ROBERT—Guard—Iowa
1923   Minneapolis Marines

**FOSTER, FREDERICK—Tackle—
Syracuse**
1922–23   Racine Legion
1924   Rochester Jeffersons
1925   Buffalo Bisons

**FOSTER, RALPH—Tackle—
Oklahoma A & M**
1945–46   Chicago Cardinals

**FOWLER, AUBREY—Back—
Arkansas**
1948   Baltimore Colts

FOX, SAMUEL—End—Ohio State
1945–46   New York Giants

FOX, TERRANCE—Back—Miami
1941   Philadelphia Eagles
1945   Philadelphia Eagles
1946   Miami Seahawks

FRAHM, HERALD—??—??
1932   Staten Island Stapletons
1935   Boston Redskins

**FRANCESCHI, PETER—Back—San
Francisco**
1946   San Francisco 49ers

FRANCIS, EUGENE—Back—Chicago
1926   Chicago Cardinals

**FRANCIS, SAMUEL—Back—
Nebraska**
1937–38   Chicago Bears
1939   Pittsburgh Steelers
1939–40   Brooklyn Dodgers

**FRANCK, GEORGE—Back—
Minnesota**
1941   New York Giants
1945–47   New York Giants

FRANK, HARRY—Back—Temple
1930   Newark

FRANK, JOSEPH—Tackle—
Georgetown
1941–42 Philadelphia Eagles
1943 Phil-Pitt

FRANKIAN, MALCOLM—End—St.
Mary's (Cal.)
1933 Boston Redskins
1934–35 New York Giants

FRANKLIN, NORMAN—Back—
Oregon State
1934 New York Giants
1935–37 Brooklyn Dodgers

FRANKLIN, PAUL—End—Franklin
College
1930–33 Chicago Bears
1935 Chicago Bears

FRANKOWSKI, RAYMOND—
Guard—Washington
1945 Green Bay Packers
1946–48 Los Angeles Dons

FRANTA, HERBERT—Tackle—St.
Thomas
1929–30 Minneapolis Redjackets
1930 Green Bay Packers

FRASER, GEORGE—Back—
Rutgers
1927 New York Yankees

FREEMAN, JOHN—Guard—Texas
1946 Brooklyn Dodgers

FREITAS, JESSE—Back—Santa Clara
1946–47 San Francisco 49ers
1948 Chicago Rockets
1949 Buffalo Bills

FRENCH, BARRY—Guard—Purdue
1947–50 Baltimore Colts
1951 Detroit Lions

FRENCH, WALTER—Back—West
Point
1922 Rochester Kodaks
1925 Pottsville Maroons

FREY, GLENN—Back—Temple
1936–37 Philadelphia Eagles

FRICK, RAYMOND—Center—
Pennsylvania
1941 Brooklyn Dodgers

FRIENDLUND, ROBERT—End—
Michigan State
1946 Philadelphia Eagles

FRIEDMAN, BENJAMIN—Back—
Michigan
1927 Cleveland Indians
1928 Detroit Wolverines
1929–31 New York Giants
1932–33 Brooklyn Dodgers

FRIEDMAN, ROBERT—Guard—
Washington
1944 Philadelphia Eagles

FRIEND, BENJAMIN—Tackle—LSU
1939 Cleveland Rams

FRIES, SHERWOOD—Guard—
Colorado State
1943 Green Bay Packers

FRITSCH, THEODORE—Back—
Stevens
1942–45 Green Bay Packers
1946 Green Bay Packers—S–F (9)
1947–50 Green Bay Packers

FRITTS, GEORGE—Tackle—
Clemson
1945 Philadelphia Eagles

FRITZ, RALPH—Guard—Michigan
1941 Philadelphia Eagles

FRKETICH, LEONARD—Tackle—
Penn State
1945 Pittsburgh Steelers

FROHM, MARTIN—Tackle—
Mississippi State
1944 Brooklyn Dodgers

FRONCZEK, ANDREW—Tackle—
Richmond
1941 Brooklyn Dodgers

FRUGONNE, JAMES—Back—
Syracuse
1925 New York Giants

FRUMP, MILTON—Guard—Ohio
Wesleyan
1930 Chicago Bears

FRUTIG, EDWARD—End—
Michigan
1941 Green Bay Packers
1945 Green Bay Packers
1945–46 Detroit Lions

FRY, WESLEY—Back—Iowa
1927 New York Yankees
1932 Staten Island Stapletons

FRYER, KENNETH—Back—West
Virginia
1944 Brooklyn Dodgers

FUQUA, RAYMOND—End—SMU
1935–36 Brooklyn Dodgers

FULLER, LAWRENCE—Back—None
1944–45 Washington Redskins
1945 Chicago Cardinals

FULTON, THEODORE—Guard—
Oglethorpe
1931–32 Brooklyn Dodgers

FURST, ANTHONY—Tackle—Dayton
1940–41 Detroit Lions
1944 Detroit Lions

* * *

**GAFFNEY, JAMES—Back—
Tennessee**
1945–47 Washington Redskins

**GAFFORD, ROY—Back—Alabama
Polytech.**
1946 Miami Seahawks
1946–48 Brooklyn Dodgers

GAGE, ROBERT—Back—Clemson
1949–50 Pittsburgh Steelers

GAGNON, ROY—Guard—Oregon
1935 Detroit Lions

**GAINER, CHARLES—End—North
Dakota**
1939 Chicago Cardinals

GALAZIN, STANLEY—Center—?
1937–39 New York Giants

**GALLAGHER, BERNARD—Guard—
Pennsylvania**
1947 Los Angeles Dons

**GALLAGHER, EDWARD—Tackle—
Washington & Jefferson**
1928 New York Yankees
1928 New York Giants

**GALLARNEAU, HUGH—Back—
Stanford**
1940–42 Chicago Bears
1945–47 Chicago Bears

**GALLOVICH, ANTHONY—Back—
Wake Forest**
1941 Cleveland Rams

GALVIN, JOHN—Back—Purdue
1947 Baltimore Colts

**GAMBINO, LUCIEN—Back—
Maryland**
1948–49 Baltimore Colts

**GANTENBEIN, MILTON—End—
Wisconsin**
1931–40 Green Bay Packers

**GARDELLA, AUGUSTUS—Back—
Holy Cross**
1922 Green Bay Packers

GARDNER, GEORGE—End—Carlisle
1923 Cleveland Indians
1924 Cleveland Bulldogs

**GARDNER, MILTON—Guard—
Wisconsin**
1921 Buffalo All American
1922–26 Green Bay Packers

**GARLIN, DONALD—Back—
Southern California**
1949–50 San Francisco 49ers

**GARNAAS, WILFORD—Back—
Minnesota**
1946–47 Pittsburgh Steelers

GARNER, ROBERT—Guard—None
1945 New York Giants

**GARRETT, ALFRED—End—
Rutgers**
1920 Akron Steels
1922 Milwaukee Badgers

**GARRETT, THURMAN—Center—
Oklahoma A & M**
1947–48 Chicago Bears

**GARRETT, WILLIAM—Guard—
Mississippi State**
1948–49 Baltimore Colts
1950 Chicago Bears

**GARVEY, EDWARD—Tackle—Notre
Dame**
1925 Chicago Bears
1927–28 New York Giants
1929 Providence Steamrollers
1930 Brooklyn Dodgers
1931 Staten Island Stapletons

GARVEY, F. ??—Tackle—Holy Cross
1925–26 Providence Steamrollers

**GARVEY, HECTOR—End—Notre
Dame**
1922–23 Chicago Bears

GARZA, DANIEL—End—Oregon
1948 New York Yankees
1951 New York Yanks

**GASPARELLA, JOSEPH—Back—
Notre Dame**
1948 Pittsburgh Steelers
1950–51 Pittsburgh Steelers
1951 Chicago Cardinals

**GATEWOOD, LESTER—Center—
Baylor**
1946–47 Green Bay Packers

GATSKI, FRANK—Center—Marshall
1946–51 Cleveland Browns

**GAUDIO, ROBERT—Guard—Ohio
State**
1947–49 Cleveland Browns
1951 Cleveland Browns

**GAUER, CHARLES—Back—
Colgate**
1943 Phil-Pitt
1944–45 Philadelphia Eagles

GAUL, FRANK—Tackle—Notre Dame
1949 New York Bulldogs

GAULKE, HAROLD—Back—None
1922 Columbus Tigers

GAUSTAD, ??—Guard—??
1922–23 Minneapolis Marines
1929 Minneapolis Redjackets

GAVIGAN, MICHAEL—Back—
St. Bonaventure
1923 Rochester Kodaks

GAVIN, FRITZ—End—Marquette
1921 Green Bay Packers
1923 Green Bay Packers

GAVIN, "BUCK"—Back—None
1920 Buffalo All Americans
1922 Buffalo All Americans
1922 Rock Island Independents
1924–25 Rock Island Independents
1926 Hammond

GAY, KENNETH—Tackle—Minnesota
1925 Buffalo Bisons
1926 Milwaukee Badgers

GAY, WILLIAM—Back—Notre Dame
1951 Chicago Cardinals

GAYER, WALTER—Tackle—
Creighton
1926 Duluth Eskimos

GELATKA, CHARLES—End—
Mississippi State
1937–40 New York Giants

GARZONI, MICHAEL—Guard—
Southern California
1947 Washington Redskins
1948 New York Giants
1948 New York Yankees

GEHRKE, CLARENCE FRED—
Back—Utah
1940 Cleveland Rams
1945 Cleveland Rams
1946–49 Los Angeles Rams
1950 San Francisco 49ers
1950 Chicago Cardinals

GENTRY, BYRON—Guard—?
1937–38 Pittsburgh Pirates
1939 Pittsburgh Steelers

GENTRY, CASSIUS—Guard—
Oklahoma
1930–31 Providence Steamrollers

GENTRY, DALE—End—Washington
State
1946–48 Los Angeles Dons

GENTRY, ELMER—Back—Tulsa
1941 Washington Redskins

GEORGE, RAYMOND—Tackle—
Southern California
1939 Detroit Lions
1940 Philadelphia Eagles

GERBER, ELWOOD—Guard—
Alabama
1942 Philadelphia Eagles
1945 Washington Redskins

GERI, JOSEPH—Back—Georgia
1949–51 Pittsburgh Steelers

GERMAN, JAMES—Back—Centre
1939 Washington Redskins
1940 Chicago Cardinals

GETCHELL, GORHAM—End—
Temple
1947 Baltimore Colts

GEYER, WILLIAM—Back—Colgate
1941–43 Chicago Bears
1946 Chicago Bears

GHECAS, LOUIS—Back—Georgetown
1941 Philadelphia Eagles

GHEE, MILTON—Back—Dartmouth
1921 Cleveland Indians

GHERSANICH, VERNON—Guard—
Alabama Polytech.
1943 Chicago Cardinals

GIANNELLI, MARIO—Guard—
Boston College
1948–51 Philadelphia Eagles

GIANNONI, JOHN—End—St. Mary's
(Cal.)
1938 Cleveland Rams

GIAVER, EINAR—Back—Georgia
Tech.
1924 Racine Legion
1925 Hammond Pros

GIBRON, ABRAHAM—Guard—
Purdue
1949 Buffalo Bills
1950–51 Cleveland Browns

GIBSON, BILLY JOE—Center—Tulsa
1942 Cleveland Rams
1943 Washington Redskins
1944 Cleveland Rams
1946–47 Brooklyn Dodgers

GIBSON, DENVER—Guard—Grove
City
1930–34 New York Giants

GIBSON, GEORGE—Guard—
Minnesota
1929 Chicago Cardinals
1930 Frankford Yellowjackets

GIBSON, PAUL—End—North Carolina State
1942   Cleveland Rams
1944   Cleveland Rams
1947–49   Buffalo Bills

GIBSON, RICHARD—Guard—Centre
1922   Louisville Colonels

GIDDENS, HERSCHEL—Tackle—Louisiana Tech.
1938   Philadelphia Eagles

GIFFORD, ROBERT—Back—Denver
1942   Brooklyn Dodgers

GIFT, WAYNE—Back—Purdue
1937   Cleveland Rams

GILBERT, WALTER—Back—Valparaiso
1923–25   Duluth Kelleys

GILDEA, DENNIS—Center—Holy Cross
1926   Hartford

GILDEA, JOHN—Back—St. Bonaventure
1935–37   Pittsburgh Pirates
1938   New York Giants

GILL, SLOKO—Guard—Youngstown
1942   Detroit Lions

GILLETTE, JAMES—Back—Virginia
1940   Cleveland Rams
1944–45   Cleveland Rams
1946   Boston Yanks
1947   Washington Redskins
1947   Green Bay Packers
1948   Detroit Lions

GILLIES, FREDERICK—Tackle—Cornell
1920–22   Chicago Cardinals
1923   Toledo Maroons
1923   Canton Bulldogs
1923–26   Chicago Cardinals
1927   Chicago Cardinals—Player-coach
1928   Chicago Cardinals

GILLO, HENRY—Back—Colgate
1922–24   Racine Legion
1925   Milwaukee Badgers
1926   Racine Legion

GILLOM, HORACE—End—Nevada
1947–50   Cleveland Browns
1951   Cleveland Browns—K

GILLORY, BYRON—Back—Texas
1949   Baltimore Colts

GILMER, HARRY—Back—Alabama
1948–51   Washington Redskins

GILSON, ROBERT—Guard—Colgate
1930   Minneapolis Redjackets
1930   Frankford Yellowjackets
1931   Brooklyn Dodgers

GIRARD, EARL—Back—Wisconsin
1948–51   Green Bay Packers

GLADCHUCK, CHESTER—Center—Boston College
1940–41   New York Giants
1946–47   New York Giants

GLAMP, JOSEPH—Back—LSU
1947–49   Pittsburgh Steelers

GLASSGOW, WILLIS—Back—Iowa
1930   Portsmouth Spartans
1931   Chicago Cardinals

GLASSMAN, MORRIS—Guard—Wilmington
1922   Columbus Tigers
1929   Buffalo Bisons

GLENN, WILLIAM—Back—Illinois Teachers
1941   Chicago Bears
1944   Chicago Bears

GLENNIE, ??—End—??
1926   Racine Legion

GLICK, EDWARD—Back—Marquette
1921–22   Green Bay Packers

GLODEN, FREDERICK—Back—Tulane
1941   Philadelphia Eagles
1946   Miami Seahawks

GODDARD, EDWARD—Back—Washington State
1936–37   Brooklyn Dodgers
1937–38   Cleveland Rams

GODFREY, HERBERT—End—Washington State
1942   Cleveland Rams

GODWIN, W.—Guard—Georgia Tech.
1929   Staten Island Stapletons

GODWIN, WILLIAM—Center—Georgia
1947–48   Boston Yanks

GOEBEL, PAUL—End—Michigan
1923–25   Columbus Tigers
1925   Chicago Bears
1926   Columbus Tigers

GOETZ, ANGUS—Tackle—Michigan
1920   Buffalo All Americans
1922   Buffalo All Americans
1923   Columbus Tigers

GOFF, CLARK—Tackle—Florida
1940   Pittsburgh Steelers

GOLDBERG, MARSHALL—Back—
 Pittsburgh
1939–43   Chicago Cardinals
1946–48   Chicago Cardinals

GOLDENBERG, CHARLES—
 Guard—Wisconsin
1933–45   Green Bay Packers

GOLDFEIN, JERSEY—Back—
 Superior State
1927   Duluth Eskimos

GOLDING, JOSEPH—Back—
 Oklahoma
1947–48   Boston Yanks
1949   New York Bulldogs
1950–51   New York Yanks

GOLDMAN, SAMUEL—End—Howard
1944–47   Boston Yanks
1948   Chicago Cardinals
1949   Detroit Lions

GOLDSBERRY, JOHN—Tackle—
 Indiana
1949–50   Chicago Cardinals

GOLEMBESKI, ANTHONY—End—
 Holy Cross
1925   Providence Steamrollers
1929   Providence Steamrollers

GOLEMGESKE, JOHN—Tackle—
 Wisconsin
1937–40   Brooklyn Dodgers

GOLLOMB, RUDOLPH—Guard—
 Wisconsin
1936   Philadelphia Eagles

GOLSEN, EUGENE—Back—
 Georgetown
1926   Louisville Colonels

GOLSEN, THOMAS—Back—
 Georgetown
1926   Louisville Colonels

GOMPERS, WILLIAM—Back—Notre
 Dame
1948   Buffalo Bills

GONDA, GEORGE—Back—Duquesne
1942   Pittsburgh Steelers
1945–46   Pittsburgh Steelers

GONYA, ROBERT—Tackle—
 Northwestern
1933–34   Philadelphia Eagles

GOODBREAD, ROYCE—Back—
 Florida
1930   Frankford Yellowjackets
1930   Minneapolis Redjackets
1931   Providence Steamrollers

GOODE, ROBERT—Back—Texas
 A & M
1949–51   Washington Redskins

GOODMAN, AUBREY—Tackle—
 Chicago
1927   Chicago Bears
1927   Chicago Cardinals

GOODMAN, HENRY—Tackle—West
 Virginia
1942   Detroit Lions

GOODNIGHT, CLYDE—End—Tulsa
1945–48   Green Bay Packers
1949–50   Washington Redskins

GOODNIGHT, OWEN—Back—
 Hardin-Simmons
1941   Cleveland Rams
1946   Chicago Bears

GOODWIN, EARL—Tackle—
 Bucknell
1928   Pottsville Maroons

GOODWIN, TOD—End—West
 Virginia
1935   New York Giants—R
1936   New York Giants

GOODYEAR, JOHN—Back—
 Marquette
1942   Washington Redskins

GOOLSBY, JAMES—End—
 Mississippi State
1940   Cleveland Rams

GORDON, LOUIS—Tackle—Illinois
1930–31   Chicago Cardinals
1931   Brooklyn Dodgers
1932–35   Chicago Cardinals
1936–37   Green Bay Packers
1938   Chicago Bears

GORE, GORDON—Back—Oklahoma
 Southwest Teachers
1938–39   Detroit Lions

GORGAL, ??—Back—Rock Island
1923   Rock Island Independents

GORGAL, KENNETH—Back—Purdue
1950   Cleveland Rams

GORGONE, PETER—Back—
 Muhlenberg
1946   New York Giants

GORINSKI, WALTER—Back—LSU
1946   Pittsburgh Steelers

GORMAN, ??—Guard—??
1922–23   Racine Legion
1924   Kenosha

GORRILL, CHARLES—End—Ohio State
1926   Columbus Tigers

GOSS, NORMAN—Tackle—Case
1923   Toledo Maroons

GOVERNALI, PAUL—Back—Columbia
1946–47   Boston Yanks
1948–49   New York Giants

GRABINSKI, THADDEUS—Center—?
1939–40   Pittsburgh Steelers

GRAHAM, ALFRED—Guard—Ohio
1925–29   Dayton Triangles
1930–31   Providence Steamrollers
1932–33   Chicago Cardinals

GRAHAM, F. ??—??
1926   Frankford Yellowjackets

GRAHAM, LESTER—Guard—??
1938   Detroit Lions

GRAHAM, LYLE—Center—Richmond
1935   Philadelphia Eagles
1941   Philadelphia Eagles

GRAHAM, MICHAEL—Back—Cincinnati
1948   Los Angeles Dons

GRAHAM, OTTO—Back—Northwestern
1946   Cleveland Browns
1947   Cleveland Browns—P   (AAFC)
1948   Cleveland Browns—P   (AAFC)
1949   Cleveland Browns—P   (AAFC)
1950–51   Cleveland Browns

GRAIN, EDWIN—Guard—Pennsylvania
1947   New York Yankees
1947–48   Baltimore Colts

GRANATO, SAMUEL—Tackle—None
1943   Brooklyn Dodgers

GRANDINETTE, GEORGE—Guard—Fordham
1943   Brooklyn Dodgers

GRANGE, GARLAND—End—Illinois
1929–31   Chicago Bears

GRANGE, HAROLD—Back—Illinois
1925   Chicago Bears
1926–27   New York Yankees
1928–34   Chicago Bears

GRANT, HARRY—End—Minnesota
1951   Philadelphia Eagles

GRANT, HUGH—Back—St. Mary's (Cal.)
1928   Chicago Cardinals

GRANT, LEONARD—Tackle—New York Univ.
1930–31   New York Giants
1932   Staten Island Stapletons
1932–37   New York Giants

GRANT, ROSS—Guard—New York Univ.
1933–34   Cincinnati Reds

GRATE, CARL—Center—Georgia
1945   New York Giants

GRAVES, RAYMOND—Center—Tennessee
1942   Philadelphia Eagles
1943   Phil-Pitt
1946   Philadelphia Eagles

GRAY, D. P.—End—Culver
1923   St. Louis Browns
1923–24   Green Bay Packers

GRAY, SAMUEL—End—Tulsa
1946–47   Pittsburgh Steelers

GRAY, WILLIAM—Guard—Oregon State
1947–48   Washington Redskins

GRAY HORSE—Back—None
1923   Oorang Indians

GREEN, E. ??—Tackle—??
1920   Canton Bulldogs
1926   Louisville Colonels
1927   Chicago Cardinals

GREEN, JOHN—End—Tulsa
1945   Philadelphia Eagles
1947   Philadelphia Eagles
1949–51   Philadelphia Eagles

GREEN, FRANK—Back—Tulsa
1934   Chicago Cardinals

GREENE, JOHN—End—Michigan
1944–50   Detroit Lions

GREENBERG, BENJAMIN—Back—Rutgers
1930   Brooklyn Dodgers

GREENFIELD, THOMAS—Center—Arizona
1939–41   Green Bay Packers

GREENHALGH, ROBERT—Back—San Francisco
1949   New York Giants

GREENLEY, NORMAN—Guard—Notre Dame
1933   Green Bay Packers
1934   Pittsburgh Pirates

GREENSHIELDS, DONN—Tackle—Pennsylvania
1932–33   Brooklyn Dodgers

GREENWOOD, DONALD—Back—
Missouri & Illinois
1945   Cleveland Rams
1946–47   Cleveland Browns

GREENWOOD, GLENN—Back—
Iowa
1924   Chicago Bears

GREFE, THEODORE—End—Notre
Dame
1945   Detroit Lions

GREGG, EDWARD—End—Kentucky
1922   Louisville Colonels

GREGORY, FRANK—Back—Williams
1924   Buffalo Bisons
1926   Detroit Panthers

GREGORY, GARLAND—Guard—
Louisiana Tech.
1946–47   San Francisco 49ers

GREGORY, JOHN—Guard—
Chattanooga
1941   Cleveland Rams

GREGORY, MICHAEL—Guard—
Denison
1931   Cleveland Indians

GRGICH, VISCO—Guard—Santa
Clara
1946–51   San Francisco 49ers

GRIFFIN, DONALD—Back—Illinois
1946   Chicago Rockets

GRIFFIN, HAROLD—Center—Iowa
1928   Green Bay Packers
1932   Portsmouth Spartans

GRIFFIN, ROBERT—Back—Baylor
1951   New York Yanks

GRIFFITH, FORREST—Back—
Kansas
1950–51   New York Giants

GRIFFITHS, HOMER—Back—Santa
Clara
1934   Chicago Cardinals

GRIFFITHS, PAUL—Guard—Penn
State
1921   Canton Bulldogs

GRIGAS, JOHN—Back—Holy Cross
1943   Chicago Cardinals
1944   Card-Pitt
1945–47   Boston Yanks

GRIGG, CECIL—Back—Dallas
1920–22   Canton Bulldogs
1927   Frankford Yellowjackets

GRIGG, FORREST—Tackle—Tulsa
1946   Buffalo Bisons
1947   Buffalo Bills
1947   Chicago Rockets
1948–51   Cleveland Browns

GRIGGS, HAROLD—Back—Wabash
1920–23   Canton Bulldogs
1925   Rochester Jeffersons
1926   Akron Steels
1926   New York Giants
1927   Frankford Yellowjackets

GRIGONIS, FRANK—Back—
Chattanooga
1942   Detroit Lions

GRIMES, GEORGE—Back—Virginia
1948   Detroit Lions

GRIMES, WILLIAM—Back—
Oklahoma A & M
1949   Los Angeles Dons
1950–51   Green Bay Packers

GROOME, JEROME—Center—Notre
Dame
1951   Chicago Cardinals

GROOMES, MELVIN—Back—
Indiana
1948–49   Detroit Lions

GROSSMAN, JOHN—Back—Rutgers
1932   Brooklyn Dodgers
1934–36   Brooklyn Dodgers

GROSSMAN, REX—Back—Indiana
1948–49   Baltimore Colts
1950   Detroit Lions

GROSVENOR, GEORGE—Back—
Colorado
1935–36   Chicago Bears
1936–37   Chicago Cardinals

GROVE, ROGER—Back—Michigan
State
1931–35   Green Bay Packers

GROVES, GEORGE—Guard—
Marquette
1946   Cleveland Browns
1947   Buffalo Bills
1948   Baltimore Colts

GROZA, LOUIS—Tackle—Ohio State
1946   Cleveland Browns—S (AAFC)
1947–49   Cleveland Browns
1950   Cleveland Browns—F (13) (NFL)
1951   Cleveland Browns

GRUBE, FRANK—End—Lafayette
1922–23   Louisville Colonels
1926   Detroit Panthers
1928   New York Yankees

GRYCO, ALBERT—Back—South Carolina
1944–45 Chicago Bears

GUARNERI, ALBERT—End— Canisius
1924 Buffalo Bisons

GUDAUSKAS, PETER—Guard— Murray State
1940 Cleveland Rams
1942 Green Bay Packers
1943–44 Chicago Bears
1945 Green Bay Packers

GUDE, HENRY—Guard—Vanderbilt
1946 Philadelphia Eagles

GUDMUNDSON, SCOTT—Back— George Washington
1944 Boston Yanks

GUFFEY, ROY—End—Oklahoma
1926 Buffalo Bisons

GULIAN, MICHAEL—Tackle— Brown
1923 Buffalo All Americans
1924 Frankford Yellowjackets
1925–27 Providence Steamrollers

GULYANICS, GEORGE—Back—None
1947–51 Chicago Bears

GUMP, ??—Guard—??
1922 Columbus Tigers

GUNDERSON, BORGE—Guard— Wisconsin
1921 Rock Island Independents

GUSSIE, MICHAEL—Guard—West Virginia
1940 Brooklyn Dodgers

GUSTAFSON, EDSEL—Center— George Washington
1947–48 Brooklyn Dodgers

GUTKNECHT, ALBERT—Guard— Niagara
1943 Brooklyn Dodgers
1944 Cleveland Rams

GUTOWSKY, LEROY—Back— Oklahoma City Univ.
1931 New York Giants
1932–33 Portsmouth Spartans
1934–38 Detroit Lions
1939 Brooklyn Dodgers

GUTTORMSEN, G. ??—Back— Washington
1926 Los Angeles

GUY, CHARLES—Center— Washington & Jefferson
1921–22 Buffalo All Americans
1923 Cleveland Indians
1925 Dayton Triangles
1925 Columbus Tigers

GUYON, JOSEPH—Back—Carlisle
1920 Canton Bulldogs
1921 Cleveland Indians
1923 Oorang Indians
1924 Rock Island Independents
1927 New York Giants

GWOSDEN, MILO—End—Pittsburgh
1925 Buffalo Bisons

* * *

HAAK, ROBERT—Tackle—Indiana
1939 Brooklyn Dodgers

HAAS, ??—Back—Wooster
1921 Cleveland Indians

HAAS, ??—Back—??
1929 Dayton Triangles

HACHTEN, WILLIAM—Guard— Stanford
1947 New York Giants

HACKENBRUCK, JOHN—Tackle— Oregon State
1940 Detroit Lions

HACKNEY, ELMER—Back—Kansas State
1940–41 Philadelphia Eagles
1941 Pittsburgh Steelers
1942–46 Detroit Lions

HADDON, ALDOUS—Back— Washington & Jefferson
1925–26 Detroit Panthers
1927–28 Providence Steamrollers
1928 Chicago Bears
1929–30 Providence Steamrollers

HAFEN, BARNARD—End—Utah
1949–50 Detroit Lions

HAGBURG, RUDOLPH—Center— West Virginia
1929 Buffalo Bisons
1930 Brooklyn Dodgers

HAGENBUCKLE, VERNON—End— Dartmouth
1926 Providence Steamrollers

HAGGERTY, JOHN—Back— Georgetown
1926–30 New York Giants
1930 Brooklyn Dodgers

HAHN, RAY—End—Bethany (Kansas)
1926 Hammond Pros

HAINES, BYRON—Back—Washington
1937   Pittsburgh Pirates

HAINES, HARRY—Tackle—Colgate
1930–31   Brooklyn Dodgers

HAINES, HENRY—Back—Penn State
1925–28   New York Giants
1929   Staten Island Stapletons
1931   Staten Island Stapletons

**HAJEK, CHARLES—Center—
Northwestern**
1934   Philadelphia Eagles

HALAS, GEORGE—End—Illinois
1920–21   Chicago Bears (Staleys) Player-
coach
1922–30   Chicago Bears—Owner-player-
coach
1931–52   Chicago Bears—Owner—Head
Coach

HALEY, ARTHUR—Back—Akron
1920   Canton Bulldogs
1923   Akron Steels

**HALICKI, EDWARD—Back—
Bucknell**
1929–30   Frankford Yellowjackets

**HALL, FORREST—Back—Duquesne,
Southern California**
1948   San Francisco 49ers

HALL, IRVING—Back—Brown
1942   Philadelphia Eagles

HALL, JOHN—Back—TCU
1940–42   Chicago Cardinals
1942   Detroit Lions
1943   Chicago Cardinals

HALL, PARKER—Back—Mississippi
1939   Cleveland Rams—P–K–V
1940–42   Cleveland Rams
1946   San Francisco 49ers

HALL, RAYMOND—Tackle—Illinois
1927   New York Yankees

**HALLADAY, RICHARD—End—
Chicago**
1922–24   Racine Legion

HALLECK, ??—Back—??
1924   Columbus Tigers

HALLECK, PAUL—Back—Ohio
1937   Cleveland Rams

HALLIDAY, JOHN—Tackle—SMU
1951   Los Angeles Rams

**HALPERN, ROBERT—Guard—
CCNY**
1930   Staten Island Stapletons
1932   Brooklyn Dodgers

**HALVERSON, WILLIAM—Tackle—
Oregon State**
1942   Philadelphia Eagles

**HAMAN, JOHN—Center—
Northwestern**
1940–41   Cleveland Rams

**HAMAS, STEVEN—Back—
Pennsylvania**
1929   Orange

**HAMBACKER, ERNEST—Back—
Bucknell**
1929   Orange

**HAMER, ERNEST—Back—Penn-
sylvania**
1924–27   Frankford Yellowjackets

**HAMILTON, RAYMOND—End—
Arkansas**
1938   Cleveland Rams
1939   Detroit Lions
1944–45   Cleveland Rams
1946–47   Los Angeles Rams

HAMITZ, LEWIS—Back—Chicago
1941   Chicago Bears

**HAMMOND, HENRY—End—
Southwestern**
1937   Chicago Bears

HANDLER, PHILIP—Guard—TCU
1930–36   Chicago Cardinals
1943   Chicago Cardinals—Head Coach
1944   Card-Pitt—Co-coach
1945   Chicago Cardinals—Head Coach
1949   Chicago Cardinals—Co-coach

**HANDLEY, RICHARD—Center—
Fresno State**
1947   San Francisco 49ers
1947   Baltimore Colts

HANKE, CARL—End—Minnesota
1923   Hammond Pros
1924–25   Chicago Cardinals

**HANKEN, RAYMOND—End—George
Washington**
1937–38   New York Giants

**HANLEY, RICHARD—Back—
Washington State**
1924   Racine Legion

**HANLON, ROBERT—Back—Notre
Dame**
1948   Chicago Cardinals
1949–50   Pittsburgh Steelers

**HANNA, ELZAPHAN—Guard—
Southern Carolina**
1945   Washington Redskins

HANNAH, HERBERT—Tackle—Alabama
1951   New York Giants

HANNEMAN, CHARLES—End—Michigan State Normal
1937–41   Detroit Lions

HANNY, FRANK—Tackle—Indiana
1923–27   Chicago Bears
1928–29   Providence Steamrollers
1930   Portsmouth Spartans
1930   Green Bay Packers

HANSEN, CLIFFORD—Back—Luther
1933   Chicago Cardinals
1935–36   Chicago Cardinals

HANSEN, DALE—Tackle—Michigan State
1948   Detroit Lions
1951   Philadelphia Eagles

HANSEN, ROSCOE—Tackle—North Carolina
1951   Philadelphia Eagles

HANSEN, WAYNE—Guard—Texas Western
1950–51   Chicago Bears

HANSON, HAROLD—Guard—Minnesota
1928–30   Frankford Yellowjackets

HANSON, JOHN—Back—Temple
1937   Brooklyn Dodgers
1938   Pittsburgh Steelers

HANSON, ROY—Back—Marquette
1921   Rock Island Independents
1923   Columbus Tigers
1923   Minneapolis Marines
1923   Green Bay Packers

HANSON, THOMAS—Back—Temple
1931   Brooklyn Dodgers
1933   Philadelphia Eagles
1934   Cincinnati Reds
1934   Philadelphia Eagles
1935   Chicago Cardinals
1935–37   Philadelphia Eagles
1938   Pittsburgh Pirates

HAPES, MERLE—Back—Mississippi
1942   New York Giants
1946   New York Giants

HARDER, MARLIN—Back—Wisconsin
1946   Chicago Cardinals
1947   Chicago Cardinals—S—F (7)
1948   Chicago Cardinals—S
1949   Chicago Cardinals—S (Tie with E. Roberts)
1950   Chicago Cardinals
1951   Detroit Lions

HARDING, ROGER—Center—California
1945   Cleveland Rams
1946   Los Angeles Rams
1947   Philadelphia Eagles
1948   Detroit Lions
1949   Green Bay Packers
1949   New York Bulldogs

HARDY, ISHAM—Guard—William & Mary
1923   Akron Steels
1926   Racine Legion

HARDY, JAMES—Back—Southern California
1946–48   Los Angeles Rams
1949–51   Chicago Cardinals

HARE, CECIL—Back—Gonzaga
1941–42   Washington Redskins
1945   Washington Redskins
1946   New York Giants

HARE, RAYMOND—Back—Gonzaga
1940–43   Washington Redskins
1944   Brooklyn Tigers
1946   New York Yankees

HARLEY, CHARLES—Back—Ohio State
1921   Chicago Bears

HARMON, HAMILTON—Center—Tulsa
1937   Chicago Cardinals

HARMON, THOMAS—Back—Michigan
1946–47   Los Angeles Rams

HARMS, ARTHUR—Tackle—Vermont
1925–27   Frankford Yellowjackets
1927   New York Giants

HARPER, MAURICE—Center—None
1937–40   Philadelphia Eagles
1941   Pittsburgh Steelers

HARRINGTON, JOHN—End—Marquette
1946   Cleveland Browns
1947   Chicago Rockets

HARRIS, AMOS—Guard—Mississippi State
1947–48   Brooklyn Dodgers

HARRIS, ELMORE—Back—Morgan
1947   Brooklyn Dodgers

HARRIS, HENRY—Back—Iowa
1937   Pittsburgh Pirates

HARRIS, HENRY—Guard—Texas
1947–48   Washington Redskins

HARRIS, JOHN—Back—Wisconsin
1920 Akron Steels
1923 Duluth Kelleys
1925–26 Green Bay Packers
1930 Portsmouth Spartans

HARRISON, J.—Tackle—Kansas State
1937 Brooklyn Dodgers

**HARRISON, EDWARD—End—
Boston College**
1927 Brooklyn Dodgers
1928 New York Giants

**HARRISON, GRANVILLE—End—
Mississippi State**
1940 New York Giants
1941 Philadelphia Eagles
1942 Detroit Lions

HART, LEON—End—Notre Dame
1950–51 Detroit Lions

HART, LESLIE—Back—Colgate
1931 Staten Island Stapletons

HARTLEY, HOWARD—Back—Duke
1948 Washington Redskins
1949–51 Pittsburgh Steelers

**HARTMAN, FREDERICK—Tackle—
Rice**
1947 Chicago Bears
1948 Philadelphia Eagles

HARTMAN, JAMES—Back—??
1936 Brooklyn Dodgers

**HARTMAN, WILLIAM—Back—
Georgia**
1938 Washington Redskins

**HARTONG, GEORGE—Guard—
Chicago**
1923 Racine Legion
1924 Chicago Cardinals

**HARTZOG, HOWARD—Tackle—
Baylor**
1928 New York Giants

**HARVEY, NORMAN—Tackle—
Detroit**
1925 Buffalo Bisons
1926 Detroit Panthers
1927 Buffalo Bisons
1928–29 Providence Steamrollers

**HASBROUCK, JOHN—Back—
Rutgers**
1921 Rochester Kodaks

**HATHAWAY, RUSSELL—Tackle—
Indiana**
1920–25 Dayton Triangles
1926–27 Pottsville Maroons
1927 Buffalo Bisons

HAUSER, HAROLD—Back—Kansas
1927 Buffalo Bisons
1930 Newark

HAVEN, JOHN—End—Hamline
1923 Duluth Kelleys

**HAVENS, CHARLES—Center—
Western Maryland**
1930 Frankford Yellowjackets

HAWS, HARVEY—Back—Dartmouth
1924–25 Frankford Yellowjackets

**HAYCRAFT, KENNETH—End—
Minnesota**
1929–30 Minneapolis Redjackets
1930 Green Bay Packers

HAYDEN, JOHN—Tackle—Arkansas
1936–38 New York Giants

**HAYDEN, KENNETH—Center—
Arkansas**
1942 Philadelphia Eagles
1943 Washington Redskins

**HAYDUK, HENRY—Guard—
Washington State**
1935 Pittsburgh Pirates
1935 Brooklyn Dodgers

HAYES, DAVID—End—Notre Dame
1921–22 Green Bay Packers

HAYES, GERALD—End—Notre Dame
1921 Rock Island Independents

HAYES, NORBERT—End—Marquette
1922 Racine Legion
1923 Green Bay Packers

HAYNES, HALL—Back—Santa Clara
1950 Washington Redskins

HAYNES, JOSEPH—Guard—Tulsa
1947 Buffalo Bills

**HAYS, GEORGE—End—St.
Bonaventure**
1950–51 Pittsburgh Steelers

**HAZELHURST, ROBERT—Back—
Denver**
1948 Boston Yanks
1949 New York Bulldogs

**HAZELWOOD, THEODORE—
Tackle—North Carolina**
1949 Chicago Hornets

**HEALY, EDWARD—Tackle—
Dartmouth**
1921–22 Rock Island Independents
1922–27 Chicago Bears

HEAP, WALTER—Back—Texas
1947–48 Los Angeles Dons

**HEARDEN, THOMAS—Back—
Notre Dame**
1924   Green Bay Packers
1927–28 Green Bay Packers

HEATER, WILLIAM—??—??
1940   Brooklyn Dodgers

HEATH, LEON—Back—Oklahoma
1951   Washington Redskins

HEATH, STANLEY—Back—Nevada
1949   Green Bay Packers

**HECHT, ALFRED—Guard—
Alabama**
1947   Chicago Rockets

HECK, ROBERT—End—Purdue
1949   Chicago Hornets

**HECKER, NORBERT—End—
Baldwin-Wallace**
1951   Los Angeles Rams

HEFTI, JAMES—Back—St. Lawrence
1947   Washington Redskins

**HEIKKENEN, RALPH—Guard—
Michigan**
1939   Brooklyn Dodgers

**HEILEMAN, CHARLES—End—Iowa
State**
1939   Chicago Bears

**HEIN, MELVIN—Center—Washington
State**
1931–37 New York Giants
1938   New York Giants—V
1939–45 New York Giants

HEIN, ROBERT—End—Kent
1947   Brooklyn Dodgers

**HEINEMAN, KENNETH—Back—
Texas Mines**
1940–41 Cleveland Rams
1943   Brooklyn Dodgers

HEINRISCH, ??—Tackle—??
1923   Racine Legion
1924   Kenosha
1926   Racine Legion
1926   Duluth Eskimos
1926   Milwaukee Badgers

**HEKKERS, GEORGE—Tackle—
Wisconsin**
1946   Miami Seahawks
1947   Baltimore Colts
1947–49 Detroit Lions

HELDT, CARL—Tackle—Purdue
1935–36 Brooklyn Dodgers

HELDT, JOHN—Center—Iowa State
1923   Columbus Tigers
1926   Columbus Tigers

**HELLER, WARREN—Back—
Pittsburgh**
1934–36 Pittsburgh Pirates

HELMS, JOHN—End—Georgia Tech.
1946   Detroit Lions

HEMERECK, ??—Center—??
1923   Columbus Tigers

**HEMPEL, WILLIAM—Tackle—John
Carroll**
1941–42 Chicago Bears

**HENDLEY, RICHARD—Back—
Clemson**
1951   Pittsburgh Steelers

**HENDREN, ROBERT—Tackle—
Southern California**
1949–51 Washington Redskins

**HENDRIAN, WARREN—Back—
Princeton**
1920   Canton Bulldogs
1921   Cleveland Indians
1922–23 Canton Bulldogs
1923   Akron Steels
1924   Green Bay Packers
1925   Rock Island Independents
1925   New York Giants

**HENKE, EDGAR—Guard—Southern
California**
1949   Los Angeles Dons
1951   San Francisco 49ers

**HENNESSEY, JEROME—End—Santa
Clara**
1950–51 Chicago Cardinals

HENRICUS, ??—Back—??
1922   Rochester Kodaks

**HENRY, WILBUR—Tackle—
Washington & Jefferson**
1920–23 Canton Bulldogs
1925   Canton Bulldogs
1925   Akron Steels
1926   New York Giants
1927–28 Pottsville Maroons
1930   Staten Island Stapletons

**HENSLEY, RICHARD—End—
Kentucky**
1949   New York Giants

HERBER, ARNOLD—Back—Regis
1930–33 Green Bay Packers
1934   Green Bay Packers—P
1935   Green Bay Packers
1936   Green Bay Packers—P
1937–39 Green Bay Packers
1944–45 New York Giants

**HERRING, HAROLD—Center—
Alabama Polytech.**
1949 Buffalo Bills
1950–51 Cleveland Browns

HERSHEY, KIRK—End—Cornell
1941 Philadelphia Eagles
1941 Cleveland Rams

HERTZ, ??—End—Carroll (Wis.)
1926 Milwaukee Badgers

HESS, ARTHUR—Back—Indiana
1922–25 Hammond Pros

**HEWITT, WILLIAM—End—
Michigan**
1932–36 Chicago Bears
1936–39 Philadelphia Eagles
1943 Phil-Pitt

**HEYWOOD, RALPH—End—
Southern Californa**
1946 Chicago Rockets
1947 Detroit Lions
1948 Boston Yanks
1949 New York Bulldogs

**HIBBS, JESSE—Tackle—Southern
California**
1931 Chicago Bears

HICKEY, HOWARD—End—Arkansas
1941 Cleveland Rams
1945 Cleveland Rams
1946–48 Los Angeles Rams

**HICKMAN, HERMAN—Guard—
Tennessee**
1933–34 Brooklyn Dodgers

**HIEMSTRA, EDWARD—Guard—
Sterling**
1942 New York Giants

**HIGGINS, LUKE—Guard—Notre
Dame**
1941 Chicago Cardinals
1947 Baltimore Colts

**HIGGINS, ROBERT—Back—Penn
State**
1920–21 Canton Bulldogs
1922 Louisville Colonels
1925 Providence Steamrollers
1925 Columbus Tigers

**HIGHTOWER, JOHN—End—Sam
Houston**
1942 Cleveland Rams
1943 Detroit Lions

HILL, CHARLES—Back—Baker
1924–25 Kansas City Cowboys

HILL, DONALD—Back—Stanford
1929 Green Bay Packers

HILL, HAROLD—End—Howard
1938–40 Brooklyn Dodgers

HILL, HARRY—Back—Oklahoma
1923 Toledo Maroons
1924–26 Kansas City Cowboys
1929 Green Bay Packers
1929 Chicago Cardinals
1931–32 Chicago Cardinals
1933 Boston Redskins

HILL, JAMES—Back—Tennessee
1951 Detroit Lions

**HILLENBRAND, WILLIAM—Back—
Indiana**
1946 Chicago Rockets
1947–48 Baltimore Colts

**HILLHOUSE, ANDREW—Back—
Brown**
1920–21 Buffalo All Americans

**HILPERT, HAROLD—Back—
Oklahoma City Univ.**
1930 New York Giants
1931 Chicago Cardinals
1933 Cincinnati Reds

**HINCHMAN, HUBERT—Back—
Butler**
1933–34 Chicago Cardinals
1934 Detroit Lions

HINKLE, CLARK—Back—Bucknell
1932–37 Green Bay Packers
1938 Green Bay Packers—S
1939 Green Bay Packers
1940 Green Bay Packers—F (9)
1941 Green Bay Packers—F (6)

HINKLE, JOHN—Back—Syracuse
1940 New York Giants
1941–42 Philadelphia Eagles
1943 Phil-Pitt
1944–47 Philadelphia Eagles

HINTE, HAROLD—End—Pittsburgh
1942 Green Bay Packers
1942 Pittsburgh Steelers

HINTON, J. W.—Back—TCU
1932 Staten Island Stapletons
Killed in East Indies on flight
mission, Dec. 10, 1944. Lt.
Col., U.S. Air Force.

HIPPA, SAMUEL—End—Dayton
1928 Dayton Triangles

**HIRSCH, EDWARD—Back—
Northwestern**
1947–49 Buffalo Bills

HIRSCH, ELROY—End—Wisconsin
1946–48 Chicago Rockets
1949–50 Los Angeles Rams
1951 Los Angeles Rams—R—S

HIX, WILLIAM—End—Arkansas
1950 Philadelphia Eagles

HOAGUE, JOSEPH—Back—Colgate
1941-42 Pittsburgh Steelers
1943 Phil-Pitt
1946 Boston Yanks

HOBBS, HOMER—Guard—Georgia
1949-50 San Francisco 49ers

**HOBSCHEID, FRANK—Guard—
Chicago**
1926 Racine Legion
1927 Chicago Bears

**HOBSON, BENJAMIN—Back—
Wabash**
1927 Buffalo Bisons

HOCK, JOHN—Tackle—Santa Clara
1950 Chicago Cardinals

HODGES, HERMAN—End—Howard
1939-42 Brooklyn Dodgers

**HOEL, ROBERT—Guard—
Pittsburgh**
1935 Pittsburgh Pirates
1938 Chicago Cardinals

HOERNER, RICHARD—Back—Iowa
1947-51 Los Angeles Rams

**HOERNSCHEMEYER, ROBERT—
Back—Indiana**
1946 Chicago Rockets
1947 Brooklyn Dodgers
1947 Chicago Rockets
1948 Brooklyn Dodgers
1949 Chicago Hornets
1950-51 Detroit Lions

**HOFFMAN, ARNOLD—Tackle—
Syracuse**
1924 Buffalo Bisons
1924 Frankford Yellowjackets
1925 Rochester Jeffersons
1925-26 Frankford Yellowjackets
1927 Pottsville Maroons

HOFFMAN, JOHN—Back—Arkansas
1949-51 Chicago Bears

**HOFFMAN, ROBERT—Back—
Southern California**
1940-41 Washington Redskins

**HOFFMAN, WAYNE—Back—
Southern California**
1946-49 Los Angeles Rams

**HOGAN, DARRELL—Guard—
Trinity**
1949-51 Pittsburgh Steelers

HOGAN, THOMAS—Back—Detroit
1924 Akron Steels
1925 Detroit Panthers
1925 Canton Bulldogs
1926 New York Giants

**HOGUE, MURRELL—Back—
Centenary**
1924 Akron Steels
1928 New York Yankees
1929-30 Chicago Cardinals
1930 Minneapolis Redjackets

**HOKUF, STEPHEN—End—
Nebraska**
1933-35 Boston Redskins

**HOLCOMB, WILLIAM—Tackle—
Texas Tech.**
1937 Pittsburgh Pirates

HOLDER, LEWIS—End—Texas
1949 Los Angeles Dons

**HOLLAR, JOHN—Back—
Appalachian State**
1948-49 Washington Redskins
1949 Detroit Lions

**HOLLERAN, THOMAS—Back—
Pittsburgh**
1923 Buffalo All Americans

**HOLLEY, KENNETH—Back—Holy
Cross**
1946 Miami Seahawks

**HOLLINGSWORTH, JOSEPH—
Back—East Kentucky State**
1949-51 Pittsburgh Steelers

HOLLQUIST, ??—Back—??
1926 Milwaukee Badgers

HOLM, ANTHONY—Back—Alabama
1930 Providence Steamrollers
1931 Portsmouth Spartans
1932 Chicago Cardinals
1933 Pittsburgh Pirates

**HOLMER, WALTER—Back—
Northwestern**
1929-30 Chicago Bears
1931-32 Chicago Cardinals
1933 Boston Redskins
1933 Pittsburgh Pirates

**HOLOVAK, MICHAEL—Back—
Boston College**
1946 Los Angeles Rams
1947-48 Chicago Bears

**HOMAN, HENRY—Back—Lebanon
Valley**
1925-30 Frankford Yellowjackets

**HONAKER, CHARLES—End—Ohio
State**
1924 Cleveland Bulldogs

**HOOD, FRANKLIN—Back—
Pittsburgh**
1933 Pittsburgh Pirates

HOOLEY, ??—Guard—??
1924 Minneapolis Marines

HOPKINS, THEODORE—End—
  Pennsylvania
1922 Columbus Tigers

HOPP, HARRY—Back—Nebraska
1940–43 Detroit Lions
1946 Miami Seahawks
1946 Buffalo Bisons
1947 Los Angeles Dons

HOPTOWIT, ALBERT—Tackle—
  Washington State
1941–45 Chicago Bears

HORNBEAK, JAY—Back—
  Washington
1935 Brooklyn Dodgers

HORNE, RICHARD—End—Oregon
1941 New York Giants
1946 Miami Seahawks
1946 Buffalo Bisons
1947 San Francisco 49ers

HORNICK, WILLIAM—Tackle—
  Tulane
1947 Pittsburgh Steelers

HORNING, CLARENCE—Tackle—
  Colgate
1920–21 Buffalo All Americans
1922–23 Toledo Maroons

HORSTMANN, ROY—Back—Purdue
1933 Boston Redskins
1934 Chicago Cardinals

HORVATH, LESLIE—Back—Ohio
  State
1947–48 Los Angeles Rams
1949 Cleveland Browns

HORWEEN, ARNOLD—Back—
  Harvard
1921–22 Chicago Cardinals
1923–24 Chicago Cardinals—Player-coach

HORWEEN, RALPH—Back—Harvard
1921–23 Chicago Cardinals

HOUGHTON, JERRY—Tackle—
  Washington State
1950 Washington Redskins
1951 Chicago Cardinals

HOUSTON, LINDELL—Guard—Ohio
  State
1946–51 Cleveland Browns

HOVIOUS, JOHN—Back—
  Mississippi
1945 New York Giants

HOWARD, ALBERT—Guard—
  Princeton
1925–26 Kansas City Cowboys
1927 Cleveland Bulldogs
1928 Detroit Wolverines
1929–30 New York Giants

HOWARD, LYNN—Back—Indiana
1921–22 Green Bay Packers

HOWARD, SHERMAN—Back—
  Nevada
1949 New York Yankees
1950–51 New York Yanks

HOWARD, WILLIAM—Back—
  Southern California
1939 Detroit Lions

HOWELL, CLARENCE—End—
  Texas A & M
1948 San Francisco 49ers

HOWELL, EARL—Back—
  Mississippi
1949 Los Angeles Dons

HOWELL, JAMES LEE—End—
  Arkansas
1937–42 New York Giants
1946–48 New York Giants

HOWELL, JOHN—Back—Nebraska
1938 Green Bay Packers

HOWELL, MILLARD—Back—
  Alabama
1937 Washington Redskins

HOWELL, WILFRED—End—
  Catholic Univ.
1929 Boston Braves

HRABETIN, FRANK—Tackle—
  Loyola (Los Angeles)
1942 Philadelphia Eagles
1946 Miami Seahawks
1946 Brooklyn Dodgers

HUBBARD, ROBERT—Tackle—
  Geneva
1927–28 New York Giants
1929–35 Green Bay Packers
1936 New York Giants
1936 Pittsburgh Pirates

HUBBARD, WESLEY—End—None
1935 Brooklyn Dodgers

HUBBELL, FRANKLIN—End—
  Tennessee
1947–49 Los Angeles Rams

HUBKA, EUGENE—Back—Temple
1947 Pittsburgh Steelers

HUDSON, R.—Back—??
1923   Minneapolis Marines
1925–26 Hammond Pros
1926   Buffalo Bisons

**HUDSON, MARTIN—Guard—
Michigan**
1931   Cleveland Indians

HUDSON, ROBERT—End—Clemson
1951   New York Giants

**HUFFINE, KENNETH—Back—
Purdue**
1921   Chicago Bears
1921–25 Dayton Triangles

**HUFFMAN, FRANK—Guard—
Marshall**
1939–41 Chicago Cardinals

**HUFFMAN, IOLAS—Tackle—Ohio
State**
1923   Cleveland Indians

**HUFFMAN, RICHARD—Tackle—
Tennessee**
1947–50 Los Angeles Rams

**HUFFMAN, VERNON—Back—
Indiana**
1937–38 Detroit Lions

**HUFFORD, DARRELL—End—
California**
1926   Los Angeles

**HUGGINS, ROY—Back—
Vanderbilt**
1944   Cleveland Rams

**HUGHES, BERNARD—Center—
Oregon**
1934–36 Chicago Cardinals
1941   Chicago Bears

**HUGHES, GEORGE—Guard—
William & Mary**
1950–51 Pittsburgh Steelers

**HUGHES, HENRY—Back—Oregon
State**
1932   Boston Braves

**HUGHES, MORRIS—Center—
Swarthmore**
1925   Pottsville Maroons

HUGHES, WILLIAM—Center—Texas
1937–40 Philadelphia Eagles
1940–41 Chicago Bears

**HUGHITT, ERNEST—Back—
Michigan**
1920–23 Buffalo All Americans
1924   Buffalo Bisons

**HUGRET, JOSEPH—End—New York
Univ.**
1933–34 Brooklyn Dodgers

**HULTMAN, VIVIAN—End—
Michigan State**
1925–26 Detroit Panthers
1927   Pottsville Maroons

**HUMBERT, RICHARD—End—
Richmond**
1941   Philadelphia Eagles
1945–49 Philadelphia Eagles

HUMBLE, WELDON—Guard—Rice
1947–50 Cleveland Browns

**HUMMELL, CHARLES—Back—
Lafayette**
1926   Providence Steamrollers
1926   Kansas City Cowboys
1926   Dayton Triangles
1927   Chicago Cardinals

HUMMON, JOHN—End—Wittenberg
1928   Dayton Triangles

HUMPHREY, PAUL—Center—Purdue
1939   Brooklyn Dodgers

**HUNEKE, CHARLES—Tackle—St.
Mary's (Texas)**
1946–47 Chicago Rockets
1947–48 Brooklyn Dodgers

**HUNSINGER, CHARLES—Back—
Florida**
1950–51 Chicago Bears

HUNT, BEN—Tackle—Alabama
1923   Toledo Maroons

HUNT, JOHN—Back—Marshall
1945   Chicago Bears

HUNTER, ??—Guard—??
1925   Hammond Pros

**HUPKE, THOMAS—Guard—
Alabama**
1934–37 Detroit Lions
1938–39 Cleveland Rams

HURLBURT, JOHN—Back—Chicago
1924–25 Chicago Cardinals

**HURLEY, GEORGE—Guard—
Washington State**
1931   Cleveland Indians
1932   Boston Braves
1933   Boston Redskins

HURST, ??—Guard—??
1924   Chicago Bears
1924   Kenosha

HURTJUN, ??—Back—??
1923   Rochester Kodaks

HUST, ALBERT—End—Tennessee
1946 Chicago Cardinals

**HUTCHINSON, ELVIN—Back—
Whittier**
1939 Detroit Lions
1942 New York Giants

**HUTCHINSON, RALPH—Tackle—
Chattanooga**
1949 New York Giants

HUTSON, DONALD—End—Alabama
1935 Green Bay Packers
1936 Green Bay Packers—R
1937 Green Bay Packers—R
1938 Green Bay Packers
1939 Green Bay Packers—R
1940 Green Bay Packers—R
1941 Green Bay Packers—R–S–V
1942 Green Bay Packers—R–S–V
1943 Green Bay Packers—R–F (3)
        (Tie with W. Cuff)
1944 Green Bay Packers—S
1945 Green Bay Packers—R

**HUTSON, MERLE—Guard—
Heidelberg**
1931 Cleveland Indians

HUTTON, LEON—Back—??
1930 Frankford Yellowjackets

* * *

**IGNATIUS, JAMES—Guard—Holy
Cross**
1935 Philadelphia Eagles

**ILLMAN, EDWARD—Back—
Montana State**
1928 Chicago Cardinals
1933 Philadelphia Eagles

ILLOWIT, ROY—Tackle—CCNY
1937 Brooklyn Dodgers

IMLAY, TALMA—Back—California
1926 Los Angeles
1927 New York Giants

**INGALLS, ROBERT, Center—
Michigan**
1942 Green Bay Packers

**INGWERSON, BERT—Tackle—
Illinois**
1920–21 Chicago Bears (Staleys)

**INTRIERI, MARNE—Guard—
Loyola (Md.)**
1932 Staten Island Stapletons
1933–34 Boston Redskins

**IPPOLITO, ANTHONY—Guard—
Purdue**
1943 Chicago Bears

IRGENS, ??—Back—??
1922–23 Minneapolis Marines

**IRVIN, BARLOW—Guard—Texas
A & M**
1926–27 Buffalo Bisons

**IRVIN, CECIL—Tackle—Davis &
Elkins**
1931 Providence Steamrollers
1932–35 New York Giants

IRWIN, DONALD—Back—Colgate
1936 Boston Redskins
1937–40 Washington Redskins

**ISAACSON, THEODORE—Tackle—
Washington**
1934–35 Chicago Cardinals

ISABEL, WILMER—Back—Ohio State
1923–24 Columbus Tigers

ISBELL, CECIL—Back—Purdue
1938–40 Green Bay Packers
1941 Green Bay Packers—P
1942 Green Bay Packers—P

**ISSELHARDT, RALPH—Guard—
Franklin**
1937 Detroit Lions
1937 Cleveland Rams

ITZEL, JOHN—Back—Pittsburgh
1945 Pittsburgh Steelers

**IVERSON, CHRISTOPHER—Back—
Oregon**
1947–48 New York Yankees
1950–51 New York Yanks

IVY, FRANK—End—Oklahoma
1940 Pittsburgh Steelers
1940–42 Chicago Cardinals
1945–47 Chicago Cardinals

* * *

**JACKSON, COLVILLE—End—
Chicago**
1921 Hammond Pros
1926 Louisville Colonels
1928–30 Providence Steamrollers

**JACKSON, DONALD—Back—North
Carolina**
1936 Philadelphia Eagles

**JACKSON, ROBERT—Back—North
Carolina**
1950–51 New York Giants

JACOBS, JACK—Back—Oklahoma
1942 Cleveland Rams
1945 Cleveland Rams
1946 Washington Redskins
1947 Green Bay Packers—K (Tie with
        F. Reagen)
1948–49 Green Bay Packers

JACOBS, MARVIN—Tackle—None
1948   Chicago Cardinals

JACUNSKI, HARRY—End—Fordham
1939–44   Green Bay Packers

JAFFUR, JOHN—Guard—Penn State
1946   Washington Redskins

JAGADE, HARRY—Back—Indiana
1949   Baltimore Colts
1951   Cleveland Browns

JAMES, GEORGE—Guard—Bucknell
1929   Frankford Yellowjackets

JAMES, THOMAS—Back—Ohio State
1948–51   Cleveland Browns

**JANECEK, CLARENCE—Guard—
Purdue**
1933   Pittsburgh Pirates

JANIAK, LEONARD—Back—Ohio
1939   Brooklyn Dodgers
1940–42   Cleveland Rams

**JANKOWSKI, EDWARD—Back—
Wisconsin**
1936–41   Green Bay Packers

**JANNISEN, RAYMOND—Tackle—
South Dakota**
1931   Green Bay Packers

**JANSANTE, VALERIO—End—
Duquesne**
1946–51   Pittsburgh Steelers
1951   Green Bay Packers

JANSING, L. ??—End—??
1922   Louisville Colonels

JAPPE, PAUL—Guard—Syracuse
1925   New York Giants
1927–28   New York Giants

**JARMOLUK, MICHAEL—Tackle—
Temple**
1946–47   Chicago Bears
1948   Boston Yanks
1949   New York Bulldogs
1950–51   Philadelphia Eagles

**JARVI, TOIMI—Back—North
Illinois State**
1944   Philadelphia Eagles
1945   Pittsburgh Steelers

**JASZEWSKI, FLOYD—Tackle—
Minnesota**
1950–51   Detroit Lions

**JAWISH, HENRY—Guard—
Georgetown**
1926   Pottsville Maroons

JEAN, WALTER—Guard—Missouri
1922–23   Akron Steels
1924   Milwaukee Badgers
1925–26   Green Bay Packers
1927   Pottsville Maroons

**JEFFERS, EDWARD—Guard—
Oklahoma A & M**
1947   Brooklyn Dodgers

**JEFFERSON, WILLIAM—Back—
Mississippi State**
1941   Detroit Lions
1942   Brooklyn Dodgers
1942   Philadelphia Eagles

**JEFFRIES, ROBERT—Guard—
Howard**
1942   Brooklyn Dodgers

**JELLEY, THOMAS—End—Miami
(Fla.)**
1951   Pittsburgh Steelers

**JENKINS, JACQUE—Back—
Vanderbilt**
1943   Washington Redskins
1946–47   Washington Redskins

**JENKINS, JONATHAN—Tackle—
Tackle—Dartmouth**
1949   Baltimore Colts
1950   New York Yanks

**JENNINGS, JOHN—Tackle—Ohio
State**
1950–51   Chicago Cardinals

JENNINGS, ??—Center—Haskell
1929   Providence Steamrollers
1930   Portsmouth Spartans

JENSEN, ROBERT—End—Iowa State
1948   Chicago Rockets
1949   Chicago Hornets
1950   Baltimore Colts

JENSVOLD, LEO—Back—Iowa
1931   Chicago Bears
1931   Cleveland Indians

**JESSUP, WILLIAM—End—
Southern California**
1951   San Francisco 49ers

JETT, JOHN—End—Wake Forest
1941   Detroit Lions

**JOCHER, ARTHUR—Guard—
Manhattan**
1940–42   Brooklyn Dodgers

JOE, LAWRENCE—Back—Penn State
1949   Buffalo Bills

JOESTING, HERBERT—Back—
Minnesota
1929–30 Minneapolis Redjackets
1930–31 Frankford Yellowjackets
1931–32 Chicago Bears

JOHNS, JAMES—Guard—Michigan
1923 Cleveland Indians
1924 Cleveland Bulldogs
1924 Minneapolis Marines

JOHNSON, ALBERT—Back—
Kentucky
1937 Brooklyn Dodgers
1938 Chicago Bears
1939–41 Chicago Cardinals
1941 Philadelphia Eagles

JOHNSON, ALVIN—Back—Hardin-
Simmons
1948 Philadelphia Eagles

JOHNSON, ARTHUR—Tackle—
Fordham
1920 Chicago Bears (Staleys)
1920 Akron Steels
1922 Rock Island Independents
1923–25 Duluth Kelleys
1926 Duluth Eskimos
1929 Orange

JOHNSON, CECIL—Back—East
Texas
1936 Brooklyn Dodgers
1937 Cleveland Rams
1939 Pittsburgh Steelers
1940–41 Chicago Cardinals
1942 Philadelphia Eagles
1943 Brooklyn Dodgers
1944 Brooklyn Tigers

JOHNSON, CLYDE—Tackle—
Kentucky
1946–47 Los Angeles Rams
1948 Los Angeles Dons

JOHNSON, FARNHAM—End—
Wisconsin & Michigan
1948 Chicago Rockets

JOHNSON, GILBERT—Back—SMU
1949 New York Yankees

JOHNSON, GLENN—Tackle—
Arizona State
1948 New York Yankees
1949 Green Bay Packers

JOHNSON, HARVEY—Back—
William & Mary
1946–49 New York Yankees
1951 New York Yanks

JOHNSON, HOWARD—Guard—
Georgia
1940–41 Green Bay Packers
Killed ninth day of Iwo Jima
invasion. Capt., U.S. Marines.

JOHNSON, JOHN—Tackle—Utah
1934–40 Detroit Lions

JOHNSON, JOSEPH—Back—
Mississippi
1948 New York Giants

JOHNSON, LAWRENCE—Center—
Haskell
1933–35 Boston Redskins
1936–39 New York Giants
1944 Washington Redskins

JOHNSON, LEON—End—Columbia
1929 Orange

JOHNSON, MARVIN—Back—San
Jose State
1951 Los Angeles Rams

JOHNSON, NATHAN—Tackle—
Illinois
1946–47 New York Yankees
1948 Chicago Rockets
1949 Chicago Hornets
1950 New York Yanks

JOHNSON, WILLIAM—Guard—
SMU
1947 Chicago Bears

JOHNSON, WILLIAM—End—
Minnesota
1940 Green Bay Packers

JOHNSON, WILLIAM—Center—
Texas A & M
1948–51 San Francisco 49ers

JOHNSOS, LUKE—End—
Northwestern
1929–36 Chicago Bears
1938 Chicago Bears
1942–45 Chicago Bears—Co-coach

JOHNSTON, CHESTER—Back—
Elmhurst
1931 Green Bay Packers
1934 St. Louis Gunners
1934–39 Green Bay Packers
1940 Pittsburgh Steelers

JOHNSTON, JAMES—Back—
Washington
1939–40 Washington Redskins
1946 Chicago Cardinals

JOHNSTON, PRESTON—Back—
SMU
1946 Miami Seahawks
1946 Buffalo Bisons

JOLLY—Tackle—None
1922 Akron Steels
1923 Oorang Indians
1923 Dayton Triangles
1929 Buffalo Bisons
1930 Brooklyn Dodgers
1931 Cleveland Indians

JONES, ARTHUR—Back—Richmond
1941 Pittsburgh Steelers
1945 Pittsburgh Steelers

JONES, BRUCE—Guard—Alabama
1927-28 Green Bay Packers
1930 Minneapolis Redjackets
1930-31 Frankford Yellowjackets
1931-32 Brooklyn Dodgers
1932 New York Giants
1933-34 Brooklyn Dodgers
1934 New York Giants

**JONES, DONALD—Back—
Washington**
1940 Philadelphia Eagles

JONES, EDGAR—Back—Pittsburgh
1945 Chicago Bears
1946-49 Cleveland Browns

JONES, ELLIS—Guard—Tulsa
1945 Boston Yanks

**JONES, ELMER—Guard—Wake
Forest**
1946 Buffalo Bisons
1947-48 Detroit Lions

**JONES, GERALD—Tackle—Notre
Dame**
1920-21 Chicago Bears (Staleys)
1923 Toledo Maroons

JONES, HARVEY—Back—Baylor
1944-45 Cleveland Rams
1947 Washington Redskins

**JONES, KENNETH—Back—
Franklin-Marshall**
1921 Akron Steels
1922 Rock Island Independents
1923 Canton Bulldogs
1924 Cleveland Bulldogs
1924 Dayton Triangles
1924 Buffalo Bisons
1925 Canton Indians

**JONES, LEWIS—Guard—
Weatherford**
1943 Brooklyn Dodgers

JONES, RALPH—End—Alabama
1946 Detroit Lions
1947 Baltimore Colts

JONES, ROBERT—Guard—Indiana
1934 Green Bay Packers

**JONES, THOMAS—Guard—
Bucknell**
1930-31 Frankford Yellowjackets
1932-36 New York Giants
1938 Green Bay Packers

**JONES, THURMAN—Back—
Abilene Christian**
1941-42 Brooklyn Dodgers

**JONES, WILLIAM—Back—Tulane &
LSU**
1946 Miami Seahawks
1946-47 Brooklyn Dodgers
1948-51 Cleveland Browns

**JONES, WILLIAM—Guard—West
Virginia Wesleyan**
1947 Brooklyn Dodgers

**JORGENSEN, CARL—Tackle—St.
Mary's (Cal.)**
1934 Green Bay Packers
1935 Philadelphia Eagles

**JORGENSEN, WAGNER—Center—St.
Mary's (Cal.)**
1936-37 Brooklyn Dodgers

JOSEPH, R.—End—Miami (Ohio)
1927 Dayton Triangles

**JOSEPH, ZERN—Center—Miami
(Ohio)**
1925 Dayton Triangles
1927 Dayton Triangles
1930 Portsmouth Spartans
1931 Cleveland Indians

JOYCE, DONALD—Tackle—Tulane
1951 Chicago Cardinals

JUDD, SAXON—End—Tulsa
1946-48 Brooklyn Dodgers

**JUNGMICHEL, HAROLD—Guard—
Texas**
1946 Miami Seahawks

**JURICH, MICHAEL—Tackle—
Denver**
1941-42 Brooklyn Dodgers

**JURKIEWICZ, WALTER—Center—
Indiana**
1946 Detroit Lions

**JUSTER, RUBIN—Tackle—
Minnesota**
1946 Boston Yanks

**JUSTICE, CHARLES—Back—North
Carolina**
1950 Washington Redskins

JUSTICE, EDWARD—Back—Gonzaga
1936 Boston Redskins
1937-42 Washington Redskins

**JUZWIK, STEPHEN—Back—Notre
Dame**
1942 Washington Redskins
1946 Buffalo Bisons
1947 Buffalo Bills
1948 Chicago Rockets

* * *

KABEALO, MICHAEL—Back—Ohio
State
1944 Cleveland Rams

KADESKY, MAX—End—Iowa
1923 Rock Island Independents

KAER, MORTON—Back—Southern
California
1931 Brooklyn Dodgers

KAHL, CYRUS—Back—North Dakota
1930 Portsmouth Spartans

KAHLER, ROBERT—Back—
Nebraska
1940–44 Green Bay Packers

KAHLER, ROYAL—Tackle—
Nebraska
1941 Pittsburgh Steelers
1942 Green Bay Packers

KAHN, EDWARD—Guard—North
Carolina
1935–36 Boston Redskins
1937 Washington Redskins
        Died of wounds in Leyte in-
        vasion, Feb. 17, 1945. Lt., U.S.
        Marines.

KAKASIC, GEORGE—Guard—
Duquesne
1936–38 Pittsburgh Pirates
1939 Pittsburgh Steelers

KAKELA, WAYNE—Center—
Minnesota
1930 Minneapolis Redjackets

KALMANIR, THOMAS—Back—
Nevada
1949–51 Los Angeles Rams

KAMP, JAMES—Tackle—Oklahoma
City Univ.
1932 Staten Island Stapletons
1933 Boston Redskins

KANE, CARL—Back—St. Louis Univ.
1936 Philadelphia Eagles

KANE, HERBERT—Tackle—Ada
Teachers (Okla.)
1944–45 New York Giants

KANYA, ROBERT—Tackle—New
York Univ.
1931–32 Staten Island Stapletons

KAPITANSKY, BERNARD—Guard—
Long Island Univ.
1942 Brooklyn Dodgers

KAPLAN, ??—Back—??
1923 Minneapolis Marines

KAPLAN, BERNARD—Guard—
Western Maryland
1935–36 New York Giants
1942 Philadelphia Eagles

KAPLANOFF, CARL—Tackle—Ohio
State
1939 Brooklyn Dodgers

KAPORCH, ALBERT—Tackle—St.
Bonaventure
1943–45 Detroit Lions

KAPTER, ALEXANDER—Guard—
Northwestern
1946 Cleveland Browns

KARAMATIC, GEORGE—Back—
Gonzaga
1938 Washington Redskins

KARCH, ROBERT—Tackle—Ohio
State
1922 Columbus Tigers

KARCHER, JAMES—Guard—Ohio
State
1936 Boston Redskins
1937–39 Washington Redskins

KARCIS, JOHN—Back—Carnegie
Tech.
1932–35 Brooklyn Dodgers
1936–38 Pittsburgh Pirates
1938–39 New York Giants
1942 Detroit Lions—Head Coach

KARMAZIN, MICHAEL—Guard—
Duke
1946–47 New York Yankees

KARNOFSKY, ABRAHAM—Back—
Arizona
1945 Philadelphia Eagles
1946 Boston Yanks

KARPOWICH, EDWARD—Tackle—
Catholic Univ.
1936–39 Pittsburgh Pirates

KARR, WILLIAM—End—West
Virginia
1933–38 Chicago Bears

KARRAS, LOUIS—Tackle—Purdue
1950–51 Washington Redskins

KARRS, JOHN—Back—Duquesne
1944 Cleveland Rams

KARSTEN, GEORGE—Center—
Indiana
1949 Detroit Lions

KARWALES, JOHN—End—Michigan
1945 Chicago Bears
1947 Chicago Bears
1947 Chicago Cardinals

KASAP, MICHAEL—Tackle—Illinois & Purdue
1947   Baltimore Colts
1947   Buffalo Bills

KASE, GEORGE—???
1936–39   Pittsburgh Pirates

KASKA, ANTHONY—Back—Illinois Wesleyan
1935   Detroit Lions
1936–38   Brooklyn Dodgers

KASKY, EDWARD—Tackle—Villanova
1942   Philadelphia Eagles

KASPER,??—Back—??
1923   Rochester Kodaks

KASSEL, CHARLES—End—Illinois
1927   Chicago Bears
1927–28   Frankford Yellowjackets
1929–33   Chicago Cardinals

KATALINES, LEO—Tackle—Catholic Univ.
1937–38   Green Bay Packers

KATRISHEN, MICHAEL—Tackle—George Washington
1947–49   Washington Redskins

KAUFMAN, JOHN—Tackle—Pennsylvania
1929   Dayton Triangles

KAVANAUGH, KENNETH—End—LSU
1940–41   Chicago Bears
1945–50   Chicago Bears

KAVEL, GEORGE—Back—Carnegie Tech.
1934   Philadelphia Eagles

KAW, EDWARD—Back—Cornell
1920   Buffalo All Americans
1924   Buffalo Bisons

KAWAL, EDWARD—Center—Illinois
1931–36   Chicago Bears
1937   Washington Redskins

KEAHEY, EULIS—Tackle—George Washington
1942   New York Giants

KEANE, JAMES—End—Iowa
1946   Chicago Bears
1947   Chicago Bears—R
1948–51   Chicago Bears

KEANE, THOMAS—Back—West Virginia
1948–51   Los Angeles Rams

KEARNS, JAMES—Tackle—Miami (Fla.)
1945   New York Giants
1946   Chicago Cardinals

KECK, STANLEY—Guard—Princeton
1923   Cleveland Indians

KEEBLE, JOSEPH—Back—UCLA
1937   Cleveland Rams

KEEFE, EMMETT—Guard—Notre Dame
1921   Green Bay Packers
1921–22   Rock Island Independents

KEEFER, JACKSON—Back—Brown
1928   Dayton Triangles

KEELING, RAYMOND—Tackle—Texas
1938–39   Philadelphia Eagles

KEEN, DELBERT—Back—Arkansas
1937–38   Philadelphia Eagles

KEENAN, JOHN—Guard—Southern Carolina
1944–45   Washington Redskins
1951   Washington Redskins

KEENE, ROBERT—Back—Detroit
1943–45   Detroit Lions

KEKERIS, JAMES—Tackle—Missouri
1947   Philadelphia Eagles
1948   Green Bay Packers

KELL, PAUL—Tackle—Notre Dame
1939–40   Green Bay Packers

KELLAGHER, WILLIAM—Back—Fordham
1946–48   Chicago Rockets

KELLEY, EDWARD—Tackle—Texas
1949   Los Angeles Dons

KELLEY, WILLIAM—End—Texas Tech.
1949   Green Bay Packers

KELLISON, JOHN—Tackle—West Virginia Wesleyan
1921   Canton Bulldogs

KELLOGG, CLARENCE—Back—St. Mary's (Cal.)
1936   Chicago Cardinals
1940   Chicago Cardinals

KELLOGG, WILLIAM—Back—Syracuse
1924   Frankford Yellowjackets
1925   Rochester Jeffersons
1926   Chicago Cardinals

KELLY, CHARLES—Back—
Northwestern
1922 Toledo Maroons
1923 Buffalo All Americans
1924–25 Duluth Kelleys
1927 Cleveland Bulldogs
1927–28 New York Yankees
1929 Orange

KELLY, ELMER—End—Wichita
1944 Chicago Bears

KELLY, JOHN SIMMS—Back—
Kentucky
1930 Brooklyn Dodgers
1932 New York Giants
1933–34 Brooklyn Dodgers
1937 Brooklyn Dodgers

KELLY, ROBERT—Back—Notre
Dame
1947–48 Los Angeles Dons
1949 Baltimore Colts

KELSCH, MOSE—Back—None
1933–34 Pittsburgh Pirates

KEMP, RAYMOND—Tackle—
Duquesne
1933 Pittsburgh Pirates

KEMPTON, HERBERT—Back—Yale
1921 Canton Bulldogs

KENDRICKS, JAMES—Tackle—
Texas A & M
1922 Toledo Maroons
1922 Canton Bulldogs
1923 Louisville Colonels
1924 Chicago Bears
1925 Hammond Pros
1925–26 Buffalo Bisons

KENNEALLY, GEORGE—End—St.
Bonaventure
1926–28 Pottsville Maroons
1929 Boston Braves
1930 Chicago Cardinals
1932 Boston Braves
1933–35 Philadelphia Eagles

KENNEDY, JOSEPH—Back—
Columbia
1925 Buffalo Bisons

KENNEDY, ROBERT—Back—
Washington State
1946–49 New York Yankees
1950 New York Yanks

KENNEDY, ROBERT—Back—North
Carolina
1949 Los Angeles Dons

KENNEDY, WILLIAM—End—
Michigan State
1942 Detroit Lions
1947 Boston Yanks

KENNY, CHARLES—Guard—San
Francisco
1947 San Francisco 49ers

KENYON, CROWELL—Guard—
Ripon
1923 Green Bay Packers

KENYON, WILLIAM—Back—
Georgetown
1925 New York Giants

KERCHER, ROBERT—End—
Georgetown
1944 Green Bay Packers

KERCHEVAL, RALPH—Back—
Kentucky
1934–37 Brooklyn Dodgers
1938 Brooklyn Dodgers—F (5) (Tie with
W. Cuff)
1939–40 Brooklyn Dodgers

KERIASOTIS, NICHOLAS—Guard—
St. Ambrose
1941–42 Chicago Bears
1945 Chicago Bears

KERN, WILLIAM—Tackle—
Pittsburgh
1929–30 Green Bay Packers

KERNS, JOHN—Tackle—Ohio
1947–49 Buffalo Bills

KERNWEIN, GRAHAM—Back—
Chicago
1926 Racine Legion
1927 Chicago Bears

KERR, WILLIAM—End—Notre
Dame
1946 Los Angeles Dons

KERRIGAN, THOMAS—Guard—
Columbia
1930 New York Giants
1930 Newark

KERSHAW, GEORGE—End—
Colgate
1949 New York Giants

KETZKO, ALEXANDER—Tackle—
Michigan State
1942 New York Giants
1943 Detroit Lions
Killed in France with Patch's
7th Army, Dec. 23, 1944. Ser-
geant, U.S. Army.

KEUPER, KENNETH—Back—
Georgia
1945–47 Green Bay Packers
1948 New York Giants

KICHEFSKI, WALTER—End—Miami (Fla.)
1940–42 Pittsburgh Steelers
1944 Card-Pitt

KIEJEL, ??—End—??
1934 Chicago Cardinals

KIELBASA, MAX—Back—Duquesne
1946 Pittsburgh Steelers

KIELEY, HOWARD—Tackle—Michigan Tech.
1923 Chicago Cardinals
1923–24 Duluth Kelleys
1926 Chicago Cardinals

KIESLING, WALTER—Guard—St. Thomas
1926–27 Duluth Eskimos
1928 Pottsville Maroons
1929–33 Chicago Cardinals
1934 Chicago Bears
1935–36 Green Bay Packers
1939–42 Pittsburgh—Head Coach
1943 Phil-Pitt—Co-coach
1944 Card-Pitt—Co-coach

KIICK, GEORGE—Back—Bucknell
1940 Pittsburgh Steelers
1945 Pittsburgh Steelers

KILBOURNE, WARREN—Tackle—Michigan
1939 Green Bay Packers

KILROY, FRANK—Tackle—Temple
1943 Phil-Pitt
1944–51 Philadelphia Eagles

KIMBLE, FRANK—End—West Virginia
1945 Pittsburgh Steelers

KIMBROUGH, JOHN—Back—Texas A & M
1946–48 Los Angeles Dons

KINARD, FRANK—Tackle—Mississippi
1938–43 Brooklyn Dodgers
1944 Brooklyn Tigers
1946–47 New York Yankees

KINARD, GEORGE—Guard—Mississippi
1941–42 Brooklyn Dodgers
1946 New York Yankees

KINDERLINE, HENRY—Center—Dayton
1920–29 Dayton Triangles

KINDT, DONALD—Back—Wisconsin
1947–51 Chicago Bears

KINEK, MICHAEL—End—Michigan State
1940 Cleveland Rams

KING, ANDREW—Back—West Virginia
1920–22 Akron Steels
1922 Rochester Kodaks
1923 St. Louis Browns
1923–24 Chicago Cardinals
1924 Racine Legion
1925 Chicago Bears
1925 Hammond Pros

KING, EDWARD—End—Boston College
1948–49 Buffalo Bills
1950 Baltimore Colts

KING, HENRY—End—Georgia
1946 Buffalo Bisons
1947 Buffalo Bills
1948 Chicago Rockets
1949 Chicago Hornets

KINGERY, WAYNE—Back—LSU
1949 Baltimore Colts

KINSCHERF, CARL—Back—Colgate
1943–44 New York Giants

KIPP, JAMES—Tackle—Montana State
1942 Detroit Lions

KIRBY, JOHN—Back—Southern California
1949 Green Bay Packers

KIRK, BERNARD—Center—Michigan
1926 Buffalo Bisons

KIRKGARD, ??—Back—??
1923 Toledo Maroons

KIRKLAND, B'HO—Guard—Alabama
1935–36 Brooklyn Dodgers

KIRKLESKI, FRANK—Back—Lafayette
1927–28 Pottsville Maroons
1929 Orange
1930 Newark
1931 Brooklyn Dodgers

KIRKMAN, ROGER—Back—Washington & Jefferson
1933–35 Philadelphia Eagles

KISH, BENJAMIN—Back—Pittsburgh
1941 Brooklyn Dodgers
1942 Philadelphia Eagles
1943 Phil-Pitt
1944–49 Philadelphia Eagles

KISIDAY, GEORGE—End—Duquesne
1948 Buffalo Bills

KISSELL, ADOLPH—Back—Boston College
1942 Chicago Bears

KISSELL, JOHN—Tackle—Boston College
1948–49 Buffalo Bills
1950–51 Cleveland Browns

KISSELL, VETO—Back—Holy Cross
1949 Buffalo Bills
1950 Baltimore Colts

KITTREDGE, PAUL—Back—Holy Cross
1929 Boston Braves

KITZMILLER, JOHN—Back—Oregon
1931 New York Giants

KIZZIRE, LEE—Back—Wyoming
1937 Detroit Lions
Killed when shot down over New Guinea, Dec. 5, 1943. Captain, U.S. Air Force.

KLAPSTEIN, EARL—Tackle—College of Pacific
1946 Pittsburgh Steelers

KLASNIC, JOHN—Back—None
1948 Brooklyn Dodgers

KLASOSKUS, ALBIN—Tackle—Holy Cross
1941 New York Giants

KLAUS, FEE—Center—None
1921 Green Bay Packers

KLENK, QUENTIN—End—Southern California
1946 Buffalo Bisons
1946 Chicago Rockets

KLEWICKI, EDWARD—End—Michigan State
1935–38 Detroit Lions

KLIEBHAN, ROGER—Back—Milwaukee Teachers
1921 Green Bay Packers

KLIMEK, ANTHONY—End—Illinois
1951 Chicago Cardinals

KLINE, HARRY—End—Emporia Teachers
1939–40 New York Giants
1942 New York Giants

KLOPPENBERG, HARRY—End—Fordham
1930 Staten Island Stapletons
1931 Brooklyn Dodgers
1933–34 Brooklyn Dodgers

KLOTOVICH, MICHAEL—Back—St. Mary's (Cal.)
1945 New York Giants

KLUG, ALFRED—Tackle—Marquette
1946 Buffalo Bisons
1947–48 Baltimore Colts

KLUMB, JOHN—End—Washington State
1939 Chicago Cardinals
1940 Detroit Lions
1940 Pittsburgh Steelers

KLUTKA, NICHOLAS—End—Florida
1946 Buffalo Bisons

KMETOVIC, PETER—Back—Stanford
1946 Philadelphia Eagles
1947 Detroit Lions

KNECHT, WILLIAM—Tackle—Xavier (Cincinnati)
1925 Dayton Triangles

KNOLLA, JOHN—Back—Creighton
1942 Chicago Cardinals
1945 Chicago Cardinals

KNOP, OSCAR—Back—Illinois
1922–23 Hammond Pros
1923–27 Chicago Bears

KNORR, LAWRENCE—End—Dayton
1942 Detroit Lions
1945 Detroit Lions

KNOX, CHARLES—Tackle—St. Edmonds
1934–36 Detroit Lions
1937 Philadelphia Eagles

KNOX, FRANK—Guard—Illinois
1935 Detroit Lions

KOBOLINSKI, STANLEY—Center—Boston College
1926 Brooklyn Dodgers

KOBROSKI, MILTON—Back—Trinity
1937 New York Giants

KOCH, GEORGE—Back—Baylor
1945 Cleveland Rams
1947 Buffalo Bills

KOCHEL, MICHAEL—Guard—Fordham
1939 Chicago Cardinals

KODBA, JOSEPH—Center—Purdue
1947 Baltimore Colts
1947 Buffalo Bills

KOEHLER, ROBERT—Back—Northwestern
1920–21 Chicago Bears (Staleys)
1921–26 Chicago Cardinals

KOENINGER, ARTHUR—Center—
Chattanooga
1932 Staten Island Stapletons
1933 Philadelphia Eagles

KOKEN, MICHAEL—Back—Notre
Dame
1933 Chicago Cardinals

KOLBERG, ELMER—Back—Oregon
State
1939–40 Philadelphia Eagles
1941 Pittsburgh Steelers

KOLESAR, ROBERT—Guard—
Michigan
1946 Cleveland Browns

KOLLS, LOUIS—Center—St.
Ambrose
1922–25 Rock Island Independents
1927 New York Yankees

KOLMAN, EDWARD—Tackle—
Temple
1940–42 Chicago Bears
1946–47 Chicago Bears
1949 New York Giants

KONDRIA, JOHN—Tackle—St.
Vincent's
1945 Pittsburgh Steelers

KONETSKY, FLOYD—End—Florida
1944–45 Cleveland Rams
1947 Baltimore Colts
1947 Buffalo Bills

KONISZEWSKI, JOHN—Tackle—
George Washington
1945–46 Washington Redskins
1948 Washington Redskins

KONOPKA, JOHN—Back—Temple
1936 Philadelphia Eagles

KOONS, JOSEPH—Center—Scranton
1941 Brooklyn Dodgers

KOPCHA, JOSEPH—Guard—
Chattanooga
1929 Chicago Bears
1932–35 Chicago Bears
1936 Detroit Lions

KOPPISCH, WALTER—Back—
Columbia
1925 Buffalo Bisons
1925–26 New York Giants

KOSEL, STANLEY—Back—Albright
1938 Brooklyn Dodgers

KOSHLAP, JULES—Back—
Georgetown
1940 Brooklyn Dodgers

KOSIKOWSKI, FRANK—End—
Marquette, Notre Dame
1948 Cleveland Browns

KOSLOWSKI, JOSEPH—Tackle—
Boston College
1925–27 Providence Steamrollers
1929 Boston Braves
1930 Providence Steamrollers

KOSLOWSKI, STANLEY—Back—
Holy Cross
1946 Miami Seahawks

KOSTIUK, MICHAEL—Tackle—
Detroit
1940 Philadelphia Eagles
1941 Cleveland Rams
1945 Detroit Lions

KOSTKA, STANLEY—Back—
Minnesota
1935 Brooklyn Dodgers

KOSTOS, ANTHONY—End—Bucknell
1927–30 Frankford Yellowjackets
1930 Minneapolis Redjackets
1931 Frankford Yellowjackets
1933 Philadelphia Eagles

KOSTOS, MARTIN—End—Bucknell
1929 Frankford Yellowjackets

KOTAL, EDWARD—Back—
Lawrence
1925–29 Green Bay Packers

KOTTLER, MARTIN—Back—Centre
1933 Pittsburgh Pirates

KOVASCY, WILLIAM—Tackle—
Illinois
1923 Hammond Pros

KOVATCH, JOHN—End—Notre
Dame
1937–38 Cleveland Rams
1941–42 Washington Redskins
1946 Washington Redskins
1947 Green Bay Packers

KOWALSKI, ADOLPH—Back—Tulsa
1947 Brooklyn Dodgers

KOWALSKI, ANTHONY—End—
Mississippi State
1943 Brooklyn Dodgers
1944 Brooklyn Tigers
1945 Boston Yanks

KOZEL, CHESTER—Tackle—
Mississippi
1947–48 Buffalo Bills
1948 Chicago Rockets

KOZIAK, MICHAEL—Guard—Notre
Dame
1924–25 Duluth Kelleys

KRACUM, GEORGE—Back—
Pittsburgh
1941   Brooklyn Dodgers

KRAEHE, OLIVER—Guard—None
1923   St. Louis Browns

KRAFT, REYNOLD—End—Illinois
1922   Minneapolis Marines

KRALL, GERARD—Back—Ohio State
1950   Detroit Lions

KRAMER, FREDERICK—Guard—
Washington State
1923–24   Minneapolis Marines
1924   Rock Island Independents
1927   New York Yankees

KRAMER, JOHN—Tackle—
Marquette
1946   Buffalo Bisons

KRANZ, KENNETH—Back—
Milwaukee State
1949   Green Bay Packers

KRAUS, FRANCIS—Tackle—Hobart
1924   Buffalo Bisons

KRAUSE, HENRY—Center—St. Louis
Univ.
1936   Brooklyn Dodgers
1937–38   Washington Redskins

KRAUSE, MAX—Back—Gonzaga
1933–36   New York Giants
1937–40   Washington Redskins

KRAUSE, PAUL—Guard—De Paul
1938   Cleveland Rams

KREINHEDER, WALTER—Guard—
Michigan
1922   Akron Steels
1923   St. Louis Browns
1925   Cleveland Indians

KRESKY, JOSEPH—Guard—
Wisconsin
1930   Green Bay Packers
1932   Boston Braves
1933–35   Philadelphia Eagles
1935   Pittsburgh Pirates

KRIEGER, EARL—Back—Ohio
1922   Columbus Tigers

KRIEGER, ROBERT—End—
Dartmouth
1940   Philadelphia Eagles
1946   Philadelphia Eagles

KRIEL, EMMETT—Guard—Baylor
1939   Philadelphia Eagles

KRING, FRANK—Back—TCU
1945   Detroit Lions

KRISTUFEK, FRANK—Tackle—
Pittsburgh
1940–41   Brooklyn Dodgers

KRIVONAK, JOSEPH—Guard—
Southern Carolina
1946   Miami Seahawks

KROL, JOSEPH—Back—West
Ontario
1945   Detroit Lions

KROUSE, RAYMOND—Tackle—
Maryland
1951   New York Giants

KRUEGER, ALBERT—Tackle—
Drake
1924   Kansas City Cowboys

KRUEGER, ALVIN—End—Southern
California
1940–42   Washington Redskins
1946   Los Angeles Dons

KRYSL, JERRY—Tackle—Kansas
State
1927   Cleveland Indians

KSIONZYK, JOHN—Back—St.
Bonaventure
1947   Los Angeles Rams

KUCHARSKI, THEODORE—End—
Holy Cross
1930   Providence Steamrollers

KUCZINSKI, BERT—End—
Pennsylvania
1943   Detroit Lions
1946   Philadelphia Eagles

KUEHL, WALTER—Back—Dubuque
1921–22   Buffalo All Americans
1923   Rock Island Independents
1924   Dayton Triangles

KUFFEL, RAYMOND—End—
Marquette
1947   Buffalo Bills
1948   Chicago Rockets
1949   Chicago Hornets

KUHARICH, JOSEPH—Guard—
Notre Dame
1940–41   Chicago Cardinals
1945   Chicago Cardinals
1952   Chicago Cardinals—Head Coach

KUICK, STANLEY—Guard—Beloit
1926   Green Bay Packers
1926   Milwaukee Badgers

KULBITSKI, VICTOR—Back—
Minnesota, Notre Dame
1946   Buffalo Bisons
1947–48   Buffalo Bills

KUPCINET, IRVING—Back—North Dakota
1935 Philadelphia Eagles

KURRASCH, ROY—End—UCLA
1947 New York Yankees
1948 Pittsburgh Steelers

KURTH, JOSEPH—Tackle—Notre Dame
1933-34 Green Bay Packers

KUSKO, JOHN—Back—Temple
1936-37 Philadelphia Eagles
1937 New York Giants

KUSSEROW, LOUIS—Back—Columbia
1949 New York Yankees
1950 New York Yanks

KUTNER, MALCOLM—End—Texas
1946-50 Chicago Cardinals

KUUSISTO, WILLIAM—Guard—Minnesota
1941-46 Green Bay Packers

KUZCO, PAUL—Back—Villanova
1929 Staten Island Stapletons

KUZMAN, JOHN—Tackle—Fordham
1941 Chicago Cardinals
1946 San Francisco 49ers
1947 Chicago Rockets

KVATERNICK, ZVONIMIR—Guard—Kansas
1934 Pittsburgh Pirates

KYLE, JOHN—Back—Indiana
1923 Cleveland Indians

KYLE, JAMES—Center—Gettysberg
1925-26 Canton Bulldogs

* * *

LABACENEER, ??—Center—??
1922 Hammond Pros

LABENGOOD, ??—Back—??
1925 Pottsville Maroons

LACH, STEPHEN—Back—Duke
1942 Chicago Cardinals
1946-47 Pittsburgh Steelers

LACKMAN, RICHARD—Back—None
1933-35 Philadelphia Eagles

LADROW, WALTER—Guard—None
1921 Green Bay Packers

LaFITTE, WILLIAM—End—Ouchita
1944 Brooklyn Tigers

LaFLEUR, JOSEPH—Back—Marquette
1922-24 Chicago Bears

LAHAR, HAROLD—Guard—Oklahoma
1940-41 Chicago Bears
1946 Buffalo Bisons
1947-48 Buffalo Bills

LAHEY, THOMAS—End—John Carroll
1946-47 Chicago Rockets

LAHR, WARREN—Back—Western Reserve
1948-51 Cleveland Browns

LAINHART, PORTER—Back—Oregon
1933 Chicago Cardinals
1933 Philadelphia Eagles

LAIRD, JAMES—Back—Colgate
1920-21 Buffalo All Americans
1921 Rochester Kodaks
1922 Buffalo All Americans
1925-28 Providence Steamrollers
1931 Staten Island Stapletons

LAJOUSKY, WILLIAM—Guard—Catholic Univ.
1936 Pittsburgh Pirates

LAMANA, PETER—Center—Boston Univ.
1947-48 Chicago Rockets

LAMAS, JOSEPH—Guard—Mt. St. Mary's
1942 Pittsburgh Steelers

LAMB, ROY—Back—Lombard
1925 Rock Island Independents
1926-27 Chicago Cardinals
1933 Chicago Cardinals

LAMB, WALTER—End—Oklahoma
1946 Chicago Bears

LAMBEAU, EARL—Back—Notre Dame
1921-29 Green Bay Packers—Player-coach
1930-49 Green Bay—Head Coach
1950-51 Chicago Cardinals—Head Coach

LAMME, EMERALD—End—Ohio Wesleyan
1931 Cleveland Indians

LAND, FREDERICK—Tackle—LSU
1948 San Francisco 49ers

LANDE, CLIFFORD—End—John Carroll
1921 Green Bay Packers

LANDRIGAN, JAMES—Tackle—Holy Cross
1947 Baltimore Colts

LANDRUM, J??—Guard—??
1922 Louisville Colonels

LANDRY, THOMAS—Back—Texas
1949 New York Yankees
1950–51 New York Giants

LANDSBERG, MORTIMER—Back—Cornell
1941 Philadelphia Eagles
1947 Los Angeles Dons

LANE, CLAYTON—Tackle—New Hampshire
1948 New York Yankees

LANE, OSCAR—Tackle—Marquette
1926 Milwaukee Badgers

LANG, ??—End—??
1929 Chicago Cardinals

LANGE, WILLIAM—Guard—Dayton
1951 Los Angeles Rams

LANGHOFF, HENRY—Back—Marquette
1922–23 Racine Legion

LANKAS, JAMES—Back—St. Mary's (Texas)
1942 Philadelphia Eagles
1943 Green Bay Packers

LANSDELL, GRANVILLE—Back—Southern California
1940 New York Giants

LANTZ, MONTGOMERY—Center—Grove City
1933 Pittsburgh Pirates

LANUM, RALPH,—Back—Illinois
1920–21 Chicago Bears (Staleys)
1922–24 Chicago Bears

LAPKA, THEODORE—End—St. Ambrose
1943–44 Washington Redskins
1946 Washington Redskins

LaPRESTA, BENJAMIN—Back—St. Louis Univ.
1933 Boston Redskins
1934 St. Louis Gunners

LAROSS, ??—End—??
1921 Chicago Cardinals

LARSON, LLOYD—Back—Wisconsin
1929 Chicago Cardinals

LARSON, O. J.—Center—Notre Dame
1922 Chicago Bears
1923–24 Milwaukee Badgers
1925 Green Bay Packers
1926 Duluth Eskimos
1929 Chicago Cardinals

LASCARI, JOHN—End—Georgetown
1942 New York Giants

LASSAHN, LOUIS—End—
1938 Pittsburgh Pirates

LATONE, ANTHONY—Back—None
1925–28 Pottsville Maroons
1929 Boston Braves
1930–31 Providence Steamrollers

LAUER, JOHN—Back—Detroit
1922 Rock Island Independents
1922 Green Bay Packers
1923 Toledo Maroons
1923 Dayton Triangles
1925–26 Detroit Panthers

LAURO, LINDELL—Back—Pittsburgh
1951 Chicago Cardinals

LAUX, THEODORE—Back—St. Joseph (Pa.)
1942 Philadelphia Eagles
1943 Phil–Pitt
1944 Philadelphia Eagles

LAVELLI, DANTE—End—Ohio State
1946 Cleveland Browns—R (AAFC)
1947–51 Cleveland Browns

LAW, HUBBARD—Guard—Sam Houston
1942 Pittsburgh Steelers
1945 Pittsburgh Steelers

LAW, JOHN—Tackle—Notre Dame
1929 Orange

LAWLER, ALLEN—Back—Texas
1948 Chicago Bears

LAWRENCE, EDWARD—Back—Brown
1929 Boston Braves
1930 Staten Island Stapletons

LAWRENCE, JAMES—Back—TCU
1936–38 Chicago Cardinals
1939 Green Bay Packers

LAWS, JOSEPH—Back—Iowa
1934–45 Green Bay Packers

LAWSON, JAMES—End—Stanford
1927 New York Yankees

LAY, RUSSELL—Guard—Michigan State
1934 Detroit Lions
1934 Cincinnati Reds
1934 St. Louis Gunners

LAYDEN, PETER—Back—Texas
1948–49 New York Yankees
1950 New York Yanks

LAYDEN, ROBERT—End—Southwestern (Kansas)
1943 Detroit Lions

LAYNE, ROBERT—Back—Texas
1948   Chicago Bears
1949   New York Bulldogs
1950–51   Detroit Lions

LAYPORT, JOHN—Back—St. Thomas
1924   Columbus Tigers
1925   Dayton Triangles

LAZETICH, MILAN—Guard— Michigan
1945   Cleveland Rams
1946–50   Los Angeles Rams

LAZETICH, WILLIAM—Back— Montana
1939   Cleveland Rams
1941–42   Cleveland Rams

LEA, PAUL—Tackle—Tulane
1951   Pittsburgh Steelers

LEAF, GARFIELD—Tackle—Syracuse
1926   Louisville Colonels

LEAPER, WESLEY—End— Wisconsin
1920   Buffalo All Americans
1921   Green Bay Packers
1923   Green Bay Packers

LEAR, LESLIE—Guard—Manitoba Univ.
1944–45   Cleveland Rams
1946   Los Angeles Rams
1947   Detroit Lions

LEARY, THOMAS—End—Fordham
1927–29   Frankford Yellowjackets
1929   Staten Island Stapletons
1930   Newark
1931   Frankford Yellowjackets

LEATHERMAN, J. D.—End— Maryland
1922   Hammond Pros

LECHNER, EDGAR—Tackle— Minnesota
1942   New York Giants

LECHTHALER, ROY—Guard— Lebanon Valley
1933   Philadelphia Eagles

LECKONBY, WILLIAM—Back—St. Lawrence
1939–41   Brooklyn Dodgers

LECTURE, JAMES—Guard— Northwestern
1946   Buffalo Bisons

LEDBETTER, CHESTER—Back— Arkansas
1932   Staten Island Stapletons
1933   Chicago Cardinals

LEDBETTER, TOY—Back— Oklahoma A & M
1950   Philadelphia Eagles

LEE, EUGENE—Center—Florida
1946   Boston Yanks

LEE, HILARY—Guard—Oklahoma
1931   Cleveland Indians
1933–34   Cincinnati Reds

LEE, JOHN—Back—Carnegie Tech.
1938   Pittsburgh Pirates
1939   Pittsburgh Steelers

LEE, WILLIAM—Tackle—Alabama
1935–37   Brooklyn Dodgers
1937–42   Green Bay Packers
1946   Green Bay Packers

LEEMANS, ALPHONSE—Back— George Washington
1936   New York Giants—G
1937–43   New York Giants

LeFEBRE, GILBERT—Back—None
1933–34   Cincinnati Reds
1935   Detroit Lions

LeFORCE, CLYDE—Back—Tulsa
1947–49   Detroit Lions

LEHECKA, JOSEPH—Back— Lafayette
1933   Frankford Yellowjackets

LEHRER, ??—Back—??
1922   Rochester Kodaks

LEICHT, JACOB—Back—Oregon
1948–49   Baltimore Colts

LEISK, WALTER—Guard—LSU
1937   Brooklyn Dodgers

LEITH, A??—Back—Pennsylvania
1926   Brooklyn Dodgers

LEMON, CLIFFORD—End—Centre
1926   Chicago Bears

LENNAN, BURGESS REID—Guard— None
1945   Washington Redskins
1947   Los Angeles Dons

LEON, ANTHONY—Guard—Alabama
1943   Washington Redskins
1944   Brooklyn Tigers
1945–46   Boston Yanks

LEONARD, JAMES—Guard—Colgate
1922–23   Chicago Cardinals
1923   Rochester Kodaks

LEONARD, JAMES—Back—Notre Dame
1934–37   Philadelphia Eagles

LEONARD, WILLIAM—End—Notre Dame
1949 Baltimore Colts

LEONETTI, ROBERT—Guard— Wake Forest
1948 Buffalo Bills
1948 Brooklyn Dodgers

LEPPER, BERNARD—Tackle—None
1920 Buffalo All Americans

LESTER, DARRELL—Center—TCU
1937-38 Green Bay Packers

LESTER, HAROLD—End—Wesleyan (Conn.)
1926 Providence Steamrollers

LETLOW, RUSSELL—Guard—San Francisco
1936-42 Green Bay Packers
1946 Green Bay Packers

LETSINGER, JAMES—Guard— Purdue
1933 Pittsburgh Pirates

LEVEY, JAMES—Back—None
1935-36 Pittsburgh Pirates

LEVY, HARVEY—Guard—Syracuse
1928 New York Giants
1928 New York Yankees

LEVY, LEONARD—Guard— Minnesota
1945 Cleveland Rams
1946 Los Angeles Rams
1947-48 Los Angeles Dons

LEWELLEN, VERNE—Back— Nebraska
1924-32 Green Bay Packers

LEWIS, ??—Back—??
1930 Portsmouth Spartans
1931 Cleveland Indians
1934 Cincinnati Reds

LEWIS, ARTHUR—Tackle—Ohio
1936 New York Giants
1938-39 Cleveland Rams

LEWIS, CLIFFORD—Back—Duke
1946-51 Cleveland Browns

LEWIS, ERNEST—Back—Colorado
1947-48 Chicago Rockets
1949 Chicago Hornets

LEWIS, WOODLEY—Back— Oregon
1950-51 Los Angeles Rams

LEYENDECKER, CHARLES— Tackle—Vanderbilt
1933 Philadelphia Eagles

LEYSENAAR, HARRY—Back— Marquette
1941 Chicago Cardinals

LIDBERG, CARL—Back—Minnesota
1926 Green Bay Packers
1929-30 Green Bay Packers

LIEBEL, FRANK—End—Norwich
1942-47 New York Giants
1948 Chicago Cardinals

LIEBERUM, DONALD—Back— Manchester (Ind.)
1942 New York Giants

LIGHTNER, JOSEPH—??—Penn State
1933 Frankford Yellowjackets

LILES, ELVIN—Guard—Oklahoma A & M
1943-45 Detroit Lions
1945 Cleveland Rams

LILLARD, JOSEPH—Back—Oregon
1932-33 Chicago Cardinals

LILLYWHITE, VERL—Back— Southern California
1948-51 San Francisco 49ers

LIND, ALBERT—Center— Northwestern
1936 Chicago Cardinals

LINDAHL, VIRGIL—Guard— Kentucky
1945 New York Giants

LINDON, LUTHER—Tackle— Kentucky
1944-45 Detroit Lions

LINDSKOG, VICTOR—Center— Stanford
1944-51 Philadelphia Eagles

LININGER, RAYMOND—Center— Ohio State
1950-51 Detroit Lions

LINNAN, FRANCIS—Tackle— Marquette
1926 Racine Legion

LINTZENICH, JOSEPH—Tackle— St. Louis Univ.
1930-31 Chicago Bears

LIO, AUGUSTINO—Guard— Georgetown
1940-43 Detroit Lions
1944-45 Boston Yanks
1946 Philadelphia Eagles

LIPSCOMB, PAUL—Tackle— Tennessee
1945-49 Green Bay Packers
1950-51 Washington Redskins

LIPSKI, JOHN—Center—Temple
1933–34 Philadelphia Eagles

**LITTLE, LOUIS—Tackle—
Pennsylvania**
1920–21 Buffalo All Americans

LITTLE TWIG—Tackle—Carlisle
1923 Oorang Indians
1924–25 Rock Island Independents
1926 Canton Bulldogs

LITTLEFIELD, CARL—Back—??
1938 Cleveland Rams
1939 Pittsburgh Steelers

**LIVINGSTON, HOWARD—Back—
None**
1944–47 New York Giants
1948–50 Washington Redskins
1950 San Francisco 49ers

**LIVINGSTON, ROBERT—Back—
Notre Dame**
1948 Chicago Rockets
1949 Chicago Hornets
1949 Buffalo Bills
1950 Baltimore Colts

**LIVINGSTON, THEODORE—
Tackle—Indiana**
1937–40 Cleveland Rams

LO BOUTWELL—Back—None
1923 Oorang Indians

**LOEPFE, RICHARD—Tackle—
Wisconsin**
1948–49 Chicago Cardinals

LOGAN, JAMES—Guard—Indiana
1942–43 Chicago Bears

LOGEL, ROBERT—End—None
1949 Buffalo Bills

LOGUS, ??—Center—??
1934 Cincinnati Reds

**LOKANC, JOSEPH—Guard—
Northwestern**
1941 Chicago Cardinals

LOLLAR, GEORGE—Back—Howard
1928 Green Bay Packers

LOLOTAI, ALBERT—Guard—Weber
1945 Washington Redskins
1946–49 Los Angeles Dons

**LOMASNEY, THOMAS—End—
Villanova**
1929 Staten Island Stapletons

LONE WOLF—Guard—Carlisle
1923 Oorang Indians

LONG, JOHN—Back—Colgate
1944–45 Chicago Bears

LONG, ROBERT—Back—Tennessee
1947 Boston Yanks

LONG, THOMAS—Guard—Ohio State
1923 Racine Legion
1925 Columbus Tigers
1925 Rochester Jeffersons
1929 Chicago Bears
1930 Frankford Yellowjackets
1931 Portsmouth Spartans

**LONG, WILLIAM—End—Oklahoma
A & M**
1949–50 Pittsburgh Steelers

**LONG TIME SLEEP (NICHOLAS
LASSA)—Center—Carlisle**
1923 Oorang Indians

**LONGO, ANTONIO—Guard—
Connecticut State**
1928 Providence Steamrollers

**LONGSTREET, ROY—Center—Iowa
State**
1926 Racine Legion

LONGUA, PAUL—End—Villanova
1929 Orange
1930 Newark

**LOOKABAUGH, JOHN—End—
Maryland**
1946–47 Washington Redskins

**LOOMIS, ACE—Back—LaCrosse
State**
1951 Green Bay Packers

LOONEY, DONALD—Back—TCU
1940 Philadelphia Eagles—R
1941–42 Pittsburgh Steelers

LORD, ??—Guard—??
1929 Staten Island Stapletons

**LOTT, JOHN—Tackle—
Bucknell**
1929 Orange
1930 Brooklyn Dodgers

LOVIN, ??—Guard—??
1929 Minneapolis Redjackets

**LOVUOLO, EDMOND—Tackle—
None**
1947 Brooklyn Dodgers

**LOVUOLO, FRANK—End—St.
Bonaventure**
1949 New York Giants

LOWE, GEORGE—End—Fordham
1920 Canton Bulldogs
1921 Cleveland Indians
1922 Buffalo All Americans
1923 Rock Island Independents
1924–25 Frankford Yellowjackets
1925 Providence Steamrollers
1926 Frankford Yellowjackets
1927 Providence Steamrollers

LOWE, WILLIAM—Back—Tennessee
1925–26 Frankford Yellowjackets

LOWERY, ??—Tackle—Ursinus
1921–23 Rochester Kodaks
1924–25 Rochester Jefferson

LOWTHER, RUSSELL—Back—
  Detroit
1944 Detroit Lions
1945 Pittsburgh Steelers

LOYD, ALEXANDER—End—
  Oklahoma A & M
1950 San Francisco 49ers

LUBRATOVICH, MILO—Tackle—
  Wisconsin
·1931–35 Brooklyn Dodgers

LUCENTE, JOHN—Back—West
  Virginia
1945 Pittsburgh Steelers

LUCKMAN, SIDNEY—Back—
  Columbia
1939–42 Chicago Bears
1943 Chicago Bears—V
1944 Chicago Bears
1945 Chicago Bears—P (Tie with S.
  Baugh)
1946–50 Chicago Bears

LUDTKE, NORMAN—Guard—John
  Carroll
1924 Green Bay Packers

LUHN, NOLAN—End—Tulsa
1945–49 Green Bay Packers

LUJACK, JOHN—Back—Notre Dame
1948–51 Chicago Bears

LUKENS, JAMES—End—Washington
  & Lee
1949 Buffalo Bisons

LUMMUS, JOHN—End—Baylor
1940–41 New York Giants
  Killed by land mine while leading
  infantry-tank attack against last
  Japanese stronghold on Iwo Jima.
  Lt., U.S. Army

LUMPKIN, ROY—Back—Georgia
  Tech.
1930–33 Portsmouth Spartans
1934 Detroit Lions
1935–37 Brooklyn Dodgers

LUND, WILLIAM—Back—Case
1946–47 Cleveland Browns

LUNDAY, KENNETH—Center—
  Arkansas
1937–41 New York Giants
1946–47 New York Giants

LUNDELL, WILBUR—End—
  Gustavus-Adolphus
1929–30 Minneapolis Redjackets
1930 Staten Island Stapletons

LUNDGREN, ??—Back—??
1923 Rock Island Independents

LUNZ, GERALD—Guard—Marquette
1925–26 Chicago Cardinals
1930 Frankford Yellowjackets

LYLE, DEWEY—Guard—Minnesota
1921–22 Rock Island Independents
1922–23 Green Bay Packers

LYMAN, DELBERT—Tackle—UCLA
1941 Green Bay Packers
1941 Cleveland Rams
1944 Cleveland Rams

LYMAN, ROY—Tackle—Nebraska
1922–23 Canton Bulldogs
1923 Cleveland Indians
1924 Cleveland Bulldogs
1925 Canton Bulldogs
1925–28 Chicago Bears
1930–31 Chicago Bears
1933–34 Chicago Bears

LYNCH, EDWARD—End—Catholic
  Univ.
1925 Columbus Tigers
1925 Rochester Jeffersons
1926 Detroit Panthers
1927 Providence Steamrollers
1929 Orange

LYONS, JOHN—Tackle—Tulsa
1929 New York Giants
1930 Portsmouth Spartans
1931 Cleveland Indians
1932–33 Brooklyn Dodgers
1934 St. Louis Gunners

* * *

MacAULIFFE, JOHN—Back—Beloit
1926 Green Bay Packers

McADAMS, DEAN—Back—
  Washington
1940–43 Brooklyn Dodgers

McAFEE, GEORGE—Back—Duke
1940–41 Chicago Bears
1945–50 Chicago Bears

McAFEE, WESLEY—Back—Duke
1941 Philadelphia Eagles

McARTHUR, JOHN—Center—St.
  Mary's (Cal.)
1926 Los Angeles
1927 Buffalo Bisons
1927–28 New York Yankees
1929 Orange
1930 Brooklyn Dodgers
1930 Frankford Yellowjackets
1930–31 Providence Steamrollers

McBRIDE, JOHN—Back—Syracuse
1925–28 New York Giants
1929 Providence Steamrollers
1930–32 Brooklyn Dodgers
1932–33 New York Giants
1935 Chicago Cardinals

**McCAIN, ROBERT—End—
Mississippi**
1946 Brooklyn Dodgers

**McCAFFERTY, DONALD—End—
Ohio State**
1946 New York Giants

**McCAFFRAY, ARTHUR—Tackle—
College of Pacific**
1946 Pittsburgh Steelers

**McCANN, ERNEST—Tackle—Penn
State**
1926 Hartford

**McCARTHY, HOWARD—Back—
Notre Dame**
1924–25 Rock Island Independents
1927 Duluth Eskimos

McCARTHY, JAMES—End—Illinois
1944 Card-Pitt
1946–47 Brooklyn Dodgers
1948 Chicago Rockets
1949 Chicago Hornets

McCAW, WILLIAM—End—Indiana
1923 Racine Legion
1926 Louisville Colonels
       Died in Service. Capt. of Infantry
       assigned to ROTC at Indiana

**McCHESNEY, ROBERT—End—
Hardin-Simmons**
1950 Philadelphia Eagles
1950–51 New York Giants

**McCHESNEY, ROBERT—End—
UCLA**
1936 Boston Redskins
1937–43 Washington Redskins

McCLAIN, CLINTON—Back—SMU
1940–41 New York Giants

McCLAIN, MAYES—Guard—Iowa
1928 New York Yankees
1930–31 Portsmouth Spartans
1931 Staten Island Stapletons

**McCLURE, ROBERT—Guard—
Nevada**
1947–48 Boston Yanks

**McCOLLUM, HARLEY—Tackle—
Tulane**
1946 New York Yankees
1947 Chicago Rockets

**McCONNELL, F. C.—Guard—Georgia
Tech.**
1927 Buffalo Bisons

**McCORMACK, MICHAEL—Tackle—
Kansas**
1951 New York Yanks

**McCORMICK, ELMER—Guard—
Canisius**
1923–25 Buffalo Bisons
1925 Frankford Yellowjackets
1926 Hartford

**McCORMICK, FELIX—Back—
Bucknell**
1929 Orange
1930 Newark

**McCORMICK, FRANK—Back—
S. Dakota**
1920 Akron Steels
1923 Buffalo All Americans
1924–25 Buffalo Bisons

**McCORMICK, LEONARD—Center—
Baylor**
1948 Baltimore Colts

**McCORMICK, WALTER—Center—
Southern California**
1948 San Francisco 49ers

McCOY, JOEL—Back—Alabama
1946 Detroit Lions

McCRARY, HURDIS—Back—Georgia
1929–33 Green Bay Packers

**McCRILLIS, EDWARD—Guard—
Brown**
1929 Boston Braves

**McCULLOUGH, HAROLD—Back—
Cornell**
1942 Brooklyn Dodgers

**McCULLOUGH, HUGH—Back—
Oklahoma**
1939 Pittsburgh Steelers
1940–41 Chicago Cardinals
1943 Phil-Pitt
1945 Boston Yanks

**McCULLOCK, J??—Guard—Holy
Cross**
1926 Brooklyn Dodgers

**McDADE, WILLIAM—Center—
Portland**
1938 Pittsburgh Pirates

**McDERMOTT, LLOYD—Tackle—
Kentucky**
1950 Detroit Lions
1950–51 Chicago Cardinals

McDONALD, DONALD—End—
Oklahoma
1940 Philadelphia Eagles
1944–46 Philadelphia Eagles
1948 New York Yankees

McDONALD, EDWARD—Back—
Duquesne
1936 Pittsburgh Pirates

McDONALD, JAMES—Back—Ohio
State
1938–39 Detroit Lions

McDONALD, JOHN—Back—
Creighton
1924 Duluth Kelleys
1925 Hammond Pros
1926 Detroit Panthers
1926 Chicago Cardinals
1928–30 Chicago Cardinals
1931 Frankford Yellowjackets

McDONALD, LESTER—End—
Nebraska
1937–39 Chicago Bears
1940 Philadelphia Eagles

McDONALD, WALTER—Center—
Utah
1935 Brooklyn Dodgers

McDONALD, WALTER—Back—
Tulane
1946 Miami Seahawks
1946–48 Brooklyn Dodgers
1949 Chicago Hornets

McDONOUGH, COLEY—Back—
Dayton
1939 Chicago Cardinals
1939 Cleveland Rams
1940 Pittsburgh Steelers
1940–41 Cleveland Rams
1944 Card-Pitt

McDONOUGH, PAUL—End—Utah
1938 Pittsburgh Pirates
1939–40 Cleveland Rams
1941 Pittsburgh Steelers

McDONOUGH, ROBERT—Guard—
Duke
1946 Philadelphia Eagles

McDOUGAL, ROBERT—Back—
Miami (Fla.)
1947 Green Bay Packers

McDOWELL, JAY—End—
Washington
1946–51 Philadelphia Eagles

McELMORE, ?—Back—Haskell
1924 Kansas City Cowboys

McELWAIN, WILLIAM—Back—
Northwestern
1924 Chicago Cardinals
1926 Chicago Cardinals

McENULTY, DOUGLAS—Back—
Wichita
1942–44 Chicago Bears

McFADDEN, BANKS—Back—
Clemson
1940 Brooklyn Dodgers

McGARRY, BERNARD—Guard—
Utah
1939–42 Cleveland Rams

McGAW, WALTER—Guard—Beloit
1926 Green Bay Packers

McGEARY, CLARENCE—Tackle—
North Dakota
1950 Green Bay Packers

McGEE, EDWARD—Tackle—Temple
1940 New York Giants
1945–46 Boston Yanks

McGEE, HOWARD—Guard—Kansas
State
1927 Cleveland Indians
1929 Staten Island Stapletons
1930 Newark
1932 Staten Island Stapletons

McGIBBONY, CHARLES—Back—
Arkansas State
1944 Brooklyn Tigers

McGILBRA, SANFORD—Tackle—
Redlands
1926 Buffalo Bisons

McGINLEY, EDWARD—Tackle—
Pennsylvania
1925 New York Giants

McGINNIS, JAMES—End—Marquette
1923–24 Milwaukee Badgers

McGIRL, LEONARD—Guard—
Missouri
1931–32 Frankford Yellowjackets
1933 Chicago Cardinals
1934 St. Louis Gunners

McGLONE, JOSEPH—Back—Harvard
1926 Providence Steamrollers

McGRATH, RICHARD—End—Holy
Cross
1922 Louisville Colonels
1927 Frankford Yellowjackets
1928 New York Yankees

McGRAW, THURMAN—Tackle—
Colorado A & M
1950–51 Detroit Lions

McGREGORY, ??—Back—??
1923   Buffalo All Americans

McGUIRK, WARREN—Tackle—
Boston College
1929–30   Providence Steamrollers

McHUGH, PAT—Back—Georgia Tech.
1947–51   Philadelphia Eagles

McILWAIN, WALTER—Back—
Illinois
1926   Racine Legion

McINERNEY, ARNOLD—Center—
Notre Dame
1920–27   Chicago Cardinals

McINTOSH, DANIEL—Back—Rhode
Island State
1925   Providence Steamrollers

McKALLIP, WILLIAM—End—
Oregon State
1931–32   Portsmouth Spartans
1934   Detroit Lions
1936   Detroit Lions

McKAY, REGIS—Back—Texas
1938   Pittsburgh Pirates
1939   Pittsburgh Steelers

McKAY, ROY—Back—Texas
1945   Green Bay Packers—K
1946   Green Bay Packers—K
1947   Green Bay Packers

McKEE, PAUL—End—Syracuse
1947–48   Washington Redskins

McKETES, ??—Back—??
1926   Hammond Pros

McLAUGHLIN, ??—Back—Villanova
1934   St. Louis Gunners

McLAUGHLIN, LEE—Guard—
Virginia
1941   Green Bay Packers

McLAUGHLIN, LEON—Center—
UCLA
1951   Los Angeles Rams

McLAUGHRY, JOHN—Back—Brown
1940   New York Giants

McLEAN, RAYMOND—Back—None
1921   Green Bay Packers

McLEAN, RAYMOND—Back—St.
Anselm's
1940–47   Chicago Bears

McLEOD, ARTHUR—Center—St.
Louis Univ.
1934   St. Louis Gunners

McLEOD, ROBERT—Back—
Dartmouth
1939   Chicago Bears

McMICHAELS, JOHN—Back—
Birmingham Southern
1944   Brooklyn Tigers

McMILLEN, JAMES—Guard—
Illinois
1923   Milwaukee Badgers
1923   Cleveland Indians
1924–28   Chicago Bears
1930–31   Chicago Bears
1931   Cleveland Indians
1935   Chicago Bears

McMILLIN, ALVIN—Back—Centre
1923   Milwaukee Badgers

McMULLEN, DANIEL—Guard—
Nebraska
1929   New York Giants

McMURDO, JAMES—Tackle—
Pittsburgh
1932   Boston Braves
1933   Boston Redskins
1934–37   Philadelphia Eagles

McNALLY, FRANK—Center—St.
Mary's
1931–34   Chicago Cardinals

McNALLY, JOHN "BLOOD"—
Back—St. John (Minn.)
1925–26   Milwaukee Badgers
1926   Duluth Eskimos
1927   Milwaukee Badgers
1927   Duluth Eskimos
1928   Pottsville Maroons
1928–36   Green Bay Packers
1937–38   Pittsburgh Pirates—Player-coach
1939   Pittsburgh Steelers—Player-coach

McNAMARA, EDMUND—Tackle—
Holy Cross
1945   Pittsburgh Steelers

McNAMARA, THOMAS—Guard—
Detroit
1923   Toledo Maroons
1925–26   Detroit Panthers

McNEIL, FRANCIS—End—
Washington & Jefferson
1932   Brooklyn Dodgers

McNELLIS, WILLIAM—Back—St.
Thomas
1927   Duluth Eskimos

McNULTY, PAUL—Back—Notre
Dame
1924–25   Chicago Cardinals

McPEAK, WILLIAM—End—
Pittsburgh
1949–51 Pittsburgh Steelers

McPHAIL, HAROLD—Back—West
Point
1934–35 Boston Redskins

McPHERSON, FORREST—Tackle—
Nebraska
1935 Chicago Bears
1935–37 Philadelphia Eagles
1943–45 Green Bay Packers

McQUADE, JOHN—Back—
Georgetown
1922 Canton Bulldogs

McQUARY, JOHN—Back—
California
1946 Los Angeles Dons

McRAE, STANLEY—Back—
Minnesota
1946 Washington Redskins

McRAVEN, WILLIAM—Back—
Murray State Teachers
1939 Cleveland Rams

McROBERTS, ??—Center—??
1925–26 Canton Bulldogs

McSHEA, ??—Guard—??
1923 Rochester Kodaks

McWHERTER, KYLE—Back—None
1920 Chicago Bears (Staleys)

McWILLIAMS, THOMAS—Back—
Mississippi State
1949 Los Angeles Rams
1950 Pittsburgh Steelers

McWILLIAMS, WILLIAM—Back—
Jordan College
1934 Detroit Lions

* * *

MAACK, HERBERT—Tackle—
Columbia
1946 Brooklyn Dodgers

MACEAU, MELVIN—Guard—
Marquette
1946–48 Cleveland Browns

MACIOSZCZYK, ARTHUR—Back—
Western Michigan
1944 Philadelphia Eagles
1947 Philadelphia Eagles
1948 Washington Redskins

MACKENROTH, JOHN—Center—
North Dakota
1938 Detroit Lions

MACKORELL, JOHN—Back—
Davidson
1935 New York Giants

MACKRIDES, WILLIAM—Back—
Nevada
1947–51 Philadelphia Eagles

MADAR, ELMER—End—Michigan
1947 Baltimore Colts

MADARIK, ELMER—Back—Detroit
1945–47 Detroit Lions
1948 Washington Redskins

MADDEN, LLOYD—Back—Colorado
Mines
1940 Chicago Cardinals

MADDOCK, ROBERT—Guard—
Notre Dame
1942 Chicago Cardinals
1946 Chicago Cardinals

MADDOX, GEORGE—Tackle—
Kansas State
1935 Green Bay Packers

MADIGAN, FRANK—Center—St.
Mary's (Minn.)
1922 Minneapolis Marines
1923 Duluth Kelleys
1924 Minneapolis Marines

MAEDA, CHESTER—Back—Colorado
State
1945 Chicago Cardinals

MAEDER, ALBERT—Tackle—
Minnesota
1929 Minneapolis Redjackets

MAGEE, JAMES—Center—
Villanova
1945–46 Boston Yanks

MAGEE, JOHN—Guard—Rice
1948–51 Philadelphia Eagles

MAGGIOLO, ACHILLE—Back—
Illinois
1948 Buffalo Bills
1949 Detroit Lions
1950 Baltimore Colts

MAGLIOLO, JOSEPH—Back—Texas
1948 New York Yankees

MAGNANI, DANTE—Back—St.
Mary's (Cal.)
1940–42 Cleveland Rams
1942–43 Chicago Bears
1946 Chicago Bears
1947–48 Los Angeles Rams
1949 Chicago Bears
1950 Detroit Lions

MAGNER, JAMES—Back—North Carolina
1931 Frankford Yellowjackets

MAGNUSSON, GLEN—Center—Northwestern
1925 Hammond Pros

MAGULICK, GEORGE—Back—St. Francis
1944 Card-Pitt

MAHAN, EDWARD—Back—Harvard
1929 Buffalo Bisons
1930 Brooklyn Dodgers

MAHAN, WALTER—Guard—West Virginia
1926 Frankford Yellowjackets

MAHER, FRANCIS—Back—Toledo
1938 Pittsburgh Pirates
1940 Pittsburgh Steelers
1941 Cleveland Rams

MAHONEY, ROGER—Back—Creighton
1923 Buffalo All Americans
1925-27 Chicago Cardinals
1928-30 Frankford Yellowjackets
1931 Chicago Cardinals

MAHRT, LOUIS—Back—Dayton
1926-27 Dayton Triangles

MAHRT, W??—Back—West Virginia
1920-25 Dayton Triangles

MAIKKULA, KENNETH—End—Connecticut
1942 New York Giants

MAILLARD, RALPH—Tackle—Creighton
1929 Chicago Bears

MAINES, THOMAS—Back—Syracuse
1946 Brooklyn Dodgers

MALCOLM, ??—Tackle—??
1926 Frankford Yellowjackets

MALCOLM, HARRY—Tackle—Washington & Jefferson
1929 Frankford Yellowjackets

MALEY, HOWARD—Back—SMU
1946-47 Boston Yanks

MALINOWSKI, EUGENE—Back—Detroit
1948 Boston Yanks

MALONE, CHARLES—End—Texas A & M
1933 Chicago Bears
1934-36 Boston Redskins
1937-40 Washington Redskins

MALONE, GROVER—Back—Notre Dame
1921 Green Bay Packers
1921 Rock Island Independents
1923 Akron Steels

MALONEY, GERALD—End—Dartmouth
1925 Providence Steamrollers
1927 New York Yankees
1929 Boston Braves

MALONEY, NORMAN—End—Purdue
1942 Washington Redskins
1948-49 San Francisco 49ers

MALLOUF, RAYMOND—Back—SMU
1941 Chicago Cardinals
1946-48 Chicago Cardinals
1949 New York Giants

MALLOY, LESTER—Back—Loyola
1931-33 Chicago Cardinals

MANCHA, VAUGHN—Center—Alabama
1948 Boston Yanks

MANDARION, MICHAEL—Center—LaSalle
1944-45 Philadelphia Eagles

MANDERS, CLARENCE—Back—Drake
1939-40 Brooklyn Dodgers
1941 Brooklyn Dodgers—G
1942-44 Brooklyn Dodgers
1945 Boston Yanks
1946 New York Yankees
1947 Buffalo Bills

MANDERS, JOHN—Back—Minnesota
1933 Chicago Bears
1934 Chicago Bears—S
1935 Chicago Bears
1936 Chicago Bears—F (7) (Tie with A. Niccolai)
1937 Chicago Bears—S—F (8)
1938-40 Chicago Bears

MANFRED, ANTHONY—Back—Holy Cross
1930 Newark

MANIACI, JOSEPH—Back—Fordham
1936-38 Brooklyn Dodgers
1939-40 Chicago Bears
1941 Cleveland Rams

MANION, JAMES—Guard—St. Thomas (Minn.)
1926-27 Duluth Eskimos

MANKAT, CARL—Guard—Colgate
1928-29 Dayton Triangles

MANLEY, LEON—Guard—Oklahoma
1950–51 Green Bay Packers

MANN, ROBERT—End—Michigan
1948–49 Detroit Lions
1950–51 Green Bay Packers

MANNING, JAMES—Back—Fordham
1926 Hartford

MANSFIELD, ??—??—??
1921 Rock Island Independents

MANSKE, EDWARD—End—Northwestern
1935 Chicago Bears
1935–36 Philadelphia Eagles
1937 Chicago Bears
1939–40 Chicago Bears

MANTELL, JOSEPH—Guard—Canisius
1924 Columbus Tigers

MANTON, TALDON—Back—TCU
1936–38 New York Giants
1938 Washington Redskins
1943 Brooklyn Dodgers

MANZINI, BAPTISTE—Center—St. Vincent's
1944–45 Philadelphia Eagles
1948 Philadelphia Eagles

MANZO, JOSEPH—Tackle—Boston College
1945 Detroit Lions

MAPLE, HOWARD—Back—Oregon State
1930 Chicago Cardinals
1934 Cincinnati Reds

MARAS, JOSEPH—Center—Duquesne
1938 Pittsburgh Pirates
1939–40 Pittsburgh Steelers

MARCHI, BASILIO—Center—New York Univ.
1934 Pittsburgh Pirates
1941–42 Philadelphia Eagles

MARCOLINI, HUGO—Back—St. Bonaventure
1948 Brooklyn Dodgers

MARCUS, ALEXANDER—End—Temple
1933 Philadelphia Eagles

MARCUS, PETER—End—Kentucky
1944 Washington Redskins

MAREFOS, ANDREW—Back—St. Mary's (Cal.)
1940–41 New York Giants
1946 Los Angeles Dons

MAREK, JOSEPH—Back—Texas A & M
1943 Brooklyn Dodgers

MARELLI, RAY—Guard—Notre Dame
1928 Chicago Cardinals

MARGARITA, HENRY—Back—Brown
1944–46 Chicago Bears

MARGUCCI, JOSEPH—Back—Southern California
1947–48 Detroit Lions

MARINO, VICTOR—Guard—Ohio State
1947 Baltimore Colts

MARION, PHILIP—Back—Michigan
1925–26 Detroit Panthers

MARK, LOUIS—End—South Carolina
1938–40 Brooklyn Dodgers
1945 Boston Yanks

MARKER, CLIFFORD—Back—Washington State
1926 Canton Bulldogs
1927 Frankford Yellowjackets
1934 Pittsburgh Pirates

MARKOV, VICTOR—Tackle—Washington
1938 Cleveland Rams

MARKS, LAWRENCE—Back—Indiana
1927 New York Yankees
1928 Green Bay Packers

MARONE, JOHN—Guard—Manhattan
1943 New York Giants

MARONIC, DUSAN—Guard—None
1944 Philadelphia Eagles
1945 Pittsburgh Steelers
1946 Chicago Bears
1945–50 Philadelphia Eagles
1951 New York Giants

MARONIC, STEPHEN—Tackle—North Carolina
1939–40 Detroit Lions

MAROTTI, LOUIS—Guard—Toledo
1943 Chicago Cardinals
1944 Card-Pitt
1945 Chicago Cardinals

MARSH, HOWARD—Back—Oklahoma
1921 Canton Bulldogs

MARSH, RICHARD—Guard—Oklahoma
1933 New York Giants

MARSHALL, CLOYD—End—New York Univ.
1925   Duluth Kelleys
1931–32   Staten Island Stapletons

MARSTERS, ALTON—Back—Dartmouth
1929   Boston Braves

MARTELL, HERMAN—End—None
1921   Green Bay Packers

MARTIN, CALEB—Tackle—Louisiana Tech.
1947   Chicago Cardinals

MARTIN, FRANK—Back—Alabama
1941   Chicago Bears
1943   Brooklyn Dodgers
1944   Brooklyn Tigers
1945   New York Giants
1945   Boston Yanks

MARTIN, HERSCHEL—Back—Missouri
1929   Staten Island Stapletons
1930   Newark
1932   Chicago Cardinals

MARTIN, JAMES—End—Notre Dame
1950   Cleveland Browns
1951   Detroit Lions

MARTIN, JOHN (PEPPER)—Kicker—None
1948   Brooklyn Dodgers

MARTIN, JOHN—Back—Oklahoma
1941–43   Chicago Cardinals
1944   Card-Pitt
1944–45   Boston Yanks

MARTIN, JOHN—Center—Navy
1947–49   Los Angeles Rams

MARTIN, VERNON—Back—Texas
1942   Pittsburgh Steelers
1945   New York Giants

MARTINEAU, EARL—Back—Minnesota
1923   Buffalo All Americans
1924–25   Rochester Jeffersons

MARTINELLI, JAMES—Center—Scranton
1946   Buffalo Bisons

MARTINKOVIC, JOHN—End—Xavier
1951   Green Bay Packers

MARTINOVICH, PHILIP—Guard—College of Pacific
1939   Detroit Lions
1940   Chicago Bears
1946–47   Brooklyn Dodgers

MASINI, LEONARD—Back—Fresno State
1947–48   San Francisco 49ers
1948   Los Angeles Dons

MASKAS, JOHN—Guard—Virginia Polytech
1947   Buffalo Bills
1949   Buffalo Bills

MASON, JOEL—End—Western Michigan
1939   Chicago Cardinals
1941–45   Green Bay Packers

MASON, SAMUEL—Back—Virginia Military Inst.
1922   Minneapolis Marines
1925   Milwaukee Badgers

MASTERS, ROBERT—Back—Baylor
1935–38   Philadelphia Eagles
1939   Pittsburgh Steelers
1941–42   Philadelphia Eagles
1942   Washington Redskins
1943   Phil-Pitt
1943–44   Chicago Bears

MASTERS, WALTER—Back—Pennsylvania
1942–43   Chicago Cardinals
1944   Card-Pitt

MASTERSON, BERNARD—Back—Nebraska
1934–40   Chicago Bears

MASTERSON, FOREST—Center—Iowa
1945   Chicago Bears

MASTERSON, ROBERT—End—Miami
1938–43   Washington Redskins
1944   Brooklyn Tigers
1945   Boston Yanks
1946   New York Yankees

MASTRANGELO, JOHN—Guard—Notre Dame
1947–48   Pittsburgh Steelers
1949   New York Yankees
1950   New York Giants

MATESIC, EDWARD—Back—Pittsburgh
1934–35   Philadelphia Eagles
1936   Pittsburgh Pirates

MATHESON, JOHN—End—Western Michigan
1943–46   Detroit Lions
1947   Chicago Bears

MATHESON, RILEY—Guard—Texas Mines
1939–42 Cleveland Rams
1943 Detroit Lions
1944–45 Cleveland Rams
1946–47 Los Angeles Rams
1948 San Francisco 49ers

MATHEWS, B. O.—End—Navy
1926 Racine Legion

MATHEWS, NED—Back—UCLA
1940–43 Detroit Lions
1945 Boston Yanks
1946 Chicago Rockets
1946–47 San Francisco 49ers

MATHEWS, RAYMOND—Back—Clemson
1951 Pittsburgh Steelers

MATHYS, CHARLES—Back—Indiana
1922–26 Green Bay Packers

MATISI, JOHN—Tackle—Duquesne
1938 Detroit Lions
1943 Brooklyn Dodgers
1946 Buffalo Bisons

MATSU, ARTHUR—Back—William & Mary
1928 Dayton Triangles

MATTEO, FRANCIS—Tackle—Syracuse
1922–23 Rochester Kodaks
1924–25 Rochester Jeffersons

MATTHEWS, CLAY—Tackle—Georgia Tech.
1950 San Francisco 49ers

MATTIFORD, JOHN—Guard—Marshall
1941 Detroit Lions

MATTINGLY, FRANCIS—Guard—Purdue
1947 Chicago Rockets

MATTIOLI, FRANCIS—Guard—Pittsburgh
1946 Pittsburgh Steelers

MATTOS, HARRY—Back—St. Mary's (Cal.)
1936 Green Bay Packers
1937 Cleveland Rams

MATTOX, MARVIN—Back—Washington & Lee
1923 Milwaukee Badgers

MATUZA, ALBERT—Center—Georgetown
1940–43 Chicago Bears
1946 Chicago Bears

MAUL, "TOUGHY"—Back—California
1926 Los Angeles

MAULDIN, STANLEY—Tackle—Texas
1946–48 Chicago Cardinals

MAVES, EARL—Back—Wisconsin
1948 Detroit Lions
1948 Baltimore Colts

MAXWELL, JOSEPH—End—Notre Dame
1927–29 Frankford Yellowjackets

MAY, JOHN—Center—Centenary
1938 Cleveland Rams

MAY, WILLIAM—Back—LSU
1937–38 Chicago Cardinals

MAYER, FRANK—Guard—Notre Dame
1927 Green Bay Packers
1927 Pottsville Maroons

MAYHEW, HAYDEN—Guard—Texas Mines
1936–38 Pittsburgh Pirates

MAYL, EUGENE—End—Notre Dame
1925 Dayton Triangles

MAYNARD, LESTER—Back—Rider
1932 Staten Island Stapletons
1933 Philadelphia Eagles

MAYNAUGH, ROLAND—Guard—St. Thomas
1924 Minneapolis Marines

MAYNE, LEWIS—Back—Texas
1946 Brooklyn Dodgers
1947 Cleveland Browns
1948 Baltimore Colts

MAZNICKI, FRANK—Back—Boston College
1941–42 Chicago Bears
1946 Chicago Bears
1947 Boston Yanks

MAZZA, VINCENT—End—Trott Vocational
1945–46 Detroit Lions
1947–49 Buffalo Bills

MEAD, JOHN—End—Wisconsin
1946–47 New York Giants

MEADE, JAMES—Back—Maryland
1939–40 Washington Redskins

MEADOWS, ERIC—Back—Pittsburgh
1923 Milwaukee Badgers

MECHAM, CURTIS—Back—Oregon
1942 Brooklyn Dodgers

**MEEKER, HERBERT—Back—
Washington State**
1930–31   Providence Steamrollers

**MEEKS, BRYANT—Center—South
Carolina**
1947–48   Pittsburgh Steelers

MEEKS, EDWARD—Back—Louisville
1922   Louisville Colonels

MEESE, WARD—End—Wabash
1922   Milwaukee Badgers
1923   St. Louis Browns
1925   Hammond Pros

**MEHELICH, CHARLES—End—
Duquesne**
1946–51   Pittsburgh Steelers

**MEHELICH,   ??—Guard—St.   Mary's
(Minn.)**
1929   Minneapolis Redjackets

**MEHRE, HENRY—Center—Notre
Dame**
1923–24   Minneapolis Marines

**MEHRINGER, PETER—Tackle—
Kansas**
1934–36   Chicago Cardinals

**MENIHARDT, GEORGE—Guard—
St. Louis Univ.**
1923   St. Louis Browns

**MEISENHEIMER, DARRELL—
Back—Oklahoma A & M**
1951   New York Yanks

MELLO, JAMES—Back—Notre Dame
1947   Boston Yanks
1948   Chicago Rockets
1948   Los Angeles Rams
1949   Detroit Lions

MELLUS, JOHN—Tackle—Villanova
1938–41   New York Giants
1946   San Francisco 49ers
1947–49   Baltimore Colts

MENEFEE, VICTOR—End—None
1921   Rock Island Independents

**MERCER, JAMES—Back—Oregon
State**
1942   New York Giants

**MERCER, KENNETH—Back—
Simpson**
1927–29   Frankford Yellowjackets

**MEREDITH, RUSSELL—Guard—
West Virginia**
1925   Cleveland Indians

**MERGENTHAL, ARTHUR—
Guard—Notre Dame**
1945   Cleveland Rams
1946   Los Angeles Rams

MERKEL, MONTE—Guard—Kansas
1942–43   Chicago Bears

**MERKLE, EDWARD—Guard—
Oklahoma A & M**
1943   Chicago Bears
1944   Washington Redskins

**MERKOVSKY, ALBERT—Tackle—
Pittsburgh**
1944   Card-Pitt
1945–46   Pittsburgh Steelers

**MERLIN, EDWARD—Guard—
Vanderbilt**
1938–39   Brooklyn Dodgers

**MERRILL, WALTER—Tackle—
Alabama**
1940–42   Brooklyn Dodgers

**MERRILAT, LOUIS—End—
West Point**
1925   Canton Bulldogs

MERTES, BERNARD—Back—Iowa
1945   Chicago Cardinals
1946   Los Angeles Dons
1947–49   Baltimore Colts

**MESAK, RICHARD—Tackle—
St. Mary's (Cal.)**
1945   Detroit Lions

**METHOD, RUSSELL—Back—North
Dakota**
1923–25   Duluth Kelleys
1926–27   Duluth Eskimos
1928   Chicago Cardinals

METRICK, ?? —Back— ??
1935   Brooklyn Dodgers

**METZGER, LOUIS—Back—
Georgetown**
1926   Louisville Colonels

**MEYER, FREDERICK—End—
Stanford**
1942   Philadelphia Eagles
1945   Philadelphia Eagles

**MEYER, GILBERT—End—Wake
Forest**
1947   Baltimore Colts

**MICHAELS, ALTON—Back—
Heidelberg**
1923–24   Akron Steels
1925   Cleveland Indians

MICHAELS, EDWARD—Guard—
Villanova
1936 Chicago Bears
1937 Washington Redskins
1943 Phil-Pitt
1944-46 Philadelphia Eagles

MICHAELS, WALTER—Guard—
Washington & Lee
1951 Green Bay Packers

MICHALSKE, AUGUST—Guard—
Penn State
1927-28 New York Yankees
1929-35 Green Bay Packers
1937 Green Bay Packers

MICKA, MICHAEL—Back—Colgate
1944-45 Washington Redskins
1945-48 Boston Yanks

MIDLER, LOUIS—Guard—
Northwestern
1939 Pittsburgh Steelers
1940 Green Bay Packers

MIELZINER, SAUL—Center—
Carnegie Tech.
1929-30 New York Giants
1931-34 Brooklyn Dodgers

MIESZKOWSKI, EDWARD—Tackle—
Notre Dame
1946-47 Brooklyn Dodgers

MIHAJLOVICH, LOUIS—End—
Minnesota
1948 Los Angeles Dons

MIHAL, JOSEPH—Tackle—Purdue
1940-41 Chicago Bears
1946 Los Angeles Dons
1947 Chicago Rockets

MIKE, ROBERT—Tackle—UCLA
1948-49 San Francisco 49ers

MIKLICH, WILLIAM—Back—Idaho
1947-48 New York Giants
1948 Detroit Lions

MIKULA, THOMAS—Back—William
& Mary
1948 Brooklyn Dodgers

MIKULAK, MICHAEL—Back—
Oregon
1934-36 Chicago Cardinals

MILAM, BARNES—Guard—Austin
1934 Philadelphia Eagles

MILAN, JOSEPH—Back—Phillips
1925 Kansas City Cowboys

MILANO, ARCH—End—St. Francis
1945 Detroit Lions

MILLER, ALFRED—Back—Harvard
1929 Boston Braves
1930 Minneapolis Redjackets

MILLER, BEN—Center—Tennessee
1946 Chicago Rockets

MILLER, CHARLES—Center—
Purdue
1932-37 Chicago Bears
1938 Green Bay Packers

MILLER, DONALD—Back—
Wisconsin
1941 Green Bay Packers

MILLER, HENRY—End—Penn State
1920-21 Buffalo All Americans
1922-23 Racine Legion
1925 Milwaukee Badgers

MILLER, JAMES—Tackle—New
York Univ.
1929-30 Staten Island Stapletons
1930 Brooklyn Dodgers
1931 Staten Island Stapletons

MILLER, JOSEPH—Back—
Pennsylvania
1923 Frankford Yellowjackets

MILLER, MILFORD—Guard—
Chaldron Normal
1932 Chicago Bears
1935 Chicago Bears
1936-37 Chicago Cardinals

MILLER, PAUL—Back—South
Dakota
1936-38 Green Bay Packers
1939-40 New York Giants

MILLER, RALPH—Tackle—Rice
1937-38 Cleveland Rams

MILLER, THOMAS—End—Hampton-
Sydney
1942 Philadelphia Eagles
1943 Phil-Pitt
1944 Philadelphia Eagles
1945 Washington Redskins
1946 Green Bay Packers

MILLMAN, ROBERT—Back—
Lafayette
1926-27 Pottsville Maroons

MILLNER, WAYNE—End—Notre
Dame
1936 Boston Redskins
1937-41 Washington Redskins
1945 Washington Redskins
1951-52 Philadelphia Eagles—Head Coach

MILLS, S??—Center—??
1922-25 Akron Steels

MILLS, THOMAS—Back—Penn State
1922-23 Green Bay Packers

MILNER, WILLIAM—Guard—Duke
1947–49 Chicago Bears
1950 New York Giants

MILSTEAD, CENTURY—Tackle—Yale
1925 New York Giants
1927–28 New York Giants

MILTON, THOMAS—End—Lake Forrest
1923 St. Louis Browns
1924 Kansas City Cowboys
1924 Green Bay Packers

MINARIK, HENRY—End—Michigan State
1951 Pittsburgh Steelers

MINICK, PAUL—Guard—Iowa
1927 Buffalo Bisons
1928–29 Green Bay Packers

MININI, FRANK—Back—San Jose State
1947–49 Chicago Bears
1949 Pittsburgh Steelers

MINISI, ANTHONY—Back—Pennsylvania
1948 New York Giants

MINTUN, JOHN—Center—None
1920 Chicago Bears (Staleys)
1923–24 Racine Legion
1925 Kansas City Cowboys
1926 Racine Legion

MISHEL, DAVID—Back—Brown
1927 Providence Steamrollers
1931 Cleveland Indians

MITCHELL, ??—Tackle—Thiel
1924 Buffalo Bisons

MITCHELL, CHARLES—Back—Tulsa
1945 Chicago Bears
1946 Green Bay Packers

MITCHELL, FONDREN—Back—Florida
1946 Miami Seahawks

MITCHELL, GRANVILLE—End—David & Elkins
1931–33 Portsmouth Spartans
1934–35 Detroit Lions
1935–36 New York Giants
1937 Brooklyn Dodgers

MITCHELL, PAUL—Tackle—Minnesota
1946–48 Los Angeles Dons
1948–49 New York Yankees
1950–51 New York Yanks

MITCHELL, ROBERT—Back—Stanford
1946–48 Los Angeles Dons

MITCHELL, THEODORE—Center—Bucknell
1929 Orange
1930 Newark

MITRICK, FRANK—Tackle—Oglethorpe
1945 Detroit Lions

MIZELL, WARNER—Back—Georgia Tech.
1931 Brooklyn Dodgers

MOAN, EMMETT—Back—West Virginia
1937 Cleveland Rams

MOBLEY, RUDOLPH—Back—Hardin-Simmons
1947 Baltimore Colts

MOE, HAROLD—Back—Oregon State
1933 Chicago Cardinals

MOHARDT, JOHN—Back—Notre Dame
1922–23 Chicago Cardinals
1924 Racine Legion
1925 Chicago Bears

MOHS, ??—End—??
1923–24 Minneapolis Marines

MOLENDA, JOHN—Back—Michigan
1927–28 New York Yankees
1929–32 Green Bay Packers
1932–35 New York Giants

MOLESWORTH, KEITH—Back—Monmouth
1931–37 Chicago Bears

MOLINET, LOUIS—Back—Cornell
1927 Frankford Yellowjackets

MOMSEN, ANTHONY—Center—Michigan
1951 Pittsburgh Steelers

MOMSEN, ROBERT—Guard—Ohio State
1951 Detroit Lions

MONACHINO, JAMES—Back—California
1951 San Francisco 49ers

MONACO, RAYMOND—Guard—Holy Cross
1944 Washington Redskins
1945 Cleveland Rams

MONAHAN, REGIS—Guard—Ohio State
1935–38 Detroit Lions
1939 Chicago Cardinals

MONFORT, AVERY—Back—New Mexico
1941 Chicago Cardinals

MONNETT, ROBERT—Back—Michigan State
1933–38 Green Bay Packers

MONT, THOMAS—Back—Maryland
1947–49 Washington Redskins

MONTGOMERY, CLIFFORD—Back—Columbia
1934 Brooklyn Dodgers

MONTGOMERY, JAMES—Tackle—Texas A & M
1946 Chicago Cardinals
1946 Detroit Lions

MONTGOMERY, RALPH—Tackle—Centre College
1923 Chicago Cardinals
1927 Frankford Yellowjackets

MONTGOMERY, WILLIAM—Tackle—St. Louis Univ.
1934 St. Louis Gunners

MOODY, WILKIE—Back—Denison
1924–25 Columbus Tigers

MOONEY, BOW TIPP—Back—Abline Christian
1944–46 Chicago Bears

MOONEY, GEORGE—Back—None
1922–24 Milwaukee Badgers

MOONEY, JAMES—End—Georgia
1930 Newark
1930–31 Brooklyn Dodgers
1933–34 Cincinnati Reds
1935 Chicago Cardinals
1935 Chicago Bears
        Killed by sniper's bullet in France, Aug. 12, 1944. Private, U.S. Army.

MOONEY, TEX—Southern California
1943 Brooklyn Dodgers

MOORE, ALLEN—Back—Loyola (Chicago)
1932 Chicago Bears
1932 Chicago Cardinals
1933 Pittsburgh Pirates
1934 Cincinnati Reds

MOORE, ALLEN—End—Texas A & M
1939 Green Bay Packers

MOORE, GEORGE—Center—Oregon
1938 Brooklyn Dodgers
1940 New York Giants

MOORE, PAUL—Back—Presbyterian
1940 Detroit Lions

MOORE, WALTER—Back—Lafayette
1927 Pottsville Maroons

MOORE, WILBUR—Back—Minnesota
1939–47 Washington Redskins

MOORE, WILLIAM—Back—Loyola (New Orleans)
1939–41 Detroit Lions

MOORE, WILLIAM—Guard—Penn State
1947–49 Pittsburgh Steelers

MORALES, GONZALES—Back—St. Mary's (Cal.)
1947–48 Pittsburgh Steelers

MORAN, DALE—Back—Carnegie Tech.
1926–27 Frankford Yellowjackets
1927 Chicago Cardinals
1928 Pottsville Maroons
1929–34 New York Giants

MORAN, JAMES—Guard—Holy Cross
1935–36 Boston Redskins

MORAN, PETER—Back—Grinnell
1925–27 Frankford Yellowjackets

MORELLI, JOHN—Guard—Georgetown
1944–45 Boston Yanks

MORGAN, ??—Back—??
1925 Kansas City Cowboys

MORGAN, BOYD—Back—Southern California
1939–40 Washington Redskins

MORGAN, JOSEPH—Tackle—Mississippi Southern
1949 San Francisco 49ers

MORGAN, WILLIAM—Tackle—Oregon
1933–36 New York Giants

MORLOCK, JOHN—Back—Marshall
1940 Detroit Lions

MORRIS, FRANCIS—Back—Boston Univ.
1942 Chicago Bears

MORRIS, GEORGE—Back—Baldwin-Wallace
1941–42 Cleveland Rams

MORRIS, GLEN—End—Colorado State
1940 Detroit Lions

MORRIS, MAX—End—Northwestern
1946–47 Chicago Rockets
1948 Brooklyn Dodgers

MORRIS, R?—Guard—Cornell
1926 Brooklyn Dodgers

MORRISEY, FRANK—Tackle—Boston College
1921 Rochester Kodaks
1922–23 Buffalo All Americans
1924 Buffalo Bisons
1924 Milwaukee Badgers

MORRISON, FRED—Back—Ohio State
1950–51 Chicago Bears

MORRISON, MAYNARD—Center—Michigan
1933–34 Brooklyn Dodgers

MORROW, JAMES—Back—Pittsburgh
1921 Canton Bulldogs
1922 Buffalo All Americans

MORROW, JOHN—Back—Alabama
1937–38 Chicago Cardinals

MORROW, ROBERT—Back—Illinois Wesleyan
1940–43 Chicago Cardinals
1945 New York Giants
1946 New York Yankees

MORROW, RUSSELL,—Center—Tennessee
1946–47 Brooklyn Dodgers

MORSE, RAYMOND—End—Oregon
1935–38 Detroit Lions
1940 Detroit Lions

MORSE, W.—Guard—??
1923 Duluth Kelleys

MORTELL, EMMETT—Back—Wisconsin
1937–39 Philadelphia Eagles

MORTON, JOHN—End—Missouri, Purdue
1945 Chicago Bears
1946 Los Angeles Dons
1947 Buffalo Bills

MORTON, LOCK—Back—Arkansas
1930 Newark

MOSCRIP, JAMES—End—Stanford
1938–39 Detroit Lions

MOSELLE, DONALD—Back—Superior Teachers
1950 Cleveland Browns
1951 Green Bay Packers

MOSER, ROBERT—Center—College of Pacific
1951 Chicago Bears

MOSES, HOWARD—End—Washington State
1933 Cincinnati Reds

MOSHER, CLURE—Center—Louisville
1942 Pittsburgh Steelers

MOSLEY, RUSSELL—Back—Alabama
1945–46 Green Bay Packers
1948 Pittsburgh Steelers

MOSS, ??—End—??
1924 Minneapolis Marines

MOSS, PAUL—End—Purdue
1933 Pittsburgh Pirates
1934 St. Louis Gunners

MOSS, PERRY—Back—Illinois
1948 Green Bay Packers

MOTE, KELLY—End—Duke
1947–49 Detroit Lions
1950–51 New York Giants

MOTL, ROBERT—End—Northwestern
1946 Chicago Rockets

MOTLEY, MARION—Back—Nevada
1946 Cleveland Browns
1947 Cleveland Browns
1948 Cleveland Browns—G (AAFC)
1949 Cleveland Browns
1950 Cleveland Browns—G (NFL)
1951 Cleveland Browns

MOTT, BUSTER—Back—Georgia
1933 Green Bay Packers
1934 Cincinnati Reds

MOYNIHAN, R?—Back—??
1927 Frankford Yellowjackets

MOYNIHAN, TIMOTHY—Center—Notre Dame
1932–33 Chicago Cardinals

MUCHA, CHARLES—Guard—Washington
1935 Chicago Bears

MUCHA, RUDOLPH—Back—
Washington
1941 Cleveland Rams
1945 Cleveland Rams
1945–46 Chicago Bears

MUEHLHEUSER, FRANK—Back—
Colgate
1948 Boston Yanks
1949 New York Bulldogs

MUELLER, E.—Guard—
Northwestern
1923–24 Racine Legion

MUELLNER, WILLIAM—End—
De Paul
1937 Chicago Cardinals

MUGG, GARVIN—Tackle—North
Texas State
1945 Detroit Lions

MUHA, JOSEPH—Back—Virginia
Military Inst.
1946–47 Philadelphia Eagles
1948 Philadelphia Eagles—K
1949–50 Philadelphia Eagles

MUIRHEAD, STANLEY—Guard—
Michigan
1924 Dayton Triangles
1924 Cleveland Bulldogs

MULBARGER, JOSEPH—Tackle—
None
1922–26 Columbus Tigers

MULDOON, M.—Tackle—St. Mary's
(Cal.)
1922 Rochester Kodaks

MULLEN, VERNE—Back—Illinois
1923 Canton Bulldogs
1924–27 Chicago Bears
1927 Chicago Cardinals
1927 Pottsville Maroons

MULLENEAUX, CARL—End—Utah
State
1938–41 Green Bay Packers
1945–46 Green Bay Packers

MULLENEAUX, LEE—Back—
Arizona
1932 New York Giants
1933–34 Cincinnati Reds
1934 St. Louis Gunners
1935–37 Pittsburgh Pirates
1938 Green Bay Packers
1938 Chicago Cardinals

MULLER, HENRY—End—California
1926 Los Angeles

MULLIGAN, GEORGE—Back—
Catholic Univ.
1936 Philadelphia Eagles

MULLINS, NOAH—Back—Kentucky
1946–49 Chicago Bears
1949 New York Giants

MULREADY, JERRY—End—North
Dakota State
1947 Chicago Rockets

MULVEY, ??—Back—??
1923 Buffalo All Americans

MUNDAY, GEORGE—Tackle—
Emporia Teachers
1931–32 New York Giants
1933–34 Cincinnati Reds

MUNDEE, FREDERICK—Tackle—
Notre Dame
1942–45 Chicago Bears

MUNGER, ??—Tackle—??
1924 Chicago Cardinals

MUNN, LYLE—End—Kansas State
1925–26 Kansas City Cowboys
1927 Cleveland Bulldogs
1928 Detroit Wolverines
1929 New York Giants

MURAKOWSKI, ARTHUR—Back—
Northwestern
1951 Detroit Lions

MURPHY, GEORGE—Back—Southern
California
1949 Los Angeles Dons

MURPHY, GEORGE—Back—
Dartmouth
1926 Columbus Tigers
1926 Racine Legion
1928 Chicago Cardinals

MURPHY, ROBERT—End—Georgia
Tech.
1940 Cleveland Rams
1941 Chicago Cardinals

MURPHY, THOMAS—Back—
Arkansas
1934 Chicago Cardinals

MURRAH, W. E.—Tackle—Texas
A & M
1922 Canton Bulldogs
1922–23 Racine Legion
1923 St. Louis Browns
1926 Duluth Eskimos

MURRAY, EARL—Guard—Purdue
1950 Baltimore Colts
1951 New York Giants

MURRAY, FRANCIS—Back—
Pennsylvania
1939–40 Philadelphia Eagles

MURRAY, JOHN—End—St. Thomas
1924 Duluth Kelleys

MURRAY, RICHARD—Tackle—
Marquette
1921–24   Green Bay Packers
1925–32   Chicago Bears

MURTAGH, GEORGE—Center—
Georgetown
1926–32   New York Giants

MUSICK, JAMES—Back—Southern
California
1932   Boston Braves
1933   Boston Redskins
1935–36   Boston Redskins

MUSSO, GEORGE—Guard—Milligan
1933–44   Chicago Bears

MUSULIN, STEPHEN—Tackle—
Pittsburgh
1938   Pittsburgh Pirates

MUTRYN, CHESTER—Back—Xavier
1946   Buffalo Bisons
1947   Buffalo Bills
1948   Buffalo Bills—S (AAFC)
1949   Buffalo Bills
1950   Baltimore Colts

MYERS, CYRIL—End—Ohio State
1922   Toledo Maroons
1923   Racine Legion
1923   Cleveland Indians
1925   Cleveland Indians
1930   Portsmouth Spartans
1931   Chicago Bears

MYERS, DAVID—Guard—New York
Univ.
1930   Staten Island Stapletons
1931   Brooklyn Dodgers

MYERS, JOHN—Back—UCLA
1948–50   Philadelphia Eagles

MYERS, THOMAS—Back—Fordham
1925   New York Giants

MYLES, ?—End—West Virginia
1929   Buffalo Bisons

* * *

NABORS, ROLAND—Center—
Texas Tech.
1948   New York Yankees

NADOLNEY, ROMANUS—Guard—
Notre Dame
1922   Green Bay Packers
1923–25   Milwaukee Badgers

NAGEL, ROSS—Tackle—St. Louis
Univ.
1941   Chicago Cardinals
1951   New York Yanks

NAGURSKI, BRONKO—Back—
Minnesota
1930–37   Chicago Bears
1943   Chicago Bears

NAIOTI, JOHN—Back—St. Francis
1942   Pittsburgh Steelers
1945   Pittsburgh Steelers

NARDI, RICHARD—Back—Ohio
State
1938   Detroit Lions
1939   Brooklyn Dodgers
1939   Pittsburgh Steelers

NARDICCI, NICHOLAS—Back—
West Virginia
1925   Cleveland Indians

NASH, ROBERT—Tackle—Rutgers
1920   Akron Steels
1920–23   Buffalo All Americans
1925   New York Giants

NASH, THOMAS—End—Georgia
1928–32   Green Bay Packers
1933–34   Brooklyn Dodgers

NATOWICH, ANDREW—Back—
Holy Cross
1944   Washington Redskins

NAUMETZ, FREDERICK—Center—
Boston College
1946–50   Los Angeles Rams

NAUMU, JOHN—Back—Southern
California
1948   Los Angeles Dons

NEACY, CLEMENT—End—Colgate
1924–26   Milwaukee Badgers
1927   Duluth Eskimos
1927   Chicago Bears
1928   Chicago Cardinals

NEAL, THOMAS—Guard—Duke
1924–26   Hammond Pros

NEAL, WILLIAM "ED"—Tackle—
Tulane, LSU
1945–51   Green Bay Packers
1951   Chicago Bears

NEGUS, FREDERICK—Center—
Wisconsin
1947–48   Chicago Rockets
1949   Chicago Hornets
1950   Chicago Bears

NEIHAUS, FRANCIS—Back—
Washington & Jefferson
1925   Akron Steels
1926   Pottsville Maroons

NEIHAUS, RALPH—Tackle—
Cincinnati
1939   Cleveland Rams

NEILL, JAMES—Back—Texas Tech.
1937 New York Giants

NELSON, ??—Center—??
1926 Hammond Pros

NELSON, DONALD—Guard—Iowa
1937 Brooklyn Dodgers

NELSON, FRANK—Back—Utah
1948 Boston Yanks
1949 New York Bulldogs

NELSON, HERBERT—End—Pennsylvania
1946 Buffalo Bisons
1947–48 Brooklyn Dodgers

NELSON, JAMES—Back—Alabama
1946 Miami Seahawks

NELSON, REED—Center—Brigham Young
1941 Detroit Lions
1945 Detroit Lions
1947 Detroit Lions

NELSON, ROBERT—Center—Baylor
1940 Detroit Lions
1945 Detroit Lions
1946–49 Los Angeles Dons

NEMECEK, ANDREW—Guard—Ohio State
1923–25 Columbus Tigers
1930 Minneapolis Redjackets
1931 Brooklyn Dodgers

NEMETH, STEPHEN—Back—Notre Dame
1945 Cleveland Rams
1946 Chicago Rockets
1947 Baltimore Colts

NERY, CARL—Guard—Duquesne
1940–41 Pittsburgh Steelers

NESBITT, RICHARD—Back—Drake
1930–33 Chicago Bears
1933 Chicago Cardinals
1934–35 Brooklyn Dodgers

NESSER, AL—End—None
1920–25 Akron Steels
1925–26 Columbus Tigers
1927–28 New York Giants
1931 Cleveland Indians

NETHERTON, W?—End—??
1922 Louisville Colonels

NEVERS, ERNEST—Back—Stanford
1926–27 Duluth Eskimos
1929–31 Chicago Cardinals—Player-coach
1939 Chicago Cardinals—Head Coach

NEWMAN, HARRY—Back—Michigan
1933–35 New York Giants

NEWMAN, OLIN—Tackle—Carnegie Tech.
1924–25 Akron Steels

NEWMAN, ROBERT—End—Illinois
1934–36 Chicago Cardinals

NEWMEYER, DONALD—Tackle—California
1926 Los Angeles

NEWASHE—Tackle—Carlisle
1923 Oorang Indians

NEWTON, CHARLES—Tackle—Washington
1939 Philadelphia Eagles

NICCOLAI, ARMAND—Tackle—Duquesne
1934 Pittsburgh Pirates
1935 Pittsburgh Pirates—F (6) (Tie with W. Smith)
1936 Pittsburgh Pirates—F (7) (Tie with J. Manders)
1937–38 Pittsburgh Pirates
1939–42 Pittsburgh Steelers

NICHOLS, ALLEN—Back—Temple
1945 Pittsburgh Steelers

NICHOLS, HAMILTON—Guard—Rice
1947–49 Chicago Cardinals
1951 Green Bay Packers

NICHOLS, RALPH—Guard—Brown
1921 Rock Island Independents
1926 Canton Bulldogs
1926 Hartford

NICHELINI, ALBERT—Back—St. Mary's
1935–36 Chicago Cardinals

NICKEL, ELBERT—End—Cincinnati
1947–51 Pittsburgh Steelers

NICKSICH, GEORGE—Guard—St. Bonaventure
1950–51 Pittsburgh Steelers

NICKSICH, MICHAEL—Back—Pittsburgh
1935 Pittsburgh Steelers

NIEDZIELA, BRUNO—Tackle—Iowa
1947 Chicago Rockets

NIELSEN, WALTER—Back—Arizona
1940 New York Giants

NIEMANN, WALTER—Center—Michigan
1922–24 Green Bay Packers

**NIEMI, LAURIE—Tackle—
Washington State**
1949–51 Washington Redskins

NILES, JERRY—Back—Iowa
1946–47 New York Giants

NISBET, DAVID—End—Washington
1933 Chicago Cardinals

NIX, ??—Tackle—Haskell
1926 Buffalo Bisons

NIX, EMERY—Back—TCU
1943 New York Giants
1946 New York Giants

**NIX, JOHN—End—Southern
California**
1950 San Francisco 49ers

NIXON, GEORGE—Back—Idaho
1942 Brooklyn Dodgers

NOBILE, LEO—Guard—Penn State
1947 Washington Redskins
1948 Pittsburgh Steelers
1949 Pittsburgh Steelers

NOBLE, DAVID—Back—Nebraska
1924 Cleveland Bulldogs
1925 Cleveland Indians
1925 Buffalo Bisons

NOLAN, EARL—Tackle—Arizona
1937 Chicago Cardinals
1938 Chicago Cardinals

NOLAN, JOHN—Guard—Santa Clara
1926 Los Angeles

NOLAN, JOHN—Tackle—Penn State
1948 Boston Yanks
1949 New York Bulldogs
1950 New York Yanks

**NOLANDER, DONALD—Center—
Minnesota**
1946 Los Angeles Dons
1947 Baltimore Colts

NOLTING, RAY—Back—Cincinnati
1936–44 Chicago Bears

**NOMELLINI, LEO—Tackle—
Minnesota**
1950–51 San Francisco 49ers

NONNEMAKER, ??—End—??
1926 Columbus Tigers

**NONNAN, GERALD—Back—
Fordham**
1921 Rochester Kodaks
1923 Rochester Kodaks
1924 Rochester Jefferson

**NOPPENBERG, JOHN—Back—
Miami (Fla.)**
1940–41 Pittsburgh Steelers
1941 Detroit Lions

NORBERG, HENRY—End—Stanford
1946–47 San Francisco 49ers
1948 Chicago Bears

NORBY, JOHN—Back—Idaho
1934 St. Louis Gunners
1934 New York Giants
1935 Brooklyn Dodgers

**NORDSTROM, HARRY—Guard—
Trinity (Conn.)**
1925 New York Giants

NORI, REINO—Back—DeKalb
1937 Brooklyn Dodgers
1938 Chicago Bears

NORGARD, AL—End—Stanford
1934 Green Bay Packers

NORMAN, ROBERT—Center—None
1945 Chicago Cardinals

**NORMAN, WILLARD—Back—
Washington & Jefferson**
1928 Pottsville Maroons

NORRIS, ??—End—??
1932 Staten Island Stapletons

**NORTH, JAMES—Tackle—Central
Washington**
1944 Washington Redskins

NORTH, JOHN—End—Vanderbilt
1948–49 Baltimore Colts

NORTH, MARTIN—Back—Carleton
1922 Minneapolis Marines
1924 Minneapolis Marines
1925 Green Bay Packers

NOSICH, JOHN—Tackle—??
1938 Pittsburgh Pirates

NOTT, DOUGLAS—Back—Detroit
1935 Detroit Lions
1935 Boston Redskins

NOVACK, EDWARD—Back—None
1921–22 Rock Island Independents
1924 Minneapolis Marines
1925 Rock Island Independents

**NOVOTNY, RAYMOND—Back—
Ashland**
1930 Portsmouth Spartans
1931 Cleveland Indians
1932 Brooklyn Dodgers

NOWAK, WALTER—End—Villanova
1944 Philadelphia Eagles

NOWASKEY, ROBERT—End—
George Washington
1940–42   Chicago Bears
1946–47   Los Angeles Dons
1948–50   Baltimore Colts

NOYES, LEONARD—Tackle—
Montana State
1938   Brooklyn Dodgers

NUGENT, ??—Back—??
1924   Cleveland Bulldogs

NUSSBAUMER, ROBERT—Back—
Michigan
1946   Green Bay Packers
1947–48   Washington Redskins
1949   Chicago Cardinals—I
1950   Chicago Cardinals
1951   Green Bay Packers

NUZUM, JERRY—Back—New
Mexico A & M
1948–51   Pittsburgh Steelers

NYDALL, MALCOLM—Back—
Minnesota
1929–30   Minneapolis Redjackets
1930–31   Frankford Yellowjackets

NYGREN, BERNARD—Back—San
Jose State
1946   Los Angeles Dons
1947   Brooklyn Dodgers

* * *

OAKES, WILLIAM—Tackle—Haskell
1921   Green Bay Packers

OBECK, VICTOR—Guard—
Springfield
1945   Chicago Cardinals
1946   Brooklyn Dodgers

OBEE, DUNCAN—Center—Dayton
1941   Detroit Lions

OBERBRUCKINGER, ??—Tackle—??
1924   Kenosha

O'BOYLE, HARRY—Back—Notre
Dame
1928   Green Bay Packers
1932   Green Bay Packers
1933   Philadelphia Eagles

O'BRIEN, DAVID—Back—TCU
1939–40   Philadelphia Eagles

O'BRIEN, GAIL—Tackle—Nebraska
1935–36   Boston Redskins

O'BRIEN, WILLIAM—Back—None
1947   Detroit Lions

OBST, HENRY—End—Syracuse
1931   Staten Island Stapletons
1933   Philadelphia Eagles

O'CONNELL, G.—Guard—Boston
College
1927   Providence Steamrollers

O'CONNELL, MILTON—End—
Penn State
1924   Chicago Bears
1924–25   Frankford Yellowjackets
1926   Hartford
1927   Providence Steamrollers

O'CONNOR, DANIEL—Guard—
Georgetown
1920   Canton Bulldogs
1920   Dayton Triangles
1921   Cleveland Indians
1921–22   Chicago Cardinals
1924   Chicago Cardinals

O'CONNOR, ROBERT—Guard—
Stanford
1935   Green Bay Packers

O'CONNOR, WILLIAM—End—Notre
Dame
1948   Buffalo Bills
1949   Cleveland Browns
1951   New York Yanks

ODEN, OLAF—Back—Brown
1925–28   Providence Steamrollers
1930–31   Providence Steamrollers
1932   Boston Braves

O'DONNELL, RICHARD—End—
Minnesota
1923   Duluth Kelleys
1924–30   Green Bay Packers
1931   Brooklyn Dodgers

ODSON, URBAN—Tackle—
Minnesota
1946–49   Green Bay Packers

OEHLER, JOHN—Center—Purdue
1933–34   Pittsburgh Pirates
1935–36   Brooklyn Dodgers

OELRICH, ARNOLD—Back—
Nebraska
1928–29   Frankford Yellowjackets
1938   Pittsburgh Pirates
1938   Chicago Bears

OESCH, VERN—Tackle—Minnesota
1936   Chicago Bears

O'HEARN, JOHN—Back—Cornell
1921   Buffalo All Americans

OHLGREN, EARL—End—Texas
A & M
1942   Green Bay Packers

O'KEEFE, THOMAS—??
1936   Cleveland Rams

OLDERSHAW, DOUGLAS—Guard—Santa Barbara
1939–41 New York Giants

OLDHAM, ??—End—??
1926 Racine Legion

OLEJNICZAK, STANLEY—Tackle—Pittsburgh
1935 Pittsburgh Pirates

OLENSKI, MITCHELL—Tackle—Alabama
1946 Miami Seahawks
1947 Detroit Lions
1948 Pittsburgh Steelers

OLIPHANT, ELMER—Back—West Point
1920–21 Buffalo All Americans

OLIVER, RICHARD—Back—Vanderbilt
1935 Pittsburgh Pirates

OLIVER, VINCENT—Back—Indiana
1945 Chicago Cardinals

OLIVER, WILLIAM—Guard—Alabama
1926 Pottsville Maroons
1927 New York Yankees

OLMSTEAD, L.—Guard—??
1922–23 Louisville Colonels

OLSEN, RALPH—End—Utah
1949 Green Bay Packers

OLSON, CARL—Tackle—UCLA
1942 Chicago Cardinals
1944 Philadelphia Eagles
1944–45 Cleveland Rams

OLSON, FORREST—Guard—Iowa
1927 New York Yankees

OLSONOSKI, LAWRENCE—Guard—Minnesota
1948–49 Green Bay Packers
1949 New York Bulldogs

OLSSON, LESTER—Guard—Mercer
1934–36 Boston Redskins
1937–38 Washington Redskins

OLSZEWSKI, ALBERT—End—Penn State & Pittsburgh
1945 Pittsburgh Steelers

OLTZ, ??—Center—Washington & Jefferson
1922–25 Hammond Pros

O'MALLEY, ROBERT—Back—Cincinnati
1950 Green Bay Packers

O'NEAL, JAMES—Guard—TCU
1946–47 Chicago Rockets

O'NEIL, ??—Center—Connecticut State
1926 Hartford

O'NEILL, THOMAS—End—St. Mary's (Minn.)
1923 Toledo Maroons
1925 Duluth Kelleys

O'NEILL, WILLIAM—Back—George Washington
1937 Cleveland Rams

OPALEWSKI, EDWARD—Tackle—Michigan Normal
1942 Detroit Lions
1944 Detroit Lions

O'QUINN, JOHN—End—Wake Forest
1950 Chicago Bears
1951 Philadelphia Eagles
1951 Chicago Bears

ORDWAY, WILLIAM—Back—N. Dakota
1939 Philadelphia Eagles

O'REILLY, ??—Guard—??
1924 Racine Legion

ORISTAGLIO, ROBERT—End—Pennsylvania
1949 Buffalo Bills
1950 Baltimore Colts
1951 Cleveland Browns

ORLICH, DANIEL—End—Nevada
1949–51 Green Bay Packers

ORMSBEE, ELLIOTT—Back—Bradley Tech.
1946 Philadelphia Eagles

O'ROURKE, CHARLES—Back—Boston College
1942 Chicago Bears
1946–47 Los Angeles Dons
1948–49 Baltimore Colts

ORTMAN, CHARLES—Back—Michigan
1951 Pittsburgh Steelers

ORWELL, ??—Back—??
1926 Milwaukee Badgers

OSBORN, ROBERT—Guard—Penn State
1921–23 Canton Bulldogs
1924 Cleveland Bulldogs
1925–28 Pottsville Maroons

OSMANSKI, JOSEPH—Back—Holy Cross
1946–49 Chicago Bears
1949 New York Bulldogs

OSMANSKI, WILLIAM—Back—Holy Cross
1939 Chicago Bears—G
1940–43 Chicago Bears
1946–47 Chicago Bears

OSS, ARNOLD—Center—Minnesota
1929 Minneapolis Redjackets

OSSOWSKI, THEODORE—Tackle— Oregon State
1947 New York Yankees

OSTENDARP, JAMES—Back— Bucknell
1950 New York Giants

O'TOOLE, WILLIAM—Guard—St. Mary's (Minn.)
1920 Chicago Cardinals
1924 Duluth Kelleys

OTTE, F. LOWELL—End—Iowa
1927 Buffalo Bisons

OTTELE, RICHARD—Back— Washington
1948 Los Angeles Dons

OTTO, A. ??—Center—??
1922–23 Louisville Colonels

OWEN, ALTON—Back—Mercer
1939 New York Giants
1942 New York Giants

OWEN, STEPHEN—Tackle—Phillips
1924–26 Kansas City Cowboys
1926–30 New York Giants
1931–32 New York Giants—Player-coach
1933–52 New York Giants—Head Coach

OWEN, VILAS—Back—LaCrosse Teachers
1942 New York Giants

OWEN, WILLIAM—Tackle— Oklahoma A & M
1927 Cleveland Bulldogs
1928 Detroit Lions
1929–36 New York Giants

OWENS, DELMER—Back—North Idaho
1947 New York Yankees

OWENS, HARRY—Guard—Lake Forest
1922 Green Bay Packers

OWENS, ISAIAH—End—Illinois
1948 Chicago Rockets

OWENS, JAMES—End—Oklahoma
1950 Baltimore Colts

OWENS, PETER—Guard—Texas Tech.
1943 Brooklyn Dodgers

PACEWIC, VINCENT—Back—San Francisco
1947 Washington Redskins

PADAN, R. ??—Back—Ohio State
1944 Cleveland Rams

PADLOW, MAX—End—Ohio State
1935 Philadelphia Eagles
1936 Cleveland Rams

PAFFRATH, ROBERT—Back— Minnesota
1946 Miami Seahawks
1946 Brooklyn Dodgers

PAGE, PAUL—Back—SMU
1949 Baltimore

PAHL, ??—Back—??
1923–24 Minneapolis Marines

PAINE, HOMER—Tackle—Oklahoma
1949 Chicago Hornets

PALAZZI, LOUIS—Center—Penn State
1946–47 New York Giants

PALM, MICHAEL—Back—Penn State
1925 New York Giants
1933 Cincinnati Reds

PALMER, CHARLES—Back— Northwestern
1924 Racine Legions
1926 Louisville Colonels

PALMER, DARRELL—Tackle—TCU
1946–48 New York Yankees
1949–51 Cleveland Browns

PALMER, LESLIE—Back—North Carolina State
1948 Philadelphia Eagles

PANCIERA, DONALD—Back—San Francisco
1949 New York Yankees
1950 Detroit Lions

PANELLI, JOHN—Back—Notre Dame
1949–50 Detroit Lions
1951 Chicago Cardinals

PANGLE, HAROLD—Back—Oregon State
1935–38 Chicago Cardinals

PANNELL, ERNEST—Tackle— Texas A & M
1941–42 Green Bay Packers
1945 Green Bay Packers

PAPACH, GEORGE—Back—Purdue
1948–49 Pittsburgh Steelers

PAPE, ORRIN—Back—Iowa
1930   Green Bay Packers
1930   Minneapolis Redjackets
1931   Providence Steamrollers
1932   Boston Braves
1933   Philadelphia Eagles

PAPIT, JOHN—Back—Virginia
1951   Washington Redskins

PAPPIO, ??—??—??
1930   Chicago Cardinals

PARDONNER, PAUL—Back—Purdue
1934-35   Chicago Cardinals

PARKER, CLARENCE—Back—Duke
1937-39   Brooklyn Dodgers
1940   Brooklyn Dodgers—V
1941   Brooklyn Dodgers

PARKER, DAVID—End—Hardin-Simmons
1941   Brooklyn Dodgers

PARKER, HOWARD—Back—SMU
1948   New York Yankees

PARKER, JOSEPH—End—Texas
1946-47   Chicago Cardinals

PARKER, RAYMOND—Back—Centenary
1935-36   Detroit Lions
1937-43   Chicago Cardinals
1949   Chicago Cardinals—Head Coach
1951-52   Detroit—Head Coach

PARKINSON, THOMAS—Back—Pittsburgh
1931   Staten Island Stapletons

PARKS, EDWARD—Center—Oklahoma
1938-40   Washington Redskins
1946   Chicago Rockets

PARMER, JAMES—Back—Oklahoma A & M
1948-51   Philadelphia Eagles

PARNELL, FREDERICK—Tackle—Colgate
1925   New York Giants
1927   New York Giants

PARRIOTT, ??—??—??
1934   Cincinnati Reds

PARRY, OWEN—Tackle—Baylor
1937-39   New York Giants

PARSEGHIAN, ARA—Back—Miami (Ohio)
1948-49   Cleveland Browns

PARSONS, EARLE—Back—Southern California
1946-47   San Francisco 49ers

PARSONS, LLOYD—Back—Gustavus-Adolphus
1941   Detroit Lions

PARTLOW, ??—Back—None
1920-23   Dayton Triangles
1923   Cleveland Indians
1924   Cleveland Bulldogs
1925-29   Dayton Triangles

PASCHAL, WILLIAM—Back—Georgia Tech.
1943   New York Giants—G
1944   New York Giants—G
1945-47   New York Giants
1947-48   Boston Yanks

PASCHKA, GORDON—Guard—Minnesota
1943   Phil-Pitt
1947   New York Giants

PASKVAN, GEORGE—Back—Wisconsin
1941   Green Bay Packers

PASQUA, BERNARD—Tackle—Southern Methodist
1941-42   Cleveland Rams
1942-43   Washington Redskins
1946   Los Angeles Rams

PASQUARIELLO, RALPH—Back—Villanova
1950   Los Angeles Rams
1951   Chicago Cardinals

PASSUELO, ??—Guard—??
1923   Columbus Tigers

PASTIN, FRANK—Guard—Waynesburg
1942   Pittsburgh Steelers

PATANELLI, MICHAEL—End—Ball State Teachers (Ind.)
1947   Brooklyn Dodgers

PATE, RUPERT—Guard—Wake Forest
1940   Chicago Cardinals
1942   Philadelphia Eagles

PATERNOSTER, ANGELO—Guard—Georgia
1943   Washington Redskins

PATRICK, FRANK—Back—Pittsburgh
1938-39   Chicago Cardinals

PATRICK, JOHN—Back—Penn State
1941   Pittsburgh Steelers
1945-46   Pittsburgh Steelers

PATT, MAURICE—End—Carnegie Tech.
1938   Detroit Lions
1939-42   Cleveland Rams

PATTERSON, PAUL—Back—Illinois
1949   Chicago Hornets

**PATTERSON, WILLIAM—Back—
Baylor**
1939   Chicago Bears
1940   Pittsburgh Steelers

PATTISON, ??—Guard—??
1924   Kenosha

PATTON, JOHN—Guard—TCU
1946–47   Philadelphia Eagles
1948   Philadelphia Eagles—F (8)
1949–50   Philadelphia Eagles
1951   Chicago Cardinals

PAYTON, ??—Back—??
1923   Rochester Kodaks
1924   Rochester Jeffersons

PAUL, DON—Center—UCLA
1948–51   Los Angeles Rams

PAUL, DON—Back—Washington State
1950–51   Chicago Cardinals

**PAULEKAS, ANTHONY—Center—
Washington & Jefferson**
1936   Green Bay Packers

**PAVELEC, THEODORE—Guard—
Detroit**
1940–43   Detroit Lions

PAVLICH, CHARLES—Guard—None
1946   San Francisco 49ers

PAYNE, OTTO—Back—Texas A & M
1937   Detroit Lions

**PEACE, LAWRENCE—Back—
Pittsburgh**
1941   Brooklyn Dodgers

PEARCE, WALTER—Back—Illinois
1920–21   Chicago Bears (Staleys)
1922   Chicago Bears
1924   Kenosha
1925   Providence Steamrollers

PEARCY, JAMES—Guard—Marshall
1946–48   Chicago Rockets
1949   Chicago Hornets

**PEARSON, ALBERT—Center—
Kansas State**
1929–34   Chicago Bears
1935–36   Chicago Cardinals

**PEARSON, LINDELL—Back—
Oklahoma**
1950–51   Detroit Lions

PEASE, GEORGE—Back—Columbia
1929   Orange

PEDERSON, JAMES—End—Augsburg
1930–31   Frankford Yellowjackets

**PEDERSON, WINFIELD—Tackle—
Minnesota**
1941   New York Giants
1945   New York Giants
1946   Boston Yanks

PEEBLES, JAMES—End—Canisius
1946–51   Washington Redskins

**PELFREY, RAYMOND—Back—East
Kentucky State**
1951   Green Bay Packers

**PENACCION, VICTOR—Tackle—
Penn State**
1930   Frankford Yellowjackets

PENSE, JAMES—Center—Arkansas
1945   Pittsburgh Steelers

PEPPER, EUGENE—Guard—Missouri
1950–51   Washington Redskins

**PERANTONI, FRANCIS—Center—
Princeton**
1948–49   New York Yankees

PERDUE, CHARLES—End—Duke
1940   Washington Redskins
1940   New York Giants
1946   Miami Seahawks
1946   Brooklyn Dodgers

PEREZ, PETER—Guard—Illinois
1945   Chicago Bears

PERINA, ROBERT—Back—Princeton
1946   New York Yankees
1947   Brooklyn Dodgers
1948   Chicago Rockets
1949–50   Chicago Bears
1950   Baltimore Colts

**PERKINS, DONALD—Back—
Plattsville Teachers**
1943–45   Green Bay Packers
1945–46   Chicago Bears

PERKO, JOHN—Guard—Duquesne
1937–38   Pittsburgh Pirates
1939–40   Pittsburgh Steelers
1944   Card-Pitt
1945–47   Pittsburgh Steelers

PERKO, JOHN—Guard—Minnesota
1946   Buffalo Bison

**PERLMAN, IRWIN—Guard—Pitts-
burgh**
1921   Cleveland Indians

**PERPICH, GEORGE—Tackle—
Georgetown**
1946   Brooklyn Dodgers
1947   Baltimore Colts

**PERROTTI, MICHAEL—Tackle—
Cincinnati**
1948–49   Los Angeles Dons

PERRY, CLAUDE—Tackle—Alabama
1927 Cleveland Bulldogs
1927–31 Green Bay Packers
1931 Brooklyn Dodgers
1932–35 Green Bay Packers

PERRY, FLETCHER—Back—None
1948 San Francisco 49ers
1949 San Francisco 49ers G (AAFC)
1950–51 San Francisco 49ers

PESHMALYAN, BARUYR—End—West Point, Yale
1922 Hammond Professionals
1924 Chicago Bears

PESSALANO, LOUIS—Tackle—Villanova
1929 Staten Island Stapletons

PETCHEL, JOHN—Back—Duquesne
1941 Cleveland Rams
1944 Cleveland Rams
1945 Pittsburgh Steelers

PETCOFF, BONI—Tackle—Ohio State
1924–26 Columbus Tigers

PETERS, FOREST—Back—Montana
1930 Providence Steamrollers
1931 Brooklyn Dodgers
1932 Chicago Cardinals

PETERSON, KENNETH—Back—Gonzaga
1935 Chicago Cardinals

PETERSON, LEONARD—End—Nebraska
1924 Kansas City Cowboys

PETERSON, LESTER—End—Texas
1932 Green Bay Packers
1933–34 Brooklyn Dodgers
1934–35 Green Bay Packers

PETERSON, NELSON—Back—West Virginia Wesleyan
1937 Washington Redskins
1938 Cleveland Rams

PETERSON, PHILIP—Back—Wisconsin
1930 Minneapolis Marines
1931 Portsmouth Spartans
1932 Green Bay Packers
1932 Chicago Bears
1932 Staten Island Stapletons
1932 Boston Braves
1934 Brooklyn Dodgers

PETERSON, RAYMOND—Back—San Francisco
1936 Detroit Lions
1937 Green Bay Packers

PETRELLA, JOHN—Back—Penn State
1945 Pittsburgh Steelers

PETRILAS, WILLIAM—End—None
1944–45 New York Giants

PETRO, STEPHEN—Guard—Pittsburgh
1940–41 Brooklyn Dodgers

PETROVICH, GEORGE—Tackle—Texas
1949–50 Chicago Cardinals

PETTY, JOHN—Back—Purdue
1942 Chicago Bears

PETTY, ROSS—Guard—Illinois
1920 Chicago Bears (Staleys)

PFANNER, EUGENE—End—Denison
1921–27 Dayton Triangles
1929 Dayton Triangles

PFOHL, ROBERT—Back—Purdue
1948–49 Baltimore Colts

PFUHL, RICHARD—Back—St. Louis Univ.
1947 Buffalo Bills

PHARMER, ARTHUR—Back—Minnesota
1930 Minneapolis Redjackets
1930–31 Frankford Yellowjackets

PHELAN, ROBERT—Back—Notre Dame
1922 Toledo Maroons
1923–24 Rock Island Independents

PHELPS, DONALD—Back—Kentucky
1950–51 Cleveland Browns

PHILLIPS, EWELL—Guard—Oklahoma Baptist
1936–37 New York Giants

PHILLIPS, GEORGE—Back—UCLA
1945 Cleveland Rams

PHILLIPS, MICHAEL—Center—Western Maryland
1947 Baltimore Colts

PIASECKY, ALBERT—End—Duke
1942 Philadelphia Eagles
1943–45 Washington Redskins

PICCOLO, WILLIAM—Center—Canisius
1943–45 New York Giants

PIEPUL, MILTON—Back—Notre
Dame
1941   Detroit Lions

PIERCE, BEMUS—Back—Carlisle
1920   Akron Steels
1923   Oorang Indians
1926   Columbus Tigers

PIERCE, DONALD—Center—Kansas
1941   Brooklyn Dodgers
1942-43   Chicago Cardinals

PIERO, ROCCO—Guard—Catholic
Univ.
1940-41   Pittsburgh Steelers
1945   Pittsburgh Steelers
1946   Buffalo Bisons
1947-49   Buffalo Bills

PIEROTTI, ALBERT—Center—
Washington & Lee
1922-24   Milwaukee Badgers
1927-28   Providence Steamrollers
1929   Boston Braves

PIERRE, JOHN—End—Pittsburgh
1945   Pittsburgh Steelers

PIFFERINI, ROBERT—Center—San
Jose State
1949   Detroit Lions

PIGGOTT, BERT—Back—Illinois
1947   Los Angeles Dons

PIGNATELLI, CARL—Back—Iowa
1931   Cleveland Indians

PIHOS, PETER—End—Indiana
1947-51   Philadelphia Eagles

PILCONIS, JOSEPH—End—Temple
1934   Philadelphia Eagles
1936-37   Philadelphia Eagles

PINCKERT, ERNEST—Back—
Southern California
1932   Boston Braves
1933-36   Boston Redskins
1937-40   Washington Redskins

PINCURA, STANLEY—Back—Ohio
State
1937-38   Cleveland Rams

PINGEL, JOHN—Back—Michigan
State
1939   Detroit Lions

PIPKIN, JOYCE—End—Arkansas
1948   New York Giants
1949   Los Angeles Dons

PIRO, HENRY—End—Syracuse
1941   Philadelphia Eagles

PISKOR, ROMAN—Tackle—Niagara
1946   New York Yankees
1947   Cleveland Browns
1948   Chicago Rockets

PITTMAN, MELVIN—Center—?
1935   Pittsburgh Pirates

PITTS, EDWIN—Back—Sing Sing
1935   Philadelphia Eagles

PIVARNICK, JOSEPH—Guard—
Notre Dame
1936   Philadelphia Eagles
1942   Brooklyn Dodgers

PLANK, ??—End—??
1929   Buffalo Bisons
1930   Brooklyn Dodgers

PLANSKY, ANTHONY—Back—
Georgetown
1928-29   New York Giants

PLASMAN, RICHARD—End—
Vanderbilt
1937-41   Chicago Bears
1944   Chicago Bears
1946-47   Chicago Cardinals

PLATUKIS, GEORGE—End—
Duquesne
1938   Pittsburgh Pirates
1939-41   Pittsburgh Steelers
1941-42   Cleveland Rams

PLUMRIDGE, THEODORE—
Center—St. John's
1926   Brooklyn Dodgers

PLUNKETT, JOSEPH—??
1920   Chicago Cardinals

PLUNKETT, WARREN—Back—
Minnesota
1941   Cleveland Rams

PODMAJERSKI, PAUL—Guard—
Illinois
1944   Chicago Bears

POHLMAN—Back—Brown
1925   Providence Steamrollers

POILLON, RICHARD—Back—
Canisius
1942   Washington Redskins
1946-49   Washington Redskins

POLONSKI, JOHN—Back—Wake
Forest
1942   Detroit Lions
1946   Los Angeles Dons
1947   Brooklyn Dodgers

POLISKI, JOHN—Tackle—Notre
Dame
1929   Chicago Bears

POLLARD, AL—Back—West Point
1951   New York Yanks
1951   Philadelphia Eagles

POLLARD, FRITZ—Back—Brown
1920–21   Akron Steels
1922   Milwaukee Badgers
1923   Hammond Pros
1925   Hammond Pros
1925   Akron Steels

POLLOCK, WILLIAM—Back—Penn.
Military Academy
1935–36   Chicago Bears
1937   Philadelphia Eagles
1942   Philadelphia Eagles

POLSFOOT, FRANCIS—End—
Washington State
1950–51   Chicago Cardinals

POOL, HAMPTON—End—Stanford
1940–43   Chicago Bears
1946   Miami Seahawks

POOLE, G. BARNEY—End—West
Point & Mississippi
1950–51   New York Yanks

POOLE, GEORGE—End—Princeton
1949   New York Yankees
1950   New York Yanks

POOLE, JAMES—End—Mississippi
1937–41   New York Giants
1945   Chicago Cardinals
1946   New York Giants

POOLE, OLIVER—End—Mississippi
1947   New York Yankees
1948   Baltimore Colts
1949   Detroit Lions

POOLE, RAY—End—Mississippi
1947–51   New York Giants

POPE, LEWIS—Back—Purdue
1931   Providence Steamrollers
1933–34   Cincinnati Reds

POPOVICH, JOHN—Back—St.
Vincent's
1944   Card-Pitt
1945   Pittsburgh Steelers

POPOVICH, MILTON—Back—
Montana
1938–42   Chicago Cardinals

POSTEL, ??—End—??
1925   Chicago Cardinals

POSTUS, ALBERT—Back—Villanova
1945   Pittsburgh Steelers

POTO, JOHN—Back—None
1947–48   Boston Yanks

POTTEIGER, EARL—Back—Ursinus
1920   Buffalo All Americans
1922   Milwaukee Badgers
1924   Kenosha
1927–28   New York Giants—Player-coach

POTTS, ROBERT—Tackle—Clemson
1926   Frankford Yellowjackets

POWELL, RICHARD—End—??
1931   New York Giants
1933–34   Cincinnati Reds

POWELL, STANCIL—Guard—
Carlisle
1923   Oorang Indians
1926   Buffalo Bisons

POWERS, JAMES—Back—Southern
California
1950–51   San Francisco 49ers

POWERS, SAMUEL—Guard—
Northern Michigan
1921   Green Bay Packers

PRATHER, DALE—End—George
Washington
1938   Cleveland Rams

PRCHLIK, JOHN—Tackle—Yale
1949–51   Detroit Lions

PREGULMAN, MERVIN—Guard—
Michigan
1946   Green Bay Packers
1947–48   Detroit Lions
1949   New York Bulldogs

PRESCOTT, HAROLD—End—
Hardin-Simmons
1946   Green Bay Packers
1947–49   Philadelphia Eagles
1949   New York Bulldogs
1949   Detroit Lions

PRESNELL, GLENN—Back—
Nebraska
1931–33   Portsmouth Spartans
1934–36   Detroit Lions

PRESSLEY, LEE—Center—Oklahoma
1945   Washington Redskins

PRESTON, PATTISON—Guard—
Wake Forest
1946–49   Chicago Bears

PREWITT, FELTON—Center—
Tulsa
1946   Buffalo Bisons
1947–48   Buffalo Bills
1949   Baltimore Colts

PRICE, CHARLES—Back—Texas
A & M
1940–41   Detroit Lions
1945   Detroit Lions
1946   Miami Seahawks

PRICE, EDWARD—Back—Tulane
1950 New York Giants
1951 New York Giants—G

PRIESTLEY, ROBERT—End—Brown
1941–42 Philadelphia Eagles

PRINCIPE, DOMINIC—Back—
Fordham
1940–41 New York Giants
1946 Brooklyn Dodgers

PRISCO, NICHOLAS—Back—Rutgers
1933 Philadelphia Eagles

PRITCHARD, ABISHA—Back—
Virginia Military Inst.
1946–51 Philadelphia Eagles
1951 New York Giants

PRITCHARD, WILLIAM—Back—
Pennsylvania
1927–28 Providence Streamrollers
1928 New York Yankees

PRITKO, STEPHEN—End—Villanova
1943 New York Giants
1944–45 Cleveland Rams
1946–47 Los Angeles Rams
1948 Boston Yanks
1949 New York Bulldogs
1949–50 Green Bay Packers

PROCHASKA, RAYMOND—End—
Nebraska
1941 Cleveland Rams

PROCTOR, DEWEY—Back—Furman
1946–47 New York Yankees
1948 Chicago Rockets
1949 New York Yankees

PROKOP, EDWARD—Back—
Georgia Tech.
1946–47 New York Yankees
1948 Chicago Rockets
1949 New York Yankees

PROKOP, JOSEPH—Back—Bradley
1948 Chicago Rockets

PROVENCIAL, KENNETH—Back—
Georgetown
1930 Frankford Yellowjackets

PROVO, FREDERICK—Back—
Washington
1948 Green Bay Packers

PUCCI, BENITO—Tackle—None
1946 Buffalo Bisons
1947 Buffalo Bills
1947 Chicago Rockets
1948 Cleveland Browns

PUDDY, HAROLD—Tackle—Oregon
State
1948 San Francisco 49ers

PUGH, MARION—Back—Texas
A & M
1940–41 New York Giants
1945 New York Giants
1946 Miami Seahawks

PUPLIS, ANDREW—Back—Notre
Dame
1943 Chicago Cardinals

PURDIN, CALVIN—Back—Tulsa
1943 Chicago Cardinals
1946 Miami Seahawks
1946 Brooklyn Dodgers

PURDY, CLAIR—Back—Brown
1920 Rochester Kodaks

PURDY, EVERETT—Back—Beloit
1922 Milwaukee Badgers
1926–27 Green Bay Packers

PYLMAN, ROBERT—Tackle—North
Dakota
1938–39 Philadelphia Eagles

PYNE, GEORGE—Tackle—Holy Cross
1931 Providence Steamrollers

* * *

QUATSE, JESS—Tackle—Pittsburgh
1933 Green Bay Packers
1933–34 Pittsburgh Pirates
1935 New York Giants

QUILLEN, FRANK—End—
Pennsylvania
1946–47 Chicago Rockets

QUILTER, CHARLES—Tackle—None
1949–50 San Francisco 49ers

QUINN, IVAN—Guard—Carroll
1921 Rock Island Independents
1924 Kansas City Cowboys

QUIRK, EDWARD—Back—Missouri
1948–51 Washington Redskins

* * *

RABORN, CARROLL—Center—SMU
1936–37 Pittsburgh Pirates

RACIS, FRANK—Guard—None
1925–28 Pottsville Maroons
1929 Boston Braves
1930 Providence Steamrollers
1931 Frankford Yellowjackets

RADICK, KENNETH—End—
Marquette
1930–31 Green Bay Packers
1931 Brooklyn Dodgers

RADO, ARTHUR—Back—Duquesne
1934 Pittsburgh Pirates

RADO, GEORGE—Guard—Duquesne
1934–38 Pittsburgh Pirates

**RADOVICH, WILLIAM—Guard—
Southern California**
1938–41   Detroit Lions
1945   Detroit Lions
1946–47   Los Angeles Dons

**RAEMER, NORBERT—Guard—
Kansas State**
1941   Brooklyn Dodgers

RAFFEL, W.—End—Pennsylvania
1932   Brooklyn Dodgers

**RAGAZZO, PHILIP—Tackle—
Western Reserve**
1938–39   Cleveland Rams
1941   Philadelphia Eagles
1945–47   New York Giants

**RAIMONDI, BENJAMIN—Back—
Indiana**
1947   New York Yankees

**RAMSEY, FRANK—Tackle—Oregon
State**
1945   Chicago Bears

**RAMSEY, GARRARD—Guard—
William & Mary**
1946–50   Chicago Cardinals

**RAMSEY, HERSCHEL—End—Texas
Tech.**
1938–40   Philadelphia Eagles
1945   Philadelphia Eagles

**RAMSEY, KNOX—Guard— William &
Mary**
1948–49   Los Angeles Dons
1950–51   Chicago Cardinals

RAMSEY, RAY—Back—Bradley
1947–48   Chicago Rockets
1948   Brooklyn Dodgers
1949   Chicago Hornets
1950–51   Chicago Cardinals

**RANDELS, HORACE—End—Kansas
State**
1926   Kansas City Cowboys
1927   Cleveland Bulldogs
1928   Detroit Lions

RANDOLPH, ??—Back—??
1923   Columbus Tigers

**RANDOLPH, CLARE—Center—
Indiana**
1930   Chicago Cardinals
1931–33   Portsmouth Spartans
1934–36   Detroit Lions

**RANDOUR, HUBERT—Back—
Pittsburgh**
1935   Pittsburgh Pirates

**RANKIN, WALTER—Back—Texas
Tech.**
1940   Chicago Cardinals
1942–43   Chicago Cardinals
1944   Card-Pitt
1945   Chicago Cardinals
1945   Cleveland Rams
1946–47   Chicago Cardinals

RANSPOT, KEITH—End—SMU
1941   Detroit Lions
1942   Green Bay Packers
1942–43   Brooklyn Dodgers
1944–45   Boston Yanks

RAPACZ, JOHN—Center—Oklahoma
1948   Chicago Rockets
1949   Chicago Hornets
1950–51   New York Giants

RAPP, HERBERT—Center—Xavier
1930   Staten Island Stapletons
1931   Staten Island Stapletons
1934   St. Louis Gunners

**RAPP, MANUEL—Back—St. Louis
Univ.**
1941   Cleveland Rams

RAPP, ROBERT—Back—none
1922–26   Columbus Tigers
1929   Buffalo Bisons

RASHLER, ??—??—??
1932   Portsmouth Spartans

**RASKOWSKI, LEO—Tackle—Ohio
State**
1932   Staten Island Stapletons
1933   Brooklyn Dodgers
1933–34   Pittsburgh Pirates
1935   Philadelphia Eagles

RATE, ??—Back—??
1923   Milwaukee Badgers

**RATICA, JOSEPH—Center—St.
Vincent's**
1939   Brooklyn Dodgers

**RATTERMAN, GEORGE—Back—
Notre Dame**
1947–49   Buffalo Bills
1950–51   New York Yanks

RAUSCH, JOHN—Back—Georgia
1949   New York Bulldogs
1950–51   New York Yanks
1951   Philadelphia Eagles

**RAUSCH, RICHARD—Guard—
Penn State**
1925   Pottsville Maroons
1928   New York Yankees

**RAVENSBURG, ROBERT—End—
Indiana**
1948–49   Chicago Cardinals

RAWLINGS, ROBERT—Back—Georgetown
1922 Buffalo All Americans

RAY, BUFORD—Tackle—Vanderbilt
1938–48 Green Bay Packers

RAYBURN, VAN—End—Tennessee
1933 Brooklyn Dodgers

READER, RUSSELL—Back—Michigan State
1947 Chicago Bears

REAGAN, FRANK—Back—Pennsylvania
1940–41 New York Giants
1946 New York Giants
1947 New York Giants—K–I (Tie with F. Seno)
1948 New York Giants
1949–51 Philadelphia Eagles

REAM, CHARLES—Tackle—Ohio State
1938 Cleveland Rams

REBSEAMAN, PAUL—Center—Centenary
1927 Pottsville Maroons

RECKMARCK, RAYMOND—Back—Syracuse
1937 Detroit Lions
1937 Brooklyn Dodgers

RED FANG—Tackle—None
1923 Oorang Indians

RED FOX—Back—None
1923 Oorang Indians

REDINGER, OTIS—Back—Colgate
1925 Canton Bulldogs

REDMAN, ?—Guard—None
1921 Dayton Triangles
1924 Dayton Triangles

REECE, DONALD—Tackle—Missouri
1946 Miami Seahawks

REED, JOSEPH—Back—LSU
1937 Chicago Cardinals
1939 Chicago Cardinals

REED, MAX—Center—Bucknell
1925 Buffalo Bisons
1926–27 Frankford Yellowjackets
1928 New York Giants

REESE, DAVID—End—Denison
1920–23 Dayton Triangles
1923 Louisville Colonels

REESE, HENRY—Center—Temple
1933–34 New York Giants
1935–37 Philadelphia Eagles
1939 Philadelphia Eagles

REESE, LLOYD—Back—Tennessee
1946 Chicago Bears
1947 Detroit Lions

REGNIER, PETER—Back—Minnesota
1922 Green Bay Packers

REICHLE, LOUIS—End—Butler
1923 Milwaukee Badgers
1926 Columbus Tigers

REICHOW, ??—Back—??
1926 Racine Legion

REID, FLOYD—Back—Georgia
1950–51 Green Bay Packers

REID, Joseph—Center—LSU
1951 Los Angeles Rams

REINHARD, ROBERT—Tackle—California
1946–50 Los Angeles Dons

REINHARD, WILLIAM—Back—California
1947–48 Los Angeles Dons

REISSIG, WILLIAM—Back—None
1938–39 Brooklyn Dodgers

REISZ, ALBERT—Back—Southeastern Louisiana
1944–45 Cleveland Rams
1946 Los Angeles Rams
1947 Buffalo Bills

REITER, WILBUR—Guard—West Virginia Wesleyan
1926–27 Dayton Triangles

REMINGTON, JOSEPH—Center—Washington State
1946 San Francisco 49ers

RENDAL, KENNETH—Back—Rutgers
1920 Akron Steels

RENFRO, RICHARD—Back—Washington State
1946 San Francisco 49ers

RENGEL, NEIL—Back—Davis & Elkins
1930 Frankford Yellowjackets

RENO, ??—End—??
1927 New York Yanks

RENTNER, ERNEST—Back—Northwestern
1934–36 Boston Redskins
1936–37 Chicago Bears

REPKO, JOSEPH—Tackle—Boston College
1946–47 Pittsburgh Steelers
1948–49 Los Angeles Rams

REUDER, ??—Center—??
1932   Staten Island Stapletons

REXER, FREEMAN—End—Tulane
1943   Chicago Cardinals
1944   Detroit Lions
1945   Chicago Cardinals

REYNOLDS, JAMES—Back—
Oklahoma A & M
1946   Pittsburgh Steelers

REYNOLDS, JAMES—Back—
Alabama Polytech.
1946   Miami Seahawks

REYNOLDS, JOHN—Center—Baylor
1937   Chicago Cardinals

REYNOLDS, OWEN—End—Georgia
1925   New York Giants

REYNOLDS, ROBERT—Center—
Stanford
1934   St. Louis Gunners
1937–38   Detroit Lions

REYNOLDS, WILLIAM—Back—
Mississippi
1944   Brooklyn Dodgers
1945   Chicago Cardinals

REZNICHAK, JOSEPH—Back—
Bucknell
1935   Pittsburgh Pirates

RHEA, FLOYD—Guard—Oregon
1943   Chicago Cardinals
1944   Brooklyn Dodgers
1945   Boston Yanks

RHEA, HUGH—Guard—Nebraska
1933   Brooklyn Dodgers

RHENQUIST, MILTON—Center—
Bethany
1924–26   Kansas City Cowboys
1927   Cleveland Indians
1928–31   Providence Steamrollers
1931   New York Giants

RHOADS, DONALD—Tackle—
Washington & Jefferson
1933   Pittsburgh Pirates
1937   Cleveland Rams

RHODEMYRE, JAY—Center—
Kentucky
1948–49   Green Bay Packers
1951   Green Bay Packers

RIBAR, FRANK—Guard—Duke
1943   Washington Redskins

RIBBLE, LORAN—Guard—
Hardin-Simmons
1934–35   Pittsburgh Pirates

RIBLETT, PAUL—End—
Pennsylvania
1932–36   Brooklyn Dodgers

RICCA, JAMES—Tackle—Georgia
1951   Washington Redskins

RICH, HERBERT—Back—Vanderbilt
1950   Baltimore Colts
1951   Los Angeles Rams

RICHARDS, ELVIN—Back—Simpson
1933–39   New York Giants

RICHARDS, HARRY—Center—
Nebraska
1927   Frankford Yellowjackets
1930   Frankford Yellowjackets

RICHARDS, RAY—Guard—Nebraska
1930   Frankford Yellowjackets
1932–33   Chicago Bears
1934   Detroit Lions
1935–36   Chicago Bears

RICHARDS, RICHARDS—Back—
Kentucky
1933   Brooklyn Dodgers

RICHESON, RAYMOND—Guard—
Alabama
1949   Chicago Hornets
1950   Pittsburgh Steelers

RICKARD, PAUL—Back—
Pittsburgh
1948   Los Angeles Rams

RIDDICK, RAYMOND—End—
Fordham
1940–42   Green Bay Packers
1946   Green Bay Packers

RIDLER, ??—Tackle—??
1931   Cleveland Indians

RIETH, WILLIAM—Center—
Carnegie Tech.
1941–42   Cleveland Rams
1944–45   Cleveland Rams

RIFENBURG, RICHARD—End—
Michigan
1950   Detroit Lions

RIFFLE, CHARLES—Guard—Notre
Dame
1944   Cleveland Rams
1946–48   New York Yankees

RIFFLE, RICHARD—Back—
Albright
1938–40   Philadelphia Eagles
1941–42   Pittsburgh Steelers

RILEY, JOHN—Tackle—
Northwestern
1933   Boston Redskins

RINGWALT, CARROLL—Center—Indiana
1931 Frankford Yellowjackets

RIORDAN, CHARLES—Back—New York Univ.
1929 Staten Island Stapletons

RISK, EDWARD—Back—Purdue
1932 Chicago Cardinals

RISLEY, ELLIOTT—Tackle—Indiana
1922–23 Hammond Pros

RISVOLD, ??—Back—??
1927–28 Chicago Cardinals

RITCHHART, DELBERT—Center—Colorado
1936–37 Detroit Lions

ROACH, JOHN—Back—Notre Dame
1927 Chicago Cardinals

ROBB, HARRY—Back—Penn State
1921–23 Canton Bulldogs
1925–26 Canton Bulldogs

ROBBINS, JOHN—Back—Pittsburgh
1938–39 Chicago Cardinals

ROBERTS, EUGENE—Back—Chattanooga
1947–48 New York Giants
1949 New York Giants–S (Tie with M. Harder)
1950 New York Giants

ROBERTS, JOHN—Back—Tulane
1934 Pittsburgh Pirates

ROBERTS, JOHN—Back—Georgia
1933–34 Philadelphia Eagles

ROBERTS, THOMAS—Tackle—DePaul
1943 New York Giants
1944–45 Chicago Bears

ROBERTS, WALCOTT—Back—Navy
1922–23 Canton Bulldogs
1924 Cleveland Bulldogs
1924 Hammond Pros
1924 Rock Island Independents
1925 Cleveland Indians
1926 Frankford Yellowjackets
1927 Pottsville Maroons
1930–32 Portsmouth Spartans
1932 Boston Braves

ROBERTSON, HARRY—Tackle—Syracuse
1922 Rochester Kodaks

ROBERTSON, JAMES—Back—Carnegie Tech.
1924–25 Akron Steels

ROBERTSON, LAKE—End—Mississippi
1945 Detroit Lions

ROBERTSON, ROBERT—Back—Southern California
1942 Brooklyn Dodgers

ROBERTSON, THOMAS—Center—Tulsa
1940–42 Brooklyn Dodgers
1946 New York Yankees

ROBESON, PAUL—End—Rutgers
1921 Akron Steels
1922 Milwaukee Badgers

ROBINSON, ??—Back—??
1923–25 Hammond Pros
1926 Louisville Colonels

ROBINSON, BURLE—End—Brigham Young
1935 Philadelphia Eagles

ROBINSON, JOHN—Tackle—Kirksville Teachers
1935–36 Brooklyn Dodgers
1936–38 Chicago Cardinals
1938 Cleveland Rams
1938 Pittsburgh Pirates

ROBL, HAROLD—Back—Oshkosh Teachers
1945 Chicago Cardinals

ROBNETT, EDWARD—Back—Texas Tech.
1947 San Francisco 49ers

ROBNETT, MARSHALL—Center—Texas A & M
1943 Chicago Cardinals
1944 Card-Pitt
1945 Chicago Cardinals

ROBUSTELLI, ANDREW—End—Arnold
1951 Los Angeles Rams

ROBY, DOUGLAS—Back—Michigan
1923 Cleveland Indians

ROCKONBACH, LYLE—Guard—Michigan State
1943 Detroit Lions

ROCKWELL, HENRY—Center—Arizona State
1940–42 Cleveland Rams
1946 Los Angeles Dons
1948 Los Angeles Dons

RODAK, MICHAEL—Guard—Western Reserve
1939–40 Cleveland Rams
1942 Pittsburgh Steelers

RODERICK, BENJAMIN—Back—Columbia
1923 Buffalo All Americans
1923 Canton Bulldogs
1926 Canton Bulldogs
1927 Buffalo Bisons

RODGERS, HOSEA—Back—North Carolina
1949 Los Angeles Dons

RODGERS, THOMAS—Tackle—Bucknell
1947 Boston Yanks

RODGERS, WALTER—Back—??
1922 Columbus Tigers

RODRIGUEZ, KELLY—Back—West Virginia Wesleyan
1929 Buffalo Bisons
1930 Frankford Yellowjackets
1930 Minneapolis Redjackets

ROEGEN, ??—Back—??
1925 Columbus Tigers

ROEPKE, JOHN—Back—Penn State
1928 Frankford Yellowjackets

ROESSLER, FRITZ—End—Marquette
1922–23 Racine Legions
1925 Milwaukee Badgers

ROGALLA, JOHN—Back—Scranton
1945 Philadelphia Eagles

ROGAS, DANIEL—Guard—Tulane
1951 Detroit Lions

ROGEL, FRANK—Back—Penn State
1950–51 Pittsburgh Steelers

ROGERS, CHARLES—Back—Pennsylvania
1927–29 Frankford Yellowjackets

ROGERS, CULLEN—Back—Texas A & M
1946 Pittsburgh Steelers

ROGERS, JOHN—Center—Notre Dame
1933–34 Cincinnati Reds

ROGERS, WILLIAM—Tackle—Villanova
1938 Chicago Cardinals
1938–40 Detroit Lions
1944 Detroit Lions

ROGGE, GEORGE—End—Iowa
1931–33 Chicago Cardinals
1934 St. Louis Gunners

ROHLEDER, GEORGE—End—Wittenberg
1925 Columbus Tigers

ROHRIG, HERMAN—Back—Nebraska
1939 Green Bay Packers
1941 Green Bay Packers
1946–47 Green Bay Packers

ROKISKY, JOHN—End—Duquesne
1946 Cleveland Browns
1947 Chicago Rockets
1948 New York Yankees

ROMAN, GEORGE—Tackle—Western Reserve
1948 Boston Yanks
1949 New York Bulldogs
1950 New York Giants

ROMANIK, STEPHEN—Back—Villanova
1950–51 Chicago Bears

ROMBOLI, RUDOLPH—Back—None
1946–48 Boston Yanks

ROMERO, RAYMOND—Guard—Kansas
1951 Philadelphia Eagles

ROMNEY, MILTON—Back—Chicago
1923–24 Racine Legion
1925–28 Chicago Bears

RONZANI, GENE—Back—Marquette
1933–38 Chicago Bears
1944–45 Chicago Bears
1950–52 Green Bay—Head Coach

ROONEY, COBB—Back—Colorado Mines
1924 Duluth Kelleys
1925 Chicago Bears
1925 Duluth Kelleys
1926–27 Duluth Eskimos
1928 New York Yankees
1929–30 Chicago Cardinals

ROONEY, JOSEPH—End—None
1923–24 Duluth Kelleys
1925 Rock Island
1926–27 Duluth Eskimos
1928 Pottsville Maroons

ROONEY, WILLIAM—Back—None
1923–25 Duluth Kelleys
1927 Duluth Eskimos
1929 Chicago Cardinals

ROSATO, SALVATORE—Back—Villanova
1945–47 Washington Redskins

ROSATTI, ROMAN—Tackle—Michigan
1923 Cleveland Indians
1924 Green Bay Packers
1926–27 Green Bay Packers
1928 New York Giants

ROSE, ALFRED—End—Texas
1929–30 Chicago Cardinals
1930 Providence Steamrollers
1930 Staten Island Stapletons
1931 Providence Steamrollers
1931–32 Chicago Cardinals
1932–36 Green Bay Packers

ROSE, EUGENE—End—Tennessee
1936 New York Giants

ROSE, EUGENE—Back—Wisconsin
1929–31 Chicago Cardinals

ROSEN, STANLEY—Back—Rutgers
1929 Buffalo Bisons

ROSENOW, AUGUST—Back—Ripon
1921 Green Bay Packers

ROSEQUIST, THEODORE—Tackle—Ohio State
1934–36 Chicago Bears
1937 Cleveland Rams

ROSKIE, KENNETH—Back—South Carolina
1946 San Francisco 49ers
1948 Detroit Lions
1948 Green Bay Packers

ROSTECK, ERNEST—Center—None
1944 Detroit Lions

ROTE, KYLE—Back—SMU
1951 New York Giants

ROTE, TOBIN—Back—Rice
1950–51 Green Bay Packers

ROTHROCK, CLIFFORD—Center—North Dakota State
1947 Chicago Rockets

ROTON, HERBERT—End—Alabama Polytech.
1937 Philadelphia Eagles

ROUDEBUSH, GEORGE—Back—Denison
1920–21 Dayton Triangles

ROUSE, STILLMAN—End—Missouri
1940 Detroit Lions

ROUSSOS, MICHAEL—Tackle—Pittsburgh
1948–49 Washington Redskins
1949 Detroit Lions

ROVINSKI, ANTHONY—Back—Holy Cross
1933 New York Giants
1934 Brooklyn Dodgers

ROWAN, ??—Back—??
1923 Louisville Colonels

ROWAN, EVERETT—End—Ohio State
1932–33 Brooklyn Dodgers
1933 Philadelphia Eagles

ROWE, HARMON—Back—San Francisco
1947–49 New York Yankees
1950–51 New York Giants

ROWE, ROBERT—Back—Colgate
1934 Detroit Lions
1935 Philadelphia Eagles

ROWLAND, BRADLEY—Back—McMurry
1951 Chicago Bears

ROY, WALLACE—End—Clemson
1921–23 Rochester Kodaks
1924–25 Rochester Jeffersons
1927 Buffalo Bisons

ROYSTON, EDWARD—Guard—Wake Forest
1948–49 New York Giants

RUBINO, ANTHONY—Guard—Wake Forest
1943 Detroit Lions
1946 Detroit Lions

RUBY, MARTIN—Tackle—Texas A & M
1946–48 Brooklyn Dodgers
1949 New York Yankees
1950 New York Yanks

RUCINSKI, EDWARD—End—Indiana
1940–41 Brooklyn Dodgers
1943 Chicago Cardinals
1944 Card-Pitt
1945–46 Chicago Cardinals

RUETZ, JOSEPH—Guard—Notre Dame
1946 Chicago Rockets
1948 Chicago Rockets
1951 Green Bay Packers

RUH, EMMETT—Back—None
1922–25 Columbus Tigers

RUKAS, JUSTIN—Guard—LSU
1936 Brooklyn Dodgers

RUNDQUIST, E. T.—Tackle—Illinois
1922 Chicago Cardinals

RUNNING DEER—End—None
1923 Oorang Indians

RUPP, JOHN—Guard—None
1920 Buffalo All Americans

RUSH, ARDEN—End—Ohio
1924 Columbus Tigers

RUSKUSKY, RAYMOND—End—St. Mary's (Cal.)
1947 New York Yankees

RUSSAS, ALBERT—Tackle—Detroit
1949 Detroit Lions

RUSSELL, DOUGLAS—Back—Kansas
1933 Philadelphia Eagles
1934 Chicago Cardinals
1935 Chicago Cardinals—G
1936–38 Chicago Cardinals
1939 Cleveland Rams

RUSSELL, FAY—Back—Northwestern
1933 New York Giants

RUSSELL, JAMES—Tackle—Temple
1936–37 Philadelphia Eagles

RUSSELL, JOHN—End—Baylor
1946–49 New York Yankees
1950 New York Yanks

RUSSELL, LLOYD—Back—Baylor
1939 Cleveland Rams

RUSSELL, REGINALD—End— Northwestern
1928 Chicago Bears

RUSSELL, TORRANCE—Tackle— Alabama Polytech.
1939–40 Washington Redskins

RUST, REGINALD—Back—Oregon State
1932 Boston Braves

RUTHSTROM, RALPH—Back—SMU
1945 Cleveland Rams
1946 Los Angeles Rams
1947–48 Washington Redskins
1949 Baltimore Colts

RUTZLER, ??—Back—??
1924 Minneapolis Marines

RYAN, DAVID—Back—Hardin- Simmons
1945–46 Detroit Lions
1948 Boston Yanks

RYAN, EDWARD—End—St. Mary's (Cal.)
1948 Pittsburgh Steelers

RYAN, JOHN—Tackle—Detroit
1924 Chicago Cardinals
1924 Rock Island Independents
1929 Chicago Bears
1929 Buffalo Bisons
1930 Portsmouth Spartans

RYAN, KENT—Back—Utah State
1938–40 Detroit Lions

RYDZEWSKI, FRANK—Tackle— Notre Dame
1922 Hammond Pros
1923 Chicago Bears
1923–25 Hammond Pros
1925 Milwaukee Badgers
1926 Hammond Pros

RYKOVICH, JULIUS—Back— Illinois
1947–48 Buffalo Bills
1948 Chicago Rockets
1949–51 Chicago Bears

RYMKUS, LOUIS—Tackle—Notre Dame
1943 Washington Redskins
1946–51 Cleveland Browns

* * *

SABADOS, ANDREW—Guard— Citadel
1939–41 Chicago Cardinals

SABAN, LOUIS—Back—Indiana
1946–49 Cleveland Browns

SABASTEANKSI, JOSEPH—Center— Fordham
1946–48 Boston Yanks
1949 New York Bulldogs

SABUCO, TINO—Center—San Francisco
1949 San Francisco 49ers

SACHS, LEONARD—End—Loyola
1921–23 Chicago Cardinals
1923 Columbus Tigers
1923–24 Milwaukee Badgers
1924–25 Hammond Pros
1926 Louisville Colonels

SACHSE, FRANCIS—Back—Texas Tech.
1942 Chicago Cardinals
1943 Brooklyn Dodgers
1944 Brooklyn Tigers
1945 Boston Yanks

SACK, JOHN—Guard—Pittsburgh
1923 Columbus Tigers

SACKSTEDER, NORMAN—Back— None
1922 Canton Bulldogs

SACRINTY, NICHOLAS—Back— Wake Forest
1947 Chicago Bears

SADOWSKY, LEONARD—Back—Ohio
1936 Cleveland Rams

SAENZ, EDWARD—Back—Southern California
1946–51 Washington Redskins

ST. JOHN, HERBERT—Guard—
Georgia
1948 Brooklyn Dodgers
1949 Chicago Hornets

SALATA, ANDREW—Guard—
Pittsburgh
1929 Orange
1930 Newark

SALATA, PAUL—End—Southern
California
1949–50 San Francisco 49ers
1950 Baltimore Colts

SALEM, EDWARD—Back—Alabama
1951 Washington Redskins

SALEMI, SAMUEL—Back—St.
Johns (N. Y.)
1928 New York Yankees

SALSCHEIDER, JOHN—Back—St.
Thomas
1949 New York Giants

SAMPLE, CHARLES—Back—Toledo
1942 Green Bay Packers
1945 Green Bay Packers

SAMPSON, ??—Back—??
1921 Dayton Triangles
1923 Minneapolis Marines

SAMUELS, DONALD—Back—Oregon
State
1949–50 Pittsburgh Steelers

SAMUELSON, CARL—Tackle—
Nebraska
1948–51 Pittsburgh Steelers

SANCHEZ, JOHN—Tackle—San
Francisco
1947 Chicago Rockets
1947 New York Yankees
1947 Detroit Lions
1947–49 Washington Redskins
1949–50 New York Giants

SANDBERG, ROY—Back—
Washington State
1926 Los Angeles

SANDBERG, SIGMUND—Tackle—
Iowa Wesleyan
1934 St. Louis Gunners
1935–37 Pittsburgh Pirates

SANDEFUR, RICHARD—Back—
Purdue
1936 Pittsburgh Pirates

SANDERS, JOHN—Back—SMU
1940–41 Pittsburgh Steelers
1943 Phil-Pitt
1944 Boston Yanks
1945 Philadelphia Eagles

SANDERS, ORBAN—Back—Texas
1946 New York Yankees—G (AAFC)
1947 New York Yankees—G–S (AAFC)
1948 New York Yankees
1950 New York Yanks—I (NFL)

SANDIFER, DANIEL—Back—
Louisana State
1948 Washington Redskins—I
1949 Washington Redskins
1950 Detroit Lions
1950 San Francisco 49ers
1950–51 Philadelphia Eagles

SANDIG, CURTIS—Back—St. Mary's
(Tex.)
1942 Pittsburgh Steelers
1946 Buffalo Bisons

SANDUSKY, JOHN—Tackle—
Villanova
1950–51 Cleveland Browns

SANDFORD, HAYWARD—End—
Alabama
1940 Washington Redskins

SANDFORD, JAMES—Tackle—
Lehigh
1924 Duluth Kelleys

SANDFORD, OTIS—Guard—LSU
1951 Chicago Cardinals

SANSEN, OLIVER—Back—Iowa
1932–35 Brooklyn Dodgers

SANZOTTA, DOMINIC—Back—
Western Reserve
1942 Detroit Lions
1946 Detroit Lions

SARAFINY, ALBERT—Center—St.
Edwards
1933 Green Bay Packers

SARAUSKY, ANTHONY—Back—
Fordham
1935–37 New York Giants
1938 Brooklyn Dodgers

SARBOE, PAUL—Back—Washington
State
1934 Boston Redskins
1934–36 Chicago Cardinals
1936 Brooklyn Dodgers

SARK, HARVEY—Guard—PHILLIPS
1931 New York Giants
1934 Cincinnati Reds

SARRATT, CHARLES—Back—
Oklahoma
1948 Detroit Lions

SARRINGHAUS, PAUL—Back—Ohio
State
1946 Chicago Cardinals
1948 Detroit Lions

SARTORI, LAWRENCE—Guard—Fordham
1942   Detroit Lions
1945   Detroit Lions

SATENSTEIN, BERNARD—Guard—New York Univ.
1929–32   Staten Island Stapletons
1933   New York Giants

SATTERFIELD, ALFRED—Tackle—Vanderbilt
1947   San Francisco 49ers

SAUER, EDWARD—Tackle—Miami (Ohio)
1920–26   Dayton Triangles

SAUER, GEORGE—Back—Nebraska
1935–37   Green Bay Packers

SAUFLEY, VICTOR—Back—SMU
1935   Pittsburgh Pirates

SAULIS, SAMUEL—Guard—None
1938   Pittsburgh Pirates

SAUNDERS, RUSSELL—Back—Southern California
1931   Green Bay Packers

SAVATSKY, OLIVER—End—Miami (Ohio)
1937   Cleveland Rams

SAVITSKY, GEORGE—Tackle—Pennsylvania
1948–49   Philadelphia Eagles

SAVOLDI, JOSEPH—Back—Notre Dame
1930   Chicago Bears

SAWYER, HERMAN—Tackle—Syracuse
1922   Rochester Kodaks
1924   Dayton Triangles

SAZIO, RALPH—Tackle—William & Mary
1948   Brooklyn Dodgers

SCAFIDE, ALBERT—Tackle—Tulane
1933   Boston Redskins

SCALISSI, THEODORE—Back—Ripon
1947   Chicago Rockets

SCALZI, JOHN—Back—Georgetown
1931   Brooklyn Dodgers

SCARDINE, ??—Back—??
1932   Chicago Cardinals

SCARRY, MICHAEL—Center—Waynesburg
1944–45   Cleveland Rams
1946–47   Cleveland Browns

SCHAAKE, ELMER—Back—Kansas
1933   Portsmouth Spartans

SCHABARUM, PETER—Back—California
1951   San Francisco 49ers

SCHAFFNIT, ??—End—??
1926   Los Angeles

SCHAMMELL, FRANCIS—Guard—Iowa
1937   Green Bay Packers

SCHARER, EDWARD—Back—Notre Dame
1926   Detroit Panthers
1927   Pottsville Maroons
1928   Detroit Wolverines

SCHEIN, JOSEPH—Tackle—Brown
1931   Providence Steamrollers

SCHELL, ??—Back—??
1924   Columbus Tigers

SCHENKER, NATHAN—Tackle—Howard
1939   Cleveland Rams

SCHERER, BERNARD—End—Nebraska
1936–38   Green Bay Packers
1939   Pittsburgh Steelers

SCHIBANOFF, ALEXANDER—Tackle—Franklin-Marshall
1942   Detroit Lions

SCHIEB, L.—Center—Washington Univ. (Mo.)
1930   Brooklyn Dodgers

SCHIECHL, JOHN—Center—Santa Clara
1940–42   Pittsburgh Steelers
1945–46   Chicago Bears
1947   San Francisco 49ers

SCHILLING, RALPH—End—Oklahoma City Univ.
1946   Washington Redskins
1946   Buffalo Bisons

SCHIMMEL, ??—Back—??
1925   Rock Island Independents

SCHLEICH, VICTOR—Tackle—Nebraska
1947   New York Yankees

SCHLINKMAN, WALTER—Back—Texas Tech.
1946–50   Green Bay Packers

SCHLUESNER, VINCENT—Tackle—Iowa
1930–31   Portsmouth Spartans

SCHMAEHL, ARTHUR—Back—None
1921   Green Bay Packers

SCHMEELK, GARRY—Tackle— Manhattan
1942   New York Giants

SCHMIDT, KERMIT—End— California Agr.
1933   Cincinnati Reds

SCHMITT, THEODORE—Center— Pittsburgh
1938–40   Philadelphia Eagles
1940   Pittsburgh Steelers

SCHNEIDER, DONALD—Back— Pennsylvania
1948   Buffalo Bills

SCHNEIDER, LEROY—Tackle— Tulane
1947   Brooklyn

SCHNEIDMAN, HERMAN—Back— Iowa
1935–39   Green Bay Packers
1940   Chicago Cardinals

SCHNELLBACHER, OTTO—Back— Kansas
1948   New York Yankees—I (AAFC)
1949   New York Yankees
1950   New York Giants
1951   New York Giants—I (NFL)

SCHNELLER, JOHN—Back— Wisconsin
1933   Portsmouth Spartans
1934–36   Detroit Lions

SCHOEMANN, ROY—Center— Marquette
1938   Green Bay Packers

SCHOLL, R. F.—Guard—Lehigh
1929   Boston Braves

SCHOTTEL, IVAN—Back— Northwest Missouri State Teachers
1946   Detroit Lions
1948   Detroit Lions

SCHROEDER, EUGENE—End— Virginia
1951   Chicago Bears

SCHROEDER, WILLIAM—Back— Wisconsin
1946–47   Chicago Rockets

SCHROLL, CHARLES—Back—LSU
1949   Buffalo Bills
1950   Detroit Lions
1951   Green Bay Packers

SCHUBER, JAMES—Back—Navy
1930   Brooklyn Dodgers

SCHUELE, JACOB—Back—Wisconsin
1939   Philadelphia Eagles

SCHUETTE, CARL—Back Marquette
1948–49   Buffalo Bills
1950–51   Green Bay Packers

SCHUETTE, PAUL—Guard— Wisconsin
1928   New York Giants
1930–32   Chicago Bears

SCHULER, WILLIAM—Tackle— Yale
1947–48   New York Giants

SCHULTZ, CHARLES—Tackle— Minnesota
1939–41   Green Bay Packers

SCHULTZ, EBERLE—Guard—Oregon State
1940   Philadelphia Eagles
1941   Pittsburgh Steelers
1942   Philadelphia Eagles
1943   Phil-Pitt
1944   Card-Pitt
1945   Cleveland Rams
1946–47   Los Angeles Rams

SCHUPBACH, O. T.—Tackle—West Texas State
1941–42   Cleveland Rams

SCHUSTER, RICHARD—End— Penn State
1925   Canton Bulldogs

SCHWAB, RAYMOND—Back— Oklahoma City Univ.
1931   New York Giants
1932   Staten Island Stapletons

SCHWALL, VICTOR—Back— Northwestern
1947–50   Chicago Cardinals

SCHWAMMEL, ADOLPH—Tackle— Oregon
1934–36   Green Bay Packers
1943–44   Green Bay Packers

SCHWARTZ, ELMER—Back— Washington State
1931   Portsmouth Spartans
1932   Chicago Cardinals
1933   Pittsburgh Pirates

SCHWARTZ, PERRY—End— California
1938–42   Brooklyn Dodgers
1946   New York Yankees

SCHWEDER, JOHN—Guard— Pennsylvania
1950   Baltimore Colts
1950   Philadelphia Eagles
1951   Pittsburgh Steelers

SCHWEIDLER, RICHARD—Back—
St. Louis Univ.
1938–39   Chicago Bears
1946   Chicago Bears

SCHWENK, WILSON—Back—
Washington (St. Louis)
1942   Chicago Cardinals
1946   Cleveland Browns
1947   Baltimore Colts
1947   Buffalo Bills
1948   New York Yankees

SCOLLARD, NICHOLAS—End—St.
Josephs
1946–48   Boston Yanks
1949   New York Bulldogs

SCOTT, CLYDE—Back—Arkansas
1949–51   Philadelphia Eagles

SCOTT, EDWARD—Guard—
Monmouth
1924   Rock Island Independents

SCOTT, JOHN—Back—Lafayette
1920–23   Buffalo All Americans

SCOTT, JOSEPH—Back—San
Francisco
1948–51   New York Giants

SCOTT, PERRY—End—Muhlenberg
1942   Detroit Lions

SCOTT, PRINCE—End—Texas Tech.
1946   Miami Seahawks

SCOTT, RALPH—Tackle—
Wisconsin
1921   Chicago Bears (Staleys)
1922–23   Chicago Bears
1923   Akron Steels
1924   Minneapolis Marines
1924–25   Chicago Bears
1927   New York Yankees
1929   Orange

SCOTT, VINCENT—Guard—Notre
Dame
1947–48   Buffalo Bills

SCRUGGS, EDWIN—End—Rice
1947–48   Brooklyn Dodgers

SEABRIGHT, CHARLES—Back—
West Virginia
1941   Cleveland Rams
1946–50   Pittsburgh Steelers

SEARS, VICTOR—Tackle—Oregon
State
1941–42   Philadelphia Eagles
1943   Phil-Pitt
1944–51   Philadelphia Eagles

SEASHOLTZ, GEORGE—Back—
Lafayette
1922   Milwaukee Badgers
1924   Kenosha

SEBASTIAN, MICHAEL—Back—
Pittsburgh
1935   Philadelphia Eagles
1935   Pittsburgh Pirates
1937   Cleveland Indians

SEBEK, NICHOLAS—Back—Indiana
1951   Washington Redskins

SEBO, SAM—Back—Syracuse
1930   Newark

SEBORG, HENRY—Back—
Kalamazoo
1930   Minneapolis Redjackets
1930–31   Frankford Yellowjackets

SECHRIST, LEONARD—Guard—
West Virginia
1924   Akron Steels
1925   Frankford Yellowjackets
1926   Hammond Pros
1926   Louisville Colonels

SECORD, JOSEPH—Center—None
1922   Green Bay Packers

SEDBROOK, LEONARD—Back—
Oklahoma City Univ.
1928   Detroit Wolverines
1929–31   New York Giants

SEEDS, ??—Back—??
1926   Canton Bulldogs

SEEMAN, GEORGE—End—Nebraska
1940   Green Bay Packers

SEIBERT, EDWARD—Guard—West
Virginia Wesleyan
1923   Hammond Pros

SEIBERT, HAROLD—Center—
Oberlin
1927   Dayton Triangles

SEIBOLD, CHAMP—Tackle—
Wisconsin
1934–38   Green Bay Packers
1940   Green Bay Packers
1942   Green Bay Packers

SEICK, EARL—Guard—Manhattan
1942   New York Giants

SEIDELSON, HARRY—Guard—
Pittsburgh
1925   Frankford Yellowjackets
1926   Akron Steels

SEIFERLING, JOHN—Back—Fresno
State
1947   Chicago Bears

SEIGEL, ??—End—??
1925 Cleveland Indians

SELF, CLARENCE—Back—Wisconsin
1949 Chicago Cardinals
1950–51 Detroit Lions

SELTZER, HARRY—Back—Morris-Harvey
1942 Detroit Lions

SEMES, BERNARD—Back—Duquesne
1944 Card-Pitt

SENN, WILLIAM—Back—Knox
1926–31 Chicago Bears
1934 St. Louis Gunners

SENO, FRANK—Back—George Washington
1943–44 Washington Redskins
1945–46 Chicago Cardinals
1947 Boston Yanks—I (Tie with F. Reagen)
1948 Boston Yanks
1949 Washington Redskins

SENSANBAUGHER, DEAN—Back—Ohio State
1948 Cleveland Browns
1949 New York Bulldogs

SERGIENKO, GEORGE—Tackle—American International
1943 Brooklyn Dodgers
1944 Brooklyn Tigers
1945 Boston Yanks
1946 Brooklyn Dodgers

SERINI, WASHINGTON—Guard—Kentucky
1948–51 Chicago Bears

SETCAVAGE, JOSEPH—Back—Duquesne
1942–43 Brooklyn Dodgers

SETRON, JOSEPH—Guard—West Virginia
1923 Cleveland Indians

SEXTON, LINWOOD—Back—Wichita
1948 Los Angeles Dons

SEYFRIT, ??—End—??
1923 Toledo Maroons
1924 Hammond Pros

SEYMOUR, ROBERT—Back—Oklahoma
1940–45 Washington Redskins
1946 Los Angeles Dons

SHAFFER, LELAND—Back—Kansas State
1933 Pittsburgh Pirates
1935–43 New York Giants
1945 New York Giants

SHANLEY, ??—Tackle—Washington U. (Mo.)
1927 Duluth Eskimos

SHAPIRO, ??—Back—??
1929 Staten Island Stapletons

SHARE, NATHAN—Guard—Tufts
1925 Providence Steamrollers

SHARKEY, EDWARD—Guard—Nevada, Duke
1947–49 New York Yankees
1950 New York Yanks

SHARP, EVERETT—Tackle—California Tech.
1944–45 Washington Redskins

SHAW, ??—Guard—??
1931 Chicago Cardinals

SHAW, CHARLES—Guard—Oklahoma A & M
1950 San Francisco 49ers

SHAW, EDWARD—Back—Nebraska
1922 Canton Bulldogs
1923 Akron Steels

SHAW, ROBERT—End—Ohio State
1945 Cleveland Rams
1946 Los Angeles Rams
1949 Los Angeles Rams
1950 Chicago Cardinals

SHEARD, ALFRED—Back—St. Lawrence
1923 Rochester Kodaks
1924–25 Rochester Jeffersons

SHEDLOSKY, EDMOND—Back—Tulsa & Fordham
1945 New York Giants

SHEEKS, PAUL—Back—South Dakota
1921–22 Akron Steels

SHELBURNE, JOHN—Back—Dartmouth
1922 Hammond Pros

SHELDON, JAMES—End—Brown
1926 Brooklyn Dodgers

SHELLOGG, ALEXANDER—Tackle—Notre Dame
1939 Brooklyn Dodgers

SHELLY, DEXTER—Back—Texas
1931 Providence Steamrollers
1931 Portsmouth Spartans
1932 Chicago Cardinals
1932–33 Green Bay Packers

SHELTON, MURRAY—End—Cornell
1920   Buffalo All Americans

SHENEFELT, PAUL—??—??
1934–35   Chicago Cardinals

SHEPHERD, WILLIAM—Back—Western Maryland
1935   Boston Redskins
1935–40   Detroit Lions

SHERMAN, AL—Back—Brooklyn College
1939–40   Chicago Bears
1943   Phil-Pitt
1944–47   Philadelphia Eagles

SHETLEY, RHOTEN—Back—Furman
1940–42   Brooklyn Dodgers
1946   Brooklyn Dodgers

SHIPKEY, JERRY—Back—UCLA
1948–51   Pittsburgh Steelers

SHIRES, ARTHUR—Back—Brooklyn College
1945   Philadelphia Eagles

SHIREY, FREDERICK—Tackle—Nebraska
1940–41   Cleveland Rams

SHIRLEY, MARION—Tackle—Oklahoma City Univ.
1948–49   New York Yankees

SHOCKLEY, ARNOLD—Guard—Southwestern State
1929   Providence Steamrollers
1929   Boston Braves

SHOEMAKER, HUBBARD—Guard—Illinois
1920–21   Chicago Bears (Staleys)

SHOENER, HAROLD—End—Iowa
1948–50   San Francisco 49ers

SHOENER, HERBERT—End—Iowa
1948–49   Washington Redskins

SHONK, JOHN—End—?
1941   Philadelphia Eagles

SHOOK, FREDERICK—Center—TCU
1940–41   Chicago Cardinals

SHOULTS, PAUL—Back—Miami (Ohio)
1949   New York Bulldogs

SHUGART, CLYDE—Guard—Iowa State
1939–44   Washington Redskins

SHULA, DONALD—John Carroll
1951   Cleveland Browns

SHULTZ, JOHN—Back—Temple
1930   Frankford Yellowjackets

SHURNAS, MARSHALL—End—Missouri
1947   Cleveland Browns

SHURTLEFF, BERTRAND—Back—Brown
1925   Providence Steamrollers
1929   Buffalo Bisons
1929   Boston Braves

SHURTZ, HUBERT—Tackle—LSU
1948   Pittsburgh Steelers

SIANO, ANTHONY—Center—Fordham
1932   Boston Braves
1934   Brooklyn Dodgers

SIDORIK, ALEXANDER—Tackle—Mississippi State
1947   Boston Yanks
1948–49   Baltimore Colts

SIEFERS, ??—End—??
1924   Hammond Pros

SIEGAL, JOHN—End—Columbia
1939–43   Chicago Bears

SIEGERT, HERBERT—Guard—Illinois
1949–51   Washington Redskins
1951   New York Yanks

SIEGFRIED, ORVILLE—Back—Washington & Jefferson
1923   St. Louis Browns

SIEGLE, JULES—Back—Northwestern
1948   New York Giants

SIEMERING, LAWRENCE—Center—San Francisco
1935–36   Boston Redskins

SIERADZKI, STEPHEN—Back—Michigan State
1948   New York Yankees
1948   Brooklyn Dodgers

SIEROCINSKI, STEPHEN—Tackle—None
1946   Boston Yanks

SIES, DALE—Guard—Pittsburgh
1921–22   Dayton Triangles
1923   Rock Island Independents
1924   Dayton Triangles

SIGILLO, DOMINIC—Tackle—Xavier (Cincinnati)
1942–44   Chicago Bears
1945   Detroit Lions

SIGNAIGO, JOSEPH—Guard—Notre Dame
1948-49   New York Yankees
1950   New York Yanks

SIGURDSON, SIGURD—End—Pacific Lutheran
1947   Baltimore Colts

SIKICH, RUDOLPH—Tackle—Minnesota
1945   Cleveland Rams

SILLIN, FRANK—Back—Western Maryland
1927-29   Dayton Triangles

SIMAS, WILLIAM—Back—St. Mary's (Cal.)
1932   Chicago Cardinals

SIMENSON, DONALD—Tackle—St. Thomas
1951   Los Angeles Rams

SIMINGTON, MILTON—Guard—Arkansas
1942   Pittsburgh Steelers
1941   Cleveland Rams

SIMMONS, JOHN—Guard—Detroit
1948   Baltimore Colts
1948   Chicago Rockets
1949-50   Detroit Lions
1950-51   Chicago Cardinals

SIMMONS, ROY—Back—Syracuse
1927   Cleveland Indians
1928   Providence Steamrollers

SIMON, ??—End—??
1924   Minneapolis Marines

SIMONETTI, LEONARD—Tackle—Tennessee
1946-48   Cleveland Browns

SIMPSON, EBER—Back—Wisconsin
1922   Toledo Maroons
1923   St. Louis Browns
1924   Kenosha

SIMS, GEORGE—Back—Baylor
1949-50   Los Angeles Rams

SINGER, WALTER—End—Syracuse
1935-36   New York Giants

SINGLETON, JOHN—Back—Wabash
1929   Dayton Triangles

SINKO, STEPHEN—Tackle—Duquesne
1934-36   Boston Redskins

SINKOVITZ, FRANK—Center—Duke
1947-51   Pittsburgh Steelers

SINKWICH, FRANK—Back—Georgia
1943   Detroit Lions
1944   Detroit Lions—K–V
1946-47   New York Yankees
1947   Baltimore Colts

SIROCHMAN, GEORGE—Guard—Duquesne
1942   Pittsburgh Steelers
1944   Detroit Lions

SISK, JOHN—Back—Marquette
1932-36   Chicago Bears

SITES, VINCENT—End—Pittsburgh
1936-37   Pittsburgh Pirates

SITKO, EMIL—Back—Notre Dame
1950   San Francisco 49ers
1951   Chicago Cardinals

SIVELL, RALPH—Guard—Alabama Polytech.
1938-42   Brooklyn Dodgers
1944-45   New York Giants
1946   Miami Seahawks

SKLADANY, LEO—End—Pittsburgh
1949   Philadelphia Eagles
1950   New York Giants

SKOZEN, STANLEY—Back—Western Reserve
1944   Cleveland Rams

SKOGLUND, ROBERT—End—Notre Dame
1947   Green Bay Packers

SKORICH, NICHOLAS—Guard—Cincinnati
1946-48   Pittsburgh Steelers

SKORONSKI, EDWARD—Center—Purdue
1935-36   Pittsburgh Pirates
1937   Brooklyn Dodgers

SKUDIN, DAVID—Guard—New York Univ.
1929   Staten Island Stapletons

SLACKFORD, DAVID—Back—Notre Dame
1921   Canton Bulldogs

SLATER, FRED—Tackle—Iowa
1922-25   Rock Island Independents
1926   Milwaukee Badgers
1927-31   Chicago Cardinals

SLATER, WALTER—Back—Tennessee
1947   Pittsburgh Steelers

SLEIGHT, ELMER—Tackle—Purdue
1930-31   Green Bay Packers

**SLIVINSKI, STEPHEN—Guard—
Washington**
1939–43   Washington Redskins

SLOAN, DWIGHT—Back—Arkansas
1938   Chicago Cardinals
1939–40   Detroit Lions

**SLOSBURG, PHILIP—Back—
Temple**
1948   Boston Yanks
1949   New York Bulldogs

SLOVAK, MARTIN—Back—Toledo
1939–41   Cleveland Rams

SMEJA, RUDOLPH—End—Michigan
1944–45   Chicago Bears
1946   Philadelphia Eagles

SMITH, BEN—End—Alabama
1933   Green Bay Packers
1934–35   Pittsburgh Pirates
1937   Washington Redskins

SMITH, BRUCE—Back—Minnesota
1945–48   Green Bay Packers
1949   Los Angeles Rams

SMITH, CHARLES—Back—Georgia
1947   Chicago Cardinals

SMITH, CLYDE—Back—Missouri
1923   Canton Bulldogs
1924   Cleveland Bulldogs
1927   Cleveland Bulldogs
1927–30   Providence Steamrollers
1930–31   Portsmouth Spartans
1933   Boston Redskins

SMITH, EARL—Tackle—Ripon
1922   Green Bay Packers
1923   Racine Legion
1923   Rock Island Independents
1923   Milwaukee Badgers
1923   Hammond Pros
1924   Racine Legion
1925   Detroit Panthers

**SMITH, EDWARD—Back—Notre
Dame**
1934   Chicago Cardinals
1936   Boston Redskins

**SMITH, ERNEST—Tackle—
Southern California**
1935–37   Green Bay Packers
1939   Green Bay Packers
1940   Detroit Lions

**SMITH, GAYLON—Back—
Southwestern Univ.**
1937–38   Pittsburgh Pirates
1939–42   Cleveland Rams
1943   Chicago Cardinals
1946   Cleveland Browns

SMITH, GEORGE—Guard—Georgia
1930   Frankford Yellowjackets

**SMITH, GEORGE—Center—
California**
1937   Washington Redskins
1940–43   Washington Redskins
1944   Brooklyn Tigers
1945   Boston Yanks
1947   San Francisco 49ers

SMITH, H?—Center—None
1921   Rochester Kodaks
1923   Rochester Kodaks
1924–25   Rochester Jeffersons

**SMITH, HOUSTON ALLEN—End—
Mississippi**
1947–48   Chicago Bears

SMITH, JAMES—Tackle—Colorado
1945   Philadelphia Eagles
1947   Los Angeles Dons

SMITH, JAMES—Back—Iowa
1948   Brooklyn Dodgers
1948   Buffalo Bills
1949   Chicago Hornets
1951   Detroit Lions

SMITH, JOHN—End—Stanford
1941   Philadelphia Eagles
1943   Washington Redskins

SMITH, JOSEPH—End—Texas Tech.
1948   Baltimore Colts

SMITH, LEO—End—??
1928   Providence Steamrollers

SMITH, MILTON—End—UCLA
1945   Philadelphia Eagles

**SMITH, OLIN—Tackle—Ohio
Wesleyan**
1924   Cleveland Bulldogs
1927–29   Providence Steamrollers

SMITH, OSCAR—Back—Texas Mines
1948   Green Bay Packers
1949   New York Bulldogs

SMITH, PAT—Back—Michigan
1920–21   Buffalo All Americans
1923   Buffalo All Americans
1924–25   Kansas City Cowboys

SMITH, RAY—Center—Missouri
1933   Philadelphia Eagles

**SMITH, REX—End—LaCrosse
Teachers**
1922   Green Bay Packers

**SMITH, RICHARD—Guard—Notre
Dame**
1927   Green Bay Packers
1929   Green Bay Packers
1930–31   New York Giants

SMITH, RILEY—Back—Alabama
1936 Boston Redskins
1937–38 Washington Redskins

SMITH, ROBERT—Back—Iowa
1949–50 Detroit Lions

SMITH, RUSSELL—Guard—Illinois
1920 Chicago Cardinals
1921 Chicago Bears (Staleys)
1923–25 Chicago Cardinals

SMITH, STUART—Back—Bucknell
1937–38 Pittsburgh Pirates

**SMITH, TRUETT—Back—Wyoming,
Mississippi State**
1950–51 Pittsburgh Steelers

**SMITH, VERDA—Back—Abilene
Christian**
1949–51 Los Angeles Rams

SMITH, WARREN—Center—Carlton
1921 Green Bay Packers

**SMITH, WILLIAM—End—
Washington**
1934 Chicago Cardinals
1935 Chicago Cardinals—F (6) (Tie
with A. Niccolai)
1936–39 Chicago Cardinals

**SMITH, WILLIAM—Tackle—North
Carolina**
1948 Chicago Rockets
1948 Los Angeles Dons

SMITH, WILLIS—Back—Idaho
1934–35 New York Giants

SMUKLER, DAVID—Back—Temple
1936–39 Philadelphia Eagles
1944 Boston Yanks

SMYTH, JAMES—Back—Centre
1926 Providence Steamrollers

SMYTH, LOUIS—Back—Texas
1922–23 Canton Bulldogs
1925 Rochester Jeffersons
1925–26 Frankford Yellowjackets

**SMYTH, WILLIAM—Tackle—
Cincinnati**
1947–50 Los Angeles Rams

SNEDDON, ROBERT—Back—Weber
1944 Washington Redskins
1945 Detroit Lions
1946 Los Angeles Dons

SNELL, GEORGE—Back—Penn State
1927 Buffalo Bisons

**SNELLING, KENNETH—Back—
UCLA**
1945 Green Bay Packers

SNOOTS, J. LEE—Back—None
1923 Columbus Tigers
1925 Columbus Tigers

SNYDER, HARRY—Back—Ohio
1929 New York Giants
1930 Staten Island
1934–35 Pittsburgh Pirates

SNYDER, ROBERT—Back—Ohio
1937–38 Cleveland Rams
1939–43 Chicago Bears
1947 Los Angeles Rams—Head Coach

SOAR, HENRY—Back—Providence
1937–44 New York Giants
1946 New York Giants

**SOBOLESKI, JOSEPH—Tackle—
Michigan**
1949 Chicago Hornets
1949 Washington Redskins
1950 Detroit Lions
1951 New York Yanks

**SOFISH, ALEXANDER—Guard—
Grove City**
1931 Providence Steamrollers

**SOHN, BENJAMIN—Guard—
Southern California**
1934 Cincinnati Reds
1941 New York Giants

**SOKOLIS, STANLEY—Tackle—
Pennsylvania**
1933 Philadelphia Eagles

**SOLTAU, GORDON—End—
Minnesota**
1950–51 San Francisco 49ers

**SOMERS, GEORGE—Tackle—
LaSalle (Pa.)**
1939–40 Philadelphia Eagles
1941–42 Pittsburgh Steelers

SOMMERS, JOHN—Center—UCLA
1947 Washington Redskins

**SONNENBERG, GUSTAVE—Guard—
Dartmouth**
1920 Buffalo All Americans
1923 Columbus Tigers
1924 Pottsville Maroons
1925–26 Detroit Panthers
1927–28 Providence Steamrollers
1930 Providence Steamrollers
Died at Great Lakes Training Station, Sept. 13, 1944. Chief Specialist,
U.S. Navy.

SORCE, ROSS—Tackle—Georgetown
1945 Pittsburgh Steelers

SORENSON, GLEN—Guard—Utah
1943–45 Green Bay Packers

SORTET, WILBUR—End—West Virginia
1933–38 Pittsburgh Pirates
1939–40 Pittsburgh Steelers

SOSSAMON, LOUIS—Center— South Carolina
1946–49 New York Yankees

SOUCHAK, FRANK—End— Pittsburgh
1939 Pittsburgh Steelers

SOUDERS, CECIL—End—Ohio State
1947–49 Detroit Lions

SPADACCINI, VICTOR—Back— Minnesota
1938–40 Cleveland Rams

SPAGNA, JOSEPH—Center—Lehigh
1920–21 Buffalo All Americans
1924–25 Frankford Yellowjackets

SPANGLER, EUGENE—Back— Tulsa
1946 Detroit Lions

SPANIEL, FRANK—Back—Notre Dame
1950 Baltimore Colts
1950 Washington Redskins

SPARKMAN, ALAN—Tackle—Texas A & M
1948–49 Los Angeles Rams

SPARKS, DAVID—Guard—South Carolina
1951 San Francisco 49ers

SPARLIS, ALBERT—Guard—UCLA
1946 Green Bay Packers

SPARR, EDWIN—Tackle—Carroll
1926 Racine Legion

SAVITAL, JAMES—Back—Oklahoma A & M
1949 Los Angeles Dons
1950 Baltimore Colts

SPEAR, GLEN—Back—Drake
1926 Kansas City Cowboys

SPECK, "DUTCH"—Guard—None
1920–23 Canton Bulldogs
1924 Akron Steels
1925–26 Canton Bulldogs

SPEEDIE, MAC—End—Utah
1946 Cleveland Browns
1947 Cleveland Browns—R (AAFC)
1948 Cleveland Browns—R (AAFC)
1949 Cleveland Browns—R (AAFC)
1950–51 Cleveland Browns

SPEEGLE, CLIFTON—Center— Oklahoma
1945 Chicago Cardinals

SPELLACY, ??—End—??
1922 Buffalo All Americans

SPELLMAN, JOHN—End—Brown
1925–31 Providence Steamrollers
1932 Boston Braves

SPENCER, ??—Guard—??
1928 Dayton Triangles
1929 Dayton Triangles

SPENCER, JOSEPH—Tackle— Oklahoma A & M
1948 Brooklyn Dodgers
1949 Cleveland Browns
1950–51 Green Bay Packers

SPETH, GEORGE—Tackle—Murray State Teachers
1942 Detroit Lions

SPIERS, ROBERT—Tackle—Ohio State
1922 Akron Steels
1925 Cleveland Indians

SPILLERS, RAYMOND—Tackle— Arkansas
1937 Philadelphia Eagles

SPINNEY, ARTHUR—End—Boston College
1950 Baltimore Colts

SPIRIDA, JOHN—End—St. Anselm's
1939–40 Washington Redskins

SPIZAK, CHARLES—Back—Carnegie Tech.
1938 Pittsburgh Pirates

SPONAUGLE, ROBERT—End— Pennsylvania
1949 New York Bulldogs

SPRINGER, HAROLD—End— Oklahoma Teachers
1945 New York Giants

SPRINGSTEEN, WILLIAM—Center— Lehigh
1925–26 Frankford Yellowjackets
1927–28 Chicago Cardinals

SPRINKLE, EDWARD—End— Hardin-Simmons
1944–51 Chicago Bears

SPRINKLE, HUBERT—Tackle— Carnegie Tech.
1924 Akron Steels
1925 Cleveland Indians

SPRUILL, JAMES—Tackle—Rice
1948–49 Baltimore Colts

SQUYRES, SEAMAN—Back—Rice
1933   Cincinnati Reds

STACCO, EDWARD—Tackle—Colgate
1947   Detroit Lions
1947–48   Washington Redskins

**STACKPOOL, JOHN—Back—
Washington**
1942   Philadelphia Eagles

STACY, JAMES—Tackle—Oklahoma
1935–37   Detroit Lions

**STAFFORD, HARRISON—Back—
Texas**
1934   New York Giants

**STAHLMAN, RICHARD—End—
Chicago**
1924   Hammond Pros
1924   Kenosha
1924–25   Akron Steels
1927   New York Giants
1930   New York Giants
1931–32   Green Bay Packers
1933   Chicago Bears

**STANDLEE, NORMAN—Back—
Stanford**
1941   Chicago Bears
1946–51   San Francisco 49ers

STANLEY, C. B.—Tackle—Tulsa
1946   Buffalo Bisons

**STANSAUK, DONALD—Tackle—
Denver**
1950–51   Green Bay Packers

STANTON, HENRY—End—Arizona
1946–47   New York Yankees

**STANTON, WILLIAM—End—
North Carolina State**
1949   Buffalo Bills

**STARK, HOWARD—Tackle—
Wisconsin**
1923   Racine Legion

**STARRET, BENJAMIN—Back—
St. Mary's (Cal.)**
1941   Pittsburgh Steelers
1941–45   Green Bay Packers

STASICA, LEO—Back—Colorado
1941   Brooklyn Dodgers
1941   Philadelphia Eagles
1943   Washington Redskins
1944   Boston Yanks

**STASICA, STANLEY—Back—South
Carolina**
1946   Miami Seahawks

**STATON, JAMES—Tackle—Wake
Forest**
1951   Washington Redskins

**STATUTO, ARTHUR—Center—
Notre Dame**
1948–49   Buffalo Bills
1950   Los Angeles Rams

**STAUTBERG, GERALD—Guard—
Cincinnati**
1951   Chicago Bears

**STAUTNER, ERNEST—Tackle—
Boston College**
1950–51   Pittsburgh Steelers

**STAUTZENBERGER, ODELL—
Guard—Texas A & M**
1949   Buffalo Bills

**STEBER, JOHN—Guard—Georgia
Tech.**
1946–50   Washington Redskins

**STEELE, ERNEST—Back—
Washington**
1942   Philadelphia Eagles
1943   Phil-Pitt
1944–48   Philadelphia Eagles

STEELE, HAROLD—Back—Syracuse
1921–22   Rochester Kodaks
1922   Akron Steels

STEEN, FRANK—End—Rice
1939   Green Bay Packers

STEEN, JAMES—Tackle—Syracuse
1935–36   Detroit Lions

STEERE, RICHARD—Tackle—Drake
1951   Philadelphia Eagles

STEFIK, ROBERT—End—Niagara
1948   Buffalo Bills

**STEIN, HERBERT—Center—
Washington & Jefferson**
1921   Buffalo All Americans
1922   Toledo Maroons
1924   Frankford Yellowjackets
1925   Pottsville Maroons
1926   Canton Bulldogs
1928   Pottsville Maroons
1929–30   Staten Island Stapletons

**STEIN, RUSSELL—Tackle—
Pittsburgh**
1922   Toledo Maroons
1924   Frankford Yellowjackets
1925   Pottsville Maroons

STEIN, WILLIAM—Guard—Fordham
1923–24   Duluth Kelleys
1925–27   Duluth Eskimos
1928   Chicago Cardinals
1931   New York Giants
1932   Brooklyn Dodgers

STEINBACH, LAURENCE—Tackle—St. Thomas
1930–31 Chicago Bears
1932 Chicago Cardinals
1933 Philadelphia

STEINER, ROY—End—Alabama
1950–51 Green Bay Packers

STEINKE, GILBERT—Back—Texas A & M
1945–48 Philadelphia Eagles

STEINKEMPER, WILLIAM—Tackle—Notre Dame
1942–43 Chicago Bears

STEINMETZ, KENNETH—Back—None
1944–45 Boston Yanks

STENN, PAUL—Tackle—Villanova
1942 New York Giants
1946 Washington Redskins
1947 Pittsburgh Steelers
1948–51 Chicago Bears

STENNET, FRED—Back—St. Mary's (Cal.)
1931 Portsmouth Spartans
1932 Chicago Cardinals

STEPHENS, JOHN—End—Marshall
1938 Cleveland Rams

STEPHENS, LESLIE—Center—Idaho
1926 Brooklyn Dodgers
1927–28 New York Yankees

STEPHENSON, DAVID—Guard—West Virginia
1950 Los Angeles Rams
1951 Green Bay Packers

STEPONOVICH, ANTHONY—Guard—Southern California
1930 Minneapolis Redjackets
1930 Frankford Yellowjackets
1933 Boston Redskins

STERNAMAN, EDWARD—Back—Illinois
1920–21 Chicago Bears (Staleys)
1923–30 Chicago Bears

STERNAMAN, JOSEPH—Back—Illinois
1922–25 Chicago Bears
1927–30 Chicago Bears

STEUBER, ROBERT—Back—Missouri
1942–43 Chicago Bears
1946 Cleveland Browns
1947 Los Angeles Dons
1948 Buffalo Bills

STEVENS, PETER—Center—Temple
1936 Philadelphia Eagles

STEVENSON, ??—??—??
1934 Cincinnati Reds

STEVENSON, ARTHUR—Guard—Fordham
1922 Columbus Tigers

STEVENSON, RALPH—Guard—Oklahoma
1940 Cleveland Rams

STEWART, ??—Guard—??
1923 Akron Steels

STEWART, CHARLES—Tackle—Carnegie Tech.
1943 Phil-Pitt

STEWART, RALPH—Center—Missouri, Notre Dame
1944 Brooklyn Tigers
1947–48 New York Yankees
1948 Baltimore Colts

STEWART, VAUGHN—Center—Alabama
1942 Brooklyn Dodgers
1943 Chicago Cardinals

STICKEL, WALTER—Tackle—Pennsylvania
1946–49 Chicago Bears
1950–51 Philadelphia Eagles

STIFLER, JAMES—End—Brown
1927 Providence Steamrollers

STILL, JAMES—Back—Georgia Tech.
1948–49 Buffalo Bills

STINCHCOMB, PETER—Back—Illinois
1921 Chicago Bears (Staleys)
1922 Chicago Bears
1923 Columbus Tigers
1926 Louisville Colonels

STOCK, HERBERT—Back—Kenyon
1924–25 Columbus Tigers

STOCKTON, HERSCHEL—Guard—Gonzaga
1937–38 Philadelphia Eagles

STOCKTON, HOUSTON—Back—Gonzaga
1925–26 Frankford Yellowjackets
1928 Frankford Yellowjackets
1929 Providence Steamrollers
1929 Boston Braves

STOFER, KENNETH—Back—Cornell
1946 Buffalo Bisons

STOFKO, EDWARD—Back—Wake Forest
1945 Pittsburgh Steelers

STOJACK, FRANK—Guard— Washington State
1935–36 Brooklyn Dodgers

STOKES, LEE—Center—Centenary
1937–39 Detroit Lions
1943 Chicago Cardinals

STOLFA, ALTON—Back—Luther
1939 Chicago Bears

STONE, WILLIAM—Back—Bradley
1949–50 Baltimore Colts
1951 Chicago Bears

STONEBRAKER, JOHN—End— Southern California
1942 Green Bay Packers

STONESIFER, DONALD—End— Northwestern
1951 Chicago Cardinals

STORER, JOHN—Back—Lehigh
1924 Frankford Yellowjackets

STORM, EDWARD—Back—Santa Clara
1934–35 Philadelphia Eagles

STOTSBERG, HAROLD—Tackle— Xavier
1930 Brooklyn Dodgers

STOUGH, GLEN—Tackle—Duke
1945 Pittsburgh Steelers

STOUT, PETER—Back—Texas Christian Univ.
1949 Washington Redskins
1951 Washington Redskins

STOVALL, RICHARD—Center— Abilene Christian
1947–48 Detroit Lions
1949 Washington Redskins

STRADER, NORMAN—Back—St. Mary's (Cal.)
1927 Chicago Cardinals
1950–51 New York Yanks—Head Coach

STRALKA, CLEMENT—Guard— Georgetown
1938–42 Washington Redskins
1945–46 Washington Redskins

STRAND, LIEF—Center—Fordham
1924 Duluth Kelleys

STRASSER, ??—End—None
1925 Canton Bulldogs

STRAUSBAUGH, JAMES—Back— Ohio State
1946 Chicago Cardinals

STRAUSS, ARTHUR—Back— Phillips
1923 Toledo Maroons
1924 Kansas City Cowboys

STRIBLING, MAJURE—End— Mississippi
1951 New York Giants

STRICKLAND, BISHOP—Back— South Carolina
1951 San Francisco 49ers

STRICKLAND, WILLIAM—Guard— Lombard
1923 Milwaukee Badgers
1923 Racine Legion

STRINGER, EUGENE—Back—John Carroll
1925 Cleveland Indians

STRINGFELLOW, JOSEPH—End— Mississippi Southern
1942 Detroit Lions

STRODE, WOODROW—End—UCLA
1946 Los Angeles Rams

STROHMEYER, GEORGE—Center— Notre Dame
1948 Brooklyn Dodgers
1949 Chicago Hornets

STROMIELLO, MICHAEL—End— Colgate
1930–32 Brooklyn Dodgers
1934 Brooklyn Dodgers

STRONG, KENNETH—Back—New York Univ.
1929–32 Staten Island Stapletons
1933–35 New York Giants
1939 New York Giants
1944 New York Giants—F (6)
1945–47 New York Giants

STROSCHEIN, BROCK—End—UCLA
1951 New York Yanks

STRUESSI, ??—Tackle—??
1926 Chicago Cardinals

STRUTT, ARTHUR—Back— Duquesne
1935–36 Pittsburgh Pirates

STRZYKALSKI, JOHN—Back— Marquette
1946–51 San Francisco 49ers

STUART, JAMES—Tackle—Oregon
1938 Washington Redskins
1941 Washington Redskins

STUART, ROY—Back—Tulsa
1941   Cleveland Rams
1943   Phil-Pitt
1943   Detroit Lions
1946   Buffalo Bisons

**STUHLDREHER, HARRY—Back—
Notre Dame**
1926   Brooklyn Dodgers

**STURGEON, CECIL—Tackle—North
Dakota State**
1941   Philadelphia Eagles

**STURGEON, LYLE—Tackle—North
Dakota State**
1937   Green Bay Packers

**STURTRIDGE, DONALD—Back—
DePaul**
1928   Chicago Bears
1929   Chicago Bears

**STYDAHAR, JOSEPH—Tackle—
West Virginia**
1936–42   Chicago Bears
1945–46   Chicago Bears
1951–52   Los Angeles Rams—Head Coach

SUCHY, PAUL—End—None
1925   Cleveland Indians

SUCIC, STEPHEN—Back—Illinois
1946   Los Angeles Rams
1947   Boston Yanks
1947–48   Detroit Lions

**SUESS, RAYMOND—Tackle—
Villanova**
1926–27   Duluth Eskimos

**SUFFRIDGE, ROBERT—Guard—
Tennessee**
1941   Philadelphia Eagles
1945   Philadelphia Eagles

**SUHEY, STEPHEN—Guard—Penn
State**
1948–49   Pittsburgh Steelers

SULAITIS, JOSEPH—Back—None
1943–45   New York Giants
1946   Boston Yanks
1947–51   New York Giants

**SULLIVAN, FRANK—Center—
Loyola (New Orleans)**
1935–39   Chicago Bears
1940   Pittsburgh Steelers

**SULLIVAN, GEORGE—Back—
Pennsylvania**
1924–25   Frankford Yellowjackets

**SULLIVAN, GEORGE—End—Notre
Dame**
1949   New York Bulldogs

**SULLIVAN, ROBERT—Back—Holy
Cross, Iowa**
1947   Pittsburgh Steelers
1948   San Francisco 49ers
1948   Brooklyn Dodgers
1948   Chicago Rockets

**SULLIVAN, WALTER—Guard—
Beloit**
1921   Green Bay Packers
1923–24   Hammond Pros

**SUMMERHAYS, ROBERT—Back—
Utah**
1949–51   Green Bay Packers

**SUMPTER, ANTHONY—Guard—
None**
1946–48   Chicago Rockets

SUNDQUIST, ??—Tackle—??
1925–26   Duluth Kelleys

**SUPULSKI, LEONARD—End—
Dickinson**
1942   Philadelphia Eagles
Killed in plane crash in Nebraska. Lt.,
U.S. Air Force.

**SURABIAN, ZAREH—Tackle—
Williams**
1927   Providence Steamrollers

**SUSEOFF, NICHOLAS—End—
Washington State**
1946–49   San Francisco 49ers

**SUSTERIC, EDWARD—Back—
Findlay**
1949   Cleveland Browns

SUTCH, GEORGE—Back—Temple
1946   Chicago Cardinals

SUTTON, JOSEPH—Back—Temple
1949   Buffalo Bills
1950–51   Philadelphia Eagles

**SVENDSEN, EARL—Guard—
Minnesota**
1937–40   Green Bay Packers
1940–43   Brooklyn Dodgers

**SVENDSEN, GEORGE—Center—
Minnesota**
1935–37   Green Bay Packers
1941   Green Bay Packers

**SVOBODA, WILLIAM—Back—
Tulane**
1950–51   Chicago Cardinals

SWAIN, ??—End—??
1926   Buffalo Bisons

SWANSON, EYAR—End—Lombard
1924   Milwaukee Badgers
1925   Rock Island Independents
1925–27   Chicago Cardinals

SWEENEY, JAMES—Tackle—
Cincinnati
1944 Chicago Bears

SWEENEY, WILLIAM—??—
Pennsylvania
1936 Cleveland Rams

SWEET, FREDERICK—Back—Brown
1925 Providence Steamrollers

SWEETLAND, FREDERICK—Tackle
—Washington & Lee
1920 Akron Steels

SWEIGER, ROBERT—Back—
Minnesota
1946–48 New York Yankees
1949 Chicago Hornets

SWIACKI, WILLIAM—End—
Columbia
1948–50 New York Giants
1951 Detroit Lions

SWISHER, ROBERT—Back—
Northwestern
1938–41 Chicago Bears
1945 Chicago Bears

SWISTOWICZ, MICHAEL—Back—
Notre Dame
1950 New York Yanks
1950 Chicago Cardinals

SYLVESTER, JOHN—Back—Temple
1947 New York Yankees
1948 Baltimore Colts

SZAFARYN, LEONARD—Tackle—
North Carolina
1949 Washington Redskins
1950 Green Bay Packers

SZAKASH, PAUL—Back—Montana
1938–42 Detroit Lions

SZOT, WALTER—Tackle—Bucknell
1946–48 Chicago Cardinals
1949–50 Pittsburgh Steelers

SZYMANSKI, FRANK—Center—
Notre Dame
1945–47 Detroit Lions
1948 Philadelphia Eagles
1949 Chicago Bears

* * *

TACKETT, DOYLE—Back—None
1946–48 Brooklyn Dodgers

TACKWELL, CHARLES—End—
Kansas State
1930–31 Frankford Yellowjackets
1931–33 Chicago Bears
1933–34 Cincinnati Reds

TAIT, ARTHUR—End—Mississippi
State
1951 New York Yanks

TALBOT, JOHN—End—Brown
1926 Providence Steamrollers

TALCOTT, DONALD—Tackle—
Nevada
1947 Philadelphia Eagles

TALIAFERRO, GEORGE—Back—
Indiana
1949 Los Angeles Dons
1950–51 New York Yanks

TALLANT, DAVID—Tackle—Grove
City
1922–25 Hammond Pros

TAMBURO, SAMUEL—End—Penn
State
1949 New York Bulldogs

TANDY, GEORGE—Center—North
Carolina
1921 Cleveland Indians

TANGUAY, JAMES—Back—New
York Univ.
1933 Pittsburgh Pirates

TANNER, HAMPTON—Tackle—
Georgia
1951 San Francisco 49ers

TANNER, JOHN—End—Center
1922 Toledo Maroons
1923–24 Cleveland Indians

TANNER, ROBERT—End—
Minnesota
1930 Frankford Yellowjackets

TARRANT, JAMES—Back—Howard,
Tennessee
1946 Miami Seahawks

TARRANT, ROBERT—End—Kansas
State Teachers
1936 New York Giants

TASEFF, CARL—Back—John Carroll
1951 Cleveland Browns

TASSOS, DAMON—Guard—Texas
A & M
1945–46 Detroit Lions
1947–49 Green Bay Packers

TATUM, JAMES—End—North
Carolina State
1938 Pittsburgh Pirates

TAUGHER, CLAUDE—Back—
Marquette
1922 Green Bay Packers

TAVENOR, JOHN—Center—Indiana
1946   Miami Seahawks
1946   Brooklyn Dodgers

TAYLOR, CHARLES—Guard—Stanford
1944   Brooklyn Dodgers
1946   Miami Seahawks

TAYLOR, ERQUIET—Guard—Alabama Polytech.
1931   Staten Island Stapletons

TAYLOR, HUGH—End—Oklahoma City Univ.
1947–51   Washington Redskins

TAYLOR, JOHN—Tackle—Ohio State
1921   Chicago Bears (Staleys)
1922   Chicago Bears
1922–23   Canton Bulldogs

TAYS, ??—Back—??
1925   Chicago Cardinals
1927   Dayton Triangles
1930   Newark
1930   Staten Island Stapletons

TEBELL, GUSTAVUS—End—Wisconsin
1923–24   Columbus Tigers

TEETER, ALAN—End—Minnesota
1932   Staten Island Stapletons

TEMPLE, MARK—Back—Oregon State
1936   Brooklyn Dodgers
1936   Boston Redskins

TENNANT, JOHN—Back—Wisconsin
1941   Pittsburgh Steelers

TENNER, ROBERT—End—Minnesota
1935   Green Bay Packers

TEPO, GEORGE—End—Fordham
1946   Boston Yanks

TERSCH, ??—Tackle—??
1922–23   Minneapolis Marines

TERESHINSKI, JOSEPH—End—Georgia
1947–51   Washington Redskins

TERLEP, GEORGE—Back—Notre Dame
1946   Buffalo Bisons
1947   Buffalo Bills
1948   Cleveland Browns

TERRELL, RAYMOND—Back—Mississippi
1946–47   Cleveland Browns
1947   Baltimore Colts

TESSER, RAYMOND—End—Carnegie Tech.
1933–35   Pittsburgh Pirates

TEVIS, LEEK—Back—Washington & Miami
1947–48   Brooklyn Dodgers

TEW, LOWELL—Back—Alabama
1948–49   New York Yankees

THACKER, ALVIN—Back—Morris-Harvey
1941   Philadelphia Eagles

THAYER, HARRY—Tackle—Tennessee
1933   Portsmouth Spartans

THIBAUT, JAMES—Back—Tulane
1946   Buffalo Bisons

THIELE, CARL—End—Denison
1920–23   Dayton Triangles

THIELSCHER, KARL—Back—Dartmouth
1920   Buffalo All Americans

THOMAS, E.—Back—Pennsylvania
1926   Hartford

THOMAS, GEORGE—Back—Oklahoma
1950–51   Washington Redskins

THOMAS, JAMES—Guard—Oklahoma
1939   Chicago Cardinals
1939   Detroit Lions

THOMAS, REX—Guard—Pennsylvania
1921   Rochester Kodaks
1922–23   Buffalo All Americans
1924   Rochester Jeffersons
1927   Cleveland Indians
1928   Detroit Wolverines
1930   Brooklyn Dodgers

THOMAS, RUSSELL—TACKLE—Ohio State
1946–49   Detroit Lions

THOMAS, WILLIAM—Back—Penn State
1924   Frankford Yellowjackets

THOMASON, JAMES—Back—Texas A & M
1945   Detroit Lions

THOMASON, JOHN—Back—Georgia Tech.
1930–34   Brooklyn Dodgers
1935–36   Philadelphia Eagles

THOMASON, ROBERT—Back—
Virginia Military Inst.
1949 Los Angeles Rams
1951 Green Bay Packers

THOMPSON, ALVIN—End—Iowa
1923–25 Rock Island Independents
1925 Kansas City Cowboys

THOMPSON, CLARENCE—Back—
Minnesota
1937 Pittsburgh Pirates

THOMPSON, D.—Guard—Redlands
1926 Los Angeles

THOMPSON, FRANKLIN—Back—
Minnesota
1937–38 Pittsburgh Pirates
1939 Green Bay Packers
1940 Pittsburgh Steelers

THOMPSON, GEORGE—Guard—
Syracuse
1922 Rochester Kodaks
1927 Buffalo Bisons

THOMPSON, HAROLD—End—
Delaware
1947–48 Brooklyn Dodgers

THOMPSON, HARRY—Guard—
UCLA
1950–51 Los Angeles Rams

THOMPSON, RUSSELL—Tackle—
Nebraska
1936–39 Chicago Bears
1940 Philadelphia

THOMPSON, THOMAS—Back—
Tulsa
1940–42 Philadelphia Eagles
1945–47 Philadelphia Eagles
1948 Philadelphia Eagles—P
1949–50 Philadelphia Eagles

THOMPSON, THOMAS—Center—
William & Mary
1949–51 Cleveland Browns

THORNHILL, CLAUDE—Tackle—
Pittsburgh
1920 Buffalo All Americans

THORNTON, RICHARD—Back—
St. Louis Univ.
1933 Philadelphia Eagles

THORNTON, ROBERT—Guard—
Santa Clara
1946–47 San Francisco 49ers

THORPE, JACK—Guard—None
1923 Oorang Indians

THORPE, JAMES—Back—Carlisle
1920 Canton Bulldogs
1921 Cleveland Indians
1922 Canton Bulldogs
1923 Oorang Indians
1924–25 Rock Island Independents
1925 New York Giants
1926 Canton Bulldogs

THORPE, WILFRED—End—
Arkansas
1940–42 Cleveland Rams

THUERK, OWEN—End—St. Joseph
(Ind.)
1940 Detroit Lions

THURBON, ROBERT—Back—
Pittsburgh
1943 Phil-Pitt
1944 Card-Pitt
1946 Buffalo Bisons

THURMAN, JOHN—Tackle—
Pennsylvania
1926 Los Angeles

TIDD, PETER—Tackle—None
1921–24 Dayton Triangles

TIDWELL, TRAVIS—Back—
Alabama Polytech.
1950–51 New York Giants

TIERNEY, FREDERICK—Guard—
Minnesota
1922 Hammond Pros
1923–24 Minneapolis Marines

TILLER, MORGAN—End—Denver
1941 Pittsburgh Steelers
1944 Boston Yanks
1945 Pittsburgh Steelers

TILLMAN, ALONZO—Center—
Oklahoma
1949 Baltimore Colts

TIMMONS, CHARLES—Back—
Clemson
1946 Brooklyn Dodgers

TINSLEY, JESS—Tackle—LSU
1929–33 Chicago Cardinals

TINSLEY, GAYNELL—End—LSU
1937 Chicago Cardinals
1938 Chicago Cardinals—R
1940 Chicago Cardinals

TINSLEY, PETER—Guard—Georgia
1938–45 Green Bay Packers

TINSLEY, ROBERT—Tackle—Baylor
1949 Los Angeles Dons

TINSLEY, SIDNEY—Back—Clemson
1945 Pittsburgh Steelers

TIPTON, HOWARD—Back—
Southern California
1933–37   Chicago Cardinals

TITCHENAL, ROBERT—Center—
San Jose State
1940–42   Washington Redskins
1946   San Francisco 49ers
1947   Los Angeles Dons

TITMAS, HERBERT—Back—
Syracuse
1931   Providence Steamrollers

TITTLE, YELVERTON—Back—
LSU
1948–50   Baltimore Colts
1951   San Francisco 49ers

TITUS, GEORGE—Center—Holy
Cross
1946   Pittsburgh Steelers

TITUS, SILAS—End—Holy Cross
1940–42   Brooklyn Dodgers
1945   Pittsburgh Steelers

TOBIN, ELGIE—End—Penn State
1920–21   Akron Steels
1925   Duluth Kelleys

TOBIN, GEORGE—Guard—Notre
Dame
1947   New York Giants

TODD, RICHARD—Back—Texas
A & M
1939–42   Washington Redskins
1945–48   Washington Redskins
1951–52   Washington—Head Coach

TOFIL, JOSEPH—End—Indiana
1942   Brooklyn Dodgers

TOLLEFSON, CHARLES—Guard—
Iowa
1944–46   Green Bay Packers

TOLLEY, ??—Guard—??
1929   Dayton Triangles

TOMAHAWK—Back—Carlisle
1923   Oorang Indians

TOMAINI, ARMY—Tackle—
Catawba
1945   New York Giants

TOMAINI, JOHN—End—Georgetown
1929   Orange
1930   Newark
1930–32   Brooklyn Dodgers

TOMASETTI, LOUIS—Back—
Bucknell
1939–40   Pittsburgh Steelers
1940–41   Philadelphia Eagles
1941   Detroit Lions
1942   Philadelphia Eagles
1946   Buffalo Bisons
1947–49   Buffalo Bills

TOMASIC, ANDREW—Back—
Temple
1942   Pittsburgh Steelers
1946   Pittsburgh Steelers

TOMLIN, THOMAS—Guard—
Syracuse
1920–21   Akron Steels
1922   Milwaukee Badgers
1925   New York Giants

TOMLINSON, RICHARD—Guard—
Kansas
1950–51   Pittsburgh Steelers

TOMMERSON, CLARENCE—Back—
Wisconsin
1938   Pittsburgh Pirates

TONELLI, ANTHONY—Center—
Southern California
1939   Detroit Lions
1940   Chicago Cardinals
1945   Chicago Cardinals

TONNEMAKER, CLAYTON—
Center—Minnesota
1950   Green Bay Packers

TOOGOOD, CHARLES—Tackle—
Nebraska
1951   Los Angeles Rams

TORGESON, LAVERN—Center—
Washington State
1951   Detroit Lions

TORRANCE, JOHN—Tackle—LSU
1939–40   Chicago Bears

TOSCANI, FRANCIS—Back—St.
Mary's (Cal.)
1932   Brooklyn Dodgers

TOSI, FLAVIO—End—Boston
College
1934–36   Boston Redskins
1939   Pittsburgh Steelers

TOTH, ZOLLIE—Back—LSU
1950–51   New York Yanks

TOWLER, DANIEL—Back—
Washington & Jefferson
1950–51   Los Angeles Rams

TRAFTON, GEORGE—Center—
Notre Dame
1920–21   Chicago Bears   (Staleys)
1922–32   Chicago Bears

TRAVIS, J. EDWARD—Tackle—
Missouri
1921   Rock Island Independents
1923   St. Louis Browns

**TRAYNOR, MICHAEL—Back—
Canisius**
1923   Buffalo All Americans
1924   Buffalo Bisons
1925   Milwaukee Badgers

**TREADAWAY, JOHN—Tackle—
Hardin-Simmons**
1947–48   New York Giants
1949   Detroit Lions

**TREBOTICH, IVAN—Back—St.
Mary's (Cal.)**
1944–45   Detroit Lions
1947   Baltimore Colts

TRIGGS, JOHN—Back—Providence
1926   Providence Steamrollers

**TRIGILIO, FRANK—Back—
Alfred & Vermont**
1946   Miami Seahawks
1946   Los Angeles Dons

**TRIPLETT, WALLACE—Back—
Penn State**
1949–50   Detroit Lions

TRIPPI, CHARLES—Back—Georgia
1947–51   Chicago Cardinals

**TRIPSON, JOHN—Tackle—
Mississippi State**
1941   Detroit Lions

**TRIPUCKA, FRANK—Back—Notre
Dame**
1949   Philadelphia Eagles
1949   Detroit Lions
1950–51   Chicago Cardinals

**TROCOLOR, ROBERT—Back—
Alabama**
1942–44   New York Giants

**TROST, MILTON—Tackle—
Marquette**
1935–39   Chicago Bears
1940   Philadelphia Eagles

TRYON, EDWARD—Back—Colgate
1927   New York Yankees

**TSUOTSOUVAS, LOUIS—Center—
Stanford**
1938   Pittsburgh Pirates
1940   Detroit Lions

**TUCKEY, RICHARD—Back—
Manhattan**
1938   Washington Redskins
1938   Cleveland Rams

**TULLY, DARRELL—Back—Texas
Teachers**
1939   Detroit Lions

TULLY, GEORGE—End—Dartmouth
1927   Frankford Yellowjackets

TUNNELL, EMLEN—Back—Iowa
1948–51   New York Giants

**TURBERT, FRANCIS—Back—
Morris-Harvey**
1942   New York Giants
1944   Boston Redskins

TURLEY, DOUGLAS—End—Scranton
1944–48   Washington Redskins

**TURLEY, WILLIAM—Back—Ohio
Wesleyan**
1935–36   Pittsburgh Pirates

**TURNBOW, GUY—Tackle—
Mississippi**
1933–34   Philadelphia Eagles

**TURNER, CLYDE—Center—Hardin-
Simmons**
1940–41   Chicago Bears
1942   Chicago Bears—I
1943–51   Chicago Bears

**TURNER, JAMES—Back—North-
western**
1923   Milwaukee Badgers

**TURNER, JAMES—Back—
Oklahoma A & M**
1935   Pittsburgh Pirates
1937   Cleveland Rams
1938–40   Washington Redskins

**TUTTLE, ORVILLE—Guard—
Oklahoma City Univ.**
1937–41   New York Giants
1946   New York Giants

**TUTTLE, RICHARD—End—
Minnesota**
1927   Green Bay Packers

**TWEDELL, FRANCIS—Guard—
Minnesota**
1939   Green Bay Packers

**TYLER, PETER—Back—Hardin-
Simmons**
1937–38   Chicago Cardinals
1938   New York Giants

TYNES, DAVID—Back—Texas
1924–25   Columbus Tigers

TYREE, JAMES—End—Oklahoma
1948   Boston Yanks

* * *

**UCOVICH, MITCHELL—Tackle—
San Jose State**
1944   Washington Redskins
1945   Chicago Cardinals

UGOCCIONI, ENRICO—End—
Kentucky
1944   Brooklyn Dodgers

ULINSKI, EDWARD—Guard—
Marshall
1946–49   Cleveland Browns

ULINSKI, HARRY—Center—
Kentucky
1950–51   Washington Redskins

ULLERY, WILLIAM—Back—Penn
State
1922   Dayton Triangles

ULRICH, HUBERT—End—Kansas
1946   Miami Seahawks

UMONT, FRANK—Tackle—None
1943–45   New York Giants

UNDERWOOD, FORREST—Tackle—
Davis & Elkins
1937   Cleveland Rams

UNDERWOOD, JOHN—Guard—
Iowa State
1923   Milwaukee Badgers
1924–25   Duluth Kelleys
1926   Duluth Eskimos
1927   Pottsville Maroons
1929   Chicago Cardinals

UNGERER, JOSEPH—Tackle—
Fordham
1944–45   Washington Redskins

URAM, ANDREW—Back—
Minnesota
1938–43   Green Bay Packers

URBAN, ALEXANDER—End—
Southern Carolina
1941   Green Bay Packers
1944–45   Green Bay Packers

URBAN, GASPER—Guard—Notre
Dame
1948   Chicago Rockets

URBAN, LUKE—End—Boston
College
1920–23   Buffalo All Americans
1924   Buffalo Bisons

UREMOVICH, EMIL—Tackle—
Indiana
1940–42   Detroit Lions
1945–46   Detroit Lions
1948   Chicago Rockets

URSELLA, REUBEN—Back—None
1921   Rock Island Independents
1924–25   Rock Island Independents
1929   Minneapolis Redjackets

USHER, EDWARD—Back—
Michigan
1921   Buffalo All Americans
1922   Rock Island Independents
1922   Green Bay Packers
1924   Green Bay Packers
1924   Kansas City Cowboys

USHER, LOUIS—Tackle—Syracuse
1921   Chicago Bears (Staleys)
1921   Rochester Kodaks
1923   Milwaukee Badgers
1923–24   Hammond Pros
1924   Milwaukee Badgers
1924   Kenosha
1926   Hammond Pros

UZDAVINIS, WALTER—End—
Fordham
1937   Cleveland Rams

* * *

VACANTI, SAMUEL—Back—
Nebraska
1947–48   Chicago Rockets
1948–49   Baltimore Colts

VAIRO, DOMINIC—End—Notre
Dame
1935   Green Bay Packers

VALENTI, JOHN—Tackle—
Pittsburgh
1935   Pittsburgh Pirates

VAN BLOCKLIN, NORMAN—Back—
Oregon
1949   Los Angeles Rams
1950   Los Angeles Rams—P
1951   Los Angeles Rams

VAN BUREN, EBERT—Back—LSU
1951   Philadelphia Eagles

VAN BUREN, STEPHEN—Back—
LSU
1944   Philadelphia Eagles
1945   Philadelphia Eagles—G–S
1946   Philadelphia Eagles
1947   Philadelphia Eagles—G
1948   Philadelphia Eagles—G
1949   Philadelphia Eagles—G
1950–51   Philadelphia Eagles

VANCE, JOSEPH—Back—Texas
1931   Brooklyn Dodgers

VANDELLO, ??—??—??
1921   Rock Island Independents

VANDEWEGHE, ALFRED—End—
William & Mary
1946   Buffalo Bisons

VAN DYKE, J?—Back—??
1922   Louisville Colonels

VAN DYNE, CHARLES—Tackle—
Missouri
1925 Buffalo Bisons

VAN EVERY, HAROLD—Back—
Minnesota
1940–41 Green Bay Packers

VAN HORNE, CHARLES—Back—
Washington & Lee
1927 Buffalo Bisons
1929 Orange

VAN SICKLE, CLYDE—Center—
Arkansas
1930 Frankford Yellowjackets
1932–33 Green Bay Packers

VANT, HULL, FREDERICK—
Guard—Minnesota
1942 Green Bay Packers

VAN TONE, ARTHUR—Back—
Mississippi
1943–45 Detroit Lions
1946 Brooklyn Dodgers

VANZO, FREDERICK—Back—
Northwestern
1938–41 Detroit Lions
1941 Chicago Cardinals

VARDIAN, JOHN—Back—None
1946 Miami Seahawks
1947–48 Baltimore Colts

VASICEK, VICTOR—Guard—Texas
1949 Buffalo Bills
1950 Los Angeles Rams

VASSAU, ??—Tackle—??
1923 Milwaukee Badgers

VAUGHN, CHARLES—Back—
Tennessee
1935–36 Detroit Lions
1936 Chicago Cardinals

VAUGHN, John—Back—Bellfont
1933–35 Pittsburgh Pirates

VAUGHN, W?—Back—SMU
1926 Buffalo Bisons

VERGARA, GEORGE—End—Notre
Dame
1925 Green Bay Packers

VERRY, NORMAN—Tackle—
Southern California
1946–47 Chicago Rockets

VESSER, JOHN—End—Idaho
1927 Chicago Cardinals
1927 Buffalo Bills
1930–31 Chicago Cardinals

VETRANO, JOSEPH—Back—
Mississippi Southern
1946–49 San Francisco 49ers

VETTER, JOHN—Back—McPherson
1942 Brooklyn Dodgers

VEXALL, ??—Back—??
1924 Duluth Kelleys

VEZMAR, WALTER—Guard—
Michigan State
1946–47 Detroit Lions

VICK, ERNEST—Back—Michigan
1924 Kenosha
1925 Chicago Bears
1927–28 Chicago Bears

VICK, RICHARD—Back—
Washington & Jefferson
1925–26 Detroit Panthers
1928 Detroit Wolverines

VIDONI, VICTOR—End—Duquesne
1935–36 Pittsburgh Pirates

VINCE, RALPH—Guard—
Washington & Jefferson
1923 Cleveland Indians
1924 Cleveland Bulldogs
1925 Cleveland Indians

VINNOLA, PAUL—Back—Santa Clara
1946 Los Angeles Dons

VISNIC, LAWRENCE—Guard—
St. Benedict's (Kansas)
1943–45 New York Giants

VODICKA, JOSEPH—Back—None
1943 Chicago Bears
1945 Chicago Bears
1945 Chicago Cardinals

VOGELAAR, CARROLL—Tackle—
San Francisco
1947–48 Boston Yanks
1949 New York Bulldogs
1950 New York Yanks

VOGOS, EVAN—Guard—Wisconsin
1946–47 Chicago Rockets
1948–49 Green Bay Packers

VOGT, ALOIS—Back—Marquette
1946 Buffalo Bisons

VOKATY, OTTO—Back—Heidelberg
1931 Cleveland Indians
1932 New York Giants
1934 Cincinnati Reds

VOLOK, WILLIAM—Guard—Tulsa
1934–39 Chicago Cardinals

VOLZ, WILBUR—Back—Missouri
1949 Buffalo Bills

VOSBERG, DONALD—End—
Marquette
1940–41   New York Giants

VOSS, WALTER—End—Detroit
1920–21   Buffalo All.Americans
1922   Rock Island Independents
1923   Toledo Maroons
1924   Green Bay Packers
1925   Detroit Panthers
1926   New York Giants
1927–28   Chicago Bears
1929   Dayton Triangles
1929   Buffalo Bisons

VUCINICH, MILTON—Center—
Stanford
1945   Chicago Bears

* * *

WADE, JAMES—Back—Oklahoma
City Univ.
1949   New York Bulldogs
1949   Los Angeles Rams

WAGER, CLINTON—End—St.
Mary's (Minn.)
1941–42   Chicago Bears
1943   Chicago Cardinals
1944   Card-Pitt
1945   Chicago Cardinals

WAGER, JOHN—Center—Carthage
1930   Newark
1931–33   Portsmouth Spartans

WAGNER, BUFFTON—Back—
Northern Michigan
1921   Green Bay Packers

WAGNER, CHARLES—End—
Columbia
1931   Brooklyn Dodgers

WAGNER, LOWELL—Back—
Southern California
1946–48   New York Yankees
1949–51   San Francisco 49ers

WAGNER, SIDNEY—Guard—
Michigan State
1936–38   Detroit Lions

WAITE, CARL—End—Georgetown
1928   Frankford Yellowjackets
1929   Orange
1930   Newark

WALDON, ??—Center—??
1934   St. Louis Gunners

WALDRON, ??—Guard—??
1927   Chicago Cardinals

WALDSMITH, RALPH—Guard—
Akron
1921   Cleveland Indians
1922   Canton Bulldogs

WALKER, EWELL DOAK—Back—
SMU
1950   Detroit Lions—S
1951   Detroit Lions

WALKER, PAUL—End—Yale
1948   New York Giants

WALKER, WILLIAM—Guard—
Virginia Military Inst.
1945   Boston Yanks

WALL, EDWARD—Back—Grove
City
1930   Frankford Yellowjackets

WALLACE, BEVERLY—Back—None
1947–49   San Francisco 49ers

WALLACE, FRED—Guard—Bethany
1923–24   Akron Steels
1925   Cleveland Indians
1926   Canton Bulldogs
1928   Chicago Bears

WALLACE, JOSEPH—End—Notre
Dame
1929   Dayton Triangles

WALLER, WILLIAM—End—
Centenary
1938   Brooklyn Dodgers

WALLNER, FREDERICK—Guard—
Notre Dame
1951   Chicago Cardinals

WALLS, WILLIAM—End—TCU
1938–43   New York Giants

WALQUIST, LAURIE—Back—
Illinois
1922–31   Chicago Bears

WALSH, WILLIAM—Center—
Notre Dame
1949–51   Pittsburgh Steelers

WALSTON, ROBERT—End—
Georgia
1951   Philadelphia Eagles

WALTERS, ??—Back—??
1924   Kenosha

WALTON, FRANK—Guard—
Pittsburgh
1934   Boston Redskins
1944–45   Washington Redskins

WANDLESS, GEORGE—Back—?
1922   Louisville

WARD, ELMER—Center—Utah
1933   Boston Redskins
1935–36   Detroit Lions

WARD, JOHN—Tackle—Southern
California
1920–21 Buffalo All Americans
1923 Dayton Triangles
1930 Frankford Yellowjackets
1930 Minneapolis Redjackets

WARD, WILLIAM—Guard—
Washington State
1946–47 Washington Redskins
1947–49 Detroit Lions

WARNER, ROBERT—Back—
Wisconsin
1927 Duluth Eskimos

WARREN, BUSIT—Back—Tennessee
1945 Philadelphia Eagles
1945 Pittsburgh Steelers

WARREN, MORRISON—Back—
Arizona State
1948 Brooklyn Dodgers

WARRINGTON, CALEB—Center—
William & Mary, Ala. Polytech.
1946–48 Brooklyn Dodgers

WASHINGTON, KENNETH—Back—
UCLA
1946–48 Los Angeles Rams

WASSERBACH, LLOYD—Tackle—
Wisconsin
1946–47 Chicago Rockets

WATERFIELD, ROBERT—Back—
UCLA
1945 Cleveland Rams—V
1946 Los Angeles Rams—P
1947–48 Los Angeles Rams
1949 Los Angeles Rams—F (9)
1950 Los Angeles Rams
1951 Los Angeles Rams—P–F (13)

WATERS, DALE—End—Florida
1931 Cleveland Indians
1932 Boston Braves
1933 Boston Redskins

WATKINS, FOSTER—Back—West
Texas State
1940–41 Philadelphia Eagles

WATKINS, GORDON—Tackle—
Georgia Tech.
1930 Frankford Yellowjackets
1931 Brooklyn Dodgers

WATSON, GRADY—Back—Texas
1922–23 Toledo Maroons
1924–25 Hammond Pros
1927 Buffalo Bisons

WATSON, JAMES—Center—College
of Pacific
1945 Washington Redskins

WATSON, JOSEPH—Center—Rice
1950 Detroit Lions

WATT, JOSEPH—Back—Syracuse
1947 Boston Yanks
1947–48 Detroit Lions
1949 New York Bulldogs

WATT, WALTER—Back—Miami
(Fla.)
1945 Chicago Cardinals

WATTERS, LEONARD—End—
Springfield
1924 Buffalo Bisons

WATTS, GEORGE—Tackle—
Appalachian State
1942 Washington Redskins

WAY, CHARLES—Back—Penn State
1921 Canton Bulldogs
1924 Frankford Yellowjackets

WEAR, ROBERT—Center—Penn
State
1942 Philadelphia Eagles

WEATHERLEY, GERALD—Center—
Rice
1950 Chicago Bears

WEATHERS, GUY—Guard—Baylor
1926 Buffalo Bisons

WEAVER, JAMES—Center—Centre
1923 Columbus Tigers
1930 Chicago Cardinals
1930 Portsmouth Spartans

WEAVER, JOHN—Guard—Miami
(Ohio)
1949 New York Bulldogs

WEBB, ??—Tackle—Genesee Wesleyan
1922 Milwaukee Badgers

WEBB, GEORGE—End—Texas Tech.
1943 Brooklyn Dodgers

WEBBER, C?—Guard—Colgate
1926 Brooklyn Dodgers

WEBBER, H?—End—Kansas State
1924–25 Kansas City Cowboys
1926 Hartford
1927 Cleveland Indians

WEBBER, HARRY—End—Nebraska
1923 Rock Island Independents
1927 Chicago Bears
1928 Green Bay Packers

WEBBER, RICHARD—Back—St.
Louis Univ.
1945 Detroit Lions

WEBSTER, FREDERICK—Back—
Colgate
1924 Racine Legion

WEDEL, RICHARD—Guard—Wake Forest
1948   Chicago Cardinals

WEDEMEYER, HERMAN—Back—St. Mary's (Cal.)
1948   Los Angeles Dons
1949   Baltimore Colts

WEEDON, DONALD—Guard—Texas
1947   Philadelphia Eagles

WEHBA, RAYMOND—End— Southern California
1943   Brooklyn Dodgers
1944   Green Bay Packers

WEIMER, HOWARD—Back— Wilmington
1929   Buffalo Bisons
1930   Brooklyn Dodgers
1931   Cleveland Indians

WEINBERG, ??—Tackle—??
1923   Cleveland Indians

WEINBERG, HENRY—Guard— Duquesne
1934   Pittsburgh Pirates

WEINER, ALBERT—Back— Muhlenberg
1934   Philadelphia Eagles

WEINER, ARTHUR—End—North Carolina
1950   New York Yanks

WEINER, BERNARD—Tackle— Kansas State
1942   Brooklyn Dodgers

WEINMEISTER, ARNOLD— Tackle—Washington
1948-49   New York Yankees
1950-51   New York Giants

WEINSTOCK, ISADORE—Back— Pittsburgh
1935   Philadelphia Eagles
1937-38   Pittsburgh Pirates

WEIR, EDWARD—Tackle—Nebraska
1926-28   Frankford Yellowjackets

WEIR, JOSEPH—Guard—Nebraska
1927   Frankford Yellowjackets

WEISGERBER, RICHARD—Back— Willamette
1938   Cleveland Rams
1938-40   Green Bay Packers
1942   Green Bay Packers

WEISS, HOWARD—Back—Wisconsin
1939-40   Detroit Lions

WEISS, JOHN—End—None
1944-47   New York Giants

WELCH, GILBERT—Back— Pittsburgh
1928   New York Yankees
1929   Providence Steamrollers

WELDON, JOHN—Back—Lafayette
1920   Buffalo All Americans

WELDON, LAWRENCE—Back— Presbyterian
1944-45   Washington Redskins

WELLER, LOUIS—Back—Haskell
1933   Boston Redskins

WELLER, TRUMAN—Tackle— Nebraska
1923   St. Louis Browns
1924   Milwaukee Badgers
1926-27   Chicago Cardinals
1928   Frankford Yellowjackets

WELLMAN, FERDINAND—Back— Purdue
1922   Rochester Kodaks

WELLS, DONALD—End—Georgia
1946-49   Green Bay Packers

WELMUS, WOODCHUCK—End— Carlisle
1923   Oorang Indians

WELSH, JAMES—Guard—Colgate
1924-25   Frankford Yellowjackets
1925-27   Pottsville Maroons

WEMPLE, DONALD—End—Colgate
1941   Brooklyn Dodgers
Killed piloting Army transport in India. Lt., U.S. Air Force.

WENDELL, MARTIN—Guard— Notre Dame
1949   Chicago Hornets

WENDLICK, JOSEPH—End— Oregon State
1940   Philadelphia Eagles
1941   Pittsburgh Steelers

WENDT, MERLE—Guard—Ohio State
1932   Chicago Cardinals

WENIG, OBE—End—Morningside
1921-22   Rock Island Independents

WENKE, ADOLPH—Tackle— Nebraska
1923   Milwaukee Badgers

WENTWORTH, SHIRLEY—Back— New Hampshire
1925   Providence Steamrollers
1929   Boston Braves

WENTZ, BYRON—Back—Penn State
1925–28 Pottsville Maroons
1929 Boston Braves
1930–31 Providence Steamrollers

WENZEL, RALPH—End—Tulane
1941 Pittsburgh Steelers

WERDER, EDWARD—Center—Penn State
1920 Buffalo All Americans

WERDER, RICHARD—Guard—Georgetown
1948 New York Yankees

WERWAISS, ??—Tackle—None
1926 Hartford

WESLEY, LECIL—Center—Alabama
1927 Providence Steamrollers
1930 Portsmouth Spartans

WEST, DAVID—Tackle—Colgate
1921 Canton Bulldogs

WEST, HODGES—Tackle—Tennessee
1941 Philadelphia Eagles

WEST, PAT—Back—Southern California
1944–45 Cleveland Rams
1946–48 Los Angeles Rams
1948 Green Bay Packers

WEST, STANLEY—Guard—Oklahoma
1950–51 Los Angeles Rams

WESTFALL, EDGAR—Back—Ohio Wesleyan
1933 Pittsburgh Pirates
1933 Boston Redskins

WESTFALL, ROBERT—Back—Michigan
1944–47 Detroit Lions

WESTOPHAL, JOSEPH—Center—Nebraska
1926 Kansas City Cowboys
1928 Detroit Wolverines
1929–30 New York Giants

WETTERLUND, CHESTER—Back—Illinois Wesleyan
1942 Chicago Cardinals
Killed flying Navy Hellcat on night patrol off New Jersey coast, Sept. 5, 1944. Lt., U.S. Navy.

WETZ, HARLAN—Tackle—Texas
1947 Brooklyn Dodgers

WETZEL, DAMON—Back—Ohio State
1935 Pittsburgh Pirates
1935 Chicago Bears

WHALEN, GERALD—Center—Canisius
1948 Buffalo Bills

WHALEN, THOMAS—Back—Catholic Univ.
1933 Pittsburgh Pirates

WHALEY, BENJAMIN—Guard—Virginia State
1949 Los Angeles Dons

WHAM, THOMAS—End—Furman
1949–51 Chicago Cardinals

WHATELY, JAMES—End—Alabama
1936–38 Brooklyn Dodgers

WHEELER, ERNEST—Back—North Dakota State
1939 Pittsburgh Steelers
1939 Chicago Cardinals
1942 Chicago Cardinals

WHEELER, LYLE—End—Ripon
1921–23 Green Bay Packers

WHELAN, THOMAS—Center—Georgetown
1920 Canton Bulldogs
1920 Chicago Cardinals
1921 Cleveland Indians
1921–24 Chicago Cardinals

WHIRE, JOHN—Back—Alabama
1933 Philadelphia Eagles

WHITE, ARTHUR—Guard—Alabama
1937–39 New York Giants
1939 Philadelphia Eagles
1940–41 Chicago Cardinals
1945 New York Giants

WHITE, BYRON—Back—Colorado
1938 Pittsburgh Pirates—G
1940 Detroit Lions—G
1941 Detroit Lions

WHITE, EUGENE—Guard—Indiana
1946 Buffalo Bisons

WHITE, JAMES—Tackle—Notre Dame
1945–50 New York Giants

WHITE, PAUL—Back—Michigan
1947 Pittsburgh Steelers

WHITE, PHILIP—End—Oklahoma
1922–23 Toledo Maroons
1923 Louisville Colonels
1925 Kansas City Cowboys
1925 New York Giants
1927 New York Giants
1927 Buffalo Bisons

WHITE, ROBERT—Back—Stanford
1951 San Francisco 49ers

WHITE, ROY—Back—Valparaiso
1924-25 Chicago Bears
1927-29 Chicago Bears

WHITE, THOMAS—Tackle—TCU
1939 Philadelphia Eagles

WHITE, WILBUR—Back—Colorado State
1935 Brooklyn Dodgers

WHITE, WILFORD—Back—Arizona State
1951 Chicago Bears

WHITED, MARVIN—Back—Oklahoma
1942 Washington Redskins
1945 Washington Redskins

WHITLOW, KENNETH—Center—Rice
1946 Miami Seahawks

WHITMAN, S. J.—Back—Tulsa
1951 Chicago Cardinals

WIATRAK, JOHN—Center—Washington
1939 Philadelphia Eagles
1939 Detroit Lions

WIBERG, OSCAR—Back—Nebraska Wesleyan
1930 New York Giants
1932 Brooklyn Dodgers
1933 Cincinnati Reds

WICKETT, LLOYD—Tackle—Oregon State
1943 Detroit Lions
1946 Detroit Lions

WIDSETH, EDWIN—Tackle—Minnesota
1938-40 New York Giants

WIEDERQUIST, CHESTER—Tackle—Washington & Jefferson
1923-24 Milwaukee Badgers
1925 Rock Island Independents
1928 Chicago Cardinals
1928 Detroit Lions
1929 Minneapolis Redjackets

WIEDICH, ??—Tackle—??
1924 Kansas City Cowboys

WIEHL, JOSEPH—Tackle—Duquesne
1935 Pittsburgh Pirates

WIESE, ROBERT—Back—Michigan
1947-48 Detroit Lions

WIESENBAUGH, HENRY—Back—Pittsburgh
1935 Pittsburgh Pirates
1935-36 Boston Redskins

WIETHE, JOHN—Guard—Xavier (Cincinnati)
1939-42 Detroit Lions

WIGGS, HUBERT—Back—Vanderbilt
1922-23 Louisville Colonels

WIGHTKIN, WILLIAM—End—Notre Dame
1950-51 Chicago Bears

WILCOX, EDWARD—Back—Swarthmore
1926 Buffalo Bisons
1926-27 Frankford Yellowjackets
1930 Staten Island Stapletons

WILDE, GEORGE—Back—Texas A & M
1947 Washington Redskins

WILDER, H. F.—Guard—Nebraska
1923 St. Louis Browns

WILDUNG, RICHARD—Guard—Minnesota
1946-51 Green Bay Packers

WILEY, JOHN—Tackle—Waynesburg
1946-50 Pittsburgh Steelers

WILGING, ??—End—??
1934 Cincinnati Reds

WILKERSON, BASIL—End—Oklahoma City Univ.
1932 Boston Braves
1934 Cincinnati Reds

WILKIN, WILBUR—Tackle—St. Mary's (Cal.)
1938-43 Washington Redskins
1946 Chicago Rockets

WILKINS, RICHARD—End—Oregon
1949 Los Angeles Dons

WILKINS, THEODORE—End—Indiana
1925 Green Bay Packers

WILKINSON, ROBERT—End—UCLA
1951 New York Giants

WILLEGALLE, HENRY—Back—Carleton
1929 Minneapolis Redjackets

WILLERT, ??—Guard—??
1922 Hammond Pros

WILLEY, NORMAN—End—Marshall
1950-51 Philadelphia Eagles

WILLIAMS, ARTHUR—Back—Connecticut State
1928-31 Providence Steamrollers

WILLIAMS, BOYD—Center—Syracuse
1947 Philadelphia Eagles

WILLIAMS, BROUGHTON—End—
Florida
1947 Chicago Bears

WILLIAMS, CY—Guard—Florida
1923 Racine Legion
1923–24 Duluth Kelleys
1924 Dayton Triangles
1925 Cleveland Indians
1925 Duluth Kelleys
1926 Duluth Eskimos
1929–30 Staten Island
1931 Brooklyn Dodgers

WILLIAMS, DONALD—Guard—
Texas
1941 Pittsburgh Steelers

WILLIAMS, ELLERY—End—Santa
Clara
1950 New York Giants

WILLIAMS, FRANK—Back—Utah
State
1948 New York Giants

WILLIAMS, GARLAND—Tackle—
Georgia
1947 Washington Redskins
1947–48 Brooklyn Dodgers

WILLIAMS, JACOB—Tackle—TCU
1933 Chicago Cardinals

WILLIAMS, JEROME—Back—
Washington State
1949–51 Los Angeles Rams

WILLIAMS, JOEL—Center—Texas
1948 San Francisco 49ers
1950 Baltimore Colts

WILLIAMS, JOHN—Center—
Alabama Polytech.
1942 Philadelphia Eagles
1946 Miami Seahawks

WILLIAMS, JOSEPH—Guard—
Lafayette
1923 Canton Bulldogs
1925–26 New York Giants
1929–32 Chicago Cardinals

WILLIAMS, REX—Center—Texas
Tech.
1945 Detroit Lions

WILLIAMS, RICHARD—Back—
Wisconsin
1921 Green Bay Packers

WILLIAMS, ROBERT—Back—Notre
Dame
1951 Chicago Bears

WILLIAMS, THEODORE—Back—
Boston College
1942 Washington Redskins

WILLIAMS, VERNON—End—
Minnesota
1921–26 Hammond Pros

WILLIAMS, WALTER—Back—
Boston Univ.
1944 Boston Yanks
1946 Chicago Rockets
1947 Boston Yanks

WILLIAMS, WINDELL—End—Rice
1948–49 Baltimore Colts

WILLIAMSON, ERNEST—Tackle—
North Carolina
1947 Washington Redskins
1948 New York Giants
1949 Los Angeles Dons

WILLIAMSON, IVAN—Tackle—
Michigan
1932 Chicago Cardinals

WILLIS, WILLIAM—Guard—Ohio
State
1946–51 Cleveland Browns

WILLSON, OSBORNE—Guard—
Pennsylvania
1933–35 Philadelphia Eagles

WILSBACH, FRANK—Guard—
Bucknell
1925 Frankford Yellowjackets

WILSON, ABRAHAM—Guard—
Washington
1928–29 Providence Steamrollers

WILSON, CAMP—Back—Tulsa
1946–49 Detroit Lions

WILSON, E. ??—Back—Penn State
1926 Hartford

WILSON, FAYE—Back—Texas A & M
1926 Buffalo Bisons
1927–31 New York Giants
1931 Green Bay Packers
1932 Portsmouth Spartans
1932 New York Giants
1933 Portsmouth Spartans
1934 Brooklyn Dodgers

WILSON, GEORGE—Back—
Washington
1927–29 Providence Steamrollers
1932 Staten Island Stapletons

WILSON, GEORGE—End—North-
western
1937–47 Chicago Bears

WILSON, GORDON—Tackle—Texas Mines
1940   Cleveland Rams
1942–43   Chicago Cardinals
1945   Chicago Cardinals

WILSON, JAMES—End—Cornell
1922   Rochester Kodaks
1922   Buffalo All Americans
1923–24   Rock Island Independents
1929–30   Minneapolis Redjackets
1930–31   Frankford Yellowjackets

WILSON, JOHN—End—Western Reserve
1938   Pittsburgh Pirates
1939–42   Cleveland Rams

WILSON, JOHN—Back—Baylor
1946–47   Los Angeles Rams

WILSON, LELAND—Back—??
1929–30   Frankford Yellowjackets

WILSON, MILTON—Tackle—Oshkosh Teachers
1921   Green Bay Packers
1923–24   Akron Steels

WILSON, OLIVER—End—SMU
1947–48   Green Bay Packers

WILSON, ROBERT—Back—SMU
1931   Green Bay Packers
1936   Brooklyn Dodgers

WILSON, WILLIAM—End—Gonzaga
1935–37   Chicago Cardinals
1938   Pittsburgh Pirates

WILSON, WILLIAM—End—San Jose State
1951   San Francisco 49ers

WIMBERLY, ABNER—End—LSU
1949   Los Angeles Dons
1950–51   Green Bay Packers

WIMBERLY, BYRON—Guard—Washington & Jefferson
1925   Detroit Panthers

WINDBURN, ??—End—??
1923   St. Louis Browns

WINKELMAN, BENJAMIN—End—Arkansas
1923–24   Milwaukee Badgers

WINKLER, BERNARD—Tackle—Texas Tech.
1948   Los Angeles Dons

WINKLER, JAMES—Tackle—Texas A & M
1951   Los Angeles Rams

WINKLER, JOSEPH—Center—Purdue
1945   Cleveland Rams

WINSLOW, ROBERT—End—Southern California
1940   Brooklyn Dodgers
1940   Detroit Lions

WINTERS, ARNOLD—Tackle—None
1941   Green Bay Packers

WINTERS, LINDELL—Back—Ohio Wesleyan
1923–24   Columbus Tigers

WISINGER, ZONAR—Guard—Pittsburgh
1926   Pottsville Maroons

WISMANN, PETER—Center—St. Louis Univ.
1949–51   San Francisco 49ers

WISTERT, ALBERT—Tackle—Michigan
1943   Phil-Pitt
1944–51   Philadelphia Eagles

WITTE, EARL—Back—Gustavus-Adolphus
1934   Green Bay Packers

WITTER, RAYMOND—Center—Syracuse
1921   Rochester Kodaks
1923   Rochester Kodaks

WITUCKI, CASIMIR—Guard—Indiana
1950–51   Washington Redskins

WIZBICKI, ALEXANDER—Back—Holy Cross
1947–49   Buffalo Bills
1950   Green Bay Packers

WOERNER, ERWIN—Tackle—Bucknell
1930   Newark

WOJCIECHOWICZ, ALEXANDER—Center—Fordham
1938–46   Detroit Lions
1946–50   Philadelphia Eagles

WOLF, RICHARD—Back—Miami (Ohio)
1923   Cleveland Indians
1924   Cleveland Bulldogs
1925   Cleveland Indians

WOLFE, HUGH—Back—Texas
1938   New York Giants

WOLTMAN, CLEMENT—Tackle—Purdue
1938–40   Philadelphia Eagles

WOOD, ??—Guard—??
1921–23   Rochester Kodaks
1924   Rochester Jeffersons
1924   Kenosha

WOODARD, RICHARD—Center—
Iowa
1949   Los Angeles Dons
1950–51   New York Giants

WOODIN, HOWARD—Guard—
Marquette
1922–31   Green Bay Packers

WOODRUFF, LEE—Back—
Mississippi
1926   Chicago Cardinals
1929   Buffalo Bisons
1931   Providence Steamrollers
1932   Boston Braves
1933   Philadelphia Eagles

WOOLFORD, BARD—Tackle—??
1922   Columbus Tigers
1924   Columbus Tigers

WORDEN, JAMES—Back—Waynes-
burgh
1945   Cleveland Rams

WORDEN, STUART—Guard—
Hampden-Sidney
1930   Brooklyn Dodgers
1932–34   Brooklyn Dodgers

WORKMAN, BLAKE—Back—Tulsa
1931   Cleveland Indians
1933   Cincinnati Reds
1934   St. Louis Gunners

WORKMAN, HARRY—Back—Ohio
State
1924   Cleveland Bulldogs

WOUDENBERG, JOHN—Tackle—
Denver
1940–42   Pittsburgh Steelers
1946–49   San Francisco 49ers

WOZNIAK, JOHN—Guard—Alabama
1948   Brooklyn Dodgers
1949   New York Yankees
1950–51   New York Yanks

WRAY, LUDLOW—Center—
Pennsylvania
1920–21   Buffalo All Americans
1922   Rochester Kodaks

WRIGHT, FRANK—Tackle—
Kentucky
1933   Brooklyn Dodgers
1935   Boston Redskins

WRIGHT, JAMES—Guard—SMU
1947   Boston Yanks

WRIGHT, JOHN—Back—Maryland
1947   Baltimore Colts

WRIGHT, THEODORE—Back—
Texas Tech.
1930   Frankford Yellowjackets
1934–35   Boston Redskins
1935   Brooklyn Dodgers

WRINKLE MEAT—Guard—None
1923   Oorang Indians

WUKITS, ALBERT—Center—
Duquesne
1943   Phil-Pitt
1944   Card-Pitt
1945   Pittsburgh Steelers
1946   Miami Seahawks
1946   Buffalo Bisons

WYCOFF, DOUGLAS—Back—
Georgia Tech.
1927   New York Giants
1929–30   Staten Island Stapletons
1931   New York Giants
1932   Staten Island Stapletons
1934   Boston Redskins

WYDO, Frank—Tackle—Cornell
1947–51   Pittsburgh Steelers

WYHONIC, JOHN—Guard—Alabama
1941   Detroit Lions
1946–47   Philadelphia Eagles
1948–49   Buffalo Bills

WYMAN, ARNOLD—Back—
Minnesota
1921   Rock Island Independents

WYNNE, CHESTER—Back—Notre
Dame
1922   Rochester Kodaks
1928   Chicago Bears
1929   Dayton Triangles

WYNNE, HARRY—End—Arkansas
1944   Boston Yanks
1945   New York Giants

* * *

YABLOK, JULIUS—Back—Colgate
1930–31   Brooklyn Dodgers
1931   Staten Island Stapletons

YABLONSKI, VENTAN—Back—
Columbia
1948–51   Chicago Cardinals

YACHANICH, Joseph—Guard—
Fordham
1946–48   New York Yankees

YAGIELLO, RAYMOND—Guard—
Catawba
1948–49   Los Angeles Rams

YARR, THOMAS—Center—Notre
Dame
1933   Chicago Cardinals

YEAGER, HOWARD—Back—Santa Barbara State
1940–41   New York Giants

YEAGER, J ??—Tackle—Lehigh
1926   Brooklyn Dodgers

YEISLEY, ??—End—??
1928   Chicago Cardinals

YEZERSKI, JOHN—Tackle— St. Mary's
1936   Brooklyn Dodgers

YOKAS, FRANK—Guard—None
1946   Los Angeles Dons
1947   Baltimore Colts

YONAKOR, JOHN—End—Notre Dame
1946–49   Cleveland Browns
1950   New York Yanks

YONAMINE, WALLACE—Back— None
1947   San Francisco 49ers

YOUEL, JAMES—Back—Iowa
1946–48   Washington Redskins
1948   Los Angeles Rams
1948   Boston Yanks

YOUNCE, LEONARD—Guard— Oregon State
1940–44   New York Giants
1946–48 . New York Giants

YOUNG, CLAUDE—Back—Illinois
1947–49   New York Yankees
1950–51   New York Yanks

YOUNG, GEORGE—End—Georgia
1946–51   Cleveland Browns

YOUNG, H. D.—End—North Dakota
1929–30   Minneapolis Redjackets
1930   Providence Steamrollers

YOUNG, L ??—Back—Detroit
1925   Dayton Triangles
1925–27   Providence Steamrollers

YOUNG, ROY—Tackle—Texas A & M
1938   Washington Redskins

YOUNG, WALTER—End—Oklahoma
1939   Brooklyn Dodgers
1940   Brooklyn Dodgers
        Killed returning from first B-29 raid over Tokyo when he dropped out of formation to cover a crippled colleague, on Jan. 9, 1945. Captain, U.S. Air Force.

YOUNG, WILLIAM—Tackle— Alabama
1937–42   Washington Redskins
1946   Washington Redskins

YOUNG, WILLIAM—Guard—Ohio State
1929   Green Bay Packers

YOUNGER, PAUL—Back—Grambling
1949–51   Los Angeles Rams

YOUNGFLEISCH, FRANCIS— Center—Villanova
1926–27   Pottsville Maroons

YOUNGSTROM, ADOLPH—Guard— Dartmouth
1920–23   Buffalo All Americans
1924–26   Buffalo Bisons
1926–27   Frankford Yellowjackets

YOVISIN, JOHN—End—Gettysburg
1944   Philadelphia Eagles

YOWARSKY, WALTER—End— Kentucky
1951   Washington Redskins

* * *

ZADWORNEY, FRANK—Back— Ohio State
1940   Brooklyn Dodgers

ZALEJSKI, ERNEST—Back—Notre Dame
1950   Baltimore Colts

ZAMLYNSKI, ZIGMOND—Back— Villanova
1946   San Francisco 49ers

ZANINELLI, SILVIO—Back— Duquesne
1934–37   Pittsburgh Pirates

ZAPUSTAS, JOSEPH—End—Fordham
1933   New York Giants

ZARNAS, AUGUSTUS—Guard—Ohio State
1938   Chicago Bears
1939   Brooklyn Dodgers
1939–40   Green Bay Packers

ZEH, RAYMOND—Back—Western Reserve
1935   Pittsburgh Pirates

ZELENCIK, FRANK—Tackle— Oglethorpe
1939   Chicago Cardinals

ZELLER, JOSEPH—Guard—Indiana
1932   Green Bay Packers
1933–38   Chicago Bears

ZENO, JOSEPH—Guard—Holy Cross
1942–44   Washington Redskins
1946–47   Boston Yanks

ZIEGLER, FRANCIS—Back—Clemson
1922   Columbus Tigers

ZIEGLER, FRANK—Back—Georgia Tech
1949–51 Philadelphia Eagles

ZIFF, D ??—End—Syracuse
1925 Rochester

ZILLY, JOHN—End—Notre Dame
1947–51 Los Angeles Rams

ZIMMERMAN, GIFFORD—Guard—Syracuse
1927–29 Dayton Triangles

ZIMMERMAN, GUY—Back—Akron
1924 Akron Steels
1925 Canton Bulldogs

ZIMMERMAN, LEROY—Back—San Jose State
1940–42 Washington Redskins
1942 Philadelphia Eagles
1943 Phil-Pitt
1944 Philadelphia Eagles
1945 Philadelphia Eagles – I
1946 Philadelphia Eagles
1947 Detroit Lions
1948 Boston Yanks

ZIMNY, ROBERT—Tackle—Indiana
1945–49 Chicago Cardinals

ZIRINSKY, WALTER—Back—Lafayette
1945 Cleveland Rams

ZIZAK, VINCENT—Tackle—Villanova
1934–37 Philadelphia Eagles

ZOLL, CARL—Guard—None
1921–22 Green Bay Packers

ZOLL, MARTIN—Guard—None
1921 Green Bay Packers

ZOLL, RICHARD—Guard—Indiana
1937–38 Cleveland Rams
1939 Green Bay Packers

ZONTINI, LOUIS—Back—Notre Dame
1940–41 Chicago Cardinals
1944 Cleveland Rams
1946 Buffalo Bisons

ZOPETTI, FRANK—Back—Duquesne
1941 Pittsburgh Steelers

ZORA, CLYDE—Guard—Notre Dame
1920–23 Chicago Cardinals

ZORICH, GEORGE—Guard—Northwestern
1944–46 Chicago Bears
1946 Miami Seahawks
1947 Baltimore Colts

ZUIDMULDER, DAVID—Back—St. Ambrose
1929–31 Green Bay Packers

ZUNKER, CHARLES—Tackle—??
1934 Cincinnati Reds

ZUPEK, ALBERT—Back—Lawrence
1946 Green Bay Packers

ZUVER, MERLE—Center—Nebraska
1930 Green Bay Packers

ZUZZIO, ANTHONY—Guard—Muhlenberg
1942 Detroit Lions

ZYNTELL, JAMES—Guard—Holy Cross
1933 New York Giants
1933–35 Philadelphia Eagles

CHAPTER 5
THE TEAMS

In modern major league football, thirty-three rather than eleven men make up the team. Limitless combinations of eleven can be made from thirty-three. There is the kick-off team; the kick-off receiving team; the team for the plunge through the middle; the team for skirting the end; the team for forward-passing in endless patterns of deception; the teams for defense against all these and more expected thrusts by the enemy; the team to kick field goals and extra points; the team to defend against them; the punting team; the punt-receiving team. Within these named there are countless combinations of men who do each factor best, so that in a league game, which averages eighty offensive and eighty defensive plays, more than a hundred different line-ups could be found on the field.

The team is the final end product of all the players and coaches listed in previous pages. The headline names, the All-Time All-Stars, are forgotten for the moment. The muscular device made up of twenty-two legs, twenty-two arms and twenty-two eyes must start and accelerate and move as one gigantic creature.

The records of those who did this best will be found at, or near, the top of the ensuing categories and break-downs.

WORLD CHAMPIONSHIP PLAY-OFFS, 1933-1951

1933	(Dec. 17 at Chicago)	Chicago Bears	23	New York Giants	21
1934	(Dec. 9 at New York)	New York Giants	30	Chicago Bears	13
1935	(Dec. 15 at Detroit)	Detroit Lions	26	New York Giants	7
1936	(Dec. 13 at New York)	Green Bay Packers	21	Boston Redskins	6
1937	(Dec. 12 at Chicago)	Washington Redskins	28	Chicago Bears	21
1938	(Dec. 11 at New York)	New York Giants	23	Green Bay Packers	17
1939	(Dec. 10 at Milwaukee)	Green Bay Packers	27	New York Giants	0
1940	(Dec. 8 at Washington)	Chicago Bears	73	Washington Redskins	0
1941	(Dec. 21 at Chicago)	Chicago Bears	37	New York Giants	9
1942	(Dec. 13 at Washington)	Washington Redskins	14	Chicago Bears	6
1943	(Dec. 26 at Chicago)	Chicago Bears	41	Washington Redskins	21
1944	(Dec. 17 at New York)	Green Bay Packers	14	New York Giants	7
1945	(Dec. 16 at Cleveland)	Cleveland Rams	15	Washington Redskins	14
1946	(Dec. 15 at New York)	Chicago Bears	24	New York Giants	14
1947	(Dec. 28 at Chicago)	Chicago Cardinals	28	Philadelphia Eagles	21
1948	(Dec. 19 at Philadelphia)	Philadelphia Eagles	7	Chicago Cardinals	0
1949	(Dec. 18 at Los Angeles)	Philadelphia Eagles	14	Los Angeles Rams	0
1950	(Dec. 24 at Cleveland)	Cleveland Browns	30	Los Angeles Rams	28
1951	(Dec. 23 at Los Angeles)	Los Angeles Rams	24	Cleveland Browns	17

WORLD CHAMPIONSHIP GAMES, 1933-1951

1933 WORLD CHAMPIONSHIP PROFESSIONAL FOOTBALL GAME

(Wrigley Field, Chicago, Ill., Dec. 17)
Attendance 26,000

Chicago Bears (23)	New York Giants (21)
Hewitt—L.E.	Badgro—L.E.
Lyman—L.T.	Grant—L.T.
Carlson—L.G.	Gibson—L.G.
Miller—C.	Hein—C.
Kopcha—R.G.	Jones—R.G.
Musso—R.T.	Owen—R.T.
Karr—R.E.	Flaherty—R.E.
Brumbaugh—Q.B.	Newman—Q.B.
Molesworth—L.H.	Strong—L.H.
Ronzani—R.H.	Burnett—R.H.
Nagurski—F.B.	Molenda—F.B.

Chicago Bears	3	3	10	7—23
New York Giants	0	7	7	7—21

Touchdowns—Karr 2, Badgro, Krause, Strong.
Points after touchdown—Strong 2, Manders 3.
Field goals—Manders 3.
Coaches—George Halas (Chicago), Stephen Owen (New York).

SUBSTITUTIONS

Chicago Bears—Manders, Grange, Richards, Sisk, Corbett.
New York Giants—Richards, Irwin, Clancy, Campbell, Krause, Canella.
Officials: Referee—Thomas Hughitt. Umpire—Robert Cohn. Head Linesman—Robert Karch. Field Judge—Dan Tehan.

THE GAME

Jack Manders opened the scoring for the Bears with a 16-yard field goal in the first quarter to touch off sixty minutes of fireworks that kept the fans standing on their chairs through most of the game.

Manders pumped another one over from 40 yards in the second period before the Giants' Harry Newman whipped a pass to Red Badgro in the end zone for the Giants' first touchdown. Strong converted and the Giants led, 7-6, at the half.

The reliable Manders banged over another field goal from 28 yards away in the third period but Newman engineered a drive for New York that ended when Max Krause plowed over from the Chicago one and Strong again converted to make it 14-9. The Bears came right back to score again on a pass from Bronko Nagurski to Bill Karr and Manders' extra point put them ahead, 16-14, as the third quarter ended.

In the last period the Giants invented a play to score again. Strong, starting from the Bears' 8-yard line, was trapped for a loss. In desperation, he lateraled to Newman, who recovered from his surprise in time to flee to the opposite side of the field. When he too was trapped he threw the ball in the general direction of the goal line—and there was Strong to catch it for a touchdown. Strong's conversion put the Giants in the lead again, 21-16. But the Bears came roaring back to the Giants' 36. Nagurski lobbed a pass over the line to Bill Hewitt, who lateraled to Bill Karr, who went the distance, thanks to an earth-shaking block which Gene Ronzani put on Strong to clear the way. Manders' conversion made it 23-21 for the Bears' victory.

1934 WORLD CHAMPIONSHIP PROFESSIONAL FOOTBALL GAME

(Polo Grounds, New York, N.Y., Dec. 9)
Attendance 35,059

New York Giants (30)	Chicago Bears (13)
Frankian—L.E.	Hewitt—L.E.
Morgan—L.T.	Lyman—L.T.
Gibson—L.G.	Pearson—L.G.
Hein—C.	Kawal—C.
Jones—R.G.	Carlson—R.G.
Irwin—R.T.	Musso—R.T.
Flaherty—R.E.	Karr—R.E.
Danowski—Q.B.	Brumbaugh—Q.B.
Burnett—L.H.	Molesworth—L.H.
Strong—R.H.	Ronzani—R.H.
Molenda—F.B.	Nagurski—F.B.

New York Giants	3	0	0	27—30
Chicago Bears	0	10	3	0—13

Touchdowns—Nagurski, Frankian, Strong 2, Danowski.

Points after touchdown—Manders, Strong 3.
Field goals—Manders 2, Strong.
Coaches—Stephen Owen (New York),
George Halas (Chicago).

SUBSTITUTIONS

New York Giants—McBride, Richards,
Owen, Grant.
Chicago Bears—Manders, Johnsos, Buss,
Sisk, Zeller, Rosequist, Masterson.
Officials: Referee—Robert Cahn. Umpire—
G. H. Lowe. Head Linesman—George
Vergara. Field Judge—O. Meyer.

THE GAME

With the temperature at nine degrees
and the Polo Grounds covered with sheet
ice, this contest became known as the
"Sneaker" game when Steve Owen, New
York coach, provided his squad with basketball shoes to open the second half and
thus brought about four touchdowns and
the rout of the Bears who had beaten the
Giants twice during the regular season.

When the game began, the Bears were
carrying a thirteen-consecutive-game winning streak and they had completed thirty-
three games in a row without defeat. But
Beattie Feathers, the sensational halfback,
and Joe Kopcha, their brilliant lineman,
were injured too severely to play (as was
Harry Newman, Giant quarterback). Still
the Bears were heavily favored to win.

Ken Strong got the Giants off on top
in the first quarter with a 38-yard field goal
which was the only score in that period.

The Bears smashed back for their
first touchdown on a one-yard plunge by
Nagurski. Manders' extra point and a field
goal by Manders gave the Bears a 10–3
lead as the half ended.

Manders booted another from the 24-
yard line in the third quarter and then the
roof fell in for the Bears.

As the last period began, the New
York team was getting used to their new
footwear. Ed Danowski started the rout
with a 28-yard pass to Ike Frankian. Mo-
ments later, Ken Strong galloped 42 yards
for another score. Then, so rapidly that the
Bears were completely lost, Danowski and
Strong ran for touchdowns to turn the game
into a track meet. Strong cashed three of
four conversion attempts and the score
ended at 30–13.

1935 WORLD CHAMPIONSHIP PROFESSIONAL FOOTBALL GAME

(Detroit University Stadium, Detroit,
Mich., Dec. 15)
Attendance 15,000

Detroit Lions (26)	New York Giants (7)
Klewicki—L.E.	Frankian—L.E.
Johnson—L.T.	Morgan—L.T.
Monahan—L.G.	Jones—L.G.
Randolph—C.	Hein—C.
Emerson—R.G.	Owen—R.G.
Christensen, G.—R.T.	Grant—R.T.
Schneller—R.E.	Goodwin—R.E.
Presnell—Q.B.	Danowski—Q.B.
Christensen, F.—L.H.	Strong—L.H.
Caddel—R.H.	Richards—R.H.
Gutowski—F.B.	Corzine—F.B.

Detroit Lions	13	0	0	13—26
New York Giants	0	7	0	0— 7

Touchdowns—Strong, Gutowsky, Clark,
Caddel, Parker.
Points after touchdown—Strong, Presnell,
Clark.
Coaches—George Clark (Detroit), Stephen
Owen (New York).

SUBSTITUTIONS

New York Giants—Ends: Singer, Mitchell;
tackle: Irwin; guards: Bellinger, Dell
Isola; backs: Newman, Shaffer, Krause.
Detroit Lions—Ends: Morse, Ebding;
tackles: Steen, Stacy; guards: Knox,
Hopke; center: Ward; backs: Clark,
Shepherd, Parker, Vaughn, Kaska.
Officials: Referee—Thomas Hughitt. Um-
pire—Robert Cahn. Head Linesman—
M. J. Meyer. Field Judge—Harry Robb.

THE GAME

The lethal power of the Detroit backfield was evident from the first kick-off
which the Lions took right back to a touchdown with Leroy "Ace" Gutowsky plowing
over from the 2-yard line. Glenn Presnell
kicked the extra point.

The Giants were unable to move successfully and Detroit scored again when
Earl "Dutch" Clark broke loose for a 40-
yard touchdown romp. Clark tried the conversion and missed.

In the second quarter, which was scoreless, the Giants smashed as far as the
Detroit 4-yard line but were unable to go

any further. The Lions led, 13–0, at the end of the half.

The Giants racked up their only score in the third quarter when Ed Danowski passed from the Detroit 42. Strong caught the ball in full stride on the 30 and went all the way, kicking the conversion to make it 13–7. But that was the end of the Giants.

In the fourth quarter, the Lions took full charge of the game, capitalizing on the New York tactics of desperation passes. George Christensen blocked a punt by Danowski and recovered the ball on the New York 26. The Lions drove to the 4 where Ernie Caddel took the ball over on his favorite reverse play. The extra point was missed. Later in the period, Raymond "Buddy" Parker intercepted Danowski's pass attempt on the Giant 32 and fled to the 9. Buddy then smashed the rest of the way for the final score and Clark picked up the extra point to make it 26–7.

1936 WORLD CHAMPIONSHIP PROFESSIONAL FOOTBALL GAME

(Polo Grounds, New York, N.Y., Dec. 13)
Attendance 29,545

Green Bay Packers (21)	Boston Redskins (6)
Gantenbein—L.E.	Millner—L.E.
Smith, Ernest—L.T.	Edwards—L.T.
Engebretsen—L.G.	Olson—L.G.
Svendsen—C.	Bausch—C.
Evans—R.G.	Karcher—R.G.
Gordon—R.T.	Barber—R.T.
Hutson—R.E.	Malone—R.E.
Bruder—Q.B.	Smith, Riley—Q.B.
Sauer—L.H.	Justice—L.H.
Herber—R.H.	Battles—R.H.
Hinkle—F.B.	Irwin—F.B.

Green Bay Packers	7	0	7	7—21
Boston Redskins	0	6	0	0— 6

Touchdowns—Hutson, Rentner, Gantenbein, Monnett.
Points after touchdown—Ernest Smith 2, Engebretsen.
Coaches—Earl Lambeau (Green Bay), Ray Flaherty (Boston).

SUBSTITUTIONS

Green Bay—Ends: Scherer, Schneidmann; tackles: Schwammel, Seibold; guards: Kiesling, Goldenberg, Paulekas; center: Butler; backs: Miller, Monnett, Laws, Clemens, Johnston, Blood (McNally).

Boston—Ends: Busich, Tosi, McChesney; tackles: O'Brien, Carroll, Sinko; center: Siemering; backs: Pinckert, Britt, Rentner, Temple, Edward Smith.

Officials: Referee—W. G. Crowell. Umpire—Robert Cahn. Head Linesman—M. J. Meyer. Field Judge—William Holleran.

THE GAME

This was the only championship game ever played on a neutral field, a situation resulting from the refusal of Boston fans to support their championship contender. Perfect weather and field conditions were in force at the Polo Grounds and the devastating Packer attack was running at full throttle.

Immediately after the kick-off, Lou Gordon recovered Riley Smith's fumble at midfield. Arnold Herber struck through the air at once, heaving a 43-yard touchdown to Don Hutson. Ernie Smith converted to give the Packers a 7-point lead before the game was three minutes old. Right after the next kick-off, the Redskins lost their great halfback, Cliff Battles, who was injured so badly he played no more that day.

The 'Skins got back in the game on the first play of the second period when "Pug" Rentner crashed over from the one-yard line to make it 7–6. Riley Smith missed the conversion.

Herber fired another long one, 52 yards to Johnny "Blood" McNally, to move the Packers to the Boston 8-yard line, and then pitched to Milt Gantenbein in the end zone in the third quarter. Smith converted. The Redskins got a setback in this period when Frank Bausch, their dynamic center, was tossed out of the game for fighting with Frank Butler.

The Packers scored once more in the last period when Monnett went over from the 2 after a Boston punt was blocked. Engebretsen converted to make it 21–6, the final score.

The gross receipts were $33,471, of which each Packer received $250, each Redskin $180.

1937 WORLD CHAMPIONSHIP PROFESSIONAL FOOTBALL GAME

(Wrigley Field, Chicago, Ill., Dec. 12)
Attendance 15,870

Washington Redskins (28)	Chicago Bears (21)
Millner—L.E.	Manske—L.E.
Edwards—L.T.	Stydahar—L.T.
Olson—L.G.	Fortmann—L.G.
Kawal—C.	Bausch—C.
Karcher—R.G.	Musso—R.G.
Barber—R.T.	Bjork—R.T.
Malone—R.E.	Wilson—R.E.
Smith, R.—Q.B.	Masterson—Q.B.
Baugh—L.H.	Nolting—L.H.
Pinckert—R.H.	Manders—R.H.
Battles—F.B.	Nagurski—F.B.

Washington Redskins	7	0	7	14—28
Chicago Bears	7	7	7	0—21

Touchdowns—Battles, Millner 2, Justice, Manders 2, Manske.
Points after touchdown—Manders 3, Riley Smith 4.
Coaches—Ray Flaherty (Washington), George Halas (Chicago).

SUBSTITUTIONS

Washington Redskins—Michaels, Justice, Carroll, Bond, Irwin, Young, Krause, Kahn, G. Smith.
Chicago Bears—Buivid, Plasman, Ronzani, McDonald, Thompson, Rentner, Francis, Molesworth, Conkwright, Feathers, Karr, Zeller, Sullivan, Trost.
Officials: Referee—W. T. Halloran. Umpire —A. W. Cochrane. Field Judge—E. F. Hughitt. Head Linesman—Bobie Cahn.

THE GAME

The Bears bumped into a young rookie by the name of Sam Baugh on this ice-covered field. He immediately began to give them nightmares. Sixteen years later he is still giving them heart attacks with a record behind him as a chronic "Bear-killer."

Cliff Battles racked up the first Redskin touchdown in the first period, scoring on a 10-yard romp through tackle. Riley Smith's conversion made it 7–0. Jack Manders pounded over for the Bears from 10 yards out and converted to tie the score.

In the second quarter, Bernie Masterson passed 20 yards to Manders for another six-pointer and Manders again converted to give the Bears a 14–7 lead at the rest period.

Baugh went through the air to Wayne Millner for 55 yards and a touchdown early in the third quarter and Smith kicked the extra point. Masterson passed 3 yards to Manske and Manders converted to put the Bears back in the lead.

The fourth quarter was all Baugh. He passed for a seventy-eight yarder to Wayne Millner for one touchdown and then to Ed Justice for 35 yards on another. Smith kicked both extra points for a final score of 28–21 to take the title to Washington.

1938 WORLD CHAMPIONSHIP PROFESSIONAL FOOTBALL GAME

(Polo Grounds, New York, N.Y., Dec. 11)
Attendance 48,120

New York Giants (23)	Green Bay Packers (17)
Poole—L.E.	Becker—L.E.
Widseth—L.T.	Seibold—L.T.
Dell Isola—L.G.	Letlow—L.G.
Hein—C.	Mulleneaux, L.—C.
Tuttle—R.G.	Goldenburg—R.G.
Parry—R.T.	Lee—R.T.
Howell—R.E.	Gantenbein—R.E.
Danowski—Q.B.	Schneidman—Q.B.
Soar—L.H.	Isbell—L.H.
Cuff—R.H.	Laws—R.H.
Shaffer—F.B.	Hinkle—F.B.

New York Giants	9	7	7	0—23
Green Bay Packers	0	14	3	0—17

Touchdowns—Leemans, Barnard, Soar, C. Mulleneaux, Hinkle.
Points after touchdown—Cuff 2, Engebretsen 2.
Coaches—Stephen Owen (New York), Earl Lambeau (Green Bay).

SUBSTITUTIONS

New York Giants—Ends: Barnard, Gelatka; tackles: Mellus, Cope; guards: Lunday, Cole, White; centers: Galazin, Johnson; backs: Leemans, Barnum, Karcis, Richards, Gildea, Burnett, Falaschi.
Green Bay Packers—Ends: Hutson, C. Mulleneaux, Scherer; tackles: Butler, Ray; guards: Johnson, Engebretsen, Tinsley; centers: Svendsen, O. Miller; backs: P. Miller, Bruder, Jankowski, Uram, Herber, Monett.
Officials: Referee—R. Cahn. Umpire—T. Thorp. Head Linesman—L. Conover. Field Judge—J. L. Meyer.

THE GAME

A real slam-bang, bruising thriller was staged for the largest crowd to turn out for a professional championship game up to that time. The entire league had played to a new high in attendance records, the average being up more than 15 percent above previous marks. The victorious Giants became the first team since 1933 (when the league was split into two divisions) to win the championship twice.

The Giants were off on top when two Green Bay punts were blocked early in the game. Ward Cuff cashed one of these for a 13-yard field goal. Tuffy Leemans smashed over from the 6 for a touchdown on the other. Gildea missed the conversion and the Giants led, 9–0, at the end of the period.

Arnie Herber launched a 50-yard pass to Carl Mulleneaux for a TD early in the second quarter and Engebretsen kicked the conversion. The Giants made it 16–7 when E. Danowski passed 20 yards to Hap Barnard in the end zone and Ward Cuff obliged with the extra point. Clark Hinkle smashed over from the 6 to lead to another conversion by Engebretsen and the Giants led, 16–14, at the half.

The Packers took the second half kick-off back to the Giant 15, where Engebretsen hoisted a field goal. The Giants stormed back to the Packer 23 from where Danowski passed to Hank Soar on the 2 and Soar plowed over for the TD. Cuff added the extra and the score was 23–17. There was no further scoring in this period nor in the next.

1939 WORLD CHAMPIONSHIP PROFESSIONAL FOOTBALL GAME

(State Fair Grounds, Milwaukee, Wis., Dec. 10)
Attendance 32,279

Green Bay Packers (27)	New York Giants (0)
Hutson—L.E.	Poole—L.E.
Ray—L.T.	Cope—L.T.
Letlow—L.G.	Dell Isola—L.G.
Svendsen—C.	Hein—C.
Goldenberg—R.G.	Tuttle—R.G.
Lee—R.T.	Mellus—R.T.
Gantenbein—R.E.	Howell—R.E.
Craig—Q.B.	Danowski—Q.B.
Isbell—L.H.	Richards—L.H.
Laws—R.H.	Cuff—R.H.
Hinkle—F.B.	Falaschi—F.B.

Green Bay Packers	7	0	10	10—27
New York Giants	0	0	0	0— 0

Touchdowns—Gantenbein, Laws, Jankowski.
Points after touchdown—Engebretsen 2, Smith.
Field goals—Engebretsen, Smith.
Coaches—Earl Lambeau (Green Bay), Stephen Owen (New York).

SUBSTITUTIONS

Green Bay Packers—Bruder, Jankowski, Tinsley, Brock, Engebretsen, Herber, Uram, Smith, Jacunski, Schultz, Balacz, Lawrence, Zarnas, Weisgerber, Moore, Greenfield.
New York Giants—Leemans, Lunday, Barnum, Burnett, Shaffer, Walls, Kline, Oldershaw, Parry, Widseth, Cole, Owen, Soar, Miller, Gelatka.
Officials: Referee—W. Halloran. Umpire—E. Cochrane. Head Linesman—T. Thorp. Field Judge—Dan Tehan.

THE GAME

This grudge game, played on dry ground but with a chill 35-mph wind making aerial sorties a bit dubious, brought sweet revenge to Green Bay, who had lost the title to the same Giants the previous year.

Arnie Herber tossed a 7-yard pass to Milt Gantenbein in the end zone and Engebretsen cashed the conversion in the first period. There was no further scoring and the Packers led, 7–0, at the half.

Engebretsen continued his scoring with a 29-yard field goal in the third period. Joe Laws then caught Cecil Isbell's 20-yard pass on the Giant 7 and scooted across. Engebretsen again converted to make it 17–0.

Late in the fourth quarter, Ernie Smith kicked a 42-yard field goal. A few plays later an interception led the Packers to the Giant 12. From there, on a double reverse, Jacunski carried to the one and, on the next play, Jankowski took it over. Smith converted and it was 27–0, the final score.

1940 WORLD CHAMPIONSHIP PROFESSIONAL FOOTBALL GAME

**(Griffith Stadium, Washington, D.C., Dec. 8)
Attendance 36,034**

Chicago Bears (73)	Washington Redskins (0)
Nowaskey—L.E.	Masterson—L.E.
Stydahar—L.T.	Wilkin—L.T.
Fortmann—L.G.	Farman—L.G.
Turner—C.	Titchenal—C.
Musso—R.G.	Slivinski—R.G.
Artoe—R.T.	Barber—R.T.
Wilson—R.E.	Malone—R.E.
Luckman—Q.B.	Krause—Q.B.
Nolting—L.H.	Baugh—L.H.
McAfee—R.H.	Justice—R.H.
Osmanski, W.—F.B.	Johnston—F.B.

Chicago Bears	21	7	26	19—73
Washington Redskins	0	0	0	0— 0

Touchdowns—Osmanski, Luckman, Maniaci, Kavanaugh, Turner, Pool, Nolting, McAfee, Clark 2, Famiglietti.
Points after touchdown—Manders, Snyder 2, Martinovich, Plasman, Stydahar, Maniaci.
Coaches—George Halas (Chicago), Ray Flaherty (Washington).

SUBSTITUTIONS

Chicago Bears—Ends: Plasman, Kavanaugh, Manders, Siegal, Martinovich, Pool, Manske; tackles: Kolman, Mihal; guards: Baisi, Forte, Torrance; center: Bausch; backs: Masterson, Sherman, Clark, Swisher, McLean, Famiglietti, Snyder, Maniaci, Manders.
Washington Redskins—Ends: Millner, McChesney, Sanford; tackles: Russell, Fisher, Parks; guards: Shugart, Stralka; centers: Andrako, Carroll; backs: Pinckert, Hoffman, Morgan, Filchock, Zimmerman, Moore, Seymour, Meade, Todd, Farkas, Hare.
Officials: Referee—William Friesell. Umpire—Harry Robb. Head Linesman—Irving Kupcinet. Field Judge—Fred Young.

THE GAME

The most fantastic exhibition of sheer football power and genius, combined with perfect timing and good luck, fashioned this championship game into one that will be mentioned with awe as long as football is played. Washington was far from an out-classed team. In fact their seasonal record was better (9 wins, 2 losses) than the Bears' (8 wins, 3 losses). They were expected to triumph. Baugh had been having his best year to date—the team was ready.

The Bears received and, on the second play, Bill Osmanski sped around his left end for 68 yards and a touchdown. Jack Manders converted. Sid Luckman scored the next with a one-yard plunge after driving the team 80 yards. Bob Snyder kicked the extra point. Joe Maniaci followed Osmanski's trail around left end for 42 yards and a TD, and Phil Martinovich cashed the conversion to make it 21–0 at the end of the quarter.

The second period was fairly quiet; the only scoring was Luckman's 30-yard pass to Ken Kavanaugh in the end zone and Snyder's second conversion.

Hampton Pool intercepted a Baugh pass to open the second half and ran 19 yards for a touchdown with Dick Plasman converting. Ray Nolting blasted for 23 yards and another score and this time Plasman missed the conversion. George McAfee then intercepted Roy Zimmerman's pass and returned 34 yards for a TD and Joe Stydahar kicked the extra point. Clyde Turner got into the act by intercepting another Zimmerman throw and rumbling 21 yards over the goal. The Redskins blocked Maniaci's conversion attempt. This made it 54–0 as the third quarter ended.

Harry Clark went around his right end for 44 yards and a TD and Gary Famiglietti missed the conversion. A few minutes later, Famiglietti atoned by smashing over from the 2 after Bulldog Turner had recovered Frank Filchock's fumble. This time, Sollie Sherman passed to Maniaci for the extra point. Clark scored the final TD from the one-yard line but the Sherman-Maniaci pass-for-conversion attempt went wild.

Ten different Bears had scored eleven touchdowns; six different players had scored seven conversions.

The gross receipts were $112,508.00, a new record at the time. Each Bear received $873.99, each Redskin $606.25. This left a pool of $4,546.45 for the members of the sectional second place clubs (Brooklyn and Green Bay).

1941 WORLD CHAMPIONSHIP PROFESSIONAL FOOTBALL GAME

(Wrigley Field, Chicago, Ill., Dec. 21)
Attendance 13,341

Chicago Bears (37)	New York Giants (9)
Plasman—L.E.	Poole—L.E.
Kolman—L.T.	Mellus—L.T.
Fortmann—L.G.	Lunday—L.G.
Turner—C.	Hein—C.
Bray—R.G.	Younce—R.G.
Artoe—R.T.	Edwards—R.T.
Siegal—R.E.	Howell—R.E.
Luckman—Q.B.	Falaschi—Q.B.
Nolting—L.H.	Franck—L.H.
Gallarneau—R.H.	Cuff—R.H.
Standlee—F.B.	Leemans—F.B.

Chicago Bears	3	6	14	14—37
New York Giants	6	0	3	0— 9

Touchdowns—Franck, Standlee, McAfee, Kavanaugh.
Points after touchdown—Snyder, Maniaci, Artoe, McLean.
Field Goals—Cuff, Snyder 3.
Coaches—George Halas (Chicago), Stephen Owen (New York).

SUBSTITUTIONS

Chicago Bears—Ends: Kavanaugh, Nowaskey, Wilson, Poole; tackles: Stydahar, Mihal, Fedorovitch; guards: Lahar, Baisi, Forte, Musso; center: Matuza; backs: Snyder, Bussey, Swisher, Clark, McLean, McAfee, Famiglietti, Maniaci, W. Osmanski.
New York Giants—Ends: Horne, Walls, Lummis; tackles: Cope, Blazine; guards: Tuttle, Sohn, Oldershaw, Edwards; centers: Gladchuk, Lunday; backs: Principe, Shaffer, Eshmont, Eakin, Yeager, McLain, Marefos, Soar.
Officials: Referee—Emil Heintz. Umpire—John Schommer. Head Linesman—Charles Berry. Field Judge—Chuck Sweeney.

THE GAME

The Giants had won eight, lost three in the East. The Bears had won ten, lost one to tie with the Green Bay Packers in the West. In the play-off game the Bears walloped the Packers 33–14. Pearl Harbor Day was only two weeks past when they met for the championship, a factor which kept the attendance down to ridiculous figures as this great Bear team prepared to break up for the duration. Young Bussey,

Bear quarterback, would be killed in action before the war was over. And Jack Lummis, New York, would die on Iwo Jima.

Bob Snyder put the Bears in front with a 14-yard field goal in the first quarter, but the Giants led after the whistle ended the period, because Tuffy Leemans had sent a 4-yard pass to George Franck, who galloped 27 more yards for the touchdown. Johnny Siegal blocked Ward Cuff's conversion attempt.

Snyder continued the long-range bombardment in the second quarter, booting a field goal from the 39 and another from the 37. There was no other scoring and the Bears led 9–6 at the half.

Ward Cuff kicked a three-pointer from the 17 to tie the score early in the third period but that was the end of the Giants. Norm Standlee smashed through right tackle for 2 yards and a TD, Snyder kicking the extra, then Standlee hit for another from 7 yards out and Joe Maniaci converted. This made it 23–9 as the fourth period opened. George McAfee then hit the line for 5 yards and another marker with Lee Artoe kicking the conversion successfully. Ken Kavanaugh added the final TD by scooping up a fumbled lateral pass from Hank Soar that was intended for Andy Marefos and racing 42 yards for the touchdown. This time Ray McLean dropkicked the conversion and it was 37–9.

The gross receipts (including radio) were $46,184.05, each Bear receiving $430.94, each Giant $288.70. This left a pool of $1,564.06 for the members of the sectional second-place clubs (Green Bay Packers and Brooklyn).

1942 WORLD CHAMPIONSHIP PROFESSIONAL FOOTBALL GAME

(Griffith Stadium, Washington, D.C., Dec. 13)
Attendance 36,006

Washington Redskins (14)	Chicago Bears (6)
Masterson—L.E.	Kolman—L.E.
Wilkin—L.T.	Nowaskey—L.T.
Farman—L.G.	Fortmann—L.G.
Aldrich—C.	Turner—C.
Slivinski—R.G.	Bray—R.G.

Young—R.T.
Cifers—R.E.
Hare, R.—Q.B.
Baugh—L.H.
Justice—R.H.
Farkas—F.B.

Artoe—R.T.
Wilson—R.E.
Luckman—Q.B.
Nolting—L.H.
Gallarneau—R.H.
Famiglietti—F.B.

Washington Redskins	0	7	7	0—14
Chicago Bears	0	6	0	0— 6

Touchdowns—Artoe, Moore, Farkas.
Points after touchdown—Masterson 2.
Coaches—Ray Flaherty (Washington),
George Halas (Chicago).

SUBSTITUTIONS

Washington Redskins—Tackles: Beinor, F.
Davis; guards: Stralka, Shugart; backs:
C. Hare, Moore, Todd, Seymour.
Chicago Bears—Ends: Siegal, Pool; tackles:
Stydahar, Hoptowit; guards: Drulis, Akin,
Musso; backs: O'Rourke, Clark, Maz-
nicki, McLean, Petty, W. Osmanski.
Officials: Referee—Ronald Gibbs. Umpire—
Carl Brubaker. Head Linesman—Charles
Berry. Field Judge—Chuck Sweeney.

THE GAME

The two top passers of the era were
at each other's throats in this championship
match, for Sam Baugh and Sid Luckman
had led their respective teams through
their best seasonal records of history. The
Bears had won all eleven of their league
contests; the Redskins had won ten and
lost but one, an early season defeat by the
New York Giants, whom they whipped later
on. Baugh at this time was still playing
halfback in a single-wing formation although the Bears had been shooting the T
for three seasons.

The first period was scoreless. In the
second, Lee Artoe snatched up a fumbled
pass from center and scampered 50 yards
for a touchdown but missed the conversion.
Baugh sent a 25-yard touchdown toss to
Wilbur Moore which led to Bob Masterson's successful conversion for a 7-6 lead,
and a half-time score of 7-6, Redskins.

In the third period, Andy Farkas, carrying the ball on ten out of twelve plays,
drove for 80 yards and a touchdown, the
scoring smash starting from the Bears' one-
yard line. Masterson again converted to
make it 14-6; the final period was scoreless.

The gross receipts (including radio)
were $113,260.40, each Redskin receiving
$965.89, each Bear $637.56. This left a
pool of $3,241.90 for members of the sec-

tional second-place clubs (Green Bay Packers and Pittsburgh Steelers).

1943 WORLD CHAMPIONSHIP PROFESSIONAL FOOTBALL GAME

(Wrigley Field, Chicago, Ill., Dec. 26)
Attendance 34,320

Chicago Bears (41)	Washington Red-skins (21)
Benton—L.E.	Masterson—L.E.
Sigillo—L.T.	Rymkus—L.T.
Fortmann—L.G.	Shugart—L.G.
Turner—C.	Smith, G.—C.
Musso—R.G.	Slivinski—R.G.
Hoptowit—R.T.	Pasqua—R.T.
Wilson—R.E.	Aguirre—R.E.
Snyder—Q.B.	Hare—Q.B.
Clark—L.H.	Seno—L.H.
Magnani—R.H.	Cafego—R.H.
Masters—F.B.	Farkas—F.B.

Chicago Bears	0	14	13	14—41
Washington Redskins	0	7	7	7—21

Touchdowns—Clark 2, Magnani 2, Nagur-
ski, Benton, Farkas 2, Aguirre.
Points after touchdown—Snyder 5, Master-
son 2, Aguirre.
Coaches—George Halas (Chicago), Arthur
Bergman (Washington).

SUBSTITUTIONS

Chicago Bears—Ends: Pool, Berry; tackles:
Steinkemper, Babartsky, Mundee; guards:
Ippolito, Logan; center: Matuza; backs:
McLean, Luckman, Famiglietti, Nagur-
ski, McEnulty, Nolting, Vodicka.
Washington Redskins—Ends: Piasecky,
Lapka; tackle: Wilkin; guards: Zeno,
Fiorentino, Leon; center: Hayden; backs:
Baugh, Seymour, Moore, Gibson, F.
Akins, Stasica.
Officials: Referee—Ronald Gibbs. Umpire—
John Kelly. Head Linesman—Charles
Berry. Field Judge—Edward Tryon.

THE GAME

Although all the teams in the league
had been depleted of most of their star
players by World War II, Sid Luckman of
the Bears and Sam Baugh of the Redskins
had kept the fans' interest high with their
spectacular passing. Against the Giants,
Luckman had fashioned the unbelievable
record of throwing for seven touchdowns in
one game and Baugh had led the Washington team to a divisional tie with the New

York Giants and then to a 28–0 victory in the play-off game.

The Bears, supposedly creaking with age, beaten previously by the Redskins during a season game, had lured the aged Bronko Nagurski out of retirement to add his thundering power to the attack, but it was Luckman's splendid passing that saved the title for the Bears. Baugh received a concussion late in the game which put the Redskins out of contention.

There was no scoring in the first period. The Redskins clicked first when Andy Farkas plowed one yard to start the second quarter and Bob Masterson converted for 7–0. Luckman fired 31 yards to Harry Clark on a screen-pass for a touchdown and Bob Snyder's extra point tied the game. The Bears led, 14–7, at the half following a 3-yard plunge for a touchdown by Nagurski and Snyder's conversion.

Luckman opened the third period with two touchdown passes, the first traveling 36 yards to Dante Magnani, the second again to Magnani for a 66-yard romp from the flat. Snyder kicked the first conversion, missed the second. The Redskins made it 27–14 at the end of the third quarter after Baugh passed 8 yards to Andy Farkas who ran 9 more for the counter. Masterson converted.

Luckman had two more TD's in his guns for the last period. He threw the first 29 yards to Jim Benton in the end zone, the second 16 yards to Harry Clark, who took it on the goal line. Bob Snyder kicked both conversions. Sam Baugh, just before he was injured, passed 26 yards to Joe Aguirre in the end zone, Aguirre kicked the point and the game ended, 41–21.

The gross receipts (including radio) were $120,500.05, of which each Bear received $1,146.87, each Redskin $765.78. This left a pool of $3,470.57 for members of the sectional second-place clubs (Green Bay Packers and New York Giants).

1944 WORLD CHAMPIONSHIP PROFESSIONAL FOOTBALL GAME

(Polo Grounds, New York, N.Y., Dec. 17)
Attendance 46,016

Green Bay Packers (14)	New York Giants (7)
Hutson—L.E.	Adams, O.—L.E.
Ray—L.T.	Cope—L.T.
Kuusisto—L.G.	Younce—L.G.
Brock, C.—C.	Hein—C.
Goldenberg—R.G.	Sivell—R.G.
Berezney—R.T.	Carroll—R.T.
Jacunski—R.E.	Liebel—R.E.
Craig—Q.B.	Calligaro—Q.B.
Comp—L.H.	Herber—L.H.
Laws—R.H.	Cuff—R.H.
Fritsch—F.B.	Livingston—F.B.

Green Bay Packers	0	14	0	0—14
New York Giants	0	0	0	7— 7

Touchdowns—Fritsch 2, Cuff.
Points after touchdown—Hutson 2, Strong.
Coaches: E. Lambeau (Green Bay), Stephen Owen (New York).

SUBSTITUTIONS

Green Bay Packers—End: Webha; tackle: Croft; guards: Tinsley, Sorenson; backs: L. Brock, Perkins, Duhart.

New York Giants—Ends: Weiss, V. Adams; tackle: Blozis; guard: Avedisian; backs: Petrilas, Paschal, Kinscherf, Sulaitis, Barker, Strong.

Officials: Referee—Ronald Gibbs. Umpire—C. H. Brubaker. Head Linesman—Charles Berry. Field Judge—Eugene Miller. Timer: W. Friesell.

THE GAME

After a scoreless first period, Ted Fritsch put the Packers ahead with a 2-yard touchdown plunge and Don Hutson converted to make it 7–0. Later in the period, Irv Comp passed to Ted Fritsch for 26 yards and another TD with Hutson's conversion giving the Green Bay team a 14–0 lead at half-time.

The third period was scoreless, but, at its end, the Giants were on the Packer one-yard line and Ward Cuff plunged across on the first play of the last quarter. Ken Strong kicked the conversion to make it 14–7 and there was no further scoring.

The gross receipts (including radio) were $146,204.15, of which each Packer received $1,449.71, each Giant $814.36. This left a pool of $8,143.84 for members of the sectional second-place teams (Philadelphia Eagles and both the Chicago Bears and Detroit Lions who tied for second in the West).

1945 WORLD CHAMPIONSHIP PROFESSIONAL FOOTBALL GAME

(Municipal Stadium, Cleveland, Ohio, Dec. 16)
Attendance 32,178

Cleveland Rams (15)	Washington Redskins (14)
Konetsky—L.E.	Millner—L.E.
Schultz—L.T.	Audet—L.T.
Matheson, R.—L.G.	Adams, J.—L.G.
Scarry—C.	Aldrich—C.
Lazetich—R.G.	Whited—R.G.
Bouley—R.T.	Ungerer—R.T.
Pritko—R.E.	Turley—R.E.
Reisz—Q.B.	Hare, C.—Q.B.
Nemeth—L.H.	Seymour—L.H.
Gillette—R.H.	Condit—R.H.
West—F.B.	Akins, F.—F.B.

Cleveland Rams	2	7	6	0—15
Washington Redskins	0	7	7	0—14

Touchdowns—Benton, Gillette, Bagarus, Seymour.
Points after touchdown—Aguirre 2, Waterfield.
Safety—Automatic.
Coaches: Adam Walsh (Cleveland), Dudley DeGroot (Washington).

SUBSTITUTIONS

Cleveland Rams—Ends: Hamilton, Hickey, Benton; tackles: Lear, Sikich, Eason; guards: Levy, Mergenthal; center: de-Lauer, Harding; backs: Waterfield, Koch, Greenwood, Gehrke.
Washington Redskins—Ends: Piasecky, Aguirre, Dye; tackles: Davis, Koniszewski; guards: Sharp, Lolotai, Hanna, Stralka; center: DeMao; backs: Bagarus, Baugh, deCorrevont, Filchock, Rosato, Todd, deFruiter.
Officials: Referee—Ronald Gibbs. Umpire—Harry Robb. Head Linesman—Charles Berry. Field Judge—William Downes.

THE GAME

It was so cold in Cleveland on the day of the game that the musical instruments froze, putting the great Redskin band out of action even before the game started. The field had been covered with mountains of straw but was slippery underfoot. The wind was strong and erratic. It was a perfect day for staying home by the fireside but no less than 32,178 eager fans appeared.

Sam Baugh attempted a pass from his end zone in the first quarter. The wind veered the ball into the goal post for an automatic safety to give the Rams a 2-point lead.

In the second period, Frank Filchock passed 26 yards to Steve Bagarus who ran 12 more for the first touchdown. Joe Aguirre converted to put the Redskins ahead 7–2. Waterfield then passed 25 yards to Jim Benton who added 12 more for a TD and Waterfield's conversion made it 9–7 at the end of the half.

In the third, Waterfield threw 39 yards to Jim Gillette, who then scored from the 14. Waterfield's conversion missed to keep it 15–7.

Filchock passed the 'Skins to within 2 points of the Rams, with an 8-yard pitch to Bob Seymour in the end zone. Aguirre again converted.

The fourth period was scoreless and the game ended 15–14.

The gross receipts (including radio and motion picture rights) were $164,542.40, of which each Ram received $1,469.74, each Redskin $902.47. This left a pool of $4,763.05 for members of the sectional second-place clubs (Philadelphia Eagles and Detroit Lions).

1946 WORLD CHAMPIONSHIP PROFESSIONAL FOOTBALL GAME

(Polo Grounds, New York, N.Y., Dec. 15)
Attendance 58,346

Chicago Bears (24)	New York Giants (14)
Kavanaugh—L.E.	Poole—L.E.
Davis, F.—L.T.	Coulter—L.T.
Mucha—L.G.	Dobelstein—L.G.
Turner—C.	Gladchuk—C.
Bray—R.G.	Young—R.G.
Jarmoluk—R.T.	White—R.T.
Wilson—R.E.	Howell—R.E.
Osmanski, J.—Q.B.	Filipowicz—Q.B.
Magnani—L.H.	Brown—L.H.
Gallarneau—R.H.	Livingston—R.H.
Osmanski, W.—F.B.	Strong—F.B.

Chicago Bears	14	0	0	10—24
New York Giants	7	0	7	0—14

Touchdowns—Kavanaugh, Magnani, Luckman, Liebel, Filipowicz.
Points after touchdown—Maznicki 3, Strong 2.

Coaches: George Halas (Chicago), Stephen Owen (New York).

SUBSTITUTIONS

Chicago Bears—Ends: Lamb, Keane, Sprinkle; tackles: Stickel, Kolman; guards: Forte, Preston, Drulis; centers: Clarkson, Schiechl; backs: Maznicki, McAfee, Perkins, Margarita, Luckman, Farris, Schweidler, McLean.

New York Giants—Ends: Mead, McCafferty, Liebel; tackles: Cope, Ragazzo, Carroll; guard: Edwards; center: De-Filippo; backs: Soar, Gorgone, Franck, Filchock, Reagan, Doolan.

Officials: Referee—Ronald Gibbs. Umpire—Carl Brubaker. Head Linesman—Charles Berry. Field Judge—William Grimberg.

THE GAME

The Bears had won the Western division championship easily with 8 wins, 2 losses and a tie. The Giants dominated the Eastern with 7 wins, 3 losses and a tie. There was considerable excitement a few days before the game when it was revealed that two New York players had been approached by Broadway characters who wanted them to control the score.

The deadly Sid Luckman-to-Ken Kavanaugh pass combination opened the scoring for the Bears in the first period with a 21-yard toss over the goal and Frank Maznicki's conversion made it 7-0. The Bears increased their lead to 14-0 when Dante Magnani intercepted Filchock's pass and raced 19 yards for the TD, then kicked the extra point. The Giants got their first touchdown in the same period when Frank Filchock passed 38 yards to Frank Liebel. Ken Strong converted.

There was no scoring in the second period.

In the third, the Giants pulled even at 14-14 when Filchock passed 5 yards for a TD to Steve Filipowicz and Strong converted.

Sid Luckman fooled the Giants completely with a "keep-it" play in the fourth quarter, running 19 yards for a touchdown and Maznicki converted again. Later in the quarter, Maznicki booted a field goal from the 26 to make the final score 24-14.

The gross receipts (including radio and motion picture rights) were $282,-955.25, a new record at the time. Each Bear received $1,975.82, each Giant $1,295.57.

This left a pool of $14,395.33 for members of the sectional second-place clubs (Philadelphia Eagles and Los Angeles Rams).

1947 WORLD CHAMPIONSHIP PROFESSIONAL FOOTBALL GAME

(Comiskey Park, Chicago, Ill., Dec. 28)
Attendance 30,759

Chicago Cardinals (28)	Philadelphia Eagles (21)
Blackburn—L.E.	Ferrante—L.E.
Plasman—L.T.	Sears—L.T.
Arms—L.G.	Patton—L.G.
Banonis—C.	Wojciechowicz—C.
Nichols—R.G.	Kilroy—R.G.
Mauldin—R.T.	Wistert—R.T.
Doolan—R.E.	Pihos—R.E.
Campbell—Q.B.	McHugh—Q.B.
Cochran—L.H.	Van Buren—L.H.
Goldberg—R.H.	Pritchard—R.H.
Rankin—F.B.	Muha—F.B.

Chicago Cardinals	7	7	7	7—28
Philadelphia Eagles	0	7	7	7—21

Touchdowns—Trippi 2, Angsman 2, McHugh, Van Buren, Craft.
Points after touchdown—Harder 4, Patton 3.
Coaches: James Conzelman (Chicago), Earle Neale (Philadelphia).

SUBSTITUTIONS

Chicago Cardinals—Ends: Parker, Kutner, Dewell; tackles: Coomer, Bulger; guards: Andros, Ramsey, Apolskis; backs: Mallouf, Dimancheff, DeCorrevont, Angsman, Harder, Christman, Trippi.

Philadelphia Eagles—Ends: Armstrong, Green, Cabrelli, Prescott; tackles: Kekeris, Douglas, McDowell, Harding; guard: Wyhonic; center: Lindskog; backs: Steele, Craft, Kish, Sherman, Thompson.

Officials: Referee—William Downs. Umpire—Harry Robb. Head Linesman—Dan Tehan. Field Judge—Harry Haines. Back Judge—Carl Rebele.

THE GAME

Philadelphia finished the season tied with the Pittsburgh Steelers, each having an 8-4 record, then won the divisional title by beating the Pittsburgh team 21-0 in the play-off. The Cardinals had won 9, lost 3. The field was fast and frozen, the weather frigid when they clashed for the championship. The new eight-man-line defense developed by coach Earle "Greasy" Neale, although highly effective all season, backfired in this game.

In the first period, Charlie Trippi squirted through tackle on a quick-opener and went 44 yards for a touchdown. Harder kicked the conversion.

In the second period, Elmer Angsman, on the same play, went 70 yards for the Cardinals' second score and Harder converted. The Eagles came back to make it 14–7 at the half after Tommy Thompson passed 53 yards to Pat McHugh, who ran 17 more to score, with Cliff Patton converting.

Charlie Trippi ran a punt back for 75 yards and a TD in the third period and Harder again converted to make it 21–7, but the Eagles countered with a 73-yard drive, Steve Van Buren scoring from the one-yard line and Patton again converting to make it 21–14.

Again on the quick-opener Elmer Angsman burst loose for his second 70-yard touchdown run in the fourth quarter and Harder converted. And again the Eagles smashed through on the ground with Russ Craft crashing from the one and Patton once more converting to end the scoring at 28–21.

The gross receipts (including radio and motion picture rights) were $159,498, of which each Cardinal received $1,132, each Eagle $754. This left a pool of $8,388 for members of the sectional second-place clubs (Chicago Bears and Pittsburgh Steelers).

1948 WORLD CHAMPIONSHIP PROFESSIONAL FOOTBALL GAME

(Shibe Park, Philadelphia, Pa., Dec. 19) Attendance 36,309

Philadelphia Eagles (7)	Chicago Cardinals (0)
Green—L.E.	Cochran—L.E.
MacDowell—L.T.	Zimny—L.T.
Maronic—L.G.	Ramsey—L.G.
Lindskog—C.	Banonis—C.
Kilroy—R.G.	Andros—R.G.
Wistert—R.T.	Bulger—R.T.
Armstrong—R.E.	Clatt—R.E.
Thompson—Q.B.	Davis—Q.B.
Steele—L.H.	Trippi—L.H.
Craft—R.H.	Angsman—R.H.
Muha—F.B.	Harder—F.B.

Philadelphia Eagles	0	0	0	7—7
Chicago Cardinals	0	0	0	0—0

Touchdown—Van Buren.
Point after touchdown—Patton.
Coaches—Earle Neale (Philadelphia), James Conzelman (Chicago).

SUBSTITUTIONS

Eagles—Ends: Ferrante, Humbert, Pihos; tackles: Sears, Douglas, Savitsky; guards: Patton, Gianelli; center: Wojciechowicz; backs: Van Buren, Pritchard, Myers, McHugh.

Cardinals—Ends: Kutner, Ravensberg, Dewell, Goldman; tackles: Coomer, Szot, Loepfe; guards: Colhouer, Nichols, Apolskis; center: Blackburn; backs: Mallouf, Dimancheff, Schwall, Goldberg, Yablonski.

Officials: Referee—Ronald Gibbs. Umpire—Sam Wilson. Head Linesman—Charles Berry. Field Judge—William F. McHugh. Back Judge—Robert C. Austin.

THE GAME

This championship has been described as having taken place in "Blizzard Bowl," the "Arctic Bowl" and otherwise in the worst conditions ever provided by nature for a football game. The field was covered with snow, the line markers were invisible, and one of the worst storms in Philadelphia history raged through the game. Referee Ronald Gibbs and his crew did a remarkable job of officiating under almost impossible conditions.

The 36,309 true fanatics who sat through the game saw the two teams struggle back and forth through the arctic conditions until Frank Kilroy recovered quarterback Ray Mallouf's fumble on the Cardinal 17-yard line in the fourth period after three scoreless sessions. It was now or never for the Eagles and they powered across for the touchdown, Steve Van Buren smashing 5 yards to score. Cliff Patton kicked the extra point to end the scoring.

The gross receipts (including radio, television and motion picture rights) were $223,622.25, of which each Eagle received $1,540.84, each Cardinals $874.39. This left a pool of $10,985.62 for members of the sectional second-place clubs (Washington Redskins and Chicago Bears).

1949 WORLD CHAMPIONSHIP PROFESSIONAL FOOTBALL GAME

(Los Angeles Memorial Coliseum, Los Angeles, Cal., Dec. 18)
Attendance 27,980

Philadelphia Eagles (14)	Los Angeles Rams (0)
Ferrante—L.E.	Fears—L.E.
Sears—L.T.	Huffman—L.T.
Patton—L.G.	Dean—L.G.
Lindskog—C.	Martin—C.
Kilroy—R.G.	Yagiello—R.G.
Wistert—R.T.	Bouley—R.T.
Pihos—R.E.	Smyth—R.E.
Thompson—Q.B.	Waterfield—Q.B.
Van Buren—L.H.	Kalmanir—L.H.
Scott—R.H.	Smith, V. T.—R.H.
Myers—F.B.	Hoerner—F.B.

Philadelphia Eagles	0 ·	7	7	0—14
Los Angeles Rams	0	0	0	0— 0

Touchdowns—Pihos, Skladany.
Points after touchdown—Patton 2.
Coaches—Earle Neal (Philadelphia), Clark Shaughnessy (Los Angeles).

SUBSTITUTIONS

Philadelphia Eagles—Ends: Armstrong, Skladany; tackles: Savitsky, McDowell, Jarmoluk; guards: Gianelli, Magee, Barnes, Maronic; centers: Wojciechowicz, Bednarik; backs: Reagen, Ziegler, Craft, Pritchard, Parmer, McHugh, Muha, Kish.
Los Angeles Rams—Ends: Fears, Hubbell, Currivan, Zilly, Shaw, Keane: tackles: Sparkman, Champagne; guards: Finlay, Lazetich; centers: Naumetz, Paul; backs: Van Brocklin, Gehrke, Hirsch, Younger, Williams, Sims, Cowhig.
Officials: Referee—Ronald Gibbs. Umpire—Joseph Crowley. Head Linesman—Charles Berry. Field Judge—William F. McHugh. Back Judge—Robert C. Austin.

THE GAME

Drenching rain on this first time the Rams had played a home game under any but the best weather conditions held the crowd down though the Philadelphia Eagles invaded the West Coast strutting a record of eleven victories, marred by only one loss to the Chicago Bears. The Rams had won eight, lost two and tied two. It was not a day for passing, a fact which hampered Bob Waterfield, throwing ace of the Rams, and added potency to the ground power of the Eagles, spearheaded by Steve Van Buren.

The game was scoreless until midway in the second quarter when Tommy Thompson, Eagle quarterback, threw one of his few passes and connected with end Pete Pihos for 31 yards and a touchdown. Cliff Patton converted and the defending champions led 7-0.

Late in the third period, Waterfield, attempting a punt from his own five, slipped, and the kick was blocked by Ed Skladany, who grabbed the loose ball for a touchdown. Patton again converted and this ended the scoring.

The gross receipts (including radio) were $149,344.80, of which each Eagle received $1094.68, each Ram $739.66. This left a pool of $7,754.12 for members of the sectional second-place clubs (Chicago Bears and Pittsburgh).

1950 WORLD CHAMPIONSHIP PROFESSIONAL FOOTBALL GAME

(Cleveland Municipal Stadium, Cleveland, Ohio, Dec. 24)
Attendance 29,751

Cleveland Browns (30)	Los Angeles Rams (28)
Speedie—L.E.	Fears—L.E.
Groza—L.T.	Huffman—L.T.
Humble—L.G.	Finlay—L.G.
Gatski—C.	Naumetz—C.
Houston—R.G.	Thompson—R.G.
Rymkus—R.T.	Reinhard—R.T.
Lavelli—R.E.	Zilly—R.E.
Graham—Q.B.	Waterfield—Q.B.
Bumgardner—L.H.	Davis, G.—L.H.
Jones, W.—R.H.	Smith, V. T.—R.H.
Motley—F.B.	Hoerner—F.B.

Cleveland Browns	7	6	7	10—30
Los Angeles Rams	14	0	14	0—28

Touchdowns—Jones, Lavelli 2, Bumgardner, Davis, Hoerner 2, Brink.
Field Goal—Groza.
Points after touchdown—Groza 3, Waterfield 4.
Coaches—Paul Brown (Cleveland), Joe Stydahar (Los Angeles).

SUBSTITUTIONS

Browns—Ends: Young, Martin, Gillom, Ford; tackles: Palmer, Grigg, Kissell, Sandusky; guards: Willis, Gibron, Agase; centers: Herring, Thompson; backs: Gorgal, Carpenter, Cole, Adamle, Lahr, James, Lewis, Moselle, Phelps.

Rams—Ends: Boyd, Brink, Smyth, Hirsch; tackles: Champagne, Bouley, guards: Stephenson, West, Vasicek, Lazetich; centers: Paul, Statuto; backs: Lewis, Towler, Williams, Barry, Keane, Kalmanir, Pasquariello, Van Brocklin, Younger.

Officials: Referee—Ronald Gibbs. Umpire—Samuel Wilson. Head Linesman—Charles Berry. Field Judge—Lloyd Brazil. Back Judge—Norman Duncan.

THE GAME

Treacherous, icy footing could not slow the action of this sixty minutes of mayhem at Cleveland Municipal Stadium. Both teams had won their divisional tie play-offs the week before, the Browns beating the Giants 8–3 after losing to them twice during the season; the Rams knocking out the Bears 24–14 after losing two to the Chicago club.

With efficient lines, evenly matched, this shaped up as a passing duel pitting Otto Graham, quarterback of the Browns. against Bob Waterfield and Norman Van Brocklin, throwing for the Rams; and as a goal kicking duel between Lou Groza of the Browns and the versatile Waterfield.

Only 27 seconds after the kick-off, Waterfield threw to Glenn Davis for 82 yards and a touchdown and converted for 7–0. Graham came right back with a completion to William "Dub" Jones and Groza converted to tie, 7–7. The Rams went ahead again, 14–7, when Hoerner plunged 3 yards to score and Waterfield converted.

In the second quarter, Graham threw another TD to Dante Lavelli, but the attempt at conversion failed when the pass from center was juggled and the Rams still led, 14–13.

Early in the second half, Graham again passed to Lavelli for a score and Groza's conversion made it 20–14. Dick Hoerner's one-yard plunge and Waterfield's conversion put the Rams ahead 21–20, and, seconds later, Larry Brink picked up Motley's fumble on the Brown 6 to score again. Waterfield converted and it was 28–20.

Graham put the Browns back in the game in the last quarter with a TD pitch to Rex Bumgardner and Groza converted for 28–27. An interception gave the Browns the ball in the closing minutes and, from the 16-yard line, with twenty-eight seconds remaining, Lou Groza booted a 3-pointer to win the game for the Browns 30–28.

The gross receipts (including radio) were $157,078.00, of which each Brown received $1,113.16, each Ram $686.44. This left a pool of $7,627.21 for members of the sectional second-place clubs (Chicago Bears and New York Giants).

1951 WORLD CHAMPIONSHIP PROFESSIONAL FOOTBALL GAME

(Los Angeles Coliseum, Los Angeles, Cal., Dec. 23) Attendance 59,475

Los Angeles Rams (24)	Cleveland Browns (17)
Fears—L.E.	Speedie—L.E.
Simensen—L.T.	Groza—L.T.
Daugherty—L.G.	Gibron—L.G.
McLaughlin—C.	Gatski—C.
Lange—R.G.	Gaudio—R.G.
Dahms—R.T.	Rymkus—R.T.
Hirsch—R.E.	Lavelli—R.E.
Waterfield—Q.B.	Graham—Q.B.
Towler—L.H.	Carpenter—L.H.
Younger—R.H.	Jones, W.—R.H.
Hoerner—F.B.	Motley—F.B.

Los Angeles Rams	0	7	7	10—24
Cleveland Browns	0	10	0	7—17

Touchdowns—Hoerner, Towler, Fears, Jones, Carpenter.

Field Goals—Waterfield, Groza.

Points after touchdown—Waterfield 3, Groza 2.

Coaches: Paul Brown (Cleveland), Joseph Stydahar (Los Angeles).

SUBSTITUTIONS

Los Angeles—Ends: Brink, Hecker, Keane, Robustelli, Boyd; tackles: Winkler, Toogood, Halliday; guards: West, Finlay, Thompson, Collier; center: Paul, Reid; backs: Van Brocklin, G. Davis, Williams, Johnson, V. Smith, Kalmanir, Lewis, Rich.

Cleveland—Ends: Young, Gillom, Ford, Oristaglio; tackles: Kissell, Palmer, Sandusky, Grigg; guards: Thompson, Agase, Willis, Houston; center: Herring; backs: Lewis, Shula, Lahr, Bumgardner, James, Taseff, Adamle, Cole, Jagade.

Officials: Referee—Ronald Gibbs. Umpire—Carl Brubaker. Head Linesman—Dan Tehan. Field Judge—William McHugh. Back Judge—Robert Austin.

THE GAME

The largest crowd in professional football history (59,475) watched in ideal weather conditions as the Los Angeles Rams, after losing the last two championship play-offs, finally beat the Browns for the first time to win the title. It was the first time the defending champions had ever lost a championship after four victorious years in the All America Football Conference and one in the NFL.

After a scoreless first period, Waterfield drove the Rams to the Cleveland one-yard line, completing two passes on the way, then gave the ball to Dick Hoerner who plowed over. Waterfield converted.

Cleveland got its first three points from a towering 52-yard field goal by Lou Groza, the longest in championship history but 2 yards short of the all-time big one of 54 yards kicked by Glenn Presnell. The Browns scored again in the second quarter on a 17-yard pass from Graham to William "Dub" Jones and Groza converted to make the score 10–7 at the half.

The Rams went ahead, 14–10 in the third period after Larry Brink's crashing tackle of Graham produced a fumble. The ball was picked up and hurried to the Brown one-yard line by Andy Robustelli. Dan Towler banged over for the touchdown and Waterfield converted.

The Browns pulled even early in the fourth period after Waterfield's 17-yard field goal had put the Rams ahead 17–10. They traveled 70 yards with the last one-yard plunge by Ken Carpenter bagging the vital points. Groza again scored the extra point.

Norman Van Brocklin, quarterbacking the Rams through most of the second half, then fired a long pass to Tom Fears behind the Brown defense for a 73-yard touchdown play which proved to be the winner. Waterfield booted his third extra point and the Rams held solidly against the Brown's frantic efforts to get the game even once more.

The gross receipts (including radio and television) were $325,970, of which each Ram received $2,108.44, each Brown $1,483.12. This left a pool of $15,655.14 for members of the sectional second-place clubs (Detroit Lions and New York Giants). All these financial scores were new records.

CHAMPIONSHIP GAME RECORDS

Most Championship Wins

7 Chicago Bears (1921, 1932, 1933, 1940, 1941, 1943, 1946)
6 Green Bay (1929, 1930, 1931, 1936, 1939, 1944)

Most Play-offs Participated In

8 Chicago Bears (1933, 1934, 1937, 1940, 1941, 1942, 1943, 1946)
New York Giants (1933, 1934, 1935, 1938, 1939, 1941, 1944, 1946)

GROUND GAINING

Most Yards Gained

2,587 Chicago Bears (8 play-offs)
1,756 New York Giants (8 play-offs)

Most Yards Gained (one game)

501 Chicago Bears vs Washington, Dec. 8, 1940
445 Chicago Bears vs Washington, Dec. 26, 1943

Fewest Yards Gained (one game)

116 Boston Redskins vs Green Bay, Dec. 13, 1936
119 Los Angeles vs Philadelphia, Dec. 18, 1949

Most Yards Gained Rushing

1,291 Chicago Bears (8 play-offs)
837 New York Giants (8 play-offs)

Most Yards Gained Rushing (one game)

382 Chicago Bears vs Washington, Dec. 8, 1940
274 Philadelphia vs Los Angeles, Dec. 18, 1949

Fewest Yards Gained Rushing (one game)

21 Los Angeles vs Philadelphia, Dec. 18, 1949
22 Washington vs Chicago Bears, Dec. 8, 1940

Most Yards Gained Passing

1,281 Chicago Bears (73 completions in 8 play-offs)

1,037 Washington (67 completions in 5 play-offs)

Most Yards Gained Passing (one game)

371 Washington vs Chicago Bears, Dec. 12, 1937 (22 completions)
312 Los Angeles vs Cleveland Browns, Dec. 24, 1950 (18 completions)

Fewest Yards Gained Passing (one game)

7 Philadelphia vs Chicago Cardinals, Dec. 19, 1948 (2 completions)
35 Chicago Cardinals vs Philadelphia, Dec. 19, 1948 (3 completions) .

FIRST DOWNS

Most First Downs

104 Chicago Bears (8 play-offs)
85 New York Giants (8 play-offs)

Most First Downs (one game)

22 Los Angeles vs Cleveland Browns, Dec. 23, 1951
Cleveland Browns vs Los Angeles, Dec. 24, 1950
Philadelphia vs Chicago Cardinals, Dec. 28, 1947

Most First Downs Rushing

66 Chicago Bears (8 play-offs)
43 New York Giants (8 play-offs)

Most First Downs Rushing (one game)

16 Philadelphia vs Chicago Cardinals, Dec. 19, 1948
14 Chicago Bears vs New York Giants, Dec. 21, 1941

Most First Downs Passing

33 Chicago Bears (8 play-offs)
32 Washington (5 play-offs)

Most First Downs Passing (one game)

16 Cleveland Browns vs Los Angeles, Dec. 23, 1951
13 Cleveland Browns vs Los Angeles, Dec. 24, 1950
12 Los Angeles vs Cleveland Browns, Dec. 24, 1950

Most First Downs by Penalty

13 New York Giants (8 play-offs)
7 Washington (5 play-offs)

FORWARD PASSING

Most Passes Completed

73 Chicago Bears (171 attempts in 8 play-offs)
67 Washington (148 attempts in 5 play-offs)

Most Passes Completed (one game)

27 Philadelphia vs Chicago Cardinals, Dec. 28, 1947 (44 attempts)
22 Washington vs Chicago Bears, Dec. 12, 1937 (40 attempts)
Cleveland Browns vs Los Angeles, Dec. 24, 1950 (33 attempts)

Fewest Passes Completed (one game)

2 Detroit vs New York Giants, Dec. 15, 1935 (5 attempts)
Philadelphia vs Chicago Cardinals, Dec. 19, 1948 (12 attempts)

Most Passes Attempted

161 Chicago Bears (73 completions in 8 play-offs)
148 Washington (67 completions in 5 play-offs)

Most Passes Attempted (one game)

51 Washington vs Chicago Bears, Dec. 8, 1940 (20 completions)
44 Philadelphia vs Chicago Cardinals, Dec. 28, 1947 (27 completions)

Fewest Passes Attempted (one game)

5 Detroit vs New York Giants, Dec. 15, 1935 (2 completions)
9 Philadelphia vs Los Angeles, Dec. 18, 1949 (5 completions)

INTERCEPTIONS

Most Passes Had Intercepted

25 New York Giants (149 attempts in 8 play-offs)
19 Washington (148 attempts in 5 play- offs)

Most Passes Had Intercepted (one game)

8 Washington vs Chicago Bears, Dec. 8, 1940 (51 attempts)
6 New York Giants vs Green Bay, Dec. 10, 1939 (26 attempts)
New York Giants vs Chicago Bears, Dec. 15, 1946 (26 attempts)

Most Passes Intercepted By

29 Chicago Bears (8 play-offs)
13 New York Giants (8 play-offs)

Most Passes Intercepted By (one game)

8 Chicago Bears vs Washington, Dec. 8, 1940
6 Green Bay vs New York Giants, Dec. 10, 1939
Chicago Bears vs New York Giants, Dec. 15, 1946

Most Yards Interceptions Returned

355 Chicago Bears (29 interceptions in 8 play-offs)
137 Green Bay (8 interceptions in 3 play-offs)

Most Yards Interceptions Returned (one game)

123   Green Bay vs New York Giants, Dec. 10, 1939 (6 interceptions)

117   Chicago Bears vs Washington, Dec. 8, 1940 (8 interceptions)

PUNTS

Most Punts

63   New York Giants (8 play-offs)

47   Chicago Bears (8 play-offs)

Most Punts (one game)

13   New York Giants vs Chicago Bears, Dec. 17, 1933

10   New York Giants vs Chicago Bears, Dec. 19, 1934

Fewest Punts (one game)

2   Chicago Bears (twice) vs Washington, Dec. 8, 1940, and vs New York Giants, Dec. 21, 1941

3   Washington vs Chicago Bears, Dec. 8, 1940

Best Punting Average

41.3 yards   Detroit (6 punts in 1 play-off)

40.7 yards   Chicago Bears (47 punts in 8 play-offs)

Best Punting Average (one game)

53.5 yards   Chicago Bears vs New York Giants, Dec. 21, 1941 (2 punts)

52.5 yards   Washington vs Chicago Bears, Dec. 13, 1942 (6 punts)

PUNT RETURNS

Most Punt Returns

19   Chicago Bears (54 punts in 8 play-offs)

17   Washington (27 punts in 5 play-offs)

Most Punt Returns (one game)

8   Green Bay vs New York Giants, Dec. 17, 1944

6   Washington vs Chicago Bears, Dec. 13, 1942

Most Yards Punts Returned

192   Chicago Bears (19 returns in 8 play-offs)

169   New York Giants (16 returns in 8 play-offs)

Most Yards Punts Returned (one game)

150   Chicago Cardinals vs Philadelphia, Dec. 28, 1947 (4 returns)

90   Detroit vs New York Giants, Dec. 15, 1935 (4 returns)

KICK-OFF RETURNS

Most Kick-offs Returned

27   New York Giants (8 play-offs)

23   Chicago Bears (8 play-offs)

Most Kick-offs Returned (one game)

8   Washington vs Chicago Bears, Dec. 8, 1940

6   New York Giants vs Chicago Bears, Dec. 17, 1933
Washington vs Chicago Bears, Dec. 26, 1943

Most Yards Kick-offs Returned

512   New York Giants (27 returns in 8 play-offs)

432   Washington (21 returns in 5 play-offs)

Most Yards Kick-offs Returned (one game)

225   Washington vs Chicago Bears, Dec. 8, 1940 (8 returns)

149   Washington vs Chicago Bears, Dec. 26, 1943 (6 returns)

PENALTIES

Most Penalties

51   Chicago Bears (420 yards in 8 play-offs)

29   New York Giants (260 yards in 8 play-offs)

Most Penalties (one game)

19   Chicago Bears vs New York Giants, Dec. 21, 1941 (80 yards)
Chicago Cardinals vs Philadelphia, Dec. 28, 1947 (98 yards)

11   New York Giants vs Green Bay, Dec. 17, 1944 (90 yards)

Fewest Penalties (one game)

1   Washington vs Chicago Bears, Dec. 12, 1937 (5 yards)
Chicago Bears vs Washington, Dec. 12, 1937 (15 yards)

Most Yards Penalized

420   Chicago Bears (51 penalties in 8 play-offs)

260   New York Giants (29 penalties in 8 play-offs)

Most Yards Penalized (one game)

102   Chicago Bears vs New York Giants, Dec. 15, 1946 (9 penalties)

98   Chicago Cardinals vs Philadelphia, Dec. 28, 1947 (10 penalties)

Fewest Yards Penalized (one game)

5   Washington vs Chicago Bears, Dec. 12, 1937 (1 penalty)

10   New York Giants vs Green Bay, Dec. 11, 1938 (2 penalties)

FUMBLES

Most Fumbles

18   Chicago Bears (8 play-offs)
16   New York Giants (8 play-offs)

Most Fumbles (one game, one team)

5   Boston Redskins vs Green Bay, Dec. 13, 1936
4   Chicago Bears vs New York Giants, Dec. 9, 1934
New York Giants vs Chicago Bears, Dec. 9, 1934
Detroit vs New York Giants, Dec. 15, 1935

Most Fumbles (one game, both teams)

8   Chicago Bears (4) vs New York Giants (4), Dec. 9, 1934
7   Boston (5) vs Green Bay (2), Dec. 13, 1936
Chicago Bears (4) vs Washington (3), Dec. 12, 1937
Detroit (4) vs New York Giants (3), Dec. 15, 1935

Fewest Fumbles (one game, one team)

0   New York Giants vs Chicago Bears, Dec. 17, 1933
Chicago Bears vs Washington, Dec. 26, 1943
Los Angeles vs Cleveland Browns, Dec. 24, 1950

Fewest Fumbles (one game, both teams)

1   New York Giants (0) vs Chicago Bears (1), Dec. 17, 1933
2   Chicago Bears (0) vs Washington (2), Dec. 26, 1943
Cleveland Rams (1) vs Washington (1), Dec. 16, 1945

Most Fumbles Recovered

22   Chicago Bears (13 own; 9 opponents; 33 opportunities in 8 play-offs)
12   Washington (9 own; 3 opponents; 25 opportunities in 5 play-offs)

Most Fumbles Recovered (one game)

7   Chicago Bears vs New York Giants (4 own; 3 opponents; 8 opportunities), Dec. 9, 1934
6   Chicago Bears vs Washington (4 own; 2 opponents; 7 opportunities), Dec. 12, 1937

Most Own Fumbles Recovered

14   Chicago Bears (out of 19 in 8 play-offs)
8   New York Giants (out of 17 in 8 play-offs)

Most Own Fumbles Recovered (one game)

4   Chicago Bears vs New York Giants (out of 4), Dec. 9, 1934
Chicago Bears vs Washington (out of 4), Dec. 12, 1937

Most Opponents Fumbles Recovered

9   Chicago Bears out of 16 in 8 play-offs)
4   New York Giants (out of 11 in 8 play-offs)

Most Opponents Recovered (one game)

3   Chicago Bears vs New York Giants (out of 4), Dec. 9, 1934
Detroit vs New York Giants (out of 4), Dec. 15, 1935
Los Angeles vs Cleveland Browns (out of 3), Dec. 24, 1950

SCORING

Most Points Scored

238   Chicago Bears (8 play-offs)
111   New York Giants (8 play-offs)

Most Points Scored (one game)

73   Chicago Bears vs Washington, Dec. 8, 1940
41   Chicago Bears vs Washington, Dec. 26, 1943

Most Points Scored (one game, both teams)

73   Chicago Bears (73) vs Washington (0), Dec. 8, 1940
62   Chicago Bears (41) vs Washington (21), Dec. 25, 1943
58   Cleveland Browns (30) vs Los Angeles (28), Dec. 24, 1950

Most Touchdowns

31   Chicago Bears (8 play-offs)
15   New York Giants (8 play-offs)

Most Touchdowns (one game)

11   Chicago Bears vs Washington, Dec. 8, 1940
6   Chicago Bears vs Washington, Dec. 26, 1943

Most Touchdowns Running

20   Chicago Bears (8 play-offs)
6   New York Giants (8 play-offs)

Most Touchdowns Running (one game)

10   Chicago Bears vs Washington, Dec. 8, 1940
4   Detroit Bears vs New York Giants, Dec. 15, 1935
Chicago Bears vs New York Giants, Dec. 21, 1941
Chicago Cardinals vs Philadelphia, Dec. 28, 1947

Most Touchdowns Passing

  11 Chicago Bears (8 play-offs)
   9 New York Giants (8 play-offs)

Most Touchdowns Passing (one game)

   5 Chicago Bears vs Washington, Dec. 26, 1943
   4 Cleveland Browns vs Los Angeles, Dec. 24, 1950

Most Extra Points

  25 Chicago Bears (8 play-offs)
  12 New York Giants (8 play-offs)

Most Extra Points (one game)

   7 Chicago Bears vs Washington, Dec. 8, 1940
   6 Chicago Bears vs Washington, Dec. 26, 1943

Most Field Goals

   9 Chicago Bears (16 attempts in 8 play-offs)

   3 Green Bay (3 attempts in 4 play-offs)
     New York Giants (7 attempts in 8 play-offs)

Most Field Goals (one game)

   3 Chicago Bears (twice) vs New York Giants, Dec. 17, 1933, and vs New York Giants, Dec. 21, 1941

Most Field Goals Attempted

  14 Chicago Bears (Made 9 in 8 play-offs)
   7 New York Giants (Made 3 in 8 play-offs)

Most Field Goals Attempted (one game)

   4 Chicago Bears vs New York Giants (thrice): Dec. 17, 1933 (made 3); Dec. 9, 1934 (made 3); Dec. 21, 1941 (made 3)

PRO BOWL RESULTS

* Played in Los Angeles
† Played in New York
‡ Played in Philadelphia

* 1938	New York Giants	13	All Stars	10
* 1939	Green Bay Packers	16	All Stars	7
* 1940	Chicago Bears	28	All Stars	14
† 1941	Chicago Bears	35	All Stars	24
‡ 1942	All Stars	17	Washington Redskins	14
* 1951	American Conference	28	National Conference	27
* 1952	National Conference	28	American Conference	13

ALL-TIME TEAM RECORDS

CONSECUTIVE PERFORMANCES

Most Consecutive Victories

  18 Chicago Bears (twice) —1933–34 and 1941–42.
  12 Green Bay—1928–29

Most Consecutive Games Won by Shutouts

   7 Detroit Lions—1934

Most Consecutive Games Without Defeat

  24 Canton—1922—(won 21, tied 3)
  23 Green Bay—1928, 1929, 1930—(won 21, tied 2)

DEFENSE

SEASON

Most Points Allowed

  462 Baltimore—1950—(12 games)
  407 Detroit—1948—(12 games)
  406 Green Bay—1950—(12 games)

Fewest Points Allowed

  20 New York Giants—1927—(13 games)
  75 New York Giants—1944—(10 games)
  79 New York Giants—1938—(11 games)

Most Yards Allowed

  5,402 Baltimore—1950
  5,220 New York Yanks—1950
  5,173 New York Yanks—1951
  4,858 Boston Yanks—1948

Fewest Yards Allowed

  1,578 Chicago Cardinals—1934
  1,703 Chicago Bears—1942

Fewest Yards Allowed Rushing

  519 Chicago Bears—1942
  558 Philadelphia—1944
  793 Phil-Pitt—1943

Fewest Yards Allowed Passing

625 Chicago Cardinals—1934
928 Boston Redskins—1934
939 Pittsburgh—1946

GAME

Fewest Yards Allowed

14 Detroit vs Chicago Cardinals, Sept. 15, 1940

Fewest Yards Allowed Rushing

Minus 53 Chicago Cardinals vs Detroit, Oct. 17, 1943
Minus 36 Chicago Bears vs Philadelphia, Nov. 19, 1939
Minus 33 Phil-Pitt vs Brooklyn, Oct. 2, 1943
Minus 29 Washington vs Cleveland, Oct. 11, 1942

Fewest Yards Allowed Passing

Minus 3 Washington vs New York Giants, Oct. 1, 1939 (6 attempts, 1 complete)
Minus 1 Chicago Bears vs Pittsburgh, Nov. 25, 1945 (20 attempts, 2 complete)
0 Several.

FIRST DOWNS

SEASON

Most First Downs (including TDs from scrimmage)

278 Los Angeles—1950— (84 rushing, 111 passing, 24 penalties, 59 TDs)
272 Los Angeles—1951— (92 rushing, 102 passing, 28 penalties, 50 TDs)
263 Chicago Bears—1947— (98 rushing, 94 passing, 18 penalties, 53 TDs)
248 Chicago Bears—1949—(91 rushing, 95 passing, 18 penalties, 44 TDs)

Fewest First Downs

68 Philadelphia—1937
75 Pittsburgh—1941

GAME

Most First Downs (one team)

34 Los Angeles vs New York Yanks, Sept. 28, 1951 (8 rushing, 16 passing, 2 penalties, 8 TDs)
32 Los Angeles vs New York Yanks, Nov. 19, 1950 (7 rushing, 17 passing, 3 penalties, 5 TDs)
   Chicago Cardinals vs New York Bulldogs, Nov. 13, 1949 (14 rushing, 7 passing, 2 penalties, 9 TDs)
   Philadelphia Eagles vs Washington Redskins, Dec. 2, 1951 (22 rushing, 4 passing, 1 penalty, 5 TDs)
31 New York Giants vs Pittsburgh, Dec. 5, 1948 (7 rushing, 19 passing, 1 penalty, 4 TDs)

Los Angeles vs Green Bay, Dec. 3, 1950 (9 rushing, 11 passing, 4 penalties, 7 TDs)

Fewest First Downs (one team)

0 Hammond vs Canton, Sept. 30, 1923 (lost, 17–0)
   Racine vs Chicago Cardinals, Oct. 3, 1926 (lost, 20–0)
   New York Giants vs Green Bay, Oct. 1, 1933 (won, 10–7)
   Pittsburgh vs Boston Redskins, Oct. 29, 1933 (won, 16–14)
   Philadelphia vs Detroit, Sept. 20, 1935 (lost, 35–0)
   New York Giants vs Washington, Sept. 27, 1942 (won, 14–7)

Most First Downs (both teams)

57 Los Angeles (32), New York Yanks (25), Nov. 19, 1950
54 New York Giants (31), Pittsburgh (23), Dec. 5, 1948

Fewest First Downs (both teams)

3 Brooklyn (1), Boston Redskins (2), Sept. 29, 1935

FORWARD PASSING

SEASON

Most Passes Completed

253 Los Angeles—1950— (attempted 453)
231 Green Bay—1951—(attempted 478)
231 Washington—1947—(attempted 416)
231 Green Bay—1951—(attempted 478)
206 Baltimore—1950—(attempted 438)
202 Washington—1948—(attempted 360)
201 Los Angeles—1948—(attempted 395)
197 Washington—1949—(attempted 378)

Fewest Passes Completed

34 Chicago Cardinals—1934— (attempted 140)
   Detroit Lions—1934— (attempted 144)
39 Boston Redskins—1934— (attempted 138)
   Philadelphia—1936— (attempted 170)

Most Passes Attempted

478 Green Bay—1951— (completed 231)
453 Los Angeles—1950— (completed 253)
438 Baltimore—1950— (completed 206)

Fewest Passes Attempted

120 Detroit Lions—1937— (completed 44)
125 New York Giants—1944— (completed 47)
126 Chicago Cardinals—1935— (completed 47)

Best Passing Efficiency

Less than 250   64%—Washington,   1945
                (146 complete, 228
                attempts)
                59%—Washington,   1940
                (144 complete, 244
                attempts)

More than 250   56.8%—Washington,   1944
                (170 complete, 299
                attempts)
                56.1%—Washington,   1948
                (202 complete, 360
                attempts)
                55.7%—Cleveland,   1951
                (151 complete, 271
                attempts)
                55.8%—Los Angeles,   1950
                (253 complete, 453
                attempts)
                55.5%—Washington,   1947
                (231 complete, 416
                attempts)

Most Passes Had Intercepted

    41   Card-Pitt—1944
    39   Chicago Cardinals—1943
    37   Detroit Lions—1943
         Green Bay Packers—1950

Fewest Passes Had Intercepted

    9   Brooklyn Dodgers—1936 (attempted
         141)
         New York Giants—1943— (attempted
         149)
    10   New York Giants—1950 (attempted
         187)

Most Touchdown Passes

    31   Los Angeles—1950
    29   Detroit—1951
    29   Chicago Bears—1947
         New York Yanks—1950
         Detroit—1951
    28   Green Bay—1942
         Chicago Bears—1943
         Washington—1947
         Los Angeles—1948

Fewest Touchdown Passes

    0   Pittsburgh—1945
    1   Detroit—1942

GAME

Most Passes Completed

    36   New York Giants vs Pittsburgh,
         Dec. 5, 1948 (attempted 53)

Most Passes Completed (both teams)

    51   Washington (26) vs Chicago Bears
         (25), Oct. 26, 1947

Most Passes Attempted

    60   Philadelphia vs Washington, Dec. 1,
         1940 (completed 33)

    59   Chicago Bears vs New York Giants,
         Oct. 23, 1949 (completed 34)

Fewest Passes Attempted

    0   Several

Most Passes Attempted (both teams)

    88   Washington (56), Los Angeles (32)
         (50 completed for 725 yards; Los
         Angeles 405, Washington 320) Dec.
         11, 1949
         Los Angeles (49), New York Yanks
         (39) (47) completed for 682 yards;
         Los Angeles 370, New York Yanks
         312) Nov. 19, 1950

Most Passes Had Intercepted (one team)

    9   Detroit Lions vs Green Bay, Oct. 24,
         1943
    8   Green Bay vs New York Giants,
         Nov. 21, 1948
         Chicago Cardinals vs Philadelphia,
         Sept. 24, 1950
    7   Several

Most Passes Had Intercepted (both teams)

    11   Several

Most Touchdown Passes (one team)

    7   Chicago Bears vs New York Giants,
         Nov. 14, 1943
    6   Several

Most Touchdown Passes (both teams)

    10   Chicago Bears (6) vs Chicago Cardi-
         nals (4), Dec. 5, 1937
    9   Several

FUMBLES

SEASON

Most Fumbles

    56   Chicago Bears—1938
    54   Philadelphia—1946
    45   Washington—1938

Fewest Fumbles

    11   Green Bay—1944
    12   Brooklyn—1934
         Detroit—1943
    13   Philadelphia—1938
         Green Bay—1942

Most Fumbles Recovered (opponents' and own)

    46   New York Giants—1946
    45   Philadelphia—1946
    44   Boston Yanks—1948
         Pittsburgh—1948

Fewest Fumbles Recovered (own)

    4   Green Bay—1944 (out of 11)
         Chicago Cardinals—1949 (out of 20)

5   Green Bay—1942 (out of 13)
    Chicago Cardinals—1948 (out of 21)
6   Chicago Bears—1950 (out of 23)

Most Opponents' Fumbles Recovered

28 Green Bay—1946 (out of 45)
    Cleveland Browns—1951 (out of 34)
27 New York Giants—1950 (out of 43)

Fewest Opponents' Fumbles Recovered

4   Philadelphia—1944
6   Brooklyn—1939
    Chicago Bears—1943
    Chicago Bears—1945
    Washington—1945

GAME

Most Fumbles (one team)

10 Phil-Pitt vs New York Giants, Oct. 9, 1943
9   Philadelphia vs Green Bay, Oct. 13, 1946
8   Several

Most Fumbles (both teams)

14 Chicago Bears (7) vs Cleveland Rams (7), Nov. 24, 1940
13 Washington (8) vs Pittsburgh (5), Nov. 4, 1937
    Philadelphia (7) vs Boston (6), Dec. 8, 1946

Most Fumbles Recovered

10 Chicago Bears (7 own, 3 opponents), vs Chicago Cardinals, Sept. 11, 1938
8   Several

Most Opponents' Fumbles Recovered

6   Several

GROUND GAINING

SEASON

Most Yards Gained

5,506   Los Angeles—1951
5,420   Los Angeles—1950
5,053   Chicago Bears—1947
4,873   Chicago Bears—1949
4,726   New York Yanks—1950
4,707   Chicago Cardinals—1948
4,679   Washington—1947

Most Yards Gained Rushing

2,885   Detroit—1936
2,763   Detroit—1934
2,607   Philadelphia—1949
2,560   Chicago Cardinals—1948

Most Yards Gained Passing

3,709   Los Angeles—1950
3,336   Washington—1947
3,296   Los Angeles—1951
3,093   Chicago Bears—1947

3,055   Chicago Bears—1949
2,894   New York Yanks—1950
2,861   Washington—1948

Fewest Yards Gained

1,481   Brooklyn—1934
1,506   Boston—1944
1,719   Pittsburgh—1945
1,843   Detroit—1941

Fewest Yards Gained Rushing

298   Philadelphia—1940
471   Boston—1944
472   Detroit—1946

Fewest Yards Gained Passing

577   Brooklyn—1934
652   Pittsburgh—1945

GAME

Most Yards Gained

735   Los Angeles vs New York Yankees, Sept. 28, 1951 (181 rushing, 554 passing)
682   Chicago Bears vs New York Giants, Nov. 14, 1943 (194 rushing, 488 passing)
636   Los Angeles vs New York Yanks, Nov. 19, 1950 (266 rushing, 370 passing)
625   Washington vs Boston, Oct. 13, 1948 (124 rushing, 501 passing)
      New York Giants vs New York Yanks, Dec. 31, 1950 (377 rushing, 248 passing)

Most Yards Gained Rushing

426   Detroit vs Pittsburgh, Nov. 4, 1934
423   New York Giants vs Baltimore, Nov. 19, 1950

Most Yards Gained Rushing and Passing

1,133   Los Angeles (266 rushing, 370 passing) vs New York Yanks (185 rushing, 312 passing), Nov. 19, 1950

Most Yards Gained Passing

554   Los Angeles vs New York Yanks, Sept. 28, 1951 (27 completions, 5 TDs)
501   Washington vs Boston Yanks, Oct. 31, 1948 (22 completions, 4 TDs)
488   Chicago Bears vs New York Giants, Nov. 14, 1943 (22 completions, 7 TDs)
468   Chicago Bears vs Chicago Cardinals, Dec. 11, 1949 (24 completions, 6 TDs)

Most Yards Gained Passing (both teams)

748   Chicago Bears (468), Chicago Cardinals (280), Dec. 11, 1949

Fewest Yards Gained

14   Chicago Cardinals vs Detroit, Sept. 15, 1940

Fewest Yards Gained Rushing

Minus 53 Detroit vs Chicago Cardinals, Oct. 17, 1943
Minus 36 Philadelphia vs Chicago Bears, Nov. 19, 1939
Minus 33 Brooklyn vs Phil-Pitt, Oct. 2, 1943

Fewest Yards Gained Passing

Minus 3 New York Giants vs Washington, Oct. 1, 1939 (6 attempts, 1 completed)
Minus 1 Pittsburgh vs Chicago Bears, Nov. 25, 1945 (20 attempts, 2 completed)
0 Several

INTERCEPTIONS

SEASON

Best Percentage of Interceptions By

17.3 Green Bay—1943 (opponents attempted 242)
15.9 Green Bay—1940 (opponents attempted 252)

Most Passes Intercepted By

42 Green Bay—1943 (opponents attempted 242)
41 New York—1951 (opponents attempted 256)
40 Green Bay—1940 (opponents attempted 252)

Fewest Passes Intercepted

8 Pittsburgh—1940 (opponents attempted 192)
10 Brooklyn—1944 (opponents attempted 181)

Most Interceptions Returned for Touchdowns

5 Green Bay—1945 (intercepted 24)
4 Several

Most Yards Interceptions Returned

656 Detroit Lions—1949 (32 interceptions)
606 Green Bay—1943 (42 interceptions)

GAME

Most Passes Intercepted By

9 Green Bay vs Detroit, Oct. 24, 1943
8 New York Giants vs Green Bay, Nov. 21, 1948
Philadelphia vs Chicago Cardinals, Sept. 24, 1950
8 New York Giants vs New York Yankees, Dec. 16, 1951

Most Passes Intercepted By (both teams)

11 Several

Most Yards Interceptions Returned

158 Chicago Cardinals vs Green Bay, Oct. 16, 1949 (4 interceptions)

PENALTIES

SEASON

Most Penalties

122 Washington—1948 (1,100 yards)
Chicago Bears—1948 (1,066 yards)
121 Chicago Bears—1944 (1,025 yards)
118 Chicago Bears—1951 (1,107 yards)
117 Cleveland Browns—1951 (1,017 yards)
110 Los Angeles—1950 (1,038 yards)
107 Chicago Bears—1947 (1,020 yards)

Fewest Penalties

19 Detroit—1937 (139 yards)
21 Boston—1935 (166 yards)

Most Yards Penalized

1,107 Chicago Bears—1951 (118 penalties)
1,100 Washington—1948 (122 penalties)
1,066 Chicago Bears—1948 (122 penalties)
1,038 Los Angeles—1950 (110 penalties)
1,025 Chicago Bears—1944 (121 penalties)

Fewest Yards Penalized

139 Detroit—1937 (19 penalties)
146 Philadelphia—1937 (25 penalties)
159 Philadelphia—1936 (24 penalties)

GAME

Most Penalties (one team)

22 Brooklyn vs Green Bay, Sept. 17, 1944 (168 yards)
Chicago Bears vs Philadelphia, Nov. 26, 1944 (170 yards)
21 Cleveland Browns vs Chicago Bears, Nov. 25, 1951 (209 yards)
18 Chicago Bears vs Los Angeles, Nov. 10, 1946 (140 yards)

Most Yards Penalized (one team)

209 Cleveland Browns vs Chicago Bears, Nov. 25, 1951 (21 penalties)
184 Green Bay vs Boston Yanks, Oct. 21, 1945 (17 penalties)
177 New York Giants vs Washington, Oct. 9, 1949 (17 penalties)
175 New York Giants vs Boston Yanks, Oct. 19, 1947 (11 penalties)

Most Yards Penalized (both teams, one game)

374 Cleveland (209), vs Chicago Bears 165, Nov. 25, 1951 (Cleveland 21, Chicago, 16)

PUNTING

SEASON

Most Punts

    113   Boston Redskins—1934
            Brooklyn—1934
    112   Boston Redskins—1935

Fewest Punts

    32   Chicago Bears—1941
    33   Washington—1945
    38   Chicago Bears—1947

GAME

Most Punts (one team)

    17   Chicago Bears vs Green Bay, Oct.
            22, 1933
    16   Chicago Cardinals vs Chicago Bears,
            Nov. 30, 1933
            Chicago Cardinals vs Detroit Lions,
            Sept. 15, 1940

Most Punts (both teams)

    31   Chicago Bears (17) vs Green Bay
            (14), Oct. 22, 1933
    29   Chicago Cardinals (15) vs Cincin-
            nati (14), Nov. 12, 1933
            Chicago Cardinals (16) vs Chicago
            Bears (13), Nov. 30, 1933

Fewest Punts

    0   New York Giants vs Chicago Bears,
            Nov. 4, 1934
            Philadelphia vs Washington, Nov.
            13, 1949

SCORING

SEASON

Most Points

    466   Los Angeles—1950— (12 games)
    396   Chicago Bears—1941— (11 games)
    395   Chicago Bears—1948— (12 games)
    392   Los Angeles—1951— (12 games)
    376   Chicago Bears—1942— (11 games)
            Philadelphia—1948— (12 games)

Most Touchdowns

    64   Los Angeles—1950— (12 games)
    56   Chicago Bears—1941— (11 games)

Most Touchdowns Rushing

    37   Chicago Bears—1941— (11 games)
    33   Los Angeles—1950— (12 games)
    32   Chicago Bears—1942— (11 games)

Most Touchdowns Passing

    31   Los Angeles—1950— (12 games)
    29   Chicago Bears—1947— (12 games)

    29   New York Yanks—1950— (12 games)
    29   Detroit Lions—1951— (12 games)

Most Points after Touchdown

    59   Los Angeles Rams—1950
    53   Chicago Cardinals—1948
    51   Chicago Bears—1948

Most Field Goals

    14   New York Giants—1939
            Cleveland—1950

Fewest Points Scored

    10   Cincinnati—1934— (8 games)

GAME

Most Points (one team)

    70   Los Angeles vs Baltimore, Oct. 22,
            1950
    65   Chicago Cardinals vs New York
            Bulldogs, Nov. 13, 1949
            Los Angeles vs Detroit, Oct. 29, 1950
    64   Philadelphia vs Cincinnati, Nov. 6,
            1934
    63   Chicago Cardinals vs New York
            Giants, Oct. 17, 1948

Most Points (both teams)

    98   Chicago Cardinals (63) vs New
            York Giants (35), Oct. 17, 1948
    97   Los Angeles (70) vs Baltimore (27),
            Oct. 22, 1950
    89   Los Angeles (52) vs New York
            Giants (37), Nov. 14, 1948
            Los Angeles (65) vs Detroit (24),
            Oct. 29, 1950

Most Points (one team, one quarter)

    41   Green Bay vs Detroit (2nd qtr),
            Oct. 7, 1945
            Los Angeles vs Detroit (3rd qtr),
            Oct. 29, 1950

Most Touchdowns (one team)

    10   Philadelphia vs Cincinnati, Nov. 6,
            1934
            Los Angeles vs Baltimore, Oct. 22,
            1950
    9   Chicago Cardinals vs Rochester,
            Oct. 7, 1923
            Chicago Cardinals vs New York
            Giants, Oct. 17, 1948
            Chicago Cardinals vs New York
            Bulldogs, Nov. 13, 1949
    8   Several

Most Touchdowns (both teams)

    14   Chicago Cardinals (9) vs New York
            Giants (5), Oct. 17, 1948
    13   Los Angeles (10) vs Baltimore (4),
            Oct. 22, 1950
    12   Several

Most Touchdowns Rushing (one team)
7   Chicago Bears vs Detroit, Oct. 19, 1941
6   Several

Most Touchdowns Passing (one team)
7   Chicago Bears vs New York Giants, Nov. 14, 1943
6   Several

Most Points after Touchdown (one team)
10 Los Angeles vs Baltimore, Oct. 22, 1950
9   Chicago Cardinals vs New York Giants, Oct. 17, 1948

Most Points after Touchdown (both teams)
14 Chicago Cardinals (9) vs New York Giants (5), Oct. 17, 1948
13 Los Angeles (10) vs Baltimore (3), Oct. 22, 1950

Most Field Goals (one team)
5   Los Angeles Rams vs Detroit Lions, Dec. 9, 1951
4   Chicago Cardinals vs Columbus, Oct. 11, 1925
    Detroit vs New York Giants, Nov. 5. 1939

LEAGUE STANDINGS

1921

	W	L	T	Pct.
Chicago Bears*	10	1	1	.909
Buffalo	9	1	2	.900
Akron	7	2	1	.778
Green Bay	6	2	2	.750
Canton	4	3	3	.571
Dayton	4	3	1	.571
Rock Island	5	4	1	.556
Chicago Cards	2	3	2	.400
Cleveland	2	6	0	.250
Rochester	2	6	0	.250
Detroit	1	7	1	.125
Columbus	0	6	0	.000
Cincinnati				.000

* Staleys

1922

	W	L	T	Pct.
Canton	10	0	2	1.000
Chicago Bears	9	3	0	.750
Chicago Cards	8	3	0	.727
Toledo	5	2	2	.714
Rock Island	4	2	1	.667
Dayton	4	3	3	.571
Green Bay	4	3	3	.571
Racine	5	4	1	.556
Buffalo	3	4	1	.429
Akron	3	4	2	.429
Milwaukee	2	4	3	.333
Marion	2	6	0	.250
Minneapolis	1	3	0	.250

Rochester, Hammond, Columbus, Louisville, Evansville .... .000

1923

	W	L	T	Pct.
Canton	11	0	1	1.000
Chicago Bears	9	2	1	.818
Green Bay	7	2	1	.778
Milwaukee	7	2	3	.778
Cleveland	3	1	3	.750
Chicago Cardinals	8	4	0	.667
Duluth	4	3	0	.571
Columbus	5	4	1	.556
Buffalo	5	4	3	.556
Racine	4	4	2	.500
Toledo	2	3	2	.400
Rock Island	2	3	3	.400
Minneapolis	2	5	2	.286
St. Louis	1	4	2	.200
Hammond	1	5	1	.167
Dayton	1	6	1	.143
Akron	1	6	0	.143

Louisville, Rochester, Oorang Indians (Marion) .... .000

1924

	W	L	T	Pct.
Cleveland	7	1	1	.875
Chicago Bears	6	1	4	.856
Frankford	11	2	1	.846
Duluth	4	1	0	.800
Rock Island	6	2	2	.750
Green Bay	7	4	0	.636
Racine	5	3	2	.625
Buffalo	6	4	4	.600
Chicago Cardinals	5	5	0	.500
Columbus	4	4	1	.500
Hammond	2	2	0	.500
Milwaukee	5	8	0	.385
Dayton	2	6	0	.250
Kansas City	2	7	0	.222
Akron	1	6	0	.143
Kenosha	0	5	1	.000
Minneapolis	0	6	0	.000
Rochester	0	7	0	.000

1925

	W	L	T	Pct.
Chicago Cardinals	11	2	1	.846
Pottsville	10	2	0	.833
Detroit	8	2	0	.800
New York	8	4	0	.667
Akron	4	2	2	.667
Frankford	13	7	0	.650
Chicago Bears	9	5	3	.643
Rock Island	5	3	3	.625
Green Bay	8	5	0	.615
Providence	6	5	1	.545

	W	L	T	Pct.
Canton	4	4	0	.500
Cleveland	5	8	1	.392
Hammond	1	3	0	.250
Kansas City	2	5	1	.286
Buffalo	1	6	2	.143
Duluth, Rochester, Milwaukee, Dayton, Columbus	....			.000

1926

	W	L	T	Pct.
Frankford	14	1	1	.933
Chicago Bears	12	1	3	.923
Pottsville	10	2	1	.833
Kansas City	8	3	0	.727
Green Bay	7	3	3	.700
Los Angeles	6	3	1	.667
New York	8	4	0	.667
Duluth	6	5	2	.545
Buffalo	4	4	2	.500
Chicago Cardinals	5	6	1	.455
Providence	5	7	0	.417
Detroit	4	6	2	.400
Hartford	3	7	0	.300
Brooklyn	3	8	0	.272
Milwaukee	2	7	0	.222
Dayton	1	4	1	.200
Akron	1	4	3	.200
Racine	1	4	0	.200
Columbus	1	6	0	.144
Canton	1	9	3	.100
Louisville	0	4	0	.000
Hammond	0	4	0	.000

1927

	W	L	T	Pct.
New York Giants	11	1	1	.917
Green Bay	7	2	1	.778
Chicago Bears	9	3	2	.750
Cleveland	8	4	1	.667
Providence	8	5	1	.615
New York Yankees	7	8	1	.467
Frankford	6	9	3	.400
Pottsville	5	8	0	.385
Chicago Cardinals	3	7	1	.300
Dayton	1	6	1	.143
Duluth	1	8	1	.111
Buffalo	0	5	0	.000

1928

	W	L	T	Pct.
Providence	8	1	2	.888
Frankford	11	3	2	.786
Detroit	7	2	1	.778
Green Bay	6	4	3	.600
Chicago Bears	7	5	1	.583
New York Giants	4	7	2	.364
New York Yankees	4	8	1	.333
Pottsville	2	8	0	.200
Chicago Cardinals	1	5	0	.167
Dayton	0	7	0	.000

1929

	W	L	T	Pct.
Green Bay	12	0	1	1.000
New York	12	1	1	.923

	W	L	T	Pct.
Frankford	9	4	5	.692
Chicago Cardinals	6	6	1	.500
Boston	4	4	0	.500
Stapleton	3	4	3	.429
Oorangs	3	4	4	.429
Providence	4	6	2	.400
Chicago Bears	4	8	2	.333
Buffalo	1	7	1	.125
Minneapolis	1	9	0	.100
Dayton	0	6	0	.000

1930

	W	L	T	Pct.
Green Bay	11	3	1	.786
New York	13	4	0	.765
Chicago Bears	9	4	1	.692
Brooklyn	7	4	1	.636
Providence	6	4	1	.600
Stapleton	5	5	2	.500
Chicago Cardinals	5	6	2	.455
Portsmouth	5	6	3	.455
Frankford	4	14	1	.222
Minneapolis	1	7	1	.125
Newark	1	10	1	.091

1931

	W	L	T	Pct.
Green Bay	12	2	0	.857
Portsmouth	11	3	0	.786
Chicago Bears	8	4	0	.667
Chicago Cardinals	5	4	0	.556
New York	6	6	1	.500
Providence	4	4	3	.500
Stapleton	4	6	1	.400
Cleveland	2	8	0	.200
Brooklyn	2	12	0	.143
Frankford	1	6	1	.143

1932

	W	L	T	Pct.
Chicago Bears	7	1	6	.875
Green Bay	10	3	1	.767
Portsmouth	6	2	4	.750
Boston	4	4	2	.500
New York	4	6	2	.400
Brooklyn	3	9	0	.250
Chicago Cardinals	2	6	2	.250
Stapleton	2	7	3	.222

1933
WESTERN DIVISION

	W	L	T	Pct.
Chicago Bears	10	2	1	.833
Portsmouth	6	5	0	.554
Green Bay	5	7	1	.418
Cincinnati	3	6	1	.333
Chicago Cardinals	1	9	1	.100

EASTERN DIVISION

	W	L	T	Pct.
New York	11	3	0	.786
Brooklyn	5	4	1	.556
Boston	5	5	2	.500
Philadelphia	3	5	1	.375
Pittsburgh	3	6	2	.333

Chicago Bears 23   New York 21

1934
EASTERN DIVISION

New York	8	5	0	.615
Boston	6	6	0	.500
Brooklyn	4	7	0	.363
Philadelphia	4	7	0	.363
Pittsburgh	2	10	0	.166

WESTERN DIVISION

Chicago Bears	13	0	0	1.000
Detroit	10	3	0	.769
Green Bay	7	6	0	.538
Chicago Cardinals	5	6	0	.454
St. Louis	1	2	0	.333
Cincinnati*	0	8	0	.000

New York 30   Chicago Bears 13

* Franchise transferred to St. Louis, Nov. 5, 1934

1935
WESTERN DIVISION

Detroit	7	3	2	.700
Green Bay	8	4	0	.667
Chicago Cardinals	6	4	2	.600
Chicago Bears	6	4	2	.600

EASTERN DIVISION

New York	9	3	0	.750
Brooklyn	5	6	1	.454
Pittsburgh	4	8	0	.333
Boston*	2	8	1	.200
Philadelphia*	2	9	0	.181

Detroit 26   New York 7

* One game cancelled

1936
WESTERN DIVISION

Green Bay	10	1	1	.909
Chicago Bears	9	3	0	.750
Detroit	8	4	0	.667
Chicago Cardinals	3	8	1	.272

EASTERN DIVISION

Boston	7	5	0	.714
Pittsburgh	6	6	0	.500
New York	5	6	1	.454
Brooklyn	3	8	1	.272
Philadelphia	1	11	0	.084

Green Bay 21   Boston 6

1937
EASTERN DIVISION

Washington	8	3	0	.727
New York	6	3	2	.667
Pittsburgh	4	7	0	.364
Brooklyn	3	7	1	.300
Philadelphia	2	8	1	.200

WESTERN DIVISION

Chicago Bears	9	1	1	.900
Green Bay	7	4	0	.636
Detroit	7	4	0	.636
Chicago Cardinals	5	5	1	.500
Cleveland	1	10	0	.091

Washington 28   Chicago Bears 21

1938
EASTERN DIVISION

New York	8	2	1	.800
Washington	6	3	2	.667
Brooklyn	4	4	3	.500
Philadelphia	5	6	0	.455
Pittsburgh	2	9	0	.182

WESTERN DIVISION

Green Bay	8	3	0	.727
Detroit	7	4	0	.636
Chicago Bears	6	5	0	.545
Cleveland	4	7	0	.364
Chicago Cardinals	2	9	0	.182

New York 23   Green Bay 17

1939
WESTERN DIVISION

Green Bay	9	2	0	.818
Chicago Bears	8	3	0	.727
Detroit	6	5	0	.545
Cleveland	5	5	1	.500
Chicago Cardinals	1	10	0	.091

EASTERN DIVISION

New York	9	1	1	.900
Washington	8	2	1	.800
Brooklyn	4	6	1	.400
Philadelphia	1	9	1	.100
Pittsburgh	1	9	1	.100

Green Bay 27   New York 0

1940
WESTERN DIVISION

Chicago Bears	8	3	0	.727
Green Bay	6	4	1	.600
Detroit	5	5	1	.500
Cleveland	4	6	1	.400
Chicago Cardinals	2	7	2	.222

EASTERN DIVISION

Washington	9	2	0	.818
Brooklyn	8	3	0	.727
New York	6	4	1	.600
Pittsburgh	2	7	2	.222
Philadelphia	1	10	0	.091

Chicago Bears 73   Washington 0

1941
WESTERN DIVISION

Chicago Bears*	10	1	0	.909
Green Bay	10	1	0	.909
Detroit	4	6	1	.400
Chicago Cardinals	3	7	1	.300
Cleveland	2	9	0	.182

EASTERN DIVISION

New York	8	3	0	.727
Brooklyn	7	4	0	.636
Washington	6	5	0	.545
Philadelphia	2	8	1	.200
Pittsburgh	1	9	1	.100

Chicago Bears   37   New York   9

* Bears defeated Green Bay 33–14 in Divisional Play-off

1942
EASTERN DIVISION

Washington	10	1	0	.909
Pittsburgh	7	4	0	.636
New York	5	5	1	.500
Brooklyn	3	8	0	.273
Philadelphia	2	9	0	.182

WESTERN DIVISION

Chicago Bears	11	0	0	1.000
Green Bay	8	2	1	.800
Cleveland	5	6	0	.455
Chicago Cardinals	3	8	0	.273
Detroit	0	11	0	.000

Washington   14   Chicago Bears   6

1943
WESTERN DIVISION

Chicago Bears	8	1	1	.889
Green Bay	7	2	1	.778
Detroit	3	6	1	.333
Chicago Cardinals	0	10	0	.000

EASTERN DIVISION

Washington*	6	3	1	.667
New York	6	3	1	.667
Phil-Pitt	5	4	1	.555
Brooklyn	2	8	0	.200

Chicago Bears   41   Washington   21

* Washington defeated New York 28–0 in Divisional Play-off

1944
WESTERN DIVISION

Green Bay	8	2	0	.800
Chicago Bears	6	3	1	.667
Detroit	6	3	1	.667
Cleveland	4	6	0	.400
Card-Pitt	0	10	0	.000

EASTERN DIVISION

New York	8	1	1	.889
Philadelphia	7	1	2	.875
Washington	6	3	1	.667
Boston	2	8	0	.200
Brooklyn	0	10	0	.000

Green Bay   14   New York   7

1945
WESTERN DIVISION

Cleveland	9	1	0	.900
Detroit	7	3	0	.700
Green Bay	6	4	0	.600
Chicago Bears	3	7	0	.300
Chicago Cardinals	1	9	0	.100

EASTERN DIVISION

Washington	8	2	0	.800
Philadelphia	7	3	0	.700
New York	3	6	1	.333
Boston	3	6	1	.333
Pittsburgh	2	8	0	.200

Cleveland   15   Washington   14

1946
WESTERN DIVISION

Chicago Bears	8	2	1	.800
Los Angeles	6	4	1	.600
Green Bay	6	5	0	.545
Chicago Cardinals	6	5	0	.545
Detroit	1	10	0	.091

EASTERN DIVISION

New York	7	3	1	.700
Philadelphia	6	5	0	.545
Washington	5	5	1	.500
Pittsburgh	5	5	1	.500
Boston	2	8	1	.200

Chicago Bears   24   New York   14

1947
WESTERN DIVISION

Chicago Cardinals	9	3	0	.750
Chicago Bears	8	4	0	.667
Green Bay	6	5	1	.545
Los Angeles	6	6	0	.500
Detroit	3	9	0	.250

EASTERN DIVISION

Philadelphia*	8	4	0	.667
Pittsburgh	8	4	0	.667
Boston	4	7	1	.364
Washington	4	8	0	.333
New York	2	8	2	.200

Chicago Cardinals   28   Philadelphia   21

* Philadelphia defeated Pittsburgh 21–0 in Divisional Play-off

1948
EASTERN DIVISION

Philadelphia	9	2	1	.818
Washington	7	5	0	.583
New York	4	8	0	.333
Pittsburgh	4	8	0	.333
Boston	3	9	0	.250

WESTERN DIVISION

Chicago Cardinals	11	1	0	.917
Chicago Bears	10	2	0	.833

Los Angeles	6	5	1	.545
Green Bay	3	9	0	.250
Detroit	2	10	0	.167

Philadelphia 7   Chicago Cardinals 0

1949
EASTERN DIVISION

Philadelphia	11	1	0	.917
Pittsburgh	6	5	1	.545
New York Giants	6	6	0	.500
Washington	4	7	1	.364
New York Bulldogs	1	10	1	.091

WESTERN DIVISION

Los Angeles	8	2	2	.800
Chicago Bears	9	3	0	.750
Chicago Cardinals	6	5	1	.545
Detroit	4	8	0	.333
Green Bay	2	10	0	.167

Philadelphia 14   Los Angeles 0

1950
AMERICAN CONFERENCE

Cleveland	10	2	0	.833
New York Giants	10	2	0	.833
Philadelphia	6	6	0	.500
Pittsburgh	6	6	0	.500
Chicago Cardinals	5	7	0	.417
Washington	3	9	0	.250

NATIONAL CONFERENCE

Los Angeles	9	3	0	.750
Chicago Bears	9	3	0	.750
New York Yanks	7	5	0	.583
Detroit	6	6	0	.500
Green Bay	3	9	0	.250
San Francisco	3	9	0	.250
Baltimore	1	11	0	.083

Cleveland 30   Los Angeles 28
Cleveland defeated New York Giants, 8–3,
in Conference Play-off
Los Angeles defeated Chicago Bears, 24–14,
in Conference Play-off

1951
NATIONAL CONFERENCE

Los Angeles	8	4	0	.667
Detroit	7	4	1	.636
San Francisco	7	4	1	.636
Chicago Bears	7	5	0	.583
Green Bay	3	9	0	.250
New York Yanks	1	9	2	.100

AMERICAN CONFERENCE

Cleveland	11	1	1	.917
New York Giants	9	2	1	.818
Washington	5	7	0	.417
Pittsburgh	4	7	1	.364
Philadelphia	4	8	0	.333
Chicago Cardinals	3	9	0	.250

Los Angeles 24   Cleveland 17

TEAM GAME RECORDS, 1920–1951

CHICAGO BEARS

1920
COACH—GEORGE S. HALAS

CHICAGO BEARS	20	Moline	0
(STALEYS)	27	Kewanee	0
	10	Rock Island	0
	10	Chicago Tigers	0
	29	Rockford	0
	20	Champaign	0
	28	Hammond	0
	0	Rock Island	0
	3	Minneapolis	0
	6	Chicago Tigers	0
	6	Cardinals	7
	10	Cardinals	0
	0	Akron	0

169   7
Won 10, Lost 1, Tied 2.

1921
COACH—GEORGE S. HALAS

CHICAGO BEARS	35	Waukegan	0
	14	Rock Island	0
	16	Rochester	13
	7	Dayton	0

CHICAGO BEARS	20	Detroit	9
	3	Rock Island	0
	22	Cleveland	7
	6	Buffalo	7
	20	Green Bay	0
	10	Buffalo	7
	10	Canton	0
	0	Cardinals	0

163   43
Won 10, Lost 1, Tied 1.

1922
COACH—GEORGE S. HALAS

CHICAGO BEARS	6	Racine	0
	10	Rock Island	6
	7	Rochester	0
	7	Buffalo	0
	6	Canton	7
	9	Dayton	0
	33	Thorp's Ind.	6
	3	Rock Island	0
	20	Akron	10
	0	Cardinals	6
	22	Toledo	0
	0	Cardinals	9

123   44
Won 9, Lost 3.

1923
COACH—GEORGE S. HALAS

CHICAGO BEARS	0	Rock Island	3
	3	Racine	0
	3	Green Bay	0
	18	Buffalo	3
	0	Canton	6
	18	Buffalo	3
	26	Oorang Inds.	0
	20	Akron	6
	7	Rock Island	3
	14	Hammond	7
	3	Cardinals	0
	0	Milwaukee	0
	29	Rock Island	7
	7	Milwaukee	7
	—		—
	148		45

Won 10, Lost 2, Tied 2.

1924
COACH—GEORGE S. HALAS

CHICAGO BEARS	0	Green Bay	5
	0	Rock Island	0
	14	Cleveland	16
	10	Racine	10
	6	Cardinals	2
	33	Frankford	3
	3	Rock Island	3
	12	Columbus	6
	3	Racine	3
	3	Green Bay	0
	21	Cardinals	0
	31	Milwaukee	14
	23	Cleveland	0
	13	Frankford	10
	6	Rock Island	7
	—		—
	178		79

Won 8, Lost 3, Tied 4.

1925
COACH—GEORGE S. HALAS

CHICAGO BEARS	0	Rock Island	0
	10	Green Bay	14
	0	Detroit	0
	28	Hammond	7
	7	Cleveland	0
	0	Cardinals	9
	6	Rock Island	0
	19	Frankford	0
	14	Detroit	0
	21	Green Bay	0
	0	Cardinals	0
	14	Columbus	13
	39	St. Louis	6
	14	Frankford	7
	—		—
	172		47

Won 9, Lost 2, Tied 3.

1925—"Post Season Red Grange Tour"

CHICAGO BEARS	19	New York	7
	19	Washington	0
	6	Providence	9

CHICAGO BEARS	0	Pittsburgh	24
	0	Detroit	21
	0	New York	9
	7	Fla. Coll'g'ns	0
	26	Tampa	3
	19	Jacksonville	6
	14	New Orleans	0
	17	L.A. Tigers	7
	14	Calif. Stars	0
	60	Portland	3
	34	Northwest	0
	—		—
	235		89

Won 10, Lost 4.

1926
COACH—GEORGE S. HALAS

CHICAGO BEARS	10	Milwaukee	7
	6	Green Bay	6
	10	Detroit	7
	7	New York	0
	16	Cardinals	0
	24	Duluth	6
	17	Akron	0
	34	Louisville	0
	10	Cardinals	0
	10	Milwaukee	7
	19	Green Bay	13
	0	Cardinals	0
	35	Canton	0
	6	Frankford	7
	9	Pottsville	7
	3	Green Bay	3
	—		—
	216		63

Won 12, Lost 1, Tied 3.

1927
COACH—GEORGE S. HALAS

CHICAGO BEARS	10	Cardinals	0
	7	Green Bay	6
	12	N.Y. Yanks	0
	14	Cleveland	12
	14	Dayton	6
	0	Providence	0
	30	Pottsville	12
	14	Green Bay	6
	7	N.Y. Giants	13
	0	Cardinals	3
	0	Frankford	0
	9	Frankford	0
	27	Duluth	0
	—		—
	144		58

Won 9, Lost 2, Tied 2.

1928
COACH—GEORGE S. HALAS

CHICAGO BEARS	15	Cardinals	0
	12	Green Bay	12
	12	Minneapolis	6
	13	N.Y. Giants	0
	6	Green Bay	16
	6	Detroit	6
	27	N.Y. Yanks	0

CHICAGO BEARS	27	Dayton	0
	13	Pottsville	6
	0	Cardinals	34
	28	Frankford	6
	0	Green Bay	6
	0	Frankford	19

| | 153 | | 111 |

Won 7, Lost 5, Tied 1.

1929
COACH—GEORGE S. HALAS

CHICAGO BEARS	19	Minneapolis	6
	0	Green Bay	23
	7	Minneapolis	6
	16	Buffalo	0
	0	Cardinals	0
	27	Minneapolis	0
	14	N.Y. Giants	26
	0	Green Bay	14
	14	Frankford	20
	0	N.Y. Giants	34
	39	Memphis	19
	6	Cardinals	40
	0	Frankford	0
	0	Green Bay	25
	9	N.Y. Giants	14

| | 151 | | 227 |

Won 5, Lost 8, Tied 2.

1930
COACH—RALPH JONES

CHICAGO BEARS	0	Brooklyn	0
	0	Green Bay	7
	20	Milwaukee	0
	26	Milwaukee	0
	0	New York	12
	32	Cardinals	6
	6	Portsmouth	7
	13	Frankford	7
	20	Minneapolis	7
	12	Green Bay	13
	12	New York	0
	6	Cardinals	0
	14	Portsmouth	6
	21	Green Bay	0
	9	Cardinals	7

| | 191 | | 72 |

Won 10, Lost 4, Tied 1.

1931
COACH—RALPH JONES

CHICAGO BEARS	21	Cleveland	0
	0	Green Bay	7
	6	New York	0
	26	Cardinals	13
	12	Frankford	13
	2	Green Bay	6
	9	Portsmouth	6
	12	New York	6
	26	Brooklyn	0
	18	Cardinals	7

| | 6 | New York | 25 |
| | 7 | Green Bay | 6 |

| | 145 | | 89 |

Won 8, Lost 4.

1932
COACH—RALPH JONES

CHICAGO BEARS	26	Cleveland	0
	0	Green Bay	0
	0	Stapleton	0
	0	Cardinals	0
	0	Green Bay	2
	13	Brooklyn	0
	27	Stapleton	7
	7	Boston	7
	28	New York	8
	13	Portsmouth	13
	35	St. Louis	0
	20	Brooklyn	0
	34	Cardinals	0
	7	Portsmouth	0
	6	New York	0
	9	Green Bay	0
	9	Portsmouth	0

| | 234 | | 37 |

Won 12, Lost 1, Tied 5.

1933
COACH—GEORGE S. HALAS

CHICAGO BEARS	14	Green Bay	7
	7	Boston	6
	10	Brooklyn	0
	12	Cardinals	9
	10	Green Bay	7
	14	New York	10
	32	Detroit	0
	0	Boston	10
	3	Philadelphia	3
	0	New York	3
	17	Portsmouth	14
	22	Cardinals	6
	17	Portsmouth	7
	7	Green Bay	6

| | 165 | | 88 |

Won 11, Lost 2, Tied 1.
Championship Game:
Chicago Bears   23   New York   21

1934
COACH—GEORGE S. HALAS

CHICAGO BEARS	21	Brooklyn	7
	28	Pittsburgh	0
	20	Cardinals	0
	10	Green Bay	6
	27	Green Bay	14
	27	New York	7
	21	Boston	0
	10	New York	9
	17	Cardinals	6
	19	Detroit	16

1934 (cont.)

CHICAGO BEARS   10   Detroit   7
                 28   Philadelphia   14
                 ———   ———
                 238   86
Won 12.
Championship Game:
Chicago Bears   13   New York   30

1935
COACH—GEORGE S. HALAS

CHICAGO BEARS   0   Green Bay   7
                 23   Pittsburgh   7
                 39   Philadelphia   0
                 24   Brooklyn   14
                 14   Green Bay   17
                 20   New York   3
                 30   Boston   14
                 0   New York   3
                 20   Detroit   20
                 2   Detroit   14
                 7   Cardinals   7
                 13   Cardinals   0
                 ———   ———
                 192   106
Won 6, Lost 4, Tied 2.

1936
COACH—GEORGE S. HALAS

CHICAGO BEARS   30   Green Bay   3
                 17   Philadelphia   0
                 27   Pittsburgh   9
                 7   Cardinals   3
                 26   Pittsburgh   7
                 12   Detroit   10
                 10   Green Bay   21
                 25   New York   7
                 26   Boston   0
                 28   Philadelphia   7
                 7   Detroit   13
                 7   Cardinals   14
                 ———   ———
                 222   94
Won 9, Lost 3.

1937
COACH—GEORGE S. HALAS

CHICAGO BEARS   14   Green Bay   2
                 7   Pittsburgh   0
                 20   Cleveland   2
                 16   Cardinals   7
                 28   Detroit   20
                 3   New York   3
                 14   Green Bay   24
                 29   Brooklyn   7
                 13   Detroit   0
                 15   Cleveland   7
                 42   Cardinals   28
                 ———   ———
                 201   100
Won 9, Lost 1, Tied 1.
Championship Game:
Chicago Bears   21   Washington   28

1938
COACH—GEORGE S. HALAS

CHICAGO BEARS   16   Cardinals   13
                 2   Green Bay   0
                 28   Philadelphia   6
                 7   Cleveland   14
                 34   Cardinals   28
                 21   Cleveland   23
                 7   Detroit   13
                 17   Green Bay   24
                 31   Washington   7
                 24   Brooklyn   6
                 7   Detroit   14
                 ———   ———
                 194   148
Won 6, Lost 5.

1939
COACH—GEORGE S. HALAS

CHICAGO BEARS   30   Cleveland   21
                 16   Green Bay   21
                 32   Pittsburgh   0
                 35   Cleveland   21
                 44   Cardinals   7
                 13   New York   16
                 0   Detroit   10
                 30   Green Bay   27
                 27   Philadelphia   14
                 48   Cardinals   7
                 ———   ———
                 275   144
Won 7, Lost 3.

1940
COACH—GEORGE S. HALAS

CHICAGO BEARS   41   Green Bay   10
                 7   Cardinals   21
                 21   Cleveland   14
                 7   Detroit   0
                 16   Brooklyn   7
                 37   New York   21
                 14   Green Bay   7
                 14   Detroit   17
                 3   Washington   7
                 47   Cleveland   25
                 31   Cardinals   23
                 ———   ———
                 238   150
Won 8, Lost 3.
Championship Game:
Chicago Bears   73   Washington   0

1941
COACH—GEORGE S. HALAS

CHICAGO BEARS   25   Green Bay   17
                 48   Cleveland   21
                 53   Cardinals   7
                 49   Detroit   0
                 34   Pittsburgh   7
                 14   Green Bay   16
                 31   Cleveland   13
                 35   Washington   21
                 24   Detroit   7

CHICAGO BEARS 49 Philadelphia 14
              34 Cardinals   24
              ——   ——
              396   147
              Won 10, Lost 1.
         Divisional Play-off:
Chicago Bears 33   Green Bay 14
         Championship Game:
Chicago Bears 34   New York 9

1942
COACHES—G. HALAS, L. JOHNSOS,
H. ANDERSON
CHICAGO BEARS 44 Green Bay   28
              21 Cleveland   7
              41 Cardinals   14
              26 New York   7
              45 Philadelphia 14
              16 Detroit   0
              35 Brooklyn   0
              38 Green Bay   7
              42 Detroit   0
              47 Cleveland   7
              21 Cardinals   7
              ——   ——
              376   91
              Won 11.
         Championship Game:
Chicago Bears 6   Washington 12

1943
COACHES—HEARTLEY ANDERSON
LUKE JOHNSOS
CHICAGO BEARS 21 Green Bay   21
              27 Detroit   21
              20 Cardinals   0
              48 Philadelphia 21
              33 Brooklyn   21
              35 Detroit   14
              21 Green Bay   7
              56 New York   7
              7   Washington   21
              35 Cardinals   24
              ——   ——
              303   157
              Won 8, Lost 1, Tied 1.
         Championship Game:
Chicago Bears 41   Washington 21

1944
COACHES—HEARTLEY ANDERSON
LUKE JOHNSOS
CHICAGO BEARS 28 Green Bay   42
              28 Washington   0
              7   Cleveland   19
              34 Card-Pitt   7
              21 Detroit   21
              28 Cleveland   21
              21 Green Bay   0
              21 Boston   7
              21 Detroit   41
              28 Philadelphia 7
              49 Card-Pitt   7
              ——   ——
              286   172
              Won 7, Lost 3, Tied 1.

1945
COACHES—HEARTLEY ANDERSON
LUKE JOHNSOS
CHICAGO BEARS 21 Green Bay   31
              0   Cleveland   17
              7   Cardinals   16
              21 Cleveland   41
              10 Detroit   16
              28 Green Bay   24
              28 Detroit   35
              21 Washington   28
              28 Pittsburgh   7
              28 Cardinals   20
              ——   ——
              192   225
              Won 3, Lost 7.

1946
COACH—GEORGE S. HALAS
CHICAGO BEARS 30 Green Bay   7
              34 Cardinals   17
              28 Los Angeles 28
              21 Philadelphia 14
              0   New York   14
              10 Green Bay   7
              27 Los Angeles 21
              24 Washington   20
              42 Detroit   6
              28 Cardinals   35
              45 Detroit   24
              ——   ——
              289   193
              Won 8, Lost 1, Tied 1.
         Championship Game:
Chicago Bears 24   New York 14

1947
COACH—GEORGE S. HALAS
CHICAGO BEARS 20 Green Bay   29
              7   Cardinals   31
              40 Philadelphia 7
              33 Detroit   24
              56 Washington   20
              28 Boston   24
              20 Green Bay   17
              41 Los Angeles 21
              49 Pittsburgh   7
              34 Detroit   14
              14 Los Angeles 17
              21 Cardinals   30
              ——   ——
              363   240
              Won 8, Lost 4.

1948
COACH—GEORGE S. HALAS
CHICAGO BEARS 45 Green Bay   7
              28 Cardinals   17
              42 Los Angeles 21
              28 Detroit   0
              7   Philadelphia 12
              35 New York   14
              21 Los Angeles   6
              7   Green Bay   6

1948 (cont.)

CHICAGO BEARS	51	Boston	17
	48	Washington	13
	42	Detroit	14
	21	Cardinals	24
	375		151

Won 10, Lost 2.

1949
COACH—GEORGE S. HALAS

CHICAGO BEARS	17	Green Bay	0
	17	Cardinals	7
	16	Los Angeles	31
	38	Philadelphia	21
	28	N.Y. Giants	35
	24	Los Angeles	27
	24	Green Bay	3
	27	Detroit	24
	31	Washington	21
	28	Detroit	7
	30	Pittsburgh	21
	52	Cardinals	21
	332		218

Won 9, Lost 3.

1950
COACH—GEORGE S. HALAS

CHICAGO BEARS	24	Los Angeles	10
	32	San Francisco	20
	21	Green Bay	30
	27	Cardinals	6
	28	Green Bay	14
	27	N.Y. Yanks	38
	35	Detroit	21
	28	N.Y. Yanks	20
	17	San Francisco	0
	24	Los Angeles	14
	10	Cardinals	20
	6	Detroit	3
	279		196

Won 9, Lost 3.
Divisional Play-off:
Chicago Bears   14   Los Angeles   24

1951
COACH—GEORGE S. HALAS

CHICAGO BEARS	31	Green Bay	20
	14	Cardinals	28
	24	N.Y. Yanks	21
	13	San Francisco	7
	28	Detroit	23
	27	Washington	0
	28	Detroit	41
	24	Green Bay	13
	21	Cleveland	42
	17	Los Angeles	42
	45	N.Y. Yanks	21
	14	Cardinals	24
	286		282

Won 7, Lost 5.

CHICAGO CARDINALS

1920
COACH—MARSHALL SMITH

CARDINALS	0	Tigers (Chi)	0
	33	Moline	0
	0	Rock Is.	7
	21	Detroit	0
	6	Tigers	3
	20	Cincinnati	0
	7	Staleys	6
	0	Staleys	10
	87		26

Won 5, Lost 2, Tied 1.

1921
COACH—JOHN DRISCOLL

CARDINALS	20	Minneapolis	20
	0	Akron	23
	7	Rock Island	14
	17	Columbus	6
	7	Hammond	0
	3	Green Bay	3
	0	Akron	7
	0	Staleys	0
	54		73

Won 2, Lost 3, Tied 3.

1922
COACH—JOHN DRISCOLL

CARDINALS	3	Milwaukee	0
	16	Green Bay	3
	3	Minneapolis	0
	37	Columbus	6
	9	Buffalo	7
	7	Akron	0
	0	Canton	7
	3	Canton	20
	3	Dayton	7
	6	Bears	0
	9	Bears	0
	96		50

Won 8, Lost 3, Tied 0.

1923
COACH—ARNOLD HORWEEN

CARDINALS	3	Buffalo	0
	60	Rochester	0
	19	Akron	0
	13	Dayton	3
	3	Canton	7
	6	Hammond	0
	10	Duluth	0
	4	Racine	10
	22	Oorang	19
	29	Rock Island	7
	0	Bears	3
	169		49

Won 8, Lost 3, Tied 0.

1924
COACH—ARNOLD HORWEEN

CARDINALS			
	17	Milwaukee	7
	13	Minneapolis	0
	0	Bears	6
	3	Hammond	6
	8	Milwaukee	17
	3	Green Bay	0
	23	Dayton	0
	13	Akron	0
	10	Racine	10
	6	Bears	21
	96		67

Won 5, Lost 4, Tied 1.

1925
COACH—NORMAN BARRY

CARDINALS			
	6	Hammond	10
	34	Milwaukee	0
	19	Columbus	9
	20	Kansas City	7
	9	Bears	0
	10	Duluth	6
	9	Green Bay	6
	23	Buffalo	6
	14	Dayton	0
	0	Bears	0
	7	Rock Island	0
	7	Pottsville	21
	158		65

Won 9, Lost 2, Tied 1.

1926
COACH—NORMAN BARRY

CARDINALS			
	14	Columbus	0
	15	Los Angeles	0
	20	Racine	6
	13	Green Bay	7
	0	Bears	16
	3	Milwaukee	2
	0	Green Bay	3
	0	Frankford	27
	0	New York	20
	0	Bears	0
	2	Kansas City	7
	65		88

Won 5, Lost 5, Tied 1.

1927
COACH—FRED GILLIES

CARDINALS			
	0	Bears	9
	19	Pottsville	7
	7	Dayton	0
	0	Green Bay	13
	6	New York	7
	6	Green Bay	6
	6	N.Y. Yanks	20
	7	N.Y. Giants	28
	3	Bears	0
	7	Cleveland	32
	61		122

Won 4, Lost 6, Tied 1.

1928
COACH—GUY CHAMBERLAIN

CARDINALS			
	0	Bears	15
	7	Dayton	0
	0	Green Bay	20
	0	N.Y. Yanks	19
	0	Bears	34
	7		88

Won 1, Lost 4, Tied 1.

1929
COACH—ERNEST NEVERS

CARDINALS			
	2	Green Bay	9
	7	Minneapolis	14
	0	Bears	0
	6	Green Bay	7
	0	Philadelphia	8
	16	Providence	0
	8	Minneapolis	0
	0	Green Bay	13
	19	Dayton	0
	40	Bears	6
	21	N.Y. Giants	24
	119		81

Won 4, Lost 5, Tied 1.

1930
COACH—ERNEST NEVERS

CARDINALS			
	0	Green Bay	14
	0	Portsmouth	0
	6	Bears	32
	13	Newark	0
	7	Providence	9
	12	New York	25
	13	Green Bay	6
	23	Portsmouth	13
	34	Frankford	7
	7	New York	13
	6	Frankford	0
	23	Portsmouth	0
	144		127

Won 6, Lost 5, Tied 1.

1931
COACH—LEROY ANDREWS
ERNEST NEVERS

CARDINALS			
	3	Portsmouth	13
	7	Green Bay	26
	13	Bears	26
	14	Brooklyn	7
	14	Cleveland	6
	21	Green Bay	13
	20	Portsmouth	19
	7	Bears	18
	21	Cleveland	0
	120		128

Won 5, Lost 4, Tied 0.

1932
COACH—JACK CHEVIGNY

CARDINALS			
	7	Green Bay	15
	7	Portsmouth	7
	0	Bears	0
	9	Boston	0
	27	Brooklyn	7
	9	Green Bay	19
	0	Brooklyn	3
	7	Stapleton	21
	0	Bears	34
	6	Boston	8
	—		—
	72		114

Won 1, Lost 6, Tied 0.

1933
COACH—PAUL SCHISSLER

CARDINALS			
	13	Pittsburgh	14
	6	Portsmouth	7
	3	Cincinnati	0
	9	Bears	12
	0	Boston	10
	0	Brooklyn	7
	6	Green Bay	14
	9	Cincinnati	12
	0	Brooklyn	3
	6	Bears	22
	0	Boston	0
	—		—
	52		101

Won 1, Lost 9, Tied 1.

1934
COACH—PAUL SCHISSLER

CARDINALS			
	9	Cincinnati	0
	0	Detroit	6
	16	Cincinnati	0
	0	Bears	20
	0	Green Bay	15
	0	Boston	9
	21	Brooklyn	0
	13	Detroit	17
	9	Green Bay	0
	6	Bears	17
	6	Green Bay	0
	—		—
	80		84

Won 5, Lost 6, Tied 0.

1935
COACH—MILAN CREIGHTON

CARDINALS			
	7	Green Bay	6
	10	Detroit	10
	3	Green Bay	0
	13	Pittsburgh	17
	14	New York	13
	7	Detroit	7
	12	Philadelphia	3
	6	Boston	0
	9	Green Bay	7
	7	Bears	7
	0	Bears	13
	—		—
	88		83

Won 6, Lost 3, Tied 2.

1936
COACH—MILAN CREIGHTON

CARDINALS			
	7	Green Bay	10
	0	Detroit	39
	0	Green Bay	24
	3	Bears	7
	6	New York	14
	10	Boston	13
	13	Philadelphia	0
	14	Pittsburgh	6
	7	Detroit	14
	14	Bears	7
	0	Green Bay	0
	—		—
	74		134

Won 3, Lost 7, Tied 1.

1937
COACH—MILAN CREIGHTON

CARDINALS			
	14	Green Bay	7
	7	Detroit	16
	21	Washington	14
	6	Philadelphia	6
	6	Cleveland	0
	13	Green Bay	34
	7	Bears	16
	13	Pittsburgh	7
	13	Cleveland	7
	7	Detroit	16
	27	Bears	42
	—		—
	134		165

Won 5, Lost 5, Tied 1.

1938
COACH—MILAN CREIGHTON

CARDINALS			
	13	Bears	16
	7	Cleveland	6
	7	Green Bay	28
	22	Green Bay	24
	0	Brooklyn	13
	28	Bears	34
	0	Detroit	10
	0	Philadelphia	7
	0	New York	6
	3	Detroit	7
	31	Cleveland	17
	—		—
	111		168

Won 2, Lost 9, Tied 0.

1939
COACH—ERNEST NEVERS

CARDINALS			
	13	Detroit	21
	10	Green Bay	14
	10	Pittsburgh	0
	3	Detroit	17
	20	Green Bay	27
	7	Bears	44
	0	Cleveland	24
	0	Cleveland	14
	7	New York	17
	7	Washington	28
	7	Bears	48
	—		—
	84		254

Won 1, Lost 10, Tied 0.

1940
COACH—JAMES CONZELMAN

CARDINALS		
7	Pittsburgh	7
0	Detroit	0
21	Bears	7
6	Green Bay	31
14	Detroit	43
21	Washington	28
14	Cleveland	26
17	Cleveland	7
7	Green Bay	28
9	Brooklyn	14
20	Bears	31
—		—
136		222

Won 2, Lost 7, Tied 2.

1941
COACH—JAMES CONZELMAN

CARDINALS		
6	Cleveland	10
14	Detroit	14
13	Green Bay	14
7	Bears	53
20	Brooklyn	6
14	Philadelphia	21
10	New York	7
9	Green Bay	17
7	Cleveland	0
3	Detroit	21
24	Bears	34
—		—
127		193

Won 3, Lost 7, Tied 1.

1942
COACH—JAMES CONZELMAN

CARDINALS		
7	Cleveland	0
13	Detroit	0
13	Green Bay	17
14	Bears	44
7	Detroit	0
3	Cleveland	7
24	Green Bay	55
0	Washington	28
3	Pittsburgh	19
7	New York	21
7	Bears	21
—		—
98		209

Won 3, Lost 8, Tied 0.

1943
COACH—PHILIP HANDLER

CARDINALS		
17	Detroit	35
7	Green Bay	28
0	Bears	20
0	Detroit	7
7	Washington	13
13	Phil-Pitt	7
0	Brooklyn	7
14	Green Bay	35
13	New York	24
24	Bears	35
—		—
95		211

Won 1, Lost 9, Tied 0.

1944 (Merged with Pittsburgh)
COACH—PHILIP HANDLER
WALTER KIESLING

CARD-PITT		
28	Cleveland	30
7	Green Bay	34
7	Bears	34
0	New York	23
20	Washington	42
6	Detroit	27
7	Detroit	21
6	Cleveland	33
20	Green Bay	35
7	Bears	49
—		—
108		328

Won 0, Lost 10, Tied 0.

1945
COACH—PHILIP HANDLER

CARDINALS		
0	Detroit	10
0	Cleveland	21
6	Philadelphia	24
16	Bears	7
0	Detroit	26
14	Green Bay	33
21	Washington	24
0	Pittsburgh	23
21	Cleveland	35
20	Bears	28
—		—
98		231

Won 1, Lost 9, Tied 0.

1946
COACH—JAMES CONZELMAN

CARDINALS		
7	Pittsburgh	14
34	Detroit	14
17	Bears	34
36	Detroit	14
24	New York	28
34	L.A. Rams	10
28	Boston	14
7	Green Bay	19
14	L.A. Rams	17
24	Green Bay	6
35	Bears	28
—		—
260		198

Won 6, Lost 5, Tied 0.

1947
COACH—JAMES CONZELMAN

CARDINALS		
45	Detroit	45
31	Bears	7
14	Green Bay	10
7	L.A. Rams	27
27	Boston	7
17	L.A. Rams	10
17	Detroit	7
21	Green Bay	20
21	Washington	45
31	New York	35
45	Philadelphia	21
30	Bears	21
—		—
306		231

Won 9, Lost 3, Tied 0.

1948
COACH—JAMES CONZELMAN

CARDINALS	21	Philadelphia	14
	17	Bears	28
	17	Green Bay	7
	63	New York	35
	49	Boston	27
	27	L.A. Rams	22
	56	Detroit	20
	24	Pittsburgh	7
	27	L.A. Rams	24
	28	Detroit	14
	42	Green Bay	7
	24	Bears	21
	___		___
	395		226

Won 11, Lost 1, Tied 0.

1949
COACH—PHILIP HANDLER
RAYMOND PARKER

CARDINALS	38	Washington	7
	7	Bears	17
	3	Philadelphia	28
	39	Green Bay	17
	7	Detroit	24
	38	N.Y. Giants	41
	42	Detroit	19
	65	N.Y. Bulldogs	20
	28	L.A. Rams	28
	41	Green Bay	21
	31	L.A. Rams	27
	21	Bears	52
	___		___
	360		301

Won 6, Lost 5, Tied 1.

1950
COACH—EARL LAMBEAU

CARDINALS	7	Philadelphia	45
	55	Baltimore	13
	6	Bears	27
	24	Cleveland	34
	38	Washington	28
	17	New York	3
	7	Cleveland	10
	21	New York	51
	14	Philadelphia	10
	17	Pittsburgh	28
	20	Bears	10
	7	Pittsburgh	28
	___		___
	254		266

Won 5, Lost 7, Tied 0.

1951
COACH—EARL LAMBEAU

CARDINALS	14	Philadelphia	17
	28	Bears	14
	17	New York	28
	3	Washington	7
	14	Pittsburgh	28
	17	Cleveland	34
	21	L.A. Rams	45
	27	San Francisco	21

CARDINALS	0	New York	10
	28	Cleveland	49
	17	Washington	20
	24	Bears	14
	___		___
	206		287

Won 3, Lost 9, Tied 0.

CLEVELAND BROWNS
(Formerly AAFC; entered NFL 1950)

1950
COACH—PAUL BROWN

CLEVELAND	35	Philadelphia	10
	31	Baltimore	0
	0	N.Y. Giants	6
	30	Pittsburgh	17
	34	Cardinals	24
	13	N.Y. Giants	17
	45	Pittsburgh	7
	10	Cardinals	7
	34	San Francisco	14
	20	Washington	14
	13	Philadelphia	7
	45	Washington	21
	___		___
	310		144

Won 10, Lost 2.
Divisional Play-off:
Cleveland 8   N.Y. Giants 3
Championship Game:
Cleveland 30   Los Angeles 28

1951
COACH—PAUL BROWN

CLEVELAND	10	San Francisco	24
	38	Los Angeles	23
	45	Washington	0
	17	Pittsburgh	0
	14	N.Y. Giants	13
	34	Chicago Cards	17
	20	Philadelphia	17
	10	N.Y. Giants	0
	42	Chicago Bears	21
	49	Chicago Cards	28
	28	Pittsburgh	0
	24	Philadelphia	9
	___		___
	331		152

Won 11, Lost 1.
Championship Game:
Cleveland 17   Los Angeles 24

DETROIT LIONS
1934
COACH—GEORGE "POTSY" CLARK

DETROIT	9	New York	0
	6	Cardinals	0
	3	Green Bay	0
	10	Philadelphia	0
	24	Boston	0

DETROIT	28	Brooklyn	0
	38	Cin.-St. L.	0
	40	Pittsburgh	7
	17	Cardinals	13
	40	Cin.-St. L.	7
	0	Green Bay	3
	16	Bears	10
	7	Bears	10
	238		59

Won 11, Lost 2.

1935
COACH—GEORGE "POTSY" CLARK

DETROIT	35	Philadelphia	0
	10	Cardinals	10
	10	Brooklyn	12
	17	Boston	7
	9	Green Bay	13
	14	Boston	0
	7	Cardinals	6
	7	Green Bay	31
	20	Green Bay	10
	20	Bears	20
	14	Bears	2
	28	Brooklyn	0
	191		111

Won 7, Lost 3, Tied 2.
Championship Game:
Detroit 26   New York   7

1936
COACH—GEORGE "POTSY" CLARK

DETROIT	39	Cardinals	0
	23	Philadelphia	0
	14	Brooklyn	7
	18	Green Bay	20
	10	Bears	12
	7	New York	14
	28	Pittsburgh	3
	38	New York	0
	14	Cardinals	7
	13	Bears	7
	17	Green Bay	26
	14	Brooklyn	6
	235		102

Won 8, Lost 4.

1937
COACH—EARL "DUTCH" CLARK

DETROIT	28	Cleveland	0
	16	Cardinals	7
	6	Green Bay	26
	7	Pittsburgh	3
	30	Brooklyn	0
	20	Bears	28
	13	Green Bay	14
	27	Cleveland	7
	17	New York	0
	16	Cardinals	7
	0	Bears	13
	180		105

Won 7, Lost 4.

1938
COACH—EARL "DUTCH" CLARK

DETROIT	16	Pittsburgh	7
	5	Washington	7
	10	Cardinals	0
	17	Cleveland	21
	17	Green Bay	7
	7	Cardinals	3
	13	Bears	7
	6	Cleveland	0
	7	Green Bay	28
	14	Bears	7
	7	Philadelphia	21
	119		108

Won 7, Lost 4.

1939
COACH—GUS HENDERSON

DETROIT	21	Cardinals	13
	27	Brooklyn	7
	17	Cardinals	3
	15	Cleveland	7
	7	Green Bay	26
	10	Bears	0
	18	New York	14
	13	Bears	23
	3	Cleveland	14
	7	Washington	31
	7	Green Bay	12
	145		150

Won 6, Lost 5.

1940
COACH—GEORGE "POTSY" CLARK

DETROIT	0	Cardinals	0
	7	Pittsburgh	10
	6	Cleveland	0
	43	Cardinals	14
	0	Bears	7
	23	Green Bay	14
	14	Washington	20
	0	Cleveland	24
	17	Bears	14
	21	Philadelphia	0
	7	Green Bay	50
	138		153

Won 5, Lost 5, Tied 1.

1941
COACH—WILLIAM EDWARDS

DETROIT	0	Green Bay	23
	7	Brooklyn	14
	14	Cardinals	14
	17	Cleveland	7
	0	Bears	49
	7	Green Bay	24
	14	Cleveland	0
	13	New York	20
	21	Philadelphia	17
	7	Bears	24
	21	Cardinals	3
	121		195

Won 4, Lost 6, Tied 1.

1942
COACH—JOHN KARCIS

DETROIT			
	0	Cardinals	13
	0	Cleveland	14
	7	Brooklyn	28
	7	Green Bay	38
	0	Cardinals	7
	7	Green Bay	28
	0	Bears	16
	7	Pittsburgh	35
	7	Cleveland	27
	0	Bears	42
	3	Washington	15
	38		263

Won 0, Lost 11.

1943
COACH—CHARLES E. DORAIS

DETROIT			
	35	Cardinals	17
	27	Brooklyn	0
	21	Bears	27
	14	Green Bay	35
	7	Cardinals	0
	6	Green Bay	27
	14	Bears	35
	0	New York	0
	20	Washington	42
	34	Phil-Pitt	35
	178		218

Won 3, Lost 6, Tied 1.

1944
COACH—CHARLES E. DORAIS

DETROIT			
	6	Green Bay	27
	19	Brooklyn	14
	17	Cleveland	20
	21	Bears	21
	0	Green Bay	14
	27	Card-Pitt	6
	21	Card-Pitt	7
	41	Bears	21
	26	Cleveland	14
	38	Boston	7
	216		151

Won 6, Lost 3, Tied 1.

1945
COACH—CHARLES E. DORAIS

DETROIT			
	10	Cardinals	0
	21	Green Bay	57
	28	Philadelphia	24
	25	Cardinals	0
	16	Bears	10
	10	Boston	9
	35	Bears	28
	14	New York	35
	21	Cleveland	28
	14	Green Bay	3
	195		194

Won 7, Lost 3.

1946
COACH—CHARLES E. DORAIS

DETROIT			
	14	Cardinals	34
	16	Washington	17
	14	Cardinals	36
	14	Los Angeles	35
	7	Green Bay	10
	20	Los Angeles	41
	17	Pittsburgh	7
	0	Green Bay	9
	6	Bears	42
	10	Boston	34
	24	Bears	45
	142		310

Won 1, Lost 10.

1947
COACH—CHARLES E. DORAIS

DETROIT			
	10	Pittsburgh	17
	21	Cardinals	45
	21	Boston	7
	13	Los Angeles	27
	24	Bears	33
	17	Green Bay	34
	35	New York	7
	7	Cardinals	17
	38	Washington	21
	17	Los Angeles	28
	14	Bears	34
	14	Green Bay	35
	231		305

Won 3, Lost 9.

1948
COACH—ALVIN N. "BO" McMILLIN

DETROIT			
	7	Los Angeles	44
	21	Green Bay	33
	14	Boston	17
	0	Bears	28
	27	Los Angeles	34
	24	Green Bay	20
	20	Cardinals	56
	21	Washington	46
	17	Pittsburgh	14
	14	Cardinals	28
	14	Bears	42
	21	Philadelphia	45
	200		407

Won 2, Lost 10.

1949
COACH—ALVIN N. "BO" McMILLIN

DETROIT			
	24	Los Angeles	27
	14	Philadelphia	22
	7	Pittsburgh	14
	10	Los Angeles	21
	24	Cardinals	7
	14	Green Bay	16
	19	Cardinals	42
	24	Bears	27
	45	N.Y. Giants	21

DETROIT	7	Bears	28
	28	N.Y. Bulldogs	27
	21	Green Bay	7
	—		—
	237		259

Won 4, Lost 8.

1950
COACH—ALVIN N. "BO" McMILLIN

DETROIT	45	Green Bay	7
	10	Pittsburgh	7
	21	N.Y. Yanks	44
	24	San Francisco	7
	28	Los Angeles	30
	27	San Francisco	28
	24	Los Angeles	65
	21	Bears	35
	24	Green Bay	21
	49	N.Y. Yanks	14
	45	Baltimore	21
	3	Bears	6
	—		—
	321		285

Won 6, Lost 6.

1951
COACH—RAYMOND PARKER

DETROIT	35	Washington	17
	37	N.Y. Yanks	10
	21	Los Angeles	27
	24	N.Y. Yanks	24
	23	Bears	28
	24	Green Bay	17
	41	Bears	28
	28	Philadelphia	7
	52	Green Bay	35
	10	San Francisco	20
	24	Los Angeles	22
	17	San Francisco	21
	—		—
	336		256

Won 7, Lost 4, Tied 1.

GREEN BAY PACKERS

1920
COACH—EARL LAMBEAU

GREEN BAY	3	Chi. Boosters	3
	56	Kaukauna	0
	3	Stambaugh	0
	25	Marinette	0
	62	DePere	0
	7	Beloit	0
	9	Milwaukee Stars	0
	3	Beloit	14
	19	Menominee	7
	26	Lapham A.C.	0
	14	Stambaugh	0
	—		—
	227		24

Won 9, Lost 1, Tied 1.

1921
COACH—EARL LAMBEAU

GREEN BAY	13	Chi. Boosters	0
	49	Rockford	0
	40	Chi. Cornhuskers	0
	7	Beloit	0
	3	Rock Island	10
	7	Minneapolis	6
	43	Evansville	6
	14	Hammond	7
	3	Cardinals	3
	0	Staleys	20
	3	Racine	3
	—		—
	182		55

Won 7, Lost 2, Tied 2.

1922
COACH—EARL LAMBEAU

GREEN BAY	0	Duluth	6
	3	Cardinals	6
	14	Rock Island	19
	6	Racine	10
	0	Milwaukee	0
	0	Rock Island	0
	3	Columbus	0
	14	Marines	6
	3	Racine	3
	13	Milwaukee	0
	10	Duluth	0
	14	Racine	0
	—		—
	80		50

Won 5, Lost 4, Tied 3.

1923
COACH—EARL LAMBEAU

GREEN BAY	10	Hibbing	0
	12	Marines	0
	0	St. Louis	0
	0	Bears	3
	12	Milwaukee	0
	3	Racine	24
	3	St. Louis	0
	10	Milwaukee	7
	16	Racine	0
	10	Duluth	0
	19	Hammond	0
	—		—
	95		34

Won 8, Lost 2, Tied 1.

1924
COACH—EARL LAMBEAU

GREEN BAY	15	Ironwood	0
	5	Bears	0
	3	Duluth	6
	0	Cardinals	3
	16	Kansas City	0
	17	Milwaukee	0
	19	Marines	0
	6	Racine	3
	13	Duluth	0
	17	Milwaukee	10

1924 (cont.)

GREEN BAY	0	Bears	3
	17	Kansas City	6
	0	Racine	7
	—		—
	128		38

Won 9, Lost 4.

1925
COACH—EARL LAMBEAU

GREEN BAY	14	Bears	10
	0	Rock Island	3
	33	Rochester	13
	20	Rock Island	0
	31	Milwaukee	0
	6	Cardinals	9
	7	Dayton	0
	7	Philadelphia	13
	0	Bears	21
	0	Pottsville	31
	14	Providence	10
	—		—
	132		110

Won 6, Lost 5.

1926
COACH—EARL LAMBEAU

GREEN BAY	79	Iron Mountain	0
	21	Detroit	0
	6	Bears	6
	7	Milwaukee	0
	7	Cardinals	13
	0	Duluth	0
	35	Racine	0
	3	Cardinals	0
	21	Milwaukee	0
	14	Louisville	0
	13	Bears	19
	14	Yellowjackets	19
	7	Detroit	0
	3	Bears	3
	—		—
	230		60

Won 8, Lost 3, Tied 3.

1927
COACH—EARL LAMBEAU

GREEN BAY	34	Milwaukee	0
	14	Dayton	0
	12	Cleveland	7
	6	Bears	7
	20	Duluth	0
	13	Cardinals	0
	13	Yankees	0
	22	Milwaukee	7
	6	Cardinals	6
	6	Dayton	0
	6	Bears	14
	17	Frankford	9
	—		—
	169		50

Won 9, Lost 2, Tied 1.

1928
COACH—EARL LAMBEAU

GREEN BAY	19	Minneapolis	0
	9	Philadelphia	19
	12	Bears	12
	0	New York	6
	20	Cardinals	0
	16	Bears	6
	17	Dayton	0
	26	Pottsville	14
	0	Yankees	0
	7	New York	0
	0	Pottsville	26
	7	Providence	7
	0	Frankford	2
	6	Bears	0
	—		—
	139		92

Won 7, Lost 4, Tied 3.

1929
COACH—EARL LAMBEAU

GREEN BAY	14	Portsmouth	0
	9	Dayton	2
	23	Bears	0
	9	Cardinals	2
	14	Frankford	2
	24	Minneapolis	0
	7	Cardinals	6
	16	Minneapolis	6
	14	Bears	0
	12	Cardinals	0
	20	New York	6
	0	Frankford	0
	25	Providence	0
	25	Bears	0
	—		—
	212		24

Won 13, Lost 0, Tied 1.

1930
COACH—EARL LAMBEAU

GREEN BAY	46	Oshkosh	0
	14	Cardinals	0
	7	Bears	0
	14	New York	7
	27	Philadelphia	12
	13	Minneapolis	0
	19	Minneapolis	0
	47	Portsmouth	13
	13	Bears	12
	6	Cardinals	13
	6	New York	13
	25	Philadelphia	7
	37	Stapleton	7
	0	Bears	21
	6	Portsmouth	6
	—		—
	273		111

Won 10, Lost 3, Tied 1.

1931
COACH—EARL LAMBEAU

GREEN BAY	26	Cleveland	0
	32	Brooklyn	6
	7	Bears	0

GREEN BAY	27	New York	7
	26	Cardinals	7
	15	Philadelphia	7
	48	Providence	20
	6	Bears	2
	26	Stapleton	0
	13	Cardinals	21
	14	New York	10
	38	Providence	7
	7	Brooklyn	0
	6	Bears	7
	—		—
	291		74

Won 12, Lost 2.

1932
COACH—EARL LAMBEAU

GREEN BAY	45	Grand Rapids	0
	15	Cardinals	7
	0	Bears	0
	13	New York	0
	15	Portsmouth	10
	2	Bears	0
	13	Brooklyn	0
	26	Stapleton	0
	19	Cardinals	9
	21	Boston	0
	0	New York	6
	7	Brooklyn	0
	21	Stapleton	3
	0	Portsmouth	19
	0	Bears	9
	—		—
	197		63

Won 11, Lost 3, Tied 1.

1933
COACH—EARL LAMBEAU

GREEN BAY	7	Boston	7
	7	Bears	14
	7	New York	10
	17	Portsmouth	0
	47	Pittsburgh	0
	7	Bears	10
	35	Philadelphia	9
	14	Cardinals	6
	0	Portsmouth	7
	7	Boston	20
	6	New York	17
	21	Stapleton	0
	10	Philadelphia	0
	6	Bears	7
	—		—
	191		107

Won 6, Lost 7, Tied 1

1934
COACH—EARL LAMBEAU

GREEN BAY	28	Ft. Atkinson	7
	19	Philadelphia	0
	10	Bears	24
	20	New York	6
	0	Detroit	3
	41	Cincinnati	0

	15	Cardinals	0
	14	Bears	27
	10	Boston	0
	3	New York	17
	0	Cardinals	9
	3	Detroit	0
	0	Cardinals	6
	21	St. Louis	14
	—		—
	184		119

Won 8, Lost 6.

1935
COACH—EARL LAMBEAU

GREEN BAY	49	LaCrosse	0
	6	Cardinals	7
	7	Bears	0
	16	New York	7
	27	Pittsburgh	0
	0	Cardinals	3
	13	Detroit	9
	17	Bears	14
	31	Detroit	7
	10	Detroit	20
	34	Pittsburgh	14
	7	Cardinals	9
	13	Philadelphia	6
	—		—
	230		96

Won 9, Lost 4.

1936
COACH—EARL LAMBEAU

GREEN BAY	10	Cardinals	7
	3	Bears	30
	24	Cardinals	0
	31	Boston	2
	20	Detroit	18
	42	Pittsburgh	10
	21	Bears	10
	7	Boston	3
	38	Brooklyn	7
	26	New York	14
	26	Detroit	17
	0	Cardinals	0
	21	Boston	6
	—		—
	269		124

Won 11, Lost 1, Tied 1.

1937
COACH—EARL LAMBEAU

GREEN BAY	7	Cardinals	14
	2	Bears	14
	26	Detroit	6
	34	Cardinals	13
	35	Cleveland	10
	35	Cleveland	7
	14	Detroit	13
	24	Bears	14
	37	Philadelphia	7
	0	New York	10
	6	Washington	14
	—		—
	220		122

Won 7, Lost 4.

1938
COACH—EARL LAMBEAU

GREEN BAY	26	Cleveland	17
	0	Bears	2
	28	Cardinals	17
	24	Cardinals	22
	7	Detroit	17
	35	Brooklyn	7
	20	Pittsburgh	0
	28	Cleveland	7
	24	Bears	17
	28	Detroit	7
	3	New York	15
	17	New York	23
	240		141

Won 8, Lost 4.

1939
COACH—EARL LAMBEAU

GREEN BAY	14	Cardinals	10
	21	Bears	16
	24	Cleveland	27
	26	Detroit	7
	24	Washington	14
	27	Bears	30
	23	Philadelphia	16
	28	Brooklyn	0
	7	Cleveland	6
	12	Detroit	7
	27	New York	0
	260		153

Won 9, Lost 2.

1940
COACH—EARL LAMBEAU

GREEN BAY	27	Philadelphia	20
	10	Bears	41
	31	Cardinals	6
	31	Cleveland	14
	14	Detroit	23
	24	Pittsburgh	3
	7	Bears	14
	28	Cardinals	7
	3	New York	7
	50	Detroit	7
	13	Cleveland	13
	238		155

Won 6, Lost 4, Tied 1.

1941
COACH—EARL LAMBEAU

GREEN BAY	23	Detroit	0
	24	Cleveland	7
	17	Bears	25
	14	Cardinals	13
	30	Brooklyn	7
	17	Cleveland	14
	24	Detroit	7
	16	Bears	14
	17	Cardinals	9

GREEN BAY	54	Pittsburgh	7
	22	Washington	17
	258		120

Won 10, Lost 1.
Divisional Play-off:
Green Bay 14   Bears 33

1942
COACH—EARL LAMBEAU

GREEN BAY	28	Bears	44
	17	Cardinals	13
	38	Detroit	7
	45	Cleveland	28
	28	Detroit	7
	55	Cardinals	24
	30	Cleveland	12
	7	Bears	38
	21	New York	21
	7	Philadelphia	0
	24	Pittsburgh	21
	300		215

Won 8, Lost 2, Tied 1.

1943
COACH—EARL LAMBEAU

GREEN BAY	21	Bears	21
	28	Cardinals	7
	35	Detroit	14
	7	Washington	33
	27	Detroit	6
	35	New York	21
	7	Bears	21
	35	Cardinals	14
	31	Brooklyn	7
	38	Phil-Pitt	28
	264		172

Won 7, Lost 2, Tied 1.

1944
COACH—EARL LAMBEAU

GREEN BAY	17	Brooklyn	7
	42	Bears	28
	27	Detroit	6
	34	Card-Pitt	7
	30	Cleveland	21
	0	Bears	21
	42	Cleveland	7
	0	New York	24
	35	Card-Pitt	20
	238		141

Won 7, Lost 2.

1945
COACH—EARL LAMBEAU

GREEN BAY	31	Bears	21
	57	Detroit	21
	14	Cleveland	27
	38	Boston	14
	33	Cardinals	14
	24	Bears	27
	7	Cleveland	20

GREEN BAY	28	Boston	0
	23	New York	14
	3	Detroit	14
	258		172

Won 6, Lost 4.

1946
COACH—EARL LAMBEAU

GREEN BAY	7	Bears	30
	17	Los Angeles	21
	19	Philadelphia	7
	17	Pittsburgh	7
	10	Detroit	7
	7	Bears	10
	19	Cardinals	7
	9	Detroit	0
	6	Cardinals	24
	20	Washington	7
	17	Los Angeles	38
	148		158

Won 6, Lost 5.

1947
COACH—EARL LAMBEAU

GREEN BAY	29	Bears	20
	17	Los Angeles	14
	10	Cardinals	14
	27	Washington	10
	34	Detroit	17
	17	Pittsburgh	18
	17	Bears	20
	20	Cardinals	21
	24	New York	24
	30	Los Angeles	10
	35	Detroit	14
	14	Philadelphia	28
	274		210

Won 6, Lost 5, Tied 1.

1948
COACH—EARL LAMBEAU

GREEN BAY	31	Boston	0
	7	Bears	45
	33	Detroit	21
	7	Cardinals	17
	16	Los Angeles	0
	7	Washington	23
	20	Detroit	24
	7	Pittsburgh	38
	6	Bears	7
	3	New York	49
	10	Los Angeles	24
	7	Cardinals	42
	154		290

Won 3, Lost 9.

1949
COACH—EARL LAMBEAU

GREEN BAY	0	Bears	17
	7	Los Angeles	48
	19	N.Y. Bulldogs	0

GREEN BAY	17	Cardinals	39
	7	Los Angeles	35
	16	Detroit	14
	3	Bears	24
	10	Giants	30
	7	Pittsburgh	30
	21	Cardinals	41
	0	Washington	30
	7	Detroit	21
	114		329

Won 2, Lost 10.

1950
COACH—GENE RONZANI

GREEN BAY	7	Detroit	45
	35	Washington	21
	31	Bears	21
	31	N.Y. Yanks	44
	14	Bears	28
	17	N.Y. Yanks	35
	21	Baltimore	41
	14	Los Angeles	45
	21	Detroit	24
	25	San Francisco	21
	14	Los Angeles	51
	14	San Francisco	30
	244		406

Won 3, Lost 9.

1951
COACH—GENE RONZANI

GREEN BAY	20	Chicago Bears	31
	35	Pittsburgh	33
	37	Philadelphia	24
	0	Los Angeles	28
	29	N.Y. Yanks	27
	17	Detroit	24
	7	Pittsburgh	28
	13	Philadelphia	24
	35	Detroit	52
	28	N.Y. Yanks	31
	19	San Francisco	31
	14	Los Angeles	42
	254		375

Won 3, Lost 9.

LOS ANGELES RAMS
(formerly Cleveland Rams, 1937–45)

1937
COACH—HUGO BEZDEK

CLEVELAND	0	Detroit	28
	21	Philadelphia	3
	7	Brooklyn	9
	0	Cardinals	6
	2	Bears	20
	10	Green Bay	35
	7	Green Bay	35
	7	Cardinals	13
	7	Detroit	27

1937 (cont.)

CLEVELAND			
	7	Washington	16
	7	Bears	15
	——		——
	75		207

Won 1, Lost 10, Tied 0.

1938
COACH—HUGO BEZDEK, ARTHUR LEWIS

CLEVELAND			
	17	Green Bay	26
	6	Cardinals	7
	13	Washington	37
	21	Detroit	17
	14	Bears	7
	23	Bears	21
	7	Green Bay	28
	0	Detroit	6
	0	New York	28
	17	Cardinals	31
	13	Pittsburgh	7
	——		——
	131		215

Won 4, Lost 7, Tied 1.

1939
COACH—EARL CLARK

CLEVELAND			
	21	Bears	30
	12	Brooklyn	23
	27	Green Bay	24
	21	Bears	35
	7	Detroit	15
	24	Cardinals	0
	14	Pittsburgh	14
	14	Cardinals	0
	14	Detroit	3
	6	Green Bay	7
	35	Philadelphia	13
	——		——
	195		164

Won 5, Lost 5, Tied 1.

1940
COACH—EARL CLARK

CLEVELAND			
	21	Philadelphia	13
	0	Detroit	6
	14	Bears	21
	14	Green Bay	31
	26	Cardinals	14
	7	Cardinals	17
	24	Detroit	0
	13	New York	0
	14	Brooklyn	29
	25	Bears	47
	13	Green Bay	13
	——		——
	171		191

Won 4, Lost 6, Tied 1.

1941
COACH—EARL CLARK

CLEVELAND			
	17	Pittsburgh	14
	10	Cardinals	6
	7	Green Bay	24
	21	Bears	48

CLEVELAND			
	7	Detroit	17
	14	Green Bay	17
	13	Washington	17
	0	Detroit	14
	13	Bears	31
	14	New York	49
	0	Cardinals	7
	——		——
	116		244

Won 2, Lost 9, Tied 0.

1942
COACH—EARL CLARK

CLEVELAND			
	0	Cardinals	7
	24	Phil-Pitt	14
	14	Detroit	0
	7	Bears	21
	14	Washington	33
	28	Green Bay	45
	7	Cardinals	3
	17	Brooklyn	0
	12	Green Bay	30
	27	Detroit	7
	0	Bears	47
	——		——
	150		207

Won 5, Lost 6, Tied 0.

1943 Suspended Operation

1944
COACH—ALDO DONELLI

CLEVELAND			
	30	Card-Pitt	28
	19	Bears	7
	20	Detroit	17
	21	Green Bay	30
	21	Bears	28
	10	Washington	14
	7	Green Bay	42
	33	Card-Pitt	6
	14	Detroit	26
	13	Philadelphia	26
	——		——
	188		224

Won 4, Lost 6, Tied 0.

1945
COACH—ADAM WALSH

CLEVELAND			
	21	Cardinals	0
	17	Bears	0
	27	Green Bay	14
	41	Bears	21
	14	Philadelphia	28
	21	New York	17
	20	Green Bay	7
	35	Cardinals	21
	28	Detroit	21
	20	Boston	7
	——		——
	244		136

Won 9, Lost 1, Tied 0.
Championship Game:
Cleveland 15   Washington 14

1946
COACH—ADAM WALSH

LOS ANGELES	14	Philadelphia	25
	21	Green Bay	17
	28	Bears	28
	35	Detroit	14
	10	Cardinals	34
	41	Detroit	20
	21	Bears	27
	17	Cardinals	14
	21	Boston	40
	31	New York	21
	38	Green Bay	17

277   257
Won 6, Lost 4, Tied 1.

1947
COACH—ROBERT SNYDER

LOS ANGELES	48	Pittsburgh	7
	14	Green Bay	17
	27	Detroit	13
	27	Cardinals	7
	7	Philadelphia	14
	10	Cardinals	17
	16	Boston	27
	21	Bears	41
	28	Detroit	17
	10	Green Bay	30
	17	Bears	14
	34	New York	10

259   214
Won 6, Lost 6, Tied 0.

1948
COACH—CLARK SHAUGHNESSY

LOS ANGELES	44	Detroit	7
	28	Philadelphia	28
	21	Bears	42
	0	Green Bay	16
	34	Detroit	27
	22	Cardinals	27
	6	Bears	21
	52	New York	37
	24	Cardinals	27
	24	Green Bay	10
	41	Washington	13
	31	Pittsburgh	14

327   269
Won 6, Lost 5, Tied 1.

1949
COACH—CLARK SHAUGHNESSY

LOS ANGELES	27	Detroit	24
	48	Green Bay	7
	31	Bears	16
	21	Detroit	10
	35	Green Bay	7
	27	Bears	24
	14	Philadelphia	38
	7	Pittsburgh	7
	28	Cardinals	28
	42	N.Y. Bulldogs	20

LOS ANGELES	27	Cardinals	31
	53	Washington	27

360   239
Won 8, Lost 2, Tied 2.
Championship Game:
Los Angeles 0   Philadelphia 14

1950
COACH—JOSEPH STYDAHAR

LOS ANGELES	20	Bears	24
	45	N.Y. Yanks	28
	35	San Francisco	14
	20	Philadelphia	56
	30	Detroit	28
	70	Baltimore	27
	65	Detroit	24
	28	San Francisco	21
	45	Green Bay	14
	43	N.Y. Yanks	35
	14	Bears	24
	51	Green Bay	14

466   309
Won 9, Lost 3, Tied 0.
Championship Game:
Los Angeles 28   Cleveland 30

1951
COACH—JOSEPH STYDAHAR

LOS ANGELES	54	N.Y. Yanks	14
	23	Cleveland	38
	27	Detroit	21
	28	Green Bay	0
	17	San Francisco	44
	23	San Francisco	16
	45	Cardinals	21
	48	N.Y. Yanks	21
	21	Washington	31
	42	Bears	17
	22	Detroit	24
	42	Green Bay	14

392   261
Won 8, Lost 4, Tied 0.
Championship Game:
Los Angeles 24   Cleveland 17

NEW YORK GIANTS

1925
COACH—ROBERT FOLWELL

N.Y. GIANTS	0	Providence	14
	3	Frankford	5
	0	Frankford	14
	7	Buffalo	0
	19	Cleveland	0
	19	Columbus	0
	13	Rochester	0
	13	Providence	12
	9	Kansas City	3
	23	Dayton	0

1925 (cont.)

N.Y. GIANTS	7	Chicago Bears	19
	9	Chicago Bears	0
	122		67

Won 8, Lost 4, Tied 0.

1926
COACH—JOSEPH ALEXANDER

N.Y. GIANTS	21	Hartford	0
	7	Providence	6
	0	Chicago Bears	7
	0	Frankford	6
	0	Frankford	6
	13	Kansas City	0
	20	Chicago Cards	0
	14	Duluth	13
	0	Los Angeles	6
	21	Providence	0
	17	Brooklyn	0
	27	Brooklyn	0
	140		44

Won 8, Lost 4, Tied 0.

1927
COACH—EARL POTTEIGER

N.Y. GIANTS	0	Cleveland	0
	19	Pottsville	0
	0	Cleveland	6
	13	Frankford	0
	27	Frankford	0
	16	Pottsville	0
	21	Duluth	0
	25	Providence	0
	19	Stapleton	0
	28	Chicago Cardinals	7
	18	Stapleton	0
	13	Chicago Bears	7
	14	N.Y. Yankees	0
	13	N.Y. Yankees	0
	226		20

Won 11, Lost 1, Tied 1. League Champion.

1928
COACH—EARL POTTEIGER

N.Y. GIANTS	7	Orange	0
	12	Pottsville	6
	6	Green Bay	6
	0	Chicago Bears	13
	0	Detroit	28
	10	N.Y. Yankees	7
	0	Frankford	0
	19	Detroit	19
	0	Green Bay	7
	0	Providence	16
	0	Stapleton	7
	13	N.Y. Yankees	19
	6	N.Y. Yankees	7
	73		135

Won 4, Lost 7, Tied 2.

1929
COACH—LEROY ANDREWS

N.Y. GIANTS	0	Orange	0
	7	Providence	0
	19	Stapleton	9
	32	Frankford	0
	19	Providence	0
	26	Chicago Bears	14
	45	Buffalo	6
	22	Orange	0
	34	Chicago Bears	0
	6	Green Bay	20
	21	Stapleton	7
	24	Chicago Cards	21
	12	Frankford	0
	31	Frankford	0
	318		77

Won 12, Lost 1, Tied 1.

1930
COACH—LEROY ANDREWS

N.Y. GIANTS	32	Newark	0
	27	Providence	7
	7	Green Bay	14
	12	Chicago Bears	0
	25	Chicago Cards	12
	53	Frankford	0
	25	Providence	0
	34	Newark	7
	9	Stapleton	7
	19	Portsmouth	6
	13	Chicago Bears	7
	13	Green Bay	6
	0	Chicago Bears	12
	6	Stapleton	7
	6	Brooklyn	7
	14	Frankford	6
	13	Brooklyn	0
	308		98

Won 13, Lost 4, Tied 0.

1931
COACH—STEPHEN OWEN

N.Y. GIANTS	14	Providence	6
	6	Portsmouth	14
	7	Green Bay	27
	0	Chicago Bears	6
	7	Stapleton	0
	27	Brooklyn	0
	14	Portsmouth	0
	13	Frankford	0
	6	Chicago Bears	12
	10	Green Bay	14
	6	Stapleton	9
	0	Providence	0
	19	Brooklyn	6
	25	Chicago Bears	6
	154		94

Won 6, Lost 6, Tied 1.

1932
COACH—STEPHEN OWEN

N.Y. GIANTS	6	Portsmouth	7
	0	Green Bay	13
	6	Boston	14
	20	Brooklyn	12
	0	Boston	0
	0	Portsmouth	6
	8	Chicago Bears	28
	27	Stapleton	7
	6	Green Bay	0
	13	Stapleton	13
	13	Brooklyn	7
	0	Chicago Bears	6
	——		——
	99		113

Won 4, Lost 6, Tied 2.

1933
COACH—STEPHEN OWEN

N.Y. GIANTS	23	Pittsburgh	2
	20	Boston	21
	10	Green Bay	7
	7	Portsmouth	17
	56	Philadelphia	0
	21	Brooklyn	7
	10	Chicago Bears	14
	13	Portsmouth	10
	7	Boston	0
	3	Chicago Bears	0
	17	Green Bay	6
	10	Brooklyn	0
	27	Pittsburgh	3
	20	Philadelphia	14
	——		——
	244		101

Won 11, Lost 3, Tied 0.
Championship Game:
N.Y. Giants 21   Chicago Bears 23

1934
COACH—STEPHEN OWEN

N.Y. GIANTS	0	Detroit	9
	6	Green Bay	20
	14	Pittsburgh	12
	16	Boston	13
	14	Brooklyn	0
	17	Philadelphia	0
	17	Philadelphia	7
	7	Chicago Bears	27
	17	Green Bay	3
	9	Chicago Bears	10
	3	Boston	0
	27	Brooklyn	0
	0	Philadelphia	6
	——		——
	147		107

Won 8, Lost 5, Tied 0.
Championship Game:
N.Y. Giants 30   Chicago Bears 13

1935
COACH—STEPHEN OWEN

| N.Y. GIANTS | 42 | Pittsburgh | 7 |
| | 7 | Green Bay | 16 |

N.Y. GIANTS	20	Boston	12
	10	Brooklyn	7
	17	Boston	6
	13	Chicago Cards	14
	3	Chicago Bears	20
	3	Chicago Bears	0
	10	Philadelphia	0
	21	Brooklyn	0
	21	Philadelphia	14
	13	Pittsburgh	0
	——		——
	170		96

Won 9, Lost 3, Tied 0.
Championship Game:
N.Y. Giants 7   Detroit Lions 26

1936
COACH—STEPHEN OWEN

N.Y. GIANTS	7	Philadelphia	10
	7	Pittsburgh	10
	7	Boston	0
	10	Brooklyn	10
	14	Chicago Cards	6
	21	Philadelphia	17
	14	Detroit	7
	7	Chicago Bears	25
	0	Detroit	38
	14	Green Bay	26
	14	Brooklyn	0
	0	Boston	14
	——		——
	115		163

Won 5, Lost 6, Tied 1.

1937
COACH—STEPHEN OWEN

N.Y. GIANTS	3	Washington	13
	10	Pittsburgh	7
	16	Philadelphia	7
	21	Philadelphia	0
	21	Brooklyn	0
	3	Chicago Bears	3
	17	Pittsburgh	0
	0	Detroit	17
	10	Green Bay	0
	13	Brooklyn	13
	14	Washington	49
	——		——
	128		109

Won 6, Lost 3, Tied 2.

1938
COACH—STEPHEN OWEN

N.Y. GIANTS	27	Pittsburgh	14
	10	Philadelphia	14
	10	Pittsburgh	13
	10	Washington	7
	17	Philadelphia	7
	28	Brooklyn	14
	6	Chicago Cards	0
	28	Cleveland	0
	15	Green Bay	3

1938 (cont.)

N.Y. GIANTS	7	Brooklyn	7
	36	Washington	0
	—		—
	194		78

Won 8, Lost 2, Tied 1.
Championship Game:
N.Y. Giants 23   Green Bay Packers 17

1939
COACH—STEPHEN OWEN

N.Y. GIANTS	13	Philadelphia	3
	0	Washington	0
	14	Pittsburgh	7
	27	Philadelphia	10
	16	Chicago Bears	13
	7	Brooklyn	6
	14	Detroit	18
	17	Chicago Cards	7
	23	Pittsburgh	7
	28	Brooklyn	7
	9	Washington	7
	—		—
	168		85

Won 9, Lost 1, Tied 1.
Championship Game:
N.Y. Giants 0   Green Bay Packers 27

1940
COACH—STEPHEN OWEN

N.Y. GIANTS	10	Pittsburgh	10
	7	Washington	21
	20	Philadelphia	14
	17	Philadelphia	7
	12	Pittsburgh	0
	21	Chicago Bears	37
	10	Brooklyn	7
	0	Cleveland	13
	7	Green Bay	3
	21	Washington	7
	6	Brooklyn	14
	—		—
	131		133

Won 6, Lost 4, Tied 1.

1941
COACH—STEPHEN OWEN

N.Y. GIANTS	24	Philadelphia	0
	17	Washington	10
	37	Pittsburgh	10
	16	Philadelphia	0
	28	Pittsburgh	7
	13	Brooklyn	16
	7	Chicago Cards	10
	20	Detroit	13
	49	Cleveland	14
	20	Washington	13
	7	Brooklyn	21
	—		—
	238		114

Won 8, Lost 3, Tied 0.
Championship Game:
N.Y. Giants 9   Chicago Bears 37

1942
COACH—STEPHEN OWEN

N.Y. GIANTS	14	Washington	7
	10	Pittsburgh	13
	35	Philadelphia	17
	7	Chicago Bears	26
	7	Brooklyn	17
	9	Pittsburgh	17
	14	Philadelphia	0
	7	Washington	14
	21	Green Bay	21
	21	Chicago Cards	7
	10	Brooklyn	0
	—		—
	155		139

Won 5, Lost 5, Tied 1.

1943
COACH—STEPHEN OWEN

N.Y. GIANTS	14	Phil-Pitt	28
	20	Brooklyn	0
	0	Detroit	0
	31	Washington	7
	42	Phil-Pitt	14
	21	Green Bay	35
	7	Chicago Bears	56
	24	Chicago Cards	13
	24	Brooklyn	7
	14	Washington	10
	—		—
	197		170

Won 6, Lost 3, Tied 1.
Divisional Play-off:
N.Y. Giants 0   Washington 28

1944
COACH—STEPHEN OWEN

N.Y. GIANTS	22	Boston	10
	14	Brooklyn	7
	23	Card-Pitt	0
	17	Philadelphia	24
	31	Boston	0
	21	Philadelphia	21
	24	Green Bay	0
	7	Brooklyn	0
	16	Washington	13
	31	Washington	0
	—		—
	206		75

Won 8, Lost 1, Tied 1.
Championship Game:
N.Y. Giants 7   Green Bay 14

1945
COACH—STEPHEN OWEN

N.Y. GIANTS	34	Pittsburgh	6
	13	Boston	13
	7	Pittsburgh	21
	14	Washington	24
	17	Cleveland	21
	17	Philadelphia	38
	35	Detroit	14
	14	Green Bay	23

N.Y. GIANTS	28	Philadelphia	21
	0	Washington	17
	___		___
	179		197

Won 3, Lost 6, Tied 1.

1946
COACH—STEPHEN OWEN

N.Y. GIANTS	17	Boston	0
	17	Pittsburgh	14
	14	Washington	24
	28	Chicago Cards	24
	14	Chicago Bears	0
	14	Philadelphia	28
	45	Philadelphia	17
	28	Boston	28
	7	Pittsburgh	0
	21	Los Angeles	31
	31	Washington	0
	___		___
	236		166

Won 7, Lost 3, Tied 1.
Championship Game:
N.Y. Giants 14   Chicago Bears 24

1947
COACH—STEPHEN OWEN

N.Y. GIANTS	7	Boston	7
	0	Philadelphia	23
	20	Washington	28
	0	Boston	14
	21	Pittsburgh	38
	7	Detroit	35
	24	Philadelphia	41
	7	Pittsburgh	24
	28	Green Bay	28
	35	Chicago Cards	31
	35	Washington	10
	10	Los Angeles	34
	___		___
	194		313

Won 2, Lost 8, Tied 2.

1948
COACH—STEPHEN OWEN

N.Y. GIANTS	27	Boston	7
	10	Washington	41
	0	Philadelphia	45
	35	Chicago Cards	63
	34	Pittsburgh	27
	14	Chicago Bears	35
	14	Philadelphia	35
	37	Los Angeles	52
	49	Green Bay	3
	28	Boston	14
	28	Pittsburgh	38
	21	Washington	28
	___		___
	287		388

Won 4, Lost 8, Tied 0.

1949
COACH—STEPHEN OWEN

N.Y. GIANTS	7	Pittsburgh	28
	38	N.Y. Bulldogs	14
	45	Washington	35
	17	Pittsburgh	21
	35	Chicago Bears	28
	41	Chicago Cards	38
	24	N.Y. Bulldogs	31
	30	Green Bay	10
	21	Detroit	45
	23	Washington	7
	3	Philadelphia	24
	3	Philadelphia	17
	___		___
	287		298

Won 6, Lost 6, Tied 0.

1950
COACH—STEPHEN OWEN

N.Y. GIANTS	18	Pittsburgh	7
	6	Cleveland	0
	21	Washington	17
	6	Pittsburgh	17
	17	Cleveland	13
	3	Chicago Cards	17
	24	Washington	21
	51	Chicago Cards	21
	55	Baltimore	20
	7	Philadelphia	3
	51	N.Y. Yanks	7
	9	Philadelphia	7
	___		___
	268		150

Won 10, Lost 2, Tied 0.
Divisional Play-off:
N.Y. Giants 3   Cleveland Browns 8

1951
COACH—STEPHEN OWEN

N.Y. GIANTS	13	Pittsburgh	13
	35	Washington	14
	28	Chicago Cards	17
	26	Philadelphia	24
	13	Cleveland	14
	37	N.Y. Yanks	31
	28	Washington	14
	0	Cleveland	10
	10	Chicago Cards	0
	14	Pittsburgh	0
	21	Philadelphia	7
	27	N.Y. Yanks	17
	___		___
	252		161

Won 9, Lost 2, Tied 1.

NEW YORK YANKS
(Formerly New York Bulldogs 1949; Boston Yanks 1944–48)

1944
COACH—HERB KOPF
BOSTON YANKS	7	Philadelphia	28
	10	New York	22
	14	Washington	21
	0	Philadelphia	38
	17	Brooklyn	14
	0	New York	31
	7	Bears	21
	13	Brooklyn	6
	7	Washington	14
	7	Detroit	38
	82		233

Won 2, Lost 8.

1945
COACH—HERB KOPF
BOSTON YANKS	28	Pittsburgh	7
	28	Washington	20
	13	New York	13
	14	Green Bay	38
	10	Pittsburgh	6
	9	Detroit	10
	7	Washington	34
	0	Green Bay	28
	7	Cleveland	20
	7	Philadelphia	35
	123		211

Won 3, Lost 6, Tied 1.

1946
COACH—HERB KOPF
BOSTON YANKS	0	New York	17
	25	Philadelphia	49
	7	Pittsburgh	16
	6	Washington	14
	7	Pittsburgh	33
	14	Cardinals	28
	14	Washington	17
	28	New York	28
	40	Los Angeles	21
	34	Detroit	10
	14	Philadelphia	40
	189		273

Won 2, Lost 8, Tied 1.

1947
COACH—MAURICE J. SMITH
BOSTON YANKS	7	New York	21
	7	Detroit	7
	14	Pittsburgh	30
	14	New York	0
	7	Cardinals	27
	24	Bears	28
	27	Los Angeles	16
	0	Philadelphia	32
	21	Philadelphia	21
	27	Washington	24

BOSTON YANKS	7	Pittsburgh	17
	13	Washington	40
	168		256

Won 4, Lost 7, Tied 1.

1948
COACH—MAURICE J. SMITH
BOSTON YANKS	0	Green Bay	31
	7	New York	27
	14	Pittsburgh	24
	17	Detroit	14
	13	Pittsburgh	7
	27	Cardinals	49
	21	Washington	59
	7	Washington	23
	0	Philadelphia	45
	17	Bears	51
	14	New York	28
	37	Philadelphia	14
	174		372

Won 3, Lost 9.

1949
COACH—CHARLES D. EWART
N.Y. BULLDOGS	0	Philadelphia	7
	14	N.Y. Giants	38
	0	Green Bay	19
	14	Washington	38
	13	Pittsburgh	24
	14	Washington	14
	31	N.Y. Giants	24
	20	Cardinals	65
	0	Philadelphia	42
	20	Los Angeles	42
	27	Detroit	28
	0	Pittsburgh	27
	153		368

Won 1, Lost 10, Tied 1.

1950
COACH—NORMAN STRADER
N.Y. YANKS	21	San Francisco	17
	28	Los Angeles	45
	44	Detroit	21
	44	Green Bay	31
	29	San Francisco	24
	35	Green Bay	17
	38	Bears	27
	20	Bears	28
	35	Los Angeles	43
	14	Detroit	49
	7	N.Y. Giants	51
	51	Baltimore	14
	366		367

Won 7, Lost 5.

1951
COACH—JAMES PHELAN
N.Y. YANKS	14	Los Angeles	54
	10	Detroit	37
	21	Chicago Bears	24
	24	Detroit	24

N.Y. YANKS	27	Green Bay	29
	31	N.Y. Giants	37
	14	San Francisco	19
	21	Los Angeles	48
	10	San Francisco	10
	31	Green Bay	28
	21	Chicago Bears	45
	17	N.Y. Giants	27
	---		---
	241		382

Won 1, Lost 9, Tied 2.

PHILADELPHIA

1933
COACH—LUDLOW WRAY

PHILADELPHIA	0	New York	56
	0	Portsmouth	25
	9	Green Bay	35
	6	Cincinnati	0
	3	Bears	3
	25	Pittsburgh	6
	20	Cincinnati	3
	0	Green Bay	10
	14	New York	20
	---		---
	77		158

Won 3, Lost 5, Tied 1.

1934
COACH—LUDLOW WRAY

PHILADELPHIA	6	Green Bay	19
	17	Pittsburgh	0
	7	Pittsburgh	9
	0	Detroit	10
	0	Boston	6
	0	New York	17
	64	Cincinnati	0
	7	Brooklyn	10
	7	Boston	14
	13	Brooklyn	0
	6	New York	0
	---		---
	127		85

Won 4, Lost 7.

1935
COACH—LUDLOW WRAY

PHILADELPHIA	7	Pittsburgh	17
	0	Detroit	35
	17	Pittsburgh	6
	0	Bears	39
	6	Brooklyn	17
	7	Boston	6
	0	Brooklyn	3
	3	Cardinals	12
	0	New York	10
	14	New York	21
	6	Green Bay	13
	---		---
	60		179

Won 2, Lost 9.

1936
COACH—LUDLOW WRAY

PHILADELPHIA	7	Brooklyn	13
	10	New York	7
	3	Boston	26
	0	Bears	17
	0	Brooklyn	18
	0	Detroit	23
	0	Pittsburgh	17
	7	Boston	17
	17	New York	21
	0	Pittsburgh	6
	0	Cardinals	13
	7	Bears	28
	---		---
	51		206

Won 1, Lost 11.

1937
COACH—LUDLOW WRAY

PHILADELPHIA	14	Pittsburgh	27
	7	Brooklyn	13
	3	Cleveland	21
	6	Cardinals	6
	7	New York	16
	14	Washington	0
	0	New York	21
	7	Washington	10
	7	Pittsburgh	16
	14	Brooklyn	10
	7	Green Bay	37
	---		---
	86		177

Won 2, Lost 8, Tied 1.

1938
COACH—BERT BELL

PHILADELPHIA	23	Washington	26
	27	Pittsburgh	7
	14	New York	10
	6	Bears	28
	7	New York	17
	14	Washington	20
	7	Cardinals	0
	7	Brooklyn	10
	14	Brooklyn	32
	14	Pittsburgh	7
	21	Detroit	7
	---		---
	154		164

Won 5, Lost 6.

1939
COACH—BERT BELL

PHILADELPHIA	0	Washington	7
	3	New York	13
	0	Brooklyn	0
	10	New York	27
	14	Brooklyn	23
	6	Washington	7
	16	Green Bay	23
	14	Bears	27
	17	Pittsburgh	14

1939 (cont.)

PHILADELPHIA	12	Pittsburgh	24
	13	Cleveland	35
	—		—
	105		200

Won 1, Lost 9, Tied 1.

1940
COACH—BERT BELL

PHILADELPHIA	20	Green Bay	27
	13	Cleveland	21
	14	New York	20
	17	Brooklyn	30
	7	New York	17
	17	Washington	34
	7	Brooklyn	21
	3	Pittsburgh	7
	0	Detroit	21
	7	Pittsburgh	0
	6	Washington	13
	—		—
	111		211

Won 1, Lost 10.

1941
COACH—EARLE NEALE

PHILADELPHIA	0	New York	24
	10	Pittsburgh	7
	13	Brooklyn	24
	0	New York	16
	17	Washington	21
	21	Cardinals	14
	6	Brooklyn	15
	7	Pittsburgh	7
	17	Detroit	21
	14	Bears	49
	14	Washington	20
	—		—
	119		218

Won 2, Lost 8, Tied 1.

1942
COACH—EARLE NEALE

PHILADELPHIA	24	Pittsburgh	14
	14	Cleveland	24
	14	Brooklyn	35
	10	Washington	14
	17	New York	35
	0	Pittsburgh	14
	14	Bears	45
	27	Washington	30
	0	New York	14
	14	Brooklyn	7
	0	Green Bay	7
	—		—
	134		239

Won 2, Lost 9.

1943
COACHES—EARLE NEALE,
    W. KIESLING

PHIL-PITT (COMBINE)	17	Brooklyn	0
	28	New York	14
	34	Cardinals	13
	21	Bears	48

PHIL-PITT (COMBINE)	14	New York	42
	14	Washington	14
	7	Brooklyn	13
	35	Detroit	34
	27	Washington	14
	28	Green Bay	38
	—		—
	225		230

Won 5, Lost 4, Tied 1.

1944
COACH—EARLE NEALE

PHILADELPHIA	28	Boston	7
	31	Washington	31
	38	Boston	0
	24	New York	17
	21	Brooklyn	7
	21	New York	21
	37	Washington	7
	7	Bears	28
	34	Brooklyn	0
	26	Cleveland	13
	—		—
	267		131

Won 7, Lost 1, Tied 2.

1945
COACH—EARLE NEALE

PHILADELPHIA	21	Cardinals	6
	24	Detroit	28
	14	Washington	24
	28	Cleveland	14
	45	Pittsburgh	3
	38	New York	17
	30	Pittsburgh	6
	16	Washington	0
	21	New York	28
	35	Boston	7
	—		—
	272		133

Won 7, Lost 3.

1946
COACH—EARLE NEALE

PHILADELPHIA	25	Los Angeles	14
	49	Boston	25
	7	Green Bay	19
	14	Bears	21
	28	Washington	24
	24	New York	14
	17	New York	45
	7	Pittsburgh	10
	10	Washington	27
	10	Pittsburgh	7
	40	Boston	14
	—		—
	231		220

Won 6, Lost 5.

1947
COACH—EARLE NEALE

PHILADELPHIA	45	Washington	42
	23	New York	0
	7	Bears	40
	24	Pittsburgh	35

PHILADELPHIA	14	Los Angeles	7
	38	Washington	14
	41	New York	24
	32	Boston	0
	14	Boston	21
	21	Pittsburgh	0
	21	Cardinals	45
	28	Green Bay	14
	308		242

Won 8, Lost 4.
Divisional Play-off:
Philadelphia 21   Pittsburgh 0
Championship Game:
Philadelphia 21   Cardinals 28

1948
COACH—EARLE NEALE

PHILADELPHIA	14	Cardinals	21
	28	Los Angeles	28
	45	New York	0
	45	Washington	0
	12	Bears	7
	34	Pittsburgh	7
	35	New York	14
	45	Boston	0
	42	Washington	21
	17	Pittsburgh	0
	14	Boston	37
	45	Detroit	21
	376		156

Won 9, Lost 2, Tied 1.
Championship Game:
Philadelphia 7   Cardinals 0

1949
COACH—EARLE NEALE

PHILADELPHIA	7	N.Y. Bulldogs	0
	22	Detroit	14
	28	Cardinals	3
	21	Bears	38
	49	Washington	14
	38	Pittsburgh	7
	38	Los Angeles	14
	44	Washington	21
	42	N.Y. Bulldogs	0
	34	Pittsburgh	17
	24	N.Y. Giants	3
	17	N.Y. Giants	3
	364		134

Won 11, Lost 1.
Championship Game:
Philadelphia 14   Los Angeles 0

1950
COACH—EARLE NEALE

PHILADELPHIA	10	Cleveland	35
	45	Cardinals	7
	56	Los Angeles	20
	24	Baltimore	14
	17	Pittsburgh	10
	35	Washington	3
	7	Pittsburgh	9

PHILADELPHIA	33	Washington	0
	10	Cardinals	14
	3	N.Y. Giants	7
	7	Cleveland	13
	7	N.Y. Giants	9
	254		141

Won 6, Lost 6.

1951
COACH—ALVIN N. McMILLIN to 10/10/51; WAYNE MILLNER

PHILADELPHIA	17	Chicago Cards	14
	21	San Francisco	14
	24	Green Bay	37
	24	N.Y. Giants	26
	23	Washington	27
	34	Pittsburgh	13
	17	Cleveland	20
	10	Detroit	28
	13	Pittsburgh	17
	35	Washington	21
	7	N.Y. Giants	21
	9	Cleveland	24
	234		262

Won 4, Lost 8.

PITTSBURGH

1933
COACH—FOREST DOUDS

PITTSBURGH	3	Brooklyn	3
	0	Brooklyn	32
	14	Cardinals	13
	0	Green Bay	47
	2	New York	23
	3	New York	27
	6	Philadelphia	25
	6	Boston	21
	16	Boston	14
	50		205

Won 3, Lost 6, Tied 2.

1934
COACH—LUBY DiMELIO

PITTSBURGH	13	Cincinnati	0
	0	Boston	7
	0	Philadelphia	17
	12	New York	14
	9	Philadelphia	7
	0	Bears	28
	0	Boston	39
	7	New York	17
	3	Brooklyn	21
	7	Detroit	40
	0	St. Louis	6
	0	Brooklyn	10
	53		206

Won 2, Lost 10.

1935
COACH—JOSEPH BACH

PITTSBURGH	17	Philadelphia	7
	7	New York	42
	7	Bears	23
	0	Green Bay	27
	6	Philadelphia	17
	17	Cardinals	13
	6	Boston	0
	7	Brooklyn	13
	16	Brooklyn	7
	14	Green Bay	34
	3	Boston	13
	0	New York	13
	—		—
	100		209

Won 4, Lost 8.

1936
COACH—JOSEPH BACH

PITTSBURGH	10	Boston	0
	10	Brooklyn	6
	10	New York	7
	9	Bears	27
	17	Philadelphia	0
	7	Bears	26
	10	Green Bay	42
	10	Brooklyn	7
	6	Philadelphia	0
	3	Detroit	28
	6	Cardinals	14
	0	Boston	30
	—		—
	98		187

Won 6, Lost 6.

1937
COACH—JOHN (BLOOD) McNALLY

PITTSBURGH	27	Philadelphia	14
	21	Brooklyn	0
	7	New York	10
	0	Bears	7
	3	Detroit	7
	20	Washington	34
	7	Cardinals	13
	16	Philadelphia	7
	0	New York	17
	21	Washington	13
	0	Brooklyn	23
	—		—
	122		145

Won 4, Lost 7.

1938
COACH—JOHN (BLOOD) McNALLY

PITTSBURGH	7	Detroit	16
	14	New York	27
	7	Philadelphia	27
	17	Brooklyn	3
	13	New York	10
	7	Brooklyn	17
	0	Green Bay	20
	0	Washington	7
	7	Philadelphia	14

PITTSBURGH	0	Washington	15
	7	Cleveland	13
	—		—
	79		169

Won 2, Lost 9.

1939
COACHES—JOHN McNALLY, WALTER KIESLING

PITTSBURGH	7	Brooklyn	12
	0	Cardinals	10
	0	Bears	32
	7	New York	14
	14	Washington	44
	14	Washington	21
	14	Cleveland	14
	13	Brooklyn	17
	7	New York	23
	14	Philadelphia	17
	24	Philadelphia	12
	—		—
	114		216

Won 1, Lost 9, Tied 1.

1940
COACH—WALTER KIESLING

PITTSBURGH	7	Cardinals	7
	10	New York	10
	10	Detroit	7
	3	Brooklyn	10
	10	Washington	40
	0	Brooklyn	21
	0	New York	12
	3	Green Bay	24
	10	Washington	37
	7	Philadelphia	3
	0	Philadelphia	7
	—		—
	60		178

Won 2, Lost 7, Tied 2.

1941
COACHES—BERT BELL, ALDO DONELLI, WALTER KIESLING

PITTSBURGH	14	Cleveland	17
	7	Philadelphia	10
	10	New York	37
	20	Washington	24
	7	New York	28
	7	Bears	34
	3	Washington	23
	7	Philadelphia	7
	14	Brooklyn	7
	7	Green Bay	54
	7	Brooklyn	35
	—		—
	103		276

Won 1, Lost 9, Tied 1.

1942
COACH—WALTER KIESLING

PITTSBURGH	14	Philadelphia	24
	14	Washington	24
	13	New York	10
	7	Brooklyn	0

PITTSBURGH	14	Philadelphia	0
	0	Washington	14
	17	New York	9
	35	Detroit	7
	19	Cardinals	3
	13	Brooklyn	0
	21	Green Bay	24
	167		115

Won 7, Lost 4.

1943
CO-COACHES—EARLE NEALE,
W. KIESLING

PHIL-PITT	17	Brooklyn	0
(STEAGLES)	28	New York	14
	21	Bears	48
	14	New York	42
	34	Cardinals	14
	14	Washington	14
	7	Brooklyn	13
	35	Detroit	34
	27	Washington	14
	28	Green Bay	38
	225		230

Won 5, Lost 4, Tied 1.

1944
CO-COACHES—PHIL HANDLER,
W. KIESLING

CARD-PITT	28	Cleveland	30
(COMBINE)	7	Green Bay	34
	7	Bears	34
	0	New York	23
	20	Washington	42
	6	Detroit	27
	7	Detroit	21
	0	Cleveland	33
	7	Bears	49
	6	Cleveland	33
	20	Green Bay	35
	108		328

Won 0, Lost 10.

1945
COACH—JAMES LEONARD

PITTSBURGH	7	Boston	28
	6	New York	34
	0	Washington	14
	21	New York	7
	6	Boston	10
	23	Cardinals	0
	6	Philadelphia	30
	7	Bears	28
	0	Washington	24
	79		220

Won 2, Lost 8.

1946
COACH—DR. JOHN B. SUTHERLAND

PITTSBURGH	14	Washington	14
	14	New York	17

PITTSBURGH	16	Boston	7
	7	Green Bay	17
	33	Boston	7
	14	Washington	7
	7	Detroit	17
	0	New York	7
	7	Philadelphia	10
	14	Cardinals	7
	10	Philadelphia	7
	136		117

Won 5, Lost 5.

1947
COACH—DR. JOHN B. SUTHERLAND

PITTSBURGH	17	Detroit	10
	7	Los Angeles	48
	26	Washington	27
	30	Boston	14
	35	Philadelphia	24
	38	New York	21
	18	Green Bay	17
	21	Washington	14
	24	New York	7
	7	Bears	49
	0	Philadelphia	21
	17	Boston	7
	0	Philadelphia	21
	240		259

Won 8, Lost 4.

1948
COACH—JOHN P. MICHELOSEN

PITTSBURGH	14	Washington	17
	24	Boston	14
	10	Washington	7
	7	Boston	13
	27	New York	34
	7	Philadelphia	34
	38	Green Bay	7
	7	Cardinals	24
	14	Detroit	17
	0	Philadelphia	17
	38	New York	28
	14	Los Angeles	31
	200		243

Won 4, Lost 8.

1949
COACH—JOHN P. MICHELOSEN

PITTSBURGH	28	N.Y. Giants	7
	14	Washington	27
	14	Detroit	7
	21	N.Y. Giants	17
	24	N.Y. Bulldogs	13
	7	Philadelphia	38
	14	Washington	27
	7	Los Angeles	7
	30	Green Bay	7
	17	Philadelphia	34
	21	Bears	30
	27	N.Y. Bulldogs	0
	224		214

Won 6, Lost 5, Tied 1.

1950
COACH—JOHN P. MICHELOSEN

PITTSBURGH	7	N.Y. Giants	18
	7	Detroit	10
	26	Washington	7
	17	Cleveland	30
	17	N.Y. Giants	6
	10	Philadelphia	17
	7	Cleveland	45
	9	Philadelphia	7
	17	Baltimore	7
	28	Cardinals	17
	7	Washington	24
	28	Cardinals	7
	—		—
	180		195

Won 6, Lost 6.

1951
COACH—JOHN P. MICHELOSEN

PITTSBURGH	13	N.Y. Giants	13
	33	Green Bay	35
	24	San Francisco	28
	0	Cleveland	17
	28	Chicago Cards	14
	13	Philadelphia	34
	28	Green Bay	7
	7	Washington	22
	17	Philadelphia	13
	0	N.Y. Giants	14
	0	Cleveland	28
	20	Washington	10
	—		—
	183		235

Won 4, Lost 7, Tied 1.

SAN FRANCISCO
(Formerly AAFC; entered NFL 1950)

1950
COACH—LAWRENCE SHAW

SAN FRANCISCO	20	Bears	32
	14	Cleveland	31
	7	Detroit	24
	21	Green Bay	25
	14	Los Angeles	35
	17	N.Y. Yanks	21
	17	Baltimore	14
	0	Bears	17
	28	Detroit	27
	30	Green Bay	14
	21	Los Angeles	28
	25	N.Y. Yanks	29
	—		—
	213		300

Won 3, Lost 9.

1951
COACH—LAWRENCE SHAW

SAN FRANCISCO	24	Cleveland	10
	14	Philadelphia	21
	28	Pittsburgh	24
	7	Chicago Bears	13
	44	Los Angeles	17

SAN FRANCISCO	16	Los Angeles	23
	19	N.Y. Yanks	14
	21	Chicago Cards	27
	10	N.Y. Yanks	10
	20	Detroit	10
	31	Green Bay	19
	21	Detroit	17
	—		—
	255		205

Won 7, Lost, 4, Tied 1.

WASHINGTON REDSKINS
(Formerly Boston Redskins 1932–1936)

1932
COACH—LUDLOW WRAY

BOSTON	0	Brooklyn	14
	7	Bears	7
	0	Cardinals	9
	6	New York	14
	7	Brooklyn	0
	0	Green Bay	21
	0	Pittsburgh	10
	0	Cardinals	9
	0	New York	0
	—		—
	20		84

Won 1, Lost 6, Tied 2.

1933
COACH—WILLIAM DIETZ

BOSTON	7	Green Bay	7
	0	Bears	7
	21	Pittsburgh	6
	21	New York	20
	0	Portsmouth	13
	10	Cardinals	0
	14	Pittsburgh	16
	10	Bears	0
	0	New York	7
	20	Green Bay	7
	0	Brooklyn	14
	0	Cardinals	0
	—		—
	103		97

Won 5, Lost 5, Tied 2.

1934
COACH—WILLIAM DIETZ

BOSTON	7	Pittsburgh	0
	6	Brooklyn	15
	13	New York	16
	39	Pittsburgh	0
	0	Detroit	24
	6	Philadelphia	0
	9	Cardinals	0
	0	Green Bay	10
	0	Bears	21
	14	Philadelphia	7
	0	New York	3
	13	Brooklyn	3
	—		—
	107		99

Won 6, Lost 6, Tied 0.

1935
COACH—EDWARD CASEY

BOSTON	7	Brooklyn	3
	14	Bears	30
	12	New York	20
	0	Cardinals	6
	0	Pittsburgh	6
	7	Detroit	17
	0	Brooklyn	0
	6	New York	17
	6	Philadelphia	7
	13	Pittsburgh	3
	65		109

Won 2, Lost 7, Tied 1.

1936
COACH—RAY FLAHERTY

BOSTON	0	Pittsburgh	10
	26	Philadelphia	3
	14	Brooklyn	3
	0	New York	7
	2	Green Bay	31
	17	Philadelphia	7
	13	Cardinals	10
	3	Green Bay	7
	0	Bears	26
	30	Brooklyn	6
	30	Pittsburgh	0
	14	New York	0
	149		110

Won 7, Lost 4, Tied 0.

1937
COACH—RAY FLAHERTY

WASHINGTON	13	New York	3
	14	Cardinals	21
	11	Brooklyn	7
	0	Philadelphia	14
	34	Pittsburgh	20
	10	Philadelphia	7
	21	Brooklyn	0
	13	Pittsburgh	21
	16	Cleveland	7
	14	Green Bay	6
	49	New York	14
	195		120

Won 8, Lost 3.
Championship Game:
Washington 28   Bears 21

1938
COACH—RAY FLAHERTY

WASHINGTON	26	Philadelphia	23
	16	Brooklyn	16
	37	Cleveland	13
	7	New York	10
	7	Detroit	5
	20	Philadelphia	14
	6	Brooklyn	6
	7	Pittsburgh	0
	7	Bears	31

WASHINGTON	15	Pittsburgh	0
	0	New York	36
	148		154

Won 6, Lost 3, Tied 2.

1939
COACH—RAY FLAHERTY

WASHINGTON	7	Philadelphia	0
	0	New York	0
	41	Brooklyn	13
	44	Pittsburgh	14
	21	Pittsburgh	14
	14	Green Bay	24
	7	Philadelphia	6
	42	Brooklyn	0
	28	Cardinals	7
	31	Detroit	7
	7	New York	9
	242		94

Won 8, Lost 2, Tied 1.

1940
COACH—RAY FLAHERTY

WASHINGTON	24	Brooklyn	17
	21	New York	7
	40	Pittsburgh	10
	28	Cardinals	21
	20	Detroit	14
	20	Philadelphia	17
	37	Pittsburgh	10
	14	Brooklyn	16
	7	Bears	3
	7	New York	21
	13	Philadelphia	6
	245		142

Won 9, Lost 2.
Championship Game:
Washington 0   Bears 73

1941
COACH—RAY FLAHERTY

WASHINGTON	10	New York	17
	3	Brooklyn	0
	24	Pittsburgh	20
	21	Philadelphia	17
	17	Cleveland	13
	23	Pittsburgh	3
	7	Brooklyn	13
	21	Bears	35
	13	New York	20
	17	Green Bay	22
	20	Philadelphia	14
	176		174

Won 6, Lost 5.

1942
COACH—RAY FLAHERTY

WASHINGTON	28	Pittsburgh	14
	7	New York	14
	14	Philadelphia	10
	33	Cleveland	14

1942 (cont.)

WASHINGTON	21	Brooklyn	10
	30	Philadelphia	27
	14	Pittsburgh	0
	28	Cardinals	0
	14	New York	7
	23	Brooklyn	3
	15	Detroit	3
	227		102

Won 10, Lost 1.
Championship Game:
Washington 14   Bears 6

1943
COACH—ARTHUR BERGMAN

WASHINGTON	27	Brooklyn	0
	33	Green Bay	7
	13	Cardinals	7
	48	Brooklyn	10
	14	Phil-Pitt	14
	42	Detroit	20
	21	Bears	7
	14	Phil-Pitt	27
	10	New York	14
	7	New York	31
	28	New York	0
	257		137

Won 7, Lost 3, Tied 1.
Championship Game:
Washington 21   Bears 41

1944
COACH—DUDLEY DeGROOT

WASHINGTON	31	Philadelphia	31
	21	Boston	14
	17	Brooklyn	14
	42	Card-Pitt	20
	14	Cleveland	10
	10	Brooklyn	0
	7	Philadelphia	37
	14	Boston	7
	13	New York	16
	0	New York	31
	169		184

Won 6, Lost 3, Tied 1.

1945
COACH—DUDLEY DeGROOT

WASHINGTON	20	Boston	28
	14	Pittsburgh	0
	24	Philadelphia	14
	24	New York	14
	24	Cardinals	21
	34	Boston	7
	28	Bears	21
	0	Philadelphia	16
	24	Pittsburgh	0
	17	New York	0
	209		121

Won 8, Lost 2.
Championship Game:
Washington 14   Cleveland 15

1946
COACH—A. GLENN EDWARDS

WASHINGTON	14	Pittsburgh	14
	17	Detroit	16
	24	New York	14
	14	Philadelphia	28
	24	Boston	6
	7	Pittsburgh	14
	17	Boston	14
	20	Bears	24
	27	Philadelphia	10
	7	Green Bay	20
	0	New York	31
	171		191

Won 5, Lost 5, Tied 1.

1947
COACH—A. GLENN EDWARDS

WASHINGTON	42	Philadelphia	45
	27	Pittsburgh	26
	28	New York	20
	10	Green Bay	27
	20	Bears	56
	14	Philadelphia	38
	14	Pittsburgh	21
	21	Detroit	38
	45	Cardinals	21
	24	Boston	27
	10	New York	35
	40	Boston	14
	295		367

Won 4, Lost 8.

1948
COACH—A. GLENN EDWARDS

WASHINGTON	17	Pittsburgh	14
	41	New York	10
	7	Pittsburgh	10
	0	Philadelphia	45
	23	Green Bay	7
	59	Boston	21
	23	Boston	7
	46	Detroit	21
	21	Philadelphia	42
	13	Bears	48
	13	Los Angeles	41
	28	New York	21
	291		287

Won 7, Lost 5.

1949
COACH—JOHN E. WHELCHEL to
11/7/49—HERMAN BALL

WASHINGTON	7	Cardinals	38
	27	Pittsburgh	14
	35	N.Y. Giants	45
	38	N.Y. Bulldogs	14
	14	Philadelphia	49

WASHINGTON	14	N.Y. Bulldogs	14
	27	Pittsburgh	14
	21	Philadelphia	44
	21	Bears	31
	7	N.Y. Giants	23
	30	Green Bay	0
	27	Los Angeles	53
	—		—
	268		339

Won 4, Lost 7, Tied 1.

1950
COACH—HERMAN BALL

WASHINGTON	35	Baltimore	14
	21	Green Bay	35
	7	Pittsburgh	26
	17	N.Y. Giants	21
	28	Cardinals	38
	3	Philadelphia	35
	21	N.Y. Giants	24
	0	Philadelphia	33
	14	Cleveland	20
	38	Baltimore	28
	24	Pittsburgh	7

WASHINGTON	21	Cleveland	45
	—		—
	229		326

Won 3, Lost 9.

1951
COACH—HERMAN BALL to 10/19/51
RICHARD TODD

WASHINGTON	17	Detroit	35
	14	N.Y. Giants	35
	0	Cleveland	45
	7	Chicago Cards	3
	27	Philadelphia	23
	0	Chicago Bears	27
	14	N.Y. Giants	28
	22	Pittsburgh	7
	31	Los Angeles	21
	21	Philadelphia	35
	20	Chicago Cards	17
	10	Pittsburgh	20
	—		—
	183		296

Won 5, Lost 7.

TEAM vs TEAM RECORDS

CHICAGO BEARS vs
CHICAGO CARDINALS

1920	Cardinals	7	Bears	6
	Bears	10	Cardinals	0
1921	Cardinals	0	Bears	0
1922	Cardinals	6	Bears	0
	Cardinals	9	Bears	0
1923	Bears	3	Cardinals	0
1924	Bears	6	Cardinals	0
	Bears	21	Cardinals	0
1925	Cardinals	9	Bears	0
	Cardinals	0	Bears	0
1926	Bears	16	Cardinals	0
	Bears	0	Cardinals	0
1927	Bears	10	Cardinals	0
	Cardinals	3	Bears	0
1928	Bears	13	Cardinals	0
	Bears	34	Cardinals	0
1929	Cardinals	0	Bears	0
	Cardinals	40	Bears	6
1930	Bears	32	Cardinals	6
	Bears	6	Cardinals	0
	Bears	9	Cardinals	7
1931	Bears	26	Cardinals	13
	Bears	18	Cardinals	7
1932	Bears	0	Cardinals	0
	Bears	34	Cardinals	0
1933	Bears	12	Cardinals	9
	Bears	22	Cardinals	6
1934	Bears	20	Cardinals	0
	Bears	17	Cardinals	6
1935	Bears	7	Cardinals	7
	Bears	13	Cardinals	0

1936	Bears	7	Cardinals	3
	Cardinals	14	Bears	7
1937	Bears	16	Cardinals	7
	Bears	42	Cardinals	28
1938	Bears	16	Cardinals	13
	Bears	34	Cardinals	28
1939	Bears	44	Cardinals	7
	Bears	48	Cardinals	7
1940	Cardinals	21	Bears	7
	Bears	31	Cardinals	23
1941	Bears	53	Cardinals	7
	Bears	34	Cardinals	24
1942	Bears	41	Cardinals	14
	Bears	21	Cardinals	7
1943	Bears	20	Cardinals	0
	Bears	35	Cardinals	24
1944	Cardinals combined with Pittsburgh			
1945	Cardinals	16	Bears	7
	Bears	28	Cardinals	20
1946	Bears	34	Cardinals	17
	Cardinals	35	Bears	28
1947	Cardinals	31	Bears	7
	Cardinals	30	Bears	21
1948	Bears	28	Cardinals	17
	Cardinals	24	Bears	21
1949	Bears	17	Cardinals	7
	Bears	52	Cardinals	21
1950	Bears	27	Cardinals	6
	Cardinals	20	Bears	10
1951	Cardinals	28	Bears	14
	Cardinals	24	Bears	14

Bears won 39; Cardinals won 16; Tied 6.

Total points: Bears 1,105; Cards 658.

CHICAGO BEARS vs DETROIT LIONS

1934	Bears	19	Detroit	16
	Bears	10	Detroit	7
1935	Detroit	20	Bears	20
	Detroit	14	Bears	2
1936	Bears	12	Detroit	10
	Detroit	13	Bears	7
1937	Bears	28	Detroit	20
	Bears	13	Detroit	0
1938	Detroit	13	Bears	7
	Detroit	14	Bears	7
1939	Detroit	10	Bears	0
	Bears	23	Detroit	13
1940	Bears	7	Detroit	0
	Detroit	17	Bears	14
1941	Bears	49	Detroit	0
	Bears	24	Detroit	7
1942	Bears	16	Detroit	0
	Bears	42	Detroit	0
1943	Bears	27	Detroit	21
	Bears	35	Detroit	14
1944	Detroit	21	Bears	21
	Detroit	41	Bears	21
1945	Detroit	16	Bears	10
	Detroit	35	Bears	28
1946	Bears	42	Detroit	6
	Bears	45	Detroit	24
1947	Bears	33	Detroit	24
	Bears	34	Detroit	14
1948	Bears	28	Detroit	0
	Bears	42	Detroit	14
1949	Bears	27	Detroit	24
	Bears	28	Detroit	7
1950	Bears	35	Detroit	21
	Bears	6	Detroit	3
1951	Bears	28	Detroit	23
	Bears	28	Detroit	41

Bears won 24; Detroit won 10; Tied 2.

Total points: Bears 818; Detroit 523.

CHICAGO BEARS vs GREEN BAY PACKERS

1921	Bears	20	Green Bay	0
1923	Bears	3	Green Bay	0
1924	Green Bay	5	Bears	0
	Bears	3	Green Bay	0
1925	Green Bay	14	Bears	10
	Bears	21	Green Bay	0
1926	Green Bay	6	Bears	6
	Bears	19	Green Bay	13
	Green Bay	3	Bears	3
1927	Bears	7	Green Bay	6
	Bears	14	Green Bay	6
1928	Green Bay	12	Bears	12
	Green Bay	16	Bears	6
	Green Bay	6	Bears	0
1929	Green Bay	23	Bears	0
	Green Bay	14	Bears	0
	Green Bay	25	Bears	0
1930	Green Bay	7	Bears	0
	Green Bay	13	Bears	12

	Bears	21	Green Bay	0
1931	Green Bay	7	Bears	0
	Green Bay	6	Bears	2
	Bears	7	Green Bay	6
1932	Green Bay	0	Bears	0
	Green Bay	2	Bears	0
	Bears	9	Green Bay	0
1933	Bears	14	Green Bay	7
	Bears	10	Green Bay	7
	Bears	7	Green Bay	6
1934	Bears	24	Green Bay	10
	Bears	27	Green Bay	14
	†Bears	10	Green Bay	6
1935	Green Bay	7	Bears	0
	Green Bay	17	Bears	14
1936	Bears	30	Green Bay	3
	Green Bay	21	Bears	10
1937	Bears	14	Green Bay	2
	Green Bay	24	Bears	14
1938	Bears	2	Green Bay	0
	Green Bay	24	Bears	17
1939	Green Bay	21	Bears	16
	Bears	30	Green Bay	27
1940	Bears	41	Green Bay	10
	Bears	14	Green Bay	7
1941	Bears	25	Green Bay	17
	Green Bay	16	Bears	14
	*Bears	33	Green Bay	14
1942	Bears	44	Green Bay	28
	Bears	38	Green Bay	7
1943	Green Bay	21	Bears	21
	Bears	21	Green Bay	7
1944	Green Bay	42	Bears	28
	Bears	21	Green Bay	0
1945	Green Bay	31	Bears	21
	Bears	28	Green Bay	24
1946	Bears	30	Green Bay	7
	Bears	10	Green Bay	7
1947	Green Bay	29	Bears	20
	Bears	20	Green Bay	17
1948	Bears	45	Green Bay	7
	Bears	7	Green Bay	6
1949	Bears	17	Green Bay	0
	Bears	24	Green Bay	3
1950	Green Bay	31	Bears	21
	Bears	28	Green Bay	14
1951	Bears	31	Green Bay	20
	Bears	24	Green Bay	13

Bears won 38; Green Bay won 23; Tied 5.

Total points: Bears, 1,030; Green Bay 758.

* Divisional Play-off
† Non-Championship Game

CHICAGO BEARS vs LOS ANGELES RAMS

1946	Los Angeles	28	Bears	28
	Bears	27	Los Angeles	21
1947	Bears	41	Los Angeles	21
	Los Angeles	17	Bears	14
1948	Bears	42	Los Angeles	21
	Bears	21	Los Angeles	6
1949	Los Angeles	31	Bears	16

1949	Los Angeles	27	Bears	24
1950	Bears	24	Los Angeles	20
	Bears	24	Los Angeles	14
	*Los Angeles	24	Bears	14
1951	Los Angeles	42	Bears	17

Bears won 6; Los Angeles won 5; Tied 1.

Total points: Bears 292; Los Angeles 272.

* Conference Play-off Game

CHICAGO BEARS vs NEW YORK GIANTS

1925	Bears	19	New York	7
	New York	9	Bears	0
1926	Bears	7	New York	0
1927	New York	13	Bears	7
1928	Bears	13	New York	0
1929	New York	26	Bears	14
	New York	14	Bears	9
	New York	34	Bears	0
1930	New York	12	Bears	0
	Bears	12	New York	0
1931	Bears	6	New York	0
	Bears	12	New York	6
	New York	25	Bears	6
1932	Bears	28	New York	8
	Bears	6	New York	0
1933	Bears	14	New York	10
	New York	3	Bears	0
	*Bears	23	New York	21
1934	Bears	27	New York	7
	Bears	10	New York	9
	*New York	30	Bears	13
1935	Bears	20	New York	3
	New York	3	Bears	0
1936	Bears	25	New York	7
1937	New York	3	Bears	3
1939	New York	16	Bears	13
1940	Bears	37	New York	21
1941	*Bears	37	New York	9
1942	Bears	26	New York	7
1943	Bears	56	New York	7
1946	New York	14	Bears	0
	*Bears	24	New York	14
1948	Bears	35	New York	14
1949	New York	35	Bears	28

Bears won 20; New York 13; Tied 1.

Total points: Bears 530; New York 387.

* Championship Play-off Game

CHICAGO BEARS vs NEW YORK YANKS

1950	Yanks	38	Bears	27
	Bears	28	Yanks	20
1951	Bears	24	Yanks	21
	Bears	45	Yanks	21

Bears won 3; Yanks won 1; Tied 0.

Total points: Bears 124; Yanks 100.

CHICAGO BEARS vs PHILADELPHIA

1933	Philadelphia	3	Bears	3
1935	Bears	39	Philadelphia	0
1936	Bears	17	Philadelphia	0
	Bears	28	Philadelphia	7
1938	Bears	28	Philadelphia	6
1939	Bears	27	Philadelphia	14
1941	Bears	49	Philadelphia	14
1942	Bears	45	Philadelphia	14
1944	Bears	28	Philadelphia	7
1946	Bears	21	Philadelphia	14
1947	Bears	40	Philadelphia	7
1948	Philadelphia	12	Bears	7
1949	Bears	38	Philadelphia	21

Bears won 11; Philadelphia won 1; Tied 1.

Total points: Bears 370; Philadelphia 119.

CHICAGO BEARS vs PITTSBURGH

1934	Bears	28	Pittsburgh	0
1935	Bears	23	Pittsburgh	7
1936	Bears	27	Pittsburgh	9
	Bears	26	Pittsburgh	6
1937	Bears	7	Pittsburgh	0
1939	Bears	32	Pittsburgh	0
1941	Bears	34	Pittsburgh	7
1945	Bears	28	Pittsburgh	7
1947	Bears	49	Pittsburgh	7
1949	Bears	30	Pittsburgh	21

Bears won 10; Pittsburgh won 0; Tied 0.

Total points: Bears 284; Pittsburgh 64.

CHICAGO BEARS vs SAN FRANCISCO 49ers

1950	Bears	32	San Francisco	14
	Bears	17	San Francisco	0
1951	Bears	13	San Francisco	7

Bears won 3; San Francisco won 0; Tied 0.

Total points: Bears 62; San Francisco 21.

CHICAGO BEARS vs WASHINGTON REDSKINS

1937	*Washington	28	Bears	21
1938	Bears	31	Washington	7
1940	Washington	7	Bears	3
	*Bears	73	Washington	0
1941	Bears	35	Washington	21
1942	*Washington	14	Bears	6
1943	Washington	21	Bears	7
	*Bears	41	Washington	21
1945	Washington	28	Bears	21
1946	Bears	24	Washington	20
1947	Bears	56	Washington	20
1948	Bears	48	Washington	13

CHICAGO BEARS vs WASHINGTON REDSKINS (cont.)

| 1949 | Bears | 31 | Washington | 21 |
| 1951 | Bears | 27 | Washington | 0 |

Bears won 9; Washington won 5; Tied 0.

Total points: Bears 424; Washington 221.

* Championship Play-off Game

CHICAGO CARDINALS vs CLEVELAND BROWNS

1950	Cleveland	34	Cardinals	24
	Cleveland	10	Cardinals	7
1951	Cleveland	34	Cardinals	17
	Cleveland	49	Cardinals	28

Cardinals won 0; Cleveland won 4; Tied 0.

Total points: Cardinals 76; Cleveland 127.

CHICAGO CARDINALS vs DETROIT LIONS

1934	Detroit	6	Cardinals	0
	Detroit	17	Cardinals	13
1935	Detroit	10	Cardinals	10
	Detroit	7	Cardinals	6
1936	Detroit	39	Cardinals	0
	Detroit	14	Cardinals	7
1937	Detroit	16	Cardinals	7
	Detroit	16	Cardinals	7
1938	Detroit	10	Cardinals	0
	Detroit	7	Cardinals	3
1939	Detroit	21	Cardinals	13
	Detroit	17	Cardinals	3
1940	Detroit	0	Cardinals	0
	Detroit	43	Cardinals	14
1941	Detroit	14	Cardinals	14
	Detroit	21	Cardinals	3
1942	Cardinals	13	Detroit	0
	Cardinals	7	Detroit	0
1943	Detroit	35	Cardinals	17
	Detroit	7	Cardinals	0
1944	Cardinals combined with Pitts.			
1945	Detroit	10	Cardinals	0
	Detroit	26	Cardinals	0
1946	Cardinals	34	Detroit	14
	Cardinals	36	Detroit	14
1947	Cardinals	45	Detroit	21
	Cardinals	17	Detroit	7
1948	Cardinals	56	Detroit	20
	Cardinals	28	Detroit	14
1949	Detroit	24	Cardinals	7
	Cardinals	42	Detroit	19

Cardinals won 9; Detroit won 18; Tied 3.

Total points: Cardinals 402; Detroit 469.

CHICAGO CARDINALS vs GREEN BAY PACKERS

1921	Cardinals	3	Green Bay	3
1922	Cardinals	16	Green Bay	3
1924	Cardinals	3	Green Bay	0
1925	Cardinals	9	Green Bay	6
1926	Cardinals	13	Green Bay	7
	Green Bay	3	Cardinals	0
1927	Green Bay	13	Cardinals	0
	Cardinals	6	Green Bay	6
1928	Green Bay	20	Cardinals	0
1929	Green Bay	9	Cardinals	2
	Green Bay	7	Cardinals	6
	Green Bay	13	Cardinals	0
1930	Green Bay	14	Cardinals	0
	Cardinals	13	Green Bay	6
1931	Green Bay	26	Cardinals	7
	Cardinals	21	Green Bay	13
1932	Green Bay	15	Cardinals	7
	Green Bay	19	Cardinals	9
1933	Green Bay	14	Cardinals	6
1934	Green Bay	15	Cardinals	0
	Cardinals	9	Green Bay	0
	Cardinals	6	Green Bay	0
1935	Cardinals	7	Green Bay	6
	Cardinals	3	Green Bay	0
	Cardinals	9	Green Bay	7
1936	Green Bay	10	Cardinals	7
	Green Bay	24	Cardinals	0
	Green Bay	0	Cardinals	0
1937	Cardinals	14	Green Bay	7
	Green Bay	34	Cardinals	13
1938	Green Bay	28	Cardinals	7
	Green Bay	24	Cardinals	22
1939	Green Bay	14	Cardinals	10
	Green Bay	27	Cardinals	20
1940	Green Bay	31	Cardinals	6
	Green Bay	28	Cardinals	7
1941	Green Bay	14	Cardinals	13
	Green Bay	17	Cardinals	9
1942	Green Bay	17	Cardinals	13
	Green Bay	55	Cardinals	24
1943	Green Bay	28	Cardinals	7
	Green Bay	35	Cardinals	14
1945	Green Bay	33	Cardinals	14
1946	Green Bay	19	Cardinals	7
	Cardinals	24	Green Bay	6
1947	Cardinals	14	Green Bay	10
	Cardinals	21	Green Bay	20
1948	Cardinals	17	Green Bay	7
	Cardinals	42	Green Bay	7
1949	Cardinals	39	Green Bay	17
	Cardinals	41	Green Bay	21

Cardinals won 19; Green Bay won 29; Tied 3.

Total points: Cardinals 560; Green Bay 758.

CHICAGO CARDINALS vs NEW YORK GIANTS

1926	New York	20	Cardinals	0
1927	New York	28	Cardinals	7
1929	New York	24	Cardinals	21
1930	New York	25	Cardinals	12
	New York	13	Cardinals	7
1935	Cardinals	14	New York	13
1936	New York	14	Cardinals	6
1938	New York	6	Cardinals	0

1939	New York	17	Cardinals	7
1941	Cardinals	10	New York	7
1942	New York	21	Cardinals	7
1943	New York	24	Cardinals	13
1946	New York	28	Cardinals	24
1947	New York	35	Cardinals	31
1948	Cardinals	63	New York	35
1949	New York	41	Cardinals	38
1950	Cardinals	17	New York	3
	New York	51	Cardinals	21
1951	New York	28	Cardinals	17
	New York	10	Cardinals	0

Cardinals won 4; New York won 16; Tied 0.

Total points: Cardinals 315; New York 443.

CHICAGO CARDINALS vs PHILADELPHIA

1935	Cardinals	12	Philadelphia	3
1936	Cardinals	13	Philadelphia	0
1937	Philadelphia	6	Cardinals	6
1938	Philadelphia	7	Cardinals	0
1941	Philadelphia	21	Cardinals	14
1945	Philadelphia	21	Cardinals	6
1947	Cardinals	45	Philadelphia	21
	*Cardinals	28	Philadelphia	21
1948	Cardinals	21	Philadelphia	14
	*Philadelphia	7	Cardinals	0
1949	Philadelphia	28	Cardinals	3
1950	Philadelphia	45	Cardinals	7
	Cardinals	14	Philadelphia	10
1951	Philadelphia	17	Cardinals	14

Cardinals won 6; Philadelphia won 7; Tied 1.

Total points: Cardinals 183; Philadelphia 221.

* Championship Play-off Game

CHICAGO CARDINALS vs PITTSBURGH STEELERS

1933	Pittsburgh	14	Cardinals	13
1935	Pittsburgh	17	Cardinals	13
1936	Cardinals	14	Pittsburgh	6
1937	Cardinals	13	Pittsburgh	7
1939	Cardinals	10	Pittsburgh	0
1940	Cardinals	7	Pittsburgh	7
1942	Pittsburgh	19	Cardinals	3
1945	Pittsburgh	23	Cardinals	0
1946	Pittsburgh	14	Cardinals	7
1948	Cardinals	24	Pittsburgh	7
1950	Pittsburgh	28	Cardinals	17
	Pittsburgh	28	Cardinals	7
1951	Pittsburgh	28	Cardinals	14

Cardinals won 4; Pittsburgh won 8; Tied 1.

Total points: Cardinals 142; Pittsburgh 198.

CHICAGO CARDINALS vs WASHINGTON REDSKINS

1937	Cardinals	21	Washington	14
1939	Washington	28	Cardinals	7
1940	Washington	28	Cardinals	21
1942	Washington	28	Cardinals	0
1943	Washington	13	Cardinals	7
1945	Washington	24	Cardinals	21
1947	Washington	45	Cardinals	21
1949	Cardinals	38	Washington	7
1950	Cardinals	38	Washington	28
1951	Washington	7	Cardinals	3
	Washington	20	Cardinals	17

Cardinals won 3; Washington won 8; Tied 0.

Total points: Cardinals 194; Washington 242.

CLEVELAND BROWNS vs SAN FRANCISCO 49ers

1950	Cleveland	34	San Francisco	14
1951	San Francisco	24	Cleveland	10

Cleveland won 1; San Francisco won 1; Tied 0.

Total points: Cleveland 44; San Francisco 38.

DETROIT LIONS vs GREEN BAY PACKERS

1934	Detroit	3	Green Bay	0
	Green Bay	3	Detroit	0
1935	Green Bay	13	Detroit	9
	Green Bay	31	Detroit	7
	Detroit	20	Green Bay	10
1936	Green Bay	20	Detroit	18
	Green Bay	26	Detroit	17
1937	Green Bay	26	Detroit	6
	Green Bay	14	Detroit	13
1938	Detroit	17	Green Bay	7
	Green Bay	28	Detroit	7
1939	Green Bay	26	Detroit	7
	Green Bay	12	Detroit	7
1940	Detroit	23	Green Bay	14
	Green Bay	50	Detroit	7
1941	Green Bay	23	Detroit	0
	Green Bay	24	Detroit	7
1942	Green Bay	38	Detroit	7
	Green Bay	28	Detroit	7
1943	Green Bay	35	Detroit	14
	Green Bay	27	Detroit	6
1944	Green Bay	27	Detroit	6
	Green Bay	14	Detroit	0
1945	Green Bay	57	Detroit	21
	Detroit	14	Green Bay	3
1946	Green Bay	10	Detroit	7
	Green Bay	9	Detroit	0
1947	Green Bay	34	Detroit	17
	Green Bay	35	Detroit	14
1948	Green Bay	33	Detroit	21
	Detroit	24	Green Bay	20
1949	Green Bay	16	Detroit	14
	Detroit	21	Green Bay	7
1950	Detroit	45	Green Bay	7
	Detroit	24	Green Bay	21

DETROIT LIONS vs
GREEN BAY PACKERS (cont.)

1951	Detroit	24	Green Bay	17
	Detroit	52	Green Bay	35

Detroit won 11; Green Bay won 26; Tied 0.

Total points: Detroit 506; Green Bay 800.

DETROIT LIONS vs
NEW YORK GIANTS

1934	Detroit	9	New York	0
1935	*Detroit	26	New York	7
1936	New York	14	Detroit	7
	Detroit	38	New York	0
1937	Detroit	17	New York	0
1939	Detroit	18	New York	14
1941	New York	20	Detroit	13
1943	New York	0	Detroit	0
1945	New York	35	Detroit	14
1947	Detroit	35	New York	7
1949	Detroit	45	New York	21

Detroit won 7; New York won 3; Tied 1.

Total points: Detroit 222; New York 118.

* Championship Play-off Game

DETROIT LIONS vs
NEW YORK YANKS

1950	Yanks	44	Detroit	21
	Detroit	49	Yanks	14
1951	Detroit	37	Yanks	10
	Detroit	24	Yanks	24

Detroit won 2; Yanks won 1; Tied 1.

Total points: Detroit 131; Yanks 92.

DETROIT LIONS vs
PHILADELPHIA EAGLES

1934	Detroit	10	Philadelphia	0
1935	Detroit	35	Philadelphia	0
1936	Detroit	23	Philadelphia	0
1938	Philadelphia	21	Detroit	7
1940	Detroit	21	Philadelphia	0
1941	Detroit	21	Philadelphia	17
1945	Detroit	28	Philadelphia	24
1948	Philadelphia	45	Detroit	21
1949	Philadelphia	22	Detroit	14
1951	Detroit	28	Philadelphia	7

Detroit won 7; Philadelphia won 3; Tied 0.

Total points: Detroit 208; Philadelphia 139.

DETROIT LIONS vs
PITTSBURGH STEELERS

1934	Detroit	40	Pittsburgh	7
1936	Detroit	28	Pittsburgh	3
1937	Detroit	7	Pittsburgh	3
1938	Detroit	16	Pittsburgh	7
1940	Pittsburgh	10	Detroit	7
1942	Pittsburgh	35	Detroit	7
1946	Detroit	17	Pittsburgh	7
1947	Pittsburgh	17	Detroit	10
1948	Detroit	17	Pittsburgh	14
1949	Pittsburgh	14	Detroit	7
1950	Detroit	10	Pittsburgh	7

Detroit won 7; Pittsburgh won 4; Tied 0.

Total points: Detroit 166; Pittsburgh 124.

DETROIT LIONS vs
SAN FRANCISCO 49ers

1950	Detroit	24	San Francisco	7
	San Francisco	28	Detroit	27
1951	San Francisco	20	Detroit	10
	San Francisco	21	Detroit	17

Detroit won 1; San Francisco won 3; Tied 0.

Total points: Detroit 78; San Francisco 76.

DETROIT LIONS vs
WASHINGTON REDSKINS

1938	Washington	7	Detroit	5
1939	Washington	31	Detroit	7
1940	Washington	20	Detroit	14
1942	Washington	15	Detroit	3
1943	Washington	42	Detroit	20
1946	Washington	17	Detroit	16
1947	Detroit	38	Washington	21
1948	Washington	46	Detroit	21
1951	Detroit	35	Washington	17

Detroit won 2; Washington won 7; Tied 0.

Total points: Detroit 159; Washington 216.

GREEN BAY PACKERS vs
NEW YORK GIANTS

1928	New York	6	Green Bay	0
	Green Bay	7	New York	0
1929	Green Bay	20	New York	6
1930	Green Bay	14	New York	7
	New York	13	Green Bay	6
1931	Green Bay	27	New York	7
	Green Bay	14	New York	10
1932	Green Bay	13	New York	0
	New York	6	Green Bay	0
1933	New York	10	Green Bay	7
	New York	17	Green Bay	6
1934	Green Bay	20	New York	6
	New York	17	Green Bay	3
1935	Green Bay	16	New York	7
1936	Green Bay	26	New York	14
1937	New York	10	Green Bay	0
1938	New York	15	Green Bay	3
	*New York	23	Green Bay	17
1939	Green Bay	27	New York	0
1940	New York	7	Green Bay	3
1942	Green Bay	21	New York	21
1943	Green Bay	35	New York	21

1944	New York	24	Green Bay	0
	*Green Bay	14	New York	7
1945	Green Bay	23	New York	14
1947	Green Bay	24	New York	24
1948	New York	49	Green Bay	3
1949	New York	30	Green Bay	10

Green Bay won 13; New York won 13; Tied 2.

Total points: Green Bay 359; New York 371.

* Championship Play-off Game

GREEN BAY PACKERS vs NEW YORK YANKS

1950	New York	44	Green Bay	31
	New York	35	Green Bay	17
1951	Green Bay	29	New York	27
	New York	31	Green Bay	28

Green Bay won 1; New York won 3; Tied 0.

Total points: Green Bay 105; New York 137.

GREEN BAY PACKERS vs PHILADELPHIA EAGLES

1933	Green Bay	35	Philadelphia	9
	Green Bay	10	Philadelphia	0
1934	Green Bay	19	Philadelphia	6
1935	Green Bay	13	Philadelphia	6
1937	Green Bay	37	Philadelphia	7
1939	Green Bay	23	Philadelphia	16
1940	Green Bay	27	Philadelphia	20
1942	Green Bay	7	Philadelphia	0
1946	Green Bay	19	Philadelphia	7
1947	Philadelphia	28	Green Bay	14
1951	Green Bay	37	Philadelphia	24

Green Bay won 10; Philadelphia won 1; Tied 1.

Total points: Green Bay 241; Philadelphia 114.

GREEN BAY PACKERS vs PITTSBURGH STEELERS

1933	Green Bay	47	Pittsburgh	0
1935	Green Bay	27	Pittsburgh	0
	Green Bay	34	Pittsburgh	14
1936	Green Bay	42	Pittsburgh	10
1938	Green Bay	20	Pittsburgh	0
1940	Green Bay	24	Pittsburgh	3
1941	Green Bay	54	Pittsburgh	7
1942	Green Bay	24	Pittsburgh	21
1946	Green Bay	17	Pittsburgh	7
1947	Pittsburgh	18	Green Bay	17
1948	Pittsburgh	38	Green Bay	7
1949	Pittsburgh	30	Green Bay	7
1951	Green Bay	35	Pittsburgh	33
	Pittsburgh	28	Green Bay	7

Green Bay won 10; Pittsburgh won 4; Tied 0.

Total points: Green Bay 362; Pittsburgh 209.

GREEN BAY PACKERS vs SAN FRANCISCO 49ers

1950	Green Bay	25	San Francisco	21
	San Francisco	30	Green Bay	14
1951	San Fransisco	31	Green Bay	19

Green Bay won 1; San Francisco won 2; Tied 0.

Total points: Green Bay 58; San Francisco 82.

GREEN BAY PACKERS vs WASHINGTON REDSKINS

1937	Washington	14	Green Bay	6
1939	Green Bay	24	Washington	14
1941	Green Bay	22	Washington	17
1943	Washington	33	Green Bay	7
1946	Green Bay	20	Washington	7
1947	Green Bay	27	Washington	10
1948	Washington	23	Green Bay	7
1949	Washington	30	Green Bay	0
1950	Green Bay	35	Washington	21

Green Bay won 5; Washington won 4; Tied 0.

Total points: Green Bay 148; Washington 169.

LOS ANGELES RAMS vs CHICAGO CARDINALS

1946	Cardinals	34	Los Angeles	10
	Los Angeles	17	Cardinals	14
1947	Los Angeles	27	Cardinals	7
	Cardinals	17	Los Angeles	10
1948	Cardinals	27	Los Angeles	22
	Cardinals	27	Los Angeles	24
1949	Cardinals	28	Los Angeles	28
	Cardinals	31	Los Angeles	27
1951	Los Angeles	45	Cardinals	21

Los Angeles won 3; Cardinals won 5; Tied 1.

Total points: Los Angeles 210; Cardinals 206.

LOS ANGELES RAMS vs CLEVELAND BROWNS

1950	*Cleveland	30	Los Angeles	28
1951	Cleveland	38	Los Angeles	23
	*Los Angeles	24	Cleveland	17

Cleveland won 2; Los Angeles won 1; Tied 0.

Total points: Cleveland 85; Los Angeles 75.

* Championship Play-off

LOS ANGELES RAMS vs DETROIT LIONS

1946	Los Angeles	35	Detroit	14
	Los Angeles	41	Detroit	20
1947	Los Angeles	27	Detroit	13
	Los Angeles	28	Detroit	17
1948	Los Angeles	44	Detroit	7
	Los Angeles	34	Detroit	27
1949	Los Angeles	27	Detroit	24
	Los Angeles	21	Detroit	10
1950	Los Angeles	30	Detroit	28
	Los Angeles	65	Detroit	24
1951	Los Angeles	27	Detroit	21
	Detroit	24	Los Angeles	22

Los Angeles won 11; Detroit won 1; Tied 0.

Total points: Los Angeles 401; Detroit 229.

LOS ANGELES RAMS vs GREEN BAY PACKERS

1946	Los Angeles	21	Green Bay	17
	Los Angeles	38	Green Bay	17
1947	Green Bay	17	Los Angeles	14
	Green Bay	30	Los Angeles	10
1948	Green Bay	16	Los Angeles	0
	Los Angeles	24	Green Bay	10
1949	Los Angeles	48	Green Bay	7
	Los Angeles	35	Green Bay	7
1950	Los Angeles	45	Green Bay	14
	Los Angeles	51	Green Bay	14
1951	Los Angeles	28	Green Bay	0
	Los Angeles	42	Green Bay	14

Los Angeles won 9; Green Bay won 3; Tied 0.

Total points: Los Angeles 356; Green Bay 163.

LOS ANGELES RAMS vs NEW YORK GIANTS

1946	Los Angeles	31	New York	21
1947	Los Angeles	34	New York	10
1948	Los Angeles	52	New York	37

Los Angeles won 3; New York won 0; Tied 0.

Total points: Los Angeles 117; New York 68.

LOS ANGELES RAMS vs NEW YORK YANKS

1950	Los Angeles	45	Yanks	28
	Los Angeles	43	Yanks	35
1951	Los Angeles	54	Yanks	14
	Los Angeles	48	Yanks	21

Los Angeles won 4; Yanks won 0; Tied 0.

Total points: Los Angeles 190; Yanks 98.

LOS ANGELES RAMS vs PHILADELPHIA EAGLES

1946	Philadelphia	25	Los Angeles	14
1947	Philadelphia	14	Los Angeles	7
1948	Philadelphia	28	Los Angeles	28
1949	Philadelphia	38	Los Angeles	14
	*Philadelphia	14	Los Angeles	0
1950	Philadelphia	56	Los Angeles	22

Los Angeles won 0; Philadelphia won 5; Tied 1.

Total points: Los Angeles 85; Philadelphia 175.

* Championship Play-off Game

LOS ANGELES RAMS vs PITTSBURGH STEELERS

1947	Los Angeles	48	Pittsburgh	7
1948	Los Angeles	31	Pittsburgh	14
1949	Los Angeles	7	Pittsburgh	7

Los Angeles won 2; Pittsburgh won 0; Tied 1.

Total points: Los Angeles 86; Pittsburgh 28.

LOS ANGELES RAMS vs SAN FRANCISCO 49ers

1950	Los Angeles	35	San Francisco	14
	Los Angeles	28	San Francisco	21
1951	San Francisco	44	Los Angeles	17
	Los Angeles	23	San Francisco	16

Los Angeles won 3; San Francisco won 1; Tied 0.

Total points: Los Angeles 103; San Francisco 95.

LOS ANGELES RAMS vs WASHINGTON REDSKINS

1948	Los Angeles	41	Washington	13
1949	Los Angeles	53	Washington	27
1951	Washington	31	Los Angeles	21

Los Angeles won 2; Washington won 1; Tied 0.

Total points: Los Angeles 115; Washington 71.

NEW YORK GIANTS vs CLEVELAND BROWNS

1950	New York	6	Cleveland	0
	New York	17	Cleveland	13
	*Cleveland	8	New York	3
1951	Cleveland	14	New York	13
	Cleveland	10	New York	0

New York won 2; Cleveland won 3; Tied 0.

Total points: New York 39; Cleveland 45.

* Conference Play-off Game

NEW YORK GIANTS vs PHILADELPHIA EAGLES

1933	New York	56	Philadelphia	0
	New York	20	Philadelphia	14
1934	New York	17	Philadelphia	0
	Philadelphia	6	New York	0
1935	New York	10	Philadelphia	0
	New York	21	Philadelphia	14
1936	Philadelphia	10	New York	7
	New York	21	Philadelphia	17
1937	New York	16	Philadelphia	7
	New York	21	Philadelphia	0
1938	Philadelphia	14	New York	10
	New York	17	Philadelphia	7
1939	New York	13	Philadelphia	3
	New York	27	Philadelphia	10
1940	New York	20	Philadelphia	14
	New York	17	Philadelphia	7
1941	New York	24	Philadelphia	0
	New York	16	Philadelphia	0
1942	New York	35	Philadelphia	17
	New York	14	Philadelphia	0
1944	Philadelphia	24	New York	17
	Philadelphia	21	New York	21
1945	Philadelphia	38	New York	17
	New York	28	Philadelphia	21
1946	Philadelphia	24	New York	14
	New York	45	Philadelphia	17
1947	Philadelphia	23	New York	0
	Philadelphia	41	New York	24
1948	Philadelphia	45	New York	0
	Philadelphia	35	New York	14
1949	Philadelphia	24	New York	3
	Philadelphia	17	New York	3
1950	New York	7	Philadelphia	3
	New York	9	Philadelphia	7
1951	New York	26	Philadelphia	24
	New York	21	Philadelphia	7

New York won 23; Philadelphia won 12; Tied 1.

Total points: New York 633; Philadelphia 511.

NEW YORK GIANTS vs PITTSBURGH STEELERS

1933	New York	23	Pittsburgh	2
	New York	27	Pittsburgh	3
1934	New York	14	Pittsburgh	12
	New York	17	Pittsburgh	7
1935	New York	42	Pittsburgh	7
	New York	13	Pittsburgh	0
1936	Pittsburgh	10	New York	7
1937	New York	10	Pittsburgh	7
	New York	17	Pittsburgh	0
1938	New York	27	Pittsburgh	14
	Pittsburgh	13	New York	10
1939	New York	14	Pittsburgh	7
	New York	23	Pittsburgh	7
1940	Pittsburgh	10	New York	10
	New York	12	Pittsburgh	0
1941	New York	37	Pittsburgh	10
	New York	28	Pittsburgh	7
1942	Pittsburgh	13	New York	10
	Pittsburgh	17	New York	9
1945	New York	34	Pittsburgh	6
	Pittsburgh	21	New York	7
1946	New York	17	Pittsburgh	14
	New York	7	Pittsburgh	0
1947	Pittsburgh	38	New York	21
	Pittsburgh	24	New York	7
1948	New York	34	Pittsburgh	27
	Pittsburgh	38	New York	28
1949	Pittsburgh	28	New York	7
	Pittsburgh	21	New York	17
1950	New York	18	Pittsburgh	7
	Pittsburgh	17	New York	6
1951	New York	13	Pittsburgh	13
	New York	14	Pittsburgh	0

New York won 20; Pittsburgh won 11; Tied 2.

Total points: New York 580; Pittsburgh 400.

NEW YORK GIANTS vs WASHINGTON REDSKINS

1937	Washington	13	New York	3
	Washington	49	New York	14
1938	New York	10	Washington	7
	New York	36	Washington	0
1939	New York	0	Washington	0
	New York	9	Washington	7
1940	Washington	21	New York	7
	New York	21	Washington	7
1941	New York	17	Washington	7
	New York	20	Washington	13
1942	New York	14	Washington	7
	Washington	14	New York	7
1943	New York	14	Washington	10
	New York	31	Washington	7
	*Washington	28	New York	0
1944	New York	16	Washington	13
	New York	31	Washington	0
1945	Washington	24	New York	14
	Washington	17	New York	0
1946	Washington	24	New York	14
	New York	31	Washington	0
1947	Washington	28	New York	20
	New York	35	Washington	10
1948	Washington	41	New York	10
	Washington	28	New York	21
1949	New York	45	Washington	35
	New York	23	Washington	7
1950	New York	21	Washington	17
	New York	24	Washington	21
1951	New York	35	Washington	14
	New York	28	Washington	14

New York won 19; Washington won 11; Tied 1.

Total points: New York 571; Washington 486.

* Divisional Play-off Game

PHILADELPHIA EAGLES vs CLEVELAND BROWNS

1950	Cleveland	35	Philadelphia	10
	Cleveland	13	Philadelphia	7
1951	Cleveland	20	Philadelphia	17
	Cleveland	24	Philadelphia	9

Philadelphia won 0; Cleveland won 4; Tied 0.

Total points: Philadelphia 43; Cleveland 92.

PHILADELPHIA EAGLES vs PITTSBURGH STEELERS

1933	Philadelphia	25	Pittsburgh	6
1934	Philadelphia	17	Pittsburgh	0
	Pittsburgh	9	Philadelphia	7
1935	Pittsburgh	17	Philadelphia	7
	Philadelphia	17	Pittsburgh	6
1936	Pittsburgh	6	Philadelphia	0
	Pittsburgh	17	Philadelphia	0
1937	Pittsburgh	27	Philadelphia	14
	Pittsburgh	16	Philadelphia	7
1938	Philadelphia	27	Pittsburgh	7
	Philadelphia	14	Pittsburgh	7
1939	Philadelphia	17	Pittsburgh	14
	Pittsburgh	24	Philadelphia	12
1940	Pittsburgh	7	Philadelphia	3
	Philadelphia	7	Pittsburgh	0
1941	Philadelphia	10	Pittsburgh	7
	Philadelphia	7	Pittsburgh	7
1942	Philadelphia	24	Pittsburgh	14
	Pittsburgh	14	Philadelphia	0
1945	Philadelphia	45	Pittsburgh	3
	Philadelphia	30	Pittsburgh	6
1946	Pittsburgh	10	Philadelphia	7
	Philadelphia	10	Pittsburgh	7
1947	Pittsburgh	35	Philadelphia	24
	Philadelphia	21	Pittsburgh	0
*	*Philadelphia	21	Pittsburgh	0
1948	Philadelphia	34	Pittsburgh	7
	Philadelphia	17	Pittsburgh	0
1949	Philadelphia	38	Pittsburgh	7
	Philadelphia	34	Pittsburgh	17
1950	Philadelphia	17	Pittsburgh	10
	Pittsburgh	9	Philadelphia	7
1951	Philadelphia	34	Pittsburgh	13
	Pittsburgh	17	Philadelphia	13

Philadelphia won 20; Pittsburgh won 13; Tied 1.

Total point: Philadelphia 567; Pittsburgh 346.

* Divisional Play-off Game

PHILADELPHIA EAGLES vs WASHINGTON REDSKINS

1937	Philadelphia	14	Washington	0
	Washington	10	Philadelphia	7

1938	Washington	26	Philadelphia	23
	Washington	20	Philadelphia	14
1939	Washington	7	Philadelphia	0
	Washington	7	Philadelphia	6
1940	Washington	34	Philadelphia	17
	Washington	13	Philadelphia	6
1941	Washington	21	Philadelphia	17
	Washington	20	Philadelphia	14
1942	Washington	14	Philadelphia	10
	Washington	30	Philadelphia	27
1944	Philadelphia	31	Washington	31
	Philadelphia	37	Washington	7
1945	Washington	24	Philadelphia	14
	Philadelphia	16	Washington	0
1946	Philadelphia	28	Washington	24
	Washington	27	Philadelphia	10
1947	Philadelphia	45	Washington	42
	Philadelphia	38	Washington	14
1948	Philadelphia	45	Washington	0
	Philadelphia	42	Washington	21
1949	Philadelphia	49	Washington	14
	Philadelphia	44	Washington	21
1950	Philadelphia	35	Washington	3
	Philadelphia	33	Washington	0
1951	Washington	27	Philadelphia	23
	Philadelphia	35	Washington	21

Philadelphia won 13; Washington won 14; Tied 1.

Total points: Philadelphia 680; Washington 478.

PITTSBURGH STEELERS vs CLEVELAND BROWNS

1950	Cleveland	30	Pittsburgh	17
	Cleveland	45	Pittsburgh	7
1951	Cleveland	17	Pittsburgh	0
	Cleveland	28	Pittsburgh	0

Pittsburgh won 0; Cleveland won 4; Tied 0.

Total points: Pittsburgh 24; Cleveland 120.

PITTSBURGH STEELERS vs WASHINGTON REDSKINS

1937	Washington	34	Pittsburgh	20
	Pittsburgh	21	Washington	13
1938	Washington	7	Pittsburgh	0
	Washington	15	Pittsburgh	0
1939	Washington	44	Pittsburgh	14
	Washington	21	Pittsburgh	14
1940	Washington	40	Pittsburgh	10
	Washington	37	Pittsburgh	10
1941	Washington	24	Pittsburgh	20
	Washington	23	Pittsburgh	3
1942	Washington	28	Pittsburgh	14
	Washington	14	Pittsburgh	0
1945	Washington	14	Pittsburgh	0
	Washington	24	Pittsburgh	0
1946	Pittsburgh	14	Washington	14
	Pittsburgh	14	Washington	7

1947	Washington	27	Pittsburgh	26
	Pittsburgh	21	Washington	14
1948	Washington	17	Pittsburgh	14
	Pittsburgh	10	Washington	7
1949	Washington	27	Pittsburgh	14
	Washington	27	Pittsburgh	14
1950	Pittsburgh	26	Washington	7
	Washington	24	Pittsburgh	7
1951	Washington	22	Pittsburgh	7
	Pittsburgh	20	Washington	10

Pittsburgh won 6; Washington won 19; Tied 1.

Total points: Pittsburgh 313; Washington 541.

WASHINGTON REDSKINS vs CLEVELAND BROWNS

1950	Cleveland	20	Washington	14
	Cleveland	45	Washington	21
1951	Cleveland	45	Washington	0

Washington won 0; Cleveland won 3; Tied 0.

Total points: Washington 35; Cleveland 110.

TEAM vs TEAM RECORDS (MERGERS)

BROOKLYN vs COMBINES

1943	Brooklyn	13	Phil-Pitt	7
	Phil-Pitt	17	Brooklyn	0

Total points: Combines 24; Brooklyn 13.

CHICAGO BEARS vs COMBINES

1943	Bears	48	Phil-Pitt	21
1944	Bears	34	Card-Pitt	7
	Bears	49	Card-Pitt	7

Bears won 3; Combines won 0; Tied 0.

Total points: Bears 131; Combines 35.

CHICAGO CARDINALS vs COMBINES

1943	Phil-Pitt	34	Cardinals	13

Cardinals won 0; Combines won 1; Tied 0.

Total points: Cardinals 34; Combines 13.

CLEVELAND RAMS vs COMBINES

1944	Cleveland	30	Card-Pitt	28
	Cleveland	33	Card-Pitt	6
1945	Cleveland	20	Yanks	7

Cleveland won 3; Combines won 0; Tied 0.

Total points: Cleveland 83; Combines 41.

DETROIT LIONS vs COMBINES

1943	Phil-Pitt	35	Detroit	34
1944	Detroit	27	Card-Pitt	6
	Detroit	21	Card-Pitt	7
1945	Detroit	10	Yanks	9

Detroit won 3; Combines 1; Tied 0.

Total points: Detroit 92; Combines 57.

GREEN BAY PACKERS vs COMBINES

1943	Green Bay	38	Phil-Pitt	28
1944	Green Bay	34	Card-Pitt	7

	Green Bay	35	Card-Pitt	20
1945	Green Bay	38	Yanks	14
	Green Bay	28	Yanks	0

Green Bay won 5; Combines won 0; Tied 0.

Total points: Green Bay 173; Combines 69.

NEW YORK GIANTS vs COMBINES

1943	Phil-Pitt	28	New York	14
	New York	42	Phil-Pitt	14
1944	New York	23	Card-Pitt	0
1945	New York	13	Yanks	13

New York won 2; Combines won 1; Tied 1.

Total points: New York 92; Combines 55.

PHILADELPHIA EAGLES vs COMBINES

1945	Philadelphia	35	Yanks	7

Philadelphia won 1; Combines won 0; Tied 0.

Total points: Philadelphia 35; Combines 0.

PITTSBURGH STEELERS vs COMBINES

1945	Yanks	28	Pittsburgh	7
	Yanks	10	Pittsburgh	6

Pittsburgh won 0; Combines won 2; Tied 0.

Total points: Pittsburgh 13; Combines 38.

WASHINGTON REDSKINS vs COMBINES

1943	Phil-Pitt	14	Washington	14
	Phil-Pitt	27	Washington	14
1944	Washington	42	Card-Pitt	20
1945	Yanks	28	Washington	20
	Washington	34	Yanks	7

Washington won 2; Combines won 2; Tied 1.

Total points: Washington 124; Combines 96.

TEAM vs TEAM RECORDS

(Discontinued Series)

BALTIMORE vs CHICAGO CARDINALS

1950 Cardinals 55 Baltimore 13

BALTIMORE vs CLEVELAND BROWNS

1950 Cleveland 31 Baltimore 0

BALTIMORE vs DETROIT LIONS

1950 Detroit 45 Baltimore 21

BALTIMORE vs GREEN BAY PACKERS

1950 Baltimore 41 Green Bay 21

BALTIMORE vs LOS ANGELES RAMS

1950 Los Angeles 70 Baltimore 27

BALTIMORE vs NEW YORK GIANTS

1950 New York 55 Baltimore 20

BALTIMORE vs NEW YORK YANKS

1950 Yanks 51 Baltimore 14

BALTIMORE vs PHILADELPHIA EAGLES

1950 Philadelphia 24 Baltimore 14

BALTIMORE vs PITTSBURGH STEELERS

1950 Pittsburgh 17 Baltimore 7

BALTIMORE vs SAN FRANCISCO 49ers

1950 San Francisco 17 Baltimore 14

BALTIMORE vs WASHINGTON REDSKINS

1950 Washington 38 Baltimore 14
     Washington 38 Baltimore 28

BOSTON REDSKINS vs BROOKLYN

1932	Brooklyn	14	Boston	0
	Boston	7	Brooklyn	0
1933	Brooklyn	14	Boston	0
1934	Brooklyn	10	Boston	6
	Boston	13	Brooklyn	3
1935	Boston	7	Brooklyn	3
	Boston	0	Brooklyn	0
1936	Boston	14	Brooklyn	3
	Boston	30	Brooklyn	3

Boston won 5; Brooklyn won 3; Tied 1.

Total points: Boston 77; Brooklyn 50.

BOSTON REDSKINS vs CHICAGO BEARS

1932	Boston	7	Bears	7
1933	Bears	7	Boston	0
	Boston	10	Bears	0
1934	Bears	21	Boston	0
1935	Bears	30	Boston	14
1936	Bears	26	Boston	0

Boston won 1; Bears won 4; Tied 1.

Total points: Boston 31; Bears 91.

BOSTON REDSKINS vs CHICAGO CARDINALS

1932	Cardinals	9	Boston	0
	Boston	8	Cardinals	6
1933	Boston	10	Cardinals	0
	Boston	0	Cardinals	0
1934	Boston	9	Cardinals	0
1935	Cardinals	6	Boston	0
1936	Boston	13	Cardinals	10

Boston won 4; Cardinals won 2; Tied 1.

Total points: Boston 40; Cardinals 31.

BOSTON REDSKINS vs DETROIT LIONS

1934	Detroit	24	Boston	0
1935	Detroit	17	Boston	7
	Detroit	14	Boston	0

Boston won 0; Detroit won 3; Tied 0.

Total points: Boston 7; Detroit 55.

BOSTON REDSKINS vs GREEN BAY PACKERS

1932	Green Bay	21	Boston	0
1933	Boston	7	Green Bay	7
	Boston	20	Green Bay	7

1934	Green Bay	10	Boston	0
1936	Green Bay	31	Boston	2
	Green Bay	7	Boston	3
	*Green Bay	21	Boston	6

Boston won 1; Green Bay won 5; Tied 1.

Total points: Boston 38; Green Bay 104.

* Championship Play-off Game

BOSTON REDSKINS vs
NEW YORK GIANTS

1932	Boston	14	New York	6
	Boston	0	New York	0
1933	Boston	21	New York	20
	New York	7	Boston	0
1934	New York	16	Boston	13
	New York	3	Boston	0
1935	New York	20	Boston	12
	New York	.17	Boston	6
1936	New York	7	Boston	0
	Boston	14	New York	0

Boston won 6; New York won 6; Tied 1.

Total points: Boston 80; New York 96.

BOSTON REDSKINS vs
PHILADELPHIA EAGLES

1934	Boston	6	Philadelphia	0
	Boston	14	Philadelphia	7
1935	Philadelphia	7	Boston	6
1936	Boston	26	Philadelphia	3
	Boston	17	Philadelphia	7

Boston won 4; Philadelphia won 1; Tied 0.

Total points: Boston 69; Philadelphia 24.

BOSTON REDSKINS vs
PITTSBURGH STEELERS

1933	Boston	21	Pittsburgh	6
	Pittsburgh	16	Boston	14
1934	Boston	7	Pittsburgh	0
	Boston	39	Pittsburgh	0
1935	Pittsburgh	6	Boston	0
	Boston	13	Pittsburgh	3
1936	Pittsburgh	10	Boston	0
	Boston	30	Pittsburgh	0

Boston won 5; Pittsburgh 3; Tied 0.

Total points: Boston 124; Pittsburgh 41.

BOSTON REDSKINS vs
PORTSMOUTH SPARTANS

1932	Portsmouth	10	Boston	0
1933	Portsmouth	13	Boston	0

Boston won 0; Portsmouth won 2; Tied 0.

Total points: Boston 0; Portsmouth 23.

BOSTON YANKS vs
BROOKLYN

1944	Boston	17	Brooklyn	14
	Boston	13	Brooklyn	6

Boston won 2; Brooklyn won 0; Tied 0.

Total points: Boston 30; Brooklyn 20.

BOSTON YANKS vs
CHICAGO BEARS

1944	Bears	21	Boston	7
1947	Bears	27	Boston	7
1948	Bears	51	Boston	17

Boston won 0; Bears won 3; Tied 0.

Total points: Boston 48; Bears 100.

BOSTON YANKS vs
CHICAGO CARDINALS

1946	Cardinals	28	Boston	14
1947	Cardinals	27	Boston	7
1948	Cardinals	49	Boston	27

Boston won 0; Cardinals won 3; Tied 0.

Total points: Boston 48; Cardinals 104.

BOSTON YANKS vs
DETROIT LIONS

1944	Detroit	38	Boston	7
1945	Detroit	10	Boston	9
1946	Boston	34	Detroit	10
1947	Detroit	21	Boston	7
1948	Boston	17	Detroit	14

Boston won 2; Detroit won 3; Tied 0.

Total points: Boston 74; Detroit 93.

BOSTON YANKS vs
GREEN BAY PACKERS

1945	Green Bay	38	Boston	14
	Green Bay	28	Boston	0

Boston won 0; Green Bay won 2; Tied 0.

Total points: Boston 14; Green Bay 66.

BOSTON YANKS vs
LOS ANGELES RAMS

1946	Boston	40	Los Angeles	21
1947	Boston	27	Los Angeles	16

Boston won 2; Los Angeles won 0; Tied 0.

Total points: Boston 67; Los Angeles 37.

BOSTON YANKS vs
NEW YORK GIANTS

1944	New York	22	Boston	10
	New York	31	Boston	0
1945	New York	13	Boston	13
1946	New York	17	Boston	0
	New York	28	Boston	28
1947	New York	7	Boston	7
	Boston	14	New York	0
1948	New York	27	Boston	7
	New York	28	Boston	14

Boston won 1; New York won 5; Tied 3.

Total points: Boston 93; New York 173.

BOSTON YANKS vs
PHILADELPHIA EAGLES

1944	Philadelphia	28	Boston	7
	Philadelphia	38	Boston	0
1945	Philadelphia	35	Boston	7
1946	Philadelphia	49	Boston	25
	Philadelphia	40	Boston	14
1947	Philadelphia	32	Boston	0
	Boston	21	Philadelphia	14
1948	Philadelphia	45	Boston	0
	Boston	37	Philadelphia	14

Boston won 2; Philadelphia won 7; Tied 0.

Total points: Boston 111; Philadelphia 295.

BOSTON YANKS vs
PITTSBURGH STEELERS

1945	Boston	28	Pittsburgh	7
	Boston	10	Pittsburgh	6
1946	Pittsburgh	16	Boston	7
	Pittsburgh	33	Boston	7
1947	Pittsburgh	30	Boston	14
	Pittsburgh	17	Boston	7
1948	Pittsburgh	24	Boston	14
	Boston	13	Pittsburgh	7

Boston won 3; Pittsburgh won 5; Tied 0.

Total points: Boston 100; Pittsburgh 140.

BOSTON YANKS vs
WASHINGTON

1944	Washington	21	Boston	14
	Washington	14	Boston	7
1945	Boston	28	Washington	20
	Washington	34	Boston	7
1946	Washington	14	Boston	6
	Washington	17	Boston	14
1947	Boston	27	Washington	24
	Washington	40	Boston	13
1948	Washington	59	Boston	21
	Washington	23	Boston	7

Boston won 2; Washington won 8; Tied 0.

Total points: Boston 144; Washington 266.

BROOKLYN vs
CHICAGO BEARS

1931	Bears	26	Brooklyn	0
1932	Bears	13	Brooklyn	0
	Bears	20	Brooklyn	0
1933	Bears	10	Brooklyn	0
1934	Bears	21	Brooklyn	7
1935	Bears	24	Brooklyn	14
1937	Bears	29	Brooklyn	7
1938	Bears	24	Brooklyn	6
1940	Bears	16	Brooklyn	7
1942	Bears	35	Brooklyn	0
1943	Bears	33	Brooklyn	21

Brooklyn won 0; Bears won 11; Tied 0.

Total points: Brooklyn 62; Bears 251.

BROOKLYN vs
CHICAGO CARDINALS

1931	Cardinals	14	Brooklyn	7
1932	Cardinals	27	Brooklyn	7
	Brooklyn	3	Cardinals	0
1933	Brooklyn	7	Cardinals	0
	Brooklyn	3	Cardinals	0
1934	Cardinals	21	Brooklyn	0
1936	Brooklyn	9	Cardinals	0
1938	Brooklyn	13	Cardinals	0
1940	Brooklyn	14	Cardinals	9
1941	Cardinals	20	Brooklyn	6
1943	Brooklyn	7	Cardinals	0

Brooklyn won 7; Cardinals 4; Tied 0.

Total points: Brooklyn 76; Cardinals 91.

BROOKLYN vs
CLEVELAND RAMS

1937	Brooklyn	9	Cleveland	7
1939	Brooklyn	23	Cleveland	12
1940	Brooklyn	29	Cleveland	14
1942	Cleveland	17	Brooklyn	0

Brooklyn won 3; Cleveland 1; Tied 0.

Total points: Brooklyn 61; Cleveland 50.

BROOKLYN vs
DETROIT LIONS

1934	Detroit	28	Brooklyn	0
1935	Brooklyn	12	Detroit	10
	Detroit	28	Brooklyn	0
1936	Detroit	14	Brooklyn	7
	Detroit	14	Brooklyn	6
1937	Detroit	30	Brooklyn	0
1939	Detroit	27	Brooklyn	7
1941	Brooklyn	14	Detroit	7
1942	Brooklyn	28	Detroit	7
1943	Detroit	27	Brooklyn	0
1944	Detroit	19	Brooklyn	14

Brooklyn won 3; Detroit won 8; Tied 0.

Total points: Brooklyn 88; Detroit 211.

BROOKLYN vs
GREEN BAY PACKERS

1931	Green Bay	7	Brooklyn	0
1932	Green Bay	7	Brooklyn	0
1936	Green Bay	38	Brooklyn	7
1938	Green Bay	35	Brooklyn	7
1939	Green Bay	28	Brooklyn	0
1941	Green Bay	30	Brooklyn	7
1943	Green Bay	31	Brooklyn	7
1944	Green Bay	14	Brooklyn	7

Brooklyn won 0; Green Bay won 8; Tied 0.

Total points: Brooklyn 35; Green Bay 190.

BROOKLYN vs
NEW YORK GIANTS

1926	New York	17	Brooklyn	0
	New York	27	Brooklyn	0
1930	Brooklyn	7	New York	6
	New York	13	Brooklyn	0
1931	New York	27	Brooklyn	0
	New York	19	Brooklyn	6
1932	New York	20	Brooklyn	12
	New York	13	Brooklyn	7
1933	New York	21	Brooklyn	7
	New York	10	Brooklyn	0
1934	New York	14	Brooklyn	0
	New York	27	Brooklyn	0
1935	New York	10	Brooklyn	7
	New York	21	Brooklyn	0
1936	Brooklyn	10	New York	10
	New York	14	Brooklyn	0
1937	New York	21	Brooklyn	0
	Brooklyn	13	New York	13
1938	New York	28	Brooklyn	14
	Brooklyn	7	New York	7
1939	New York	7	Brooklyn	6
	New York	28	Brooklyn	7
1940	New York	10	Brooklyn	7
	Brooklyn	14	New York	6
1941	Brooklyn	16	New York	13
	Brooklyn	21	New York	7
1942	Brooklyn	17	New York	7
	New York	10	Brooklyn	0
1943	New York	20	Brooklyn	0
	New York	24	Brooklyn	7
1944	New York	14	Brooklyn	7
	New York	7	Brooklyn	0

Brooklyn won 5; New York won 24; Tied 3.

Total points: Brooklyn 192; New York 49.

BROOKLYN vs
PHILADELPHIA EAGLES

1934	Brooklyn	10	Philadelphia	7
	Philadelphia	13	Brooklyn	0
1935	Brooklyn	17	Philadelphia	6
	Brooklyn	3	Philadelphia	0
1936	Brooklyn	18	Philadelphia	0
	Brooklyn	13	Philadelphia	7
1937	Brooklyn	13	Philadelphia	7
	Philadelphia	14	Brooklyn	10
1938	Brooklyn	10	Philadelphia	7
	Brooklyn	32	Philadelphia	14
1939	Philadelphia	0	Brooklyn	0
	Brooklyn	23	Philadelphia	14
1940	Brooklyn	30	Philadelphia	17
	Brooklyn	21	Philadelphia	7
1941	Brooklyn	24	Philadelphia	13
	Brooklyn	15	Philadelphia	6
1942	Brooklyn	35	Philadelphia	14
	Philadelphia	14	Brooklyn	7
1944	Philadelphia	21	Brooklyn	7
	Philadelphia	34	Brooklyn	0

Brooklyn won 14; Philadelphia won 5; Tied 1.

Total points: Brooklyn 288; Philadelphia 215.

BROOKLYN vs
PITTSBURGH STEELERS

1933	Brooklyn	3	Pittsburgh	3
	Brooklyn	32	Pittsburgh	0
1934	Brooklyn	21	Pittsburgh	3
	Brooklyn	10	Pittsburgh	0
1935	Brooklyn	13	Pittsburgh	7
	Pittsburgh	16	Brooklyn	7
1936	Pittsburgh	10	Brooklyn	6
	Pittsburgh	10	Brooklyn	7
1937	Pittsburgh	21	Brooklyn	0
	Brooklyn	23	Pittsburgh	0
1939	Pittsburgh	17	Brooklyn	3
	Brooklyn	17	Pittsburgh	7
1939	Brooklyn	12	Pittsburgh	7
	Brooklyn	17	Pittsburgh	13
1940	Brooklyn	10	Pittsburgh	3
	Brooklyn	21	Pittsburgh	0
1941	Pittsburgh	14	Brooklyn	7
	Brooklyn	35	Pittsburgh	7
1942	Pittsburgh	7	Brooklyn	0
	Pittsburgh	13	Brooklyn	0

Brooklyn won 11; Pittsburgh won 8; Tied 1.

Total points: Brooklyn 244; Pittsburgh 158.

BROOKLYN vs
PORTSMOUTH SPARTANS

1930	Portsmouth	14	Brooklyn	0
1931	Portsmouth	19	Brooklyn	0
1932	Portsmouth	17	Brooklyn	7

Brooklyn won 0; Portsmouth won 3; Tied 0.

Total points: Brooklyn 7; Portsmouth 50.

BROOKLYN vs
WASHINGTON REDSKINS

1937	Washington	11	Brooklyn	7
	Washington	21	Brooklyn	0
1938	Washington	16	Brooklyn	16
	Washington	6	Brooklyn	6
1939	Washington	41	Brooklyn	13

BROOKLYN vs
WASHINGTON REDSKINS (cont.)

1939	Washington	42	Brooklyn	0
1940	Washington	24	Brooklyn	17
	Brooklyn	16	Washington	14
1941	Washington	3	Brooklyn	0
	Brooklyn	13	Washington	7
1942	Washington	21	Brooklyn	10
	Washington	23	Brooklyn	3
1943	Washington	27	Brooklyn	0
	Washington	48	Brooklyn	10
1944	Washington	17	Brooklyn.	14
	Washington	10	Brooklyn	0

Brooklyn won 2; Washington 12; Tied 2.

Total points: Brooklyn 125; Washington 331.

CINCINNATI
(Part of 1934 Season)

Pittsburgh	13	Cincinnati	0
Cardinals	9	Cincinnati	0
Cardinals	16	Cincinnati	0
Bears	21	Cincinnati	3
Bears	41	Cincinnati	7
Green Bay	41	Cincinnati	0
Detroit	38	Cincinnati	0
Philadelphia	64	Cincinnati	0

Cincinnati won 0; Opponents won 8; Tied 0.

Total points: Cincinnati 10; Opponents 243.

CLEVELAND RAMS vs
BOSTON YANKS

1945	Cleveland	20	Boston	7

CLEVELAND RAMS vs
CHICAGO BEARS

1937	Bears	20	Cleveland	2
	Bears	15	Cleveland	7
1938	Cleveland	14	Bears	7
	Cleveland	23	Bears	21
1939	Bears	30	Cleveland	21
	Bears	35	Cleveland	21
1940	Bears	21	Cleveland	14
	Bears	47	Cleveland	25
1941	Bears	48	Cleveland	21
	Bears	31	Cleveland	13
1942	Bears	21	Cleveland	7
	Bears	47	Cleveland	0
1944	Cleveland	19	Bears	7
	Bears	28	Cleveland	21
1945	Cleveland	17	Bears	0
	Cleveland	41	Bears	21

Cleveland won 5; Bears won 11; Tied 0.

Total points: Cleveland 266; Bears 399.

CLEVELAND RAMS vs
CHICAGO CARDINALS

1937	Cardinals	6	Cleveland	0
	Cardinals	13	Cleveland	7
1938	Cardinals	7	Cleveland	6
	Cardinals	31	Cleveland	17
1939	Cleveland	24	Cardinals	0
	Cleveland	14	Cardinals	0
1940	Cleveland	26	Cardinals	14
	Cardinals	17	Cleveland	7
1941	Cleveland	10	Cardinals	6
	Cardinals	7	Cleveland	0
1942	Cardinals	7	Cleveland	0
	Cleveland	7	Cardinals	3
1945	Cleveland	21	Cardinals	0
	Cleveland	35	Cardinals	21

Cleveland won 7; Cardinals won 7; Tied 0.
Total points: Cleveland 174; Cardinals 132.

CLEVELAND RAMS vs
DETROIT LIONS

1937	Detroit	28	Cleveland	0
	Detroit	27	Cleveland	7
1938	Cleveland	21	Detroit	17
	Detroit	6	Cleveland	0
1939	Detroit	15	Cleveland	7
	Cleveland	14	Detroit	3
1940	Detroit	6	Cleveland	0
	Cleveland	24	Detroit	0
1941	Detroit	17	Cleveland	7
	Detroit	14	Cleveland	0
1942	Cleveland	14	Detroit	0
	Cleveland	27	Detroit	7
1944	Cleveland	20	Detroit	17
	Detroit	26	Cleveland	14
1945	Cleveland	28	Detroit	21

Cleveland won 7; Detroit won 8; Tied 0.
Total points: Cleveland 183; Detroit 204.

CLEVELAND RAMS vs
GREEN BAY PACKERS

1937	Green Bay	35	Cleveland	10
	Green Bay	35	Cleveland	7
1938	Green Bay	26	Cleveland	17
	Green Bay	28	Cleveland	7
1939	Cleveland	27	Green Bay	24
	Green Bay	7	Cleveland	6
1940	Green Bay	31	Cleveland	14
	Green Bay	13	Cleveland	13
1941	Green Bay	24	Cleveland	7
	Green Bay	17	Cleveland	14
1942	Green Bay	45	Cleveland	28
	Green Bay	30	Cleveland	12
1944	Green Bay	30	Cleveland	21
	Green Bay	42	Cleveland	7
1945	Cleveland	27	Green Bay	14
	Cleveland	20	Green Bay	7

Cleveland won 3; Green Bay won 12; Tied 1.

Total points: Cleveland 237; Green Bay 408.

CLEVELAND RAMS vs NEW YORK GIANTS

1938	New York	28	Cleveland	0
1940	Cleveland	13	New York	0
1941	New York	49	Cleveland	14
1945	Cleveland	21	New York	17

Cleveland won 2; New York won 2; Tied 0.

Total points: Cleveland 48; New York 94.

CLEVELAND RAMS vs PHILADELPHIA EAGLES

1937	Cleveland	21	Philadelphia	3
1939	Cleveland	35	Philadelphia	13
1940	Cleveland	21	Philadelphia	13
1942	Cleveland	24	Philadelphia	14
1944	Philadelphia	26	Cleveland	13
1945	Philadelphia	28	Cleveland	14

Cleveland won 4; Philadelphia won 2; Tied 0.

Total points: Cleveland 128; Philadelphia 97.

CLEVELAND RAMS vs PITTSBURGH STEELERS

1938	Cleveland	13	Pittsburgh	7
1939	Cleveland	14	Pittsburgh	14
1941	Cleveland	17	Pittsburgh	14

Cleveland won 2; Pittsburgh won 0; Tied 1.

Total points: Cleveland 44; Pittsburgh 35.

CLEVELAND RAMS vs WASHINGTON REDSKINS

1937	Washington	16	Cleveland	7
1938	Washington	37	Cleveland	13
1941	Washington	17	Cleveland	13
1942	Washington	33	Cleveland	14
1944	Washington	14	Cleveland	10
1945	*Cleveland	15	Washington	14

Cleveland won 1; Washington won 5; Tied 0.

Total points: Cleveland 72; Washington 131.

* Championship Play-off Game

NEW YORK BULLDOGS vs CHICAGO CARDINALS

| 1949 | Cardinals | 65 | Bulldogs | 20 |

NEW YORK BULLDOGS vs DETROIT LIONS

| 1949 | Detroit | 28 | Bulldogs | 27 |

NEW YORK BULLDOGS vs GREEN BAY PACKERS

| 1949 | Green Bay | 19 | Bulldogs | 0 |

NEW YORK BULLDOGS vs LOS ANGELES RAMS

| 1949 | Los Angeles | 42 | Bulldogs | 20 |

NEW YORK BULLDOGS vs NEW YORK GIANTS

| 1949 | Giants | 38 | Bulldogs | 14 |
| | Bulldogs | 31 | Giants | 24 |

NEW YORK BULLDOGS vs PHILADELPHIA EAGLES

| 1949 | Philadelphia | 7 | Bulldogs | 0 |
| | Philadelphia | 42 | Bulldogs | 0 |

NEW YORK BULLDOGS vs PITTSBURGH STEELERS

| 1949 | Pittsburgh | 24 | Bulldogs | 13 |
| | Pittsburgh | 27 | Bulldogs | 0 |

NEW YORK BULLDOGS vs WASHINGTON REDSKINS

| 1949 | Washington | 38 | Bulldogs | 14 |
| | Washington | 14 | Bulldogs | 14 |

NEW YORK YANKS vs BALTIMORE COLTS

| 1950 | Yanks | 51 | Colts | 14 |

NEW YORK YANKS vs CHICAGO BEARS

1950	Yanks	38	Bears	27
	Bears	28	Yanks	20
1951	Bears	24	Yanks	21
	Bears	45	Yanks	21

Yanks won 1; Bears won 3; Tied 0.

Total points: Yanks 100; Bears 124.

NEW YORK YANKS vs DETROIT LIONS

1950	Yanks	44	Detroit	21
	Detroit	49	Yanks	14
1951	Detroit	37	Yanks	10
	Detroit	24	Yanks	24

Yanks won 1; Detroit won 2; Tied 1.

Total points: Yanks 92; Detroit 131.

NEW YORK YANKS vs GREEN BAY PACKERS

1950	Yanks	44	Green Bay	31
	Yanks	35	Green Bay	17
1951	Green Bay	29	Yanks	27
	Yanks	31	Green Bay	28

Yanks won 3; Green Bay won 1; Tied 0.
Total points: Yanks 137; Green Bay 105.

NEW YORK YANKS vs LOS ANGELES RAMS

1950	Los Angeles	45	Yanks	28
	Los Angeles	43	Yanks	35
1951	Los Angeles	54	Yanks	14
	Los Angeles	48	Yanks	21

Yanks won 0; Los Angeles won 4; Tied 0.

Total points: Yanks 98; Los Angeles 190.

NEW YORK YANKS vs NEW YORK GIANTS

1950	Giants	51	Yanks	7
1951	Giants	37	Yanks	31
	Giants	27	Yanks	17

Yanks won 0; Giants won 3; Tied 0.

Total points: Yanks 55; Giants 115.

NEW YORK YANKS vs SAN FRANCISCO FORTY NINERS

1950	Yanks	21	San Francisco	17
	Yanks	29	San Francisco	24
1951	San Francisco	19	Yanks	14
	San Francisco	10	Yanks	10

Yanks won 2; S.F. won 1; Tied 1.

Total points: Yanks 74; S.F. 70.

PORTSMOUTH vs CHICAGO BEARS

1930	Portsmouth	7	Bears	6
	Bears	14	Portsmouth	6
1931	Bears	9	Portsmouth	6
	Portsmouth	3	Bears	0
1932	Portsmouth	13	Bears	13
	Portsmouth	7	Bears	7
	*Bears	9	Portsmouth	0
1933	Bears	17	Portsmouth	14
	Bears	17	Portsmouth	7

Portsmouth won 2; Bears won 5; Tied 2.

Total points: Portsmouth 63; Bears 92.

* Championship Play-off (Played in Chicago Stadium; indoors)

PORTSMOUTH vs CHICAGO CARDINALS

1930	Portsmouth	0	Cardinals	0
	Cardinals	23	Portsmouth	0

1931	Cardinals	20	Portsmouth	19
1932	Cardinals	7	Portsmouth	7
1933	Portsmouth	7	Cardinals	6

Portsmouth won 1; Cardinals won 2; Tied 2.

Total points: Portsmouth 33; Cardinals 56.

PORTSMOUTH vs GREEN BAY PACKERS

1930	Green Bay	47	Portsmouth	13
	Green Bay	6	Portsmouth	6
1932	Green Bay	15	Portsmouth	10
	Portsmouth	19	Green Bay	0
1933	Green Bay	17	Portsmouth	0
	Portsmouth	7	Green Bay	0

Portsmouth won 2; Green Bay won 3; Tied 1.

Total points: Portsmouth 55; Green Bay 85.

PORTSMOUTH vs NEW YORK GIANTS

1930	New York	19	Portsmouth	6
1931	Portsmouth	14	New York	6
	New York	14	Portsmouth	0
1932	Portsmouth	7	New York	0
	Portsmouth	6	New York	0
1933	Portsmouth	17	New York	7
	New York	13	Portsmouth	10

Portsmouth won 4; New York won 3; Tied 0.

Total points: Portsmouth 60; New York 59.

PORTSMOUTH vs PHILADELPHIA EAGLES

1933	Portsmouth	25	Philadelphia	0

ST. LOUIS
(Part of 1934 Season)

St. Louis	6	Pittsburgh	0
Detroit	40	St. Louis	7
Green Bay	21	St. Louis	14

St. Louis won 1; Opponents won 2; Tied 0.

Total points: St. Louis 27; Opponents 61.

TEAM DEPARTMENTAL CHAMPIONS

FORWARD PASSING

		Attempts	Completed	Efficiency
1951	Cleveland	271	151	55.7
1950	Los Angeles Rams	*453	*253	55.8
1949	Los Angeles Rams	366	192	52.5

1948	New York Giants	363	191	52.6
1947	Washington Redskins	416	231	55.5
1946	Los Angeles Rams	326	153	46.9
1945	Washington Redskins	228	146	*64.0
1944	Washington Redskins	299	170	56.8
1943	Washington Redskins	254	139	54.7
1942	Washintgon Redskins	257	137	53.3
1941	Green Bay Packers	253	133	52.6
1940	Washington Redskins	244	144	59.0
1939	Cleveland Rams	253	127	50.1
1938	Chicago Cardinals	240	114	47.5
1937	Washington Redskins	222	99	44.5
1936	Green Bay Packers	255	108	42.3
1935	New York Giants	154	69	44.8
1934	New York Giants	154	63	40.9
1933	Brooklyn Dodgers	169	79	46.7
1932	New York Giants	188	87	46.2
1931	Green Bay Packers	230	93	40.4

* League Record

POINTS SCORED

			Games
1951	Los Angeles Rams	392	12
1950	Los Angeles Rams	*466	12
1949	Philadelphia Eagles	364	12
1948	Chicago Cardinals	395	12
1947	Chicago Bears	363	12
1946	Chicago Bears	289	11
1945	Philadelphia Eagles	272	10
1944	Philadelphia Eagles	267	10
1943	Chicago Bears	303	10
1942	Chicago Bears	376	11
1941	Chicago Bears	396	11
1940	Washington Redskins	245	11
1939	Chicago Bears	298	11
1938	Green Bay Packers	223	11
1937	Green Bay Packers	220	11
1936	Green Bay Packers	248	12
1935	Chicago Bears	192	12
1934	Chicago Bears	286	13
1933	New York Giants	244	14
1932	Green Bay Packers	152	14

* League Record

TOTAL YARDS GAINED

1951	Los Angeles Rams	*5,506
1950	Los Angeles Rams	5,420
1949	Chicago Bears	4,873
1948	Chicago Cardinals	4,694
1947	Chicago Bears	5,053
1946	Los Angeles Rams	3,763
1945	Washington Redskins	3,549
1944	Chicago Bears	3,239
1943	Chicago Bears	4,045
1942	Chicago Bears	3,900
1941	Chicago Bears	4,265
1940	Green Bay Packers	3,400
1939	Chicago Bears	3,988
1938	Green Bay Packers	3,037
1937	Green Bay Packers	3,201
1936	Detroit Lions	3,703

1935	Chicago Bears	3,454
1934	Chicago Bears	3,750
1933	New York Giants	2,970
1932	Chicago Bears	2,755

* League Record

YARDS GAINED PASSING

1951	Los Angeles Rams	3,296
1950	Los Angeles Rams	*3,709
1949	Chicago Bears	3,055
1948	Washington Redskins	2,861
1947	Washington Redskins	3,336
1946	Los Angeles Rams	2,080
1945	Cleveland Rams	1,857
1944	Washington Redskins	2,021
1943	Chicago Bears	2,310
1942	Green Bay Packers	2,407
1941	Chicago Bears	2,002
1940	Washington Redskins	1,887
1939	Chicago Bears	1,965
1938	Washington Redskins	1,536
1937	Green Bay Packers	1,398
1936	Green Bay Packers	1,629
1935	Green Bay Packers	1,416
1934	Green Bay Packers	1,165
1933	New York Giants	1,335
1932	Chicago Bears	1,013

* League Record

YARDS GAINED RUSHING

1951	Chicago Bears	2,408
1950	New York Giants	2,336
1949	Philadelphia Eagles	2,607
1948	Chicago Cardinals	2,560
1947	Los Angeles Rams	2,171
1946	Green Bay Packers	1,765
1945	Cleveland Rams	1,714
1944	Philadelphia Eagles	1,663
1943	Phil-Pitt "Steagles"	1,730
1942	Chicago Bears	1,881

YARDS GAINED RUSHING (cont.)

1941	Chicago Bears	2,156
1940	Chicago Bears	1,818
1939	Chicago Bears	2,043
1938	Detroit Lions	1,893
1937	Detroit Lions	2,074

1936	Detroit Lions	*2,885
1935	Chicago Bears	2,096
1934	Detroit Lions	2,763
1933	Boston Redskins	2,367
1932	Chicago Bears	1,770

* League Record

THEY COVER THE GAMES

National Football League games are important to more than a hundred million Americans. To take the story to that vast audience is the pleasant duty of these men, fans themselves, who cover the league games by newspaper, radio, and television reporting.

CHICAGO BEARS AND CHICAGO CARDINALS

Chicago Tribune—Arch Ward, Ed Prell, Harry Warren, Bob Cromie

Chicago Daily News—John Carmichael, Howie Roberts, Jack Ryan

Chicago Sun & Times—Gene Kessler, Bruce Morrison, Joe Agrella

Chicago Herald-American—Leo Fischer, Harry McNamara, Warren Brown, Jim Enright

Associated Press—Charles Dunkley

International News Service—Jerry Liska, Charles Chamberlain

United Press—Edward Sainsbury

Radio—Bob Elson, Joe Boland, Bert Wilson

TV—Harold "Red" Grange, Jack Brickhouse

CLEVELAND BROWNS

Cleveland Plain Dealer—Gordon Cobbledick, Harold Sauerbrei, Chuck Heato

Cleveland Press—Franklin Lewis, Bob Yonkers, Henry Andrews

Cleveland News—Herman Goldstein, Hal Lebovitz

Radio—Bob Neal

TV—Clay Dopp

DALLAS TEXANS

Dallas Times-Herald—Louis Cox, Jere Hayes

Dallas News—William Rives, Charles Burton

DETROIT LIONS

Detroit Free Press—Lyall Smith, Bob Latshaw

Detroit Times—Bob Murphy, Bob McClellan

Detroit News—Harry Salsinger, Sam Greene, Watson Spoelstra

Radio—Van Patrick, Don Wattrick

GREEN BAY PACKERS

Green Bay Press-Gazette—Art Daley

Milwaukee Sentinel—Stoney McGlynn, Lloyd Larson

Milwaukee Journal—Oliver Kuechle

Madison State Journal—Roundy Coughlin

Associated Press—Chris Edmonds

Radio—Larry Clark, Tony Flynn

LOS ANGELES RAMS

Los Angeles Times—Frank Finch

Los Angeles Examiner—Bob Oates

Los Angeles Mirror—Max Stiles

Los Angeles Daily News—Art Rense

Los Angeles Herald-Express—John Old

Associated Press—Bob Myers

International News—Chuck Panama

United Press—Al Kahn

Radio—Bob Kelley

TV—Tom Harmon

NEW YORK GIANTS

New York Times—Lou Effrat, Joe Sheehan, Art Daley

New York Tribune—Bill Lauder, Rud Rennie, Red Smith, Bob Cooke

New York Daily News—Jim Powers, Gene Ward

New York Daily Mirror—Dan Parker, Ken Smith, Harold Weissman

New York Post—Al Buck

New York Journal-American—Max Kase, Bill Corum, Dave Eisenberg
New York World-Telegram & Sun—Joe Williams, Joe King
Brooklyn Eagle—Harold Burr
Long Island Press & Star-Journal—Don Smith, Murray Janoff
Newark News—Ed Friel
Radio—Marty Glickman, Chris Schenkel
TV—Harry Wismer

PHILADELPHIA EAGLES

Philadelphia Enquirer—Frank O'Gara
Philadelphia Bulletin—Hugh Brown
Philadelphia Daily News—Ed Delaney
Associated Press—Ralph Bernstein
International News—Tony Zecca
United Press—Russell Green
Radio—Bill Campbell, Bill Sears
TV—Byrum Saam

PITTSBURGH STEELERS

Pittsburgh Sun Telegraph—Harry Keck, Tom Birks
Pittsburgh Press—Chester Smith, Pat Livingston
Pittsburgh Post Gazette—Al Abrams, Jack Sell
Associated Press—Joe Bradis
United Press—Rudy Cernkovic

International News Service—John Golightly
Radio and TV—Joe Tucker

SAN FRANCISCO 49ers

San Francisco Chronicle—Bill Leiser, Bruce Lee, Will Conolly, Art Rosenbaum
San Francisco News—Bud Spencer, Bill Anderson, Roger Williams
San Francisco Call-Bulletin—Jack McDonald, Peter Tehaney
San Francisco Examiner—Prescott Sullivan, Harry Borba
Oakland Tribune—Alan Ward, Wally Willis
Radio—Wilson "Bud" Foster

WASHINGTON REDSKINS

Washington Star—Lewis Atchison, Frances Stann
Washington Post—Morris Siegel, Shirley Povich, Bus Ham
Washington Times-Herald—Al Costello, Dick O'Brien, Bob Addie
Washington Daily News—Dave Slattery, Everett Gardner
Associated Press—Art Edson
International News—Earle Marckres
United Press—Bob Serling
Radio—Mel Allen, Jim Gibbons, Bob Wolff, Arch McDonald, Arthur Bergman, Tony Wakeman, Ray Michaels
TV—Mel Allen, Bob Roth, Jim Simpson

SEATING DIAGRAMS OF NFL STADIUMS

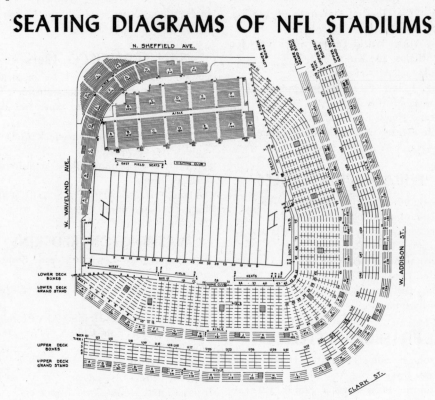

WRIGLEY FIELD, CHICAGO—HOME OF THE BEARS

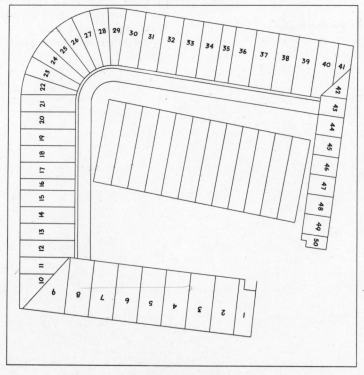

COMISKEY PARK, CHICAGO—HOME OF THE CARDINALS

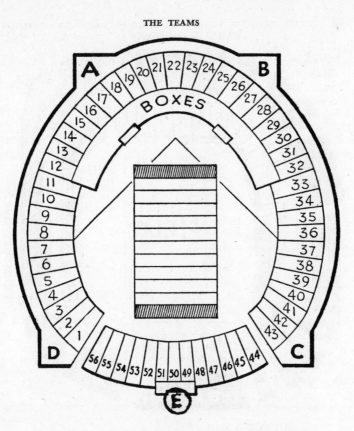

MUNICIPAL STADIUM, CLEVELAND—HOME OF THE BROWNS

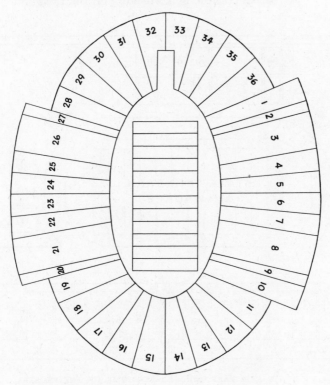

COTTON BOWL, DALLAS—HOME OF THE TEXANS

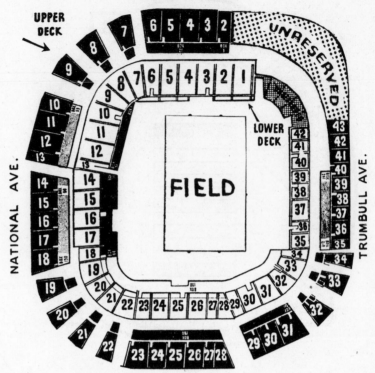

BRIGGS STADIUM, DETROIT—HOME OF THE LIONS

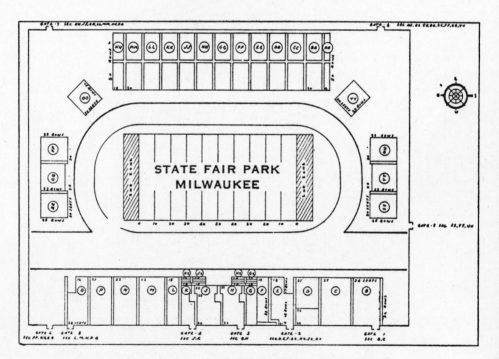

STATE FAIR PARK, MILWAUKEE—HOME OF THE PACKERS

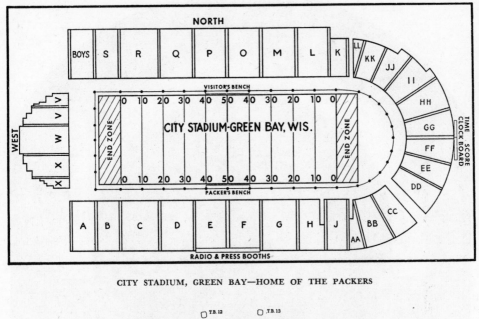

CITY STADIUM, GREEN BAY—HOME OF THE PACKERS

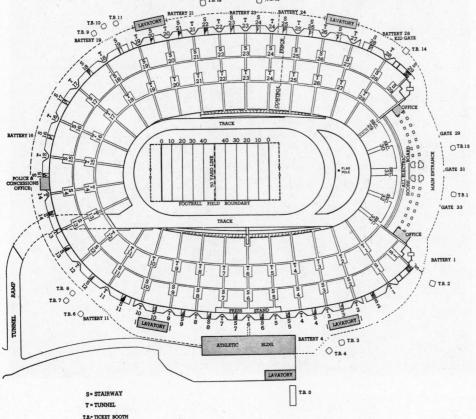

MEMORIAL COLISEUM, LOS ANGELES—HOME OF THE RAMS

POLO GROUNDS, NEW YORK CITY—HOME OF THE GIANTS

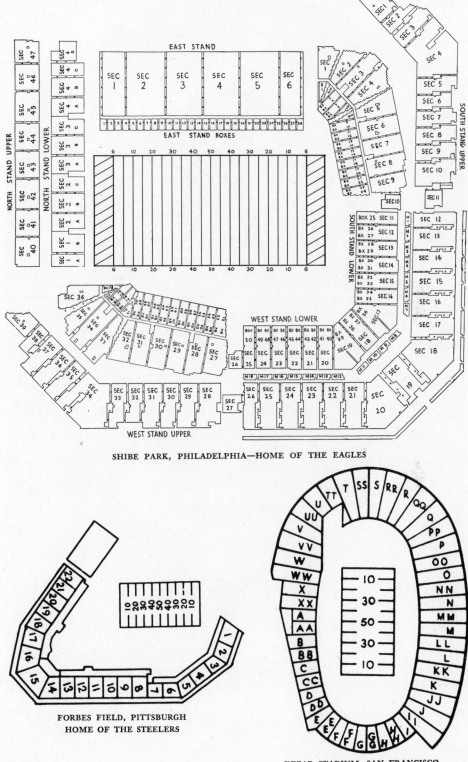

SHIBE PARK, PHILADELPHIA—HOME OF THE EAGLES

FORBES FIELD, PITTSBURGH
HOME OF THE STEELERS

KEZAR STADIUM, SAN FRANCISCO
HOME OF THE 49ERS

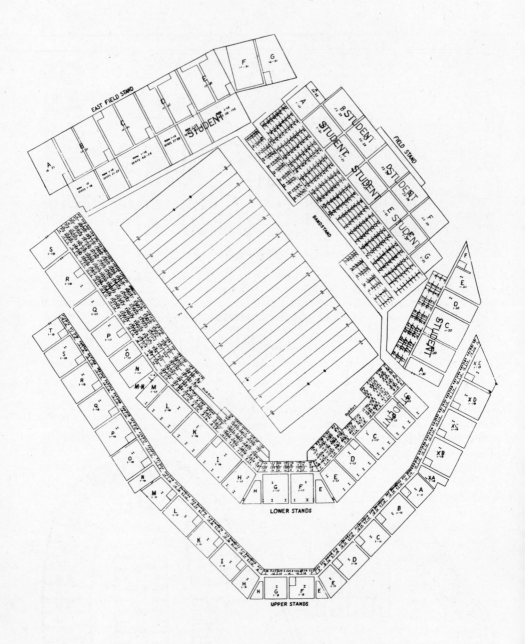

GRIFFITH STADIUM, WASHINGTON—HOME OF THE REDSKINS

Tribune Studio

CHAPTER 6
THE
ALL-STAR
GAME
THE COLLEGE ALL-STAR
FOOTBALL SERIES
By ARCH WARD
Sports Editor, Chicago *Tribune*

Figures can be overpowering and we'll begin the story of the glamorous College All-Star series by submitting some. They, more than all the adjectives dear to the heart of a sportswriter, give a picture of the spectacle's tremendous impact on American athletics.

The eighteen games through 1951 were witnessed by 1,537,740 spectators, an average of 85,430 per game. Gross receipts totaled $4,356,689.76. To charities has gone $1,043,478.77.

The eighteenth annual game was witnessed by an estimated fifty million on television screens in a hook-up of forty-eight stations stretching from Jacksonville, Fla., and Birmingham, Ala., in the South, to Minneapolis in the North, from Omaha and Kansas City west to the Pacific coast, and into the major cities in the East. There were five hundred radio outlets and the armed forces sent a word story of the game around the world, wherever our troops were stationed. Requests for the top-priced tickets at $7 exceeded the supply by more than twenty-five thousand. Eight thousand rooters came from Cleveland to watch their Browns beat the Collegians, 33–0.

This is a quick presentation of the game which has thrilled the nation's fans since 1934, when the series was inaugurated. The greatest college players of the last eighteen years and most of the finest professionals have engaged in the intriguing pro versus college gridiron arguments.

This glamorous event in American football was conceived primarily as a means of raising money to help the poor. It has come through war and peace, depression and prosperity, as the top attraction in its field. Invariably it draws one of the largest crowds to see a football game, collegiate or professional, each season. No other event lures so many coaches, newspapermen, and athletic directors. And no other game pulls its audience from so vast an area. Nearly every state in the union is represented—as are many foreign countries—in the stacks of ticket applications.

During World War II, other sports extravaganzas, even including the major league baseball All-Star game, became casualties. But the All-Star football game had its most prosperous years and some of its most exciting contests after the United States entered the conflict. The All-Star game's survival was due, in no small measure, to the co-operation of the Army Air Force and the various collegiate conferences, which permitted use of undergraduates at a time when talent was scarce. In normal times, only athletes whose college eligibility has ended are invited to join the All-Star squad.

From the launching of the game in 1934, until 1942, the net revenue was divided equally among the United Charities, the Catholic Charities and the Jewish Charities of Chicago. In 1943, 1944 and 1945, profits of the enterprise were donated to war charities, such as the Army Air Force Aid Society and the Chicago Servicemen's centers, which made Chicago known as the most hospitable of all cities to the men in uniform.

We are grateful for the support the All-Star game has received, from both professional and collegiate football. A large percentage of football players among graduating seniors sign annually with the twelve National Football League clubs, whose owners relinquish the outstanding ones to the All-Star squad. The game, of course, has great exploitation value for the league.

The All-Star series is sponsored by Chicago Tribune Charities, Inc., which also sponsors the Golden Gloves competition. It, of course, is a non-profit organization.

Each year a staff of a half dozen or more collegiate coaches drill the stars assembled from all over the country. The present training site is Delafield, Wis., eighty miles from Chicago, and the squad is housed in St. John's Military Academy, whose facilities and cool climate are ideal for the rigid three weeks of preparation.

The game is held in August and the team which won the National League title the previous season automatically qualifies to meet the collegians. The All-Star game marks the first appearance of the professional team which comes into the new season as champion.

Invitation to the All-Star squad is the goal of most college players. In this day of commercialism we like to emphasize that it's the honor, not the money, which beckons to the young men. Each player, from the most gifted All-American quarterback to the linemen, receives $150 and expenses. Players prize the All-Star sweaters and blankets and the thrill of playing under the bright lights of Soldier Field. From the start, the $150 payment has been in effect.

Thrills have piled on thrills down the years to create a montage. But, in the blending of mental pictures from the floodlighted field, we still can clearly see the little giant, Eddie LeBaron, of the 1950 All-Star team, dancing away from tacklers, retreating far back—so far it seemed he would be nailed in his own end zone by on-rushing Philadelphia Eagles. Then we see Eddie finally throwing the ball and Charley "Choo Choo" Justice of North Carolina fielding it at about where the line of scrimmage had been and dashing 35 yards to score.

That was the most spectacular play in all the games contested to date. A 31-yard sprint by Justice had started the Collegians on their way to a touchdown in the first quarter against the startled Eagles, who had walloped the All-Stars the year before, 33–0. Later in the game, Justice rambled 47 yards. Sportswriters voted him the most valuable All-Star in the game. But if ever two awards were justified, that was the night, because College of the Pacific's LeBaron, five feet eight inches tall, was a mental giant among physical giants. After the game he joined the Marines and soon afterwards was fighting, and was later wounded, in Korea.

The professionals have won ten of the games, the Collegians six. The other two were ties. That's a respectable showing for the All-Stars against championship units. But never has the game been advanced primarily as a test of skill and strength between rival units. It is presented more as a spectacle, the grand and gala opening of the football season with all its pageantry and excitement. Fans thrill as much to the inter-mission musical shows as to the action on the field.

And it's the one game of the year when we are as rabid a fan as any in the vast reaches of the gray mass of concrete and steel off the shores of Lake Michigan!

ALL-STAR GAMES, 1934-1952

1934	Chicago Bears	0	All-Stars	0
1935	Chicago Bears	5	All-Stars	0
1936	Detroit Lions	7	All-Stars	7
1937	All-Stars	6	Green Bay Packers	0
1938	All-Stars	28	Washington Redskins	16
1939	New York Giants	9	All-Stars	0
1940	Green Bay Packers	45	All-Stars	28
1941	Chicago Bears	37	All-Stars	13
1942	Chicago Bears	21	All-Stars	0
1943	All-Stars	27	Washington Redskins	7
1944	Chicago Bears	24	All-Stars	21
1945	Green Bay Packers	19	All-Stars	7
1946	All-Stars	16	Los Angeles Rams	0
1947	All-Stars	16	Chicago Bears	0
1948	Chicago Cardinals	28	All-Stars	0
1949	Philadelphia Eagles	38	All-Stars	0
1950	All-Stars	17	Philadelphia Eagles	7
1951	Cleveland Browns	33	All-Stars	0
1952	Los Angeles Rams	10	All-Stars	7

1934 CHICAGO ALL-STAR GAME

(Soldier Field, Chicago, Ill., Aug. 31, 1934)

Attendance 79,432

Chicago Bears (0)		College All-Stars (0)
Hewitt	L.E.	Manske (Northwestern)
Lyman	L.T.	Krause (Notre Dame)
Carlson	L.G.	Walton (Pittsburgh)
Miller	C.	Bernard (Michigan)
Zeller	R.G.	Febel (Purdue)
Musso	R.T.	Schwammel (Oregon)
Johnsos	R.E.	Skladany (Pittsburgh)
Brumbaugh	Q.B.	Griffith (Southern California)
Ronzani	L.H.	Feathers (Tennessee)
Corbett	R.H.	Laws (Iowa)
Nagurski	F.B.	Mikulak (Oregon)

Chicago Bears	0	0	0	0—0
College All-Stars	0	0	0	0—0

Coaches—George Halas (Bears), Noble Kizer (Purdue).

SUBSTITUTIONS

Chicago Bears—Ends: Karr, Becker; tackle: Buss; guard: Kopcha, Zizak; center: Kawal; backs: Grange, Manders, Sisk, Westray.

All-Stars—Ends: Smith (Washington), Gillman (Ohio State), Canrinus (St. Mary's); tackles: Crawford (Duke), Mehringer (Kansas), Krueger (Marquette), Rosenquist (Ohio State), Maneikis (Chicago); guards: Jones (Indiana), Hupke (Alabama); centers: Vuchinich (Ohio State), Gorman (Notre Dame); backs: Everhardus (Michigan), Cook (Illinois), Pardonner (Purdue), Sebastian (Pittsburgh), Hecker (Purdue), Lukats (Notre Dame), Montgomery (Columbia), Sauer (Nebraska), Cramer (Ohio State).

Officials: Referee—James Masker. Umpire—John Schommer. Field judge—Wilfred Smith. Head Linesman—J. J. Lipp.

THE GAME

The spirit and enthusiasm of the first of the brilliant lines of College All-Star squads held the methodical precision of the Chicago Bears, professional football champions, to a scoreless tie.

The Bears, who perhaps did not take their assignment too seriously, twice threatened to score after the All-Stars fumbled on reaching the major leaguers' 13-yard line the first time they had the ball. A 20-yard pass, Corbett to Ronzani, put the ball on the collegians' 10-yard line, late in the first quarter, but Corbett's wild lateral was recovered by the All-Stars' Schwammel.

Late in the third quarter, the All-Stars' Bill Smith missed a field goal from near midfield.

In the fourth period, the Bears reached the All-Stars' 26, aided by Red Grange's 22-yard pass to Johnnie Sisk, but the attack bogged down. Late in the game, Smith tried another field goal, this one from the Bears' 38, but it was low.

1935 CHICAGO ALL-STAR GAME

(Soldier Field, Chicago, Ill., Aug. 29, 1935)

Attendance 77,450

Chicago Bears (5)		College All-Stars (0)
Hewitt	L.E.	Hutson (Alabama)
Buss	L.T.	Blazine (Illinois Wesleyan)
Richards	L.G.	Monahan (Ohio State)
Kawal	C.	Shotwell (Pittsburgh)
Kopcha	R.G.	Bevan (Minnesota)
Musso	R.T.	Barber (San Francisco)
Karr	R.E.	Fuqua (So. Methodist)
Masterson	Q.B.	Munjas (Pittsburgh)
Feathers	L.H.	Shepherd (West. Maryland)
Sisk	R.H.	Nichelini (St. Mary's)
Manders	F.B.	Kostka (Minnesota)

Chicago Bears	3	0	0	2—5
College All-Stars	0	0	0	0—0

Field Goal—Manders. Safety—Shepherd.
Coaches—Frank Thomas (Alabama), George Halas (Chicago Bears).

SUBSTITUTIONS

Chicago Bears—Ends: Johnsos, Becker, Crawford: tackles: Trost, Rosequist; guard: Carlson; center: Miller; backs: Dunlop, Corbett, Pollock, Ronzani, Nagurski.

All-Stars—Ends: Morse (Oregon), Borden (Fordham), Larson (Minnesota), Leeper (Northwestern); tackles: Steen (Syracuse), Lee (Alabama), Bengston (Minnesota); guards: Mucha (Washington), Gundlach (Harvard), Barclay (No. Carolina), Schiarelli (Notre Dame); centers: Siemering (San Francisco), Ford (Michigan), backs: Salatino (Santa Clara), Regeczi (Michigan), Lund (Minnesota), Borries (Navy), Wetzel (Ohio State).

Officials: Referee—James Masker. Umpire—John Schommer. Field Judge—Wilfred Smith. Head Linesman—J. J. Lipp.

THE GAME

Jack Manders' 27-yard field goal from placement late in the first quarter, plus a safety in the fourth period, gave the Chicago Bears a 5 to 0 triumph over the All-Americans before a rain-soaked crowd of 77,450 in Soldier Field.

Thus, after two games in the brilliant series, not a single touchdown had been scored. The Bears were in command most of the time, but in the fifth minute of the final quarter, Alabama's Don Hutson all but got away for a touchdown on a stirring end around play. This threat, sparked by Hutson's 17-yard dash to the Bears' 8, ended after the collegians had reached the 5.

It was after the All-Stars had stemmed a Bear drive on their 3-yard line that Manders, following a 15-yard penalty for holding against the professionals, booted a field goal from the 27.

Beattie Feathers was the top ball-toter for the Bears, with 42 yards on 9 attempts. Bill Shepherd of Western Maryland gained 44 yards in 11 thrusts for the All-Stars.

1936 CHICAGO ALL-STAR GAME

(Soldier Field, Chicago, Ill., Sept. 3, 1936)

Attendance 76,000

Detroit Lions (7)		College All-Stars (7)
Klewicki	L.E.	Millner (Notre Dame)
Johnson	L.T.	Smith, R. (Minnesota)
Knox	L.G.	Tangora (Northwestern)
Randolph	C.	Jones (Ohio)
Emerson	R.G.	Oesch (Minnesota)
Christensen, G.	R.T.	Spain (S.M.U.)
Schneller	R.E.	Topping (Stanford)
Clark	Q.B.	Smith, R. (Alabama)
Christensen, F.	L.H.	Berwanger (Chicago)
Caddel	R.H.	Shakespeare (Notre Dame)
Parker	F.B.	Beise (Minnesota)

Detroit Lions	0	0	0	7—7
College All-Stars	0	7	0	0—7

Touchdowns—Caddel, LeVoir.
Points after touchdown—Clark, Fromhart.
Coaches—George Clark (Detroit), Bernie Bierman (Minnesota).

SUBSTITUTIONS

Detroit Lions—Ends: Ebding, Morse; tackle: Stacy; guards: Hupke, Monahan; center: Ritchart; backs: Presnell, White, Gutowsky, Shepherd, Nori.
All-Stars—Ends: Rees (Ohio State), Loebs (Purdue); tackles: Reynolds (Stanford), Stydahar (W. Virginia), Lutz (California); guards: Fortmann (Colgate), Gryboski (Illinois), Karcher (Ohio State); centers: Lind (Northwestern), Rennebohn (Minnesota); backs: Seidel (Minnesota), Fromhart (Notre Dame), Leemans (George Washintgon), Cruice (Northwestern), LeVoir (Minnesota), Crayne (Iowa), Maniaci (Fordham), Layden (Notre Dame), Lawrence (T.C.U.), Wilson (S.M.U.), Elser (Notre Dame).
Officials: Referee—Robert Cahn. Umpire—H. G. Hedges. Head Linesman—Ernest Vick. Field Judge—Maurice Meyer.

THE GAME

The College All-Stars marched 61 yards for a touchdown in the second period, and it wasn't until midway in the fourth quarter that the Detroit Lions matched those seven points for the second tie in the series, 7–7. The game was as even as the score indicated. Only five passes were completed, four of them by the collegians.

After a scoreless first quarter, the collegians scored when LeVoir went inside tackle for 17 yards. Fromhart added the point.

The third period was also scoreless; but in the fourth, the Lions recovered Leeman's fumble on their own 29 and drove home for the touchdown. Ernie Caddel going the last 10 yards on a lateral from Frank Christensen. "Dutch" Clark drop-kicked the extra point.

1937 CHICAGO ALL-STAR GAME

(Soldier Field, Chicago, Ill., Sept. 1, 1937)

Attendance 84,560

Green Bay Packers (0)		College All-Stars (6)
Hutson	L.E.	Tinsley (L.S.U.)
Smith	L.T.	Widseth (Minnesota)

Engebretsen	L.G.	Starcevich (Washington)
Svendsen, G.	C.	Svendsen, E. (Minnesota)
Evans	R.G.	Reid (Northwestern)
Gordon	R.T.	Daniell (Pittsburgh)
Gantenbein	R.E.	Wendt (Ohio State)
Bruder	Q.B.	Huffman (Indiana)
Sauer	L.H.	LaRue (Pittsburgh)
Herber	R.H.	Drake (Purdue)
Hinkle	F.B.	Francis (Nebraska)

| Green Bay Packers | 0 | 0 | 0 | 0—0 |
| College All-Stars | 6 | 0 | 0 | 0—6 |

Touchdowns—Tinsley (L.S.U.).
Coaches—Earl Lambeau (Green Bay), Bernie Bierman (Minnesota).

SUBSTITUTIONS

Green Bay Packers—Ends: Becker, Scherer; tackle: Butler; guards: Seibold, Michalske, Goldenberg, Schwammel, Letlow; center: Lester; back: Schneidman, Miller, Monnett, Laws, Johnson.

College All-Stars—Ends: Antil (Minnesota), Deutsch (St. Benedict's), Galatka (Mississippi State), Stromberg (Army); tackles: Dennerlein (St. Mary's), Bjork (Oregon), Henrion (Carnegie Tech), Kopczak (Notre Dame), Steinkemper (Notre Dame); guards: Lautar (Notre Dame), Bassi (Santa Clara), I. Smith (Ohio State), Dahlgren (Michigan State); centers: Basrak (Duquesne), Wiatrak (Washington); backs: Wilkinson (Minnesota), Baugh (T.C.U.), Agett (Michigan State), Wilke (Notre Dame), Cardwell (Nebraska), Jankowski (Wisconsin), Toth (Northwestern), Danbom (Notre Dame), Glassford (Pittsburgh), Haines (Washington).

Officials: Referee—Robert Cahn. Umpire—John Schommer. Field Judge—Joseph Magidsohn. Head Linesman—Maurice Meyer.

THE GAME

Samuel Adrian Baugh, a name which since became immortal in major league football, scored his first touchdown-pass against the Packers in this defensive thriller. Sixteen years later, Baugh held nearly every passing mark in the records and was still throwing them.

Baugh pitched one to Gaynell Tinsley from the Packer 47 in the first period. Tinsley caught it on the 25 and eluded both Hank Bruder and Joe Laws to score for the All-Stars.

There was no further scoring although both Arnold Herber and Bobby Monnett bombarded the collegians' defense trying to hit Don Hutson, or one of their other great receivers, to retrieve the game. But the defense was solid and Baugh's brilliant punting kept the Packers back on their heels until the final gun.

1938 CHICAGO ALL-STAR GAME

(Soldier Field, Chicago, Ill., Aug. 31, 1938)

Attendance 74,250

Washington Redskins (16)		College All-Stars (28)
Millner	L.E.	Schwartz (California)
Edwards	L.T.	Shirey (Nebraska)
Olsson	L.G.	Routt (Texas A & M)
Carroll	C.	Wolf (Ohio State)
Karcher	R.G.	Monsky (Alabama)
Barber	R.T.	Markov (Washington)
Malone	R.E.	Sweeney (Notre Dame)
Smith, R.	Q.B.	Puplis (Notre Dame)
Baugh	L.H.	Isbell (Purdue)
Pinckert	R.H.	Uram (Minnesota)
Krause	F.B.	Patrick (Pittsburgh)

| Washington Redskins | 7 | 3 | 0 | 6—16 |
| College All-Stars | 3 | 0 | 12 | 13—28 |

Touchdowns—Kovatch, Dougherty, Davis C., Uram, Krause, Karamatic.
Points after touchdown—Patrick, R. Smith.
Field Goals—McDonald, R. Smith.
Coaches—Ray Flaherty (Washington), Alvin N. "Bo" McMillin (All-Stars).

SUBSTITUTIONS

Washington Redskins—Ends: McChesney, Moore; tackles: Wilkin, Bond; guards: Young, Kahn; center: Parks; backs: Tuckey, Justice, Karamatic.

College All-Stars—Ends: Kovatch (Northwestern), P. Smith (Oklahoma), Birr (Indiana), Zachary (Purdue), Benton (Arkansas), Gustitus (St. Ambrose), Wolfe (Texas); tackles: Kinard (Mississippi), Kevorkian (Harvard), Babartsky (Fordham), Ryba (Alabama), Dixon (Boston U.); guards: Zarnas (Ohio State), Kuharich (Notre Dame), Reutz (Notre Dame), Calvano (Northwestern), Hoptowit (Washington State); centers: Nebel (Xavier), McCarty (Notre Dame), Dougherty (Santa Clara), Wegner (Northwestern), Gallagher (Yale); backs: McDonald (Ohio State), Vanzo (Northwestern), Davis (Indiana), J. White (Princeton), Spadaccini (Minnesota), Gmitro (Minnesota), B. White (Colorado), Rohm (L.S.U.), Heap (Northwestern), Coffis (Stanford), Calhoun (Loyola, N.O.), Kilgrow (Alabama), Popovich (Montana), Hackney (Duke).

Officials: Referee—Thomas Hughitt. Umpire—E. C. Krieger. Field Judge—Lawrence Conover. Head Linesman—Fred Gardner.

THE GAME

For the first time in the series, offensive power ruled under the lights of Soldier Field as Cecil Isbell of Purdue led the All-Stars to a 28–16 triumph over the Washington Redskins. Baugh, the Redskin star, was handicapped by an ankle injury, but it is doubtful that this was a vital factor.

In the first quarter, Fred Shirey of Nebraska intercepted Baugh's pass and ran to the Redskin 11, where Jim McDonald booted a field goal to put the Collegians ahead. The 'Skins came back 73 yards, Max Krause going over for a touchdown from the four and Riley Smith adding the extra point for 7–3 as the period ended.

Smith kicked a 23-yard field goal in the second period and the Redskins led, 10–3, at the half.

The All-Stars scored two touchdowns in the third. Isbell passed 39 yards to John Kovatch for the first and Phil Dougherty intercepted Karamatic's pass to run 40 yards for the second. Both extra point attempts failed.

Corby Davis crashed over from the Redskin 4 on the first play of the fourth quarter after Baugh's punt had been blocked. Again the point was missed, making it 21–10. Baugh connected with Riley Smith to move to the All-Star one and Karamatic smashed for the touchdown. Andy Uram later scored again for the All-Stars when he intercepted Dick Tuckey's pass and scampered 40 yards.

1939 CHICAGO ALL-STAR GAME

(Soldier Field, Chicago, Ill., Aug. 30, 1939)

Attendance 81,456

New York Giants (9)		College All-Stars (0)
Poole	L.T.	Wyatt (Tennessee)
Cope	L.E.	Mihal (Purdue)
Dell Isola	L.G.	Twedell (Minnesota)
Hein	C.	Brock, C. (Nebraska)
Tuttle	R.G.	Heikkinen (Michigan)
Mellus	R.T.	Haak (Indiana)
Howell	R.E.	Brown (Notre Dame)
Danowski	Q.B.	O'Brien (T.C.U.)
Cuff	L.H.	Goldberg (Pittsburgh)
Shaffer	R.H.	McLeod (Dartmouth)
Karcis	F.B.	Weiss (Wisconsin)

New York Giants	3	3	0	3—9
College All-Stars	0	0	0	0—0

Field Goals—Strong 2, Cuff.

Coaches—Steve Owen (New York), Elmer Layden (All-Stars).

SUBSTITUTIONS

New York Giants—Ends: Hanken, Walls; tackles: Widseth, Parry; guards: White, Lunday; center: Johnson; backs: Barnum, Burnett, Leemans, Falaschi, Strong.

College All-Stars—Ends: Jacunski (Fordham), Daddio (Pittsburgh), Young (Oklahoma), Coughlan (Santa Clara), Manders (Drake), Wysocki (Villanova), Wemple (Colgate); tackles: Wolff (Santa Clara), Beinor (Notre Dame), Voigts (Northwestern), Hale (T.C.U.), Schoenbaum (Ohio State); guards: Bock (Ohio State), Hovland (Wisconsin), Bell (Minnesota); centers: Hill (Duke), Kochel (Fordham), Aldrich (T.C.U.), Humphrey (Purdue); backs: Faust (Minnesota), Bottari (California), Osmanski (Holy Cross), Pingel (Michigan State), Patterson (Baylor), Sherman (Chicago), Jefferson (Northwestern), Seidel (Columbia), Buhler (Minnesota), Hofer (Notre Dame), Brunner (Tulane).

Officials: Referee—William Halloran. Umpire—Fred Young. Head Linesman—Lawrence Conover. Field Judge—Jay Wyatt.

THE GAME

The New York Giants, making their debut in the series, played the type of game expected of them—one featuring a rock-ribbed defense, and patience to wait for the breaks. They won the game with three field goals while holding the All-Stars scoreless.

Ward Cuff lofted the first one over from 27 yards out in the first period.

Ken Strong kicked the next, this one from 22 yards in the second quarter.

There was no scoring in the third quarter, and Strong wound up the scoring with a 33-yard shot in the last period.

Bill Osmanski of Holy Cross and Billy Patterson of Baylor were outstanding performers for the collegians.

1940 CHICAGO ALL-STAR GAME

(Soldier Field, Chicago, Ill., Aug. 29, 1940)

Attendance 84,567

Green Bay Packers (45)		College All-Stars (28)
Hutson	L.E.	Fisk (U.S.C.)
Ray	L.T.	Cutlich (Northwestern)
Letlow	L.G.	Logan (Indiana)
Svendsen, E.	C.	Turner (Hardin-Simmons)
Goldenberg	R.G.	Smith, H. (U.S.C.)
Lee	R.T.	Harvey (Notre Dame)
Gantenbein	R.E.	Sarkkinen (Ohio State)
Craig	Q.B.	Schindler (U.S.C.)
Isbell	L.H.	Kinnick (Iowa)
Laws	R.H.	Brock, L. (Purdue)
Hinkle	F.B.	Thesing (Notre Dame)

Green Bay Packers	14	14	7	10—45
College All-Stars	7	14	0	7—28

Touchdowns—Hutson 3, Mulleneaux, Uram, Isbell, Schindler 2, Washington, McFadden.

Points after touchdown—E. Smith 4, Engebretsen, Hutson, Kinnard 3, Kellogg.

Field Goal—E. Smith.

Coaches—Earl Lambeau (Green Bay), Dr. Edward Anderson (All-Stars).

SUBSTITUTIONS

Green Bay Packers—Ends: Mulleneaux, Jacunski, Berry, Temple; tackles: E. Smith, Schultz, Kell, Seibold, Kilbourne; guards: P. Tinsley, Zarnas, Engebretsen, Johnson, Midler, Marlin; centers: C. Brock, Greenfield; backs: Uram, Schneidman, Jankowski, Herber, Buhler, Balazs, Lawrence, Weisberger, Gillette, Feathers.

College All-Stars—Ends: Ivy (Oklahoma), Kavanaugh (L.S.U.), Anahu (Santa Clara),

Gustafson (Penn), Winslow (U.S.C.), Seeman (Nebraska); tackles: Artoe (Cal), Kolman (Temple), Anderson (Stanford), Pedersen (Minnesota); guards: Brewer (Illinois), Waldorf (Missouri), Method (Northwestern), Riffle (Notre Dame), Morino (Ohio State); centers: Schiechl (Santa Clara), Haman (Northwestern), Kopcha (Chattanooga); backs: Van Every (Minnesota), Emmons (Oregon), Kellogg (Tulane), Hoffman (U.S.C.), Washington (U.C.L.A.), McFadden (Clemson), Heineman (Texas Mines), Sheridan (Notre Dame).

Officials: Referee—Robie Cahn. Umpire—Blake. Head Linesman—Reese. Field Judge—Taylor.

THE GAME

This was a free-scoring thriller with the collegians holding on gamely through the first half, then fading before the power and experience of the devastating Packer squad.

Ambrose Schindler opened the scoring for the All-Stars by smashing over from the one-yard line in the first period. Nile Kinnick kicked the conversion. Cecil Isbell fired a 60-yard pass to Don Hutson who ran 30 more to score for the Packers. Ernie Smith's conversion evened the score at 7–7. Isbell then passed 26 yards to Carl Mulleneaux in the end zone and Smith added the extra point.

Kenny Washington smashed over from a foot away in the second period and Bobby Kellogg's conversion evened the score at 14–14. Arnie Herber passed 18 yards to Andy Uram who scampered 42 more for a touchdown and Tiny Engebretsen converted. Isbell followed with a 35-yard pass to Hutson in the end zone and Smith booted the dividend. Nile Kinnick fired a pass of 38 yards to Banks McFadden who galloped the remaining 28 to touchdown country and Kinnick kicked the conversion to make it 28–21 at the half.

In the third period, Herber passed 29 yards to Hutson in the end zone and Smith converted. The All-Stars were held scoreless in this quarter.

Schindler crashed over from the one in the fourth period and Kinnick again converted. Ernie Smith booted a field goal for the Packers from the 34. Cecil Isbell ran 4 yards on a reverse for a TD and Hutson booted the extra point to make the final score 45–28.

Ambrose Schindler was chosen for the first Chicago *Tribune* award as the most valuable All-Star player.

1941 CHICAGO ALL-STAR GAME

(Soldier Field, Chicago, Ill., Aug. 28, 1941)

Attendance 98,203

Chicago Bears (37)		College All-Stars (13)
Plasman	L.E.	Rankin (Purdue)
Stydahar	L.T.	Pannell (Texas A & M)
Fortmann	L.G.	Lio (Georgetown)
Turner	C.	Mucha (Washington)
Musso	R.G.	O'Boyle (Tulane)
Artoe	R.T.	Drahos (Cornell)
Wilson	R.E.	Rucinski (Indiana)
Luckman *Columbia*	Q.B.	Evashevski (Michigan)
Nolting	L.H.	Harmon (Michigan)
McAfee	R.H.	Franck (Minnesota)
Osmanski, W.	F.B.	Paskvan (Wisconsin)

Chicago Bears	6	7	3	21—37
College All-Stars	6	0	0	7—13

Touchdowns—Kavanaugh, Clark 2, McAfee, Nowaskey, Franck, Robinson.
Points after touchdown—Manders 4, Lio.
Field goal—Artoe.
Coaches—George Halas (Chicago), Carl Snavely (All-Stars).

SUBSTITUTIONS

Chicago Bears—Ends: Kavanaugh, Manders, Nowaskey, Pool, Siegel; tackles: Kolman, Mihal, Federovitch; guards: Baisi, Forte, Bray, Lahar; center: Buck; backs: Swisher, Bussey, Clark, Martin, McLean, Lee, Monfort, Famiglietti, Maniaci.

College All-Stars—Ends: Elrod (Miss. State), Severin (N. Carolina), Vosberg (Marquette), Frutig (Michigan), Bodney (Tulane), Darnell (Duke), Uremovich (Indiana), Prochaska (Nebraska); tackles: Hartman (Rice), Routt (Texas A & M), Ruffa (Duke), Pavelec (Detroit); guards: Lokanc (Northwestern), Bucchianeri (Indiana), Sogn (U.S.C.), Alfson (Nebraska), Osa (Bradley), Kerasiotis (St. Andrews); centers: Whitlow (Rice), Hiemenz (Northwestern), Osterman (Notre Dame); backs: Matuszczak (Cornell), Thomson (Texas A & M), Paffrath (Minnesota), Schulte (Rockhurst), Christman (Missouri), McAdams (Washington), Jones (Richmond), O'Rourke (Boston College), Mallouf (S.M.U.), Rohrig (Nebraska), Gallarneau (Stanford), Robinson (U.C.L.A.), Banta (U.S.C.), Eshmont (Fordham), Standlee (Stanford), Piepul (Notre Dame), Davis (Duke), Kracum (Pittsburgh), McGannon (Notre Dame), Allerdice (Princeton).

Officials: Referee—W. H. Friesell. Umpire—John Schommer. Head Linesman—Ernie Vick. Field Judge—Frank Lane.

THE GAME

This All-Star squad was loaded but it was up against the fabulous Bear champions of 1940 who had exploded for the 73-0 annihilation of the Washington Redskins the previous fall. It was a case of a "good little team" facing a "good big team" and the one-sided result was inevitable.

Sid Luckman passed 27 yards to Ken Kavanaugh who ran 7 more for a touchdown to open the scoring in the first period. Jack Mander's try for the extra point was blocked by Ernie Pannell. Tom Harmon passed 22 yards to George Franck in the end zone to put the All-Stars even. This conversion attempt by Tony Ruffa was blocked by Joe Stydahar to end the quarter at 6-6.

Harry Clark plunged over from the 1 to score again for the Bears and Manders conversion was successful to end the half, 13-6.

In the third period Lee Artoe booted a 46-yard field goal for the Bears.

The All-Stars fell apart in the final period, after Charley O'Rourke tossed a touchdown to Jack Robinson who ran an additional 7 yards to score. (This was the same Jackie Robinson who later became the first Negro accepted as such in major league baseball, brilliant second baseman of the Brooklyn Dodgers.) Augie Lio kicked the conversion and the score was 16-13. The Bears opened the throttle then with Harry Clark smashing over from the 1 to set up Manders' conversion for 23-13. Luckman passed to McAfee in the flat and George ran 25 yards for another score with Manders again cashing the extra point. Young Bussey then passed 9 yards to Bob Nowaskey, Manders converted again, and the final score was 37-13.

George Franck of Minnesota was chosen for the Chicago *Tribune* award as the most valuable All-Star player. He later joined the New York Giants.

1942 CHICAGO ALL-STAR GAME

(Soldier Field, Chicago, Ill., Aug. 28, 1942)

Attendance 101,103

Chicago Bears (21)		College All-Stars (0)
Siegal	L.E.	Kutner (Texas)
Kolman	L.T.	Daniell (Ohio State)
Fortmann	L.G.	Jeffries (Missouri)
Turner	C.	Banonis (Detroit)
Bray	R.G.	Crimmins (Notre Dame)
Artoe	R.T.	Blozis (Georgetown)
Pool	R.E.	Ringer (Minnesota)

Luckman	Q.B.	Erdlitz (Northwestern)
Nolting	L.H.	Smith, B. (Minnesota)
Gallarneau	R.H.	Juzwik (Notre Dame)
Osmanski, W.	F.B.	Graf (Ohio State)

Chicago Bears	7	7	7	0 = 21
College All-Stars	0	0	0	0 = 0

Touchdowns—Gallarneau 2, Pool.
Points after touchdown—Stydahar 3.
Coaches—George Halas (Chicago), Robert Zuppke (All-Stars).

SUBSTITUTIONS

Chicago Bears—Ends: Nowaskey, Wilson; tackles: Stydahar, Hoptowit; guards: Drulis, Musso, Akin; center: Matuza; backs: Bussey, O'Rourke, Clark, McLean, Maznicki, Geyer, Famiglietti, Petty, Morris.

College All-Stars—Ends: Fitch (Minnesota), Rast (Alabama), Stanton (Arizona), Elbi (Notre Dame), Ringer (Minnesota), Meyer (Stanford), Kovatch (Notre Dame); tackles: Bauman (Northwestern), Odson (Minnesota), Eason (Oklahoma), Herndon (Nebraska), Lillis (Notre Dame); guards: Frankowski (Washington), Maddock (Notre Dame), Abel (Nebraska), Pukema (Minnesota), Sartori (Fordham); centers: Ingalls (Michigan), Gude (Vanderbilt), Lindskog (Stanford); backs: Cheatham (Auburn), Farris (Wisconsin), Hargrave (Notre Dame), Dudley (Virginia), Jacobs (Oklahoma), Moser (Texas A & M), Kmetovic (Stanford), Robertson (U.S.C.), Westfall (Michigan), Sweiger (Minnesota).

Officials: Referee—Ronald Gibbs. Umpire—E. C. Krieger. Head Linesman—Charles Berry. Field Judge—William Blake.

THE GAME

Although the great Bear team was about to disintegrate because of the demands of World War II, this squad still had enough inherent power to romp at will over the All-Stars. The comparatively small score was a restrained demonstration of the capabilities of the Halas crew.

Hugh Gallarneau plunged 4 yards for a touchdown in the first period and Joe Stydahar kicked the conversion.

In the second quarter, Young Bussey passed 24 yards into the end zone to Hampton Pool and Stydahar converted again to make it 14–0 at the half.

Hugh Gallarneau smashed for 8 yards and another TD in the third period and Stydahar's third conversion ended the scoring to make the final 21–0.

Tragedy was stalking two of the players. Young Bussey of the Bears was to die on the first day of the Lingayen invasion in the Philippines. Al Blozis of the All-Stars, who played for a while with the New York Giants, was to be killed by German machine-gun fire in the Vosges Mountains of France.

Bruce Smith was chosen as winner of the Chicago *Tribune* award as the most valuable All-Star player. He later became a member of the Green Bay Packers.

1943 CHICAGO ALL-STAR GAME
(Dyche Stadium, Evanston, Ill., Aug. 25, 1943)
Attendance 48,437

Washington Redskins (7)		College All-Stars (27)
Masterson	L.E.	Pihos (Indiana)
Wilkin	L.T.	Wistert (Michigan)
Farman	L.G.	Bucek (Texas A & M)
Smith	C.	Lindskog (Stanford)
Slivinski	R.G.	Ramsey (William and Mary)
Shugart	R.T.	Wildung (Minnesota)
McChesney	R.E.	Huber (Notre Dame)
Hare, C.	Q.B.	Renfrom (Washington State)
Baugh	L.H.	Graham (Northwestern)
Moore	R.H.	Steuber (Missouri)
Seymour	F.B.	Harder (Wisconsin)

Washington Redskins	0	7	0	0— 7
College All-Stars	7	7	6	7—27

Touchdowns—Harder 2, Graham, Steuber, Aguirre.
Points after touchdown—Harder 2, Graham, Masterson.
Coaches—Arthur "Dutch" Bergman (Washington), Harry Stuhldreher (All-Stars).

SUBSTITUTIONS

Washington Redskins—Ends: Aguirre, Haloupek; tackles: Pasqua, Bentz, Zeno; guards: Leon, Florentino; centers: Carroll, Nolander; backs: Jenkins, Zimmerman, Bagarus, Masters, Farkas.

College All-Stars—Ends: Susoeff (Wash. State), Lister (Missouri), Smeja (Michigan), Currivan (Boston College), Sizemore (Furman), Karwales (Michigan); tackles: Kapter (Northwestern), Rhea (Oregon), Werkheiser (Duquesne), Barwegan (Purdue), Ashcom (Oregon), Irish (Arizona); centers: Remington (Wash. State), Ziemba (Notre Dame); backs: Farris (Wisconsin), Zapals (Texas A & M), Kennedy (Wash. State), Youel (Iowa), Trippi (Georgia), Dobbs (Tulsa), Silovich (Minnesota), Dewar (Indiana), Fenton (Mich. State), James (Ohio State), Filipowicz (Fordham), Clatt (Notre Dame), McKay (Texas).

Officials: Referee—E. F. Hughitt. Umpire—Dr. Raymond Huegel. Head Linesman—Charles Berry. Field Judge—Lloyd Larson.

THE GAME

The Redskins, under a new coach, were not even close to ready for this All-Star squad which contained a swarm of the professional stars of the future. Several of the All-Star recruits were to be top players in the NFL for the next decade.

Bob Steuber opened the scoring for the All-Stars when he scampered 50 yards on a punt return for a touchdown and Pat Harder made it 7–0 with the conversion.

Sam Baugh helped tie it up for the Redskins in the second by passing 5 yards to Joe Aguirre in the end zone for a touchdown. Bob Masterson converted. Later in the period Glen Dobbs threw 20 yards to Harder over the goal. Harder booted the extra point and it was 14–7 at the half.

In the third period, Otto Graham intercepted Sam Baugh's pass and ran 97 yards for a TD. Harder's conversion was blocked.

Harder ran 33 yards through tackle for a touchdown in the fourth quarter and Graham's conversion made it 27–7 for the final score.

Marlin "Pat" Harder was chosen for the Chicago *Tribune* award as the most valuable player of the All-Stars. He was to play again as a collegian in the 1946 game and then join the Chicago Cardinals to become, with Charley Trippi, Marshall Goldberg and Paul Christman, the "Dream Backfield" of the 1947 champions coached by Jim Conzelman.

1944 CHICAGO ALL-STAR GAME

(Dyche Stadium, Evanston, Ill., Aug. 30, 1944)

Attendance 49,246

Chicago Bears (24)		College All-Stars (21)
Benton	L.E.	Dugger (Ohio State)
Sigillo	L.T.	Willis (Ohio State)
Gudauskas	L.G.	Barwegan (Purdue)
Turner	C.	Tavener (Indiana)
Zorich	R.G.	Houston (Ohio State)
Hoptowit	R.T.	Zimny (Indiana)
Wilson	R.E.	Yonakor (Notre Dame)
Long	Q.B.	Saban (Indiana)
Nolting	L.H.	Dobbs (Tulsa)
McEnulty	R.H.	Trippi (Georgia)
Famiglietti	F.B.	Miller (Notre Dame)

Chicago Bears	0	14	7	3—24
College All-Stars	14	0	7	0—21

Touchdowns—Benton, Famiglietti, McLean, Miller, Tavener, Saban.
Points after touchdown—Saban 3, Gudauskas 3.
Field goal—Gudauskas.
Coaches—Heartley Anderson and Luke Johnsos (Chicago), Lynn Waldorf (All-Stars).

SUBSTITUTIONS

Chicago Bears—Ends: Berry, Smeja; tackles: Sweeney, Barbartsky; guards: Sprinkle, Musso; center: Mundee; backs: Luckman, Margarita, Mooney, McLean, Masters, Simonich.
College All-Stars—Ends: Huber (Notre Dame), Sizemore (Furman); tackles: McCafferty (Ohio State), Barnes (L.S.U.); guards: Jones (Tulsa), Kolesar (Michigan), Jabbusch (Ohio State), Hecht (Alabama), Gaziano (Holy Cross); center: Appleby (Ohio State); backs: Keuper (Georgia), Hillenbrand (Indiana), Jacoby (Indiana), Ford (Tulsa), Layden (Texas).
Officials: Referee—Ronald Gibbs. Umpire—E. C. Krieger. Head Linesman—John Kelly. Field Judge—H. C. Hedges.

THE GAME

The great Bear teams of the early 1940's were completely wrecked by war at this point in history. Only Luckman, Turner, Wilson and McLean were left to carry on the battle of the gridiron. Coach George Halas was in the Pacific with the Navy and the players were scattered all over the world. The Bears were lucky to squeak out a win on a last-period field goal.

The All-Stars scored first when Glen Dobbs passed 4 yards to Creighton Miller for a touchdown and Lou Saban booted the conversion. Still in the first period, John Tavener recovered Dobbs' fumble and ran 12 yards for another score which Saban again converted to make it 14-0.

The Bears evened it up in the second quarter. Gary Famiglietti crashed 3 yards for the first score and Sid Luckman passed 12 yards to Jim Benton for another. Pete Gudauskas kicked both extra points and it was 14-14 at the half.

Saban plunged over from one yard away to score again for the All-Stars and kicked the conversion. The Bears pulled even when Ray McLean scampered 19 yards through tackle to score and Gudauskas again added the dividend.

In the last period, Gudauskas booted a field goal from the 13 to give the Bears a 24-21 victory.

Glen Dobbs of Tulsa was chosen winner of the Chicago *Tribune* award as the most valuable player on the All-Stars. He returned to play in the All-Star game of 1947 before joining the Los Angeles Dons of the All America Football Conference.

1945 CHICAGO ALL-STAR GAME

(Soldier Field, Chicago. Ill., Aug. 30, 1945)

Attendance 92,753

Green Bay Packers (19)		College All-Stars (7)
Hutson	L.E.	Cook (Alabama)
Ray	L.T.	Zimmy (Indiana)
Kuusisto	L.G.	Tassos (Texas A & M)
Brock, C.	C.	Warrington (Auburn)
Goldenberg	R.G.	Burgeis (Tulsa)
Berezney	R.T.	Foster (Oklahoma A & M)
Mason	R.E.	Huber (Notre Dame)
Craig	Q.B.	Mitchell (Tulsa)
Comp	L.H.	Trippi (Georgia)
Brock, L.	R.H.	Greenwood (Illinois)
Fritsch	F.B.	Kennedy (Washington State)

Green Bay Packers	3	9	0	7—19
College All-Stars	0	7	0	0— 7

Touchdowns—McKay, Hutson, Scollard.
Points after touchdown—Hutson 2, Harmon.
Field goal—Hutson.
Safety—Kennedy.
Coaches—Earl Lambeau (Green Bay), Bernie Bierman (All-Stars).

SUBSTITUTIONS

Green Bay Packers—Ends: Goodnight, Jacunski, Luhn, Urban; tackles: Adams, Croft; guards: Tollefson, P. Tinsley; Sorenson, Bucchianeri; center: Flowers; backs: Starret, Akins, Laws, McKay, Rohrig, Perkins.

College All-Stars—Ends: Scollard (St. Joseph), Karmazin (Wake Forest), Sizemore (Furman), Lamb (Oklahoma), Dugger (Ohio State), McCafferty (Ohio State); tackles: Willis (Ohio State), Bentz (Tulane), Bell (Indiana), Crawford (Tennessee), Johnson (Kentucky); guards: Calcagni (Pennsylvania), Colhouer (Oklahoma A & M), Brown (Tennessee), Coffee (Indiana), Enich (Marquette), Jones (Tulsa), Buda (Tulsa); centers: Speegle (Oklahoma), Silovich (Marquette), Appleby (Ohio State); backs: Meek (Tennessee), Long (Tennessee), Stryzkalski (Marquette), Shedlosky (Tulsa), Moss (Tulane), Harmon (Michigan), Bondli (Pittsburgh), Horvath (Ohio State), Yates (Texas A & M), Allen (Pennsylvania), Schlinkman (Texas Tech), Singer (Arizona).

Officials: Referee—Ronald Gibbs. Umpire—E. C. Krieger. Head Linesman—John Kelly. Field Judge—William Blake.

THE GAME

In a hard-fought game, the champion Packers ground out a victory over a hard-fighting All-Star team that made them earn every point and every yard. Because of war, neither the pros nor the All-Stars were of their usual caliber.

The great Don Hutson opened the scoring for Green Bay in the first period with a 12-yard field goal.

The Packers benefited from an unusual safety in the second when Bob Kennedy intercepted Irv Comp's pass, ran forward to his own 2-yard line, then fled back of his own goal and was trapped for a safety. Later in the quarter, Herman Rohrig passed 30 yards to Roy McKay in the end zone and Hutson added the extra point to make it 12-0. Kennedy atoned for his lapse before the period was over when he threw a 28-yard pass to Nick Scollard, who scampered 35 more yards for a touchdown. Tom Harmon added the conversion, to make the score 12-7 at the half.

There was no scoring in the third period. In the fourth, Don Hutson intercepted a pass by Perry Moss and raced 85 yards for a touchdown, then added the extra point himself to end the game at 19-7.

Charley Trippi of Georgia was voted the Chicago *Tribune* award as the most valuable player of the All-Stars. He was soon taken into the Army, then returned to Georgia for another appearance in the All-Star game of 1947 before joining the Chicago Cardinals.

1946 CHICAGO ALL-STAR GAME

(Soldier Field, Chicago, Ill., Aug. 23, 1946)
Attendance 97,380

Los Angeles Rams (0)		College All-Stars (16)
Hickey	L.E.	Russell (Baylor)
Schultz	L.T.	Ruby (Texas A & M)
Matheson	L.G.	Grgich (Santa Clara)
DeLauer	C.	Godwin (Georgia)
Lazetich	R.G.	Ramsey (William and Mary)
Bouley	R.T.	Palmer (T.C.U.)
Pritko	R.E.	Heywood (U.S.C.)
Waterfield	Q.B.	Graham (Northwestern)
Gehrke	L.H.	Hillenbrand (Indiana)
Gillette	R.H.	Jones, W. (Tulane)
West	F.B.	Harder (Wisconsin)

| Los Angeles Rams | 0 | 0 | 0 | 0— 0 |
| College All-Stars | 7 | 0 | 7 | 2—16 |

Touchdowns—Hirsch 2.
Points after touchdown—Harder 2.
Safety—Against Washington of Los Angeles.
Coaches—Adam Walsh (Los Angeles), Alvin N. "Bo" McMillin (All-Stars).

SUBSTITUTIONS

Los Angeles Rams—Ends: Benton, Shaw, McDowell, Hamilton, Strode, Hightower; tackles: Eason, Johnson, Pasqua; guards: Mergenthal, Levy, Lear, Fawcett; centers: Naumetz, Harding, Scrubbs; backs: Reisz, Hardy, Washington, Farmer, Harmon, Banta, Wilson, Koch, Ruthstrom, Holovak, Sucic, Hoffman.
College All-Stars—Ends: Scollard (St. Joseph), Fitch (Minnesota), Morris (Northwestern), Yonakor (Notre Dame), P. Walker (Yale), Hasse (Amherst); tackles: Blandin (Tulane), Verry (U.S.C.), Stanley (Tulsa), Olenski (Alabama), Mitchell (Minnesota), Mieczkowski (Notre Dame); guards: Jungmichel (Texas), Kapter (Northwestern), Vogds (Wisconsin); centers: Pregulman (Michigan), Blackburn (Rice), Coleman (Notre Dame), Tavener (Indiana); backs: Hoernschemeyer (Indiana), Dekdebrun (Cornell), Dancewicz (Notre Dame), B. Walker (Yale), Hirsch (Wisconsin), Gafford (Auburn), Angsman (Notre Dame), Reynolds (Oklahoma A & M), Hankins (Oklahoma A & M), Doss (Texas), Nussbaumer (Michigan), Griffin (Illinois), Breslin (Michigan State), Saban (Indiana), Johnson (William and Mary).
Officials: Referee—Tom Dowd. Umpire—R. W. Finsterwald. Field Judge—William Blake. Head Linesman—Lloyd Brazil.

THE GAME

The Los Angeles Rams, who had won their championship in the Cleveland Municipal Stadium with the temperature at five degrees below zero, were colder than that when they faced this hopped-up squad of All-Stars. They were held scoreless while the collegians won comfortably, thanks to the sparkling running of Elroy "Crazy Legs" Hirsch of Wisconsin.

In the first period, Hirsch scampered 68 yards around his right for a touchdown and Pat Harder added the conversion. There was no scoring in the second quarter and the half ended 7–0.

Otto Graham fired a 38-yard pass to Hirsch in the second quarter for the second TD, and Harder again converted to put the All-Stars ahead 14–0.

In the fourth period, with the Rams on their own 13, Kenny Washington was smeared behind his own goal by Paul Walker for a safety, and the game ended 16–0.

Elroy Hirsch was chosen for the Chicago *Tribune* award to the most valuable All-Star player and reported immediately to the Chicago Rockets of the All America Football Conference.

1947 CHICAGO ALL-STAR GAME

(Soldier Field, Chicago, Ill., Aug. 22, 1947)

Attendance 80,054

Chicago Bears (0)		College All-Stars (16)
Kavanaugh	L.E.	Skoglund (Notre Dame)
Davis, F.	L.T.	Barwegan (Purdue)
Drulis	L.G.	Haase (Illinois)
Turner	C.	Cannady (Indiana)
Bray	R.G.	Humble (Rice)
Stickel	R.T.	Mastrangelo (Notre Dame)
Sprinkle	R.E.	Tereshinski (Georgia)
Luckman	Q.B.	Ratterman (Notre Dame)
McLean	L.H.	Young (Illinois)
Gallarneau	R.H.	Blanchard (Army)
Osmanski, J.	F.B.	Adamle (Ohio State)

| Chicago Bears | 0 | 0 | 0 | 0— 0 |
| College All-Stars | 13 | 0 | 3 | 0—16 |

Touchdowns—Mello, Zilly.
Points after touchdown—Case.
Field Goal—Case.
Coaches—George Halas (Chicago), Frank Leahy (All-Stars).

SUBSTITUTIONS

Chicago Bears—Ends: Wilson, F. Johnson, Karwales, Keane; tackles: Kolman, Ecker, Jarmoluk, Hartman; guards: Milner, W. Johnson, Preston; center: Clarkson; backs: Sacrinty, Seiferling, Gulyanics, Geyer, McAfee, Mullen, W. Osmanski, Holovak.

College All-Stars—Ends: Skoglund (Notre Dame), Souders (Ohio State), Poole (Mississippi), Zilly (Notre Dame), Scruggs (Rice), Hayes (Army), Baldwin (U.C.L.A.); tackles: Biles (Army), Moore (Penn State), Niedziela (Iowa), Esser (Wisconsin), Deal (Indiana), Cooper (Tulsa); guards: McBride (Notre Dame), Harris (Miss. State), Alvarez (Dartmouth), Hirsch (Northwestern), Collins (Texas), Clemons (St. Mary's), Knotts (Duke); centers: Cannady (Indiana), Gustafson (George Washington), Kodba (Purdue), Gray (Oregon State), Hellinghausen (Tulsa); backs: Tucker (Army), Cowhig (Notre Dame), Roberts (Chattanooga), Case (U.C.L.A.), Blanchard (Army), Trippi (Georgia), Rykovich (Illinois), Smith (Georgia), Adamle (Ohio State), Raimondi (Indiana), Cody (Purdue).

Officials: Referee—Carl Rebele. Umpire—Rollie Barnum. Head Linesman—Charles Berry. Field Judge—William Blake.

THE GAME

The Chicago Bears were far from their traditional top form for this contest and a series of surprising fumbles and miscues kept them continually back on their heels. The All-Star squad was heavy with talent and took advantage of many breaks to score a spectacular upset.

Jim Mello plowed over from the 6 to score in the first period and the score remained 6–0 when Ernie Case's conversion attempt was blocked. Later in the period, George Ratterman passed 36 yards to John Zilly for a touchdown and this time Case kicked the conversion. There was no scoring in the second period and the All-Stars led by 13–0 at the half.

Ernie Case booted a 21-yard field goal in the third period and that ended the scoring to give the All-Stars a 16–0 victory.

Claude "Buddy" Young of Illinois was chosen to receive the Chicago *Tribune* award as the most valuable All-Star player and reported immediately to the New York Yankees, at that time a member of the All America Football Conference.

1948 CHICAGO ALL-STAR GAME

(Soldier Field, Chicago, Ill., Aug. 20, 1948)

Attendance 101,220

Chicago Cardinals (28)		College All-Stars (0)
Dewell	L.E.	Cleary (Southern California)
Bulger	L.T.	Connor (Notre Dame)
Arms	L.G.	Weinmeister (Washington)
Banonis	C.	Scott (Navy)
Ramsey, G.	R.G.	Brown (Indiana)
Mauldin	R.T.	Czarobski (Notre Dame)
Kutner	R.E.	Ford (Michigan)
Christman	Q.B.	Lujack (Notre Dame)
Trippi	L.H.	Chappuis (Michigan)
Goldberg	R.H.	Conerly (Mississippi)
Harder	F.B.	Elliott (Michigan)

Chicago Cardinals	7	7	0	14—28
College All-Stars	0	0	0	0— 0

Touchdowns—Angsman, Schwall, Banonis, Trippi.
Points after touchdown—Harder 4.
Coaches—James Conzelman (Chicago), Frank Leahy (All-Stars).

SUBSTITUTIONS

Chicago Cardinals—Ends: Dove, Liebel, Ravensberg, Sortal, Doolan, Goldman; tackles: Szot, Coomer, Loepfe, Zimny, Jacobs; guards: Andros, Colhouer, Apolskis, Nichols; centers: Blackburn; backs: Eikenberg, Mallouf, Hanlon, Cochran, Dimancheff, deCorrevont, J. Davis, Schwall, Hollar, Angsman, Yablonski, Clatt.

College All-Stars—Ends: Fears (U.C.L.A.), Swiacki (Columbia), O'Connor (Notre Dame), Mann (Michigan), D. Foldberg (Army), Baumgardner (Texas), North (Vanderbilt), Halliday (S.M.U.), Maloney (Purdue), Owens (Illinois), Edwards (Georgia), Potsklan (Penn State); tackles: Yagiello (Catawba), Pritula (Michigan), Agase (Illinois), Urban (Notre Dame), Sullivan (Notre Dame), R. Davis (Georgia), Carrett (Miss. State), Prchlik (Yale), Smith (N. Carolina), Edwards (T.C.U.), Savitsky (Pennsylvania); guards: Suhey (Penn State), Werder (Georgetown), Wozniak (Alabama), Signaigo (Notre Dame), DiFrancesca (Northwestern), Olsonoski (Minnesota), O'Connor (Notre Dame), Gianelli (Boston College); centers: Nabors (Texas Tech.), Statuto (Notre Dame), Rhodemyre (Kentucky), White (Michigan), Strohmeyer (Notre Dame), Rapacz (Oklahoma); backs: Gray (U.S.C.), Gompers (Notre Dame), Mathews (Georgia Tech.), Sandifer (L.S.U.), Maves (Wisconsin), Wedemeyer (St. Mary's), Cline (Ohio State), Simmons (Notre Dame), Layne (Texas), Luongo (Pennsylvania).

Officials: Referee—William Downes. Umpire—Lylo Clarno. Head Linesman—Dan Tehan. Field Judge—William Blake.

THE GAME

The Chicago Cardinals were out to avenge the humiliating defeat suffered by the Chicago Bears in the previous game and were inspired as only Jim Conzelman could inspire men. They made a shambles of an All-Star team that was loaded with talent but seemed to lack teamwork and cohesion.

Elmer Angsman cracked over from the 2 in the first period and Pat Harder converted to give the Cardinals a 7–0 lead.

In the second quarter, Vic Schwall raced 14 yards through tackle for a touchdown and Harder converted to make it 14–0 at the half.

There was no scoring in the third period, but, early in the fourth, Vince Banonis intercepted Perry Moss's pass and raced 31 yards for the touchdown, Harder again converting. Later, Ray Mallouf passed 13 yards to Charley Trippi in the end zone and Harder's fourth conversion made the final score 28–0.

Jay Rhodemeyre, center from the University of Kentucky, was chosen for the Chicago *Tribune* award as the most valuable All-Star player and reported immediately to the Green Bay Packers.

1949 CHICAGO ALL-STAR GAME

(Soldier Field, Chicago, Ill., Aug. 12, 1949)

Attendance 93,780

Philadelphia Eagles (38)		College All-Stars (0)
Ferrante	L.E.	Poole (Mississippi)
Sears	L.T.	Petrovich (Texas U.)
Patton	L.G.	Wendell (Notre Dame)
Lindskog	C.	Bednarik (Pennsylvania)
Kilroy	R.G.	Fischer (Notre Dame)
Wistert	R.T.	DeRogatis (Duke)
Pihos	R.E.	Sheehan (Missouri)
Thompson	Q.B.	Mitchell (Oklahoma)
Van Buren, S.	L.H.	Taliaferro (Indiana)
Pritchard	R.H.	Williams (Washington State)
Muha	F.B.	Geri (Georgia)

Philadelphia Eagles	0	17	7	14—38
College All-Stars	0	0	0	0— 0

Touchdowns—Van Buren, Craft, Pihos, Doss, Armstrong.
Points after touchdown—Patton 5.
Field goal—Patton.

Coaches—Earl Neale (Eagles), College All-Stars, Charles "Bud" Wilkinson (Oklahoma).

SUBSTITUTIONS

Philadelphia Eagles—Ends: Armstrong, Prescott, Skladany, DiRenzo, Humbert, Green, Laster; tackles: Douglas, Savitsky, MacDowell, Hamberger; guards: Barnes, Maronic, Fusci, Magee, Gianelli; centers: Wojciechowicz, Szymanski, Donley, Yanelli; backs: Mackrides, Craft, Reagen, Ziegler, McHugh, Parmer, Pugh, Doss, Myers, Kish.

College All-Stars—Ends: Wimberly (Louisiana State), Brodnax (Georgia Tech.), O'Brien (Tulane), Cain (Alabama), Canady (Arkansas), Gagne (Minnesota); tackles: O'Reilly (Purdue), Niemi (Wash. State), Szafaryn (N. Carolina), Maddock (Northwestern), Bryant (Army); guards: Burris (Oklahoma), Stautzenberger (Texas A & M), Steffy (Army); centers: Walsh (Notre Dame), Sarkisian (Northwestern), Thompson (William and Mary), McCurry (Mich. State); backs: Tripucka (Notre Dame), Van Brocklin (Oregon), Elliott (Michigan), Di Marco (Iowa), Stuart (Army), Sims (Baylor), Guerro (Mich. State), Sullivan (Dartmouth), Doll (U.S.C.), Davis (Miss. State), Scott (Arkansas), McWilliams (Miss. State), Goode (Texas A & M), Rowan (Army), Jagade (Indiana), Benrick (Wisconsin), Greathouse (Oklahoma).

Officials: Referee—Ronald Gibbs. Umpire—M. G. Volz. Head Linesman—Charles Berry. Field Judge—Lawrence Ely. Alternates—William Downes, E. C. Curtis.

THE GAME

The Philadelphia Eagles were hot and relentless for this one. They piled up the score without pity and the All-Stars, although boasting several future professional stars, were outclassed.

After a scoreless first period, Steve Van Buren went over for the first touchdown from the one-yard line and Cliff Patton cashed the conversion to make it 7–0. Patton then kicked a field goal from the 14. Before the half ended, Russ Craft crashed over from the 4, Patton converted, and it was 17–0 at the rest period.

Tommy Thompson passed into the end zone to Pete Pihos in the third and Patton's conversion made it 24–0.

In the fourth quarter, Noble Doss plunged over from the 4, Patton again obliging with the extra point. Later in the period, Bill Mackrides passed 13 yards to Neill Armstrong and Patton's fifth conversion made the final score 38–0.

Bill Fischer of Notre Dame was chosen winner of the Chicago *Tribune* award as the most valuable All-Star player and reported immediately to the Chicago Cardinals.

1950 CHICAGO ALL-STAR GAME

(Soldier Field, Chicago, Ill., Aug. 11, 1950)

Attendance 88,885

Philadelphia Eagles (7)		College All-Stars (17)
Ferrante	L.E.	Weiner (North Carolina)
Sears	L.T.	Campora (College of the Pacific)
Patton	L.G.	Payne (Georgia)
Lindskog	C.	Tonnemaker (Minnesota)
Kilroy	R.G.	Hughes (William and Mary)
Wistert	R.T.	Manley (Oklahoma)
Pihos	R.E.	Martin (Notre Dame)
Thompson	Q.B.	Tidwell (Auburn)
Van Buren, S.	L.H.	Walker, D. (Southern Methodist)
Scott	R.H.	Haynes (Santa Clara)
Muha	F.B.	Morrison (Ohio State)

Philadelphia Eagles	0	0	0	7— 7
College All-Stars	7	7	0	3—17

Touchdowns—Pasquierello, Justice, Van Buren.
Points after touchdown—Soltau 2, Patton.
Field Goal—Soltau.
Coaches—Earle Neale, Edward Anderson.

SUBSTITUTIONS

Philadelphia Eagles—Ends: Armstrong, Green, Skladany, Hix, Willey, Humbert; tackles: Barnes, MacDowell, Jarmoluk; guards: Magee, Gianelli, Maronic; centers: Bednarik, Wojciechowicz; backs: Panciera, Reagen, Ziegler, Craft, Sutton, Parmer, Pritchard, Myers, Sanders.

All-Stars—Ends: Ison (Baylor), Hart (Notre Dame), Owens (Oklahoma), Soltau (Minnesota), Kersulis (Illinois), Wightkin (Notre Dame), McChesney (Hardin-Simmons), Rowe (Dartmouth); tackles: Nomellini (Minnesota), Sandusky (Villanova), Karras (Purdue), Creekmur (William and Mary), Kiilsgaard (Idaho); guards: Bagdon (Michigan State), Crawford (Mississippi), Winslow (Iowa), West (Oklahoma), Schweder (Pennsylvania); centers: Fuchs (Mississippi), Watson (Rice), Ulinski (Kentucky), Novak (Nebraska); backs: Burk (Baylor), LeBaron (College of the Pacific), Justice (N. Carolina), Chandnois (Michigan State), Chollet (Cornell), Swistowicz (Notre Dame), Hunsinger (Florida), Coutre (Notre Dame), Carpenter (Oregon State), Thomas (Oklahoma), Kempthorn (Michigan), Svoboda (Tulane), Pasquariello (Villanova), Murakowski (Northwestern), Mitchell (Stanford).

Officials: Referee—Emil Heintz. Umpire—John Wilson. Head Linesman—Charles Berry. Field Judge—William Blake. Alternates—William Downes, E. C. Krieger.

THE GAME

Inspired by the brilliant ball-handling of quarterback Eddie LeBaron and the elusive running of Charley "Choo-Choo" Justice, the All-Stars dominated the game throughout, the Eagles appearing sluggish and far off on their timing.

The All-Stars scored in the first period when Ralph Pasquariello smashed over from the 2 and Gordon Soltau converted.

In the second quarter, LeBaron passed to Justice for 35 yards and a touchdown, Soltau again converting to make it 14-0 at the half.

The third period was scoreless and the Eagles finally avoided a shutout in the last quarter when Steve Van Buren plunged over from one yard and Cliff Patton kicked the conversion.

Soltau put the game on ice for the All-Stars with a field goal from the 23 late in the quarter.

Charles Justice was chosen winner of the Chicago *Tribune* trophy as the most valuable All-Star player of the game and reported to the Washington Redskins. Eddie LeBaron, beaten in the ballot by a narrow margin, was also drafted by Washington but reported to the U.S. Marine Corps instead. Before the 1951 game was played, he had been wounded in Korea.

1951 CHICAGO ALL-STAR GAME

(Soldier Field, Chicago, Ill., Aug. 17, 1951)

Attendance 92,180

Cleveland Browns (33)		College All-Stars (0)
Speedie	L.E.	Stonesifer (Northwestern)
Groza	L.T.	Gain (Kentucky)
Gibron	L.G.	McFadin (Texas)
Gatski	C.	Groom (Notre Dame)
Houston	R.G.	Lynch (Illinois)
Rymkus	R.T.	McCormack (Kansas)
Lavelli	R.E.	Wilkinson (U.C.L.A.)
Graham	Q.B.	Williams (Notre Dame)
Bumgardner	L.H.	White (Arizona State)
Jones, W.	R.H.	Rote (S.M.U.)
Motley	F.B.	Dufek (Michigan)

Cleveland Browns	2	10	7	14—33
College All-Stars	0	0	0	0— 0

Touchdowns—Jones 2, Lavelli, Cole.
Points after touchdown—Groza 4.

Field Goal—Groza.
Safety—Williams.
Coaches—Paul Brown (Cleveland), Herman Hickman (Yale).

SUBSTITUTIONS

Cleveland Browns—Ends: Young, Gillom, Ford, Oristaglio; tackles: Kissell, Palmer, Grigg, Sandusky, Donovan; guards: Agase, Michaels, Schroll; centers: Herring, Thompson; backs: Lewis, Shula, Lahr, Carpenter, Loomis, James, Moselle, Adamle, Jagade, Cole.

College All-Stars—Ends: Allis (Michigan), Sherrod (Tennessee), Felker (Marquette), Schroeder (Virginia), Minarik (Michigan State), Pfeifer (Fordham), Wingate (Maryland); tackles: Krouse (Maryland), Joyce (Tulane), Stroud (Tennessee), Wahl (Michigan), Carapella (Miami, Fla.), Jackson (Texas), Tate (Illinois), Yowarsky (Kentucky); guards: Dodrill (Colorado A & M), Lemonick (Pennsylvania), Doyle (Tulane); centers: Moser (College of Pacific), Vohaska (Illinois), Holdash (N. Carolina), Rowden (Maryland); backs: Bagnell (Pennsylvania), Grandelius (Michigan State), Egler (Colgate), Ortmann (Michigan), Nagle (Nebraska), Douglass (Illinois), Hill (Tennessee), Konz (L.S.U.), Volm (Marquette), Gay (Notre Dame), Boydstun (Baylor), Campbell (Wyoming), Dottley (Mississippi).

Officials: Referee—Ronald Gibbs. Umpire—Ernest Vick. Head Linesman—Charles Berry. Field Judge—Jay Berwanger. Alternates—William Downes, Herbert Steiger.

THE GAME

The Cleveland Browns completed their amazing cycle of triumphs with a smashing 33–0 decision over the All-Stars. It followed four straight conference pennants in the All America Football Conference and the 1950 Championship of the National Football League. The game was no-contest although the All-Stars had plenty of talent. Cleveland defense dominated the game and the major leaguers scored almost at will.

In the first period, Kyle Rote's fumble was recovered in the end zone by Bob Williams to give Cleveland the first two points.

"Dub" Jones crashed 2 yards for a touchdown in the second period. Lou Groza kicked the point and later booted a 20-yard field goal for a 12–0 half-time lead.

Jones scored again, this time from the 3, to open the third quarter and Groza again converted.

In the last period, Otto Graham passed 10 yards to Dante Lavelli and 8 yards to Emerson Cole. Groza cashed both extra points.

Lewis "Bud" McFadin of Texas was chosen winner of the Chicago *Tribune* award as the most valuable All-Star player and retired after this game.

1952 CHICAGO ALL-STAR GAME

(Soldier Field, Chicago, Ill., Aug. 15, 1952)

Attendance 90,000 (est)

Los Angeles Rams (10)		College All-Stars (7)
Fears	L.E.	Sugar (Purdue)
Simensen	L.T.	Mitchell (UCLA)
Daugherty	L.G.	Coleman (Michigan)
McLaughlin	C.	Richter (Cal.)
Lange	R.G.	Ward (Maryland)
Dahms	R.T.	Pearman (Tennessee)
Hirsch	R.E.	Howton (Rice)
Waterfield	Q.B.	Parilli (Kentucky)
Towler	L.H.	Janowicz (Ohio State)
Smith, V.	R.H.	McElhenny (Washington)
Myers	F.B.	Boerio (Illinois)

Los Angeles Rams	0	0	0	10—10
College All-Stars	0	7	0	0— 7

Touchdowns—Younger (Los Angeles) ; Janowicz (All-Stars) .
Points after touchdowns—Waterfield (Los Angeles) ; Janowicz (All-Stars) .
Field Goal—Waterfield (Los Angeles) .
Coaches—Joseph Stydahar (Los Angeles), Bobby Dodds (Geo Tech) .

SUBSTITUTIONS

Los Angeles—Ends: Lane, Kreuger, Brink, Robustelli, Smith, F., Hacker, N.; tackles:
Toogood, Dees, Green, Teeuws, Winkler, Casner; guards: Nanni, Putnam, Fry, Hor-
rell, West; center: Paul; backs: Van Brocklin, Lewis, Quinlan, Williams, Kalmanir,
Johnson, Ferguson, Towler, Younger, Reed, Townsend, Rich, English, Hecker, R.
All-Stars—Ends: Brewster (Purdue) , Howton (Rice), Gandee (Ohio State), O'Donahue
(Wisconsin), Carey (Michigan State), Lemmon (Cal.) , Faverty (Wisconsin) , McColl
(Stanford), Thomas (Oregon State); tackles: Moss (Maryland), Mitchell (UCLA) ,
Pearman (Tennessee) , Snyder (Georgia Tech) , Johnson (Michigan), Coleman
(Michigan), Weatherall (Oklahoma) , George (Wake Forest), Campbell (Georgia),
Williams (Arkansas), Marchetti (San Francisco), Toneff (Notre Dame) ; guards: Price
(Texas Tech) , Beck (Georgia Tech), Macrae (Northwestern), Clark (Oregon State) ,
Forester (SMU); centers: Kinson (Missouri) , Mosely (Kentucky), Griffin (Arkansas);
backs: Dorow (Michigan State) , Karras (Illinois), Gifford (S. Cal.), Matson (San
Francisco) , Flowers (TCU), Wade (Vanderbilt), Crawford (Georgia Tech) , Lauricella
(Tennessee), Dooley (Miami, Fla.), Rechichar (Tennessee), Petitbon (Notre Dame) ,
Kensler (Maryland) , Reichardt (Iowa), Modzelewski (Maryland), Hughes (Michigan
State) , Toler (San Francisco), Tarasovic (LSU).
Officials: Referee—Ronald Gibbs. Umpire—Don Elser. Head Linesman—Dan Tehan.
Field Judge—Dave Noble. Alternates—William Downes (NFL); Lyle Clarno (Bradley).

THE GAME

Rain had drenched the field during the afternoon and continued to fall through
most of the game. The All-Stars outplayed the Rams during the scoreless first period, as
well as the second when Vic Janowicz (Ohio State) plunged three yards to score the first
TD, then placekicked the conversion to give the Stars a 7–0 halftime lead.

The third period was scoreless, but, with time running out, the Rams shifted into
high gear for the final fifteen minutes to save the game. An interference penalty called
against the Stars on their own seven-yard line on a pass play from Van Brocklin to Volney
Quinlan, gave the Rams the break they needed. Van Brocklin quickly pitched to Paul
"Tank" Younger for the score and Waterfield converted.

With seven minutes to play, Bob Waterfield kicked a 31-yard field goal to win the
game.

Vito Parilli, of Kentucky, was chosen to receive the Chicago *Tribune* award as the
most valuable All-Star and reported immediately to the Green Bay Packers.

CHAPTER 7

THE ALL AMERICA FOOTBALL CONFERENCE

At the end of World War II, rumors were heard that a new professional football league was being formed. They disturbed the owners of the veteran National Football League who were jubilantly welcoming the return of several hundred players who had been in service—collegians who had gone directly from the campus to uniform as well as other products of the war-time boon in sports.

Out of these rumors, and a few false starts, came the All America Football Conference, organized by Arch Ward, sports editor of the Chicago *Tribune,* father of the All-Star football and All-Star baseball games, the man who raised Golden Glove boxing to unprecedented heights through inter-city and international bouts.

National Football League owners, painfully aware of the struggle they had gone through to establish the big league game from the days of 300 fans to crowds of more than 100,000, preferred to ignore both the rumors and the plans. They knew that, in spite of a quarter-century of progress, only four of their franchises could show an over-all profit, while dozens had fallen by the wayside. They said it was financial suicide to try to start another league, basing their opinion on these facts: that they had the best parks in the best cities; that they had the best coaches and the best players; that pro football was not a sound business for investment, particularly for beginners.

Ward's explanation was indicative of his promotional ability: "A man doesn't stand still," he said. "He either goes ahead or slips back. I could see several groups attempting to organize a new league, and, because football has always been the sport closest to my heart, I wanted to see the new group organized properly."

Those were the factors behind the professional football "war" of 1945–1949. It lasted four seasons. It was termed ruinous and catastrophic. It was hailed as the greatest boon the game has ever experienced.

The truth was somewhere between these extremes. It was a boon to the players with salaries forced upward by the law of supply and demand. It was ruinous to several owners who found that fans are fickle and are sure to support only a winner. It attracted to the major league game the most brilliant playing personnel ever assembled in one organization, and they remained after peace came, before the 1950 season. The rumblings, bickering and war-talk between the two leagues accomplished something else, intangible but vitally important to the growth of the game; they focused attention on professional football, created hundreds of thousands of new fans. Before the war it was almost impossible to find the results, even in single agate line, in Monday's papers; now entire pages are devoted to the thrilling stories, games are carried by radio and television from coast to coast. Each year more fans became fanatic devotees of professional contests.

When peace finally came, to start the 1950 season, it was generally recognized that the best college team would have little, if any, chance against an average professional team; that major league football had provided the game's most interesting advances such as the platoon system, the fifth official, the intricate development of the T-formation; that major league football was on a par with major league baseball, and perhaps more evenly balanced than big league baseball.

These facts had not been accepted by the general public previously.

It is doubtful that such developments were foreseen by the six men who met secretly in a St. Louis hotel room on June 4, 1944, to discuss the formation of the new group and to choose its name.

Ward, who had power of attorney for Arthur B. McBride of Cleveland, met with Sam Cordovano of Buffalo, Jack Keeshin of Chicago, Christy Walsh of Los Angeles, Ray Ryan of New York, and A. J. "Tony" Morabito of San Francisco. Cordovano, Walsh and Ryan had departed by the time the first game was played and Keeshin dropped out after the first season, but both McBride and Morabito—whose teams were powerhouses in the AAFC—were still very much in evidence in the NFL in 1952.

Three months after the original meeting, representatives of the same half-dozen clubs met with "Gene" Tunney, who was interested in starting a club in Baltimore. (He, too, withdrew before the year was out, nearly two years before the first game was played.) Rules and regulations were adopted, player contracts drawn up, and James H. Crowley, formerly one of the "Four Horsemen" of Notre Dame, was elected president and commissioner. Mrs. Lou Gehrig was named secretary, Cordovano treasurer, at a meeting in April, 1945, a year and a half before a game was played. Buffalo, Chicago, Cleveland, Los Angeles, Miami and San Francisco were officially admitted to the AAFC and were followed, six months later, by Brooklyn, headed by William D. Cox.

It was during that April meeting that Paul E. Brown, later to coach the Cleveland Browns, was appointed, along with Jack Keeshin, to try to set up a working agreement with Elmer Layden, then Commissioner of the NFL.

They were unsuccessful, and it was at that time that Layden issued his widely quoted, and even more widely misunderstood statement: "Let them get a football and play a game and then maybe we'll have something to talk about." It is a matter of record that, after Layden was no longer commissioner, and the AAFC had weathered a couple of seasons that were spectacularly successful for a few teams and equally disastrous to others, Layden stated that, in his opinion, the time had come for the NFL to recognize the AAFC.

On October 23, 1945, announcement was made that Christy Walsh had withdrawn from the Los Angeles Dons organization and had been replaced by a syndicate, headed by Don Ameche, and including Ben F. Lindheimer, Louis B. Mayer, Lloyd Wright, Norman W. Church and Daniel F. Rice. This syndicate strengthened the embryo league enormously. Six weeks later another bombshell exploded when Daniel R. Topping stated that he was transferring his NFL club to the new conference because of inability to work out satisfactory dates and territorial agreements with the New York Giants. Topping had been operating in Brooklyn, but now, as part-owner of the Yankee Stadium and the baseball Yankees, he preferred to have his football team paying rent to his own corporation.

This move brought the conference to full strength with eight clubs: Buffalo (James F. Breuil who had replaced Cordovano as principle owner) ; Brooklyn (Cox) ; Chicago (Keeshin) ; Cleveland (McBride) ; Los Angeles (Lindheimer, principal stock-holder) ; Miami (Harvey Hester) ; New York (Topping) ; San Francisco (Morabito). The roster of coaches was completed with Dudley DeGroot at Los Angeles, Dr. Mal Stevens at Brooklyn, Sam Cordovano at Buffalo, Dick Hanley at Chicago, Paul Brown at Cleveland, Jack Meagher at Miami, Ray Flaherty at New York, and Lawrence Shaw at San Francisco. Only Flaherty had previous major league experience. Cordovano resigned before the first season opened and was replaced by Lowell "Red" Dawson.

The first season, 1946, developed a pattern which was to remain static through the four years of the AAFC's existence. Cleveland dominated the Western Division without serious contention except from the San Francisco 49ers who were never quite good enough; the Eastern Division failed to develop any consistent team; its best was thrashed in four championship games by the Cleveland Browns. More than one hundred former

National Football League players had joined the AAFC, but the Conference failed to shine artistically from lack of experienced major league coaching. Cleveland won four titles, trouncing the New York Yankees in 1946, the same team in 1947, the Buffalo Bills in 1948 and San Francisco in 1949 (when the divisions had been abandoned because only seven teams played the season).

Owners and coaches had appeared and disappeared in the less successful locations. Admiral Jonas Ingram had been named commissioner in 1947 to succeed Crowley, who took over the Chicago Rocket coaching job for a few months. Ingram later gave way to O. O. Kessing in 1949, just before peace was made with the older NFL.

Prodigal intra-league bidding for top college stars was taking its toll in both leagues, and, just after the seasons ended in 1948, committees from the AAFC and NFL met in Philadelphia for "cease-fire" discussion. Nothing definite was decided at this time but the door cracked open wide enough to assure some kind of agreement in the near future. It was a year later that the AAFC was disbanded with Cleveland, San Francisco and Baltimore joining the NFL as complete units and the balance of the other players being put in a pool from which they were later drafted by the thirteen—at that time—clubs of the new NFL.

This consolidation of talent meant depth and balance for major league football. In the first season of the combined operation, the teams were so evenly matched that divisional tie play-offs were necessary in both sections of the NFL before the Cleveland Browns, still following the victory pattern, won the world championship from the Los Angeles Rams, 30–28, in a hair-raising game that was not decided until Lou Groza kicked a field goal for the Browns with eighteen seconds remaining in the game.

Baltimore, unable to develop either an acceptable team or fan support, departed after one disastrous season and the league assumed the more workable pattern of twelve franchises divided into two "Conferences," the "American" and "National."

The war had left countless casualties, particularly financial, but the American football fan had benefited by the development of the most exciting spectacle on the American sporting scene—a true major league schedule of football played at its roughest, most thrilling, best.

ROSTER OF COACHES

BALTIMORE COLTS

1947	Cecil Isbell
1948	Cecil Isbell
1949	Cecil Isbell
	Walter Driskill

BROOKLYN DODGERS

1946	Dr. Malcolm Stevens
	Thomas Scott
	Cliff Battles
1947	Cliff Battles
1948	Carl Voyles
1949	Disbanded

BROOKLYN—NEW YORK YANKEES

1946	Ray Flaherty
1947	Ray Flaherty
1948	Ray Flaherty
	Norman Strader
1949	Norman Strader

BUFFALO BILLS (BISONS)

1946	Lowell Dawson
1947	Lowell Dawson
1948	Lowell Dawson
1949	Lowell Dawson
	Clem Crowe

CHICAGO HORNETS (ROCKETS)

1946	Richard Hanley
	Robert Dove, Ned Mathews, Wilbur Wilkin, Pat Boland
1947	James H. Crowley
	Hampton Pool
1948	Edward McKeever
1949	Ray Flaherty

CLEVELAND BROWNS

1946	Paul E. Brown
1947	Paul E. Brown
1948	Paul E. Brown
1949	Paul E. Brown

LOS ANGELES DONS		**SAN FRANCISCO 49ers**
1946	Dudley DeGroot	1946 Lawrence T. Shaw
1947	Dudley DeGroot	1947 Lawrence T. Shaw
	Mel Hein, and Ted Shipkey	1948 Lawrence T. Shaw
1948	James M. Phelan	1949 Lawrence T. Shaw
1949	James M. Phelan	

MIAMI SEAHAWKS

1946   Jack Meagher
Hampton Pool

STATISTICAL CHAMPIONS

BALL CARRYING

1949	Fletcher Perry, San Francisco *FB*	783 yards
1948	Marion Motley, Cleveland *FB*	964 yards
1947	Orban Sanders, New York	1,432 yards
1946	Orban Sanders, New York	709 yards

FIELD GOALS

1949	Howard Johnson, New York	7
1948	Rex Grossman, Baltimore	10
1947	Ben Agajanian, Los Angeles	15
1946	Louis Groza, Cleveland	13

FORWARD PASSING

		Atts.	Comp.	Yds.
1949	Otto Graham, Cleveland	285	161	2,785
1948	Otto Graham, Cleveland	333	173	2,713
1947	Otto Graham, Cleveland	269	163	2,753
1946	*Glenn Dobbs, Brooklyn	269	135	1,886
	*Otto Graham, Cleveland	174	95	1,834

* Co-Champions

PASS RECEIVING

		Comp.	Yds.
1949	Mac Speedie, Cleveland	40	843
1948	Mac Speedie, Cleveland	58	816
1947	Mac Speedie, Cleveland	67	1,146
1946	Dante Lavelli, Cleveland	40	843

PUNTING

		Atts.	Ave. Yds.
1948	Glenn Dobbs, Los Angeles	68	49.1
1947	John Colmer, Brooklyn	56	44.7
1946	Glenn Dobbs	80	47.8

SCORING

		TDs	FG	XPTs	Total
1949	Alyn Beals, San Francisco	12	1	0	73
1948	Chester Mutryn, Buffalo	16	0	0	96
1947	Orban Sanders, New York	19	0	0	114
1946	Lou Groza, Cleveland	0	13	45	84

FINAL STANDINGS

1949

	W	L	T	Pct.
Cleveland	9	1	2	.900
San Francisco	9	3	0	.750
Bklyn-N.Y.	8	4	0	.667
Buffalo	5	5	2	.500
Chicago	4	8	0	.333
Los Angeles	4	8	0	.333
Baltimore	1	11	0	.083

Championship Game—
Cleveland 21, San Francisco 7

1948

WESTERN DIVISION

	W	L	T	Pct.
Cleveland	14	0	0	1.000
San Francisco	12	2	0	.857
Los Angeles	7	7	0	.500
Chicago	1	13	0	.071

EASTERN DIVISION

	W	L	T	Pct.
Buffalo	8*	7	0	.533
Baltimore	7	8*	0	.467
New York	6	8	0	.429
Brooklyn	2	12	0	.143

* Includes divisional play-off
Championship Game—
Cleveland 49, Buffalo 7
Championship Game—Cleveland 49, Buffalo 7

Otto Graham QB
Jim Brown HB
Motley FB

1947

WESTERN DIVISION

	W	L	T	Pct.
Cleveland	12	1	1	.923
San Francisco	8	4	2	.667
Los Angeles	7	7	0	.500
Chicago	1	13	0	.071

EASTERN DIVISION

	W	L	T	Pct.
New York	11	2	1	.846
Buffalo	8	4	2	.667
Brooklyn	3	10	1	.231
Baltimore	2	11	1	.154

Championship Game—
Cleveland 14, New York 3

1946

WESTERN DIVISION

	W	L	T	Pct.
Cleveland	12	2	0	.857
San Francisco	9	5	0	.643
Los Angeles	7	5	2	.583
Chicago	5	6	3	.455

EASTERN DIVISION

	W	L	T	Pct.
New York	10	3	1	.769
Brooklyn	3	10	1	.231
Buffalo	3	10	1	.231
Miami	3	11	0	.154

Championship Game—
Cleveland 14, New York 9

COLLEGES AND THEIR PLAYERS

The following pages list all major league football players (since 1920) under the names of the colleges which produced them. Here also are players who attended no college, or whose background is obscured. It must be admitted too that a few mastodons of the early days sometimes coyly added the name of a prominent university to their own without going through the formality of becoming a student thereof, thereby clouding the scene from the standpoint of research in later years. This will explain why some last names have universities attached but lack first names, for all colleges were queried about the identity of these athletes.

These same players are listed under the Player Roster, along with their playing records and any departmental championships they earned. In the General Index, those of them who made some permanent contribution to fame are also found. The latter would be those who still hold all-time records recognized by the National Football League; those who have played in Championship or College All-Star Games; those who are otherwise mentioned in the narrative contained in this book.

Some interesting facts have emerged from this breakdown by colleges to prove that quantity of production does not always mean quality; that several of the finest players of history have been produced by colleges which never see their names in the banner headlines of the papers.

Of the thirty-three men listed on the All-Time All-Star Team (see page 56), Geneva, Gonzaga, Dickinson, St. Thomas, Milligan and Bucknell can take bows as sweeping as UCLA, Southern California, the Big Ten teams and Notre Dame. The number one most valuable football player of recorded eternity, Sam Baugh, came from Texas Christian University.

On this all-time team, it is interesting to note, thirty-one colleges hold down the thirty-three positions, with only Alabama and Washington State repeating. Many schools which have been accused of flagrant professionalism are not represented at all—and some are. The ancient and honorable Ivy League, which, in recent years, is obviously guilty of outright amateurism, has one man on the team, the Columbia product, Mr. Luckman. Otherwise players have come from east to west and north to south to make their names in the big game, and the amazing fact to the writer is that the big league scouts have managed to scratch them out of the mire of overenthusiastic publicity perennially given to certain colleges and all their players, whether they can play football or not. Even now, many of these scrap-book heroes do obtain contracts far beyond their ability to deliver, but within a few weeks their shortcomings are known and they fade quickly from the scene.

Numerically, as might be expected, Notre Dame, with 151 candidates, leads the list. Minnesota with 82 is second, then Ohio State with 74. A surprise entry comes fourth—Pittsburgh with 71, and even more unexpected is Marquette in sixth place with 58. Of the twenty colleges which lead the list in quantity of production of professional players, the Big Ten holds nine places.

It is crystal clear from this analysis that no lazy big league scout can safely park himself in any one particular stadium, nor section of the country, and hope to bite his initials on the stars of the future. He may decide to haunt the Big Ten fields, the stadium at South Bend, Indiana, and later learn that there was another Cal Hubbard at Geneva, another Clark Hinkle at Bucknell, another George Musso at Milligan, another Bill Dudley at Virginia, another Bulldog Turner at Hardin-Simmons, another Dutch Clark at Colorado, to haunt him in an enemy uniform in the years to come. The scouts, nameless and shadowy men that they are, deserve a sincere salute from every football fan for the excellent overall job they do in this respect, refusing to be swayed by the exorbitant claims of All American selectors and the appalling over-emphasis that certain schools receive from gullible sports editors.

Here, for the benefit of nostalgic alumni, and serious researchers of all descriptions, are the 354 colleges which have produced the heroes of the National Football League. Attached too is the writer's deep gratitude to the perspiring registrars of the colleges who helped to build this listing.

PLAYERS BY COLLEGES

ABILENE CHRISTIAN
Jones, Thurman
Mooney, Bow Tipp
Smith, Verda
Stovall, Richard

AKRON UNIVERSITY
Bierce, Bruce
Daum, Carl
Haley, Arthur
Waldsmith, Ralph
Zimmerman, Guy

ALABAMA UNIVERSITY
Avery, Don
Bostick, Lewis
Bowdoin, James
Brown, David
Buckler, William
Bushby, Sherrill
Cain, James
Chambers, William
Cook, Theodore
Craft, Russell
Davis, Frederick
DeShane, Charles
Domnanovich, Joseph
Eberdt, Jess
Fichman, Leon
Gerber, Elwood
Gilmer, Harry
Hannah, Herbert
Hecht, Alfred
Holm, Anthony
Howell, Millard
Hunt, Ben
Hupke, Thomas
Hutson, Donald
Jones, Bruce
Jones, Ralph
Kirkland, B'ho
Leon, Anthony
Mancha, Vaughn
Lee, William
McCoy, Joel
Martin, Frank
Merrill, Walter
Morrow, John
Mosley, Russell
Nelson, James
Olenski, Mitchell
Oliver, William
Perry, Claude
Richeson, Ray
Salem, Edward
Sanford, Hayward
Smith, Ben
Smith, Riley
Steiner, Roy
Stewart, Vaughn
Tew, Lowell
Trocolor, Robert
Wesley, Lecil
Whately, James
Whire, John
White, Arthur
Wozniak, John
Wyhonic, John
Young, William

ALBRIGHT
Barkman, Ralph
Disend, Leo
Durko, John
Kosel, Stanley
Riffle, Richard

ALFRED
Trigilio, Frank

AMERICAN
Sergienko, George

ANNAPOLIS
Bartos, Joseph
Carney, Arthur
Chase, Ben
Denfield, Frank
Duden, Richard
Martin, John
Mathews, B. O.
Roberts, Walcott
Schuber, James

APPALACHIAN STATE
Hollar, John
Watts, George

ARIZONA STATE
Johnson, Glenn
McGibbony, Charles
Rockwell, Henry
Warren, Morrison
White, Wilford

ARIZONA UNIVERSITY
Banjavic, Emil
Corbitt, John
Enke, Fred
Greenfield, Thomas
Karnofsky, Abraham
Mulleneaux, Lee
Nielsen, Walter
Nolan, Earl
Stanton, Henry

ARKANSAS UNIVERSITY
Adams, O'Neal
Bagby, Herman
Baldwin, Alton
Barker, Hubert
Benton, James
Britt, Maurice
Brown, William
Campbell, Leon
Casey, Albert
Cato, Ralph
Corgan, Charles
Creighton, Milan
Eakin, Kay
Forte, Robert
Fowler, Aubrey
Hamilton, Ray
Hayden, John
Hayden, Kenneth
Hickey, Howard
Hix, William
Hoffman, John
Howell, James Lee
Keen, Delbert
Ledbetter, Chester
Lunday, Kenneth
Morton, Lock
Murphy, Thomas
Pense, James
Pipkin, Joyce
Scott, Clyde
Simington, Milton
Sloan, Dwight
Spillers, Ray
Thorpe, Wilfred
Van Sickle, Clyde
Winkelman, Ben
Wynne, Harry

ARMOUR INSTITUTE
Cary, Joseph

ARNOLD
Robustelli, Andrew

ASHLAND
Novotny, Raymond

AUBURN (ALA. POLYTECH)
Arial, David
Bulger, Chester
Cheatham, Lloyd
Cochran, Thomas
Cremer, Theodore
Deal, Rufus
Gafford, Roy
Ghersanich, Vernon
Harper, Maurice
Herring, Harold
Milam, Barnes
Reynolds, James
Roton, Herbert
Russell, Torrance
Sivell, J. Ralph
Taylor, Erquiet
Tidwell, Travis
Warrington, Caleb
Williams, John

AUGSBERG
Pederson, James

BAKER UNIVERSITY
Hill, Charles

BALDWIN–WALLACE
Caldwell, Cyril
Hecker, Norbert
Morris, George

BALL STATE TEACHERS
Patanelli, Michael

BAYLOR
Akin, Leonard
Barnett, Solon
Boyd, Samuel
Bradshaw, Wesley
Brazell, Carl
Burk, Adrian
Crain, Milton
Edwards, William
Gatewood, Lester
Griffin, Robert
Hartzog, Howard
Jones, Harvey
Koch, George
Kriel, Emmett
Lummus, John
McCormick, Leonard
Masters, Robert
Nelson, Robert
Parry, Owen
Patterson, William
Reynolds, John
Russell, John
Russell, Lloyd
Sims, George
Tinsley, Robert
Weathers, Guy
Wilson, John

BELLFONT
Vaughn, John

BELOIT
Buckeye, Garland
Dahlgren, George
Darling, Bernard
Dumore, William
Kuick, Stanley
MacAuliffe, John
McGaw, Walter
Purdy, Everett
Sullivan, Walter

BETHANY
Broadlet, Karl
Hahn, Ray
Rhenquist, Milton
Wallace, Fred

BIRMINGHAM SOUTHERN
McMichaels, John

BOSTON COLLEGE
Ananis, Vito
Bouley, Gilbert
Canale, Rocco
Cannava, Anthony
Connolly, Harry
Cronin, John
Cronin, William
Currivan, Donald
Dell Isola, John
Donahue, James
Donovan, Arthur
Druze, John
Dubinski, Walter
Fiorentino, Albert
Giannelli, Mario
Gladchuk, Chester
Harrison, Edward
Holovak, Michael
King, Edward
Kissell, Adolph
Kissell, John
Kobolinski, Stanley
Koslowski, Joseph
McGurik, Warren
Manzo, Frank
Maznicki, Frank
Morrisey, Frank
Naumetz, Fred
O'Connell, G.

O'Rourke, Charles
Repko, Joseph
Spinney, Arthur
Stautner, Ernest
Tosi, Flavio
Urban, Luke
Williams, Theodore

BOSTON UNIVERSITY
Dixon, Felix
Dorfman, Arthur
Famiglietti, Gary
Lamana, Peter
Morris, Francis
Williams, Walter

BRADLEY
Carlson, Roy
Ormsbee, Elliott
Prokop, Joseph
Ramsey, Ray
Stone, William

BRIGHAM YOUNG
Berry, Rex
Chamberlain, Garth
Nelson, Reed
Robinson, Burle

BROOKLYN COLLEGE
Sherman, Al
Shires, Arthur

BROWN
Annan, Duncan
Brace, Robert
Broda, Harold
Colo, Don
Cornsweet, Albert
Eckstein, Adolph
Edwards, C. H.
Gulian, Michael
Hall, Irving
Hillhouse, Andrew
Keefer, Jackson
Lawrence, Edward
McCrillis, Edward
McLaughry, John
Margarita, Henry
Mishel, David
Nichols, Ralph
Oden, Olaf
Pohlman, John
Pollard, Fritz
Priestley, Robert
Purdy, Clair
Schein, Joseph
Sheldon, James
Shurtleff, Bertrand
Spellman, John
Stifler, James
Sweet, Frederick
Talbot, John

BUCKNELL
Bollinger, Edward
Bowser, Arda
Brumbaugh, Justin
Conti, Enio
Dayhoff, Harry
Ellor, A.
Goodwin, Earl
Halicki, Edward
Hambacker, Ernest
Hinkle, Clark
James, George
Jones, Thomas
Kiick, George
Kostos, Anthony
Kostos, Martin
Lott, John
McCormick, Felix
Mitchell, Theodore
Ostendarp, James
Reed, Max
Reznichak, Joseph
Rodgers, Thomas
Smith, Stuart
Szot, Walter
Tomasetti, Louis
Wilsbach, Frank
Woerner, Erwin

BUFFALO
Ailinger, James

BUTLER
Cavosie, Joseph
Elser, Earl

Hinchman, Hubert
Reichle, Louis

CALIFORNIA AGGIES
Schmidt, Kermit

CALIFORNIA TECH
Sharp, Everett

CALIFORNIA U.
Agler, Harry
Baker, Jon
Celeri, Robert
Cullom, James
Eaton, Louis
Evans, John
Harding, Roger
Hufford, Darrell
Imlay, Talma
McQuary, John
Maul,
Monachino, James
Muller, Henry
Newmeyer, Donald
Reinhard, Robert
Reinhard, William
Schabarum, Peter
Schwartz, Perry
Smith, George
Wagner, Lowell

CAMERON JR.
Sumpter, Anthony

CANISIUS
Burt, Russell
Carr, Harlan
Colella, Thomas
Collins, John
Doyle, Edward
Feist, Louis
Guarneri, Albert
McCormick, Elmer
Mantell, Joseph
Peebles, James
Piccolo, William
Poillon, Richard
Trayner, Michael
Whalen, Gerald

CARLETON
Norton, Martin
Smith, Warren
Willegalle, Henry

CARLISLE
Barrel
Calac, Peter
Guyon, Joseph
Little Twig
Lone Wolf
Long Time Sleep
 (Nikolas Lassa)
Newashe
Pierce, Bemus
Powell, Stancil
Thorpe, James
Tomahawk
Welmus, Woodchuck

CARNEGIE TECH
Carnelly, Ray
Condit, Merlyn
Croft, Thurman
Dobrus, Peter
Donahue, W.
Flanagan, Latham
Karcis, John
Kavel, George
Lee, John
Mielziner, Saul
Moran, Dale
Newman, Olin
Patt, Maurice
Rieth, William
Robertson, James
Spizak, Charles
Sprinkle, Hubert
Stewart, Charles
Tesser, Ray

CARROLL COLLEGE
Bizer, Herbert
Buck, Arthur
Hempel, William
Hertz,
Lande, Clifford
Ludtke, Norman

Quinn, Ivan
Sparr, Edwin

CARTHAGE
Wager, John

CASE
Goss, Norman
Lund, William

CATAWBA
Tomaini, Army
Yagiello, Ray

CATHOLIC UNIVERSITY
Ambrose, John
Augusterfer, Eugene
Connell, James
Connor, William
Eberts, Bernard
Howell, Wilfred
Karpowich, Edward
Katalines, Leo
Lajousky, William
Lynch, Edward
Mulligan, George
Piero, Rocco
Whalen, Thomas

CENTENARY
Baker, Conway
Baldwin, Jack
Bohlmann, Frank
Flenniken, Max
Hogue, Murrel
May, John
Parker, Raymond
Rebseaman, Paul
Stoker, Lee
Waller, William

CENTRAL WASHINGTON
North, James

CENTRE COLLEGE
Baxter, Ernest
German, James
Gibson, Richard
Kottler, Martin
Lemon, Clifton
McMillin, Alvin
Montgomery, Ralph
Smythe, James
Tanner, John
Weaver, James

CHALDRON NORMAL
Miller, Milford

CHATTANOOGA UNIV.
Braidwood, Charles
Gregory, Jack
Grigonis, Frank
Hutchinson, Ralph
Koeninger, Arthur
Kopcha, Joseph
Roberts, Eugene

CHICAGO UNIV.
Bryant, John
Busse, Ellis
DesJardins, Paul
Folz, Arthur
Francis, Eugene
Goodman, Aubrey
Halladay, Richard
Hamitz, Lewis
Hartong, George
Hobscheid, Frank
Hurlburt, John
Jackson, Colville
Kernwein, Graham
Romney, Milton
Stahlman, Richard

CINCINNATI
Blake, Thomas
Feldhaus, William
Graham, Michael
Neihaus, Ralph
Nickel, Elbie
Nolting, Ray
O'Malley, Robert
Perrotti, Michael
Skorich, Nicholas
Smyth, William
Stautberg, Gerald
Sweeney, James

CITADEL
Sabados, Andrew

CITY COLLEGE, N.Y.
Halpern, Robert
Illowit, Roy

CLEMSON
Bryant, Lowell
Cone, Fred
Folk, Richard
Fritts, George
Gage, Robert
Hendley, Richard
Hudson, Robert
McFadden, Banks
Mathews, Ray
Potts, Robert
Roy, Wallace
Timmons, Charles
Tinsley, Sidney
Ziegler, Francis

COLGATE
Abell, Earl
Abruzzino, Frank
Anderson, Oscar
Anderson, Winston
Batorski, John
Cabrelli, Lawrence
Chesbro, Marcel
Crowthers, Rae
Crowthers, Saville
Duckworth, Joseph
Dufft, James
Fortmann, Daniel
Gauer, Charles
Geyer, William
Gillo, Henry
Gilson, Robert
Haines, Harry
Hart, J. Leslie
Hoague, Joseph
Horning, Clarence
Irwin, Donald
Kershaw, George
Kinscherf, Carl
Laird, James
Leonard, James
Long, John
Mankat, Carl
Micka, Michael
Muehlheuser, Frank
Neacy, Clement
Parnell, Fred
Redinger, Otis
Rowe, Robert
Stacco, Edward
Stromiello, Michael
Tryon, Edward
Webber, C.
Webster, Fred
Welsh, James
Wemple, Donald
West, David
Yablok, Julius

COLORADO A. & M.
Christiansen, John
Dodrill, Dale
McGraw, Thurman

COLORADO MINES
Madden, Lloyd
Rooney, Cobb

COLORADO STATE
Clay, Roy
Fries, Sherwood
Maeda, Chester
Morris, Glen
White, Wilbur

COLORADO UNIV.
Briggs, Paul
Caranci, Roland
Clark, Earl
Clay, Walter
Fena, Joseph
Grosvenor, George
Lewis, Ernest
Ritchard, Delbert
Smith, James
Stasica, Leo
White, Byron

COLUMBIA
Armstrong, John
Bleeker, Malcolm

Cordavano, Samuel
Cuneo, Edward
Field, Richard
Governali, Paul
Johnson, Leon
Kennedy, Joseph
Kerrigan, Thomas
Kisiday, George
Koppisch, Walter
Kusserow, Lou
Luckman, Sidney
Maack, Herbert
Montgomery, Clifford
Pease, George
Roderick, Benjamin
Siegal, John
Swiacki, William
Wagner, Charles
Yablonski, Ventan

COMPTON JR.
Perry, Fletcher
Wallace, Beverly

CONNECTICUT STATE
Maikkula, Kenneth
O'Neil,
Williams, Arthur

CORNELL
Barna, George
Berryman, Robert
Daukas, Louis
Dekdebrun, Allen
Douglas, Benjamin
Ebersole, H. L.
Flynn, Frank
Gillies, Fred
Hershey, Kirk
Kaw, Edward
Landsburg, Mortimer
McCullough, Harold
Molinet, Louis
Morris, R.
O'Hearn, John
Shelton, Murray
Stofer, Kenneth
Wilson, James
Wydo, Frank

CREIGHTON
Bertoglio, James
Borak, Fritz
Cemore, Anthony
Fitzgibbons, Paul
Gayer, Walter
Knolla, John
McDonald, John
Mahoney, Roger
Maillard, Ralph

CULVER
Gray, D. P.

DALLAS UNIVERSITY
Grigg, Cecil

DARTMOUTH
Burke, Charles
Crowley, Joseph
Daukas, Nicholas
Diehl, Carl
Ghee, Milton
Hagenbuckle, Vernon
Haws, Harvey
Healy, Edward
Jenkins, Jonathan
Krieger, Robert
McLeod, Robert
Maloney, Gerald
Marsters, Alton
Murphy, George
Shelburne, John
Sonnenberg, Gustave
Thielscher, Karl
Tully, George
Youngstrom, Adolph

DAVIDSON
Mackorell, John

DAVIS & ELKINS
Corzine, Lester
Federovich, John
Irvin, Cecil
Mitchell, Granville
Rengel, Neil
Underwood, Forrest

DAYTON UNIVERSITY
Achui, Walter
Belanich, William
Cabrina, August
Dellinger,
Duffy, Patrick
Furst, Anthony
Hippa, Samuel
Kinderdine, Henry
Knorr, Lawrence
Lange, William
McDonough, Coley
Mahrt, Louis
Obee, Duncan
Partlow,

DEKALB
Behan, Charles
Nori, Reino

DELAWARE
Thompson, Harold

DENISON
Becker, John
Calhoun, Eric
Gregory, Michael
Moody, Wilkie
Phanner, Eugene
Reese, David
Roudebush, George
Thiele, Carl

DENVER UNIVERSITY
Balog, Robert
Browning, Gregory
Dreher, Ferdinand
Gifford, Robert
Hazelhurst, Robert
Jurich, Michael
Stansauk, Donald
Tiller, Morgan
Woudenberg, John

DE PAUL
Apolskis, Charles
Boedecker, William
Cherne, Harold
Dowling, Patrick
Fiske, Max
Krause, Paul
Muellner, William
Roberts, Thomas

DE PAUW
Fortune, Burnell
Sturtridge, Donald

DETROIT UNIVERSITY
Andrusking, Sigmund
Banonis, Vincent
Barrett, John
Bucher, Frank
Cassidy, William
Ciago, Walter
Cooper, Harold
Ellis, Walter
Farkas, Andrew
Harvey, Norman
Hogan, Thomas
Keene, Robert
Kostiuk, Michael
Lauer, John
Lowther, Russell
McNamara, Thomas
Madarik, Elmer
Malinowski, Eugene
Nott, Douglas
Pavelec, Theodore
Russas, Al
Ryan, John
Simmons, John
Voss, Walter
Young, L.

DICKINSON
Behman, Russell
Books, Robert
Supulski, Leonard

DRAKE
Bienemann, Thomas
Brindley, Walter
Don Carlos, J. E.
Krueger, Albert
Manders, Clarence
Nesbitt, Richard
Spear, Glen
Steere, Richard

DUBUQUE
Kuehl, Walter

DUKE
Allen, Louis
Bailey, Edgar
Cox, William
Crawford, Frederick
DeRogatis, Albert
Hartley, Howard
Karmazin, Michael
Lach, Steven
Lewis, Clifford
McAfee, George
McAfee, Wesley
McDonough, Robert
Milner, William
Mote, Kelly
Neal, Thomas
Parker, Clarence
Perdue, Charles
Piasecky, Al
Ribar, Frank
Sharkey, Edward
Sinkovitz, Frank
Stough, Glen

DULUTH CATHEDRAL
Bratt, George

DUQUESNE
Basrak, Michael
Bonotto, John
Brumbaugh, Boyd
Cibulas, Joseph
Ciccone, Benjamin
Corbo, Thomas
DeCarbo, Nicholas
DeMao, Albert
DePaul, Henry
Gonda, George
Hall, Forrest
Jansante, Valerio
Kakasic, George
Karrs, John
Kemp, Ray
Kielbasa, Max
McDonald, Edward
Maras, Joseph
Matisis, John
Mehelich, Charles
Nery, Carl
Niccolai, Armand
Perko, John
Petchell, John
Platukis, George
Rado, Arthur
Rado, George
Rokisky, John
Semes, Bernard
Setcavage, Joseph
Sinko, Steven
Sirochman, George
Strutt, Arthur
Vidoni, Victor
Weinberg, Henry
Wiehl, Joseph
Wukits, Albert
Zaninelli, Silvio
Zopetti, Frank

EAST CENTRAL
Capps, Walter

E. KENTUCKY STATE
Hollingsworth, Joseph
Pelfrey, Ray

EAST TEXAS TEACHERS
Johnson, Cecil
Tully, Darrell

ELLISVILLE JR.
Gulyanics, George

ELMHURST
Johnston, Chester

ELON
Boone, Robert
Bradley, Harold

EMPORIA TEACHERS
Burnett, Dale
Campbell, Glenn
Kline, Harry
Munday, George

FINDLAY
Susteric, Edward

FLORIDA
Brumbaugh, Carl
Crabtree, Clyde
Dempsey, Frank
Duhart, Paul
Goff, Clark
Goodbread, Royce
Hunsinger, Charles
Klutka, Nicholas
Konetsky, Floyd
Lee, Eugene
Mitchell, Fondren
Waters, Dale
Williams, Broughton
Williams, Cyrus

FORDHAM
Babartsky, Albert
Berezney, Paul
Bissell, Frederick
Blumenstock, James
Borden, Lester
Brennan, Paul
Cannela, John
Cheverko, George
Danowski, Edward
DeFillipo, Louis
Dennery, Vincent
Eshmont, Leonard
Feaster, William
Filipowicz, Steven
Grandinette, George
Jacunski, Harry
Johnson, Arthur
Kellagher, William
Kloppenberg, Harry
Kochel, Michael
Kuzman, John
Leary, Thomas
Lowe, George
Maniaci, Joseph
Manning, James
Myers, Thomas
Noonan, Gerald
Principe, Dominic
Riddick, Raymond
Sabasteanski, Joseph
Sarausky, Anthony
Sartori, Lawrence
Siano, Anthony
Stein, William
Stevenson, Arthur
Strand, Lief
Tepo, George
Ungerer, Joseph
Uzdavinis, Walter
Wojciechowicz, Alex
Yackanich, Joseph
Zapustas, Joseph

FT. HAYS, TEACHERS
Reissig, William

FRANKLIN
Franklin, Paul
Isselhardt, Ralph

FRANKLIN MARSHALL
Jones, Kenneth
Schibanoff, Alex

FRESNO STATE
Handley, Richard
Masini, Leonard
Seiferling, John

FULLERTON JR.
Livingston, Howard

FURMAN
Proctor, Dewey
Shetley, Rhoten
Wham, Thomas

GENESEE WESLEYAN
Webb,

GENEVA
Davis, Sylvester
Hubbard, Robert

GEORGE WASHINGTON
Butkus, Carl
Fedora, Walter
Gudmundson, Scott

Gustafson, Edsel
Hanken, Ray
Katrishen, Michael
Keahey, Eulis
Koniszewski, John
Leemans, Alphonse
Nash, Thomas
Nowaskey, Robert
O'Neill, William
Prather, Dale
Seno, Frank

GEORGETOWN
Barron, James
Blozis, Al
Castiglia, James
Comstock, Rudolph
Connaughton, Harry
Corcoran, Thomas
Cullen, Thomas
Doolan, John
Dubofsky, Maurice
Dwyer, Robert
Flavin, John
Frank, Joseph
Ghecas, Louis
Golsen, Eugene
Golsen, Thomas
Hagerty, John
Itzel, John
Jawish, Henry
Kenyon, William
Kercher, Robert
Koshlap, Jules
Lascari, John
Lio, Augustino
McQuade, John
Matuza, Albert
Metzger, Louis
Morelli, John
Murtagh, George
O'Connor, Daniel
Perpich, George
Plansky, Anthony
Provencial, Kenneth
Rawlings, Robert
Scalzi, John
Sorce, Ross
Stralka, Clement
Tomaini, John
Waite, Carl
Werder, Richard
Whelan, Thomas

GEORGIA TECH
Davis, Robert
Duke, Paul
Giaver, Einar
Godwin, W.
Helms, John
Lumpkin, Roy
McConnell, F. C.
McHugh, Pat
Matthews, Clay
Mizell, Warner
Murphy, Robert
Paschal, William
Prokop, Edward
Steber, John
Still, James
Thomason, John
Watkins, Gordon
Wycoff, Douglas
Ziegler, Frank

GEORGIA UNIVERSITY
Conger, Melvin
Davis, R. Lamar
Davis, Van
Dickens, Marion
Donaldson, John
Dudish, Andrew
Edwards, Daniel
Ehrhardt, Clyde
Ellenson, Eugene
Feher, Nicholas
Fordham, James
Geri, Joseph
Godwin, William
Grate, Carl
Hartman, William
Hobbs, Homer
Johnson, Howard
Keuper, Kenneth
King, Henry
McCrary, Hurdis
Mooney, James
Mott, Buster
Paternoster, Angelo

Rausch, John
Reid, Floyd
Reynolds, Owen
Ricca, James
Roberts, John
St. John, Herbert
Sinkwich, Frank
Smith, Charles
Smith, George
Tanner, Hampton
Tereshinski, Joseph
Tinsley, Peter
Trippi, Charles
Walston, Robert
Wells, Donald
Williams, Garland
Young, George

GETTYSBURG
Kyle, James
Yovisin, John

GONZAGA
Ashmore, Roger
Bellinger, Robert
Brian, William
Cahoon, Ivan
Canadeo, Anthony
Cyre, Hector
Flaherty, Ray
Hare, Cecil
Hare, Ray
Justice, Edward
Karamatic, George
Krause, Max
Peterson, Kenneth
Stockton, Herschel
Stockton, Houston
Wilson, William

GRAMBLING
Younger, Paul

GRINNELL
Moran, Peter

GROVE CITY
Brian, Harry
Critchfield, Lawrence
Gibson, Denver
Lantz, Montgomery
Sofish, Alexander
Tallant, David
Wall, Edward

GUSTAVUS ADOLPHUS
Butcher, Wendell
Lundell, Wilbur
Parsons, Lloyd
Witte, Earl

HAMLINE
Cramer, Carl
Eliason, Donald
Haven, John

HAMPTON INSTITUTE
Casey, Thomas

HAMPTON SIDNEY
Miller, Thomas
Worden, Stuart

HARDIN–SIMMONS
Bennett, Earl
Burrus, Harry
Cherry, Edgar
Crowell, Odis
Davenport, Wayne
Evans, Murray
Goodnight, Owen
Johnson, Alvin
McChesney, Robert
Mobley, Rudolph
Parker, David
Prescott, Harold
Ribble, Loran
Ryan, David
Sprinkle, Edward
Treadaway, John
Turner, Clyde
Tyler, Peter

HARVARD
Burnham, Stanley
Casey, Edward
Clark, Charles
Dadman, Harrie

Evans, Earl
Horween, Arnold*
Horween, Ralph*
McGlone, Joseph
Mahan, Edward
Miller, Alfred
*Played as "McMahon"

HASKELL
Crow, Orien
Elkins, Fait
Jennings,
Johnson, Lawrence
McElmore,
Nix,
Oakes, William
Weller, Louis

HEIDELBERG
Hutson, Merle
Michaels, Alton
Vokaty, Otto

HOBART
Kraus, Francis

HOLY CROSS
Brawley, Edward
Brennan, Leo
Britt, Edward
Cahill, Ronald
Carton, Charles
Clancy, Stuart
Cregar, William
Digris, Bernard
Fitzgerald, Donald
Gardella, Augustus
Garvey, F.
Gildea, Dennis
Golembeske, Anthony
Grigas, John
Holley, Kenneth
Ignatius, James
Kissell, Veto
Kittredge, Paul
Klasoskus, Albin
Koslowski, Stanley
Kucharski, Theodore
Landrigan, James
McCulloch, J.
McGrath, Richard
McNamara, Edmund
Manfreda, Anthony
Monaco, Raymond
Moran, James
Natowich, Andrew
Osmanski, Joseph
Osmanski, William
Pyne, George
Rovinski, Anthony
Sullivan, Robert
Titus, George
Titus, Silas
Wizbicki, Alexander
Zeno, Joseph
Zyntell, James

HOUSTON
Barnhart, Daniel

HOWARD
Cooper, Norman
Goldman, Samuel
Hill, Harold
Hodges, Herman
Jeffries, Robert
Lollar, George
Schenker, Nathan
Tarrant, James

IDAHO
Bucklin, Thomas
Fitzke, Robert
Miklich, William
Nixon, George
Norby, John
Owens, Delmer
Smith, Willis
Stephens, Leslie
Vesser, John

ILLINOIS TEACHERS
Glenn, William

ILLINOIS UNIVERSITY
Agase, Alexander
Bernhardt, George
Berry, Gilbert
Bingaman, Lester

Britton, Earl
Burdick, Lloyd
Cook, David
Corcoran, Gerald
Crangle, John
Daugherty, Russell
Depler, John
Drayer, Clarence
Gordon, Louis
Grange, Garland
Grange, Harold
Griffin, Donald
Halas, George
Hall, Raymond
Ingwersen, Bert
Johnson, Nathan
Kasap, Michael
Kassel, Charles
Kawal, Edward
Klimek, Anthony
Knop, Oscar
Knox, Frank
Kovacsy, William
Kraft, Reynold
Lanum, Ralph
McCarthy, James
McIlwain, Walter
McMillen, James
Maggioli, Achille
Morris, G. Max
Moss, Perry
Mullen, Vern
Owens, Isaiah
Patterson, Paul
Pearce, Walter
Perez, Peter
Petty, Ross
Piggott, Bert
Podmajerski, Paul
Rundquist, E. T.
Rykovich, Julius
Shoemaker, Hubbard
Siegert, Herbert
Smith, Russell
Sternaman, Edward
Sternaman, Joseph
Stichcomb, Peter
Sucic, Steven
Walquist, Laurie
Young, Claude

ILLINOIS WESLEYAN
Blazine, Anthony
Kaska, Anthony
Morrow, Robert
Newman, Robert
Wetterlund, Chester

INDIANA
Addams, Abraham
Bell, Edward
Bennett, Charles
Bernoski, Daniel
Brown, Howard
Bucchianeri, Amadeo
Cannady, John
Cowan, Robert
Davis, Corbett
Dewar, James
Filchock, Frank
Goldsberry, John
Groomes, Melvin
Grossman, Rex
Haak, Robert
Hanny, Frank
Hathaway, Russell
Hess, Arthur
Hillenbrand, William
Hoernschmeyer, Robert
Howard, Lynn
Huffman, Vernon
Jagade, Harry
Jones, Robert
Jurkewicz, Walter
Karsten, George
Kyle, John
Livingston, Theodore
Logan, James
McCaw, William
Marks, Lawrence
Mathys, Charles
Oliver, Vincent
Pihos, Peter
Raimondi, Benjamin
Randolph, Clare
Ravensburg, Robert
Ringwalt, Carroll
Risley, Elliott
Rucinski, Edward

Saban, Louis
Sebek, Nicholas
Taliaferro, George
Tavenor, John
Tofil, Joseph
Uremovich, Emil
White, Eugene
Wilkins, Theodore
Witucki, Casimir
Zeller, Joseph
Zimny, Robert
Zoll, Richard

IOWA STATE
Barker, Richard
Doran, James
Heileman, Charles
Heldt, John
Jensen, Robert
Longstreet, Roy
Shugart, Clyde
Underwood, John

IOWA UNIVERSITY
Balazs, Frank
Belding, Lester
Couppee, Albert
Crayne, Richard
Deskin, Versil
Ely, Harold
Evans, Richard
Farmer, Thomas
Farrott, Shipley
Fisher, Darrell
Fleckenstein, William
Fosdick, Robert
Fry, Wesley
Glassgow, Willis
Greenwood, Glenn
Griffin, Harold
Harris, Henry
Hoerner, Richard
Jensvold, Leo
Kadesky, Max
Keane, James
Laws, Joseph
McClain, Mayes
Masterson, Forest
Mertes, Bernard
Minick, Paul
Nelson, Donald
Niedziela, Bruno
Niles, Jerry
Olson, Forrest
Otte, F. Lowell
Pape, Orrin
Pignatelli, Carl
Rogge, George
Sandberg, Sigmund
Sansen, Oliver
Schammel, Francis
Schluesner, Vincent
Schneidman, Herman
Shoener, Harold
Shoener, Herbert
Slater, Fred
Smith, James
Smith, Robert
Thompson, Alvin
Tollefson, Charles
Tunnell, Emlen
Woodard, Richard
Youel, James

ITHACA COLLEGE
D'Orazio, Joseph

JOHN CARROLL
Armstrong, Graham
Ecker, Enrique
Lahey, Thomas
Shula, Donald
Stringer, Eugene
Taseff, Carl

JORDAN
McWilliams, William

KALAMAZOO
Casteel, Miles
Seborg, Henry

KANSAS AGGIES
Feather, E. E.

KANSAS STATE
Cronkhite, Henry
Hackney, Elmer
Harrison, J.

Krysl, Jerry
McGee, Howard
Maddox, George
Munn, Lyle
Pearson, Albert
Raemer, Norbert
Randels, Horace
Shaffer, Leland
Tackwell, Charles
Webber, H.
Weiner, Bernard

KANSAS STATE TEACHERS
Andrews, Leroy
Tarrant, Robert

KANSAS UNIVERSITY
Amberg, John
Bausch, Frank
Black, Charles
Bushby, Thomas
Detweiler, John
Ettinger, Donald
Evans, Ray
Griffith, Forrest
Hauser, Harold
Kvaternick, Zvonimir
McCormack, Michael
Mehringer, Peter
Merkel, Monte
Pierce, Donald
Romero, Ray
Russell, Douglas
Schaake, Elmer
Schnellbacher, Otto
Tomlinson, Richard
Ulrich, Hubert

KENT STATE
DeWeese, Byrne
Hein, Robert

KENTUCKY STATE
Anderson, Ezzret
Bass, William

KENTUCKY UNIVERSITY
Allen, Ermal
Blanda, George
Davis, Robert
Eibner, John
Gregg, Edward
Hensley, Richard
Johnson, Albert
Johnson, Clyde
Kelly, John Simms
Kercheval, Ralph
Lindahl, Virgil
Lindon, Luther
McDermott, Lloyd
Marcus, Peter
Mullins, Noah
Phelps, Donald
Rhodemyre, Jay
Richards, Richard
Serini, Washington
Ugoccioni, Enrico
Ulinski, Harry
Wright, Frank
Yowarsky, Walter

KENYON
Stock, Herbert

KIRKSVILLE TEACHERS
Robinson, John

KNOX
Bridgeford, Lane
Senn, William

LaCROSSE STATE
TEACHERS
Loomis, Ace
Owen, Vilas
Smith, Rex

LAFAYETTE
Bednar, Albert
Berry, Charles
Brennan, Matthew
Budd, John
Deibel, Arthur
Elliott, Wallace
Ernst, John
Farrell, J. T.
Ford, Adrian
Grube, Frank
Kirkleski, Frank

Lehecka, Joseph
Millman, Robert
Moore, Walter
Scott, John
Seasholtz, George
Weldon, John
Williams, Joseph
Zirinsky, Walter

LAKE FOREST
Biolo, John
Milton, Thomas
Owens, Henry

LA SALLE
Mandarion, Michael
Sommers, George

LAWRENCE
Basing, Myrton
Kotal, Edward
Zupek, Albert

LEBANON VALLEY
Homan, Henry
Lechthaler, Roy

LEHIGH
Davidovitz, Arthur
Sanford, James
Scholl, R. F.
Spagna, Joseph
Springsteen, William
Storer, John
Yeager, J.

LOMBARD
Lamb, Roy
Strickland, William
Swanson, Eyar

LONG ISLAND UNIVERSITY
Kapitansky, Bernard

LOUISIANA STATE UNIV.
Barnes, Walter
Barrett, Jeffrey
Burkett, Jeffrey
Bussey, Young
Cason, James
Champagne, Edward
Coates, Ray
Coffee, James
Collins, Albin
Collins, Ray
Cormier, Ulysses
Friend, Benjamin
Glamp, Joseph
Gorinski, Walter
Jones, William
Kavanaugh, Kenneth
Kingery, Wayne
Land, Fred
Leisk, Wardell
May, William
Neal, William
Reed, Joseph
Reid, Joseph
Rukas, Justin
Sandifer, Daniel
Sanford, Otis
Schroll, Charles
Shurtz, Hubert
Tinsley, Gaynell
Tinsley, Jess
Tittle, Yelverton
Torrance, John
Toth, Zollie
Van Buren, Ebert
Van Buren, Steven
Wimberly, Abner

LOUISIANA TECH
Doherty, George
Giddens, Herschel
Gregory, Garland
Martin, Caleb

LOUISVILLE
Meeks, Edward
Mosher, Clure

LOYOLA (CHICAGO)
Berwick, Edward
Bush, R. M.
Malloy, Lester
Moore, Allen
Sachs, Leonard

LOYOLA (MARYLAND)
Intrieri, Marne

LOYOLA (NEW ORLEANS)
Moore, William
Sullivan, Frank

LOYOLA (LOS ANGELES)
Boyd, Robert
Brito, Eugene
Dempsey, John
Dwyer, John
Elsey, Earl
Ferris, Neil
Hrabetin, Frank

LUTHER
Hansen, Clifford
Stolfa, Alton

MANCHESTER
Banet, Herbert
Lieberum, Donald

MANHATTAN
Damiani, Francis
Jocher, Arthur
Marone, John
Schmeelk, Garry
Seick, Earl
Tuckey, Richard

MANITOBA
Lear, Leslie

MARQUETTE
Apolskis, Raymond
Aspatore, Edward
Becker, Wayland
Bentzien, Alfred
Bergin, William
Bilda, Richard
Braden, David
Buivid, Raymond
Bultman, Arthur
Busler, Raymond
Butler, William
Carlson, Ray
Cronin, Thomas
Cuff, Ward
Curtin, Donald
Davis, Paul
Dilweg, Lavern
Douglas, George
Duford, Wilfred
Dunn, Joseph
Elliott, Burton
Enich, Steven
Fahay, John
Faye, Allen
Felker, Arthur
Flaherty, Richard
Gavin, Fritz
Glick, Edward
Goodyear, John
Groves, George
Hanson, Ray
Harrington, John
Hayes, Norbert
Klug, Alfred
Kosikowski, Frank
Kramer, John
Kuffel, Raymond
LaFleur, Joseph
Lane, Oscar
Langhoff, Henry
Leysenaar, Harry
Linnan, Francis
Lunz, Gerald
McGinnis, James
Maceau, Melvin
Murray, Richard
Radick, Kenneth
Roessler, Fritz
Ronzani, Gene
Schoemann, Roy
Schuette, Carl
Sisk, John
Strzykalski, John
Taugher, Claude
Trost, Milton
Vogt, Alois
Vosberg, Donald
Woodin, Howard

MARSHALL
Adkins, Robert
Brown, William

Gatski, Frank
Huffman, Frank
Hunt, John
Mattiford, John
Morlock, John
Pearcy, James
Stephens, John
Ulinski, Edward
Willey, Norman

MARYLAND STATE
Fletcher, Andrew

MARYLAND UNIVERSITY
Brewer, Brooke
Dryden,
Gambino, Lucien
Krouse, Ray
Leatherman, J. D.
Lookabaugh, John
Meade, James
Mont, Thomas
Wright, John

McMURRY
Cowan, Leslie
Rowland, Bradley

McPHERSON
Vetter, John

MERCER
Olsson, Lester
Owen, Alton

MIAMI (FLA.)
Carapella, Al
DeMarco, Mario
Fox, Terrance
Jelley, Thomas
Kearns, James
Kichefski, Walter
McDougal, Robert
Masterson, Robert
Noppenberg, John
Tevis, Leek
Watt, Walter

MIAMI (OHIO)
Buchanan, Stephen
Crawford, Kenneth
Joseph, A.
Joseph, Z.
Parseghian, Ara
Sauer, Edward
Savatsky, Oliver
Shoults, Paul
Weaver, John
Wolf, Richard

MICHIGAN STATE
Allman, Stanley
Bagdon, Edward
Beckley, Arthur
Blacklock, Hugh
Bruckner, Leslie
Buss, Arthur
Butler, Frank
Chandnois, Lynn
Dibble, Dorne
Diehl, David
Friedlund, Robert
Grove, Roger
Hansen, Dale
Hultman, Vivian
Johnson, Farnham
Kennedy, William
Ketzko, Alexander
Kinek, Michael
Klewicki, Edward
Lay, Russell
Minarik, Henry
Monnett, Robert
Pingel, John
Reader, Russell
Rockonbach, Lyle
Sieradzki, Stephen
Vezmar, Walter
Wagner, Sidney

MICHIGAN STATE NORMAL
Hanneman, Charles
Opalewski, Edward

MICHIGAN TECH
Kieley, Howard

MICHIGAN UNIVERSITY
Auer, Howard

Babcock, Samuel
Bernard, Charles
Brennan, John
Callahan, Robert
Carpenter, John
Chappuis, Robert
Daley, William
Dawley, Fred
Draveling, Leo
Dworsky, Daniel
Ford, Leonard
Friedman, Benjamin
Fritz, Ralph
Frutig, Edward
Goebel, Paul
Goetz, Angus
Greene, John
Harmon, Thomas
Heikkinen, Ralph
Hewitt, William
Hirsch, Elroy
Hudson, Martin
Hughitt, Ernest
Ingalls, Robert
Johns, James
Karwales, John
Kilbourne, Warren
Kirk, Bernard
Kolesar, Robert
Kreinheder, Walter
Lazetich, Milan
Madar, Elmer
Mann, Robert
Marion, Philip
Molenda, John
Morrison, Maynard
Monsen, Anthony
Muirhead, Stanley
Newman, Harry
Nieman, Walter
Nussbaumer, Robert
Ortman, Charles
Pregulman, Mervin
Rifenburg, Richard
Roby, Douglas
Rosatti, Roman
Smeja, Rudolph
Smith, Pat
Soboleski, Joseph
Vick, Ernest
Westfall, Robert
White, Paul
Wiese, Robert
Williamson, Ivan
Wistert, Albert
Usher, Edward

MILLIGAN
Carpe, Joseph
Corbett, George
Musso, George

MILWAUKEE TEACHERS
Kliebhan, Roger
Kranz, Kenneth

MINNESOTA
Abramson, George
Alfonse, Jules
Baston, Albert
Baumgartner, William
Beson, Warren
Billman, John
Bisbee, Bertin
Bjorklund, Robert
Buhler, Lawrence
Christianson, Martin
Clow, H.
Dunigan, Merton
Dunnigan, Walter
Faunce, Everett
Faust, George
Franck, George
Garnaas, Wilford
Gay, Kenneth
Gibson, George
Grant, Harry
Hanke, Carl
Hanson, Harold
Haycraft, Kenneth
Jaszewski, Floyd
Joesting, Herbert
Johnson, William
Juster, Rubin
Kakela, Wayne
Kostka, Stanley
Kulbitski, Victor
Kuusisto, William
Lechner, Edgar

Levy, Leonard
Lidberg, Carl
Lyle, Dewey
McRae, Stanley
Maeder, Albert
Manders, John
Martineau, Earl
Mihajlovich, Louis
Mitchell, Paul
Moore, Wilbur
Nagurski, Bronko
Nolander, Donald
Nomellini, Leo
Nydall, Malcolm
O'Donnell, Richard
Odson, Urban
Oech, Vern
Olsonoski, Lawrence
Oss, Arnold
Paffrath, Robert
Paschka, Gordon
Pederson, Win
Perko, John
Pharmer, Arthur
Plunkett, Warren
Regnier, Peter
Schultz, Charles
Sikich, Rudolph
Smith, Bruce
Soltau, Gordon
Spadaccini, Victor
Svendsen, Earl
Svendsen, George
Sweiger, Robert
Tanner, Robert
Tenner, Robert
Teeter, Alan
Thompson, Clarence
Thompson, Franklin
Tierney, Frederick
Tonnemaker, Clayton
Tuttle, Richard
Twedell, Francis
Uram, Andrew
Van Every, Harold
Van Hull, Frederick
Widseth, Edwin
Wildung, Richard
Williams, Vernon
Wyman, Arnold

MISSISSIPPI SOUTHERN
Morgan, Joseph
Stringfellow, Joseph
Van Tone, Arthur
Vetrano, Joseph

MISSISSIPPI STATE
Armstrong, Charles
Black, John
Blount, Lamar
Champion, James
Corley, Elbert
Davis, Harper
Frohm, Martin
Garrett, William
Gelatka, Charles
Goolsby, James
Harris, Amos
Harrison, Granville
Jefferson, William
Kowalski, Anthony
McWilliams, Thomas
Sidorik, Alexander
Smith, Truett
Tait, Arthur
Tripson, John

MISSISSIPPI UNIVERSITY
Bilbo, Jonathan
Bernard, David
Britt, Oscar
Conerly, Charles
Dale, Roland
Dodson, Leslie
Dottley, John
Erickson, William
Farragut, Kenneth
Hall, L. Parker
Hapes, Merle
Hovious, John
Howell, Earl
Johnson, Joseph
Kinard, Frank
Kinard, George
Kozel, Chester
McCain, Robert
Poole, G. Barney
Poole, James

Poole, Oliver
Poole, Ray
Reynolds, William
Robertson, Lake
Smith, Houston Allen
Stribling, Majure
Terrell, Raymond
Turnbow, Guy
Woodruff, Lee

MISSOURI UNIVERSITY
Bacchus, Carl
Blumer, Herbert
Christman, Paul
Collins, Paul
Copley, Charles
Greenwood, Donald
Jean, Walter
Kekeris, James
McGirl, Leonard
Martin, Herschel
Morton, John
Pepper, Eugene
Quirk, Edward
Reece, Donald
Rouse, Stillman
Shurnas, Marshall
Smith, Clyde
Smith, Ray
Steuber, Robert
Stewart, Ralph
Travis, J. Edward
Van Dyne, Charles
Volz, Wilbur

MONMOUTH
Earp, Francis
Molesworth, Keith
Scott, Edward

MONTANA STATE
Cosner, Donald
Forte, Aldo
Illman, Edward
Kipp, James
Lazetich, William
Noyes, Leonard
Peters, Forest
Popovich, Milton
Szakash, Paul

MORGAN
Harris, Elmore

MORNINGSIDE
Wenig, Obe

MORRIS HARVEY
Adams, Verlin
Jones, William
Seltzer, Harry
Thacker, Alvin
Turbert, Francis

MT. ST. MARY'S
Ferko, John
Lamas, Joseph

MUHLENBERG
Averno, Sisto
Borrelli, Nicholas
Gorgone, Peter
Scott, L. Perry
Weiner, Albert
Zuzzio, Anthony

MURRAY STATE TEACHERS
Gudauskas, Peter
McRaven, William
Speth, George

NEBRASKA STATE TEACHERS
Blessing, Paul

NEBRASKA UNIVERSITY
Alfson, Warren
Ashburne, Clifford
Bassett, Herbert
Berquist, Jay
Bloodgood, Elbert
Broadstone, Marion
Brock, Charles
Byler, Joseph
Callahan, William
Cardwell, Joseph
Cardwell, Lloyd
Chamberlain, Guy
DeFruiter, Robert
DeWitz, Herbert

Doyle, Theodore
Fischer, Cletus
Francis, Samuel
Hokuf, Steven
Hopp, Harry
Howell, John
Kahler, Robert
Kahler, Royal
Lewellen, Verne
Lyman, Roy
McDonald, Lester
McMullen, Daniel
McPherson, Forrest
Masterson, Bernard
Noble, David
O'Brien, Gail
Oelrich, Arnold
Peterson, Leonard
Presnell, Glenn
Prochaska, Ray
Rhea, Hugh
Richards, Harry
Richards, Raymond
Rohrig, Herman
Samuelson, Carl
Sauer, George
Scherer, Bernard
Schleich, Victor
Seeman, George
Shaw, Edward
Shirey, Frederick
Thompson, Russell
Toogood, Charles
Vacanti, Samuel
Webber, Harry
Weir, Edward
Weir, Joseph
Weller, Truman
Wenke, Adolph
Westopal, Joseph
Wilder, H. F.
Zuver, Merle

NEBRASKA WESLEYAN
Wiberg, Oscar

NEVADA
Afflis, Richard
Carroll, Victor
Clark, Arthur
Gillom, Horace
Heath, Stanley
Howard, Sherman
Kalmanir, Thomas
Lane, Clayton
McClure, Robert
Mackrides, William
Motley, Marion
Orlich, Daniel
Talcott, Donald
Wentworth, Shirley

NEW MEXICO
Agajanian, Benjamin
Montfort, Avery

NEW MEXICO A & M
Nuzum, Jerry

NEW YORK UNIVERSITY
Barabee, Robert
Briante, Frank
Brown, Frederick
Buckley, Edward
Bunvan, John
Chalmers, George
Concannon, Ernest
Dunn, R.
Follet, Beryl
Grant, Leonard
Grant, Ross
Hugret, Joseph
Kanya, Robert
Marchi, Basilio
Marshall, Cloyd
Miller, James
Myers, David
Riordan, Charles
Satenstein, Bernard
Skudkin, David
Strong, Kenneth
Tanguay, James

NIAGARA
Deremer, Arthur
DeSantis, Daniel
Gutknecht, Albert
Piskor, Roman
Stefik, Robert

N. CAROLINA A & I
Jackson, Robert

N. CAROLINA STATE
Brown, John
Coon, Edward
Farrar, Vincent
Gibson, Paul
Palmer, Leslie
Stanton, William
Tatum, James

N. CAROLINA UNIVERSITY
Barclay, George
Bartos, Henry
Berry, Connie Mack
Burnette, Thomas
Camp, James
Cara, Dominic
Faircloth, Arthur
Hansen, Roscoe
Hazelwood, Theodore
Jackson, Donald
Justice, Charles
Kahn, Edward
Kennedy, Robert
Magner, James
Mark, Louis
Maronic, Steven
Rodgers, Hosea
Smith, William
Szafaryn, Leonard
Tandy, George
Weiner, Arthur
Williamson, Ernest

N. DAKOTA
Felber, Frederick
Gainor, Charles
Kahl, Cyrus
Kupcinet, Irving
McGeary, Clarence
Mackenroth, John
Method, Russell
Muready, Jerry
Ordway, William
Pylman, Robert
Rothrock, Clifford
Sturgeon, Cecil
Sturgeon, Lyle
Wheeler, Ernest
Young, H. D.

N. ILLINOIS STATE
Brink, Lawrence
Jarvi, Toimi

N. MICHIGAN
Powers, Samuel
Wagner, Buffton

N. TEXAS
Abbey, Joseph
Cooper, James
Mugg, Garvin

NORTHWESTERN
Aschenbrenner, Frank
Baker, Frank
Bauman, Alfred
Benson, George
Blumenthal, Morris
Bruder, Henry
DeCorrevont, William
DeStefano, Frederick
Driscoll, John
Engebretsen, Paul
Erdlitz, Richard
Erickson, Michael
Fencl, Richard
Gonya, Robert
Graham, Otto
Hajek, Charles
Haman, John
Hirsch, Edward
Holmer, Walter
Johnsos, Luke
Kapter, Alexander
Kelly, Charles
Koehler, Robert
Lecture, James
Lind, Albert
Lokanc, Joseph
McElwain, William
Magnusson, Glenn
Manske, Edward
Midler, Louis

Motl, Robert
Mueller, E.
Murakowski, Arthur
Palmer, Charles
Rentner, Ernest
Riley, John
Russell, Fay
Russell, Reginald
Schwall, Victor
Siegle, Jules
Stonesifer, Donald
Swisher, Robert
Tuner, James
Vanzo, Frederick
Wilson, George
Zorich, George

NORTHWESTERN MISSOURI STATE TEACHERS
Schottel, Ivan

NORWICH
Liebel, Frank

NOTRE DAME
Adams, John
Anderson, Edward
Anderson, Heartley
Angsman, Elmer
Bagarus, Steven
Bahan, Leonard
Banas, Steven
Barry, Norman
Baujan, Harry
Beinor, J. Edward
Berezney, Peter
Bertelli, Angelo
Brill, Martin
Brutz, James
Carberry, Glenn
Cardinal, Frank
Cifelli, August
Clatt, Corwin
Coleman, Herbert
Connor, George
Corgan, Michael
Cotton, Forrest
Coughlin, Frank
Coutre, Lawrence
Cowhig, Gerard
Crimmins, Bernard
Culver, Alvin
Czarobski, Zygmont
Dancewicz, Frank
David, Robert
DeClere,
Dove, Robert
Duggan, Edward
Ebli, Raymond
Edwards, Eugene
Eichenlaub, Raymond
Enright, Rex
Evans, Frederick
Feeney, Francis
Fischer, William
Fitzgerald, Freeman
Garvey, Edward
Garvey, Hector
Gasparella, Joseph
Gaul, Frank
Gay, William
Gompers, William
Greenley, Norman
Grefe, Theodore
Groom, Jerome
Hanlon, Robert
Hart, Leon
Hayes, David
Hayes, Gerald
Hearden, Thomas
Higgins, Luke
Jones, Gerald
Juzwik, Steven
Keefe, Emmett
Kell, Paul
Kelly, Robert
Kerr, William
Koken, Michael
Kovatch, John
Koziak, Michael
Kuharich, Joseph
Kurth, Joseph
Lambeau, Earl
Larson, O. J.
Law, John
Leonard, James
Leonard, William
Livingstone, Robert
Lujack, John

McCarthy, Howard
McInerney, Arnold
McNulty, Paul
Maddock, Robert
Malone, Grover
Marelli, Raymond
Martin, James
Mastrangelo, John
Mayer, Frank
Mayl, Eugene
Maxwell, Joseph
Mehre, Henry
Mello, James
Mergenthal, Arthur
Mieszkowski, Edward
Millner, Wayne
Mohardt, John
Moynihan, Timothy
Mundee, Frederick
Nadolney, Roman
Nemeth, Steven
O'Boyle, Harry
O'Connor, William
Panelli, John
Phelan, Robert
Piepul, Milton
Pivarnik, Joseph
Poliski, John
Puplis, Andrew
Ratterman, George
Ridzewski, Frank
Riffle, Charles
Roach, John
Rogers, John
Ruetz, Joseph
Rymkus, Louis
Savoldi, Joseph
Scharer, Edward
Scott, Vincent
Shellogg, Alec
Signaigo, Joseph
Sitko, Emil
Skoglund, Robert
Slackford, Fritz
Smith, Edward
Smith, Richard
Spaniel, Frank
Statuto, Arthur
Steinkemper, William
Strohmeyer, George
Stuhldreyer, Harry
Sullivan, George
Swistowicz, Michael
Szymanski, Frank
Terlep, George
Tobin, George
Trafton, George
Tripucka, Frank
Urban, Gasper
Vairo, Dominic
Vegara, George
Wallace, Joseph
Wallner, Frederick
Walsh, William
Wendell, Martin
White, James
Wightkin, William
Williams, Robert
Wynne, Chester
Yarr, Thomas
Yonakor, John
Zalejski, Ernest
Zilly, John
Zontini, Louis
Zora, Clyde

OBERLIN
Cooper, William
Seibert, Harold

OCCIDENTAL
Beebe, Keith

OGLETHORPE
Fulton, Theodore
Mitrick, Frank
Zelencik, Frank

OHIO NORTHERN
Conley, John

OHIO STATE
Adamle, Anthony
Andrako, Stephen
Ash, Julian
Bettridge, John
Bradley, R. T.
Busich, Samuel
Cheroke, George

Clair, Frank
Clark, Myers
Cline, Oliver
Cumisky, Frank
Cunningham, Harold
Daniell, James
Dean, Harold
Dellerba, Spiro
DiPierro, Raymond
Dow, Elwood
Dugger, John
Emerick, Robert
Fekete, Eugene
Flanagan, Richard
Flowers, James
Fox, Samuel
Gaudio, Robert
Gorrill, Charles
Groza, Louis
Harley, Charles
Honaker, Charles
Horvath, Leslie
Houston, Lindell
Huffman, Iolas
Isabel, Wilmer
James, Thomas
Jennings, John
Kabealo, Michael
Kaplanoff, Carl
Karch, Robert
Karcher, James
Krall, Gerard
Lavelli, Dante
Lininger, Raymond
Long, Thomas
McCafferty, Donald
McDonald, James
Marino, Victor
Michaels, Alton
Momsen, Robert
Monaha, Regis
Morrison, Frederick
Myers, Cyril
Nardi, Richard
Nemeck, Andrew
Padan, R.
Padlow, Max
Petcoff, Boni
Pincura, Stanley
Raskowski, Leo
Ream, Charles
Rosequist, Theodore
Rowan, Everett
Sarringhaus, Paul
Sensanbaugher, Dean
Shaw, Robert
Souders, Cecil
Spiers, Robert
Strausbaugh, James
Taylor, John
Thomas, Russell
Wendt, Merle
Wetzel, Damon
Willis, William
Workman, Harry
Young, William
Zadworney, Frank
Zarnas, Augustus

OHIO UNIVERSITY
Adams, Chester
Duvall, Earl
Graham, Alfred
Halleck, Paul
Janiak, Leonard
Kerns, John
Krieger, Earl
Lewis, Arthur
Rush, Arden
Sadowsky, Leonard
Snyder, Harry
Snyder, Robert

OHIO WESLEYAN
Edler, Robert
Frump, Milton
Lamme, Emerald
Smith, Olin
Turley, William
Westfall, Edgar
Winters, Lingel

OKLAHOMA A. & M.
Aldridge, Benjamin
Arms, Lloyd
Armstrong, Neil
Ault, Wayne
Buffington, Harry
Fenimore, Robert

Foster, Ralph
Garrett, Thurman
Grimes, William
Jeffers, Edward
Ledbetter, Toy
Liles, Elvin
Long, William
Loyd, Alexander
Meisenheimer, Darrell
Merkle, Edward
Owen, William
Parmer, James
Reynolds, James
Shaw, Charles
Spavital, James
Spencer, Joseph
Turner, James

OKLAHOMA BAPTIST
Phillips, Ewell

**OKLAHOMA CITY
UNIVERSITY**
Allen, Carl
Gutowsky, Leroy
Hilpert, Harold
Kamp, James
Schilling, Ralph
Schwab, Raymond
Shirley, Marion
Taylor, Hugh
Tuttle, Orville
Wade, James
Wilkerson, Basil

OKLAHOMA S. W. TEACHERS
Gore, Gordon
Kane, Herbert
Springer, Harold

OKLAHOMA UNIVERSITY
Allton, Joseph
Andros, Plato
Breedon, William
Bristow, Gordon
Brockman, Edward
Burris, Paul
Campbell, William
Clark, Beryl
Colhouer, J. C.
Conkright, William
Coppage, Alton
Cox, Robert
Crowder, Earl
Cullen, Ronald
Duggan, Gilford
Dunlap, Robert
Eason, Roger
Edmundson, Van
Ellstrom, Marvin
Gentry, Cassius
Golding, Joseph
Guffey, Roy
Heath, Leon
Hill, Harry
Ivy, Frank
Jacobs, Jack
Lahar, Harold
Lamb, Walter
Lee, Hilary
McCullough, Hugh
McDonald, Donald
Manley, Leon
Marsh, Howard
Marsh, Richard
Martin, John
Owens, James
Paine, Homer
Parks, Edward
Pearson, Lindell
Pressley, Lee
Rapacz, John
Sarratt, Charles
Seymour, Robert
Speegle, Clifton
Stacy, James
Stevenson, Ralph
Thomas, George
Thomas, James
Tillman, Alonzo
Tyree, James
West, Stanley
White, Philip
Whited, Marvin
Young, Walter

OMAHA UNIVERSITY
Arenas, Joseph

OREGON STATE
Austin, William
Bergerson, Gilbert
Biancone, John
Carlson, Jules
Durdan, Donald
Evansen, Paul
Franklin, Norman
Gray, William
Hackenbruck, John
Halverson, William
Hughes, Henry
Kolberg, Elmer
McKallip, William
Maple, Howard
Mercer, James
More, Harold
Ossowski, Theodore
Pangle, Harold
Puddy, Harold
Ramsey, Frank
Rust, Reginald
Samuels, Donald
Schultz, Eberle
Sears, Victor
Temple, Mark
Wendlick, Joseph
Wickett, Lloyd
Younce, Leonard

OREGON UNIVERSITY
Bjork, Delbert
Carpenter, Kenneth
Carter, Ross
Chapman, Harmon
Christensen, George
Culwell, Val
Cuppoletti, Bree
Daugherty, Richard
Eagle, Alexander
Ecklund, Bradley
Elliott, Charles
Emmons, Franklin
Field, Harry
Gagnon, Roy
Garza, Daniel
Horne, Richard
Hughes, Bernard
Iverson, Christopher
Kitzmiller, John
Lainhart, Porter
Leicht, Jacob
Lewis, Woodley
Lillard, Joseph
Mecham, Curtis
Mikulak, Michael
Moore, George
Morgan, William
Morse, Raymond
Rhea, Floyd
Schwammel, Adolph
Stuart, James
Van Brocklin, Norman
Wilkins, Richard

OSHKOSH TEACHERS
Robl, Harold
Wilson, Milton

OTTERBEIN
Agler, Robert
Davis, Paul
Faust, Richard

OUCHITA
LaFitte, William

PACIFIC, COLLEGE OF
Campora, Donald
Klapstein, Earl
McCaffray, Arthur
Martinovich, Philip
Moser, Robert
Watson, James

PACIFIC LUTHERAN
Sigurdson, Sigurd

PENN STATE
Cherundulo, Charles
Conover, Lawrence
Davis, Robert
Drazenovich, Charles
Durkota, Jeffrey
Eschbach, Herbert
Filak, John
Frketich, Leonard
Griffiths, Paul
Haines, Henry

Hamas, Steven
Higgins, Robert
Jaffur, John
Joe, Lawrence
Lightner, Joseph
McCann, Ernest
Michalske, August
Miller, Henry
Mills, Thomas
Moore, William
Nobile, Leo
Nolan, John
O'Connell, Milton
Olszewski, Albert
Osborn, Robert
Palazzi, Louis
Palm, Michael
Patrick, John
Penaccion, Victor
Petrella, John
Pritchard, William
Rauch, Richard
Robb, Harry
Roepke, John
Rogel, Frank
Schuster, Richard
Snell, George
Suhey, Steven
Tamburo, Samuel
Thomas, William
Tobin, L.
Triplett, Wallace
Ullery, William
Way, Charles
Wear, Robert
Wentz, Byron
Werder, Edward
Wilson, E.

PENN UNIVERSITY
Allen, Edward
Bednarik, Charles
Calcagni, Ralph
Chesney, Chester
Craig, C.
Dieter, Herbert
Fiedler, William
Frick, Ray
Gallagher, Bernard
Grain, Edwin
Greenshields, Donn
Hamer, Ernest
Hopkins, Theodore
Kaufman, John
Kuczinski, Bert
Leith, A.
Little, Louis
McGinley, Edward
Masters, Walter
Milan, Joseph
Miller, Joseph
Minisi, Anthony
Murray, Francis
Nelson, Herbert
Oristaglio, Robert
Quillen, Frank
Raffel, W.
Reagan, Frank
Riblett, Paul
Rogers, Charles
Savitsky, George
Schneider, Donald
Schweder, John
Sokolis, Stanley
Sponaugle, Robert
Stickel, Walter
Sullivan, George
Sweeney, William
Thomas, E.
Thomas, Rex
Thurman, John
Willson, Osborne
Wray, Ludlow

PHILLIPS UNIVERSITY
Owen, Stephen
Sark, Harvey
Strauss, Arthur

PITTSBURGH
Adams, Peter
Ashbaugh, William
Bohren, Karl
Bonelli, Ernest
Boswell, Charles
Cassiano, Richard
Chase, Ralph
Chickerneo, John
Clark, James

Collins, Paul
Cosgrove, Thomas
Cuba, Paul
Daddio, Louis
Dailey, T.
Daniell, Averell
Durishan, John
Dutton, William
Edgar, William
Fife, Ralph
Flanagan, William
Goldberg, Marshall
Gwosden, Milo
Heller, Warren
Hinte, Harold
Hoel, Robert
Holleran, Thomas
Hood, Franklin
Jones, Edgar
Kern, William
Kish, Benjamin
Kracum, George
Kristufek, Frank
Lauro, Lindell
McMurdo, James
McPeak, William
Matesic, Edward
Mattioli, Francis
Meadows, Eric
Merkovsky, Albert
Morrow, James
Musulin, Steven
Nicksick, Michael
Olezniczak, Stanley
Parkinson, Thomas
Patrick, Frank
Peace, Lawrence
Perlman, Irwin
Petro, Steven
Pierre, John
Quatse, Jess
Randour, Hubert
Rickards, Paul
Robbins, John
Roussos, Michael
Sack, John
Salata, Andrew
Schmitt, Theodore
Sebastian, Michael
Siedelson, Harry
Sies, Dale
Sites, Vincent
Skladany, Leo
Souchak, Frank
Stein, Russell
Thornhill, Claude
Thurbon, Robert
Valenti, John
Walton, Frank
Weinstock, Isadore
Welch, Gilbert
Wiesenbaugh, Henry
Wisinger, Zonar

PLATTSVILLE TEACHERS
Perkins, Donald

PORTLAND
Barrett, Emmett
Beil, Lawrence
Dunstan, Elwyn
McDade, William

PRESBYTERIAN
Moore, Paul
Weldon, Lawrence

PRINCETON
Beattie, Robert
Drews, Theodore
Hendrian, Warren
Howard, Albert
Keck, Stanley
Perantoni, J. Francis
Perina, Robert
Poole, George

PROVIDENCE
Avedisian, Charles
Dagata, Frederick
Soar, Henry
Triggs, John

PURDUE
Barbolak, Peter
Barwegan, Richard
Berne, William
Birk, Ferdinand
Boland, George

Brock, J. Louis
Buksar, George
Burmeister, Forrest
Carman, Edmund
Claypool, Ralph
Cody, Edward
Combs, William
DeMoss, Robert
Dimancheff, Boris
Drake, John
Duggins, G. Herbert
Fleischman, Godfrey
French, Barry
Galvin, John
Gibron, Abraham
Gift, Wayne
Gorgal, Kenneth
Heck, Robert
Heldt, Carl
Horstmann, Roy
Huffine, Kenneth
Humphrey, Paul
Ippolito, Anthony
Isbell, Cecil
Janecek, Clarence
Karras, Louis
Kodba, Joseph
Letsinger, James
Maloney, Norman
Mattingly, Francis
Mihal, Joseph
Miller, Charles
Moss, Paul
Murray, Earl
Oehler, John
Papach, George
Pardonner, Paul
Petty, John
Pfohl, Robert
Pope, Lewis
Risk, Edward
Sandefur, Richard
Skoronski, Edward
Sleight, Elmer
Wellman, Ferdinand
Winkler, Joseph
Woltman, Clement

REDLANDS
McGilbra, Sanford
Thompson, D.

REGIS
Herber, Arnold

RHODE ISLAND STATE
Abbruzzi, Louis
Cure, Armand
McIntosh, Daniel

RICE INSTITUTE
Blackburn, William
Boettcher, Frederick
Brick, Shirley
Brumley, Robert
Cordill, Oliver
Eikenberg, Virgil
Hartman, Frederick
Humble, Weldon
Magee, John
Miller, Ralph
Nichols, Hamilton
Rote, Tobin
Scruggs, Edwin
Spruill, James
Squyres, Seaman
Steen, Frank
Watson, Joseph
Weatherly, Gerald
Whitlow, Kenneth
Williams, Wendell

RICHMOND
Fronczek, Andrew
Graham, S. Lyle
Humbert, Richard
Jones, Arthur

RIDER
Maynard, Lester

RIPON
Croft, Milburn
Kenyon, Crowell
Rosenow, August
Scalissi, Theodore
Smith, Earl
Wheeler, Lyle

RUTGERS
Alexander, John
Benkert, Henry
Burkhardt, A.
Crowl, R.
Fraser, George
Garrett, Alfred
Greenberg, Benjamin
Grossman, John
Hasbrouck, John
Nash, Robert
Prisco, Nicholas
Rendall, Kenneth
Robeson, Paul
Rosen, Stanley

ST. AMBROSE
Lapka, Theodore
Keriasotis, Nicholas
Kolls, Louis
Zuidmulder, David

ST. ANSELM'S
McLean, Raymond
Spirida, John

ST. BENEDICT'S
Comp, Irvin
Visnic, Lawrence

ST. BONAVENTURE
Butler, John
Gavigan, Michael
Gildae, John
Hays, George
Kaporch, Anbert
Kenneally, George
Ksionzyk, John
Lovuolo, Frank
Marcolini, Hugo
Nicksich, George

ST. EDMONDS
Knox, Charles

ST. EDWARDS
Sarafiny, Albert

ST. FRANCIS
Bova, Anthony
Magulick, George
Milano, Arch
Naioti, John

ST. JOHNS (MINN.)
Carlson, Irvin
Caywood, Lester
McNally, John "Blood"

ST. JOHNS (NEW YORK)
Salemi, Samuel

ST. JOSEPH'S (IND.)
Scollard, Nicholas
Thuerk, Owen

ST. JOSEPH'S (PA.)
Laux, Theodore

ST. LAWRENCE
Hefti, James
Leckonby, William
Sheard, Alfred

ST. LOUIS
Arenz, Arnold
Drury, Lyle
Kane, Carl
Krause, Henry
LaPresta, Benjamin
Lintzenich, Joseph
McLeod, Arthur
Menihardt, George
Montgomery, William
Nagel, Ross
Pfuhl, Richard
Rapp, Manuel
Schweidler, Richard
Thornton, Richard
Webber, Richard
Wismann, Peter

ST. MARY'S (CAL.)
Aguirre, Joseph
Austin, James
Brovelli, Angelo
Callen, Frank
Clemons, Raymond
Compagno, Anthony

Conlee, Gerald
Crowe, Paul
Dennerlien, Gerald
Dowd, Jerry
Ebding, Harry
Falkenstein, Anthony
Flagerman, John
Frankian, Malcolm
Giannoni, John
Grant, Hugh
Jorgenson, Carl
Jorgenson, Wagner
Kellogg, Clarence
Klotovich, Michael
McArthur, John
McNally, Frank
Magnani, Dante
Marefos, Andrew
Mattos, Harry
Mesak, Richard
Morales, Gonzales
Muldoon, M.
Nichelini, Al
Ruskusky, Raymond
Ryan, Edward
Simas, William
Starrett, Benjamin
Stennet, Frederick
Strader, Norman
Toscani, Francis
Trebotich, Ivan
Wedemeyer, Herman
Wilkin, Wilbur
Yezerski, John

ST. MARY'S (MINN.)
Madigan, Frank
Mehelich,
O'Neill, Thomas
O'Toole, William
Wager, Clinton

ST. MARY'S (TEXAS)
Bettencourt, Lawrence
Huneke, Charles
Lankas, James
Sandig, Curtis

ST. THOMAS
Baril, Adrian
Franta, Herbert
Kiesling, Walter
Layport, John
McNellis, William
Manion, James
Maynaugh, Roland
Murray, John
Salscheider, John
Simensen, Donald
Steinbach, Laurence

ST. VINCENT'S
Foltz, Vernon
Kondria, John
Manzini, Baptiste
Popovich, John
Ratica, Joseph

SAM HOUSTON
Hightower, John
Law, Hubbard

SAN DIEGO STATE
Dahms, Thomas

SAN FRANCISCO
Barber, Ernest
Barber, James
Franceschi, Peter
Greenhalgh, Robert
Kenny, Charles
Pacewic, Vincent
Panciera, Donal
Peterson, Raymond
Letlow, Russell
Rowe, Harmon
Sabuco, Tino
Sanchez, John
Scott, Joseph
Siemering, Lawrence
Vogelaar, Carroll

SAN JOSE STATE
Birlem, Keith
Collier, Floyd
Crisler, Harold
Dow, Harley
Johnson, Marvin
Minini, Frank

Nygren, Bernard
Pifferini, Robert
Titchenal, Robert
Ucovich, Mitchell
Wilson, William
Zimmerman, Leroy

SANTA BARBARA
Cathcart, Royal
Cathcart, Samuel
Oldershaw, Douglas
Yeager, Howard

SANTA CLARA
Artoe, Lee
Bassi, Richard
Beals, Alyn
Casanega, Kenneth
Cope, Frank
Dougherty, Philip
Falaschi, Nello
Forrest, Edward
Freitas, Jesse
Grgich, Visco
Haynes, Hall
Hennessey, Jerome
Hock, John
Nolan, John
Schiechl, John
Storm, Edward
Thornton, Robert
Vinnola, Paul
Williams, Ellery

SCRANTON
Eiden, Edmund
Koons, Joseph
Martinelli, James
Rogalla, John
Turley, Douglas

SIMPSON
Mercer, Kenneth
Richards, Elvin

S. CAROLINA
Blackwell, Harold
Craig, Lawrence
Grygo, Al
Hanna, Elzaphan
Keenan, John
Krivonak, Joseph
Meeks, Bryant
Roskie, Kenneth
Sparks, David
Sossamon, Louis
Stasica, Stanley
Strickland, Bishop
Urban, Alexander

S. DAKOTA STATE
Arndt, Alfred
Barber, Mark
Beasey, John
Crakes, Joseph
Engelmann, Wuert
Erickson, Weldon
Jannisen, Raymond
McCormick, Frank
Miller, Paul
Sheeks, Paul

SOUTHEASTERN LOUISIANA
Campion, Thomas
Davis, Jerome
Reisz, Albert

SOUTHERN CALIFORNIA
Apsit, Marger
Audet, Earl
Badgro, Morris
Baker, Roy
Banta, Herbert
Barrager, Nathan
Bleeker, Melvin
Burke, Donald
Chantiles, Thomas
Clark, Donald
Cleary, Paul
Clemens, Calvin
Danehe, Richard
Davis, Joseph
DeLauer, Robert
Doll, Donald
Dunn, Coye
Elston, Arthur
Fisher, Robert
Fisk, William
Fletcher, Oliver

Garlin, Donald
Garzoni, Michael
George, Raymond
Griffiths, Homer
Hardy, James
Hendren, Robert
Henke, Edgar
Heywood, Ralph
Hibbs, Jesse
Hoffman, Robert
Hoffman, Wayne
Howard, William
Jessup, William
Kaer, Morton
Kirby, John
Klenk, Quentin
Krueger, Alvin
Lansdell, Granville
Lillywhite, Verl
McCormick, Walter
Margucci, Joseph
Mooney, Tex
Morgan, Boyd
Murphy, George
Musick, James
Naumu, John
Nix, John
Parsons, Earle
Pinckert, Ernest
Powers, James
Radovich, William
Robertson, Robert
Saenz, Edward
Salata, Paul
Saunders, Russell
Smith, Ernest
Sohn, Benjamin
Steponovich, Anthony
Stonebraker, John
Tipton, Howard
Tonelli, Anthony
Verry, Norman
Ward, John
Wehba, Raymond
West, Pat
Winslow, Robert

SOUTHERN METHODIST
Baxter, Lloyd
Bedford, William
Booth, Clarence
Bray, Maurice
Carter, Joseph
Clement, John
Collier, Robert
Croft, Abe
Dean, Thomas
Dewell, William
Ethridge, Joseph
Fawcett, Jacob
Fuqua, Raymond
Halliday, John
Johnson, Gilbert
Johnson, William
Johnston, L. Preston
McClain, Clinton
Maley, Howard
Mallouf, Raymond
Page, Paul
Parker, Howard
Pasqua, Joseph
Raborn, Carroll
Ranspot, Keith
Rote, Kyle
Ruthstrom, Ralph
Sanders, John
Sauflev, Victor
Vaughn, W.
Walker, Ewell Doak
Wilson, Oliver
Wilson, Robert
Wright, James

SOUTHWESTERN
Hammond, Henry
Layden, Robert
Shockley, Arnold
Smith, Gaylon

SPRINGFIELD
Civiletto, Frank
Obeck, Victor
Watters, Leonard

STANFORD
Albert, Frank
Anderson, Stanley
Artman, Corwan
Banducci, Bruno

Boensch, Frederick
Bove, John
Caddel, Ernest
Calvelli, Anthony
Cavelli, Anthony
Cox, James
Gallarneau, Hugh
Hachten, William
Hill, Donald
Kmetovic, Peter
Lawson, James
Lindskog, Victor
Meyer, Frederick
Mitchell, Robert
Moscrip, James
Nevers, Ernest
Norberg, Henry
Norgard, Al
O'Connor, Robert
Pool, J. Hampton
Reynolds, Robert
Smith, John
Stnadlee, Norman
Taylor, Charles
Tsoutsouvas, Louis
Vucinich, Milton
White, Robert

STERLING
Hiemstra, Edward

STEVENS POINT
Fritsch, Theodore

SUPERIOR STATE
Engstrom, G.
Goldfein, Jersey
Moselle, Don

SWARTHMORE
Clime, Benjamin
Hughes, Morris
Wilcox, Edward

SYRACUSE
Abbott, L.
Albanese, Vincent
Alexander, Joseph
Archoski, Julius
Barbuti, Raymond
Bayley, John
Biggs, Carl
Braney, John
Cobb, Alfred
Constantine, Irving
Courtney, Gerard
Culver, Frank
Dooley, John
Dve, Lester
Ellis, Lawrence
Fallon, Michael
Fishel, Richard
Foley, James
Forsyth, Charles
Foster, Frederick
Frugonne, James
Hinkle, Jack
Hoffman, Arnold
Jappe, Paul
Kellogg, William
Leaf, Garfield
Levv, Harvey
McBride, John
McKee, Paul
Maines, Thomas
Matteo, Francis
Obst, Henry
Piro, Henry
Reckmarck, Raymond
Robertson, Harry
Sawyer, Herman
Sebo, Samuel
Simmons, Roy
Singer, Walter
Steele, Harold
Steen, James
Thompson, George
Titmas, Herbert
Tomlin, Thomas
Usher, Louis
Watt, Joseph
Williams, Boyd
Witter, Ray
Ziff, D.
Zimmerman, Gifford

TEMPLE
Batinski, Stanley
Brahm, Lawrence

Brunski, Andrew
Davidson, William
Drulis, Charles
Frank, Harry
Frey, Glenn
Getchell, C. Gorham
Hanson, John
Hanson, Thomas
Hubka, Eugene
Jarmoluk, Michael
Kilroy, Frank
Kolman, Edward
Konopka, John
Kusko, John
Lipski, John
McGee, Edward
Marcus, Alexander
Nichols, Allen
Pilconis, Joseph
Reese, Henry
Russell, James
Shults, John
Slosburg, Philip
Smukler, David
Stevens, Peter
Sutch, George
Sutton, Joseph
Sylvester, John
Tomasio, Andrew

TENNESSEE
Bartholomew, Samuel
Brandau, Arthur
Butler, John
Cafego, George
Cifers, Edward
Cifers, Robert
Clay, Boyd
Crawford, Denver
Dobelstein, Robert
Feathers, Beattie
Gaffney, James
Graves, Raymond
Hickman, Herman
Hill, James
Hubbell, Franklin
Huffman, Richard
Hust, Albert
Lipscomb, Paul
Long, Robert
Lowe, William
Miller, Benjamin
Morrow, Russell
Rayburn, Van
Reese, Lloyd
Rose, Eugene
Simonetti, Leonard
Slater, Walter
Suffridge, Robert
Tarrant, James
Thayer, Harry
Vaughan, Charles
Warren, Buist
West, Hodges

TEXAS A. & I.
Steinke, Gilbert

TEXAS A. & M.
Allison, James
Britt, Rankin
Bucek, Felix
Clarkson, Stuart
Coston, Frederick
Ellis, Herbert
Goode, Robert
Howell, Clarence
Irvin, Barlow
Johnson, William
Kendricks, James
Kimbrough, John
Malone, Charles
Marek, Joseph
Montgomery, James
Moore, Allen
Murrah, W. E.
Ohlgren, Earl
Pannell, Ernest
Payne, Otto
Price, Charles
Pugh, Marion
Robnett, Marshall
Rogers, Cullen
Ruby, Martin
Sparkman, Alan
Stautzenberger, Odell
Tassos, Damon
Thomason, James
Todd, Richard

Wilde, George
Wilson, Fay
Winkler, James
Young, Roy

TEXAS CHRISTIAN UNIV.
Aldrich, Charles
Alford, Herbert
Baugh, Samuel
Brown, George
Casper, Charles
Cox, Norman
Douglass, Astynax
Edwards, Weldon
Ellis, Drew
Evans, Lon
Hall, John
Handler, Philip
Hinton, J. W.
Kring, Frank
Lawrence, James
Lester, Darrell
Looney, Donald
Manton, Taldon
Nix, Emery
O'Brien, David
O'Neal, James
Palmer, Darrell
Patton, John
Shook, Frederick
Stout, Peter
Walls, William
White, Thomas
Williams, Jacob

TEXAS MINES
Cotton, Russell
Evans, Raymond
Heineman, Kenneth
Matheson, Riley
Mayhew, Hayden
Smith, Oscar
Wilson, Gordon

TEXAS TEACHERS
Davis, Gaines
Wright, Theodore

TEXAS TECH
Alford, Eugene
Barnard, Charles
Baze, Winford
Bryant, Robert
Davis, William
Dowell, "Mule"
Earhart, Ralph
Flowers, Robert
Holcomb, William
Kelley, William
Nabors, Ronald
Neill, James
Owens, Peter
Ramsay, Herschel
Rankin, Walter
Robnett, Edward
Sachse, Francis
Schlinkman, Walter
Scott, Prince
Smith, Joseph
Webb, George
Williams, Rex
Winkler, Bernard

TEXAS UNIVERSITY
Arnold, Jay
Baumgardner, Max
Bechtol, Hubert
Callahan, J. R.
Canady, James
Clay, Randall
Collins, William
Conner, Emerson
Connolly, William
Doss, Noble
Eckhardt, Oscar
Emerson, Grover
Freeman, John
Gillory, Byron
Harris, Henry
Heap, Walter
Holder, Lewis
Hughes, William
Jungmichel, Harold
Keeling, Raymond
Kelley, Edward
Kutner, Malcolm
Landry, Thomas
Lawler, Allen
Layden, Peter

Layne, Robert
McKay, Regis
McKay, Roy
Magliolo, Joseph
Martin, Vernon
Mauldin, Stanley
Mayne, Lewis
Parker, Joseph
Peterson, Lester
Petrovich, George
Rose, Alfred
Sanders, Orban
Shelley, Dexter
Symth, Louis
Stafford, Harrison
Tynes, David
Vance, Joseph
Vasicek, Victor
Watson, Grady
Weedon, Donald
Wetz, Harlan
Williams, Donald
Williams, Joel
Wolfe, Hugh

TEXAS WESTERN
Hansen, Wayne

THIEL
Christman, Floyd
Mitchell,

TOLEDO
Cole, Emerson
Maher, Francis
Marotti, Louis
Sample, Charles
Slovak, Martin

TRINITY (CONN.)
Kobrosky, Milton
Nordstrom, Harry

TRINITY ((TEX.)
Cole, Peter
Hogan, Darrell

TROTT VOCATIONAL
Mazza, Vincent

TUFTS
Doane, Joseph
Share, Nathan

TULANE
Bentz, Roman
Bladin, Ernest
Bodenger, Maurey
Comer, Martin
Gloden, Frederick
Hornick, William
Joce, Donald
Lea, Paul
McCollum, Harley
McDonald, Walter
Price, Edward
Rexer, Freeman
Roberts, John
Schneider, Leroy
Svoboda, William
Thibaut, James
Wenzel, Ralph

TULSA UNIVERSITY
Barry, Paul
Bernstein, Joseph
Boone, J. R.
Brown, Hardy
Buda, Carl
Burgess, Glenn
Dobbs, Glenn
Finks, James
Gentry, Elmer
Gibson, Billy Joe
Goodnight, Clyde
Gray, Samuel
Green, John
Greene, Frank
Crigg, Forrest
Harmon, Hamilton
Haynes, Joseph
Jones, Ellis
Judd, Saxon
Kowalski, Adolphe
LeForce, Clyde
Luhn, Nolan
Lyons, John
Mitchell, Charles
Prewitt, Felto

Purdin, Calvin
Robertson, Thomas
Rogas, Daniel
Scafide, Albert
Shedlosky, Edmond
Spangler, Eugene
Stanley, G. B.
Stuart, Roy
Thompson, Thomas
Volok, William
Whitman, S. J.
Wilson, Camp
Workman, Blake

U. C. L. A.
Baldwin, Burr
Boyer, Verdi
Cantor, Leo
Case, Ernest
Fears, Thomas
Fenenbock, Charles
Finlay, John
Keeble, Joseph
Kurrasch, Roy
Lyman, Del
McChesney, Robert
McLaughlin, Leon
Mathews, Ned
Mike, Robert
Myers, John
Olson, Carl
Paul, Don
Phillips, George
Shipkey, Jerry
Smith, Milton
Snelling, Kenneth
Sommers, John
Sparlis, Albert
Strode, Woodrow
Stroschein, Brock
Thompson, Harry
Washington, Kenneth
Waterfield, Robert
Wilkinson, Robert

URSINUS
Bassman, Herman
Lowery,
Potteiger, Earl
Mulleneaux, Carl

UTAH STATE
Ryan, Kent
Sorenson, Glen
Williams, Frank

UTAH UNIVERSITY
Christensen, Frank
Clark, Wayne
Croft, Win
Gehrke, Clarence
Hafen, Banard
Johnson, John
McDonald, Walter
McDonough, Paul
McGarry, Bernard
Nelson, D. Frank
Olsen, Ralph
Speedie, Mac
Summerhavs, Robert
Ward, Elmer

VALPARAISO
Cearing, Lloyd
Gilbert, Walter
White, Roy

VANDERBILT
Agee, Samuel
Beasley, Turman
Bomar, Lynn
Cooper, Kenneth
Gude, Henry
Huggins, Roy
Jenkins, Jacque
Leyendecker, Charles
Merlin, Edward
North, John
Oliver, Richard
Plasman, Richard
Ray, Bufford
Rich, Herbert
Satterfield, Alfren
Wiggs, Hubert

VERMONT
Harms, Arthur
Trigilio, Frank

VILLANOVA
Andrulewicz, Theodore
August, Edward
Basca, Michael
Berrang, Edward
Brazingsky, Samuel
Brown, Daniel
Chisick, Andrew
D'Alonzo, Peter
DeFilippo, David
Ferry, Louis
Finn, John
Kasky, Edward
Kuzco, Paul
Lomasney, Thomas
Longua, Paul
McLaughlin,
Magee, James
Mellus, John
Michaels, Edward
Nowak, Walter
Padloski, Chester
Pasquariello, Ralph
Pessalano, Louis
Postus, Al
Pritko, Steven
Rogers, William
Romanik, Steven
Rosato, Salvatore
Sandusky, John
Stenn, Paul
Suess, Raymond
Youngfleisch, Francis
Zamlynski, Zygmond
Zizak, Vincent

VIRGINIA MILITARY INST.
Barber, Benjamin
Mason, Samuel
Maha, Joseph
Pritchard, Abisha
Thomason, Robert
Walker, William

VIRGINIA POLYTECH INST.
Maskas, John

VIRGINIA UNIVERSITY
Baldwin, George
Churchman, Charles
Dudley, William
Elliott, Carlton
Gillette, James
Grimes, George
McLaughlin, Lee
Papit, John
Schroeder, Eugene
Whaley, Benjamin

WABASH
Bacon, Francis
Griggs, Harold
Hobson, Benjamin
Meere, Ward
Singleton, John

WAKE FOREST
Barbour, Wesley
Bradley, Edward
Cochran, John
Crabtree, Clement
Dowda, Harry
Duncan, James
Gallovich, Anthony
Jett, John
Jones, Elmer
Leonetti, Robert
Meyer, Gilbert
O'Quinn, John
Pate, Rupert
Polanski, John
Preston, Pattison
Royston, Edward
Rubino, Anthony
Sacrinty, Nicholas
Staton, James
Stofko, Edward
Wedel, Richard

WASHINGTON (ST. LOUIS)
Bertagnolli, Libero
Bukant, Joseph
Conzelman, James
Schieb,
Schwenk, Wilson

WASHINGTON STATE
Akins, Albert

Akins, Frank
Bell, Kay
Burks, Joseph
Edwards, Albert Glen
Farman, Richard
Gentry, Dale
Goddard, Edward
Godfrey, Herbert
Hanley, Richard
Hayduk, Henry
Hein, Melvin
Hoptowit, Al
Houghton, Jerry
Hurley, George
Kennedy, Robert
Klumb, John
Kramer, Frederick
Marker, Clifford
Meeker, Herbert
Moses, Howard
Niemi, Laurie
Paul, Donald
Polsfoot, Francis
Remington, Joseph
Renfro, Richard
Sandberg, Roy
Sarboe, Paul
Schwartz, Elmer
Stojack, Frank
Suseoff, Nicholas
Torgeson, Lavern
Ward, William
Williams, Jerome

WASHINGTON UNIVERSITY
Bond, Charles
Bond, Randal
Brett, Edward
Bruce, Gail
Cook, Edward
Deeks, Donald
Erickson, Carleton
Fennema, Carl
Frankowski, Raymond
Friedman, Robert
Guttormsen, G.
Haines, Byron
Hornbeak, Jay
Isaacson, Theodore
Johnston, James
Jones, Donald
McAdams, Dean
McDowell, Jay
Markov, Victor
Mucha, Charles
Mucha, Rudolph
Newton, Charles
Nisbet, David
Ottele, Richard
Provo, Frederick
Slivinski, Steven
Smith, William
Stackpool, John
Steele, Ernest
Tevis, Leek
Weinmeister, Arnold
Wiater, John
Wilson, Abraham
Wilson, George

WASHINGTON & JEFFERSON
Berrehsen, William
Bliss, Homer
Carroll, Edward
Clements, George
Crook, Albert
Demas, George
Douds, Forrest
Edwards, Leslie
Fleming, Malcolm
Guy, Charles
Gallagher, Edward
Haddon, Aldous
Henry, Wilbur
Kirkman, Roger
McNeil, Francis
Malcolm, Harry
Neihaus, Francis
Norman, Willard
Oltz,
Paulekas, Anthony
Rhoads, Donald
Siegfried, Orville
Stein, Herbert
Towler, Daniel
Vick, R.
Vince, Ralph
Wiederquist, Chester
Wimberly, Byron

WASHINGTON & LEE
Boyda, Michael
Brenkhart, William
Cameron, Edmund
Chipley, William
Lukens, James
Mattox, Marvin
Michaels, Walter
Pierotti, Albert
Sweetland, Frederick
Van Horne, Charles

WAYNESBURG
Pastin, Frank
Scarry, Michael
Wiley, John
Worden, James

WEATHERFORD
Jones, Lewis

WEBER
Lolatai, Albert
Sneddon, Robert

WESLEYAN (CONN.)
Lester, Harold

WEST LIBERTY TEACHERS
Campiglio, Robert

WESTERN MARYLAND
Benson, Alvin
Campofreda, Nicholas
Havens, Charles
Kaplan, Bernard
Phillips, Michael
Shepherd, William
Sillin, Frank

WESTERN MICHIGAN
Bray, Raymond
Macioszczyk, Arthur
Mason, Joel
Matheson, John

WESTERN ONTARIO
Krol, Joseph

WEST POINT
Cagle, Christian
Coulter, DeWitt
Davidson, Garrison
Davis, Glen
Dibbs, John
Foldberg, Henry
French, Walter
McPhail, Harold
Merrilat, Louis
Oliphant, Elmer
Peshmalyan, Baruyr
Pollard, Al

WEST TEXAS STATE TEACHERS
Box, Cloyce
Cross, William
Schupbach, O. T.
Watkins, Foster

WEST VIRGINIA
Anderson, William
Atty, Alexander
Bailey, James
Bailey, Russell
Baisi, Albert
Barnum, Robert
Beck, Carl
Brewster, James
Bruder, Woodie
Bumgardner, Rex
Clark, Harry
Dolly, John
Fryer, Kenneth
Goodman, Harry
Goodwin, Tod
Gussie, Michael
Hagburg, Rudolph
Karr, William
Keane, Thomas
Kimble, Frank
King, Andrew
Lucente, John
Mahan, Walter
Mahrt, W.
Meredith, Russell
Moan, Emmett
Myles,
Nardicci, Nicholas

Seabright, Charles
Sechrist, Leonard
Setron, Joseph
Sortet, Wilbur
Stephenson, David
Stydahar, Joseph

WEST VIRGINIA WESLEYAN
Barnum, Leonard
Battles, Clifford
Blondin, Thomas
Bullman, Gail
Kellison, John
Peterson, Nelson
Reiter, Wilbur
Rodriguez, Kelly
Seibert, Edward

WESTMINSTER
Boyd, Walter

WESTERN RESERVE
Badaczewski, John
Belicheck, Stephen
Booth, Richard
Lahr, Warren
Ragazzo, Philip
Rodak, Michael
Roman, George
Sanzotta, Dominic
Skoczen, Stanley
Wilson, John
Zeh, Raymond

WHITTIER
Finch, Olin
Hutchinson, Elvin

WICHITA
Brill, Harold
Dugan, Leonard
Kelly, Elmer
McEnulty, Douglas
Sexton, Linwood

WILLAMETTE
Weisgerber, Richard

WILLIAM & MARY
Brown, Thomas
Charles, Winston
Cloud, John
Clowes, John
Creekmur, Louis
Douglas, Otis
Forkovitch, Nicholas
Hardy, Isham
Hughes, George
Johnson, Harvey
Matsu, Arthur
Mikula, Thomas
Ramsey, Garrard
Ramsey, Knox
Sazio, Ralph
Thompson, Thomas
Vandeweghe, Alfred

WILLIAMS
Boynton, Benjamin
Clement, Alexander
Gregory, Frank
Surabian, Zareh

WILMINGTON
Bonowitz, Elliott
Egan, Richard
Glassman, Morris
Weimer, Howard

WISCONSIN
Albrecht, Arthur
Albright, William
Atwood, John
Barr, Wallace
Bieberstein, Adolph
Brumm, Roman
Buck, Howard
Calligaro, Leonard
Cook, James
Davis, Ralph
Dreyer, Walter
Eckle, Robert
Elliott, Alvah
Esser, Clarence
Farris, Thomas
Gantenbein, Milton
Gardner, Milton
Girard, Earl
Goldenburg, Charles

Golemgeske, John
Gollomb, Rudolph
Gunderson, Borge
Harder, Marlin
Harris, John
Hekkers, George
Kankowski, Edward
Kindt, Donald
Kresky, Joseph
Larson, Lloyd
Leaper, Wesley
Loepfe, Richard
Lubratovich, Milo
Maves, Earl
Mead, John
Miller, Donald
Mortell, Emmett
Negus, Frederick
Paskvan, George
Peterson, Philip
Rose, Eugene
Schneller, John
Schroeder, William
Schuele, Jacob
Schuette, Paul
Scott, Ralph
Seibold, Champ
Self, Clarence
Simpson, Eber
Stark, Howard
Tebell, Gustavus
Tennant, John
Tommerson, Clarence
Vogos, Evan
Warner, Robert
Wasserbach, Lloyd
Weiss, Howard
Williams, Richard

WITTENBERG
Burgner, Earl
Hummon, John
Rohleder, George

WOOSTER
Flattery, William
Haas,

WYOMING UNIVERSITY
Kizzire, Lee

XAVIER
Bucklew, Philip
Knecht, William
Martinovic, John
Mutryn, Chester
Rapp, Herbert
Sigillo, Dominic
Stotsberg, Harold
Wiethe, John

YALE
Barzilauskas, Francis
Caldwell, Bruce
Kempton, Herbert
Milstead, Century
Peshmalyan, Baruyr
Prchlik, John
Schuler, William
Walker, Paul

YOUNGSTOWN
Aiello, Anthony
Campana, Al
Gill, Sloko

**NO COLLEGE &
    COLLEGE UNKNOWN**
Aberson, Clifford—NC
Abrams, Nathan—NC
Adams,
Argus, Robert—NC
Armstrong,
Arrowhead
Bachmaier,—NC
Balatti, Edward—NC
Bancroft,
Barle, Louis
Bartaanen, William—NC
Batchelor,
Bauer,
Beeming,
Belden, Charles—NC
Benton,
Bernard,
Besta,
Big Bear
Big Twig

Black Bear
Blailock,
Boldt, S
Boyle, William—NC
Bramhall, Arthur—NC
Brannan,
Bruncklacher,
Buffalo
Buland, Walter—NC
Burnside
Campbell, Donald
Card, J. Harper
Cardarelli, Carl—NC
Carey, Joseph—NC
Carr, Edwin—NC
Chicken, Frederick—NC
Christensen,
Clark, "Butch"
Clayton, Donald
Cleve,
Colmer, John—NC
Comer,
Connors,
Conrad,
Cooker,
Coomer, Joseph—NC
Corn, Joseph—NC
Cortemeglia, Christopher—NC
Croft,
Curzon,
Darby,
Davis, Raymond
Deadeye
Demmy,—NC
Dickey, Leonard—NC
Dobliet,
Dobrey, E. A.
Doehring, John—NC
Doloway, Clifford
Donelli, Allan—NC
Doolan,
Dressen, Charles—NC
Eagle Feather
Eiden,
Emslie,
Englund, Harry—NC
Fagioli, Carl—NC
Failing,
Falcon, Gilbert—NC
Ferguson,
Fernia,
Ferrante, Jack—NC
Fetz, Gustave—NC
Fisher, Everett
Frahm, Herald
Fuller, Lawrence—NC
Galazin, Stanley
Gardner,
Garner, Robert
Gaulke, Harold
Gaustad,
Gavin, Buck—NC
Gentry, Byron
Glennie,
Gorgal,
Gorman,
Grabinski, Thaddeus
Graham, F.
Graham, Lester
Granato, Samuel—NC
Gray Horse
Green, E.
Gump,
Haas,
Halleck,
Hartman, James
Heater, William
Heinrisch,
Hemerek,
Henricus,
Hollquist,
Hooley,
Hubbard, Wesley—NC
Hudson, R.
Hummell
Hunter,
Hurst,
Hurtjun,
Hutton, Leon
Irgens,
Jacobs, Marvin—NC
Jansing, L.
Jolly
Kaplan,
Kase, George
Kasper,
Kelsch, Mose—NC
Kiejel,
Kirkgard,

Klasnic, John—NC
Klaus, Fee—NC
Kraehe, Oliver—NC
Labaceneer,
Labengood
Lackman, Richard—NC
Ladrow, Walter—NC
Landrum, J.
Lang,
Laross,
Lassahn, Louis
Latone, Anthony—NC
LeFebre, Gilbert—NC
Lehrer,
Lennan, Reid—NC
Lepper, Bernard—NC
Levey, James—NC
Lewis,
Littlefield, Carl
Lo Boutwell
Logel, Robert—NC
Logus,
Longo,
Lord,
Lovin,
Lovuolo, Edmond—NC
Lundgren,
McLean, Raymond—NC
McGregory,
McKetes,
McRoberts,
McShea,
McWherter, Kyle—NC
Malcolm, C.
Martell, Herman—NC
Martin, John—NC
Menepee, Victor—NC
Metrick,
Mills, S.
Minturn, John—NC
Mohs,
Mooney, George—NC
Morgan,
Morse, W.
Moss,
Moynihan, R.
Mulbarger, Joseph—NC
Mulvey,
Munger,
Nelson,
Nesser, Al—NC
Netherton, W.
Nonnemaker,
Norman, Robert—NC
Norris,
Nosich, John
Novack, Edward—NC
Nugent,
Oberbruckinger,
O'Brien, William—NC
O'Keefe, Thomas

Oldham,
Olmstead, L.
O'Reilly,
Orwell,
Otto, A.
Pahl,
Pappio,
Parriott,
Passuelo,
Pattison,
Pavlich, Charles—NC
Payton,
Petrilas, William—NC
Pittman, Melvin
Pitts, Edwin—NC
Plank,
Plumridge, Theodore
Plunkett, Joseph
Pollock, William—NC
Postel,
Poto, John—NC
Powell, Richard
Pucci, Benito—NC
Racis, Frank—NC
Randolph,
Rapp,
Rapp, Robert—NC
Rashler,
Rate,
Red Fang
Red Fox
Redman,
Reichow,
Reno,
Reuder,
Ridler,
Riggins,
Risvold,
Robinson,
Rodgers, Walter
Roegen,
Romboli, Rudolph—NC
Rooney, Joseph—NC
Rooney, William—NC
Rosteck, Ernest—NC
Rowan,
Ruh, Emmett—NC
Running Deer
Rupp, John—NC
Rutzler,
Quilter, Charles—NC
Sacksteder, Norman—NC
Sampson,
Saulis, Samuel
Scardine,
Schaffnit,
Schell,
Schimmel,
Schmaehl, Arthur—NC
Secord, Joseph—NC
Sedbrook, Leonard

Seeds,
Seyfrit,
Shanley,
Shapiro,
Shaw,
Shenefelt, Paul
Shonk, John
Siefers,
Sierocenski, Stephen—NC
Simon,
Smith, H.
Smith, Leo
Snoots, J. Lee—NC
Speck, "Dutch"—NC
Spellacy,
Spencer,
Steinmetz, Kenneth—NC
Stevenson,
Stewart,
Strasser,
Struessi,
Suchy, Paul—NC
Sulaitis, Joseph—NC
Sundquist,
Swain,
Tackett, Doyle—NC
Tays,
Tersch,
Thorpe, Jack—NC
Tidd, Peter—NC
Tolley,
Umont, Frank—NC
Ursella, Reuben—NC
Van Dyke, J.
Vandello,
Vardian, John—NC
Vassau,
Vexall,
Vodicka, Joseph—NC
Waldon,
Waldron,
Walters,
Wandless, George
Weinberg,
Weiss, John—NC
Werwaiss,
Wiedich,
Wilging,
Willert,
Wilson, Leland
Windburn,
Winters, Arnold—NC
Wolford, Bard
Wood,
Wrinkle Meat
Yeisley,
Yokas, Frank—NC
Yonamine, Wallace—NC
Zoll, Carl—NC
Zoll, Martin—NC
Zunker, Charles—NC

INDEX